T0180427

Lecture Notes in Computer Science   11997

More information about this series at http://www.springer.com/series/7407

Ulrich Schwardmann · Christian Boehme ·
Dora B. Heras et al. (Eds.)

Euro-Par 2019: Parallel Processing Workshops

Euro-Par 2019 International Workshops
Göttingen, Germany, August 26–30, 2019
Revised Selected Papers

 Springer

Editors
Ulrich Schwardmann 🆔
Gesellschaft für Wissenschaftliche
Datenverarbeitung mbH
Göttingen, Germany

Christian Boehme
Gesellschaft für Wissenschaftliche
Datenverarbeitung mbH
Göttingen, Germany

Dora B. Heras
CiTIUS
Santiago de Compostela, Spain

Workshop Editors *see next page*

ISSN 0302-9743 ISSN 1611-3349 (electronic)
Lecture Notes in Computer Science
ISBN 978-3-030-48339-5 ISBN 978-3-030-48340-1 (eBook)
https://doi.org/10.1007/978-3-030-48340-1

LNCS Sublibrary: SL1 – Theoretical Computer Science and General Issues

This Springer imprint is published by the registered company Springer Nature Switzerland AG
The registered company address is: Gewerbestrasse 11, 6330 Cham, Switzerland

Workshop Editors

Auto-DaSP

Valeria Cardellini
University of Rome Tor Vergata
Italy
cardellini@ing.uniroma2.it

COLOC

Emmanuel Jeannot
Inria Bordeaux
France
emmanuel.jeannot@inria.fr

F2C-DP

Antonio Salis
Engineering Sardegna
Italy
antonio.salis@eng.it

FPDAPP

Claudio Schifanella
University of Turin
Italy
schi@di.unito.it

HeteroPar

Ravi Reddy Manumachu
University College Dublin
Ireland
ravi.manumachu@ucd.ie

HPCN

Dieter Schwamborn
DLR-AS
Germany
Dieter.Schwamborn@dlr.de

LSDVE

Laura Ricci
University of Pisa
Italy
laura.ricci@unipi.it

ParaMo

Oh Sangyoon
Ajou University
South Korea
syoh@ajou.ac.kr

PMACS

Thomas Gruber
RRZE, Friedrich-Alexander-Universität
Erlangen-Nürnberg
Germany
thomas.gruber@fau.de

PDCLifeS

Laura Antonelli
ICAR-CNR
Italy
laura.antonelli@icar.cnr.it

Resilience

Stephen L. Scott
Tennessee Technological University
USA
sscott@tntech.edu

Preface

Euro-Par is an annual, international conference in Europe, covering all aspects of parallel and distributed processing. These range from theory to practice, from the smallest to the largest parallel and distributed systems and infrastructures, from fundamental computational problems to full-fledged applications, from architecture, compiler, language, and interface design and implementation, to tools, support infrastructures, and application performance aspects. The Euro-Par conference itself is complemented by a workshop program, where workshops dedicated to more specialized themes, cross-cutting issues, and upcoming trends and paradigms can be easily and conveniently organized with little administrative overhead.

12 workshop proposals were submitted to Euro-Par 2019, and after a careful revision process, which was led by the workshop co-chairs, all of them were accepted. 11 workshops received sufficient paper contributions and took place during the two days before Euro-Par 2019. The program included the following 11 workshops:

1. Workshop on Autonomic Solutions for Parallel and Distributed Data Stream Processing (AUTO-DaSP)
2. Workshop on Data Locality (COLOC)
3. Workshop on Fog-to-Cloud Distributed Processing (F2C-DP)
4. Workshop on Future Perspective of Decentralized Applications (FPDAPP)
5. Workshop on Algorithms, Models, and Tools for Parallel Computing on Heterogeneous Platforms (HeteroPar)
6. Workshop on High Performance Computing and Networking in Aerospace (HPCN)
7. Workshop on Large-Scale Distributed Virtual Environments (LSDVE)
8. International Workshop on Parallel Programming (ParaMo)
9. Workshop on Parallel and Distributed Computing for Life Sciences: Algorithms, Methodologies, and Tools (PDCLifeS)
10. Performance Monitoring and Analysis of Cluster Systems (PMACS)
11. Workshop on Resiliency in High Performance Computing with Clouds, Grids, and Clusters (Resilience)

All workshops together received a total of 77 submissions from 31 different countries. Each workshop had an independent Program Committee, which was in charge of selecting the papers. The workshop papers received 3.7 reviews per paper on average. Out of the 77 submissions, 54 papers were selected to be presented at the workshops. One of the accepted papers was not included in the final proceedings because the authors decided to withdraw it. Thus, the acceptance rate was 70%.

This year Euro-Par 2019 also introduced a poster track as a new format to attract young researchers to the Euro-Par community. The poster call was aimed especially at young scientists and was accompanied by a mentoring session, which provided young contributors the opportunity to discuss their research findings with established researchers. 15 posters related to ongoing projects covering subjects of parallel and distributed computing were submitted, and 10 were finally accepted leading to an acceptance rate of 66%. Short papers for these accepted posters were submitted and are also part of the proceedings as a separate chapter.

The success of the Euro-Par workshops and the poster track depends on the work of many individuals and organizations. We therefore thank all workshop organizers and reviewers for the time and effort they devoted. We would also like to express our gratitude to the members of the Organizing Committee and the local staff, especially the volunteer PhD students, who helped us. Sincere thanks are due to Springer for their help in publishing the proceedings.

We would also like to thank all the participants, panelists, and keynote speakers of the Euro-Par workshops for their contributions to a productive meeting. It was a pleasure to organize and host the Euro-Par 2019 workshops in Göttingen, Germany.

March 2020   Ulrich Schwardmann
                                                        Christian Boehme
                                                        Dora B. Heras

Organization

Euro-Par 2019 Steering Committee

Chair

Luc Bougé   ENS Rennes, France

Co-chair

Fernando Silva   University of Porto, Portugal

Full Members

Marco Aldinucci   University of Turin, Italy
Dora Blanco Heras   CiTIUS, Santiago de Compostela, Spain
Emmanuel Jeannot   LaBRI, Inria Bordeaux, France
Christos Kaklamanis   Computer Technology Institute, Greece
Paul Kelly   Imperial College, UK
Thomas Ludwig   University of Hamburg, Germany
Tomàs Margalef   Autonomous University of Barcelona, Spain
Wolfgang Nagel   Dresden University of Technology, Germany
Francisco F. Rivera   CiTIUS, Santiago de Compostela, Spain
Rizos Sakellariou   The University of Manchester, UK
Henk Sips   Delft University of Technology, The Netherlands
Domenico Talia   University of Calabria, Italy
Jesper Larsson Träff   Vienna University of Technology, Austria
Denis Trystram   Grenoble Institute of Technology, France
Felix Wolf   Technische Universität Darmstadt, Germany

Honorary Members

Christian Lengauer   University of Passau, Germany
Ron Perrott   Oxford e-Research Centre, UK
Karl Dieter   Reinartz University of Erlangen-Nuremberg, Germany

Observer

Ramin Yahyapour   GWDG, University of Göttingen, Germany

Euro-Par 2019 Organizing Committee

Chair

Ramin Yahyapour   GWDG, University of Göttingen, Germany

Workshops

Ulrich Schwardmann	GWDG, Germany
Christian Boehme	GWDG, Germany
Dora B. Heras	University of Pisa, Italy, and CiTIUS, Santiago de Compostela, Spain

Logistics

Martina Brücher	GWDG, Germany

Additional Reviewers

Abdelhafez, Hazem
Agrawal, Prateek
Antonelli, Laura
Badia, Jose M.
Barbara, Fadi
Campanile, Raffaele
Cannataro, Mario
Catalan, Sandra
Cuomo, Salvatore
De Salve, Andrea
Di Napoli, Claudia
Dubovitskaya, Alevtina
Fuerlinger, Karl
Galizia, Antonella
Geiser, Georg
Guerreiro, João
Guffanti, Alberto
Guidi, Barbara

Guzzi, Pietro Hiram
Jägersküpper, Jens
Maddalena, Lucia
Maple, Carsten
Mercanti, Ivan
Neves, Nuno
Nobre, Ricardo
Oliva, Gennaro
Sangiovanni, Mara
Saurabh, Nishant
Schiano Di Cola, Vincenzo
Schneider, Ralf
Talia, Domenico
Tao, Dingwen
Taticchi, Carlo
Tonellotto, Nicola
Veltri, Pierangelo

Contents

**FPDAPP - Workshop on Future Perspective
of Decentralised Applications**

**HeteroPar - Workshop on Algorithms, Models and Tools for Parallel
Computing on Heterogeneous Platforms**

Auto-DASP - Workshop on Autonomic Solutions for Parallel and Distributed Data Stream Processing

Workshop on Autonomic Solutions for Parallel and Distributed Data Stream Processing (Auto-DaSP)

Workshop Description

Auto-DaSP is a forum for researchers and practitioners working on parallel and autonomic solutions for Data Stream Processing applications, frameworks, and programming support tools. The data streaming domain belongs to the Big Data ecosystem, where the so-called data velocity, i.e., the rate at which data arrive at the system for processing, represents one of the most challenging aspects to be addressed in the design of applications and frameworks. High-volume data streams can be efficiently handled through the adoption of novel high-performance solutions targeting today's commodity parallel hardware. However, despite the large computing power offered by the affordable hardware available nowadays, high-performance data streaming solutions need to be equipped with smart logics in order to adapt the framework/application configuration to rapidly changing execution conditions and workloads. This turns out in mechanisms and strategies to adapt the queries and operators placement policies, intra-operator parallelism degree, scheduling strategies, load shedding rate and so forth, and fosters novel interdisciplinary approaches that exploit Control Theory and Artificial Intelligence methods. The workshop calls the attention of the data stream processing and the distributed and parallel computing research communities in order to stimulate integrated approaches between these two disciplines.

The third edition of the International Workshop on Autonomic Solutions for Parallel and Distributed Data Stream Processing (Auto-DaSP 2019) was held in Göttingen, Germany. Auto-DaSP 2019 and all previous editions of the workshop were organized in conjunction with the Euro-Par annual series of international conferences. The format of the workshop included an invited presentation by Prof. Marco Aldinucci (University of Turin, Italy) titled "The European High-Performance Computing EuroHPC JU initiative explained," followed by technical presentations of accepted papers, and concluded with a tutorial session by Dr. Daniele De Sensi (University of Pisa, Italy) titled "Adding autonomic and power-aware capabilities to parallel streaming applications with the Nornir framework."

The workshop was attended by around 15 people on average. This year we received five submissions for reviews, and all of them were accepted to be presented at the workshop after an accurate and thorough peer-review process. The review process focused on the quality of the papers, their scientific novelty, and applicability to existing Data Stream Processing problems and frameworks. The acceptance of the papers was the result of the reviewers' discussion and agreement.

Finally, we would like to thank the Auto-DaSP 2019 Program Committee, whose members made the workshop possible with their rigorous and timely review process. We would also like to thank Euro-Par for hosting the workshop, and the Euro-Par workshop chairs for the valuable help and support.

Organization

Program Chairs

Valeria Cardellini	University of Rome Tor Vergata, Italy
Gabriele Mencagli	University of Pisa, Italy
Massimo Torquati	University of Pisa, Italy

Program Committee

Marcos Assuncao	Inria, LIP, ENS Lyon, France
Tiziano De Matteis	ETH Zurich, Switzerland
Daniele De Sensi	University of Pisa, Italy
Dalvan Griebler	PUCRS/SETREM, Brazil
Matteo Nardelli	University of Rome Tor Vergata, Italy
Marco Danelutto	University of Pisa, Italy
J. Daniel Garcia	University Carlos III of Madrid, Spain
Marco Aldinucci	University of Torino, Italy
Daniele Bonetta	Oracle Labs, Switzerland
Daniele Buono	IBM, USA
Dave Lillethun	Seattle University, USA

Parallelization of Massive Multiway Stream Joins on Manycore CPUs

Constantin Pohl[✉][iD] and Kai-Uwe Sattler[iD]

Databases and Information Systems Group, TU Ilmenau, Ilmenau, Germany
{constantin.pohl,kus}@tu-ilmenau.de

Abstract. Joining a high number of data streams efficiently in terms of required memory and CPU time still poses a challenge. While binary join trees are very common in database systems, they are mostly unusable for streaming queries with tight latency constraints when the number of streaming sources is increasing. Multiway stream joins, on the other hand, are very suitable for this task since they are mostly independent of the non-optimal ordering of join operators or huge intermediate join results.

In this paper, we discuss challenges but also opportunities for multiway stream joins for modern hardware, especially manycore processors. We describe different parallelization and optimization strategies to allow a streaming query to join up to 256 streams on a single CPU while keeping individual tuple response time and also memory footprint low. Our results show that a multiway join can perform magnitudes faster than a binary join tree. In addition, further tuning for efficient parallelism can improve performance again for a factor up to a magnitude.

Keywords: Multiway · Join · Stream processing · Manycore · Xeon Phi

1 Introduction

Smart devices connected with each other are in the ascendant today, often simply referred to as IoT. Gathering information from those devices and correlating it for further processing can be found anywhere, like for smart homes, networks, or industry. Current solutions often store all collected data into cloud services for later analytics, since the amount of data and information is huge. Nevertheless, lots of research is done recently for processing this data *online* in real-time via different stream processing systems.

In this paper, we aim to join huge numbers of data streams from different independent sources. The main challenge lies in efficient parallelism to keep response time for individual tuples low. Binary join operator trees usually save intermediate join results or pointers in own tables for probing at a higher level in the tree, leading to an intense memory overhead the deeper the tree gets. Even the response time can become very bad if a tuple has to be joined and inserted repeatedly up the whole tree before producing any final join result.

© Springer Nature Switzerland AG 2020
U. Schwardmann et al. (Eds.): Euro-Par 2019 Workshops, LNCS 11997, pp. 5–16, 2020.
https://doi.org/10.1007/978-3-030-48340-1_1

Therefore, we focus on multiway stream join algorithms, since a join operator that has access to all input streams provides many opportunities to optimize latency and its memory footprint. A key for good performance is the avoidance of materialized intermediate results as well as long join probe sequences that would fail anyway because of a missing key match in one of the tables. Our general approach follows the *AMJoin* algorithm [5], where joins are only performed when success is guaranteed. We investigated different ways of parallelization and added optimizations for a multiway join, leading to drastic performance improvements overall. Our measurements are taken on a Xeon Phi *Knights Landing* (KNL) manycore CPU, which allows us to scale our join implementation up to 256 concurrently running input streams, showing the effectiveness of our approach. In this paper, we answer the following questions:

– How bad becomes a binary join operator tree compared to a multiway join algorithm under high numbers of data streams that must be joined?
– Which opportunities are given by a multiway join to allow efficient scaling on a manycore processor?
– How to parallelize a multiway join without harming performance through necessary synchronization efforts?

2   Related Work

One of the first non-blocking **binary** join algorithms was the Pipelining Hash Join from Wilschut et al. [11], later referred to as *Symmetric Hash Join* (SHJ). It builds and probes two hash tables continuously as elements from two streams arrive, producing results immediately. In general, the SHJ is a good choice because of its simple but effective algorithm, further described in Sect. 3.1. In this paper, we will use our implementation[1] of the SHJ as a candidate for a binary join between two input streams.

Based on the SHJ, the later *XJoin* from Urhan et al. [9] solved the problem of hash tables that do not fit into main memory. Instead of simply storing tuples of a stream inside one big hash table, tuples are inserted into partitions consisting of a memory-resident and a disk-resident portion, allowing to switch tuples between RAM and disk. The key idea behind this work is to use possible delays from a dynamic data stream (where less or no tuples arrive) for processing disk-resident tuples.

Other non-blocking binary join algorithms of the last decade focused on the exploitation of modern hardware, like GPUs or multicore CPUs. The *CellJoin* from Gedik et al. [3] partitions the window of one stream, assigning partitions to available CPU cores. Teubner et al. [8] developed the *Handshake Join*, where windows from both stream sources are joined in local partitions by cores close to each other. Buono et al. [2] investigated parallelization strategies for both of these algorithms with respect to multicore CPUs and sliding windows, however, a demonstration of performance for a multiway join execution (hypercubes) was

---

[1] Open source, implemented in *PipeFabric*: https://github.com/dbis-ilm/pipefabric.

left for future work. On the GPU side, the *HELLS-Join* was proposed by Karnagel et al. [4] to utilize the high bandwidth and processing power for joining large windows.

One prominent example for early **multiway** stream joins is the *MJoin* from Viglas et al. [10], extending the idea of the SHJ and XJoin in such a way that it accepts more than two input streams. This allows on the one hand to avoid deep binary trees that would possibly lead to very bad latencies of individual tuples. On the other hand, join reordering is not necessary, which is a fundamental optimization problem also for relational database systems until nowadays.

The *AMJoin* from Kwon et al. [5] picks up the idea of the MJoin, extending it with additional data structures to guarantee join execution only when a result can be computed successfully. In this paper, we enhanced the AMJoin algorithm (further described in Sect. 3.2) for massive parallelism provided by manycore CPUs, leading to the **OptAMJoin** algorithm. It should be mentioned that a related join concept can also be found for relational database systems joining tables instead of streams, using *Concise Hash Tables* (CHT) [1].

We decided to stick with the AMJoin, since it allows joining different[2] streams algorithmically independent from the underlying hardware. For the rest of this work, we assume that streams have different schemas and cannot simply be unified together into single streams.

3   Binary vs. Multiway Stream Join

The goal of both join variants is obviously the same. Two or more data streams provide tuples continuously and the join operator has to match partners, often based on key values. The main difference to relational joins is the requirement to be *non-blocking*, which means that a stream join must produce results even when more tuples are incoming in future. If the number of streams is more than two, binary join operators have to cascade, where the output of a join is the input of the next join (see Fig. 1, tables are denoted as T_x, while x describes the stream(s) whose tuples are stored in T).

While this is common in relational database systems even for hundreds of tables, it poses a serious challenge for stream processing under strong latency constraints. Multiway joins, on the other hand, can connect all inputs in one single operator (see Fig. 2), allowing a much better *scaling out* theoretically. This scaling can be achieved by addressing the order of probes as well as the materialization of intermediate results efficiently. For the evaluation in Sect. 5, we use the previously mentioned *SHJ* as a representation of a typical binary stream join operator and the enhanced *AMJoin* algorithm as multiway join, along with optimizations and different parallelization schemas to improve performance.

---

[2] For instance, assume each of $n > 2$ streams has a different tuple schema.

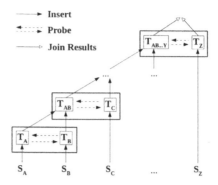

Fig. 1. Binary join tree (SHJ)

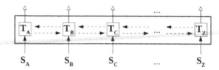

Fig. 2. Basic multiway stream join

3.1 SHJ

The SHJ uses two hash tables internally for storing incoming tuples. When a tuple arrives from any of the two sources, the algorithm basically follows three steps:

- Inserting the tuple in the corresponding hash table,
- probing the other hash table afterward for matches,
- materializing the joined result tuples, if matches were found.

If window semantics are applied, which means that a tuple is invalidated later and will not contribute to future join results anymore, deletions are also occurring for the hash tables. It is a simple but effective algorithm, even it is not very well suited for joining many concurrent sources because of its limitation on exactly two input streams, leading to deep trees otherwise (see Fig. 1). The deeper a tree gets, the worse the individual response time and memory footprint become.

3.2 AMJoin

The key concept of the AMJoin is the complete avoidance of unnecessary join probes as well as no materialization of intermediate results. It guarantees that a probe is only executed when a final join result will be produced, therefore no intermediate results are stored, overall contention is kept low, and join ordering does not matter (all tuples from each source are stored only once). This is achieved by one additional data structure, the so-called *Bit-vector Hash Table* (BiHT) which stores pairs of join key hash values $h(k)$ and bit vectors v, one vector v_k per hashed key. Each bit vector v_k stores one bit per input stream, indicating whether the join key from the stream is present (1) or absent (0). Obviously, a join can successfully be executed only if all bits in a vector are set to 1. Since the AMJoin extends the MJoin, it also contains a memory overflow mechanism where tuples are spilled to disk when the main memory size is exceeded. However, for our later experiments, we omit this phase since it is not notably influenced by parallelization strategies of this paper.

4   Optimization Techniques

In the original paper from Kwon et al. [5], the AMJoin was executed on a two-core CPU with 4 GB RAM. In their experiments, they set the number of input streams to 5. With these settings, the contention problem of concurrently running streams on different CPU cores was mostly avoided. Our implementation follows the general idea of the AMJoin along with major additions, leading to an *optimized version* being able to scale up to hundreds of streams with minimal synchronization and memory overhead.

4.1   OptAMJoin

The main changes in our optimized implementation base on the following observations:

(1) Bit Vector vs. Atomic Counter. For a join success, all bits in the vector must be 1. If there is a 0 anywhere in the vector, the current join step can be aborted (mismatch) regardless of the bit position in the vector (where the 0 was found). This leads to the possibility of using a single counter that is incremented and decremented in a threadsafe way. This allows join probes to check if the counter is equal to the number of input streams instead of iterating over (many) concurrently accessed bits. In addition, it reduces the memory usage for higher stream numbers. However, this assumption is only true for primary key join attributes, else thread-local handling of duplicates is necessary to avoid wrong counter results.

If a stream fails and does not deliver tuples, no join output will be produced (since a position in the bit vector will never be 1 and the counter will miss an increment). To solve that problem, it is also possible to specify a counter threshold to execute outer joins (leaving a missing value as *null* or using dummy elements) to enforce a join after a timeout of a stream.

(2) Hash Table vs. Array. Usually, tuples are stored in a hash table for fast insertions, lookups, and deletions. Nevertheless, if the key distribution is dense enough, it can be very beneficial to use a simple array instead of a hash table [6]. Payloads of tuples can be stored at the key position in the array, greatly reducing necessary memory usage since the key is not stored anymore. Further redirections of pointers to buckets in the hash table are also avoided, improving execution time. If the key distribution becomes sparse, however, many array positions stay empty, wasting memory without compression techniques.

(3) Locks/Latches vs. Lock-Free Containers. Under high contention of many threads accessing and modifying the same values, synchronization via locking reduces the parallelism advantage tremendously. Even if collisions on individual elements may be rare, acquiring and releasing locks or latches unnecessarily hurts performance. There are many implementations available for lock-free concurrent data structures (e.g. Intel TBB) that are well suited to parallelize the AMJoin.

In our later experiments, we run both versions of the AMJoin, our implementation of the original work as well as our optimized version, OptAMJoin, with further enhancements regarding parallelization.

4.2   Parallelization Strategies

To achieve good performance results on modern CPUs, it is inevitable to utilize multiple cores for processing. This is even more important for manycore CPUs since high core numbers usually lead to low clock rates and thus to bad single-threaded execution times. However, the parallelization of stream joins poses new challenges mainly because of the non-blocking property. A stream join is executed continuously, so there are no phases that can be finished one after another.

In this section, we describe three parallelization strategies that can be applied to a multiway stream join, namely *data parallelism*, the *SPSC paradigm*, and *shared data structures*. They can also be combined basically, however, for our evaluation we use them separately under the assumption that each stream producing tuples has its own thread.

(1) Data Parallelism. To reduce the pressure of many concurrent data sources delivering tuples to a single multiway join operator, it is possible to partition incoming tuples based on their join attribute value. This allows running multiple instances of the join in parallel, each responsible for a certain key range (see Fig. 3).

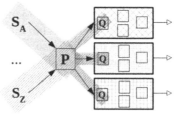

Fig. 3. Data parallelism

The advantage of this strategy is that no synchronization between join instances (the squared boxes in Fig. 3) is necessary and the amount of work can easily be distributed and scaled out. On the other hand, achieving a good load balancing can be difficult, especially in skewed streams. There are approaches to solve the load balancing problem, though. In addition, the partitioning step P requires additional computations and also efficient tuple exchange to partitions (Q), else synchronization efforts are necessary within a join instance.

(2) SPSC Paradigm. The *Single Producer, Single Consumer* (SPSC) concept is well known in the field of lock-free programming. It means that only one thread is writing into a data structure while only one other thread is reading from it. A common example is the SPSC queue, often realized as a ring buffer, avoiding locks on a higher level completely. Figure 4 shows the fundamental idea for the multiway join.

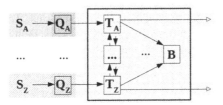

Fig. 4. SPSC paradigm

When each data stream is running independently by a separate thread, it is possible to add an SPSC queue Q per stream to efficiently exchange tuples between streams and the join operator (run by one single thread). The advantage is that the join can be managed without any further internal synchronization, avoiding the contention dilemma when scaling out to many input streams. Nevertheless, it adds a potential delay in processing for the SPSC queues and the join operator thread can be overwhelmed when streams are bursty or in too high numbers.

(3) Shared Data Structures. A very straightforward idea is to share the data structures like hash tables and BiHT between all input streams (see Fig. 5).

Any overhead through additional data structures (like exchange queues) or computational efforts (partitioning) can be avoided. This comes with a cost, efficient synchronization is an absolute necessity to primarily achieve correct results (no duplicates or missing join results) and secondarily get good scaling performance for high stream numbers. For our experiments, we use lock-free concurrent hash tables and vectors from Intel TBB to minimize blocking time for threads.

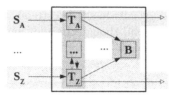

Fig. 5. Shared data structures

5   Experimental Evaluation

In this section, we demonstrate the effectiveness of our parallelization techniques as well as our optimizations, along with the assumption that binary join trees are not suitable for joining many concurrent data streams. To allow a high scaling and pressure without interferences through network delays between sockets or machines, we use a manycore CPU with 64 cores, further described below.

5.1   Setup

On the hardware side, we ran all experiments on a Xeon Phi KNL 7210 processor, which has 64 cores supporting up to 4 threads each. It is clocked up to 1.5 GHz, has 96 GB DDR4 main memory size, and utilizes the AVX512 instruction set. The cluster mode is set to SNC4, while the MCDRAM is configured in flat mode. All code is compiled with the Intel compiler version 17.0.6, most important flags set are $-O3$ and $-xMIC_AVX512$. Our measurements are taken from our stream processing engine *PipeFabric*[3]. All tuples are fully allocated in main memory (no disk involved). The measurements start when the first tuple is produced by any stream and stopped when all expected join results are materialized.

5.2   Workload and Test Cases

Since we focus on joining many independent data streams, the query only contains the join operation and can be formulated like the following (Stream SQL):

SELECT *
FROM Stream $S_1, S_2, ... , S_{N-1}, S_N$
SLIDING WINDOW(1000000)
WHERE S_1.key = S_2.key
    AND ...
    AND S_{N-1}.key = S_N.key

For the join, we distinguish between a concatenation of SHJ operators (binary join tree), the AMJoin, and the optimized variant, OptAMJoin, that includes all optimization techniques from Sect. 4.1 (like using arrays instead of tables). In addition, we use the different parallelization strategies from the previous Sect. 4.2

---

[3] Open Source https://github.com/dbis-ilm/pipefabric.

on all join algorithms. For reducing the possible result space going through all combinations of joins, parallelization strategies, and parameters, we decided to discard variants that do not contribute to new insights.

The tuples per stream are shuffled individually, therefore it is guaranteed that each stream produces tuples in an order completely independent from other streams. One million tuples per stream are kept relevant by using a sliding window operator, which invalidates the oldest tuple for each new tuple that arrives after window size is reached. Tuples from input streams are <key,value> pairs with 8 byte each, joining directly over equal keys (equi-join[4]) with one million distinct key values, beginning with zero and incrementing by one. The binary join tree with SHJ operators is realized as an optimal left deep tree since this structure is easily expendable without hitting performance gaps (e.g. when the tree finally grows up a new level, becoming imbalanced) and because left deep trees are also often found in the literature [7]. The maximum number of streams is 256 since the KNL supports a maximum of 256 threads running in parallel (hyperthreading).

We further distinguish between weak and strong scaling. Weak scaling is achieved by running each stream as a single thread, increasing the number of streams to join. For strong scaling, we fixed the stream number to 8. Based on the scale factor, we spawn multiple instances of join queries running independently, concatenating their results under synchronization., i.e. a scale factor of 4 means that 4 times a join between 8 streams is performed at the same time, merging results of all four instances.

5.3   Results and Discussion

First, we increase the number of threads and measure the overall latency per joined output tuple, following the *shared data structures* parallelization. Each input tuple produces exactly one joined output tuple independent from the stream number. To give an example, if 100 streams are joined and each stream produces one million tuples, the join will produce one million final results. However, for the sake of simplicity we do not consider distractions of window semantics (e.g. a key is invalidated by one stream before the same key arrives on another stream). Figure 6 contains the results of our measurements for weak and strong scaling.

While the performance of a single SHJ operator is comparable to a 2-way join (obviously), the average latency per output tuple increases drastically when the binary join tree gets deeper. Each tuple that arrives from one stream has to traverse the join operators sequentially - in the best case, it has only to join with one table for final results (top of the tree), in the worst case it has to be probed and joined $n - 1$ times (with n being the number of stream sources) for cases where the tuple arrives at the bottom of the tree and its key has matches in all other hash tables. After reaching 96 streams with the SHJ, the main memory capacity of 96 GB is exceeded (out of memory) because of storing all intermediate tuples.

---

[4] Theta-joins are possible by comparing to other bitvectors also, but they would require more computational efforts as well as more synchronization.

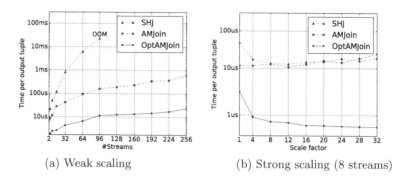

(a) Weak scaling (b) Strong scaling (8 streams)

Fig. 6. Execution of joins under varying numbers of threads

The AMJoin scales much better since it avoids unnecessary probes and just updates the BiHT after it is inserted into its corresponding hash table. With our optimizations, the OptAMJoin behavior is similar to the original AMJoin but approximately one magnitude faster. It is clear that the performance can only get worse with more data streams since the degree of contention and computational efforts for joining is constantly rising. Adding more threads to the same join (strong scaling) leads to a performance improvement for the optimized AMJoin, but the SHJ, as well as original AMJoin, cannot benefit that much due to locks and more expensive synchronized accesses. In addition, NUMA effects occur for high numbers of threads (due to the KNL architecture), since threads share the same tables and vectors under strong scaling.

Next, we measured the behavior for OptAMJoin using all parallelization techniques from the previous section. We omit results of both other algorithms for reasons of space, however, the overall performance of the different parallelization strategies has similar behavior. While increasing the number of input streams, the number of partitions for the *data parallelism* strategy is fixed to 4 partitions. Each of the four partitions is controlled by a single thread, while all stream threads write their tuples into the partition queues (as shown in Fig. 3). Our results for weak and strong scaling can be found in Fig. 7.

Interestingly, the variant of using SPSC queues is closely equal to the partitioning strategy in terms of performance for Fig. 7a. This means that a single thread is able to insert and update its join state independent from the number of streams, at least until 256. The lock-free shared data structures provide the best performance, since the chance of collision within a hash table is rare, especially when keys are shuffled and randomly arriving. The strong scaling shown in Fig. 7b finally shows a difference between data parallelism and the usage of SPSC queues. For a scale factor of more than 20, however, this can be explained by the number of real threads used. For data parallelism with 8 streams and 4 partitions, 12 threads are used per scale factor. With 256 threads on the KNL, context switching starts when scaling to more than $\frac{256}{12}$ (=21) query instances.

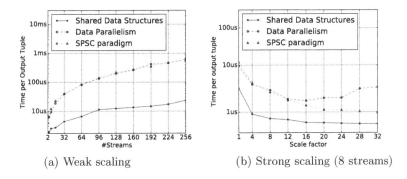

(a) Weak scaling   (b) Strong scaling (8 streams)

Fig. 7. Parallelization strategies for OptAMJoin

Finally, we analyzed the amount of memory used to run a join over a various stream number, assuming one million tuples per input stream. The overall calculated numbers can be found in Table 1. It can easily be seen that a binary join tree with the materialization of intermediate results (SHJ) is no good candidate for scaling out on a manycore CPU.

Table 1. Memory footprint for data structures [GB]

Streams	SHJ	AMJoin	OptAMJoin
2	0.260	0.253	0.106
8	1.646	0.745	0.419
16	4.328	1.400	0.836
64	40.449	5.334	3.339
256	528.253	21.079	13.353

Based on our results, we can summarize that a multiway stream join with fully shared data structures delivers the best performance overall. This may change with skewed streams where some key values appear on a higher frequency, increasing contention. Nevertheless, a multiway join is absolutely superior to a binary join tree for high stream numbers that cannot simply be unified.

6 Conclusion

In this paper, we investigated stream join performance for manycore CPUs, posing the challenge of efficient parallelization of joins on high stream numbers. While binary join algorithms can be found in literature frequently, fulfilling their role even for joining a few streams sequentially, they fail any latency requirements when the number of different streams to join goes up. Based on the idea of minimizing avoidable join steps, especially joining intermediate results that are never used for final join tuples, we analyzed the AMJoin from Kwon et al. [5] since it looks very promising to scale out on modern hardware.

We optimized the implementation regarding memory usage and response time on the basis of our insights, being able to reduce the memory footprint by around 40% and execution time roughly up to a magnitude. In addition to the optimizations, we described three different strategies to parallelize the multiway join operator. Although the straightforward idea of sharing all data structures between all threads shows superior performance, there might be use cases (skewness, further scaling) where the other techniques will shine.

In our future work, we would like to investigate the impact of high-bandwidth memory (HBM) on the various data structures used in the multiway join operators, since the KNL processor has 16 GB HBM available which was currently unused for our measurements. Furthermore, instead of tuple-wise processing for minimized individual tuple latency, we plan to add batching support for joining where latency constraints are not that relevant overall. This allows improving the utilization of the AVX512 registers through vectorization, ideally resulting in an even better performance advantage.

References

1. Barber, R., et al.: Memory-efficient hash joins. PVLDB **8**(4), 353–364 (2014)
2. Buono, D., Matteis, T.D., Mencagli, G.: A high-throughput and low-latency parallelization of window-based stream joins on multicores. In: IEEE ISPA, pp. 117–126 (2014)
3. Gedik, B., Bordawekar, R., Yu, P.S.: Cell join: a parallel stream join operator for the cell processor. VLDB J. **18**(2), 501–519 (2009)
4. Karnagel, T., Habich, D., Schlegel, B., Lehner, W.: The HELLS-join: a heterogeneous stream join for extremely large windows. In: DaMoN, p. 2 (2013)
5. Kwon, T., Kim, H.G., Kim, M., Son, J.H.: AMJoin: an advanced join algorithm for multiple data streams using a bit-vector hash table. IEICE Trans. **92−D**(7), 1429–1434 (2009)
6. Schuh, S., Chen, X., Dittrich, J.: An experimental comparison of thirteen relational equi-joins in main memory. In: SIGMOD, pp. 1961–1976 (2016)
7. Selinger, P.G., Astrahan, M.M., Chamberlin, D.D., Lorie, R.A., Price, T.G.: Access path selection in a relational database management system. In: SIGMOD, pp. 23–34 (1979)
8. Teubner, J., Müller, R.: How soccer players would do stream joins. In: SIGMOD, pp. 625–636 (2011)
9. Urhan, T., Franklin, M.J.: XJoin: a reactively-scheduled pipelined join operator. IEEE Data Eng. Bull. **23**(2), 27–33 (2000)
10. Viglas, S., Naughton, J.F., Burger, J.: Maximizing the output rate of multi-way join queries over streaming information sources. In: VLDB, pp. 285–296 (2003)
11. Wilschut, A.N., Apers, P.M.G.: Dataflow query execution in a parallel main-memory environment. In: PDIS, pp. 68–77 (1991)

Adaptive Crown Scheduling for Streaming Tasks on Many-Core Systems with Discrete DVFS

Christoph Kessler[1] , Sebastian Litzinger[2(✉)] , and Jörg Keller[2]

[1] Linköping University, Linköping, Sweden
christoph.kessler@liu.se
[2] FernUniversität in Hagen, Hagen, Germany
{sebastian.litzinger,joerg.keller}@fernuni-hagen.de

Abstract. We consider temperature-aware, energy-efficient scheduling of streaming applications with parallelizable tasks and throughput requirement on multi-/many-core embedded devices with discrete dynamic voltage and frequency scaling (DVFS). Given the few available discrete frequency levels, we provide the task schedule in a conservative and a relaxed form so that using them adaptively decreases power consumption, i.e. lowers chip temperature, without hurting throughput in the long run. We support our proposal by a toolchain to compute the schedules and evaluate the power reduction with synthetic task sets.

Keywords: Streaming task graphs · Energy-efficient scheduling · Frequency scaling · Temperature control · Embedded multicore

1 Introduction

Data stream processing is an important computation paradigm in edge computing devices for the Internet of Things. A continuous stream of data elements coming from data sensors should be processed as close to the data source as possible, due to its high volume and velocity. An example is the continuous preprocessing of camera or vehicle sensor data. Such devices are often constrained both in power usage (battery driven and/or using passive cooling), communication bandwidth/latency, and available memory. With high raw data rates but limited data storage available, data must be compacted at low power consumption on the device before sending it to a central observer, e.g. some cloud server. Low-power designs favor many-core designs with lots of simple cores running at moderate frequency, which often can be selected by the application.

Stream processing programs are usually expressed as a graph of persistent streaming tasks that read in packets of data from their input channels, process one packet at a time, and write a packet of output data to output channels, thus forwarding it to data consumer tasks or to the program's result channel(s). By providing sufficient FIFO buffering capacity along all channels (thus following

© Springer Nature Switzerland AG 2020
U. Schwardmann et al. (Eds.): Euro-Par 2019 Workshops, LNCS 11997, pp. 17–29, 2020.
https://doi.org/10.1007/978-3-030-48340-1_2

the Kahn Process Network model [9]), the stream program execution can be software-pipelined such that all instances of streaming tasks for different data packets in the same round in the steady state of the pipeline can execute concurrently (see Fig. 1). On a many-core system, these can then be scheduled to different cores or core groups so that the makespan for one round is kept low and the workload is well balanced. Streaming tasks perform a certain amount of work per input packet and can be internally parallel, i.e., run on multiple cores to speed up one instance of their execution. For example, a *moldable* task can use any number of cores that must be determined before the task is executed.

We consider the static scheduling problem for the steady state of the streaming pipeline, i.e., for a set of independent streaming task instances, see Fig. 1. This problem includes three subproblems: determining the core allocation for each moldable task, its mapping to a core subset, and selection of its execution frequency.[1] Core allocation and frequency selection impact a task's execution time and energy usage, while the mapping impacts the entire schedule's load balance and thus its makespan, which also impacts the overall energy consumption (as idle cores also take some energy and imbalance may enforce higher frequency to meet deadlines). If the program should keep a certain (average) processing rate over time, this translates into a certain makespan per steady state round. Given this user requirement, the goal is to minimize the overall energy consumption.

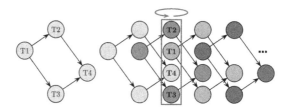

Fig. 1. Left: A streaming task graph with 4 streaming tasks. Right: The red box shows the steady state of the software-pipelined execution, where all task instances in one round are independent, i.e. belong to different instances of the graph.

The three subproblems are strongly interdependent and any consecutive approach considering them one at a time can thus introduce inefficiencies. *Crown scheduling* [12] is a scheduling technique for one round of the steady state that solves core allocation, mapping and frequency selection together, either by solving an integer linear programming model generated from the task and machine descriptions, or by using heuristics. By unique temporal ordering of core subset use (cf. Fig. 2), the puzzle problem is avoided. Based on previous work on power modeling e.g. for the ARM big.LITTLE architecture [5], we found that

---

[1] Moreover, the executions of the mapped tasks must be ordered in time in a kind of "puzzle" such that the total execution time is minimized or below a given threshold.

the need to select from a fixed, small set of discrete voltage/frequency levels has the largest impact on the resulting schedule's energy consumption.

To relax this limitation in crown scheduling, we provide *two*, structurally similar, crown schedules: a *conservative* schedule, which respects the makespan constraint (required average throughput rate) but possibly leads to increased chip temperature when high frequency levels are used by many tasks, and a *relaxed* schedule that slightly increases the acceptable makespan (i.e., reduces the throughput) in favor of selecting a lower frequency level for some tasks, thus being more energy-efficient. At runtime, a simple dynamic control mechanism adaptively switches between the conservative and relaxed schedule to maintain, on average, the best combination of data processing rate and energy efficiency, thus operating on average at lower power (and thus lower chip temperature). The dynamic switching also allows to dynamically adapt the schedule's power usage to the current chip temperature to avoid temperature problems when unforeseen external factors influence temperature (e.g., direct sunshine exposure).

In particular, we make the following contributions: We identify key properties of streaming tasks that impact throughput and energy efficiency, and present both optimal and greedy algorithms that derive a relaxed crown schedule from a conservative crown schedule. We present the control mechanism for dynamically switching between the schedules, and show how to make it adaptive to the current chip temperature. Finally, we demonstrate the potential for improving energy efficiency over the conservative schedule for a number of synthetic benchmarks and a real-world power model for ARM A15 cores in big.LITTLE processors.

The remainder of this paper is organized as follows: Sect. 2 introduces the processor, task and power models and the crown scheduling principle. Section 3 explains how the conservative and relaxed crown schedule to be used in our approach are determined. Section 4 describes the adaptive control algorithm and extends it for temperature-aware scheduling. In Sect. 5, we present preliminary results. Related work is discussed in Sect. 6. Section 7 concludes the paper.

2   Background

Processor Model. We are given a generic multi-/many-core CPU architecture with p cores. Let $P = \{P_1, ..., P_p\}$ denote the set of all p cores available[2]. We assume that the $K > 1$ frequency levels of each of the p cores can be set independently at runtime to any value in the discrete frequency set $F = \{f_1, .., f_K\}$, with index set $F' = \{1..K\}$. Frequencies f_k are normalized relative to the lowest possible frequency, i.e., $f_1 = 1$. We assume that the voltage is automatically co-scaled for each frequency level to its minimal possible value. We assume that the runtime of any task performing work λ scales with the frequency $f \in F$, i.e., is proportional to λ/f, which is true for computational loads (see e.g. experiments in Holmbacka *et al.* [5]). In order to model computations that are less sensitive to frequency scaling, we will model the runtime for each task depending on the task's type.

---

[2] Heterogeneous cores are possible, but we assume identical cores here for simplicity.

Task Model. We are given n task instances $T = \{\tau_1, ..., \tau_n\}$ to be executed in one round of the steady state of the software pipeline for a streaming task set. Given an expected throughput goal such as X rounds (e.g., input images processed) per second for the steady state of the pipeline, being faster than $M = 1/X$ seconds per round is of no use and we instead optimize for energy under the (soft) deadline constraint that each round has M time units to finish execution.

A task τ_j performs λ_j *work*, i.e., the work it needs to achieve takes λ_j units of time when running on one core at the lowest possible frequency. A task τ_j is *moldable, partially moldable* or *sequential*, depending on its specified *maximum width*, i.e., the maximum number W_j of cores that can participate in running task τ_j in parallel. If τ_j is *moldable*, it can run on any strictly positive, unbounded integer number of cores ($W_j = \infty$), but it cannot allocate more or fewer cores dynamically, i.e., while the application is running. If τ_j is *partially moldable*, then its maximum width $W_j \geq 2$ is finite. Finally, if task τ_j is *sequential*, then it can run only on one core ($W_j = 1$). Each task also has a task type tt_j from a set V of known task types. Here, we define tasks τ_j with $tt_j = 0$ as memory-bound. They are not affected by frequency switching like computation-bound tasks.

Let $e_j(q)$ be the given *parallel efficiency* of task τ_j (i.e., parallel speedup divided by the number of used cores) when running on $1 \leq q \leq W_j$ cores. The parallel efficiency can either be measured or derived from algorithmic task properties, such as predicted non-parallelizable work and predicted communication/synchronization overhead in relation to parallelizable computational work (cf. Sect. 5). By convention, we have $e_j(1) = 1$ for any task τ_j; in most cases, we can expect $0 < e_j(q) < 1$ for all $q > 1$, but allow $e_j(q) \geq 1$ for $q > 1$ to denote, e.g., speedup anomalies. In particular, we do *not* assume e_j to decrease monotonically. Where context allows, we write j to denote τ_j.

Time, Power and Energy Model. The optimization problem consists in assigning to each task $\tau_j \in T$ a number w_j of cores ($w_j \leq W_j$), a core subset $R_j \in P$ (where $|R_j| = w_j$) and a frequency $f_j \in F$ so that all tasks τ_j complete before the deadline M, and minimizing the overall energy consumption. We model the average power consumption of a moldable task empirically, based on samples taken by micro-benchmarking on a real processor (e.g. for A15 in [5]), provided in a table indexed by task type, frequency, and number of cores used.

For task τ_j, the energy consumption depends on τ_j's power consumption, the number of cores w_j running it and its execution time with w_j cores at frequency f_j. If task τ_j runs with w_j cores at frequency $f_j \in F$, then its execution time is

$$t_j(w_j, f_j) = \frac{\lambda_j}{f_j \cdot e_j(w_j) \cdot w_j} \tag{1}$$

if it is a computational task. We replace f_j by $\min\{f_j, f_{K/2}\}$ for memory-bound tasks to indicate that it will not profit from high frequencies.

A task's energy consumption is its average power multiplied with its execution time and the number of cores it runs on. The total energy consumption of a scheduled task set is the sum of energy consumed at idle time[3] and the accumulated energy consumption of all tasks. The optimization target is to arrange the tasks in such a way over the cores and the runtime that a non-overlapping execution meets the deadline and minimizes energy consumption.

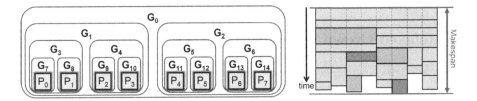

Fig. 2. Left: The core partitioning of a classic crown scheduler (a balanced binary crown) for 8 cores. — Right: A crown schedule for an 8-core machine.

Crown Scheduling is a scheduling technique that introduces a structural constraint on core allocation in order to make the joint optimization of core allocation, mapping and frequency level assignment for the task instances in the steady state of the streaming pipeline computationally feasible [12]. Crown schedulers hierarchically partition the set of p cores of a target architecture by recursive binary decomposition into $2p - 1$ core groups $G_0, ..., G_{2p-2}$ (see Fig. 2), where a core group includes cores and all associated hardware resources such as caches or local memories shared or owned by cores in the group. The *root group* G_0 includes all p cores. It is decomposed into 2 disjoint subgroups (for a balanced binary decomposition, of $p/2$ cores each), and so on until we obtain p subgroups of 1 core each. We refer to the set of all core groups defined by such tree-based decomposition as the *crown*. Figure 2 shows a balanced binary *crown* for $p = 8$ cores, containing 15 core groups of 4 different sizes.

A crown schedule maps each streaming task to exactly one of the $2p - 1$ core groups, thus allocating to it all the cores of that group. The crown structure and in particular the restriction of the number of possible core allocation sizes from p to $\log_2 p$ for each task reduces the number of possible mapping targets from 2^p to $2p - 1 = O(p)$ different core subsets, and therefore limits considerably the solution search space. Moreover, within one round of the steady state of the streaming pipeline, every core group and every core execute its assigned (instances of) streaming tasks in the (same) order of *non-increasing width* (see Fig. 2 (right)), which eliminates external fragmentation (idle times due to waiting for other cores to start a new parallel task) between tasks *within* the schedule for one round of the steady state, and also makes frequency assignment of a task mapped to one core group independent of the frequency assignment of any task mapped to a disjoint (e.g., sibling) core group. Melot *et al.* [13] show that the penalty due to this artificial restriction on core allocation may be significant in contrived worst case scenarios but is negligible for practical task sets.

---

[3] We do not model the idle power further as it did not play a role in our experiments.

Like other frequency-aware static schedulers for parallel tasks (cf. Sect. 6), crown scheduling must bow to the necessity to use one of the discrete frequency levels for each task. The loss in energy efficiency compared to an ideal solution based on continuous frequencies will be significant when the number of tasks is small and there are only few DVFS levels to choose from. In this work, we present a general method for crown schedules to overcome this limitation.

3   Relaxed Crown Schedule Adaptation

A conservative crown schedule will fulfill the deadline constraint, i.e., the time for one round will not exceed the user-specified limit M. Due to the few available discrete frequency levels, a conservative crown schedule is likely to contain significant idle times, especially for streaming programs with few tasks. In many cases, this implies that the makespan is actually lower than the deadline M (i.e., the schedule overfulfills the throughput requirement).

Crown scheduling does not minimize makespan but energy. We denote the energy consumption of the previous schedule by E^*. We can derive a makespan-optimal schedule for energy budget E^* by using an integer linear program where energy as target function and deadline as constraint for makespan are exchanged. From the resulting makespan $M^* = (1 - \epsilon)M$, we derive $\epsilon = 1 - M^*/M$. We use this S^c as the *conservative* crown schedule from now on. Alternatively, we could iteratively run the crown scheduler in a binary search loop (with some timeout limit). By that, we find the largest $\epsilon > 0$ such that the makespan of some valid crown schedule S^c does not exceed $(1 - \epsilon)M$ while its energy is not higher than the energy E^* of the initial crown schedule returned for deadline M.

Next, we derive a *relaxed* crown schedule S^r from S^c. We do this by first computing M', the smallest makespan obtained by decreasing the operating frequency level for any single task by one. We again compute an energy-optimal crown schedule S^r for deadline M', with allocation and mapping of tasks identical to S^c. This makes it easier to switch between schedules and keeps the switching overhead very low as no migration of tasks and the associated data (e.g., channel buffers) across cores or core groups is required, which also minimizes unwanted side effects such as change of cache hit rate.

Alternatively, we can also greedily reduce the frequency for one or several tasks by one level, while keeping core allocations and the mapping unchanged for all tasks. For that purpose, we consider some task properties in S^c that are expected to have a possibly large impact on time and/or energy and thus can be used as indicators to select tasks for which to decrease execution frequency:

- *Number of cores w_j* used by a task j. This property is relevant because scaling wider tasks affects more (ideally, all) cores, preserving load balance also in the scaled schedule at least for the core group this task is mapped to.
- Task *type*. This is relevant because arithmetics-intensive tasks are more sensitive to frequency scaling than memory-intensive tasks.

- Task *frequency level* f_j assigned in S^c. A task that is running on a high frequency level in S^c has more potential for power and temperature reduction than a task with a low execution frequency, as power reduces only little at low frequency ranges e.g. due to growing importance of static power consumption. For example, for the A15 cores in the big.LITTLE architecture we found in earlier work [5] that only for the three topmost frequency levels (1.6 GHz, 1.4 GHz, 1.2 GHz) scaling down to a lower frequency level yields benefits in energy consumption – when scaling further, the slight power reduction is more than compensated by significantly longer execution time. Since we do not consider static power, these findings do not necessarily apply here. Therefore, we do not impose any restrictions on frequency choice.
- Task *workload* λ_j. This is relevant because tasks performing more work have a larger impact on execution time and energy cost than lightweight tasks.

From these properties, a cumulative preference score can be computed task-wise. Alternatively, for each task j we can compute the energy reduction

$$\Delta E_j = t_j(w_j, f_j)P(f_j, tt_j) - t_j(w_j, f_{j-1})P(f_{j-1}, tt_j)$$

achieved by reducing the execution frequency level by one. We first sort the tasks in decreasing order of the chosen criterion (cumulative preference score or ΔE_j), but exclude all tasks where f_j is already low. Then we apply the following greedy algorithm that treats tasks in the order just established: The currently considered task's frequency is lowered from f_j to the next lower level, and the increase in execution time of the schedule is determined. If the resulting execution time exceeds $\max\{(1+\varepsilon)M, M'\}$, then the algorithm stops.[4] Likewise, we calculate the energy savings ΔE_j, and if ΔE_j is negative (e.g. due to static energy), we skip this task for scaling down.

Determining the increase of the execution time involves exploring the tree of the core groups (each node annotated with the time span from the group's start time till completion of all dependent leaf groups), starting from the group comprising the currently considered task towards the root group (where the makespan is increased), and updating parent group annotation if the group's increased annotation is larger than its sibling's annotation.[5] The resulting relaxed crown schedule S^r will, in general, violate the strict makespan constraint but use less energy as some tasks now run at a lower frequency level.

---

[4] Checking against M' essentially amounts to examining whether the ranking criterion places the task at the top of list for which the makespan increase is smallest when lowering operating frequency by one level. Since $(1 - \epsilon)M > M'$ is possible, the chances for a relaxed schedule differing from the conservative one increase when not solely focusing on M' for the extended deadline calculation.

[5] This can be avoided by treating the tasks in the order of the core group they are mapped to, and apply the above sorting only within each group. As long as only tasks of groups 1 and 2 are modified, one can simply add up the increase in runtimes.

4   Adaptive Schedule Selection

At runtime we switch between the conservative and the relaxed schedule, in
the first hand in order to maintain an average throughput goal. The algorithm
maintains the sliding average throughput over the last $Q > 1$ rounds executed,
which ideally should be $1/M$ (recall that throughput is the number of rounds per
second). If the average throughput falls below a certain tolerance limit $1/M - \delta$,
the algorithm switches to the conservative schedule; if the average throughput
grows beyond $1/M + \delta$, the algorithm switches back to the relaxed schedule. We
denote by α the fraction of rounds where S^c is used: $\alpha = (M - \hat{M})/(M^* - \hat{M})$,
$\hat{M}$ being the makespan of the relaxed schedule. From the knowledge of E^*, M^*,
$\hat{E}$, $\hat{M}$, and α, where $\hat{E}$ is the energy consumption under the relaxed schedule,
we can compute the average power consumption.

Some processors allow to temporarily exceed the Thermal Design Point of
the chip by high frequency levels, such as turbo-mode frequencies. The chip can
sustain the high power dissipation only for a short amount of time before it needs
to run at significantly lower frequency again to cool down. A chip temperature
sensor allows to check if the current chip temperature is still safe or close to the
critical temperature θ_{max} where the chip material may take damage.

We can extend the simple control algorithm above to check the temperature
when deciding about the schedule variant for the next round and, if the temperature is too close to θ_{max} (by some δ), choose the relaxed schedule regardless of
the throughput penalty, as the safe operation of the chip should have priority
over a slight degradation in quality of service in soft realtime scenarios.

The temperature-aware dynamic adaptation of the schedule variant selection
also allows to react to unforeseen temporary changes in the chip temperature
that are caused by factors outside the control of the static scheduler, for example
due to fluctuations in external air cooling or high sunlight exposure of the device.

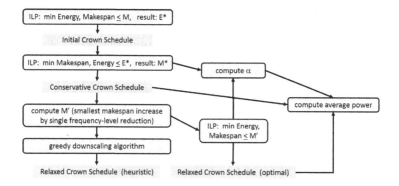

Fig. 3. Workflow for the experimental evaluation

5   Preliminary Results

For our experiments, we have implemented the workflow described in Sect. 3 and depicted in Fig. 3. The experiments are based on synthetic task sets of varying cardinality and different machine sizes. We chose task sets with few tasks, i.e., $n = 2, 3, 4$, because if there are many tasks, we expect the conservative schedule's makespan to be very close to the deadline. We used $p = 8$ for most experiments, only for $n = 3$ we also tested for $p = 16$ and 32. For each combination, we have created 10 task sets consisting of memory-intensive tasks and 10 task sets where the task type is randomly selected from { BRANCH, FMULT, SIMD, MATMUL} (uniformly distributed). The tasks' maximum width W_j is set to the machine size p so as to facilitate feasible schedules under tight deadline constraints. For all tasks, the parallel efficiency is determined as follows, cf. [12]:

$$e_j(q) = \begin{cases} 1 & \text{for } q = 1, \\ 1 - 0.3\frac{q^2}{(W_j)^2} & \text{for } 1 < q \leq W_j, \\ 0.000001 & \text{for } q > W_j, \end{cases}$$

where τ_j is executed on q cores. The deadline M is computed in the style of [12]:

$$M = d \cdot \frac{\sum_j \frac{\lambda_j}{p \cdot f_{max}} + 2\sum_j \frac{\lambda_j}{p \cdot f_{min}}}{2}.$$

Here, f_{min} and f_{max} are the A15 core's minimum and maximum operating frequencies, i.e. 0.6 GHz and 1.6 GHz. We set $d = 0.75$ for $n = 2$ and $d = 0.65$ for $n \in \{3, 4\}$, leading to tight deadlines and thus high operating frequencies, which constitutes the scenario our method has been designed for. For sets of memory-intensive tasks however, $d = 1.2$ for $n = 2$ and $d = 1.05$ for $n \in \{3, 4\}$ since higher frequencies do not yield shorter runtimes and thus deadlines cannot be as tight as for other task types. All tools, the heuristic scheduler, and all ILPs have been implemented in Python, the latter using the gurobipy module and the Gurobi 8.1.0 solver. The toolchain to compute and evaluate the schedules was executed on an AMD Ryzen 7 2700X with 8 physical cores and SMT.

It can be observed that in all cases, the second ILP does not decrease the schedule's makespan, which means that the conservative schedule is already determined by the first ILP – for the task sets considered here. Furthermore, it becomes clear that increasing the machine size does not have any influence on energy consumption (keep in mind that $\forall j : W_j = p$). Accordingly, the optimal schedulers' behaviour does not differ (they simply scale up the schedule with increasing machine size). This mostly holds true for the heuristic scheduler as well, except for one task set treated differently on 8 or 16 cores as opposed to 32 cores. Since the difference between machine sizes is marginal, we restrict the subsequent considerations to the experiments with an 8-core machine. Furthermore, the two task ordering proposals for the heuristic scheduler from Sect. 4 deliver the same results for all examined task sets of the non-memory-intensive type. We therefore refrain from further experiments with both approaches and exclusively use the ΔE_j criterion for sets of memory-intensive tasks.

To explore the extent to which chip temperature can be influenced by alteration of the schedule, we determine the decrease in average power consumption when alternately using S^c and S^r, compared to using S^c alone. In addition, we compare results from the heuristic compared to the optimal scheduler. Table 1 shows the ratio of average power when switching between optimal schedules to average power when solely running by S^c. As one can see, the fewer tasks a task set contains, the higher a decrease in average power consumption results. It is to be expected that for more than 4 tasks, average power consumption of the two-schedule approach will further approximate average power consumption of the conservative-only approach, up to the point where there is no significant difference in average power consumption which would justify proceeding with the proposed technique. Many times though, a streaming application will contain only a few tasks, in which case going with two schedules and switching between them can yield moderate benefits (2–12%). Interestingly, the average ratio of execution of S^c does not seem to be connected to the achievable reduction of average power consumption. The task type has a notable impact on the average power reduction potential (which decreases with growing number of tasks). This is due to the fact that memory-intensive tasks run on lower frequency levels from the beginning, as higher frequencies do not award a runtime advantage but increase energy consumption. The number of relaxed schedules that equal the corresponding conservative schedule is cleary higher for task sets comprising memory-intensive tasks (11 vs. 3). In total, 14 out of 60 optimal relaxed schedules equal their conservative counterpart. Thus, in most cases, the additional computational resources are not spent in vain.

Table 1. Average power consumption ratios of S^c plus S^r versus S^c, and execution ratios of the conservative schedule for various task set cardinalities and task types.

# tasks	Task types	Avg. power ratio	Exec. ratio cons
2	Other	0.883	0.471
	Memory	0.932	0.700
3	Other	0.927	0.464
	Memory	0.961	0.655
4	Other	0.956	0.603
	Memory	0.976	0.762

Regarding the performance of the heuristic scheduler, one must acknowledge that often the resulting schedule does not deviate from S^c. This especially holds true for the larger task sets. For those containing 2 tasks, 11 out of 20 schedules delivered an advantage over S^c. It should be noted however that for another 7 cases, S^r equals S^c. When considering task sets of size 2 the heuristic scheduler achieved optimality in 16 out of 20 cases. All in all, its performance is not satisfactory though, and measures must be devised to strengthen its competitiveness.

6   Related Work

Hällis et al. [4] clearly demonstrate that the ambient temperature influences core power consumption, but do not consider reacting to changes in ambient temperature. Mohaqeqi et al. [14] consider scheduling for variable ambient temperature, and provide different schedules for different ambient temperature ranges, with the goal to minimize the fraction of tasks that miss their deadline. In contrast, the present work targets streaming applications with a throughput requirement on application level, instead of different deadlines for individual tasks. Chrobak et al. [2] study throughput optimization depending on the heat contribution of individual tasks when the operating system tries to keep chip temperature constant, but do not consider ambient temperature. Coskun et al. [3] study dynamic scheduling algorithms at operating system level that improve the temporal and spatial temperature profile of the chip, to increase reliability. Jia et al. [7] investigate how time slices given to tasks can be dynamically scaled depending on the thermal characteristics of tasks, in order to decrease chip temperature. Chantem et al. [1] use integer linear programming to assign and schedule tasks to an MPSoC given real-time constraints, and their approach achieves lower chip temperature compared to competing approaches. They use a steady-state analysis, i.e. do not target changes in environment. Rajan and Yu [15] prove that going at maximum possible performance until a temperature threshold is met, and subsequent throttling, i.e. reduction of speed, is the best that can be achieved at system level for some temperature models. Hence, they support our approach at a more general level. Jayaseelan and Mitra [6] partition tasks into hot and cold sets, depending on their thermal characteristics, and manage chip temperature by controlling the amount of processor time provided to the hot and cold tasks, while satisfying soft real-time requirements.

Krzywda et al. [10] investigate the influence of number of virtual machines and resources per virtual machine (horizontal and vertical scaling) plus the use of DVFS and minimization of idle time for energy reduction on the servers running those virtual machines with a webserver application. In contrast, our research considers energy minimization and performance adaptation on streaming applications with real-time throughput requirements. Jin et al. [8] integrate DVFS and energy-efficient task scheduling into YARN (a Hadoop scheduler utilized for real-time processing). In contrast, our work focuses on streaming tasks with predictable workload and runtime. Stavrinides and Karatza [16] discuss energy-aware scheduling of real-time workflows. Yet the tasks in those workflows are sequential with exponentially distributed runtime. De Matteis and Mencagli [11] consider workload fluctuation in data stream processing and present proactive strategies to adapt number of cores and processing frequency. In contrast, we focus on predictable workloads and allocate given processing resources.

For a review of frequency-aware schedulers for moldable parallel tasks and a quantitative comparison with crown scheduling we refer to Melot *et al.* [12,13].

7   Conclusions

For the combined problem of core allocation, mapping and DVFS scaling for energy-optimized execution of software-pipelined streaming task graphs on a many-core processor, we have presented a general and automatic method that extends the static crown scheduling technique by an adaptive dynamic control mechanism. This allows to reduce the negative impact due to the few available discrete DVFS levels on the energy usage of crown schedules by switching between a conservative and a relaxed crown schedule that only differ in some tasks' frequency levels. The approach works with moldable tasks (i.e., does not assume malleable tasks) and does not rely on preemptive scheduling of task instances, i.e., could even be used in bare-hardware scenarios without any OS overhead. Our experimental evaluation using energy profiles taken from a real-world embedded multicore platform shows that there exists a moderate but significant potential for energy savings by our adaptive method compared to the original crown scheduling solution, which already outperformed other optimal and heuristic scheduling methods for moldable streaming tasks of the literature in terms of optimization time and energy efficiency [12,13].

References

1. Chantem, T., Hu, X., Dick, R.: Temperature-aware scheduling and assignment for hard real-time applications on MPSoCs. IEEE Trans. VLSI Syst. **19**(10), 1884–1897 (2011)
2. Chrobak, M., Dürr, C., Hurand, M., Robert, J.: Algorithms for temperature-aware task scheduling in microprocessor systems. In: 4th International Conference on Algorithmic Aspects in Information and Management (AAIM), pp. 120–130 (2008)
3. Coskun, A., Simunic Rosing, T., Whisnant, K.: Temperature aware task scheduling in MPSoCs. In: Design, Automation and Test in Europe, pp. 1659–1664 (2007)
4. Hällis, F., Holmbacka, S., Lafond, S., Lilius, J.: Thermal Influence on the energy efficiency of workload consolidation in many-core architecture. In: 24th Tyrrhenian International Workshop on Digital Communications (2013)
5. Holmbacka, S., Keller, J.: Workload type-aware scheduling on big.LITTLE platforms. In: 17th International Conference on Algorithms and Architectures for Parallel Processing (ICA3PP), pp. 3–17 (2018)
6. Jayaseelan, R., Mitra, T.: Temperature aware scheduling for embedded processors. J. Low Power Electron. **5**(3), 363–372 (2009)
7. Jia, G., Yuan, Y., Wan, J., Jiang, C., Li, X., Dai, D.: Temperature-aware scheduling based on dynamic time-slice scaling. In: 14th International Conference on Algorithms and Architectures for Parallel Processing (ICA3PP), pp. 310–322 (2014)
8. Jin, P., Hao, X., Wang, X., Yue, L.: Energy-efficient task scheduling for CPU-intensive streaming jobs on Hadoop. IEEE Trans. Parallel Distrib. Syst. **30**(6), 1298–1311 (2019)
9. Kahn, G.: The semantics of a simple language for parallel programming. In: IFIP Congress on Information Processing, North-Holland, pp. 471–475 (1974)
10. Krzywda, J., Ali-Eldin, A., Carlson, T.E., Östberg, P.O., Elmroth, E.: Power-performance tradeoffs in data center servers: DVFS, CPU pinning, horizontal, and vertical scaling. Fut. Gener. Comput. Syst. **81**, 114–128 (2018)

11. Matteis, T.D., Mencagli, G.: Proactive elasticity and energy awareness in data stream processing. J. Syst. Softw. **127**, 302–319 (2017)
12. Melot, N., Kessler, C., Keller, J., Eitschberger, P.: Fast crown scheduling heuristics for energy-efficient mapping and scaling of moldable streaming tasks on manycore systems. ACM Trans. Archit. Code Optim. **11**(4), 62:1–62:24 (2015)
13. Melot, N., Kessler, C., Keller, J., Eitschberger, P.: Co-optimizing core allocation, mapping and DVFS in streaming programs with moldable tasks for energy efficient execution on manycore architectures. In: 19th International Conference on Application Concurrency to System Design (ACSD), pp. 63–72 (2019)
14. Mohaqeqi,, M., Kargahi, M., Gharedaghi, F.: Temperature-aware speed scheduling in periodic real-time systems. CSI J. Comput. Sci. Eng. **12**(2), 36–46 (2014)
15. Rajan, D., Yu, P.: Temperature-aware scheduling: when is system-throttling good enough? In: 9th International Conference on Web-Age Information Management, pp. 397–404 (2008)
16. Stavrinides, G.L., Karatza, H.D.: Energy-aware scheduling of real-time workflow applications in clouds utilizing DVFS and approximate computations. In: 6th International Conference on Future Internet of Things and Cloud, pp. 33–40 (2018)

Minimizing Self-adaptation Overhead in Parallel Stream Processing for Multi-cores

Adriano Vogel[1]($\boxtimes$) (ID), Dalvan Griebler[1,3] (ID), Marco Danelutto[2] (ID),
and Luiz Gustavo Fernandes[1] (ID)

[1] School of Technology, Pontifical Catholic University of Rio Grande do Sul,
Porto Alegre, Brazil
{adriano.vogel,dalvan.griebler}@edu.pucrs.br, luiz.fernandes@pucrs.br
[2] Department of Computer Science, University of Pisa, Pisa, Italy
[3] Laboratory of Advanced Research on Cloud Computing (LARCC),
Três de Maio Faculty (SETREM), Três de Maio, Brazil

Abstract. Stream processing paradigm is present in several applications that apply computations over continuous data flowing in the form of streams (*e.g.*, video feeds, image, and data analytics). Employing self-adaptivity to stream processing applications can provide higher-level programming abstractions and autonomic resource management. However, there are cases where the performance is suboptimal. In this paper, the goal is to optimize parallelism adaptations in terms of stability and accuracy, which can improve the performance of parallel stream processing applications. Therefore, we present a new optimized self-adaptive strategy that is experimentally evaluated. The proposed solution provided high-level programming abstractions, reduced the adaptation overhead, and achieved a competitive performance with the best static executions.

Keywords: Parallel programming · Stream parallelism · Self-adaptive parallelism · Autonomic computing

1 Introduction

Nowadays, the increasing number of devices producing data on real-time demands effective programming models. Stream processing systems [2] emerged as a potential solution for improving the processing of continuous flows of data. The amount of stream processing applications is increasing, which requires efficient solutions to meet the challenges regarding a properly exploitation of parallelism and provide higher level programming abstractions. Moreover, processing data in real time is still requiring continuous performance optimization.

The characteristics of stream processing applications vary depending on the data source and computations but may have several common characteristics. One of the most highlighted aspects is the continuous and unbounded arrival of data items [2]. In stream processing, an item can be seen as a task coming from a given

U. Schwardmann et al. (Eds.): Euro-Par 2019 Workshops, LNCS 11997, pp. 30–41, 2020.
https://doi.org/10.1007/978-3-030-48340-1_3

data source (e.g., camera, radar). Parallelism is an opportunity to process faster those data items, so increasing the overall performance. In the context of this study, we refer to parallelism as the possibility to concurrently perform different operations over independent stream items. Currently, parallelism is important because our computer architectures have multiple processing units placed on a chip. Although parallelism is an opportunity to improve performance, the applications must be implemented for exploiting the available hardware parallelism.

From the application programmers perspective, introducing parallel routines to their systems tends to be a complex and time-consuming activity. Consequently, programming abstractions were provided for reducing the application programmers' burden. Moreover, in order to abstract the definition of error-prone parameters, we have proposed self-adaptivity [12] and service-level objectives (SLOs) [7] for autonomously managing the executions at run-time. However, performance losses (compared to the best performing static executions) occurred in applications using the self-adaptive strategies [7,12]. Therefore, in this work we aim at providing the following contributions:

- A new optimized strategy for self-adapting the degree of parallelism when the programmer/user sets a target performance. The previous implementation [7, 12] was extended to better encompass the SASO(*stability, accuracy, settling time and overshoot*) properties [8], mainly for stability and short settling times. Consequently, the precision and performance were improved.
- A comprehensive validation of our solution for parallel programming abstractions. The evaluation performed compares the new strategy to static executions considering variant application characteristics and workload trends.

This paper is organized as follows. Section 2 provides the scenario of this study. Section 3 describes the proposed solution. Then, Sect. 4 shows the experimental results. Finally, Sect. 5 concludes the paper.

2 Context

This section highlights this study's scenario. The next sections show related works and SPar (Sect. 2.2). Then, we present SPar's self-adaptive part.

2.1 Related Work

A set of studies have evaluated how to determine the optimal number of replicas in parallel applications, but only a few tackled this problem considering the specific characteristics of stream processing. The study of Sensi *et al.* [11] targets stream systems, aiming to predict performance and power consumption using linear regression learning. Their goal was to manage power consumption and maintain proper performance. The execution is managed by their programming interface and runtime called *NORNIR*, which adapts the system at run-time (number of cores and clocks frequency). Matteis and Mencagli [9] provided elastic properties for data stream processing, their goal was to improve performance and energy consumption. Their proposed model was implemented along with the FastFlow runtime, using one controller thread for monitoring the infrastructure and environment and for triggering changes.

Gedik *et al.* [3] use the term elastic auto-parallelization attempting to find and parallelize profitable regions. They also implemented parallelism adaptation at run-time. Gedik *et al.* [3] propose an elastic auto-parallelization solution, which adjusts the number of parallel channels to achieve high throughput without wasting resources. It was implemented by requiring the programmer to define a threshold and a congestion index. These arguments are used in order to control the execution and apply adaptation. Selva *et al.* [10] introduce an approach related to adaptation at run-time for the StreamIt language. They extended StreamIt in order to allow the programmer to specify the desired throughput. Moreover, the implementation covered an application and system monitor for detecting the throughput and potential system bottlenecks.

Our research differs from existing papers because we provide a self-adaptive degree of parallelism support to the SPar DSL. Like [11] and [9], we use the Fast-Flow framework as the runtime library. However, [11] and [9] address energy consumption while we focus particularly on stream parallelism abstractions. Another relevant contrast of our solution is that it executes within the first stage, not requiring an additional thread to manage the execution. Avoiding the use of an additional thread is important for reducing the consumption of resources and potentially causing less overhead. Moreover, our strategy is a ready-to-use strategy in such a way that it does not require to install external libraries nor include code parts. While Gedik *et al.* [3] and Selva *et al.* [10] address distributed stream systems, our approach targets stream parallelism in shared-memory multi-core environments for parallelism abstraction. Moreover, the algorithm implementations of related works are arguably not sufficiently abstracted for application programmers, thus we aim at providing additional abstractions for non-experts in parallelism. A relevant aspect addressed in our work that is not covered by the related ones is a proper measurement of the adaptivity overhead. To assess the actual impact of using the self-adaptive strategy, we measure the performance and memory consumption comparing the executions to the regular static ones.

2.2   SPar Overview

SPar is a C++ internal Domain-Specific Language (DSL) that aims at simplifying parallelization of sequential programs targeting multi-core systems [4]. SPar enables parallelism in a stream fashion by providing a standard C++11 annotation language, which intends to prevent sequential source code rewriting/refactoring. Parallel execution is enabled with a compiler that performs source-to-source transformations generating parallel code compatible with FastFlow [1].

SPar's language provides five standard C++ attributes representing stream parallelism characteristics. Listing 1.1 gives a representation of the SPar's attributes. The **ToStream** attribute marks the beginning of a stream parallel region, which is the code block between the **ToStream** and the first **Stage** (lines 1 and 3). Additional *Stages* may be placed within the *ToStream* region.

Another attribute is the *Input* that is used by programmers to set the data that is processed in the given stream region. On the other hand, the *Output* attribute is used to define the variable that produces a result. *Replicate* refers to the number of replicas in a replicated stage, which can be seen as the degree of parallelism, consequently, the number of replicas and degree of parallelism are used interchangeably. Listing 1.1 shows a code block where the data format is "string" and the input is received by reading a file in line 3. A given computation is performed in line 6. In line 5, the attribute *Replicate* sets the second stage to use a degree of parallelism of 4 replicas, which is static degree of parallelism used during the entire execution. In line 8 an output is produced accordingly to the computations performed.

Figure 1 shows the respective activity graph compatible with the annotations added on Listing 1.1. In fact, the annotations result in a runtime with a parallel execution composed of 3 stages. Such an execution represents a Farm pattern, where the first sequential stage is the emitter, the second stage is replicated, and the last stage is the collector.

```
[[spar::ToStream]] while(1){
  std::string data;
  read_in(data);
  if(stream_in.eof()) break;
  [[spar::Stage,spar::Input(data),spar::
      Output(data),spar::Replicate(4)]]
  { compute(data); }
  [[spar::Stage,spar::Input(data)]]
  { write_out(data); }
}
```

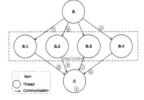

Listing 1.1. SPar Language.   **Fig. 1.** Parallel activity graph.

2.3 Self-adaptive Parallelism Management in SPar

As viewed in the previous section, in SPar the `Replicate` attribute is a static value used during the entire program's execution. However, if the stream processing application presents fluctuations (*e.g.,* performance, environment, or input rates), this static execution can lead to inefficient resources usage (waste) or poor performance. Consequently, we studied how to introduce profitability for fission dynamics [2] on the SPar replicated stages.

A set of **properties** and interests can be included when designing a self-adaptive strategy. **SASO** are the most relevant properties [8]. A system is *stable* if it produces the same configurations every time under a given condition. A system is *accurate* if the "measured output converges (or becomes sufficiently close) to the reference input" [8]. A system is expected to present *short settling times* by quickly responding to changes and reaching an optimal state. A strategy should also avoid *overshooting* by using precisely the resources needed. Moreover, to avoid oscillation in the number of replicas, our self-adaptive strategies are designed using a threshold value to compare different performance indicators. In this study, when the strategy infers that two values are significantly different, it is because they have a contrast higher than 20% (a threshold), such value was ascertained in [7,12] as a suitable one for stream processing applications.

One of the most relevant performance metrics for stream processing applications is throughput, which defines how many items are processed in a given time interval. Considering the complexities related to defining parallelism parameters, provide a performance goal can be considered presumably easier for application programmers. Consequently, we studied ways to handle the configuration challenges and abstract them from programmers for a transparent degree of parallelism. However, in the stream processing context, an effective mechanism is required to change a program's execution on-the-fly without the need to recompile or rerun. To this end, we studied SPar's runtime to find techniques to change the number of replicas at run-time. Hence, we implemented a strategy that adapts the degree of parallelism based on the application's throughput.

In this implemented strategy [7,12], the decision whether to change the degree of parallelism is based on the target throughput (user defined) and the actual measured throughput. This previous strategy continuously monitors the application throughput and, when necessary, it attempts to optimize the execution for the next iteration. The regulator was implemented within the first stage, which is the entity that actually applies the parallelism regulation. In Listing 1.2 is shown an example of the SPar's language that supports the self-adaptive part, the difference compared to the Listing 1.1 is that the definition of the number of replicas in the *Replicate* attribute is no longer required. Additionally, Fig. 2 shows a representation of the parallel runtime, with the self-adaptive strategy that controls the application execution at run-time.

```
[[spar::ToStream]] while(1){
  std::string data;
  read_in(data);
  if(stream_in.eof()) break;
  [[spar::Stage,spar::Input(data),spar::
     Output(data),spar::Replicate()]]
  { compute(data); }
  [[spar::Stage,spar::Input(data)]]
  { write_out(data); }
}
```

Listing 1.2. SPar code example.   Fig. 2. Self-adaptive strategy.

The validation of this self-adaptive strategy showed that comparing only the target (expected) and measured (actual) throughput sometimes resulted in too many and frequent reconfigurations, which in some events caused performance instability. For efficiency purpose, the number of replicas was reduced when the actual throughput was significantly higher than the target one. The throughput oscillations and peaks induced the regulator to reduce the number of replicas. But, it was notable that when the unstable workload trend passed, using fewer replicas sometimes caused a lower performance than the target one. Also, this previous strategy increased 1 or 2 replicas while the throughput was smaller than the target, which resulted in settling times higher than the ideal one.

3 A New Strategy for Self-adaptive Parallelism

Here we present a new strategy that aims at reducing the overhead by better encompassing the SASO properties. The scope of this work is limited in some aspects, we are not discussing the problem of thread placement, which may be tackled in the future. Also, the self-adaptive strategy works by default on stateless replicated stages, a stateful stage would require the control by other means. The self-adaptive strategy uses a maximum number of replicas according to machine hardware, defining it to one application thread per hardware thread. The strategy also counts threads used in sequential application stages.

In Sect. 2.3 we presented the first self-adaptive strategy, where we identified opportunities for improvement. We extensively analyzed the root causes and elaborated mechanisms to improve it, resulting in a new optimized strategy for handling the stability and performance violations. Figure 3 shows a high-level representation of the steps performed by the new strategy's regulator that performs the decision-making. In order to respond to fluctuation, the decision is expected to periodically iterate the steps: execute, decide, apply changes, and sleep. The time interval between iterations is set to 1 s, which a value that gives a balance between responsiveness and stability.

The regulator checks if the current throughput is significantly lower than the target one. If true, it enters the **Decision 1 (D1)** for increasing the number of replicas (**R**) with the following steps: 1) detects the machine processing capabilities; 2) calculates the percentage that each processor has from the total processing capability; 3) calculates the percentage of difference between actual and target throughput; 4) according to the percentage of the difference and the

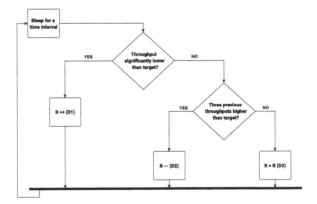

Fig. 3. High-level representation of the Decision-Making.

processing power that each processor holds (from step 2), the regulator estimates how many replicas should be added. Consequently, if the actual throughput is extremely lower than the target, this new strategy attempts to increase the throughput by adding several replicas in one step (the previous strategy added 1 or 2 per step), such a decision has the potential to reduce the setting time. The regulator also checks if the current and previous throughputs are higher than the target one. If false, it applies **Decision 3 (D3)** maintaining the same number of replicas. But, if this condition is true, the regulator applies **Decision 2 (D2)** that decreases the number of replicas. Pursuing stability and avoiding frequent/unprofitable changes, three previous throughputs are compared to the target throughput (the previous strategy considered only one).

The new strategy was compared to the existing one. The adaptive part was included in Lane Detection application, details regarding the application and tested machine are presented in Sect. 4. Figure 4(a) shows the throughput of a serial execution of Lane Detection with the tested video file Input-1 (260 MB), which characterizes the load and shows the usual throughput fluctuations in stream processing, between 2 and 9 frames per second (FPS). Some frames require more (or less) time to be processed resulting in load fluctuations, significant fluctuation can be viewed around the second 180 with throughput falling and increasing after 600 s in another workload phase.

Figure 4(b) characterizes the previous strategy and the new one with a target throughput of 30 FPS. The top part shows the measured throughput, where the new strategy had a stabler throughput that resulted in less throughput violations. Moreover, the lower graph referring to the number of replicas highlights the stability of the new strategy. The previous strategy reconfigured the number of replicas too many times causing additional throughput instability. Regarding the settling time, it is possible to note that between the seconds 40 and 60 of Fig. 4(b) a new workload phase required parallelism reconfiguration. The new strategy reacted faster by adding 9 replicas that increased the throughput. The execution of the new strategy ended before due to its higher throughput.

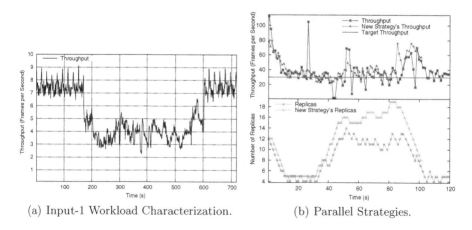

(a) Input-1 Workload Characterization.   (b) Parallel Strategies.

Fig. 4. Lane Detection Characterization - Sequential execution (Left) and parallel strategies (Right).

4   Self-adaptive Strategy Evaluation

In this section, we evaluate the self-adaptive strategy by comparing it to the hand-coded static parallel applications. Here we present the final throughput that in an entire execution is a result considering the number of processed items divided by the total time taken. Observe that it is different from the previous performance characterization, where the throughput was collected at run-time.

Real-world applicability was the key criterion used to select the two applications. **Lane Detection**, which is used on autonomous vehicles to detect road lanes. The parallel version using SPar and the application workflow details can be found in [5]. **Bzip2:** is a data compression application that uses Burrows-Wheeler algorithm for sorting and Huffman coding. This application is built on top of libbzip2. Its parallel version using SPar is described in [6]. Therefore, our tested applications have different stream processing characteristics.

4.1   Test Environment

The machine used was equipped with memory 32 GB–2133 MHz and a dual-socket Intel(R) Xeon(R) CPU 2.40 GHz (12 cores-24 threads). The operating system used was Ubuntu Server, G++ version 5.4.0 with the -O3 flag. This environment was dedicated to these experiments, thus no other application was executing at the same time. All parallel code versions used the on-demand scheduling policy, which provides a suitable scenario for stream processing with finer granularity, and a better load balancing. The results presented are the arithmetic mean of 10 executions. The standard deviation is also presented in the graphs.

4.2   Performance

The self-adaptive strategy is compared to regular parallel executions that use a static number of replicas, ranging in this machine from 2 to 24 replicas. It is important to note that in this evaluation we only considered performance. The self-adaptive strategy tends to have a more elaborated execution with monitoring and adaptations. Thus, the control overhead may reduce the overall performance.

Figure 5 shows the results of Lane Detection using Input-1, presented in Fig. 4(a). In the static executions, the throughput increased as more replicas were added until it reached the maximum performance of the application. It is notable some performance oscillations in the static executions between 10 and 21 replicas. These events were caused by the combination of this input load oscillations and the ordering performed in the last stage. When the load is too unbalanced (items have significant computing time differences), there will be more unordered items in the last stage, where a single thread has to reorder the items along with its operations (*e.g.*, write). Therefore, it becomes a bottleneck when there is such a combination of load oscillations and ordering requirements.

In the used machine, the self-adaptive execution started using 12 replicas, since it is the number of available physical cores collected by the parallelism regulator. The throughput from self-adaptive executions is the same for all replicas

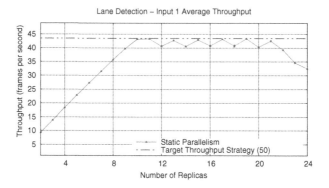

Fig. 5. Average throughput of Lane Detection Input-1.

since any number of replicas could be used during the execution. The performance of the self-adaptive strategy with a target performance was as good as the best static parallelism configurations. This demonstrates that even with the additional parts implemented, the self-adaptive strategy can achieve a performance similar to the best static executions that have no control or adaptability with respect to the number of replicas.

Figure 6 shows the throughput of Lane Detection with Input-2 (a video file 5.25 MB - 640 × 360 pixels). In this case, the static executions achieved the best performance with more replicas (17 to 22). The proposed self-adaptive strategy again achieved a throughput competitive with the best peaks of static executions.

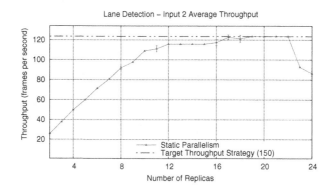

Fig. 6. Average throughput of Lane Detection Input-2.

Figure 7 shows the throughput of the self-adaptive strategy and static executions on the Pbzip2 application. The input used on Pbzip2 is a file with 6.3 GB with a dump of all the abstracts from the English Wikipedia, previously used in [11]. The proposed self-adaptive strategy performed similar to 22 static replicas, but with 23 replicas the static parallelism execution was slightly better. The static executions show the impact of the number of replicas on performance. It is notable that in this application, the best throughput was achieved with 23 static replicas, this number of replicas in the same machine resulted in significant performance losses in the Lane Detection application. Consequently, even with the executions with a static degree of parallelism, it is possible to identify contrasts in the impact of the number of replicas in applications' performance. Moreover, although the standard deviation was plotted, it is difficult to identify deviation since it was minimal.

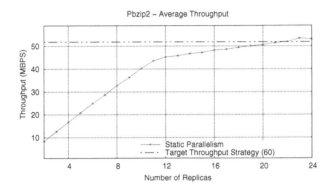

Fig. 7. Average throughput of Pbzip2.

4.3 Memory Consumption

Several aspects of the execution are relevant to evaluate the strategies' executions. Noteworthy, the memory usage is relevant for evaluating the amount of resources that a given program demands in order to run. The total memory usage was collected by the UPL (Utility Performance Library)[1] library and the results are shown as an average of the executions.

Figure 8 shows the memory usage of the execution from Lane Detection using Input-1, which is the only memory results shown due to space constraints. The result is similar to other workload and applications. Figure 8 illustrates how the number of replicas impacts on memory usage. Although the self-adaptive strategy has additional processing parts that could use additional memory, it consumed less memory than the static execution with more than 12 replicas. It is also worth noting a variation in memory consumption on the static execution with more than 12 replicas, this aspect is caused by a combination of the load unbalance of threads and by the ordering constraint. The results from memory usage of the self-adaptive strategies demonstrated no additional resource demands, which is relevant for running under a low overhead.

---

[1] https://github.com/dalvangriebler/upl.

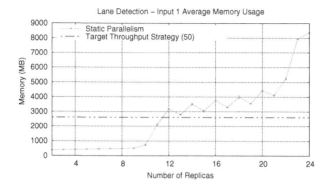

Fig. 8. Average memory usage of Lane Detection Input-1.

5   Conclusion

In this study, we presented a new optimized self-adaptive strategy. SASO properties were better encompassed in the new strategy's decision making, resulting in additional stability and performance. Furthermore, real-world applications were used for assessing the overhead of the new strategy compared to static executions. The results show that the proposed strategy achieved a great performance, competitive to best static cases. Hence, the self-adaptive strategy increased the level of abstraction without compromising the performance. Consequently, real-world stream processing applications can benefit from the proposed solution.

It is important to note that our work is limited in some aspects. For instance, the performance trend can be different in other applications or machines. Moreover, we have seen that adding more replicas tends to increase the performance, but in some scenarios, this may result in overhead/contention. Hence, the trend between processing power and throughput may be reverse in specific cases.

Finally, in the future we intend to extend this study to other real-world applications and port the strategy to run in distributed cluster environments including cloud and fog, increasing the flexibility with an elastic infrastructure.

Acknowledgment. This study was financed in part by the Coordenação de Aperfeiçoamento de Pessoal de Nivel Superior - Brasil (CAPES) - Finance Code 001, Univ. of Pisa PRA_2018_66 "DECLware: Declarative methodologies for designing and deploying applications", the FAPERGS 01/2017-ARD project called ParaElastic (No. 17/2551-0000871-5), and the Universal MCTIC/CNPq N° 28/2018 project called SParCloud (No. 437693/2018-0).

References

1. Aldinucci, M., Danelutto, M., Kilpatrick, P., Torquati, M.: Fastflow: High-Level and Efficient Streaming on Multicore, chap. 13, pp. 261–280. Wiley-Blackwell (2014)

2. Andrade, H., Gedik, B., Turaga, D.: Fundamentals of Stream Processing: Application Design, Systems, and Analytics. Cambridge University Press, Cambridge (2014)
3. Gedik, B., Schneider, S., Hirzel, M., Wu, K.L.: Elastic scaling for datastream processing. IEEE Trans. Parallel Distrib. Syst. **25**(6), 1447–1463 (2014)
4. Griebler, D., Danelutto, M., Torquati, M., Fernandes, L.G.: SPar: a DSL for high-level and productive stream parallelism. Parallel Process. Lett. **27**(01), 1740005 (2017)
5. Griebler, D., Hoffmann, R.B., Danelutto, M., Fernandes, L.G.: Higher-level parallelism abstractions for video applications with SPar. In: Parallel Computing is Everywhere, Proceedings of the International Conference on Parallel Computing, ParCo 2017, pp. 698–707. IOS Press, Bologna, September 2017
6. Griebler, D., Hoffmann, R.B., Danelutto, M., Fernandes, L.G.: High-level and productive stream parallelism for dedup, ferret, and Bzip2. Int. J. Parallel Prog. **47**(2), 253–271 (2018). https://doi.org/10.1007/s10766-018-0558-x
7. Griebler, D., Vogel, A., De Sensi, D., Danelutto, M., Fernandes, L.G.: Simplifying and implementing service level objectives for stream parallelism. J. Supercomput. (2019). https://doi.org/10.1007/s11227-019-02914-6
8. Hellerstein, J.L., Diao, Y., Parekh, S., Tilbury, D.M.: Feedback Control of Computing Systems. Wiley, Chichester (2004)
9. Matteis, T.D., Mencagli, G.: Keep calm and react with foresight: strategies for low-latency and energy-efficient elastic data stream processing. In: Proceedings of the ACM Symposium on Principles and Practice of Parallel Programming, pp. 13:1–13:12 (2016)
10. Selva, M., Morel, L., Marquet, K., Frenot, S.: A monitoring system for runtime adaptations of streaming applications. In: Proceedings of the Euromicro Conference on Parallel, Distributed and Network-based Processing, pp. 27–34 (2015)
11. Sensi, D.D., Torquati, M., Danelutto, M.: A reconfiguration algorithm for power-aware parallel applications. ACM Trans. Architect. Code Optim. **13**(4), 43:1–43:25 (2016)
12. Vogel, A., Griebler, D., De Sensi, D., Danelutto, M., Fernandes, L.G.: Autonomic and latency-aware degree of parallelism management in SPar. In: Mencagli, G., et al. (eds.) Euro-Par 2018. LNCS, vol. 11339, pp. 28–39. Springer, Cham (2019). https://doi.org/10.1007/978-3-030-10549-5_3

A Fully Decentralized Autoscaling Algorithm for Stream Processing Applications

Mehdi Mokhtar Belkhiria and Cédric Tedeschi[✉]

Univ Rennes, Inria, CNRS, IRISA, Rennes, France
mehdi.belkhiria@irisa.fr, cedric.tedeschi@inria.fr

Abstract. Stream Processing deals with the efficient, real-time processing of continuous streams of data. Stream Processing engines ease the development and deployment of such applications which are commonly pipelines of operators to be traversed by each data item. Due to the varying velocity of the streams, autoscaling is needed to dynamically adapt the number of instances of each operator. With the advent of geographically-dispersed computing platforms such as Fog platforms, operators are dispersed accordingly, and autoscaling needs to be decentralized as well. In this paper, we propose an algorithm allowing for scaling decisions to be taken and enforced in a fully-decentralized way. In particular, in spite of scaling actions being triggered concurrently, each operator maintains a view of its neighbours in the graph so as no data message is lost. The protocol is detailed and its correctness discussed. Its performance is captured through early simulation experiments.

Keywords: Stream Processing · Decentralized Management · Autoscaling

1 Introduction

The need for near real-time processing of continuously produced data led to the development of the Stream Processing (SP) computing paradigm. A stream processing application is typically a graph of operators that each data item will traverse, data processing being pipelined. Stream Processing is becoming ubiquitous and is being applied in many domains, ranging from social media to military applications. Stream Processing Engines (SPEs) have been proposed to ease the development of these applications and their deployment over utility computing platforms [5,14,19]. From the data perspective, each data item traverses the graph of operators. From the processing perspective, each operator collects the data stream from its predecessors in the graph, applies its own transformation and creates a new stream of data, sent to its successors in the graph. Operators have different costs, for instance in terms of processing time and CPU utilization.

Parallelism within Stream Processing applications can be achieved in different manners. The first one, already mentioned, is pipeline parallelism: data

U. Schwardmann et al. (Eds.): Euro-Par 2019 Workshops, LNCS 11997, pp. 42–53, 2020.
https://doi.org/10.1007/978-3-030-48340-1_4

items can be processed concurrently on different portions of the graph. The second one is data parallelism: if stateless or partitioned, an operator can process several data items at the same time, provided it is scaled accordingly. Because the input data stream generally varies in size over time, this scaling needs to be adjusted dynamically in time so as to be able to ensure parallelism while minimising computing resource waste. This mechanism, referred to as *autoscaling*, is commonly designed and implemented in SPEs as a side system taking glocal decisions about the scaling (in or out) of operators based on real-time metrics collected about operators and the current stream velocity.

Assuming a dedicated, centralized autoscaling subsystem can become difficult in geographically dispersed platforms, such as Edge or Fog computing platforms. Such platforms are becoming realities and typically support mobile-based or IoT-based applications where Stream Processing is the adequate computing paradigm to be used [21]. Moving Stream Processing to the edge brings new challenges due to the very essence of these platforms: they gather a lot of small, geographically-dispersed computing resources. Accurately monitoring such platforms in a centralized fashion becomes difficult due to the constraints on both network and computing resources.

In this paper, we assume a distributed deployment of the graph of operators. The infrastructure gathers geographically-dispersed compute nodes and each operator is placed over a compute node which is potentially distant from the compute nodes hosting its predecessor and successor operators in the graph. Consequently, each operator needs to maintain the addresses of the compute nodes hosting their neighbours in the graph. We also assume no central scaling authority is available and that operators take their own scaling decisions independently from each others. Then, as instances (or *replicas*) of operators appear and disappear at many places of the operators dynamically, one challenge is to be able to maintain on each operator a correct view of its predecessors and successors so that no message is lost: wrongly assume some node is still the host of one instance of one of our successor may cause one operator to send some message to a deleted instance, causing in turn data loss.

The contribution of this paper is a fully-decentralized algorithm where scaling decisions are taken independently and the graph maintained so as to ensure no data message is lost. Operators exist in a dynamically adjusted number of *instances*. Each instance takes its own probabilistic scale-in or scale-out decisions, based on local monitoring so as to globally converge towards the *right* number of instances in regard to the current velocity level for this operator. Each time it decides a scaling operator, an instance also triggers a protocol to ensure the correct maintenance of the graph in spite of concurrent scale decisions.

Related work is presented in Sect. 2. In Sect. 3, the system model used to describe applications and platforms considered is given. Our decentralized scaling protocol, including the scaling policy in both in and out cases, as well as a sketch of proof regarding correctness facing concurrency is presented in Sect. 4. Simulation results are given in Sect. 5.

2   Related Work

Autoscaling in stream processing has been the subject of a recent series of works [2,12] addressing i) the dynamic nature of the velocity of the data stream, and ii) the difficulty of estimating prior to execution the computation cost of the operators, that can vary significantly from one operator to another. The scaling problem can be tackled either statically, *i.e.*, prior to the actual deployment of the application or online, so as to dynamically adapt the amount of computing power dedicated to each operator.

Static approaches typically rely on the prior-to-execution analysis of the graph so as to infer its *optimal* parallelization. Schneider et al. [18] propose a heuristic-based traversal of the graph so as to group operators together in different *parallel areas*, each area being a contiguous set of stateless operators, stateful operators being considered here again as not trivial to parallelize. While this static analysis is a necessary first step, it is unable to find a continuously accurate level of parallelism able when facing changes in the velocity of the incoming data stream. Accuracy refers here to the ability to find the right amount of instances, and avoid both over and under-provisioning.

Dynamic scaling generally relies on three operations: fusion, fission, and deletion [12]. *Fusion* refers to the merging of two contiguous operators hosted by two different compute nodes, into a single compute node. While this increases the load on the compute node chosen, *fusion* primarily targets the reduction of the network load by keeping within one node the traffic initially traversing the network links between the two nodes. Fusion is not a scaling action *per se*, and relates more to a consolidation of the placement of operators over the compute nodes. *Fission* (or *scale-out*) refers to operators' duplication: a new instance of operator gets started. It increases the level of parallelism of this operator provided the new thread or process spawned to support it leverages computing resources that were not fully used prior to the fission (Fission can rely over either vertical or horizontal scaling, again relating to a placement problem [16,17]). Note that, in practice, the fission mechanism is influenced by the *statefulness* of the operator: Maintaining the state of a stateful operator when it is fissioned requires to merge the partial states maintained independently over the instances. Statefulness is an issue in scaling but not our primary concern here. *Deletion* (or *scale-in*) is fission's inverse operation. It consists in removing running instances of a given operator, typically when the operator's incoming load gets reduced.

In practice, dynamic scaling systems typically rely on two elements [8,10,11, 15,20]: i) a centralized subsystem collecting up-to-date information about the network traffic and available resources, so as to be able to take relevant decisions to optimize a certain performance metric, and ii) a scaling policy to decide *when* to trigger a scale-out, scale-in or reconfiguration. Some of these works focus on monitoring the CPU utilization so as to detect bottlenecks and trigger a scaling-out phase, in particular for partitioned stateful operators, which requires to split and migrate the state of the operator between the evolving set of instances [8]. Some works rely on a model-based predictive approach [15]. Designed as an extension of Storm [19], T-Storm [20] introduces a mechanism of dynamic load rebalance triggered periodically, with a focus on trying to reduce internode communication by grouping operators). Aniello et al. proposes a similar approach [1]. StreamCloud [11] provides a set of techniques to identify parallelizable zones of operators into which the whole graph is split, zones being delimited by stateful operators. The splitting algorithm shares some similarities with the work in [18]: each zone can be parallelized independently. Yet, on top of this splitting mechanism, dynamic scheduling is introduced to balance the load at the entry point of each zone. Finally, some work combines fission and deletion so as to continuously satisfy the SASO properties (Settling time, Accuracy, Stability, Overshoot) [10]. The requirement is to be able to dynamically allocate the right amount instances ensuring the performance of the system (accuracy), that this number is reached quickly (settling time), that it does not oscillate artificially (stability) and that no resource is used uselessly (overshoot). While their objectives are similar to those of the present work, they still rely over a centralized authority to monitor the system, decide on the scaling operations and enforce them. The present work offers a decentralized vision of the problem.

Decentralizing the management of stream processing frameworks has been the subject of different works [4,6,7,13,17]. DEPAS [4] is not specifically targeted at stream processing and focus on a multi-cloud infrastructure with local schedulers taking decisions independently. The similarity between DEPAS and the present work stands in that autonomous instances take scaling decisions based on a probabilistic policy. Yet, our main focus is also different: we are mainly interested in providing a graph maintenance algorithm minimizing downtime. More specifically targeted at stream processing, Pietzuch et al. [17] proposed a Stream-Based Overlay Network (SBON) that allows to map stream processing operators over the physical network. Hochreiter et al. [13] devise an architectural model to deploy distributed stream processing applications. Finally, Cardellini et al. [6,7] proposed a hierarchical approach to the autoscaling problem, following a hierarchical approach combining a threshold-based local scaling decision with a central coordination mechanism to solve conflicts between decisions taken independently and limit the number of reconfigurations.

Autoscaling generally assumes a pause-and-restart: when a scaling operation takes place, the application is paused. It gets restarted once the reconfiguration is over. Reconfiguration is needed in particular when dealing with the scaling of partitioned stateful operators which requires to split and migrate its state dynamically. In the following, assuming stateless operators, we devise a fully-decentralized autoscaling protocol that does not require to pause data processing during reconfigurations. While making the problem easier, assuming stateless operators appear to be a reasonable first step. To our knowledge, no such fully-decentralized proper protocol was proposed assuming neither stateful, nor stateless protocols.

3   System Model

Platform Model. We consider a distributed system composed of an unbounded set of (geographically dispersed) homogeneous compute nodes. These nodes can be either physical nodes or virtual machines. We do not consider how compute nodes are allocated, we assume they are made available through some Cloud API. We abstract out the addition of a new node through the `addSibling()` primitive which implicitly knows the information about the current operator to be instanciated. In practice, *homogeneity* means that all virtual machines allocated have the same size. Compute nodes are assumed reliable: they can be deallocated, but cannot crash. Nodes communicate in a partially synchronous model [9] using FIFO reliable channels: A message reaches its destination in a finite time, and two messages sent through the same channel are processed in the same order they were sent. Sending a message is done through the `send(type, ctnt, dest)` non-blocking method. `type` denotes the message type and `ctnt` its content. `ctnt` actual structure varies depenting on `type`. `dest` is the address of the destination node. The higher-level communication primitive `sendAll(type, ctnt, dests)` sends the same message to all nodes in `dests`.

Application Model. We consider stream processing applications represented as directed pipelines in which vertices represent operators to be applied on each input record and edges represent streams between these operators. We assume stateless operators. At starting time, each operator is launched on one particular compute nodes, and each compute node hosts a single replica. Then, the scaling mechanism can add or remove replicas. Each replica of an operator is referred to as an *operator instance* (OI) in the following. OIs running the same operator are referred to as *siblings*. The load of an operator is shared equally between all of its instances. Each operator O_i can exist in several instances $OI_i j$ where i is the id of the operator and j the id of the instance. In the example of Fig. 1, the pipeline is made of three operators. At some point, scaling out introduced two new instances for the middle operator. The application follows a purely distributed configuration: due to the geographic dispersion of nodes and for the sake of scalability, the view of the graph on each instance is limited to the instances of their successor and predecessor operators.

4   Scaling Algorithm

The algorithm proposed and described in this section enables each OI to decide locally and independently when to get duplicated or deleted. The algorithm is run periodically on each OI (with possibly different frequencies). The algorithm starts with the decision phase in which the OI checks its current load. Assuming OIs are homogeneous and the load fairly distributed amongst instances, OIs are able to take uncoordinated decisions leading to a global accurate number of instances. Once an OI decides to get duplicated or deleted, it actually executes the action planned and ensures its neighbours are informed of it. Section 4.1 details the decision process and Sect. 4.2 gives the details of the maintenance protocol enforcing the decision taken.

4.1 Scaling Decision

Duplication Decision. Let C denote the capacity of the nodes, i.e. the number of records they can process per time unit. Let l_t the current load experienced by the OI, *i.e*, the number of records received during the last time unit. r, with $0 < r \le 1$ denotes the desired load level of operators, typically a parameter set by the user. It represents the targeted ratio between load and capacity of each node. The objective for an OI is to find

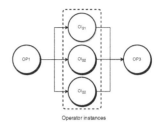

Operator instances

Fig. 1. Scaling a 3-stage pipeline.

the replication factor to be applied to itself so all OIs for this operator globally reach a load level of r. The desired load for an OI is $r \times C$, which means that this OI needs to be scaled with a factor of $\frac{l_t}{r \times C}$. Note that this factor will be concurrently calculated and applied by each OI for this operator. This means that the OI will need to get duplicated $\frac{l_t}{r \times C} - 1$ times. If $p < 1$, it is interpreted as a duplication probability: the node will get duplicated with probability p. Otherwise, the node will get duplicated $\lfloor p \rfloor$ times and then one final time with probability $p - \lfloor p \rfloor$.

Deletion Decision. The inverse decision, triggered when the load is below a certain threshold, follows the same principle. Yet, the factor calculated in this case is a probability. Note that there is a risk that all OIs for a given operator take this decision at the approximate same time, leading to a collective termination, and to the disappearance of this operator. This problem is solved by introducing a particular node (called the *operator keeper*) that cannot terminates itself whatever its load. The deletion/duplication factor is materialized through the `getProbability(C, r, l_t)` function. The `applyProba(p: real)` function transforms a probability into a boolean stating whether the deletion or duplication action will actually take place.

4.2 Scaling Protocol

Algorithm 1 gives the pseudo-code of the protocol triggered once the duplication decision has been taken. It takes two extra inputs: i) $thres_\uparrow$, the value above which the load level triggers the duplication policy, and ii) the list of successors and predecessors of the current OI. The first part of the algorithm consists in calculating the amount of duplication needed to reach the targeted load ratio r (in Lines 2–4). From Lines 5 to Lines 7, the calculated amount of nodes get started. Newly spawned OIs are not yet `active`: they are idle, waiting for a message of the current node to initialize its neighbors and start processing incoming data, which is stored in some entry queue in the meantime. The current node, in Lines 9–11, spreads the information about the new nodes to its own neighbors. A counter of the expected number of responses is initialized. To validate the duplication and actually initialize the new, initially idle, nodes, the OI needs to collect the acknowledgement of all of its neighbors.

Algorithm 1. Scale-out protocol.

Input: $thres_\uparrow$: threshold
Input: $succs, preds$: arrays of successors and predecessors
  1: **procedure** $opScaleOut()$
  2:     $p \leftarrow getProbability(C, r, l_t)$
  3:     $newAddrs \leftarrow []$
  4:     $n \leftarrow \lfloor p \rfloor + applyProba(p)$
  5:     **if** $n > 1$ **then**
  6:         **for** $i \leftarrow 1$ **to** n **do**
  7:             $newAddrs.add(addSibling())$
  8:         **end for**
  9:         $sendInformation(\text{``duplication''}, succs, preds, newAddrs)$
 10:         $nbAck \leftarrow 0$
 11:         $nbAckExpected \leftarrow |succs| + |preds|$
 12:     **end if**
 13: **upon** receipt **of** ($\text{``duplication''}, addrs$) **from** p
 14:     **if** $p \in succs$ **then**
 15:         **if** isActive **then**
 16:             $succs = succs \cup addrs$
 17:         **else**
 18:             $succsToAdd = succsToAdd \cup addrs$
 19:         **end if**
 20:     **else if** $p \in preds$ **then**
 21:         **if** isActive **then**
 22:             $preds = preds \cup addrs$
 23:         **else**
 24:             $predsToAdd = predsToAdd \cup addrs$
 25:         **end if**
 26:     $send(\text{``duplication\_ack''}, p)$
 27: **upon** receipt **of** ($\text{``duplication\_ack''}$)
 28:     $nbAck + +$
 29:     **if** $nbAck = nbAckExpected$ **then**
 30:         **for each** $newSibling$ **in** $newAddrs$ **do**
 31:             $send(\text{``start''}, succs, preds, newSibling)$
 32:         **end for**
 33:     **end if**
 34: **upon** receipt **of** ($\text{``start''}, succs\_, preds\_$) **from** p
 35:     $succs = succs\_ \cup succsToAdd \setminus succsToDelete$
 36:     $preds = preds\_ \cup predsToAdd \setminus predsToDelete$
 37:     $isActive \leftarrow true$

Lines 14–19 shows the case of a *duplication* message coming from a successor: new predecessors addresses are added to the corresponding set. If the node receiving the message is itself not yet *active*, i.e., it is itself a new node waiting for its *start* message, it will store the new neighbour in a particular *succsToAdd* set containing future neighbors: the node may store incoming data but cannot yet send data to its successors to avoid lost tuples, as reviewed in Sect. 4.3. Then, in Lines 20–25, the case of a duplication message received from a predecessor is processed similarly. Finally, the node acknowledges the message to the duplicating node by sending a *duplication_ack* message. Once all acknowledgements have been received by the duplicating OI, the new nodes can become active and start processing records. To this end, in Line 31 of Algorithm 1, the duplicating OI sends a *start* message to all of its new siblings. On receipt—refer to

Lines 35–36)—the new siblings initialize the sets of their neighbors by combining the sets sent by the duplicating OI and the possible information received in the meantime, stored in *ToAdd and *ToDelete variables.

Let us now review the similar termination protocol, detailed in Algorithm 2. The algorithm first shows how the current OI ensures that every node pertained by the deletion (its neighbours) is informed. On receipt of this upcoming termination information, we again have to consider two cases, depending whether the receiving node is active or not: if it is, then the node is simply removed from the list of its neighbors (either from *pred* or *succ*) and an acknowledgement is sent back. Otherwise, the node is stored in a *to be deleted* set of nodes, that will be taken into account at starting time. The final step consists, on the node about to terminate, to count the number of acknowledgements. As discussed in Sect. 4.3, the terminating node must wait for all the acknowledgement of the nodes it considers as neighbors. Once it is done, it flushes its data queue and triggers its own termination.

Algorithm 2. Scale-in protocol.

Input: $thres_\downarrow$: threshold
```
 1: procedure operatorScale − In()
 2:    p ← getProbability(C, r, l_t)
 3:    if applyProba(p) then
 4:       sendInformation("deletion", succs, preds, me)
 5:       nbAck ← 0; nbAckExpected ← |succs| + |preds|
 6:    end if
 7: upon receipt of ("deletion", addr) from p
 8:    if P ∈ succs then
 9:       if isActive then
10:          succs ← succs \ addr
11:       else
12:          succsToDelete ← succsToDelete ∪ addr
13:       end if
14:    else if p ∈ preds then
15:       if isActive then
16:          preds ← preds \ addr
17:       else
18:          predsToDelete ← predsToDelete ∪ addr
19:       end if
20:    send("deletion_ack", p)
21: upon receipt of ("deletion_ack")
22:    nbAck + +
23:    if nbAck = nbAckExpected then
24:       terminate() // wait current tuples to be processed
25: end if
```

The global algorithm checks periodically the current load *vs* the thresholds and starts the corresponding algorithm as needed, each OI, except the operator keepers, doing that independently at possibly different times.

4.3   Correctness

A graph is said *stable* when for every OI, the set of its successors is equal to the set of OI having it as a predecessor, and the same goes reversing successors and predecessors. In such a situation, following that nodes are reliable and that messages reach their destination in a finite time, no tuple is lost.

Let us now review the possible perturbations in this graph. The simplest case is a single duplication triggered in a stable graph. Recall that new nodes are first spawned (through `addSibling()`) and become `active` once they have received a *start* message. Yet, a spawned not-yet-active node can store incoming data messages: becoming active means that it will start process them and send the result to its successors. Note that a node needs to know where to send messages (its successors) but does not need to know its predecessors to receive messages from them. For instance, using message-oriented middleware, does not require a node to know where the messages are coming from to receive them. We simply need to be sure that nodes to which messages are sent have been spawned. Clearly, starting from a stable graph, successors of the new instances are already running when the new instances become active. Also, when predecessors of the new instances receive the notification about them, new instances are already spawne, since calls to `addSibling()` are made (and return) before the information is sent to the predecessors. After this period of instability, everyone has received and updated its sets of neighbours so the graph becomes stable again. Having multiple concurrent duplication processes on different OIs of an operator does not bring any difficulty, OIs processing messages one by one.

Let us now study the deletion of a single node at a time starting from a stable graph. Messages could be lost in case the predecessors of the deleted node keep sending message to it. As per the algorithm, to trigger the actual termination (calling `terminate()`), a node needs to receive acks from its predecessors. These acks are sent only after the `deletion` message has been received. What we assume here is that before sending the `deletion_ack` message, an OI communicates with its data processing layer so as to inform it of the upcoming deletion. The data processing layer takes it into account by stopping emitting messages to the about-to-be-deleted OI. Yet, the last message sent contains a particular *last message* stamp. The `terminate()` primitive is assumed to return only after these specifically marked messages has been received from each predecessor, ensuring no message is lost. Neighbors of the deleting node are informed of the deletion and their sets of neighbours are updated, so the graph becomes stable again. Multiple concurrent deletions do not bring any more difficulty.

Let us now study the case of having concurrent duplication and deletion. If triggered by nodes that are not neighbours, this does not bring any particular difficulty. If they are triggered by nodes that are not neighbours, this is not a problem either. A more difficult case to check is when two neighbouring nodes N1 and N2 take these antagonist actions. Say N2 is amongst the successors of N1. Assume N1 triggers a duplication while N2 triggers its own termination. Consequently, N1 sends a `duplication` message while N2 sends a `deletion` message at the approximate same time. Let us assume that N2's deletion message takes far longer to reach N1 than N1's message to reach N2. Assuming channels are FIFO we distinguish two cases: The first case is when N2 sends the `deletion` message before processing N1's duplication message. In this case, due to the

FIFO assumption, N1 will first receive N2's deletion message and remove N2 from its set of successors, so that, once N1 receives all of the `duplication_ack` from its neighbours (including N2), N1 will send the starting message to the new OI with a set of successors not including N2, leading both N1 and the new OI to not consider N2 as a successor. The second case is when N2 processes the `duplication` message sent by M1 before sending its own `deletion` message. In this case, N2 sends the *duplication_ack* message before the `deletion` message. So they will arrive in this order on N1. On receipt of the first message, N1 still considers N2 as a neighbour for the future OI and may send it to the new OI at starting time. Yet it is not a problem, as N2 now knows about the new OI and will send its deletion message also to it. While not yet active, the new OI will receive the deletion message and keep the information that N2 is to be deleted from the successors at starting time, as enforced by Line 12 in Algorithm 1.

The case of two concurrent duplications is simpler. In case each duplication message arrives before the other one is processed, each node will learn its new neighbour independently and start its new OI with the information of that new neighbours' OI. The case of two concurrent deletions is solved similarly.

5 Simulation Results

We developed a discrete-time simulator in Java. Each time step t sees the following operations: a subset of the nodes test the conditions for triggering a scaling operation. In case the protocol is initiated, the first message (`duplication` or `deletion`) is received by the neighbours of the initiating node. Then, messages sent at step t are processed at step $t + 1$ and new resulting messages are sent as per the protocol, to be processed at time $t + 2$, and so on. A scale-out operation spans three steps, and a scale-in one spans two. The variation of the workload is modelled by a stochastic process, mimicking a Brownian motion, which allows us to evaluate our algorithm with a quick yet swift variation of the workload. The graph tested is a pipeline composed of 5 operators, each operator having a workload evolving independently. Initially, each operator is duplicated on 7 OIs. Compute nodes hosting OIs have a processing capacity of processing 500 tuples per time step. The other parameters are: $r = 0.7$, $thres_\downarrow = 0.6$, and $thres_\uparrow = 0.8$. Nodes try to start the scaling protocol every 5 steps.

Our algorithm's ability to quickly reach an adequate number of instances through local decisions is illustrated by Fig. 2. The blue curve shows the aggregated number of tuples globally received by all the nodes in the pipeline, and the red curve shows how the total number of OIs (whatever the operator they are an instance of) evolved during the experiment. Firstly, we observe that the number of nodes decreases with the decline of the workload during the first 25 iterations. Then, it increases until reaching the peak of 114 nodes at iteration 104 quickly after the load itself reached the peak of 40396 tuples per step at iteration 100. Then, the load (and consequently the number of OIs) does not fluctuate significantly. Secondly, we observe that the number of nodes can scale quickly. The delay between a variation in the load and the adaptation can is

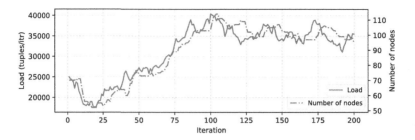

Fig. 2. Number of nodes *vs* load.

small most of the time, in spite of the decentralized and asynchronous nature of the scaling mechanism. Nodes, without coordination, based on decisions taken locally, are able to start or remove nodes in a *batch* fashion, the burden of starting or removing these nodes being shared by the existing nodes. Remind also that this graph shows the global number of instances for all the operators. This number may vary differently from one operator to another one. More simulation results are available in a research report [3].

6   Conclusion

This paper presented a fully decentralized autoscaling algorithm for stream processing applications. The algorithm relies on independent, local autoscaling decisions taken by operators having only a partial view of the load and maintaining only a local view of the graph. Future work will consist in relaxing some of the assumptions regarding the algorithm, in particular the fault model and the statelessness of operators. On the validation side, more simulations are needed to better capture the protocol's behaviour, tune correctly its parameters (for instance to avoid oscillations), and compare it to a centralized baseline. Also, the prototype of a decentralized stream processing engine is being developed, including the scaling algorithm presented.

Acknowledgements. This project was partially funded by ANR grant ASTRID SESAME ANR-16-ASTR-0026-02.

References

1. Aniello, L., Baldoni, R., Querzoni, L.: Adaptive online scheduling in storm. In: Proceedings of the 7th ACM International Conference on Distributed Event-Based Systems (DEBS 2013), Arlington, USA, pp. 207–218. ACM (2013)
2. de Assunção, M.D., Veith, A.D.S., Buyya, R.: Distributed data stream processing and edge computing: a survey on resource elasticity and future directions. J. Netw. Comput. Appl. **103**, 1–17 (2018)
3. Belkhiria, M., Tedeschi, C.: Decentralized scaling for stream processing engines, May 2019. working paper or preprint. https://hal.inria.fr/hal-02127609

4. Calcavecchia, N.M., Caprarescu, B.A., Di Nitto, E., Dubois, D.J., Petcu, D.: DEPAS: a decentralized probabilistic algorithm for auto-scaling. Computing **94**(8), 701–730 (2012). https://doi.org/10.1007/s00607-012-0198-8

5. Carbone, P., Katsifodimos, A., Ewen, S., Markl, V., Haridi, S., Tzoumas, K.: Apache flink ^{TM}: stream and batch processing in a single engine. IEEE Data Eng. Bull. **38**(4), 28–38 (2015)

6. Cardellini, V., Grassi, V., Lo Presti, F., Nardelli, M.: Distributed QoS-aware scheduling in storm. In: Proceedings of the 9th ACM International Conference on Distributed Event-Based Systems, DEBS 2015, pp. 344–347. ACM (2015)

7. Cardellini, V., Presti, F.L., Nardelli, M., Russo, G.R.: Decentralized self-adaptation for elastic data stream processing. Future Gener. Comput. Syst. **87**, 171–185 (2018)

8. Castro Fernandez, R., Migliavacca, M., Kalyvianaki, E., Pietzuch, P.: Integrating scale out and fault tolerance in stream processing using operator state management. In: ACM SIGMOD 2013, pp. 725–736. ACM, New York (2013)

9. Dwork, C., Lynch, N., Stockmeyer, L.: Consensus in the presence of partial synchrony. J. ACM **35**(2), 288–323 (1988)

10. Gedik, B., Schneider, S., Hirzel, M., Wu, K.: Elastic scaling for data stream processing. IEEE Trans. Parallel Distrib. Syst. **25**(6), 1447–1463 (2014)

11. Gulisano, V., Jiménez-Peris, R., Patiño-Martínez, M., Soriente, C., Valduriez, P.: StreamCloud: an elastic and scalable data streaming system. IEEE Trans. Parallel Distrib. Syst. **23**(12), 2351–2365 (2012)

12. Hirzel, M., Soulé, R., Schneider, S., Gedik, B., Grimm, R.: A catalog of stream processing optimizations. ACM Comput. Surv. **46**(4), 46:1–46:34 (2014)

13. Hochreiner, C., Vögler, M., Schulte, S., Dustdar, S.: Elastic stream processing for the internet of things. In: 2016 IEEE 9th International Conference on Cloud Computing (CLOUD), pp. 100–107, June 2016. https://doi.org/10.1109/CLOUD.2016.0023

14. Kulkarni, S., et al.: Twitter heron: stream processing at scale. In: Proceedings of the 2015 ACM SIGMOD International Conference on Management of Data, SIGMOD 2015, pp. 239–250. ACM, New York (2015)

15. Matteis, T.D., Mencagli, G.: Elastic scaling for distributed latency-sensitive data stream operators. In: Proceedings of the 25th Euromicro International Conference on Parallel, Distributed and Network-Based Processing (PDP 2017), pp. 61–68 (2017)

16. Peng, B., Hosseini, M., Hong, Z., Farivar, R., Campbell, R.: R-storm: resource-aware scheduling in storm. In: Proceedings of the 16th Annual Middleware Conference, Middleware 2015, pp. 149–161. ACM, New York (2015)

17. Pietzuch, P., Ledlie, J., Shneidman, J., Roussopoulos, M., Welsh, M., Seltzer, M.: Network-aware operator placement for stream-processing systems. In: 22nd International Conference on Data Engineering (ICDE 2006), p. 49, April 2006

18. Schneider, S., Hirzel, M., Gedik, B., Wu, K.: Auto-parallelizing stateful distributed streaming applications. In: International Conference on Parallel Architectures and Compilation Techniques, PACT 2012, Minneapolis, USA, pp. 53–64, September 2012

19. Toshniwal, A., et al.: Storm@Twitter. In: International Conference on Management of Data (SIGMOD 2014), Snowbird, USA, pp. 147–156, June 2014

20. Xu, J., Chen, Z., Tang, J., Su, S.: T-storm: traffic-aware online scheduling in storm. In: IEEE 34th International Conference on Distributed Computing Systems (2014)

21. Yousefpour, A., et al.: All one needs to know about fog computing and related edge computing paradigms: a complete survey. CoRR abs/1808.05283 (2018)

Transparent Autonomicity for OpenMP Applications

Daniele De Sensi$^{(\boxtimes)}$ ⓘ and Marco Danelutto

Computer Science Department, University of Pisa, Pisa, Italy
{desensi,marcod}@di.unipi.it
http://pages.di.unipi.it/desensi, http://pages.di.unipi.it/marcod

Abstract. One of the key needs of an autonomic computing system is the ability to monitor the application performance with minimal intrusiveness and performance overhead. Several solutions have been proposed, differing in terms of effort required by the application programmers to add autonomic capabilities to their applications. In this work we extend the NORNIR autonomic framework, allowing it to transparently monitor OpenMP applications thanks to the novel OpenMP Tools (OMPT) API. By using this interface, we are able to transparently transfer performance monitoring information from the application to the NORNIR framework. This does not require any manual intervention by the programmer, which can seamlessly control an already existing application, enforcing any performance and/or power consumption requirement. We evaluate our approach on some real applications from the PARSEC and NAS benchmarks, showing that our solution introduces a negligible performance overhead, while being able to correctly control applications' performance and power consumption.

Keywords: Power-aware computing · Autonomic computing · OpenMP · Power capping

1 Introduction

Adding autonomic capabilities to applications is an important feature of modern computing systems. Indeed, being able to automatically tune the application according to the user requirements would allow an optimal usage of the computing resources, with a consequent reduction of their power consumption. Autonomic capabilities are usually added to applications by having a separate entity (a *manager*) which periodically monitors the application and decides the action to take (e.g. reduce the resources allocated to the application) according to some requirements specified by the user. Such requirements can be usually expressed in terms of performance, power consumption, reliability, and others.

For performance monitoring purposes, interactions between the autonomic manager and the application can be implemented in several ways. The simplest solution would be to modify the application inserting some instrumentation

© Springer Nature Switzerland AG 2020
U. Schwardmann et al. (Eds.): Euro-Par 2019 Workshops, LNCS 11997, pp. 54–64, 2020.
https://doi.org/10.1007/978-3-030-48340-1_5

calls, which would collect the performance of the application and communicate this information to the autonomic manager, for example by using the *Heartbeat API* [15] or the NORNIR framework [9]. However, it is not always possible to modify the source code of the application, and this additional effort could discourage application programmers, limiting the adoption of such autonomic tools. On the other hand, other solutions monitor application performances without requiring any modification to the application source code. For example, this can be implemented by modifying the application binary to add instrumentation calls, either by using dynamic instrumentation tools like *PIN* [14] or by using static istrumentation tools such as *Maqao* [6] or *Dyninst* [7]. Alternatively, application performance may be inferred by analyzing performance counters (such as the number of instructions executed per time unit). However, by using such approach it would be difficult for the user to relate this performance information to the actual application performance (for example in terms of number of stream elements processed per time unit). Eventually, a last class of solutions modifies neither the application source code nor its binary, while still being able to monitor real application performance. These solutions can be used on applications implemented with specific programming frameworks, and interact with the runtime used by the application [10,18], for example by intercepting some runtime calls.

In this work we will focus on this last class of solutions, by extending the NORNIR autonomic framework, allowing it to transparently interact with OpenMP applications. We will analyze our solution on different applications from the PARSEC [8] and NAS [5] benchmarks, showing that our implementation introduces a negligible performance overhead, while at the same time allowing the user to set arbitrary performance and power consumption requirements on such applications.

The rest of this paper is structured as follows. Section 2 briefly describes some existing works addressing autonomicity in OpenMP applications. In Sect. 3 we provide some background about the NORNIR framework and the OMPT API, which will be used to intercept OpenMP calls. In Sect. 4 we will describe the design and implementation of our solution and in Sect. 5 we will perform the experimental evaluation. Eventually, Sect. 6 concludes this work and outlines possible future developments.

2   Related Work

Different works deal with autonomic solutions for controlling performance and power consumption of applications, according to user requirements. In this section we will focus on the existing works targeting OpenMP applications.

Li et al. [13] target hybrid MPI/OpenMP applications, proposing an algorithm which applies Dynamic Voltage and Frequency Scaling (DVFS) and Dynamic Concurrency Throttling (DCT) to improve the energy efficiency of such applications. However, manual instrumentation by the programmer is required, and no explicit performance and/or power consumption requirements can be specified by the user.

Other works [3,17] propose extensions to the OpenMP annotations, to express explicit requirements in terms of power consumption, energy, or performance. Although such approaches are more expressive than the one presented in this work, they require to modify and recompile the application source code.

Wang et al. [18] apply clock modulation and DCT to OpenMP applications to reduce their energy consumption. On the other hand, in our work we interface OpenMP applications to the NORNIR framework, allowing to enforce arbitrary constraints in terms of power consumption and performance, by using not only DCT and clock modulation but also DVFS and other mechanisms provided by the NORNIR framework. Moreover, whereas in the work by Want et al. [18] the selection of the optimal concurrency level is done through a complete exploration of the search space, by using NORNIR different algorithms can be applied to avoid such full exploration, thus reducing the time required to find the optimal resources configuration.

In addition to the aforementioned limitations, all the described approaches are implemented ad-hoc and do not rely on any general purpose autonomic framework. On the contrary, our approach relies on NORNIR, extending the perks of the framework (e.g. the possibility to easily implement new autonomic algorithm) to any OpenMP application.

3   Background

In this section we provide some background about the NORNIR framework and the OMPT API.

3.1   Nornir

NORNIR[1] [9] is a framework for power-aware computing, providing the possibility to control performance and power consumption of applications running on shared memory multicore machines. NORNIR provides a set of algorithms to control performance and power consumption of applications, in order to enforce requirements specified by the user. Internally, NORNIR abstracts many low-level aspects related to interaction with both the underlying hardware and the application, and it can be easily customized by adding new control algorithms. NORNIR acts according to the *Monitor, Analyze, Plan, Execute* (MAPE) loop. At each iteration of the MAPE loop (also known as *control step*), the application performance and power consumption is monitored, then appropriate decisions based on these observations are taken, and eventually these decisions are applied in the *Execute* phase. The MAPE loop is executed by a *manager* entity, which is executed as a separate thread/process.

To perform the *Monitor* and *Execute* phases, the NORNIR *manager* needs to interact both with the machine it is running on, but also with the application it is controlling. To interact with the underlying hardware, NORNIR relies

---

[1] https://github.com/DanieleDeSensi/nornir.

on the MAMMUT library [11], which abstracts in an object-oriented fashion the available hardware control knobs and monitoring interfaces. This allows an easy exploitation of many features required in power-aware autonomic computing, such as scaling the clock frequency of the cores, monitoring the power consumption, dynamically turning off CPUs, etc. On the other hand, to interact with the application, multiple possibilities are provided by NORNIR:

Black-box. With this kind of interaction, the source code of the controlled application does not need to be modified, and NORNIR will monitor application performance by using hardware performance counters (e.g. number of instructions executed per time unit).

Instrumentation. If users are willing to modify the application to be controlled, they could insert some instrumentation calls in the source code of the application, to track application progress (e.g., in streaming applications, the number of stream elements processed per time unit). Although this is more intrusive than the *Black-box* approach, in this case the user can express the performance requirements in a more meaningful way, rather than expressing them in terms of CPU instructions.

Runtime. In some cases, NORNIR can directly interact with the runtime of the application, not requiring any modification to the application code but at the same time being able to collect high-level performance metrics, such as number of stream elements processed per time unit. Moreover, in this case it is also possible to exploit more efficient actuators, such as the *concurrency throttling* knob, which allows NORNIR to dynamically change the number of threads used by the application. Currently, NORNIR provides this possibility only for applications implemented using the *FastFlow* framework [2]. In this work, we will extend this possibility also to applications using OpenMP.

Nornir API. Lastly, NORNIR also provides a programming API to implement parallel applications, relying on a runtime based on *Fastflow* [2]. This approach allows a fine-grained control on the application, but it is also the most intrusive one, since it requires the user to rewrite the application by using a different programming framework.

NORNIR limitations mostly depend on the limitation of the algorithms used for the *Analyze* and *Plan* phases. For example, one common assumption made by these algorithms is that the application can reasonably balance the workload among the threads. If this is not the case, this could affect the accuracy of these algorithms.

3.2   OMPT

The OpenMP Tools API (OMPT) [4,12] is an Application Programming Interface for first-party performance tools. By using OMPT, it is possible to track different events during the lifetime of an OpenMP application, such as tasks creation and destruction, OpenMP initialization, synchronizations, and others. To intercept these events, the OMPT user must define callbacks which will be invoked every time one of these events occurs. Then, these callbacks can be either statically linked to the application when it is compiled, or they can be dynamically loaded by specifying the dynamic library containing such user-defined callbacks in the LD_PRELOAD environment variable. By tracking these events, it would be possible to monitor the application progress and performance (e.g., in terms of number of OpenMP tasks executed per time unit), which is what is needed by NORNIR to monitor an application and to apply autonomic decisions.

4   Design and Implementation

In this section we will describe how NORNIR has been extended to transparently monitor OpenMP applications. First, because the OMPT API is not yet provided by most OpenMP implementations, we rely on an experimental LLVM-based implementation [1]. To interface the NORNIR *manager* to the OpenMP application, we first intercept the initialization of the OpenMP application by using the OMPT API. When OpenMP is initialized, the *manager* is created and started as an external process. The *manager* will execute the MAPE loop and, at each iteration of the MAPE loop, in the *monitor* phase it will collect the application performance by sending a request to the application process. Every time a task is created, the event will be intercepted through OMPT. If a request by the NORNIR manager was present, then the number of tasks executed per time unit will be communicated to the manager, otherwise the number of executed tasks will be stored locally. This interaction between the application and the *manager* is implemented by using the RIFF library, which is a small library (provided by NORNIR) for monitoring application performance, which was already used for *Instrumentation* interactions (see Sect. 3.1). This exchange between the OpenMP application and the NORNIR manager is depicted in Fig. 1.

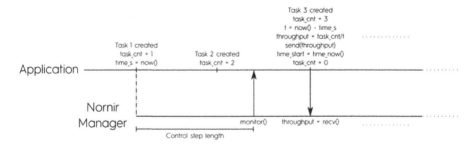

Fig. 1. Interaction between the OpenMP application and the NORNIR manager.

However, this approach would not work for applications composed only of a single OpenMP parallel loop. In this case, the OpenMP runtime would create a number of tasks equal to the number of cores available on the machine, and then each task will execute different chunks of loop iterations. Since tasks are

Listing 1.1. Nornir configuration file

```xml
<?xml version="1.0" encoding="UTF-8"?>
<nornirParameters>
<requirements>
    <throughput>100</throughput>
</requirements>
</nornirParameters>
```

created only once, we would not be able to track application progress. To address this problem, we also need to track the events associated to the scheduling of chunks of loop iterations. However, this type of callbacks is not defined by the OMPT API specification. For this reason, we extended the LLVM-based OMPT implementation to also track the scheduling of chunks of iterations in OpenMP parallel loops. This modified OpenMP implementation has been released as open source [16] and is used by NORNIR by default. It is worth remarking that if the application is composed of a single parallel loop and if static scheduling is used, then we would have the same problem, since only one chunk per thread will be generated, and we will not be able to track application progress.

To impose specific performance and power consumption requirements, the user needs first to build an XML file containing, among others, the minimum performance required (in terms of tasks or loop iterations processed per second) and the maximum allowed power consumption. The path of this file must be then specified in the `NORNIR_OMP_PARAMETERS` environment variable. For example, if the user wants his/her OpenMP application to execute 100 loop iterations per second, the XML file like the one in Listing 1.1 should be provided.

Then, the user needs to specify the path of the NORNIR dynamic library and of the modified OpenMP implementation in the `LD_PRELOAD` environment variable. This process is wrapped in a script which is provided by NORNIR and which sets these paths in a proper way according to the way NORNIR was installed. For example, to run the `foo` OpenMP application enforcing the requirements specified in the `config.xml` configuration file, it is sufficient to run the command: `nornir_openmp foo config.xml`.

It is worth mentioning that the same approach could also be adopted for other frameworks (e.g. Intel TBB). To do that, we should locate the points in the runtime code where we could track application progress (e.g. where tasks are created), and then insert instrumentation calls in the same way we did for OpenMP. This could be either done by using similar profiling API, or by actually modifying the runtime source code.

5 Experiments

In this section we first evaluate the overhead introduced by NORNIR (which also includes the overhead for intercepting OpenMP events). Then, we will show

how by applying our approach it is possible to transparently enforce arbitrary performance and power consumption requirements on OpenMP applications. For our analysis we selected the *blackscholes* and *bodytrack* benchmarks from the PARSEC benchmark suite [8] and the *bt* and *cg* applications from the NAS benchmark [5]. We used the *native* input for the PARSEC applications, the class B input for *bt* and the class C input for *cg*. All the experiments have been executed on a Dual-socket NUMA machine with two Intel Xeon E5-2695 Ivy Bridge CPUs running at 2.40 GHz featuring 24 hyper-threaded cores (12 per socket). Each hyper-threaded core has 32KB private L1, 256KB private L2 and 30MB of L3 shared with the cores on the same socket. The machine has 64GB of DDR3 RAM. We did not use the hyper-threading, and the applications used at most 24 cores in our experiments. The software environment consists of Linux 3.14.49 x86_64 shipped with CentOS 7.1 and gcc version 4.8.5.

Every experiment has been executed a number of times, until the 95% confidence interval from the mean was lower than the 5% of the mean. We report the entire distribution of results as a *boxplot* (e.g. see Fig. 2), where the upper and lower borders of the box represent the third ($Q3$) and first ($Q1$) quartile respectively. Being IQR the interquartile range (i.e. $Q3 - Q1$), the upper and lower whiskers represent the largest sample lower than $Q3 + 1.5 \cdot IQR$ and the smallest sample greater than $Q1 - 1.5 \cdot IQR$. All the points outside these whiskers are considered to be outliers and are plotted individually. The line inside the box represents the median and the small diamond represents the mean.

5.1   Overhead

To measure the overhead introduced by NORNIR and OMPT, we first executed the applications in their default configuration (denoted as *Default*), without any kind of instrumentation and without enabling OMPT. Then, we use OMPT but we do not communicate any data to NORNIR (denoted as *OMPT*). Eventually, we attach NORNIR to the application, but we do not change its configuration. In this way, we can separately measure the overhead introduced by OMPT to intercept OpenMP calls and the overhead introduced by NORNIR plus OMPT, including the overhead to communicate performance information between the application and the NORNIR manager. We report the results of this analysis in Fig. 2. We report on the x-axis the different applications, and on the y-axis the application throughput (in terms of tasks/iterations executed per time unit). The throughput is normalized with respect to the median throughout of the default execution (the higher the better), so that values lower than one represent a lower throughput with respect to the default execution.

As we can see from both the medians and the means, while for *blackscholes* and *bodytrack* there are no relevant differences, for *bt* and *cg* we have some performance degradation. For *bt*, the performance degradation is less then 10%, which however seems to be caused by OMPT rather than by the communication of the performance information to NORNIR. On the contrary, for *cg* we have an overhead lower than 5%, which the data show to be caused by NORNIR.

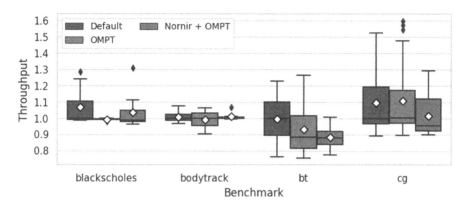

Fig. 2. Throughput comparison between the default execution and the execution where NORNIR and OMPT are used. Throughput is normalized with respect to the default execution. The higher the better.

5.2   Throughput and Power Consumption Requirements

We now analyze the ability of NORNIR to set explicit performance and power consumption requirements, by using the performance information extracted with OMPT. To enforce performance and power consumption requirements we used one of the several algorithms provided by NORNIR (ANALYTICAL_FULL). This algorithm tunes the number of cores used by the application and their clock frequency, searching for a configuration which satisfies the requirements expressed by the user. To avoid biases due to the selection of a specific requirement, we perform our test for different requirements. For example, being T the application throughput, we set as throughput requirements $0.2 \cdot T$, $0.4 \cdot T$, ..., T. A similar approach has been adopted for power consumption requirements[2].

We report in Fig. 3 the results of this evaluation for performance requirements. We show on the x-axis the performance requirements expressed as a percentage of the maximum performance. On the y-axis we show the obtained performance normalized with respect to the requirement. Namely, 1.0 represents the requirement and values higher or equal than one mean that NORNIR was able to satisfy the requirement. As shown in the plot, we were able to run the application so that its throughput is higher or equal than that required by the user. In almost all the cases (with the exception of *bt* and *cg* on the 40% requirement), the achieved throughput was at most 20% higher than the user requirement.

Similarly, in Fig. 4 we report the results of the evaluation for power consumption requirements. We show on the x-axis the power consumption requirements expressed as a percentage of the maximum power consumption. On the y-axis we report the obtained power consumption normalized with respect to the requirement. Namely, 1.0 represents the requirement and values lower or equal than one

---

[2] For power consumption requirements, we do not consider the 0.2 requirement since it can never be enforced, not even by using only one core at minimum clock frequency.

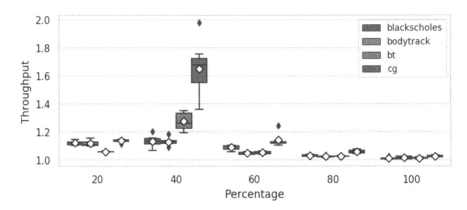

Fig. 3. Performance of the analyzed applications under different performance requirements. On the x-axis the performance requirements expressed as a percentage of the maximum performance. On the y-axis the obtained performance normalized with respect to the requirement (i.e. values higher than one mean that NORNIR was able to satisfy the requirement).

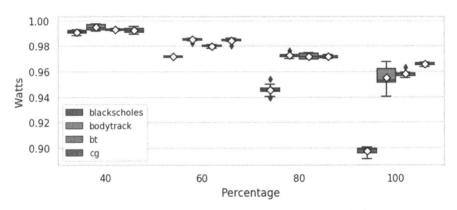

Fig. 4. Power consumption of the analyzed applications under different power consumption requirements. On the x-axis the power consumption requirements expressed as a percentage of the maximum power consumption. On the y-axis the obtained power consumption normalized with respect to the requirement (i.e. values lower than one mean that NORNIR was able to satisfy the requirement).

mean that NORNIR was able to satisfy the power consumption requirement. Also in this case we were able to correctly enforce the user requirements, having a power consumption which is always lower or equal to that specified by the user. In all the cases except one (*blackscholes* for the 100% requirement), NORNIR was able to find a configuration characterized by a power consumption at most 5% lower than that required by the user.

6   Conclusions and Future Work

When designing autonomic solutions, a relevant design decision is related to the way in which the application performance is monitored. Several solutions are possible, each requiring a different effort to the application programmer. In this work we analyze the possibility to intercept different events in OpenMP applications to track their performance. Such solution would not require any effort to the application programmer.

To implement this process we relied on the OMPT API, which allowed us to track OpenMP applications and to interface them to the NORNIR framework, allowing us to transparently set arbitrary performance and power consumption requirements on existing applications. To correctly monitor applications composed of a single parallel loop, we modified the OMPT backend to also track the scheduling of chunks of iterations in parallel loops. Moreover, all the developed code has been integrated into NORNIR, which is a publicly available open-source framework. Eventually, we showed that the introduced performance overhead is negligible and that we can correctly enforce arbitrary requirements.

In the future, we would like to extend the interaction with OpenMP also to the *execute* phase of the MAPE loop, by dynamically changing the number of threads used by the OpenMP runtime. Moreover, we would like to monitor the performance at a finer granularity, for example by intercepting individual iterations of the parallel loop rather than the scheduling of chunks of iterations.

Acknowledgement. This work has been partially supported by Univ. of Pisa PRA_2018_66 DECLware: Declarative methodologies for designing and deploying applications.

References

1. LLVM runtime with experimental changes for OMPT (2019). https://github.com/OpenMPToolsInterface/LLVM-openmp. Accessed 12 June 2019
2. Aldinucci, M., Danelutto, M., Kilpatrick, P., Torquati, M.: Fastflow: high-level and efficient streaming on multicore, pp. 261-280. John Wiley and Sons Ltd. (2017). Chapter 13
3. Alessi, F., Thoman, P., Georgakoudis, G., Fahringer, T., Nikolopoulos, D.S.: Application-level energy awareness for OpenMP. In: Terboven, C., de Supinski, B.R., Reble, P., Chapman, B.M., Müller, M.S. (eds.) IWOMP 2015. LNCS, vol. 9342, pp. 219–232. Springer, Cham (2015). https://doi.org/10.1007/978-3-319-24595-9_16
4. Eichenberger, M.S.A., Mellor-Crummey, J.: OpenMP Technical Report 2 on the OMPT Interface (2019). https://www.openmp.org/wp-content/uploads/ompt-tr2.pdf/. Accessed 12 June 2019
5. Bailey, D.H., et al.: The NAS parallel benchmarks - summary and preliminary results. In: Proceedings of the 1991 ACM/IEEE Conference on Supercomputing, New York, NY, USA, pp. 158–165. ACM (1991)

6. Barthou, D., Charif Rubial, A., Jalby, W., Koliai, S., Valensi, C.: Performance tuning of x86 OpenMP codes with MAQAO. In: Müller, M., Resch, M., Schulz, A., Nagel, W. (eds.) Tools for High Performance Computing 2009, pp. 95–113. Springer, Berlin (2010). https://doi.org/10.1007/978-3-642-11261-4_7

7. Bernat, A.R., Miller, B.P.: Anywhere, any-time binary instrumentation. In: Proceedings of the 10th ACM SIGPLAN-SIGSOFT Workshop on Program Analysis for Software Tools (PASTE 2011), pp. 9–16. ACM (2011)

8. Bienia, C., Kumar, S., Singh, J.P., Li, K.: The PARSEC benchmark suite: characterization and architectural implications. In 17th International Conference on Parallel Architectures and Compilation Techniques, pp. 72–81. ACM (2008)

9. De Sensi, D., De Matteis, T., Danelutto, M.: Simplifying self-adaptive and power-aware computing with nornir. Future Gener. Comput. Syst. **87**, 136–151 (2018)

10. De Sensi, D., Torquati, M., Danelutto, M.: A reconfiguration algorithm for power-aware parallel applications. ACM Trans. Archit. Code Optim. **13**(4), 43:1–43:25 (2016)

11. De Sensi, D., Torquati, M., Danelutto, M.: Mammut: high-level management of system knobs and sensors. SoftwareX **6**, 150–154 (2017)

12. Eichenberger, A.E., et al.: OMPT: an OpenMP tools application programming interface for performance analysis. In: Rendell, A.P., Chapman, B.M., Müller, M.S. (eds.) IWOMP 2013. LNCS, vol. 8122, pp. 171–185. Springer, Heidelberg (2013). https://doi.org/10.1007/978-3-642-40698-0_13

13. Li, D., de Supinski, B.R., Schulz, M., Cameron, K., Nikolopoulos, D.S.: Hybrid MPI/openMP power-aware computing. In: 2010 IEEE International Symposium on Parallel Distributed Processing (IPDPS), pp. 1–12, April 2010

14. Luk, C.-K., et al.: Pin: building customized program analysis tools with dynamic instrumentation. SIGPLAN Not. **40**(6), 190–200 (2005)

15. Maggio, M., Hoffmann, H., Santambrogio, M.D., Agarwal, A., Leva, A.: Controlling software applications via resource allocation within the heartbeats framework. In: 49th IEEE Conference on Decision and Control (CDC), pp. 3736–3741. IEEE, December 2010

16. De Sensi, D.: Chunk scheduling callbacks for OMPT (2019). https://github.com/DanieleDeSensi/LLVM-openmp. Accessed 12 June 2019

17. Shafik, R.A., Das, A., Yang, S., Merrett, G., Al-Hashimi, B.M.: Adaptive energy minimization of openMP parallel applications on many-core systems. In: Proceedings of the 6th Workshop on Parallel Programming and Run-Time Management Techniques for Many-core Architectures (PARMA-DITAM 2015), New York, NY, USA, pp. 19–24. ACM (2015)

18. Wang, W., Porterfield, A., Cavazos, J., Bhalachandra, S.: Using per-loop CPU clock modulation for energy efficiency in openMP applications. In: 2015 44th International Conference on Parallel Processing, pp. 629–638, September 2015

COLOC - Workshop on Data Locality

Workshop on Data Locality (COLOC)

Workshop Description

A well-known handicap for HPC applications running on modern highly parallelized and heterogeneous HPC platforms is that an increasing amount of time is spent in communication and data transfers; thus, it is necessary to design, implement, and validate new approaches to optimize process placement and data locality management. COLOC is a forum held to foster collaboration between and contribution from HPC application developers interested in exploring new ways to optimize their code; HPC centers and clusters managers to enhance cluster usage and application efficiency; as well as academics and researchers in scientific computing.

The different areas or research interest include, but are not limited to:

- Modeling node topology
- Modeling network and communication
- Performance analysis of applications to understand affinity
- Affinity metrics
- Runtime support for extracting affinity from application
- Code analysis in order to understand communication pattern
- Algorithm to improve locality
- Language, abstraction, and compiler support for data locality
- Data structure and library support to better manage memory access
- Runtime-system and dynamic locality management
- System-scale locality optimization
- Validating locality optimization at thread or process level
- Memory management
- Locality management in large-scale application

We received three submissions and accepted two. They are both published in these proceedings. The workshop also featured two invited talks:

- "Programming for Data Locality and Parallelism" by Didem Unat, Koç University, Turkey
- "Application Characterization with Cache-Aware Rooine Model" by Leonel Sousa, INESC-ID and Universidade de Lisboa, Portugal

The workshop also featured the SPPEXA http://www.sppexa.de Poster Session on Data Locality. Karl Fürlinger (LMU München, Germany) was the poster chair. Eight posters were accepted and presented by young researchers. The SPPEXA project gave travel grants to the presenters. The list of posters are as follows:

- Camille Coti, Laure Petrucci, and Daniel Alberto Torres Gonzalez: "Process scheduling on volatile nodes for fault-tolerant linear algebra"
- Wesley Smith and Chen Ding: "Relational Theory of Locality"
- Bert Wesarg, Matthias Werner, and Pascal Jungblut: "MEPHISTO - Metaprogramming for Heterogeneous Distributed Systems"

- Pascal Jungblut: "Locality and Node-Level Parallelism within the PGAS Model"
- Dimitris Floros, Alexandros-Stavros Iliopoulos, Nikos Pitsianis, and Xiaobai Sun: "Multi-level Data Translocation for Faster Processing of Scattered Data on Shared-Memory Computers"
- Moritz Beutel and Robert Strzodka: "Hierarchical Tilings in Temporal Blocking"
- Christoph Klein and Robert Strzodka: "Operator Splittings on GPUs"
- Roger Kowalewski. "Shared-Memory Locality in Tasking-Based MPI All-to-All Communication"

Organization

Program Chair

Emmanuel Jeannot   Inria, France

Program Committee

George Bosilca	UTK, USA
Florina Ciorba	University of Basel, Switzerland
Matthias Diener	University of Illinois at Urbana-Champaign, USA
Anshu Dubey	Argonne National Laboratory, USA
Karl Fuerlinger	LMU München, Germany
Brice Goglin	Inria, France
Aleksandar Ilic	INESC-ID/IST, Universidade de Lisboa, Portugal
Vitus Leung	Sandia National Laboratory, USA
Hatem Ltaief	KAUST, Saudi Arabia
Allen Malony	University of Oregon, USA
Naoya Maruyama	LLNL, USA
Lawrence Mitchell	Durham University, UK
Hartmut Mix	Technische Universität Dresden, Germany
Marc Perache	CEA, France
Eric Petit	Intel, France
Didem Unat	Koç University, Turkey

Optimizing Memory Bandwidth Efficiency with User-Preferred Kernel Merge

Nabeeh Jumah[1(✉)] and Julian Kunkel[2]

[1] Universität Hamburg, Hamburg, Germany
`Jumah@informatik.uni-hamburg.de`
[2] University of Reading, Reading, UK
`j.m.kunkel@reading.ac.uk`

Abstract. Earth system modeling computations use stencils extensively while running many kernels. Optimal coding of the stencils is essential to efficiently use memory bandwidth of an underlying hardware. This is important as stencil computations are memory bound.

Even when the code within one kernel is written to optimally use the memory bandwidth, there are still opportunities for further optimization at the inter-kernel level. Stencils naturally exhibit data locality, and executing a sequence of stencils within separate kernels could waste caching capabilities. Interprocedural optimizations such as merging of kernels bears the potential to improve the use of the caches. However, due to semantic restrictions, it is difficult to achieve on general purpose languages.

Some tools were developed to automatically fuse loops instead of the manual optimization. However, scientists still implement fusion in different levels of loop nests manually to find optimal performance. To allow scientists to still apply loop fusions equal to manual loop fusion, we develop a technique to automatically analyze the code and allow scientists to select their preferred fusions by providing automatic dependency analysis and code transformation; this also bears the potential for automatic tools that make smart choices on behalf of the user. Our work is done using GGDML language extensions which enables performance portability over different architectures using a single source code.

Keywords: HPC · Earth system modeling · Software development

1 Introduction

Earth system modeling codes consist of many kernels, in which stencil operations are applied. Values of variables at spatially-neighboring points are read to evaluate some variable at some point in space. Neighborhoods give an opportunity to use the locality of data through caches. On the other hand, the arithmetic intensity of such computations is low, which makes them memory bound.

Efforts on optimizing operations within a kernel that applies a stencil operation is essential to optimize code performance, however, it is not sufficient. Taking into account the relationships between the consecutive kernels, it is sometimes possible to still improve performance. Reusing the data across stencil operations while still in caches makes this possible.

© Springer Nature Switzerland AG 2020
U. Schwardmann et al. (Eds.): Euro-Par 2019 Workshops, LNCS 11997, pp. 69–81, 2020.
https://doi.org/10.1007/978-3-030-48340-1_6

To exploit this inter-kernel possibilities, data dependencies should be applied to guarantee computation correctness. After making sure that a loop fusion does not impair the code in terms of computation correctness, the code should be transformed to apply the fusion. Instead of doing such effort by a programmer, tools have been developed to automatically apply such optimization.

Nested loops allow fusing loops in different combinations. Automatic loop fusions do not allow testing a specific set of loop fusions, which scientists would evaluate, may be to try other possible optimizations. We see such cases, e.g. where an outer loop encloses a set of consecutive second level nest each of which contains another inner loop, with many kernels fused in more complicated structure.

To allow scientists to still exploit loop fusion possibilities, while doing minimal effort, we develop a technique to apply preferred loop fusions that operates on the higher-level code abstraction of a domain-specific language. The **main contribution** of this work is a technique to automatically identify possible loop fusions with the necessary data dependency analysis, and apply the fusions which the user prefers. To maximize the benefit of this effort, we also allow automatic analysis for inter-module function inlining possibilities. This allows to fuse loops among different files within the source code.

2   Related Work

In this section, we review some research efforts which applied loop fusion in different ways and development contexts.

Data Re-use and Loop Restructuring: An optimization algorithm to reuse data was presented in [16], where loop nests were transformed by interchange, reversal, skewing, and tiling. Loop fusion and distribution to improve data locality was used in [9] besides to optimizing loop parallelism. A cost model that computes the spatial and the temporal reuse of cache lines was used in [10] to enable compiler optimizations using data locality. The authors used loop fusion as one of the transformations besides to loop permutation, distribution, and reversal.

Applicability of Loop Fusion: Fusion concept was used to serve optimization in different fields where performance is a main concern. An algorithm was presented in [5] in which loop fusion is used to reduce the use of temporary arrays. This effort was used to reduce the access to memory in data dominated applications like multimedia applications. Also, loop fusion was used for the purpose of energy consumption optimization. Fusion was proposed also to reduce the energy consumption [15] and improve the efficiency of power use on GPUs.

Compiler optimizations to exploit the efficiency of the GPUs computational power for the data warehousing applications were proposed in [18]. The benefits of the loop fission and fusion on relational algebra operators are also evaluated. Again we see the code fissions and fusions in the same field in [17] where the split and fused loops are dynamically scheduled on CUDA streams and dispatched to the GPUs to improve the performance when running queries.

Automatic Loop Fusion Tools: Manual loop fusion is time consuming. Automatic fusion was the alternative in many efforts. A source-to-source compiler was presented in [4] to automatically apply fusion. Other efforts focused on the identification of opportunities to apply loop fusion and to estimate its benefits like [11]. This effort presented a dataflow-based framework that analyzes a provided code to identify multi-kernel optimization opportunities and data management. The framework can then estimate the performance on GPUs without running it.

Finite difference method was also subject to the automatic analysis for fusion [13], where the space of possible kernel fusions is explored to find an optimal kernel fusion. Projections of the performance are done to get to the optimal kernel fusion. The authors again proposed a framework [14] to automatically transform stencil codes written in CUDA to exploit the data locality among multiple kernels. A compiler were also used in [3] to automatically fuse loops. CUDA kernel fusion was done on BLAS-1 and BLAS-2 routines.

Loop Fusion Through DSLs: Other efforts, e.g. [1] used DSLs which were designed to allow code generation of fused loops. Gridtools provides a DSL to specify stencil operations in a way that allows the user to define a computation in stages within the source code. The code generation process makes use of this information to exploit the data locality.

Directives are used in HybridFortran [12] to control the granularity of code. HybridFortran was developed to allow the user to port existing CPU code to GPUs by annotating the code with directives. The HybridFortran directives allow the tools to generate the code with the suitable granularity based on the target machine.

In contrast, **with our method**, the user does not need to manually fuse loops to apply the desired fusions. The tools handle the data dependency analysis, and the code transformation. Users choose from a list of automatically-detected fusion opportunities. So, in comparison to automatic, our technique enables scientists to have the flexibility to apply preferred fusions. But also, in comparison to manual fusion, scientists need to do less effort.

3   Methodology

We implemented the inlining and loop fusion procedures in the tool that translates GGDML [8] code to general purpose code. The tool runs automatic detection of inlining and fusion opportunities and shows a list to the user. When the user chooses an optimization from this list, the tool transforms the code automatically.

To evaluate the technique, we prepared a code that solves the shallow water equations [2] using the finite difference method[1]. The source code is written in the GGDML language extensions [8], which allows architecture-independent high-level code. The GGDML source-to-source translation technique [6] was used to generate and optimize the code for the different architectures and configurations.

---

[1] Refer to https://github.com/aimes-project/ShallowWaterEquations.

3.1 GGDML and the Code Translation

GGDML is a set of language extensions that provides performance portability for earth system modeling. Code is written with a high-level scientific abstraction of the problem as seen in Listing 1.1. A single source code can be translated into different targets by applying user-specified code schemata for different architectures. Typically, these schemata are developed by scientific programmers that understand code domain and the machine architecture. The key benefit is that these schemata and configuration files are used by many different kernels while the translation needs to be specified only once.

Listing 1.1. Example mixed GGDML and C code

```
float EDGE 2D f_U;
float EDGE 2D f_UT;
...
foreach e in grid
{
    f_U[e]=f_U[e]+f_UT[e]*dt;
}
```

This code updates the value of the X component of the velocity on the edges of the grid. It reflects the mathematical equation without optimization details.

GGDML code is translated for a specific machine based on a configuration description. Different optimization procedures, e.g memory layout transformations [7], are applied during the code translation process. Different configuration file sections guide the translation tool to apply the optimization procedures.

3.2 Inlining and Loop Fusion

The tools parse the different code files into AST structures. Inlining possibilities are checked by the tool by analysis of calls and function bodies. A call to a function, the body of which is defined even in a different code file, could be a candidate for inlining. Close loops traversing same ranges are also analyzed for loop fusion possibilities. This analysis includes all data dependencies within loops, and possibilities to move code that resides between loops. If the loop fusion analysis is found to keep consistency of code, the fusion is listed as a candidate fusion. Inlining and fusion candidates are listed for the user to choose what to apply. According to user choice, the tool automatically uses analysis information to apply necessary transformations, including handling necessary variables, moving code around, transforming loops etc.

3.3 Code Structure and Merging

The standard code is the baseline for which we compare the performance improvements. In this modularized code, every kernel includes the necessary mathematical operations and expressions to update exactly one field. This code is easy to understand and maintain, and includes eight kernels updating: the two components of the flux: (the kernels are) $flux1$ and $flux2$, the tendencies of the two components of the velocity: $compute\_u\_tendency$ and $compute\_v\_tendency$, the tendency of the surface level: $compute\_h\_tendency$, the two components of the velocity: $update\_u$ and $update\_v$, and the surface level: $update\_h$.

To create the merged code, the mathematical operations were remapped into three kernels such that the mathematical operations still keep the order to ensure correct computation. The merged code includes three kernels: $flux\_and\_tendencies$, $velocities$, and $compute\_surface$.

Performance-aware users typically perform such code merging manually in the expense of readability. E.g., in a popular numerical weather prediction model, there is a single function with 2,000 LoC.

3.4 Performance Assessment

C codes with OpenMP/OpenACC were generated from the DSL representation to investigate behavior on multi-core processors, GPUs, and vector engines. The experiments are designed to understand the use of the memory bandwidth and exploiting caching/registers. To assess the performance, we derive behavioral models from the code and validate the models using monitoring tools. 'Likwid', NVIDIA's 'nvprof', and NEC's 'ftrace' tools were used on multi-core CPUs, GPUs, and vector engines respectively.

4 Evaluation

The test application solves the shallow water equations on a 2D regular grid with cyclic boundary conditions[2]. The application uses an explicit time stepping scheme in which all eight fields are updated once in each time step.

The multi-core processor experiments were run on dual socket Broadwell nodes with Intel(R) Xeon(R) CPU E5-2697 v4 @ 2.30 GHz processor. We used the Intel (ICC 17.0.5) C compiler. The GPU experiments are run on the Tesla P100 with 16 GB memory and PCIe interconnect to the host. We used the PGI (17.7.0) C compiler. The vector engine experiments were run on SX-Aurora TSUBASA vector engine using the NCC (1.3.0) C compiler.

Various more experiments have been made on other generations of GPUs and CPUs showing similar results – we selected the results conducted on the latest generation of hardware that we had access to.

4.1 Multi-core Processors

First, we evaluate the code generated for Broadwell with different grid widths. The results before and after blocking (block size of 20000) are shown in Fig. 1.

Merging the kernels results in the expected code optimization reducing the necessary memory traffic over all grid widths. Without blocking, the results of the

---

[2] Refer to https://github.com/aimes-project/ShallowWaterEquations.

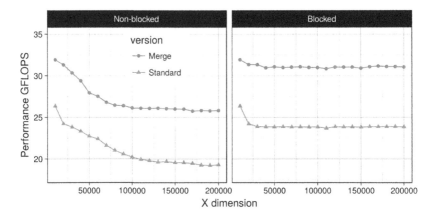

Fig. 1. Variable grid width with/o blocking on Broadwell

measurements show that the performance decreased with wider grids since the capacity of the caches is exhausted. Appropriate blocking eliminates performance loss. Given that the data are stored as single precision floating point, and that the maximum number of fields to access within a kernel is eight, the 20000 block width means the cache holds 0.61 MB per grid row. The processor has 2.5 MB L3 cache per core. Therefore, the 20000 blocking factor guarantees that more than two grid rows, and hence all the elements of the stencil (both in X and Y dimensions) are still in the L3 caches.

To better understand kernel merging and blocking relationship, we varied the block sizes. We fixed the grid width to 100k cells in the X dimension. We tested blocking with two categories of block sizes: powers of two ranging from 32 to 65536, and multiples of 1,000 from 1,000 to 10,000. Results are in Fig. 2. Kernel merge provided performance improvement over all the tested blocking factors except very small/large factors.

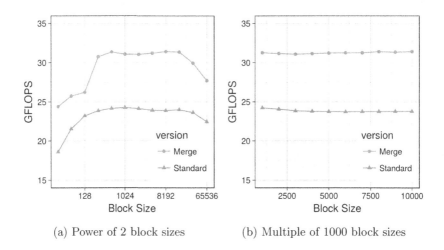

(a) Power of 2 block sizes   (b) Multiple of 1000 block sizes

Fig. 2. Different block sizes on Broadwell

Theoretical Analysis: To understand the data movement between the cores and the main memory we instrumented the code with 'Likwid'. The measured metrics and values for the different kernels are shown in Table 1.

The kernels are bound by the memory bandwidth. Theoretical max. memory bandwidth of the Broadwell processor is $76.8\,GB/s^3$. The kernels are optimized to read each variable only once from memory. For example the kernel $flux1$ accesses the memory to read two fields –reused more than once– and update one field. Multiplying the number of bytes accessed per grid cell by the grid dimensions and the time steps, this kernel needs to access 1491 GB during an application run. To compare with the measured values, if we multiply the kernel's runtime (26.86 s) by the measured memory bandwidth (61.22 GB/s), we find that the kernel accessed 1605 GB which is close to the theoretical calculations.

The achieved memory throughput of the code is close to the optimum. As long as we access the minimum amount of data in the memory with a high percentage of max memory bandwidth, the only way to optimize the code further is to decrease number of memory accesses for the application level.

In the standard code version, we need 33 accesses to the main memory for each grid cell in each time step. The arithmetic intensity of the code is 0.45 FLOP/Byte. Given the peak processor performance (2.3 GHz · 18 cores · 16 Single FP/core · 2) and the memory bandwidth (76.8 GB/s), the threshold arithmetic intensity to achieve the peak performance is 17.25 FLOP/Byte. The arithmetic intensity of the code is far from this threshold intensity, which explains why the achieved performance is far from the peak performance of the processor. Optimizations must increase the arithmetic intensity to increase the performance of the application.

What we gain in the merged code is reusing the values of some fields while they are still in the caches or the processor registers instead of reading them from the memory. This reduces the number of accesses to the main memory from 33 accesses to 24 accesses for each grid cell in each time step. This way, we can increase the intensity of the code to 0.63 FLOP/Byte. This is an increase by about 37% which explains the performance gain we can observe in the diagrams.

4.2   GPUs

To understand data movement between the GPU threads and the device memory, we prepared experiments for the P100 GPU. We record the performance measurements for the application with different grid widths (see Fig. 3). Without blocking, the performance decreases over the tested grid widths with and without merge. However, merged code performance degrades faster after the grid width of 110k. Performance drops beyond the standard code around the grid width of 140k. This is a result of the cache limitation on the GPU as a merged kernel accesses more variables per grid cell. A kernel that accesses 8

---

[3] The streaming benchmark 'stream_sp_mem_avx' from the 'Likwid' tools measured 67 GBytes/s on the processor.

Table 1. Likwid profiles on Broadwell for all kernels and both code versions

Kernel	Time (s)	GFLOPS	Memory bandwidth (GB/s)
flux1	26.9	11.2	59.8
flux2	26.6	11.3	62.8
compute_U_tendency	41.3	41.2	62.3
update_U	19.5	10.3	62.8
compute_V_tendency	46.4	36.7	61.8
update_V	19.3	10.3	63.3
compute_H_tendency	26.6	11.3	62.9
update_H	19.8	10.1	62.4
Standard_code	226.3	23.8	62.2
flux_and_tendencies	96.9	41.3	59.5
velocities	39.6	10.1	61.3
compute_surface	40.6	12.3	60.7
Merged_code	177.0	31.0	60.2

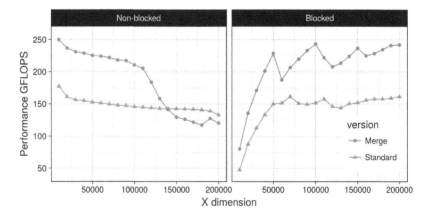

Fig. 3. Different grid widths on P100 GPU

fields on a grid that is 140k wide, where each field needs 4 bytes per cell, needs
4.27 MB, which exceeds the 4 MB L2 cache of the P100 GPU.

The blocking version (20k block size) does not exhibit the sharp drop over
wider grids, and the merged code is better over the tested grid widths. This is a
result of fitting the kernel data within the caches (remember that the 20k row
in a block needs 0.61 MB for a kernel that accesses 8 fields).

To investigate further the impact of the kernel merging along with blocking,
we test different block sizes again (see Fig. 4). In general, kernel merging improves
performance with all the tested block sizes. Optimal block sizes are around 10k.
Smaller (and larger) block sizes harm the performance for both code versions.

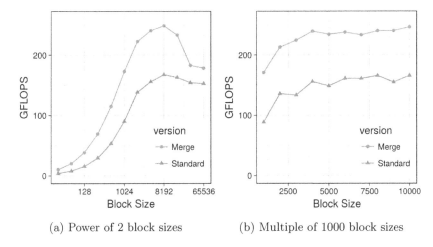

(a) Power of 2 block sizes   (b) Multiple of 1000 block sizes

Fig. 4. Different block sizes on P100 GPU

Theoretical Analysis: To gain a deeper understanding the 'nvprof' tool is used to collect different metrics. Table 2 shows the kernels measured memory throughput and accessed data volumes. Execution times and GFLOPS are also shown.

The measured data volumes that kernels access show data reuse at warp level. For example, the *flux*1 kernel accesses the device memory to read two fields – reused within the kernel – and updates one field. The memory access is coalesced, thus, the theoretical estimation of the data volume that the threads

Table 2. Kernels measurements in both code versions on P100 GPU

Kernel	Memory throughput (GB/s)	Data volume (GB)	Kernel time (s)	GFLOPS
flux1	447	1,175	2.63	114
flux2	478	1,570	3.29	91
compute_u_tendency	358	3,338	9.33	225
update_u	376	1,126	2.99	67
compute_v_tendency	374	4,195	11.22	196
update_v	376	1,126	3.00	67
compute_h_tendency	333	1,588	4.77	105
update_h	387	1,126	2.91	69
Standard_code	380	15,244	40.13	149
flux_and_tendencies	396	5,970	15.08	325
velocities	360	2,268	6.31	63
compute_surface	403	2,303	5.71	123
Merged_code	389	10,542	27.11	221

should access during the runtime of the kernel should be 12 bytes multiplied by the grid size and by the count of the time steps, which gives 1117 GB. In comparison, the computed value based on the 'nvprof' measurements is 1175 GB as shown in the table which is close to our expectation.

All kernels are memory bound. The measured memory throughput of the P100 on the test nodes was measured with a CUDA STREAM benchmark yielding about 498 GB/s. The memory throughput that was measured for the kernels shows high percentages (67%–96%) of the streaming memory throughput. Reducing device memory access leads to focus on the application-level optimization.

The data access is coalesced in all the kernels, before and after merging. With data reuse (coalescing means data is in cache), the standard kernels access the device memory 38 times · grid cells · time steps in total. However, the merged kernels reduce the accesses to 26. The numbers of the accesses look different from those of the Broadwell because the scheduling of the work on GPU threads is different, and hence the caching of the data is different. The access reduction explains the performance improvement between the two code versions (221 GFLOPS:149 GFLOPS) as the arithmetic intensity is shifted from 0.39 to 0.58 through merging.

4.3   Vector Engines

On Aurora vector engine, we vary the grid width from 10k to 100k and measure the performance (see Fig. 5). Merging improved performance over all the grid widths. Performance is not dropping without blocking (at least at the chosen grid widths).

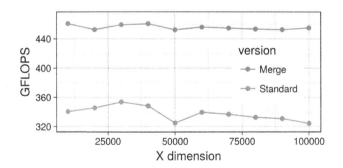

Fig. 5. Different grid widths on NEC Aurora vector engine

To understand the performance NEC's 'ftrace' tool is used (see Table 3). The theoretical memory bandwidth of the vector engine is 1.2 TB/s. Based on the 'ftrace' measurements, the computed values of the memory throughput show that all the kernels run with a high percentage of the memory bandwidth (80%) before and after the kernel merging.

The performance ratio before and after the kernel merging is 453 GFLOPS: 322 GFLOPS. This result is roughly the ratio of the arithmetic intensities which we discussed in the multi-core processor results (0.63:0.45).

5 Summary

With manual fusion, a 2k LOC function represents a challenge for scientists to find and test optimal fusions, while automatic fusion does not allow this flexibility. In this work, we presented a technique to replace manual and automatic loop fusion with a new genuine alternative. Code is automatically analyzed for fusion opportunities, and function inlining is also detected across source files. A list of possibilities is given to the user. Based on the user preferences, code transformation is applied based on the inlining/fusion that the user chooses.

GGDML was used to develop high-level code that can be translated into different architectures. This shallow water equations solver was then translated and executed on multi-core processors, GPUs, and vector engines.

Table 3. Kernel measurements of both code versions on the NEC Aurora

Kernel	Time (s)	GFLOPS	Memory throughput (GB/s)
flux1	1.30	230	858
flux2	1.51	199	989
compute_U_tendency	5.29	359	986
update_U	1.21	166	927
compute_V_tendency	5.22	384	1,001
update_V	1.21	165	924
compute_H_tendency	1.52	330	984
update_H	1.20	167	934
Standard_code	18.63	322	961
flux_and_tendencies	8.40	500	911
velocities	2.43	165	922
compute_surface	2.31	303	940
Merged_code	13.25	453	911

The results show the success of the technique to improve the efficiency of the use of the memory bandwidth on the different architectures. Scientists can apply the fusions (even across source files) and test any set of loop fusions as they prefer. As a future work, we plan to explore exploiting temporal locality between timesteps using the semantics of GGDML, and to explore using machine learning to recommend fusion sequences.

Acknowledgements. This work was supported in part by the German Research Foundation (DFG) through the Priority Programme 1648 Software for Exascale Computing SPPEXA (GZ: LU 1353/11-1). We also thank the 'Regionales Rechenzentrum Erlangen' (RRZE) at Friedrich-Alexander-Universität Erlangen-Nürnberg (FAU), the Swiss National Supercomputing Center (CSCS), and NEC Deutschland, who provided access to their machines to run the experiments. We also thank Prof. John Thuburn – University of Exeter, for his help to develop the code of the shallow water equations.

References

1. CSCS GridTools. https://github.com/GridTools/gridtools
2. Casulli, V.: Semi-implicit finite difference methods for the two-dimensional shallow water equations. J. Comput. Phys. **86**(1), 56–74 (1990)
3. Filipovič, J., Madzin, M., Fousek, J., Matyska, L.: Optimizing CUDA code by kernel fusion: application on BLAS. J. Supercomput. **71**(10), 3934–3957 (2015)
4. Fousek, J., Filipovič, J., Madzin, M.: Automatic fusions of CUDA-GPU kernels for parallel map. ACM SIGARCH Comput. Archit. News **39**(4), 98–99 (2011)
5. Fraboulet, A., Kodary, K., Mignotte, A.: Loop fusion for memory space optimization. In: Proceedings of the 14th International Symposium on Systems Synthesis, pp. 95–100. ACM (2001)
6. Jum'ah, N., Kunkel, J.: Performance portability of earth system models with user-controlled GGDML code translation. In: Yokota, R., Weiland, M., Shalf, J., Alam, S. (eds.) ISC High Performance 2018. LNCS, vol. 11203, pp. 693–710. Springer, Cham (2018). https://doi.org/10.1007/978-3-030-02465-9_50
7. Jumah, N., Kunkel, J.: Automatic vectorization of stencil codes with the GGDML language extensions. In: Proceedings of the 5th Workshop on Programming Models for SIMD/Vector Processing, WPMVP 2019, pp. 2:1–2:7. ACM, New York (2019)
8. Jumah, N., Kunkel, J.M., Zängl, G., Yashiro, H., Dubos, T., Meurdesoif, T.: GGDML: icosahedral models language extensions. J. Comput. Sci. Technol. Updates **4**(1), 1–10 (2017)
9. Kennedy, K., McKinley, K.S.: Maximizing loop parallelism and improving data locality via loop fusion and distribution. In: Banerjee, U., Gelernter, D., Nicolau, A., Padua, D. (eds.) LCPC 1993. LNCS, vol. 768, pp. 301–320. Springer, Heidelberg (1994). https://doi.org/10.1007/3-540-57659-2_18
10. McKinley, K.S., Carr, S., Tseng, C.-W.: Improving data locality with loop transformations. ACM Trans. Program. Lang. Syst. (TOPLAS) **18**(4), 424–453 (1996)
11. Meng, J., Morozov, V.A., Vishwanath, V., Kumaran, K.: Dataflow-driven GPU performance projection for multi-kernel transformations. In: Proceedings of the International Conference on High Performance Computing, Networking, Storage and Analysis, p. 82. IEEE Computer Society Press (2012)
12. Müller, M., Aoki, T.: Hybrid Fortran: high productivity GPU porting framework applied to Japanese weather prediction model. arXiv preprint arXiv:1710.08616 (2017)
13. Wahib, M., Maruyama, N.: Scalable kernel fusion for memory-bound GPU applications. In: Proceedings of the International Conference for High Performance Computing, Networking, Storage and Analysis, pp. 191–202. IEEE Press (2014)
14. Wahib, M., Maruyama, N.: Automated GPU kernel transformations in large-scale production stencil applications. In: Proceedings of the 24th International Symposium on High-Performance Parallel and Distributed Computing, pp. 259–270. ACM (2015)

15. Wang, G., Lin, Y., Yi, W.: Kernel fusion: an effective method for better power effi-
    ciency on multithreaded GPU. In: 2010 IEEE/ACM International Conference on
    Cyber, Physical and Social Computing (CPSCom), Green Computing and Com-
    munications (GreenCom), pp. 344–350. IEEE (2010)
16. Wolf, M.E., Lam, M.S.: A data locality optimizing algorithm. In: ACM SIGPLAN
    Notices, vol. 26, pp. 30–44. ACM (1991)
17. Wu, H., Cadambi, S., Chakradhar, S.T.: Optimizing data warehousing applications
    for GPUs using dynamic stream scheduling and dispatch of fused and split kernels.
    US Patent 8,990,827, 24 March 2015
18. Wu, H., Diamos, G., Wang, J., Cadambi, S., Yalamanchili, S., Chakradhar, S.:
    Optimizing data warehousing applications for GPUs using kernel fusion/fission.
    In: 2012 IEEE 26th International Parallel and Distributed Processing Symposium
    Workshops & PhD Forum (IPDPSW), pp. 2433–2442. IEEE (2012)

Opportunities for Partitioning Non-volatile Memory DIMMs Between Co-scheduled Jobs on HPC Nodes

Brice Goglin[✉] and Andrès Rubio Proaño

Inria, LaBRI, Univ. Bordeaux, Talence, France
{brice.goglin,andres.rubio}@inria.fr

Abstract. The emergence of non-volatile memory DIMMs such as Intel Optane DCPMM blurs the gap between usual volatile memory and persistent storage by enabling byte-accessible persistent memory with reasonable performance. This new hardware supports many possible use cases for high-performance applications, from high performance storage to very-high-capacity volatile memory (terabytes). However the numerous ways to configure the memory subsystem raises the question of how to configure nodes to satisfy applications' needs (memory, storage, fault tolerance, *etc.*).

We focus on the issue of partitioning HPC nodes with NVDIMMs in the context of co-scheduling multiple jobs. We show that the basic NVDIMM configuration modes would require node reboots and expensive hardware configuration. Moreover it does not allow the co-scheduling of all kinds of jobs, and it does not always allow locality to be taken into account during resource allocation.

Then we show that using 1-Level-Memory and the Device DAX mode by default is a good compromise. It may be easily used and partitioned for storage and memory-bound applications with locality awareness.

Keywords: Non volatile memory DIMM · NVDIMM · DAX · Partitioning · Co-scheduling · Locality

1 Introduction

Computing nodes are increasing complex, with tens of cores. Co-scheduling multiple jobs on such nodes is a useful strategy for making sure all powered-on cores are used in HPC centers. However sharing nodes between multiple jobs also comes with issues such as contention in the memory subsystem or cache pollution. Resource partitioning is an interesting way to avoid such issues thanks to operating system features such as Linux Cgroups.

The emergence of non-volatile memory DIMMs such as recently announced Intel Optane DC Persistent Memory brings new possible strategies for data management in HPC applications. Indeed they support multiple hardware and software configurations spanning from huge volatile capacities to high-performance storage, that may be used as burst buffers or for recovery after fault.

© Springer Nature Switzerland AG 2020
U. Schwardmann et al. (Eds.): Euro-Par 2019 Workshops, LNCS 11997, pp. 82–94, 2020.
https://doi.org/10.1007/978-3-030-48340-1_7

We focus in this paper on the co-scheduling of jobs with different needs, and on the partitioning of these new hardware resources between them. We compare the possible hardware configurations and advocate for the use of the 1-Level-Memory mode with namespaces and explicit NUMA memory management.

The rest of this paper is organized as follows. We present the upcoming NVDIMM hardware in Sect. 2 and discuss its possible hardware and software configurations. Co-scheduling jobs with different requirements is then discussed in Sect. 3 before we explain how to partition resources between them in Sect. 4. Before concluding, related works are discussed in Sect. 5.

2 Background

Non-volatile memory DIMMs is a promising emerging technology that is expected to blur the longstanding separation between usual volatile memory and persistent storage [5]. It supports both with good performance and offers multiple ways to be used by software.

2.1 Hardware

Non-volatile memory DIMMs have been available for several years as DDR DIMMs with a battery so as to save data to a flash backup on power loss. However software support was not ready until recently. Intel recently announced the availability of Optane DataCenter Persistent Memory Module (DCPMM) and competitors are working on offering similar technologies in the near future. These memory DIMMs are inserted in usual memory slots just like normal DIMMs (DDR) as depicted in Fig. 1.

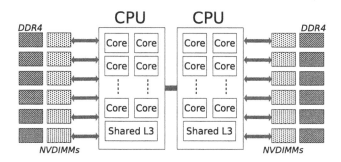

Fig. 1. Dual-socket Xeon platform with 6 channels per processor, with one Optane DCPMM and one DDR each.

Optane DCPMMs can be configured as individual *Regions* or as *Interleaved Regions*. Interleaving implies that the entire region data is lost whenever a single NVDIMM fails. However, interleaving is still expected to be used by default because it increases the memory bandwidth by using multiple channels simultaneously. Non-interleaved regions are expected to be useful for separating small, independent jobs such as virtual machines.

Besides regions, Intel hardware introduces in latest Xeon processor (*Cascade Lake*) a way to use Optane DCPMM as normal (volatile) memory [2]. Each DCPMM can be partitioned between *Memory Mode* (to be used as a large pool of volatile memory) and *App Direct* (for persistent storage) [14]. This configuration is performed in the BIOS or using tools such as `ipmctl` and requires a reboot.

2.2   Memory Mode and 2-Level-Memory

Latest Xeon processors may be configured in *2-Level-Memory* mode (2LM). It exposes the *Memory Mode* part of NVDIMMs as volatile memory and uses DDR as a *Memory-side Cache* in front of it, as shown in Fig. 2. This mode is convenient for applications that require lots of RAM (up to $6\times 512\,$GB DCPMM per socket with current hardware).

Fig. 2. 2-Level-Memory mode (2LM) uses DDR as a *Memory-side Cache* in front of the *Memory Mode* part of NVDIMMs exposed as normal volatile memory.

Unfortunately this mode does not bring the exact same performance as a pure DDR [8]. One reason is that each DDR cache is direct-mapped, which is known to perform inconsistently over time [12].[1]

In this 2LM mode, the *App Direct* part of NVDIMMs is exposed as storage just like in 1LM mode. We detail this storage mode in the next section.

2.3   App Direct and 1-Level-Memory for Storage

Latest Xeon processors may also be configured in *1-Level-Memory* mode (1LM) which puts back DDR as the main volatile memory as show on Fig. 3. The *Memory Mode* part of NVDIMMs is not usable anymore. The *App Direct* part is exposed as a *Persistent Memory Regions* (called *region* in the reminder of this paper) that may be used as a disk (e.g. `/dev/pmem1`). However this disk is directly byte-accessible by the processor. Contrary of usual disks, there is no need to copy disk blocks in memory (in the kernel page-cache) before actually accessing those bytes. This mode is called DAX (*Direct Access*) in Linux and Windows. It enables the mapping of the actual backend data directly in application virtual memory and the use of load and stores. This avoids the need for intermediate copy and page-cache allocations.

---

[1] Linux kernel version 5.2 will mitigate this issue by shuffling the list of free pages. https://lkml.org/lkml/2019/2/1/15.

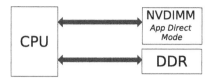

Fig. 3. 1-Level-Memory mode (1LM) uses DDR as the main memory while NVDIMMs are exposed as a persistent memory region that is usually used as storage.

1-Level-Memory has several interesting use cases for HPC applications, ranging from local disks as burst buffers [7], to recovering memory contents after a fault thanks to persistence. When a modern filesystem is used to store data in the App Direct part of NVDIMMs, the region is actually configured in *FSDAX* mode in Linux (*File System DAX*). Applications may use these files as usual. However, optimal performance requires application to be modified for DAX: they should stop using explicit file access (read/write requires a copy) and rather map files in virtual memory instead (to directly access data).

Accessing the App Direct part of NVDIMMs (either in 1LM or 2LM) never goes through an intermediate DDR cache, hence performance is lower [1,8,15]. However 1LM latency is better than 2LM in case of cache-miss because there is no need to lookup the data in the DDR cache [11].

2.4 Device DAX and kmem Additional NUMA Nodes

Although FSDAX is expected to be used in the vast majority of cases because it exposes persistent storage as a normal filesystem, App Direct regions may also be useful without a filesystem. This mode is called *Device DAX* in Linux. It exposes a mmap'able linear space where applications may manually store their datasets without the structure and help of a file system. It was designed to expose large regions of non-volatile memories to specific applications such as virtual machines, but we are going to show in this paper that it is actually much more useful than this.

Device DAX requires significant rework of applications because they have to manually separate independent data without the help of independent files. However we explained in Sect. 2.3 that DAX requires applications to be rewritten to benefit from improved performance (map files instead of read/write). Hence we believe additional application changes for supporting Device DAX are not a significant hurdle.

Partitioning Device DAX between different jobs indeed requires synchronization between jobs. We will explain in Sect. 4.2 how resource managers may solve this issue using namespaces. Partitioning between different tasks of a job is where application developers will have to update their code to use different parts of a Device DAX for different datasets.

Device DAX brings an important feature since Linux 5.1: the *kmem* DAX driver can expose NVDIMM pages as an additional NUMA node where applications can allocate memory as usual [6], as depicted in Fig. 4. This may be

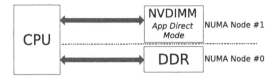

Fig. 4. When the App Direct part of NVDIMMs is managed by the kmem device DAX driver in Linux, it appears as an additional NUMA node.

considered similar to Intel Xeon Phi *Flat* mode where both fast and slow memories are exposed as separate NUMA nodes.[2] It means that applications now have to manually allocate in one of the nodes depending on the required performance for each dataset. This requires more work from application developers but provides more flexibility than 2LM and possibly higher performance [3]. Indeed developers have to choose between pure DDR (faster than NVDIMMs with DDR cache) and pure NVDIMM (slower) [8,15].

2.5   Locality of NVDIMMs

NVDIMMs being attached to processors through memory slots, their access performance suffers from locality like normal DDR memory, *i.e.* accessing a NVDIMM is faster from the CPU where it is attached. Optane DCPMM performance being lower than DDR, one may expect these NUMA effects to be negligible. Unfortunately, there are actual higher [10] which means applications must take locality into account when choosing their target NVDIMMs.

This is obviously true for 1LM because NVDIMMs are accessed by the processor like DDR. But it is also true for 2LM because the DDR-cache acts as a *Memory-side Cache*: accesses to NVDIMMs of another CPU are cached in the DDR cache of that CPU, they are not cached locally.

3   Co-scheduling Jobs with Memory and Storage Needs

Modern HPC nodes feature lots of cores and memory. They are therefore good candidates for co-scheduling several small jobs. Unfortunately node sharing raises multiple issues in terms of performance [13]. Hence we now explain how to partition nodes equipped with NVDIMMs.

3.1   Hardware Partitioning in 2LM

We explained in the previous section that partitioning is possible in most configurations. However we assumed the hardware configuration matches the job

---

[2] NVDIMMs 1LM and 2LM modes are similar to KNL *Flat* and *Cache* modes. However, NVDIMMs do not enable a KNL-like *Hybrid* mode: KNL could partition the fast memory (MCDRAM) between cache and normal memory. NVDIMMs rather allow partitioning the slow memory between cached (by the fast memory, DDR) and uncached.

requirements. We now look at the case where some jobs want a 2LM configuration (Memory Mode for large amounts of volatile memory) and some others
want 1LM (App Direct for persistent storage). The only way to have both Memory Mode and App Direct available at the same time in a machine is to configure
the processors in 2LM (see Sects. 2.2 and 2.3, and Fig. 5).

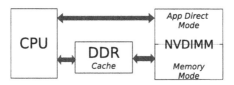

Fig. 5. 2-Level-Memory enables exposing both Memory Mode as DDR-cached main
memory and App Direct as storage.

However this configuration has major drawbacks: First, the administrators
would have to choose a good ratio for NVDIMM partitioning between Memory Mode and App Direct. This ratio depends on the needs of all jobs that will
be scheduled simultaneously on a node, and setting up the ratio requires a reboot
of the node.[3]

Secondly, locality issues arise as shown in Fig. 6: If a socket is allocated to a
1LM job, its local NVDIMMs should be entirely set in App Direct. However it
means there is no local memory anymore: both local DDR and NVDIMM cannot
be used as volatile memory (DDR is entirely used as a cache; NVDIMMs are
entirely used as App Direct). Cores of this socket would therefore use remote
memory, which incurs bad performance as explained in Sect. 2.5.

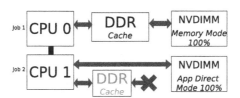

Fig. 6. Allocating one socket to a job that wants 100% Memory Mode and the other
socket to a job that wants 100% App Direct causes the latter to have no local memory
anymore, and its DDR cache is useless.

In the end, we believe using 2LM to share a node with such different jobs
is not a good idea and we do not expect significant improvements in future
hardware platforms. Administrators would rather create one set of 1LM nodes

---

[3] Additionally a 32G granularity seems to constrain possible ratios in hardware.

and a separate set of 2LM nodes[4] and possibly reconfigure, reboot and move some nodes from one set to another depending on users' needs. However we will now show how 1LM may actually offer a more flexible solution.

3.2 Flexible Co-scheduling with 1LM and kmem NUMA Nodes

We explained in the previous section that 2LM requirements incur too many drawbacks. Therefore we propose not to use 2LM anymore. As explained in Sect. 2.4, Device DAX may be exposed as additional NUMA nodes. This provides lots of volatile memory that 2LM applications require but requires application developers to explicitly manage allocation between fast and slow memory. We believe that this additional work for developers is a good trade-off because of the flexibility it provides to users and administrators.

Hence we propose the following strategy:

1) NVDIMMs are configured 100% in App Direct and processors are in 1LM mode.
2) NVDIMM regions are configured as Device DAX by default in the Linux configuration (may be used for persistent storage as a single file).
3a) An application that cannot work without multiple files may request the reconfiguration of a region as FSDAX.[5]
3b) An application that needs lots of volatile memory may request the reconfiguration of a region as an additional NUMA node through the kmem driver.[6]

This solution does not bring locality issues because each CPU still has its local DDR explicitly available, while its local NVDIMMs may be exposed in the mode that matches the local job needs. Besides, this approach is on par with current Linux kernel development towards exposing both DDR and PMEM as explicit NUMA nodes and having ways to migrate hot pages between fast and slow memory[7].

Table 1 summarizes the advantage of our proposal compared to 2LM memory presented in the previous Section.

Table 1. Advantages and drawbacks of 2LM and 1LM modes for co-scheduling jobs.

CPU config	2-Level-Memory	1-Level-Memory
NVDIMM config	Memory Mode ratio depends on jobs Reboot required for updating	100% App Direct
Fast/slow memory management	Automatic (DDR Cache)	Manual & Flexible (NUMA)
Storage management	Limited to App Direct ratio	OK
Locality	May miss local memory	OK

---

[4] This is similar to what happened in many KNL clusters: some nodes were in Cache mode, others in Flat mode.
[5] Using the `ndctl` command-line tool, which does not require a reboot.
[6] Using the `daxctl` command-line tool, which does not require a reboot.
[7] https://lwn.net/Articles/787418/.

4   Fine-Grain Partitioning Between HPC Jobs

We showed in the previous section that 1LM is a good trade-off enabling flexibility with respect to application needs and memory management. We now explain how to actually partition and expose different kinds of memory between jobs at fine grain.

HPC resource managers may already use Linux *Cgroups* for partitioning CPUs between jobs [4], as well as NUMA nodes (individual nodes or amounts of memory may be dedicated to each group). This work may already be applied to partition NVDIMM-based NUMA nodes, either in 2LM or kmem nodes in 1LM.

However, when a single Device DAX is used, there is no way to partition it between multiple jobs. This is an issue that we will now address.

4.1   NVDIMM Hardware Partitioning

As explained in Sect. 2.1, each NVDIMM (its App Direct part) may be exposed as an individual region or it may be interleaved with others (see Fig. 7). Each region is exposed as a different FSDAX, Device DAX or NUMA node in Linux, which may be allocated to different jobs by the administrator. However, with only 6 channels per CPU and 1 single DCPMM per channel (128, 256 or 512 GB each), there are very few possibilities for partitioning. Moreover, modifying regions requires a long reconfiguration process (minutes) and a reboot. Hence we do not think this is a good way to partition NVDIMMs between jobs.

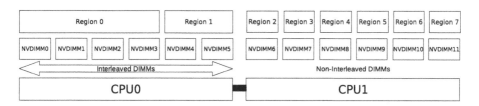

Fig. 7. Partitioning NVDIMMs using Regions and Interleaving. On the first processor two interleaved regions use respectively 4 and 2 NVDIMMs. On the second processor, all NVDIMMs are exposed as individual non-interleaved regions.

4.2   Multi-DAX and Namespace-Based Software Partitioning

We believe that partitioning should rather be applied in software on top of persistent memory regions. Indeed, each region may be split into different *Namespaces* that are configured by the administrator without requiring a reboot [14].[8] Hence we believe that the hardware configuration should consist in one interleaved

---

[8] Using the `ndctl` command-line tool again.

region per locality domain (CPU or SubNUMA Cluster, for good NUMA locality). The resource manager would then use namespaces for partitioning those static regions dynamically on job allocation. We observed a 1-gigabyte minimal granularity for this partitioning on our platform, and we believe this is sufficient for current HPC jobs on platforms with tens of hundreds of GB of memory.

Hence we propose to extend our strategy from Sect. 3.2:

1) NVDIMMs are configured 100% in App Direct and processors are in 1LM mode. **NVDIMM regions are interleaved at CPU level (or Sub-NUMA Cluster).**
2) **Jobs request one or several region namespaces from the resource manager. Namespaces** are configured as Device DAX by default in the Linux configuration (may be used for persistent storage as a single file).
3) **Jobs specify how each namespace should be configured, as shown in** Fig. 8.

3a) An application that cannot work without multiple files may request the reconfiguration **of a namespace** as FSDAX.

3b) An application that needs lots of volatile memory may request the reconfiguration **of a namespace** as an additional NUMA node through the kmem driver.

If multiple namespaces from the same physical region are exposed as NUMA node, they are actually exposed as a single NUMA node[9] Fortunately, Linux Cgroups may be used to partition the memory of that shared NUMA node between jobs.

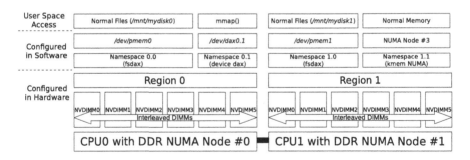

Fig. 8. Using namespaces to partition regions between jobs requiring FSDAX, Device DAX or NUMA nodes. Each processor is configured with a single interleaved region. Software splits them between namespaces that may be configured according to jobs requirements.

One may wonder whether using namespaces to partition a single region into multiple DAX incurs a performance penalty. Figure 9 shows that the overhead is negligible. Indeed processes only map DAX pages in their virtual address

---

[9] Each persistent memory region corresponds to a unique NUMA node in ACPI tables.

spaces and access them as regular memory. The actual overhead of using multiple namespaces is their creation during job prologue (a couple of minutes).

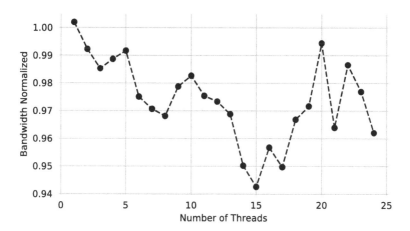

Fig. 9. Performance of the STREAM Triad benchmark when using one Device DAX per thread (in a single region), normalized to using the same Device DAX for all threads.

4.3   DAX Locality

Finally, we look at how locality information is exposed in our proposed strategy. Indeed, even if the resource manager tries its best to allocate local namespaces to jobs, there is no guarantee that it will always be possible, and we explained in Sect. 2.5 that locality matters to performance of NVDIMMs. Hence, there is a need for the resource manager and the application to gather locality information about the different software handles that correspond to NVDIMMs.

When NVDIMMs are exposed as additional NUMA nodes, we implemented in hwloc a way to find out the corresponding local CPUs and DDR by looking at NUMA distances and memory target-initiator information in Linux.[10] Figure 10 depicts an example of such configuration.

For other cases (FSDAX, Device DAX and raw namespace), the information exposed by Linux is currently incomplete: only one local DDR node is reported even if there are multiple of them. For instance, in Fig. 10, they would be reported as close to NUMA node #0 only (SubNUMA Cluster) instead of both #0 and #1 (entire Package). We are currently working with kernel developers to expose the correct information[11].

---

[10] This code is currently in hwloc git master and will be published in the upcoming 2.1 release.

[11] https://lists.01.org/pipermail/linux-nvdimm/2019-April/020822.html.

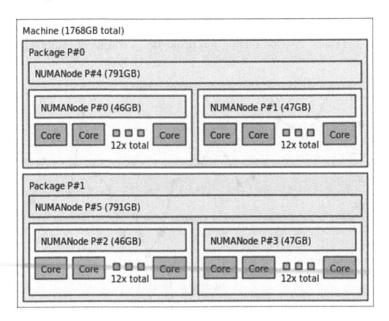

Fig. 10. hwloc's lstopo representation of a platform with NVDIMMs exposed as additional NUMA nodes using the kmem DAX driver. Each processor has one local DDR NUMA node per SubNUMA Cluster (e.g. #0 and #1) and a single NVDIMM NUMA node (e.g. #4). Hence each core has two local memories.

5   Related Works

HPC nodes are growing, causing co-scheduling to become necessary as soon as applications do not scale well to many cores. Indeed it is better to fill powered-on nodes rather than powering up yet another partially-used node. However previous work has shown than node sharing raises several performance issues, especially in the memory subsystem [13]. Many resources may be partitioned in software to avoid processes disturbing each others.

Resource managers such as SLURM are usually in charge of allocating cores and memory to jobs. They now use techniques such as Linux Cgroups for partitioning these resources between jobs [4] or containers [17]. Cache partitioning also appeared in recent processors as a way to also avoid co-existing cache pollution between applications [9]. However it is currently not supported by DDR caches in 2LM. Fortunately, we explained that we do not believe that 2LM is a sensible choice for HPC nodes.

When NVDIMMs are used as persistent storage, the resource manager is in charge of allocating this local storage to jobs. Like any local disk in computing nodes, these FSDAX may be provisioned by the manager, for instance as explicit or automatic burst buffers [7,16]. This local storage may also be used as a high-performance temporary storage between different jobs [7] for instance for in-situ analysis.

All these techniques are compatible with our proposal for partitioning non-volatile memory since we apply the partitioning when launching jobs (in the job prologue) and not in hardware.

6   Conclusion and Future Work

Non-volatile memory DIMMs are a promising technology that blurs the separation between volatile memory and persistent storage. We studied the different ways to use Intel Optane DCPMM and showed that supporting different use cases for different application needs requires careful hardware configuration. We explained why we think 2-Level-Memory is not a convenient solution for locality-aware partitioning of NVDIMMs between jobs. We showed why 1-Level-Memory looks like a better approach with more flexibility for memory allocation, easier configuration for the administrator and resource managers, and better locality.

Future work includes exposing better locality information from the Linux kernel to the resource managers and applications, as well as exposing in hwloc some information about the different kinds of NUMA nodes to ease application allocation policies. We are also looking at implementing our proposed ideas inside a resource manager such as SLURM.

References

1. Intel 64 and IA-32 Architectures Optimization Reference Manual, Section 11.2 - Device Characteristics of Intel Optane DC Persistent Memory Module, April 2019
2. Arafa, M., et al.: Cascade lake: next generation Intel Xeon scalable processor. IEEE Micro **39**(2), 29–36 (2019)
3. Barnes, T., et al.: Evaluating and optimizing the NERSC Workload on Knights Landing. In: 2016 7th International Workshop on Performance Modeling, Benchmarking and Simulation of High Performance Computer Systems (PMBS), pp. 43–53, November 2016. https://doi.org/10.1109/PMBS.2016.010
4. Georgiou, Y., Hautreux, M.: SLURM Resources isolation through Cgroups. SLURM USER Group(2011)
5. Götze, P., van Renen, A., Lersch, L., Leis, V., Oukid, I.: Data management on non-volatile memory: a perspective. Datenbank-Spektrum **18**(3), 171–182 (2018). https://doi.org/10.1007/s13222-018-0301-1
6. Hansen, D.: Allow persistent memory to be used like normal RAM. Linux Weekly News, January 2019. https://lwn.net/Articles/777212/
7. Henseler, D., Landsteiner, B., Petesch, D., Wright, C., Wright, N.J.: Architecture and design of cray DataWarp. In: Cray User Group Conference, London, UK, May 2016
8. Izraelevitz, J., et al.: Basic performance measurements of the Intel Optane DC persistent memory module. CoRR (2019). http://arxiv.org/abs/1903.05714
9. Lin, J., Lu, Q., Ding, X., Zhang, Z., Zhang, X., Sadayappan, P.: Gaining insights into multicore cache partitioning: Bridging the gap between simulation and real systems. In: IEEE 14th International Symposium on High Performance Computer Architecture (HPCA), pp. 367–378. IEEE (2008)

10. Liu, J., Chen, S.: Initial experience with 3D XPoint main memory. In: Joint Workshop of HardBD and Active, held in Conjunction with ICDE, Macau, China (2019)
11. Looi, L.: Intel Optane DC Persistent Memory Performance Overview. Tech Field Day Exclusive At Intel Data-Centric Innovation Day, April 2019. https://www.youtube.com/watch?v=UTVt_AZmWjM
12. NERSC: KNL Cache Mode Performance. https://www.nersc.gov/research-and-development/knl-cache-mode-performance-coe/
13. Simakov, N.A., et al.: A quantitative analysis of node sharing on HPC clusters using XDMoD application kernels. In: Proceedings of the XSEDE16 Conference on Diversity, Big Data, and Science at Scale, pp. 32:1–32:8. ACM, New York (2016). https://doi.org/10.1145/2949550.2949553
14. Upadhyayula, U., Scargall, S.: Introduction to Persistent Memory Configuration and Analysis Tools. In: Storage Developer Conference. Santa Clara, CA, September 2018
15. van Renen, A., Vogel, L., Leis, V., Neumann, T., Kemper, A.: Persistent memory I/O primitives. arXiv e-prints, April 2019. http://arxiv.org/abs/1904.01614
16. Wang, T., Mohror, K., Moody, A., Sato, K., Yu, W.: An ephemeral burst-buffer file system for scientific applications. In: SC 2016: Proceedings of the International Conference for High Performance Computing, Networking, Storage and Analysis, pp. 807–818, November 2016. https://doi.org/10.1109/SC.2016.68
17. Zounmevo, J.A., et al.: A container-based approach to OS specialization for Exascale computing. In: International Workshop on Container Technologies and Container Clouds (WoC) (2015)

F2C-DP - Workshop on Fog-to-Cloud Distributed Processing

Workshop on Fog-to-Cloud Distributed Processing (F2C-DP)

Workshop Description

Future service execution in different domains (e.g. smart cities, e-health, smart transportation, etc.), will rely on a large and highly heterogeneous set of distributed devices, located from the edge to the cloud, empowering the development of innovative services. In such envisioned scenario, the main objective for the workshop was to set the ground for researchers, scientists, and members of the industrial community to interact with each other, fueling new discussions in the emerging area coming out when shifting distributed services execution towards the edge. Analyzing the way existing programming models and distributed processing strategies may support such a scenario and to what extent these solutions should be extended or just replaced, is also fundamental to support the expected evolution in edge computing. The workshop aimed at bringing together the community of researchers interested in new applications, architectures, programming models, applications and systems based on these computing environments, with emphasis on research topics like Machine and Deep Learning, Blockchain, Function as a Service, Security, and Privacy. The workshop was organized with the support of the mF2C, a H2020 funded project, and was the third edition, that was held in Göttingen, Germany, in conjunction with the Euro-Par annual series of international conferences.

The workshop format included a keynote speaker, technical presentations, and a panel. The workshop received five submissions, from authors belonging to seven distinct countries. Each of them were reviewed at least three times. The Program Committee took into account the relevance of the papers to the workshop, the technical merit, the potential impact, and the originality and novelty. From these submissions, and taking into account the reviews, four papers were selected for presentation at the workshop (80% acceptance ratio). The papers focused on different aspects of the Fog to Cloud computing platforms: application requirements and specifications, architecture, programming models, deployment with containers, security, and privacy in a Fog-to-Cloud environment. The workshop included also a keynote presentation and a panel that discussed emerging trends, technologies, challenges, and business scenarios in Fog-to-Cloud architectures. We would like to thank the Euro-Par organizers for their support in the organization, specially to the Euro-Par workshop chairs: Dora Blanco, Christian Boehme, and Ulrich Schwardmann. We would like to also thank Massimo Villari (University of Messina, Italy) for his excellent keynote presentation and Fabrizio Marozzo (University of Calabria, Italy) for his participation in the panel, as well as all the Program Committee members.

Organization

Organizing Committee

Rosa M. Badia	Barcelona Supercomputing Center, Spain
Xavier Masip	Universitat Politècnica de Catalunya, Spain
Admela Jukan	Technical University of Braunschweig, Germany
Ana Juan Ferrer	ATOS Research, Spain

Program Chair

Antonio Salis	Engineering Sardegna, Italy

Program Committee

Toni Cortes	Barcelona Supercomputing Center, Spain
Jens Jensen	Sciences and Technology Facilities Council, UK
Roberto Cascella	ECSO, Belgium
Eduardo Quinones	Barcelona Supercomputing Center, Spain
Domenico Talia	University of Calabria, Italy
Erez Hadad	IBM, Israel
Anna Queralt	Barcelona Supercomputing Center, Spain
David Carrera	Universitat Politècnica de Catalunya, Spain
Daniele Lezzi	Barcelona Supercomputing Center, Spain

Security and Privacy Management in a Fog-to-Cloud Environment

Antonio Salis[1]([⊠]) [iD], Jens Jensen[2] [iD], Roberto Bulla[1],
Glauco Mancini[1] [iD], and Paolo Cocco[1]

[1] Engineering Sardegna Srl, Loc. Sa Illetta, SS195 km 2,3, 09123 Cagliari, Italy
{antonio.salis,roberto.bulla,glauco.mancini,
paolo.cocco}@eng.it
[2] UK Research and Innovation/STFC RAL, Didcot, UK
jens.jensen@stfc.ac.uk

Abstract. Security and privacy are a concern in many Internet of Things environments, particularly when anyone can connect their device into it. We demonstrate and discuss the security in an airport environment where users are guided to through security, to their flight, or to shops or other points of interest, which in turn should reduce the stress of the user's stay in the airport. The challenge is not just that any user can connect their phone but also to ensure that personal data is handled correctly - in particular, users must be tracked by the infrastructure in order to guide them. Built on a fog-to-cloud platform developed by the Horizon2020-funded mF2C project, we discuss the steps towards a full implementation in a real airport, and the kind of security assessment that is required to persuade an airport to deploy a pervasive user-facing infrastructure without compromising - and hopefully improving - airport security, fulfilling GDPR compliance.

Keywords: Cloud computing · Fog computing · Fog-to-cloud · Distributed systems · IoT · Proximity marketing · Security · Privacy · GDPR

1 Introduction

We are facing a tremendous advance in systems architectures and business around Internet of Things (IoT). First, the installed base of IoT devices is growing constantly, and the latest forecasts estimates around 31 billion devices worldwide, with an expected annual economic impact of about $12T, by 2025 [1]. The foreseen scenario includes smart cities, factories, transportation and logistics, large retail and healthcare.

Another aspect that has galvanized interest is the increasing capabilities of devices, such as "smart" connection boxes deployed in many homes, high capacity mobile end-user devices and powerful wireless networks, used at the edge of the Internet. Typically, a smart device relies on cloud services for extra processing capabilities (think of Amazon Alexa, Google Connected Home Assistant, etc.), where data is sent to a cloud for processing and the results sent back. This can be considered a new computing paradigm, particularly where computation stays as close to the edge as possible, "fog computing" (a diffuse cloud).

© Springer Nature Switzerland AG 2020
U. Schwardmann et al. (Eds.): Euro-Par 2019 Workshops, LNCS 11997, pp. 99–111, 2020.
https://doi.org/10.1007/978-3-030-48340-1_8

In this edge-first computing approach [2, 3], edge devices are the starting point of computing, where people work and live, and processing is done locally until the required load in terms of processing and storage exceeds the capacity of the devices. Then the processing and data are "osmotically" moved to more powerful devices in proximity [4], the fog nodes, which, in turn, can offload processing onto the cloud [5].

In this paper we present a traveler guidance service, in the setting of an airport, implemented following the fog-to-cloud approach of the mF2C project[1]. The service acts as a "smart hub" to provide real time information in a public environment [5]. A prototype has been implemented that collects data from the passengers and provides information to enable proximity marketing (shops, restaurants, etc.), while preserving the privacy and security of data owners [6], and augmented by analytics computed in the cloud. This setting could be reused in other public domains like train stations, shopping centers, etc. to constitute a building block for a smart city implementation. Initially deployed in a cloud-based testbed, the prototype was validated with data from Cagliari airport.

This paper is structured as follows. Section 2 introduces the security and privacy issues in the IoT ecosystem in general. Section 3 describes the mF2C system and the Airport Use Case, Sect. 4 describes the security features coming from the mF2C framework and the specific features implemented in the use case. Section 5 presents the experimental results related to the security check of the Use Case, finally, Sect. 6 concludes the paper.

2   Security in an IoT Ecosystem

IoT security is important: a compromise can be expensive, embarrassing, lose customers, or even compromise airport security. In an **IoT proxy** attack, IoT devices (mobile phones, in our case) are used as entry point or resources to attack selected targets; the hacked resource can be compromised and used to launch a DDoS[2] attack. In a **IoT direct** attacks, the IoT device could be subject to attacks with the aim of disrupting the IoT itself, for instance compromising passenger information or triggering a fire alarm.

To fully identify the whole list of threats, it's useful to classify the type of attacks in the following categories [7]:

- Access of information, where the only purpose of the hacker is to get private information without any impact in the integrity and availability of such information;
- Temporarily disrupt activity, where the hacker want to disrupt accessibility to information;
- Change code, files or information, where the hacker intends to modify code, data or files, with a resulting relevant impact;
- Destroy the target, where the hacker intends to attack the core resources of the target, with potentially major impact.

---

[1] https://www.mf2c-project.eu/.

[2] Distributed Denial of Service attack.

There are many reasons that determine the growing of cybersecurity threats:

Scalability and surface of risk – with a large scale deployment of IoT devices, the surface of attack will be wider, and the likelihood of exploit, e.g. through an unpatched device, or a weak password, will be higher. Finding one weak point could be sufficient for the attacker who steals information, or it could provide a springboard for further attacks;

Energy and computing constraints – IoT devices have limited capabilities, sometimes the energy saving is a major priority in codes and protocols, leaving room to vulnerabilities;

Physical accessibility – IoT devices are more often deployed in open environments, so easily accessible and susceptible to be tampered;

Protocol communication weaknesses – IoT device rely on specific communication protocols, some are IP-based mostly based on UDP, others are non-IP protocols (e.g. Zigbee) that often have specific weaknesses like unencrypted data transmission;

Manageability and human factor - the huge number of deployed device pose a serious issue in terms of manageability. The task of securing such a complex and heterogeneous networks is quite challenging. Then human factors can amplify any potential weaknesses of IoT networks;

Cognitive bias - many people underestimate risks, and may perceive their devices as simple and not containing sensitive information.

Any IoT platform must thus provide privacy and security models that address the relevant risks, and design countermeasures for these risks.

3   Fog Hub in Airport Use Case

The airport application is built on the mF2C platform, an open, secure, decentralized, multi-stakeholder management framework for F2C (Fog-to-Cloud) computing. This approach is taken in order to benefit from the platform's features of novel programming models, privacy and security, data storage techniques, service creation, brokerage solutions, SLA policies, and resource orchestration methods [8–10], and thus to reduce the effort required to build and interconnect the airport application. The mF2C project is funded through the EC Horizon 2020 program, and brings together relevant industry and academic players in the cloud sector.

As mentioned in the introduction, the service is designed to guide travelers through the airport "obstacles" – check-in, security, passport control, and the departure gate, while offering them tailored access to airport services – food, gifts, books, etc. [11, 12], as in Fig. 1. Service offers are anonymous, based on a recommender system that groups users with similar interests. Wi-fi signals are used to track the location of the traveler; and a cloud service tracks departure time, time to walk to gate, gate changes, etc., thus making the traveler's journey less stressful.

Conversely, the service could offer benefits to the airport as well, not just through "optimized" use of shops, but also by helping people with special needs (limited mobility, travelling with young children), by identifying bottlenecks as they form, and could help handle emergencies (a passenger being sick, lost children, etc.).

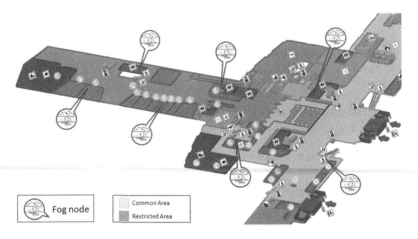

Fig. 1. Use case scenario in the airport

3.1   The mF2C Fog-to-Cloud Platform Architecture

The mF2C fog architecture is illustrated in Fig. 2. At the cloud level, containerization, virtualization, orchestration provide resource-efficient management in the top layer, while the fog infrastructure below can be dynamic and heterogeneous. Processes can be deployed by the cloud to the edges of the network, near the IoT sensors and actuators, and computation and data is fed "upwards" in the architecture as needed.

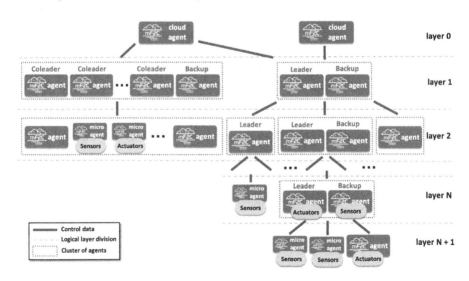

Fig. 2. mF2C architecture

An mF2C "agent" implements the management functionalities in every component within the system which is capable of running an agent. Devices that are not able to run the mF2C agent – typically at the very edge – send data to the nearest agent which then collects, processes and distributes it. One agent is selected to act as "Leader" in order to manage resources and coordinate resource usage of the fog nodes around it.

3.2 Implementing Airport System on the mF2C Platform

In the architecture described in the previous section, the airport system is implemented as depicted in Fig. 3:

- The cloud layer is based on an OpenStack[3] instance, wired connected with the fog layers. The cloud layer provides scalable computing power for machine learning algorithms used for the (Collaborative Filtering) recommendation system and manage the long term data storage and analysis;
- The first fog layer acts as aggregator, based on a NuvlaBox mini[4] and two U55 Mini PC both with 8 GB RAM, that provide real-time computing and storage resources to the edge elements, manage proximity events, airport flight events and information, recommender data cache and support admin dashboard with relevant reports;
- A second fog layer, which acts as access node, is based on seven RaspberryPi3[5] with 1 GB RAM, that provide session management, communications with and fast response to the edge devices, running the object (traveler) tracking and proximity application;
- Finally, the edge layer consists of the travelers' Android[6] smartphones, connected to the access node with Wi-Fi, and using an app to interact with the system.

All fog devices in the airport area are positioned in order to create a grid for Wi-Fi coverage. Appropriate algorithms that evaluate relative Wi-Fi signal strengths are used internally in the Android app to calculate the passenger's position.

---

[3] https://www.openstack.org/.

[4] http://www.sixsq.com/products/nuvlabox/.

[5] https://www.raspberrypi.org/products/raspberry-pi-3-model-b/.

[6] Initially, only Android is supported.

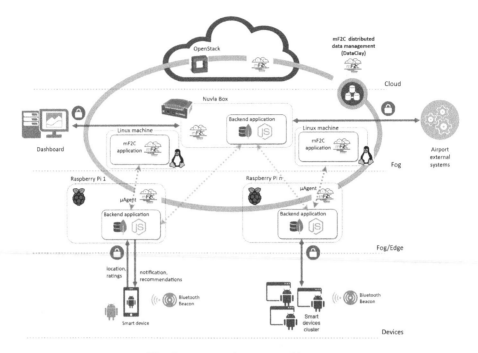

Fig. 3. Use case 3 system architecture

4 Security Architecture of the Airport Use Case

In Sect. 2, we briefly outlined security topics in an IoT scenario. In the airport specifically, the mF2C platform comes with built-in security, which can be leveraged and adapted to implement security for the application. The goals are:

- Protect the system from disruptions (network loss, denial of service).
- Protect the individual user's privacy, by letting them choose how much data to share and only using aggregated and anonymized data beyond the user's domain.
- Protect the airport – the system should not compromise any of the airport's security features.
- Protect other participants – airport shops, airport staff – from "nefarious use" of the mF2C application. A malicious user with knowledge of the system might try, for example, to generate a fake discount voucher for a shop.

4.1 mF2C Platform Security

Figure 4 shows the architecture again, but highlighting the security measures. The foundation of this is a Public Key Infrastructure (PKI) with a Certification Authority (CA) running as a service in the cloud. In fact, in our example, there will be three distinct PKIs which by default do not trust each other.

1. Fixed infrastructure services that support the mF2C platform and applications have their own PKI, with long-lived credentials. Examples of these services include web services endpoints and the CA.
2. The Agents (Sect. 3.1), that provide the dynamic resources and capabilities of the mF2C infrastructure – including a leader and backup, have credentials from a different PKI, which, in a production environment, uses shorter-lived credentials.
3. The recommender application has access to a third PKI which generates credentials only for the airport recommender application.

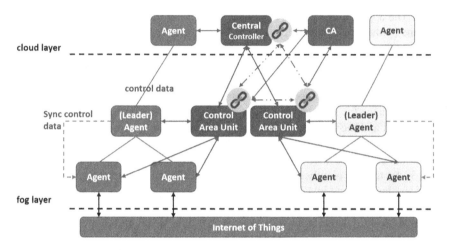

Fig. 4. mF2C security features

The three main reasons for separating the PKIs from each other are: First, a compromise of an application credential does not lead directly to an attack against the platform. Secondly, application specific data is protected with its own PKI, and the platform could in principle serve other use cases at the same time, with the same agents, without risking the unauthorized disclosure of application data. Finally, the CAs for the different PKIs can have different issuance policies and access controls. For example, anyone bringing a device into the airport with mF2C software installed on it, could become an agent, but should not have access to recommender data (using the application PKI), nor should they be able to impersonate a platform endpoint (which use the infrastructure PKI).

Thus, the agent will be distributed with the trust anchors for the infrastructure and for the other agents; whereas the application would typically come only with its own trust anchor.

We have mentioned that the CA service (issuing credentials to applicants according to its policy) runs in the cloud, which would allow users to get their application running before they reach the airport – the user will register and the application obtains its credential. In case the user has not performed this step prior to reaching the airport, it is necessary to let their phone contact the cloud to register the user and obtain a credential. However, we cannot, in general, give a device unfettered access to the Internet, as this may violate the airport's security policy. For this purpose, a special endpoint called, for historical reasons, the Control Area Unit (CAU, Fig. 4) is provided; it is able to receive a certificate signing request from an agent in the fog area and obtain a certificate for it from the service in the cloud. Currently, a separate CAU instance is needed for each PKI.

4.2   Use Case Security

Starting at the edge, all passengers install and use an Android app to interact with the system. The app as a first step presents a privacy notice describing the use of personal data done by the app, and users can decide how much data to share – sharing more data may lead to better recommendations [12]. According to Android best practices[7], neither the device MAC address nor other hardware information are used to identify the app, so no Personal Identifiable Information (PII) are collected without the user's consent. Instead, a random UUID is generated to uniquely identify the app in the system. This identifier remains the same even if the app is killed and then restarted, while if the app is uninstalled and then reinstalled, or if app data are cleared, a new random UUID will be generated. The other information collected by the app are location, traveler flight number (if they choose to share it) and a scoring on the user's inferred interests (Sect. 3). So the app is fully compliant with the GDPR [6] requirements; moreover, the risk of sniffing PII data in a Wi-Fi environment is quite low, since all PII is encrypted using the PKI (Sect. 4.1).

The Android app interacts with second fog layer nodes through an HTTPS web service. This connection is established using both client and server certificates signed by the application CA. The use of a client certificate allows the fog nodes to recognize and trust the app. Once the app has logged in the system, a mechanism based on signed JWT [13] (JSON Web Token) is used to reference the app in subsequent API server calls. The JWT expires after 24 h, after which the app must repeat the login.

The Android apk (Android application package) file is generated according to Google's recommendations with code obfuscation to prevent reverse engineering. The app is distributed as a separate apk file, thus currently not available through the Google Play store. In a future (commercial) step, an official release of the app will be published on Google Play store – it is expected that each airport that deploys it will want its own customized look and feel of the app. Further best practices on app security will be adopted, for example the use of SafetyNet APIs[8].

Backend applications hosted on all fog layers nodes (including Nuvlabox) and in the cloud instance communicate with each other for data synchronization and aggregation through secure channels – and also in a private network within fog cluster - using certificates signed by the application CA. Each backend application instance has a unique identifier that is hashed together with a pre-shared secret to obtain an identity key (ID key). This identity key is used when sending data to other nodes. A receiving

---

[7] https://developer.android.com/training/articles/user-data-ids.

[8] https://developer.android.com/training/safetynet.

node takes the identifier of the sending application and computes the hash using the pre-shared secret. If the hash matches the identity key of the sending node, the receiving node accepts incoming data. The mechanism based on identity keys avoids the use of a different client certificate for each node. The pre-shared secret used for hashing is never used in communications between nodes, and could be stolen only having access to the device in which the application is installed (Fig. 5).

On the "dashboard," given that there are no personal data involved; the current solution implements a simple user/password authentication, while in the future commercial solution it will incorporate a hierarchy of users with roles and permissions, authentication and authorization – for example, parents may be authorized to track their children, and a group of friends might authorize information sharing with each other. Another obvious extension could also let users authenticate with existing ids (e.g. Microsoft Live, Google, Facebook, on the assumption that most users would have at least one of these, but with username/password as a backup for users who do not want to use these) - for our purposes, we do not need any attributes other than a persistent identifier, but users might choose to share their email address through a social media identity provider. Additionally, the registration could optionally register a credit card number, or possibly even eIDAS[9] if this would benefit travelers (e.g. quicker identity checks). User authorization for use of their data would be delegated through the JWT token [13–15].

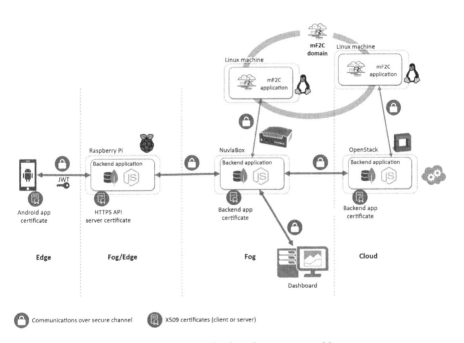

Fig. 5. Secure communications in use-case architecture

---

[9] https://www.eid.as/home/.

Regarding the use of certificates, for the commercial solution we foresee the following options:

a) Manage an internal custom root CA (as today), using certificates signed by it both in the client and server applications;
b) Use Open Source packages such as Let's Encrypt, for CA management;
c) Adapt the current software to take advantage of mF2C CA/CAU built-in capabilities.

The final point that requires attention in the use case architecture is the wireless communications between smartphones and access nodes (RPi). In order to perform a fraudulent usage, an intruder should be within the Wi-Fi range, have downloaded the app and extracted the client certificate. After that, in order to act on behalf of another device, the attacker must generate the same app identifier, but the probability to generate the same random UUID owned by another device is negligible. This probability is further reduced by performing a periodic cleaning of identifiers and data not actively used within a reasonable amount of time, which is a recommended practice. In any case, however, an attacker could get only anonymized data.

5   Experimental Results and Benefits from MF2C

Supposing that the mF2C platform would guarantee the security of the system in fog and cloud, we will run penetration tests at the edge with appropriate tools, so we will check wi-fi communications and peer devices to demonstrate that rPIs are properly protected.

A security testing procedure has been defined for the use case. As primary software tool the KALI distribution has been chosen as it offers a wide range of tools for the most common attacks and is also available on both VM and container to be easily executed by a client on any operating environment. KALI requires a wireless network card that can be set in monitoring mode to operate.

The security testing procedure is divided into the following steps:

- Planning – Gather Information
- Execution – Post Authentication
- Execution – Unauthorized Access Attempts
- Post Execution – Reporting

Planning – Gather Information
Testing starts with a site survey, a security specialist moves with devices and antennas within the defined perimeter to collect information on the wireless signal within the environment: the FERN WIFI tool is used in order to detect the scope of coverage of the Access Points (APs) of the application, detect other AP and other boundary information. It is useful to determine the areas outside the airport area where the wi-fi signal is present: if these areas were available to the public they would be an area of potential attack. In addition, the NMAP tool allows to collect info on all detected APs in terms of hardware, OS and software on the AP, with related models and versions.

This information is useful to determine if vulnerabilities are known on such hardware and software. During this survey, all textual information should be collected and entered into the dictionary for subsequent verification.

The KISMET tool helps in verifying if the channel is open or closed, and the signal is transmitted in clear or encrypted, in case evaluating which data are potentially exposed to disclosure.

Execution – Post Authentication

The next step is oriented to verify security aspects as a regular user. The policies related to network segregation (e.g. guest network separated from internal network) have to be verified. It also verifies the availability and security of the administrative access login. NMAP is used in this case to determine the reachability of the various devices, open ports and potential vulnerabilities.

Execution – Unauthorized Access Attempts

The security specialist with the appropriate tools tries to gain unauthorized access to the wireless network, proceeding to attacks of various kinds (but, obviously, with the authorization of the service provider.) The goal is to determine the possibility that an unauthorized person can gain access to the wireless network, relying on one of the weaknesses such as weak protocols, default or weak administrative credentials, software known vulnerabilities, WPA misconfiguration, etc. or others determined in the previous steps.

KISMET is used together with GIS Kismet for Access Control Attacks such as MAC spoofing, AP/ Client misconfiguration, unauthorized association, or AIREPLAY-NG for Integrity Attacks such as data frame injection, WEP injections, Data Replay, Vector Replay Attacks.

The FERN WIFI tool allows instead Confidentiality Attacks as eavesdropping, as well as Authentication Attacks like cracking key WEP or WPA–PreShare Key, password cracks, identity steal and information of wi-fi clients or VPN login cracking, LEAP cracking and password speculation.

Post Execution – Reporting

At the end of tests a detailed report is generated, showing a map of the environment, with the positions of the APs and relative coverage area and all the hardware and software details detected, vulnerabilities detected (actions to reproduce them and any remediation actions), risk assessment, critical elements detected, documented with traces and screenshots.

The entire procedure was successfully run in the internal testbed; the tests will be repeated at the airport as soon as the solution is released (provided the airport permits it).

6 Conclusions and Next Steps

Traveling can be stressful and it is common to have to allow several hours in order to get boarding passes, pass security, several identity checks, and, on the other end, baggage collection, more identity checks, customs, and onward travel. Implementing a service which can guide the user through these necessary activities can make the journey less stressful, particularly for users with special needs such as those traveling with young children or people with disabilities. We have presented an early version of such a system, intended for deployment initially in Cagliari airport. Based on the fog-to-cloud computing paradigm implemented by the mF2C project in a general platform, it implements an Android app which lets the users choose how much to share (e.g. interests, flight data) and anonymously provides them with guidance and location-aware offers. As with all IoT applications, both security and usability of the security is a concern that must be addressed, or users would not trust the platform with their data – it would be disastrous for the user to miss the flight or lose personal data due to a malfunctioning or compromised airport app. We have already demonstrated security features, and plan to continue to improve security and functionality through the real-life deployment in Cagliari, leading, ultimately, to a commercial product that can be offered to other airports.

Acknowledgments. This work is supported by the H2020 mF2C project (730929).

References

1. Boston Consulting Group, Internet of Things market to reach $267B by 2020 (2017)
2. Garcia Lopez, P., et al.: Edge-centric computing: vision and challenges. In ACM SIGCOMM Computer Communication Review, vol. 45, no. 5, pp. 37–42, October 2015
3. Salis, A., Mancini, G.: Making use of a smart fog hub to develop new services in airports. In: Heras, D.B., Bougé, L. (eds.) Euro-Par 2017. LNCS, vol. 10659, pp. 338–347. Springer, Cham (2018). https://doi.org/10.1007/978-3-319-75178-8_28
4. Villari, M., Fazio, M., Dudstar, S., Rana, O., Ranjan, R.: Osmotic computing: a new paradigm for edge/cloud integration. IEEE Cloud Comput. **3**, 76–83 (2016)
5. Salis, A., Jensen, J., Bulla, R.., Mancini, G., Cocco, P.: Anatomy of a fog-to-cloud distributed recommendation system in airports. In: Proceedings of the IEEE/ACM International Conference on Utility and Cloud Computing, pp. 272–277 (2018)
6. Regulation (EU) 2016/679 of the European Parliament and of the Council of 27 April 2016. https://eur-lex.europa.eu/legal-content/EN/TXT/PDF/?uri=CELEX:32016R0679
7. Ziegler, S.: Internet of Things Security and Data Protection. Springer, Cham (2019). https://doi.org/10.1007/978-3-030-04984-3
8. Lordan, F., Lezzi, D., Ejarque, J., Badia, R.M.: An architecture for programming distributed applications on fog to cloud systems. In: Heras, D.B., Bougé, L. (eds.) Euro-Par 2017. LNCS, vol. 10659, pp. 325–337. Springer, Cham (2018). https://doi.org/10.1007/978-3-319-75178-8_27
9. Martì, J., Queralt, A., Gasull, D., Barcelo, A., Costa, J.J., Cortes, T.: Dataclay: a distributed data store for effective inter-player data sharing. J. Syst. Softw. **131**, 129–145 (2017)
10. Masip-Bruin, X. et al.: mF2C: towards a coordinated management of the IoT-fog-cloud continuum. In: Proceedings of the ACM Smartobjects 2018 (MobiHoc) Conference (2018)
11. Salis, A., Mancini, G., Bulla, R., Cocco, P., Lezzi, D., Lordan, F.: Benefits of a fog-to-cloud approach in proximity marketing. In: Mencagli, G., et al. (eds.) Euro-Par 2018. LNCS, vol. 11339, pp. 239–250. Springer, Cham (2019). https://doi.org/10.1007/978-3-030-10549-5_19
12. Salis, A., Bulla, R., Mancini, G., Cocco, P., Jensen, J.: Anatomy of a fog-to-cloud distributed recommendation system in airports. In: UCC Companion, pp. 272–277 (2018)

13. Jones, M., Bradley, J., Sakimura, N.: RFC 7519: JSON Web Token (JWT), IETF May 2015. https://www.rfc-editor.org/rfc/rfc7519.txt, https://doi.org/10.17487/rfc7519
14. Hardt, D. (ed.): RFC 6749: The OAuth2 Authorization Framework, IETF October 2012. https://www.rfc-editor.org/rfc/rfc6749.txt, https://doi.org/10.17487/rfc6749
15. Jones, M., Campbell, B., Mortimore, C.: RFC 7523: JWT Profile for OAuth 2.0 Client Authentication and Authorization Grants, IETF May 2015. https://www.rfc-editor.org/rfc/rfc7523.txt, https://doi.org/10.17487/rfc7523

On the Similarities and Differences Between the Cloud, Fog and the Edge

Sašo Stanovnik$^{(\boxtimes)}$ and Matija Cankar

XLAB Research, XLAB d.o.o., Ljubljana, Slovenia
{saso.stanovnik,matija.cankar}@xlab.si

Abstract. The field of edge and fog computing is growing, but there are still many inconsistent and loosely–defined terms in current literature. With many articles comparing theoretical architectures and evaluating implementations, there is a need to understand the underlying meaning of information condensed into fog, edge, and similar terms. Through our review of current literature, we discuss these differences and extract key characteristics for basic concepts that appear throughout. The similarities to existing IaaS, PaaS and SaaS models are presented, contrasted against similar models modified for the specifics of edge devices and workloads.

We also evaluate the different aspects existing evaluation and comparison works investigate, including the compute, networking, storage, security, and ease–of–use capabilities of the target implementations. Following that, we make a broad overview of currently available commercial and open–source platforms implementing the edge or fog paradigms, identifying key players, successful niche actors and general trends for feature–level and technical development of these platforms.

Keywords: Fog · Edge · IoT · Platform · Comparison · Overview · Definition

1 Introduction

Computing resources can be made available in a number of ways. Using the *grid* as a somewhat low–level abstraction predates using the *cloud* as a more high–level abstraction to computing resources, and the latter is, at the moment, the most popular method of delegating computational resources. With consumer–focused and low–powered machines becoming capable of an increasing number of non–trivial tasks, there is often a desire to take advantage of that capacity to perform computation more optimally, e.g. by increasing data locality.

Extending from the cloud, edge computing and, more recently, fog computing have appeared as terms for describing such architectures. The differences are

---

This work is supported by the European Union through the Horizon 2020 research and innovation programme under grant 730929.

U. Schwardmann et al. (Eds.): Euro-Par 2019 Workshops, LNCS 11997, pp. 112–123, 2020.
https://doi.org/10.1007/978-3-030-48340-1_9

not immediately apparent however, and different sources have sometimes subtly, sometimes very prominently, differing view on what each should encompass.

Our goals are to identify similarities and differences in the approaches to handling the different layers of the fog/edge computing architectures and to make a comparison of existing research and solutions. We will begin by exploring and clarifying commonly used terms in Sect. 2, then continue on to explore the levels of overall management of platforms in literature in Sect. 3. Following that, we provide an overview of current literature in Sect. 4 and conclude with an overview of currently available proprietary and open–source platforms in Sect. 5.

2   Commonly Used Terms

Many terms used in this field are used frequently, without a clear consensus on what, specifically, they mean. This complicates interpreting existing literature, where different researchers have slightly different views on the boundaries between layers, which, while always overlapping, can differ significantly.

Most of these terms are not technical and are used primarily in marketing and, even there, are established to varying degrees. They condense many technical details into a well–recognised word that is a generally correct description of the concept, but lacks the specificity needed to recognise and understand the issue in–depth.

2.1   The Cloud

Although a term that is already established, it is useful to define the key characteristics that researchers in the field describe with this term, as not all may be immediately obvious when compressed into a single word.

Mainly the term concerns the abstraction of physical or virtual resources, made available through a managed interface. The location, specific configuration and ownership of the resources themselves should not matter, other than for their performance characteristics or for differences in billing models.

2.2   Fog, Edge and IoT

These are terms widely used, but problematic in terms of overlap. The somewhat recently emerged field of cloud IoT providers sometimes covers all three aspects, seldom well–defined and mostly used interchangeably. The research into these platforms exhibits the same, with authors' interpretation implicit and specific to a single application.

This work attempts to non–authoritatively define the scope of each of these terms, based on our cumulative understanding of the field rather than based on any specific research. The basic constraint is that we attempt to classify devices into a single category, which provides multiple opportunities to evaluate differences and overlaps.

In a larger picture, the *fog*, *edge* and *IoT* layers, joined by the *cloud*, form a hierarchical relationship with a single, likely distributed cloud at the top, followed by multiple fogs, each containing multiple edge devices, connected to even more IoT devices.

The only layer the standalone existence of which does not make sense is the fog layer, as this is, usually, a bridging layer connecting multiple edge devices and the cloud and, almost by definition, must include edge devices. IoT devices are of little use on their own and edge computing–capable devices, on their own, already exist in the form of personal computers.

2.3   Proposed Understanding of the Architecture

To try to establish an understanding and to define terms used in subsequent sections, we present our definition of the above terms. This layout is summarised in Fig. 1.

Starting from the bottom layer of IoT devices, these are commonly defined as sensors and actuators that interact with the environment. The definition we use is slightly stricter in that we require them to not run a traditional operating system. This excludes powerful single board computers such as the Raspberry Pi, but includes microcontrollers, simple sensors communicating over one wire and Bluetooth–based sensor packages.

This is the first instance of overlap between the IoT and edge layers. The Raspberry Pi in particular, having GPIO pins available to connect to the physical world is often considered an IoT device because of that fact, but can also act as an edge device. The differentiating factor is only the software that runs on them and, subsequently, the role they take in the overall architecture.

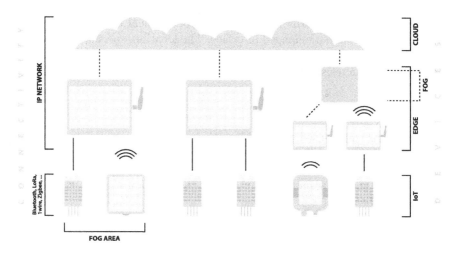

Fig. 1. Hierarchical architecture summary.

Edge devices are, in our definition, devices capable of IP–based networking, running an operating system offering remote configuration, connectivity, and being able to run applications on–demand. They also connect to devices hierarchically below them, possibly using non–IP–based networks such as Bluetooth [4] or Thread [22]. Apart from bridging different connections, providing computational power is a major role of these devices because of them being relatively computationally powerful. Examples of such devices are single board computers, laptops and industrial gateways. Mobile phones could also be considered edge devices, but as they are not configurable enough to be equivalent to others, we do not include them in this definition.

The most ambiguously defined is the layer of fog devices. It is very similar to the edge layer and can be viewed as its vertical extension—there is very little difference between the edge and the fog. As it is used in current literature, it most often is a general–purpose term used for devices between the topmost cloud layer and another layer below them, with the primary differentiator being their primary role in bridging logical connections. We believe this does not differ from the edge layer in any significant aspect.

However, there is a distinction between a *fog layer* as described above and a *fog area*, and that is where the term is useful. The *fog area* is a geographically–based group of devices, including devices on all layers except the cloud. This grouping may be static or dynamic, depending on the properties of the devices—an example is inter–vehicle communication, where edge nodes are mobile. This grouping allows reasoning about larger–scale device locality which solely edge do not encompass.

Lastly, there is the cloud layer, which was already described. One may note that devices such as routers, are not included, even though they must be present for any meaningful infrastructure as described to exist. They are a supporting mechanism present on all layers, but are sometimes replaced by alternative connection mechanisms that the edge layer provides.

3 Levels of Management of Edge Architectures

Apart from the overall architecture, there are also different ways of managing devices and functionalities in edge architectures. In the cloud, IaaS, PaaS and SaaS are the most common solution types. At the edge, no such type has emerged to be the most prominent.

Similar terms exist in this field. Things-aaS [1] and Smart Object-aaS [6] are concepts of exposing sensors, actuators and devices to the network by providing managed bridges as an interface between a traditional networked component and *things* that may or may not have been originally designed to connect to a network as a managed object. Sensing-aaS [6,18] and Sensing and Actuation-aaS [1,6,15] are similar concepts, but deal with exposing the sensing and/or actuation capabilities of devices rather than the devices themselves, providing a further abstraction layer between data sources and data consumers. Data-aaS, City Infrastructure-aaS are examples of different terms for more or less the same concept, shared between all previously mentioned terms: making some kind of data available over the network in a managed system. Existing research on this will be presented in Sect. 4.

The cloud IaaS, PaaS and SaaS concepts can be somewhat extended to the edge. With the exception of SaaS, which is focused on end–user applications, concepts of both IaaS and SaaS can be found in, for example, Sensing-aaS, where sensors are abstracted and exposed in the same way as computing resources.

Classically, the main difference between IaaS and PaaS is that the former allows direct use of hardware resources, albeit virtualised or somehow isolated, while the latter offers an abstracted development platform and software lifecycle and hides the actual underlying hardware [8].

To transfer IaaS and PaaS to the area of edge devices, we need to know the benefits and drawbacks to using devices not situated in traditional data centre environments, which offer security, power management and a reliable hardware deployment setting.

Placing devices at the edge, for example in a factory floor or throughout an airport provides no redundancy found in a data center—there is only a single power supply with no external management and a single network link with potentially low-performing upstream equipment. Additionally, physical security is an issue as devices are placed where anyone, potentially even the general public, can access them. This presents a difficult issue in hardware and network security, as new threat models need to be considered that have previously been ignored.

On the other hand, there are application-specific benefits that placing devices *in situ* bring. A factory often lacks the necessary infrastructure for a proper data centre, an airport may have its own data centre but require smart sensing devices to analyse data from customers or even manage point–of–sale terminals [19]. Even with the lack of local device redundancy, in an event of a wider network outage, the local network could be retained, offering a limited set of functionalities locally.

An extension of that is a reduction of decision-making latency that can be achieved by not contacting a distant server through a WAN but instead making decisions on the edge device, where network latency can be several orders of magnitude lower, enabling applications where real-time decisions are crucial. The data security aspect could also be important: privacy constraints could limit data transfer to a cloud service. In this case, having devices capable of processing data in a compliant location could be the only way for an application to operate.

4   Existing Research

Research related to the cloud computing and IoT paradigms is reasonably old, with them being started to be widely explored in the mid 2000s. The more recent field of fog and edge computing has emerged in the early 2010s.

On the industrial side, existing providers of cloud platforms have begun to implement and support IoT platforms as an extension to their business, attaching additional IoT– and edge–focused functionalities to their existing solutions. Due to this, work on edge computing platforms and comparisons between existing solutions has begun to increase.

Grid computing was considered a predecessor to the IaaS, PaaS and SaaS models. Whereas the grid was considered useful for a small number computationally expensive tasks, the benefits of the cloud were considered as the capability to provide scalability to a large number of heterogeneous tasks, not necessarily compute–intensive. A cloud is considered to have the following properties:

– self-service, with no administrator intervention for general usage,
– broad, homogenous network access,
– resource pooling, multi-tenancy, possibly via virtualisation,
– elasticity and scalability and
– resource usage measurement, possibly used for billing.

4.1   Related Work

Recent work has been mostly focused on integration strategies for platforms. Because comparing platforms in–depth is difficult at best, most research does not include any comprehensive evaluation, but instead focuses on purely theoretical methods or a simple proof of concept [6].

Papers appear mostly in workshops or conferences rather than journals, which relates to the relative immaturity of the field. Publications are spread across around 30 sources [6], with no single one seeming prevalent. More thorough evaluation methods are desired, as 15% of evaluations are done on a purely theoretical basis and another 40% are extremely simple single-purpose proof of concept applications. Types of proposals for new platforms can be categorised into the following groups:

– architecture: purely theoretical proposals,
– platform: implementations supporting the development and execution of applications in hardware or in software,
– framework: software directly used in the development process and
– middleware: services applications use.

The IoT layer is nearly always included [9] within existing platform as articles—the edge is seldom used solely for computation. This makes sense, as only relocating computation, without data–generating components near it, brings little benefit.

Approaches to integrating low–level devices are various: one project integrates the sensors directly into existing modules in OpenStack [15,21], while another tries to adhere to the UNIX philosophy of *everything is a file*, and maps sensors to filesystem objects [5]. Both resemble IaaS in that they only expose resources as primitives, but do not otherwise provide added services. Authors claim language independence and liken their approach to the one in the Raspberry Pi platform, which exposes GPIO pins as special filesystem objects.

In research of the edge and the fog, authors largely equate the two [1,13]. This is done either explicitly, or implicitly without even mentioning the edge layer—using the fog to include its functionalities. Sources do agree, however, on the features a fog should provide:

- storage, or some kind of persistance mechanism for data,
- networking, or a way to connect devices between separate networks and
- computational offloading.

Providing storage can be done in many ways. The only important characteristics are that there must be a way to submit and retrieve data to and from the solution, as edge devices might not necessarily have the capability to have local instances of databases.

Networking can be provided either as an overlay network for transparent connectivity–this would provide an IaaS–like service. There may be a higher–level mechanism for logical connections, akin to PaaS, such as a distributed message queue, which applications could explicitly conform to and use.

An important and often overlooked aspect of edge networking is ensuring reliability. Compared to data centres, where one can assume that while reliability of equipment and connections is high, at the edge devices are in uncontrolled environments with using reliable hardware. Network connections are not fault tolerant and handling this unreliability must be done at the software level, or more specifically, at the level of the platform devices are connected to. Applications must be able to persist through network connection loss and, ideally, provide functionality even in cases with no connection to the global Internet.

Offloading of computation is necessarily present in fog or edge computation scenarios for them to be useful to lower layers. How this is implemented is flexible, ranging from grid computing–like solutions, to only spawning whole applications on other nodes and subsequently communicating with them, possibly speculatively if there is a demand for responsiveness.

Data locality is frequently used in the context of this computation [11]. Used in terms of a single computer, this means cache hits and misses but in a distributed environment that edge devices provide, it is used for processing data that resides on the local node, without it being fetched over the network. Lessons learned from grid distributed computing apply here—not all workloads are necessarily sutable for this. Calculating an easily parallelisable task, such as the mean value of a dataset, is simple, however if the computation is not trivially parallelisable, challenges due to the relatively high network latency between edge nodes arise, which must be solved differently than grid computing problems, which exist in controlled environments.

The reduction of latency, particularly computation and decision–making, is most often the primary benefit pointed out for edge infrastructures [1]. While the balance between data transfer speed and processing speed needs to be achieved, there are use–cases where this may be useful.

5   Existing Solutions

There are a myriad of platforms supporting IoT and edge computing workloads. We have selected 32 for an evaluation. This will not be an in–depth comparison— the goal is to understand the variety of functionalities, as advertised, of this limited set of platforms. This is definitely not a comprehensive list of solutions in this niche. The products listed have been sourced through browsing review papers, web searches for similar platforms and through platforms already known to the authors.

We have chosen around 25 metrics for comparison. These mostly concern categorisation and boolean feature availability and scope, pricing scheme, and general popularity. This information has been condensed into a table in Fig. 2. In the following text, we will refer to these platforms by either their name or by their sequential number in the first (index) column.

A basic comparison is the type of the platform, classified into IaaS, PaaS and SaaS. Existing cloud provider features can easily be categorised into these three groups, but this is not the case for edge computing platforms, where there is not much variety. Essentially, most platforms use a PaaS model, providing tools to the developer to explicitly use when developing, often resulting in vendor lock–in. SaaS platforms exist for end–user solutions and IaaS platforms are the rarest. The platform focused most on the style of IaaS was Cisco Jasper [7], which focuses on device connectivity.

Most platforms are deployed as a service managed by the provider, with some being available to completely self–host. The vast majority of open–source components are able to be self–hosted, and about half of the others offer the ability to host a component on a private infrastructure, connecting to the global cloud deployment.

Even the platforms that offer edge computing devices (11, 15, 16, 18, 20, 22, 30, 31, 32) or software that connects to an existing cloud only allow for a single additional layer of devices. Using the layers defined in 2, the cloud layer is always available, with the optional gateways acting as the edge layer as an intermediary to IoT devices. There is no platform that offers a variable number of layers, or the ability to have more than three layers.

Integrations for platforms from providers with existing cloud solutions (10, 12, 14, 15, 29, 30, 31, 32) are mostly for inventory and access management and data pipelines. This enables processing data and integrating into existing applications using the wider cloud platform, but almost all solutions offer analytics, triggers and a web dashboard out–of–the–box. An interesting exception is MathWorks ThingSpeak [14], which offers data processing through MATLAB, an existing desktop product instead.

Most platforms, except (7, 11, 18, 21, 22, 25, 30, 31, 32), focus solely on IoT, which means only focusing on acquiring and processing sensor data, either without or with limited ability to run other computation or applications on the platform. About a third are generalised to be able to operate under the edge computing paradigm to varying degrees—these are mostly the ones also offering an edge gateway solution. Within the IoT-focused frameworks, there is not often

Provider	Main type	Open source	Self hosted	Provider integration	Analytics / triggers	Has Official GW devices	Official languages	Comm protocols	IoT focus	IoT Segment focus	Authn/z	Alt. network	Offline funct.	Pricing	Year	Docs
1 Carriots/Altair SmartWorks	PaaS	no	optional	no	yes, no	no	Java, Groovy	REST, MQTT	yes	none	API key	Sigfox, LoRa	no	30 day trial, quote	2011	open, moderate
2 Exosite Murano	SaaS	no	optional	no	yes, yes	no	Lua	REST, MQTT, ws	yes	none	API key	no	no	quote	2009	open, moderate
3 Grovestreams	SaaS	no	optional	no	yes, yes	no	/	REST	yes	none	API key	no	no	free tier, per I/O, users	2011	open, very limited
4 Realkme.io/ioBridge	SaaS	no	no	no	yes, yes	no	proprietary, JS	REST	yes	none	API key	no	no	quote	2008	open, very limited
5 Sensorcloud	SaaS	no	no	no	yes, yes	no	proprietary	REST	yes	none	API key	yes	no	free tier, per transaction, alert	2011	open, moderate
6 Tempoiq	SaaS	no	no	no	yes, yes	no	Python, JS, Ruby, Java, C#	REST, MQTT	yes	none	API key	no	no	trial, quote	2016	open, limited
7 Thingworx	SaaS	no	optional	no	yes, yes	no	C, C#, Java, ObjC	REST, MQTT	no	Industry 4.0	API key, LDAP	no	no	trial, quote	2014	videos
8 Wookit	SaaS	no	no	no	yes, no	no	/	REST	yes	none	API key, OAuth2	no	no	quote	2011	open, very limited
9 Lelylan	PaaS	yes	yes	no	no, yes	no	/	REST, MQTT, ws	yes	none	API key	no	no	open source	2011	open, moderate
10 Mainwoks Thingspeak	SaaS	yes	optional	no	yes, yes	no	C, Python	REST	yes	none	API key	no	no	trial, per I/O	2010	open, extensive
11 Stack4Things	IaaS	yes	yes	no	yes, yes	no	/	REST, CoAP	no	none	API key	no	no	open source	2014	open, very limited
12 C3 IoT	SaaS	no	no	yes	yes, n/a	no	n/a	n/a	no	Industry 4.0	n/a	no	no	open source	2016	closed
13 Parse Platform	PaaS	yes	yes	no	yes, yes	no	ObjC, JS, Java, .NET, PHP	REST	yes	none	API key	no	no	open source	2011	open, extensive
14 Salesforce IoT	SaaS	no	no	yes	yes, n/a	no	JS, Java, ObjC, C	REST	yes	Salesforce	OAuth2	no	no	quote	2015	closed
15 Oracle IoT Cloud	PaaS	no	no	yes	yes, yes	no	C++, ObjC, Java	REST	yes	none	OAuth2	no	no	per cpu/hour	2017	open, extensive
16 Kaa	SaaS	yes	optional	no	yes, yes	no	Java, PHP, C#, ObjC, py, JS, Ruby	MQTT, CoAP	yes	none	user/pass, OAuth2	no	no	trial, hosted, self-hosted	2014	open, extensive
17 Temboo	PaaS	no	no	no	yes, yes	no	Arduino	REST, MQTT, CoAP	yes	Industry 4.0	user/pass, OAuth2	no	no	trial, quote	2006	open, extensive
18 Ayla IoT Fabric	PaaS	no	no	no	yes, yes	yes	RTOS	n/a	no	none	n/a	BLE, Z-Wave, Zigbee	no	quote	2010	closed
19 ThethingsIO	PaaS	partial	optional	no	yes, yes	no	/	REST, MQTT	yes	none	API key	LoRa, NB-IoT, Sigfox	no	trial, quote, per device/message	2013	open, extensive
20 OpenRemote	PaaS	yes	yes	no	no, yes	no	Java	REST, SNMP, 1wire	yes	smart home	API key	no	yes	open source, quote	2016	open, extensive
21 Cisco Jasper	IaaS	no	no	no	yes, yes	n/a	n/a	n/a	no	none	n/a	NB-IoT	no	quote	2004	closed
22 Cumulocity	PaaS	no	gateway	no	yes, yes	yes	Java, C++, C#	REST, MQTT	no	none	user/pass	LoRa, Sigfox	yes	trial, quote, per device	2010	open, extensive
23 Cloudplugs	PaaS	partial	optional	no	yes, yes	no	Java, C, JS, ObjC, Python	REST, MQTT, ws	yes	Industry 4.0	user/pass	LoRa, BLE, Z-Wave	no	quote	2014	partially open, extensive
24 FIWARE	PaaS	yes	yes	no	no, yes	a lot	Java, JS, py	REST, MQTT	no	none	API key	no	no	open source	2011	open, limited
25 OpenMTC	PaaS	yes	yes	no	yes, yes	no	/	REST, MQTT, AMQP, CoAP	no	none	API key	Zigbee	no	trial, quote, per device	2017	open, extensive
26 Sitewhere	SaaS	yes	yes	no	yes, yes	no	Java	REST, MQTT	yes	none	API key	no	no	community, quote	2010	open, limited
27 Kura	PaaS	yes	yes	no	no, no	no	/	REST, MQTT	yes	smart home	API key	no	no	open source	2013	open, moderate
28 Node-RED	PaaS	yes	yes	no	yes, yes	no	visual, JS	REST, MQTT	yes	none	API key	no	no	open source	2013	open, extensive
29 IBM Watson IoT	SaaS	no	no	yes	yes, yes	a lot	n/a	n/a	yes	none	n/a	no	no	per instance, feature, quote	2015	closed
30 AWS IoT	PaaS	no	gateway	yes	yes, yes	a lot	Java, .NET, JS, PHP, py, Ruby, Go, C++	REST, MQTT, ws	no	none	cert	no	yes	per call, device, action, tx	2017	open, extensive
31 GCP IoT /Xively	PaaS	no	gateway	yes	yes, yes	a lot	Java, JS, py, C++	REST, MQTT	no	none	cert	no	yes	per call, data, tx	2017	open, moderate
32 Azure IoT	PaaS	partial	gateway	yes	yes, yes	a lot	Java, .NET, JS, py, C	REST, MQTT, AMQP	no	none	API key, cert, SASL	no	yes	per unit, action, message, device	2016	open, very extensive

Fig. 2. Summary platform comparison table.

a focus on a specific segment of the industry, but about a quarter do: mostly focusing on targeting Industry 4.0, with some also explicitly targeting the smart home market.

5.1   Technical Details

Around half of the platforms (see the *Official devices* column in Fig. 2) offer some kind of explicit support for IoT devices in the form of usage tutorials or real–time operating system support. The most commonly supported platforms are Arduino and Raspberry Pi, with larger or more focused industrial providers also supporting more specialised devices. Frameworks excelling in this category are Cumulocity [20], AWS IoT [2], Google Cloud Platform IoT [10] and Azure IoT [16], particularly the latter, offering an exceptionally large number of devices with software and hardware integrations.

All platforms offer a programming language-agnostic way to interface with the platform with an HTTP API. Other *official* programming languages differ by platform, but Java, Python, C, C# and Javascript are most frequently supported. The presence of SDKs and examples are correlated with platform popularity.

The most common mechanism for securing, authenticating and authorising transmissions is the combination of an API key along with TLS encryption. This is sometimes used in an OAuth2 context or, less frequently, with HTTP Basic authentication. A common configuration is per–device X.509 certificates, serving the dual purpose of inventory management.

Alternative networking protocols are seldom supported. They are, in order of decreasing frequency of support: LoRa, Sigfox, ZigBee, Bluetooth, Z-Wave and NB-IoT. Gateway devices offer this connection bridging capability, particularly for transmitting sensor data. Kaa IoT [12] is the only platform offering explicit support for battery management by batching updates, while AWS IoT and Azure IoT stand out with explicit support for intermittent connectivity, offering a subset of functionalities locally.

5.2   Pricing and Popularity

Pricing varies greatly between the platforms. Open source components are offered for free or with paid plans for hosted solutions, while others have various methods of managing costs. Some have bulk packages with quotas, others have prices scaling with the number of connected devices. Typical of platforms provided by companies with existing cloud services are very verbose pricing plans, charging by the number of actions performed, API calls or bytes transferred in very small increments. A number of the projects, particularly those not generally popular, do not have public pricing plans, instead requiring a direct contact for a pricing inquiry.

We measured popularity through Google Trends and categorised platforms into 5 groups of popularity based on their current or historical popularity and growth rate. The groups are descriptive with their members being fairly similar among themselves, but their popularity quantifier is subjective. We make no claim to the quality of the platforms through this metric, but recognise that community support and the availability of documentation are very important for development. The categories are, excluding platforms which do not appear on Google Trends at all:

1. very high popularity: Node-RED, AWS IoT, GCP IoT, Azure IoT
2. high popularity: Thingworx, Mathworks Thingspeak, FIWARE
3. low popularity: ioBridge, C3 IoT, Salesforce IoT, Temboo, OpenRemote, Cisco Jasper, Cumulocity

4. very low popularity: Oracle IoT Cloud, Kaa, Sitewhere
5. extremely low popularity: Grovestreams, Tempoiq, Lelylan, thethings.io, Cloudplugs

There are a few platforms that stand out from others in particular aspects. As mentioned before, Cisco Jasper is the only platform focused purely on infrastructure management. Ayla IoT Fabric [3] and OpenRemote [17] are the only frameworks offering data sharing between users—the idea being that multiple users connect their devices into a wider network, giving each themselves the possibility of selectively sharing sensor data with other users.

AWS IoT, GCP IoT and Azure IoT are seemingly the most mature and popular products, objectively offering the most features, with integrations into the wider platforms of their respective providers.

6   Conclusion

We have discussed to different approaches to understanding cloud, fog, edge and IoT architectures, reviewed relevant literature and investigated the platforms currently available on the market.

The differences in the interpretation and understanding of especially the terms of *fog* and *edge* were large, as different sources place functionalities into different groups. These overlap, so there is no definitive agreement on a precise definition of the terms, but we have managed to identify key features sources use when referencing them.

Levels of conformance to established IaaS/PaaS/SaaS styles were also considered, finding a large overlap but not a definitive mapping. In existing literature, there is a large variety of approaches to building new systems. Evaluating them leaves much to be desired, though, as comparisons are frequently very shallow.

Existing solutions do not cover the area of fog computing, but some support for edge computing is present, frequently in the form of edge gateways supporting delegating functionality from the cloud. We have identified the key characteristics of a multitude of commercial and open–source platforms and found that there are clear leaders in functionalities, but there exist leaders in specific niches targeting specific needs.

Our work is ongoing with these being our initial results. In the future, we plan to make a more detailed and methodological comparison, with a PoC implementation in some of the most platforms.

References

1. Aazam, M., Zeadally, S., Harras, K.A.: Fog computing architecture, evaluation, and future research directions, **56**(5), 46–52. https://doi.org/10.1109/MCOM.2018.1700707, https://ieeexplore.ieee.org/document/8360849/
2. Amazon Web Services: IoT Apps and Solutions. https://aws.amazon.com/iot/
3. Ayla Networks Inc.: IoT Software Companies. https://www.aylanetworks.com/

4. Bluetooth SIG Inc.: Bluetooth Technology Website. https://www.bluetooth.com/
5. Bruneo, D., Distefano, S., Longo, F., Merlino, G., Puliafito, A.: I/Ocloud: adding an IoT dimension to cloud infrastructures, **51**(1), 57–65. https://doi.org/10.1109/MC.2018.1151016, http://ieeexplore.ieee.org/document/8267996/
6. Cavalcante, E.: On the interplay of Internet of Things and Cloud Computing: a systematic mapping study, **89–90**, 17–33. https://doi.org/10.1016/j.comcom.2016.03.012, https://linkinghub.elsevier.com/retrieve/pii/S0140366416300706
7. Cisco Systems Inc.: Cisco Jasper. https://www.jasper.com/
8. Dillon, T., Wu, C., Chang, E.: Cloud computing: issues and challenges. In: 2010 24th IEEE International Conference on Advanced Information Networking and Applications, pp. 27–33. IEEE. https://doi.org/10.1109/AINA.2010.187, http://ieeexplore.ieee.org/document/5474674/
9. Díaz, M., Martín, C., Rubio, B.: State-of-the-art, challenges, and open issues in the integration of Internet of things and cloud computing, **67**, 99–117. https://doi.org/10.1016/j.jnca.2016.01.010, https://linkinghub.elsevier.com/retrieve/pii/S108480451600028X
10. Google Inc.: Google Cloud IoT. https://cloud.google.com/solutions/iot/
11. Jiang, Y., Huang, Z., Tsang, D.H.K.: Challenges and solutions in fog computing orchestration, **32**(3), 122–129. https://doi.org/10.1109/MNET.2017.1700271, https://ieeexplore.ieee.org/document/8121864/
12. KaaIoT Technologies: Kaa Enterprise IoT Platform. https://www.kaaproject.org/
13. Mahmud, R., Kotagiri, R., Buyya, R.: Fog computing: a taxonomy, survey and future directions. In: Di Martino, B., Li, K.-C., Yang, L.T., Esposito, A. (eds.) Internet of Everything. IT, pp. 103–130. Springer, Singapore (2018). https://doi.org/10.1007/978-981-10-5861-5_5
14. MathWorks Inc.: ThingSpeak Internet of Things. https://thingspeak.com/
15. Merlino, G., Bruneo, D., Distefano, S., Longo, F., Puliafito, A.: Stack4Things: integrating IoT with OpenStack in a Smart City context. In: 2014 International Conference on Smart Computing Workshops, pp. 21–28. IEEE. https://doi.org/10.1109/SMARTCOMP-W.2014.7046678
16. Microsoft Corp.: Azure IoT. https://azure.microsoft.com/en-us/overview/iot/
17. OpenRemote: Open Source for Internet of Things. http://www.openremote.com/
18. Perera, C., Zaslavsky, A., Christen, P., Georgakopoulos, D.: Sensing as a service model for smart cities supported by Internet of Things (2014)
19. Salis, A., Mancini, G., Bulla, R., Cocco, P., Lezzi, D., Lordan, F.: Benefits of a fog-to-cloud approach in proximity marketing. In: Mencagli, G., et al. (eds.) Euro-Par 2018. LNCS, vol. 11339, pp. 239–250. Springer, Cham (2019). https://doi.org/10.1007/978-3-030-10549-5_19
20. Software AG: Cumulocity IoT. https://www.softwareag.cloud/site/product/cumulocity-iot.html
21. The OpenStack Project: OpenStack. https://www.openstack.org/
22. Thread Group: Thread. https://www.threadgroup.org/

TDM Edge Gateway: A Flexible Microservice-Based Edge Gateway Architecture for Heterogeneous Sensors

Massimo Gaggero$^{(\boxtimes)}$ ⓘ, Giovanni Busonera ⓘ, Luca Pireddu ⓘ,
and Gianluigi Zanetti ⓘ

CRS4 - Center for Advanced Studies, Research and Development in Sardinia,
Loc. Piscina Manna, Edificio 1, 09050 Pula, CA, Italy
{massimo.gaggero,giovanni.busonera,luca.pireddu,
gianluigi.zanetti}@crs4.it
http://www.crs4.it

Abstract. How to effectively handle heterogeneous data sources is one of the main challenges in the design of large-scale research computing platforms to collect, analyze and integrate data from IoT sensors. The platform must seamlessly support the integration of myriads of data formats and communication protocols, many being introduced after the platform has been deployed. Edge gateways, devices deployed at the *edge* of the network near the sensors, communicate with measurement stations using their proper protocol, receive and translate the messages to a standardized format, forward the data to the processing platform and provide local data buffering and preprocessing. In this work we present the *TDM Edge Gateway* architecture, which we have developed to be used in research contexts to meet the requirements of being self-built, low-cost, and compatible with current or future connected sensors.

The architecture is based on a microservice-oriented design implemented with software containerization and leverages publish/subscribe Inter Process Communication to ensure modularity and resiliency. Costs and construction simplicity are ensured by adopting the popular Raspberry Pi Single Board Computer. The resulting platform is lean, flexible and easy to expand and integrate. It does not pose constraints on programming languages to use and relies on standard protocols and data models.

Keywords: Edge computing · Sensor networks · Embedded · FIWARE

1 Introduction

The spread of internet-connected devices has proven to be an important and boundless source of data for the development of new services in different

This work was supported by the TDM project funded by Sardinian Regional Authorities under grant agreement POR FESR 2014–2020 Azione 1.2 (D. 66/14 13.12.2016 S3-ICT).

To the memory of Dr. Gianluigi Zanetti.

U. Schwardmann et al. (Eds.): Euro-Par 2019 Workshops, LNCS 11997, pp. 124–135, 2020.
https://doi.org/10.1007/978-3-030-48340-1_10

application domains, from industry to transportation, health-care, home & comfort and entertainment. These devices are potentially an excellent source of data for the scientific research too, but the use of closed and proprietary components and the impossibility to export the acquired data makes them unsuitable for effective research data acquisition applications. At the same time, self-built low-budget sensors voluntarily installed and operated by private citizens are an alternative, growing opportunity for research to access large amounts of valuable data. While volunteer project participants cover the affordable deployment and maintenance costs, they receive in return the results and services provided by the research – environmental monitoring, weather and power-consumption forecasting, visualization and statistics. However, using these kinds of devices poses important issues to the data collecting infrastructure from the point of view of security, reliability and, especially, device heterogeneity.

In this paper we describe a novel architecture of an Edge Device for heterogeneous and distributed data acquisition that we have developed for research applications. Its primary purpose is to translate sensor-specific data to a standard FIWARE-compliant data model [7] and form a bridge between the sensors' native communication protocols and the computing platform. Unlike existing platforms, the TDM Edge Gateway is designed with a lean and simple architecture based on common standards and light protocols for component interaction (e.g., FIWARE and MQTT), and it avoids defining custom APIs and restricting the implementation options for extensions.

Various application scenarios are supported:

- edge device with no user interaction for data acquisition in buildings, plants and farmlands;
- edge station in private home with local data viewing and possible interaction with central facility;
- mobile edge gateway that can provide store-and-forward capabilities for resource constrained sensors.

The fundamental requirements for this Edge Gateway are *flexibility* and *robustness*. The Edge Gateway must guarantee seamless integration of future sensors and applications without affecting those already present. The adoption of a microservice-oriented approach provides the required modularity [6]: the various functionalities provided by the device are distributed among different separate micro applications, each only implementing one service. Microservices are delivered by means of *lightweight software containers* packaged with all the required files and libraries. Microservices and containerization also provide robustness: a broken module does not directly affect the whole system or taint others executable contexts, while incompatible libraries are kept separated among different containers [11]. Another point of robustness in our design is represented by the use of the *publish/subscribe* paradigm for data exchange between microservices. This asynchronous communication pattern allows the different applications to work even if there are no sender or receiver modules alive, and addition or removal of microservices does not require a system reboot or a message-routing reconfiguration. Again, module failures are not propagated by means of socket errors, timeouts or service unavailability.

This Edge Gateway has been developed, tested and its deployment in research context is currently underway withing the context of the "Tessuto Digitale Metropolitano"[1] (TDM) research project that aims to develop innovative applications for Smart Cities in the fields of Weather Safety and Nowcasting, Citizen Energy Awareness, and Large Dataset Visualization for Cultural Heritage. These vertical applications depend on a mixture of data from different sources – from satellites to meteorological radar, and particularly to weather, air and energy sensors distributed over the Metropolitan Area of Cagliari. To facilitate the recruitment of volunteer sensor deployers for the project, the sensors platform was chosen to be low-cost, ready-made and available, open source and open hardware. Moreover, given that all the developed code, documentation and Reference Designs have been made available to the public as open source, the creation and adoption of new sensors and the interest of diverse research fields are encouraged too. Thus, the Edge Gateway must bridge a multitude of sensor formats and protocols to our Lambda-architecture platform for storage and processing. One distinctive feature of TDM Edge Gateway is that it is natively *FIWARE compliant*. FIWARE [7] is *"a curated framework of Open Source platform components to accelerate the development of smart solutions"*. It provides a common set of Open Source APIs for data exchange, the *Next Generation Service Interface*, software components for IoT and Big Data integration, and a large set of *harmonized data models*. Given the portability and interoperability they provide to the infrastructure for Smart Cities and Smart Solutions, the FIWARE NGSI API has also been adopted by the Open and Agile Smart Cities (OASC) network for the integration of services among the cities taking part in the initiative.

The rest of the paper is structured as follows. In Sect. 2 we describe the architecture of our Edge Gateway and its components, while the developed system, its testbed and deployment is explained in Sect. 3. Section 4 discusses the state of the art of this specific research field and Sect. 5 concludes the manuscript summarizing its contribution and proposing future developments.

2   TDM Edge Gateway Architecture

The TDM Edge Gateway follows a microservice-based design. The functionality it provides is distributed across separate micro-applications deployed as Docker [4] containers on the edge device. Data exchange between microservices is performed asynchronously through the publish/subscribe MQTT protocol. MQTT is also used to forward data from the Edge Gateway to the acquisition and processing platform using an encrypted and authenticated channel. In addition, data is also written to a local InfluxDB instance. From here it can be queried by applications running directly on the Edge Gateway, such as the dashboard (Fig. 1).

---

[1] http://www.tdm-project.it/.

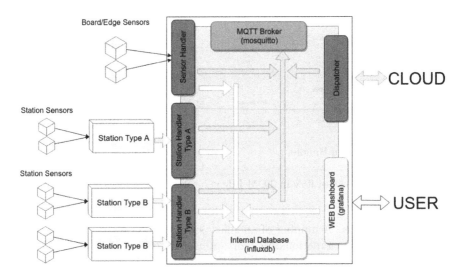

Fig. 1. Edge Gateway architecture

TDM Edge Gateway microservices are divided into three roles: *handlers, consumer* or *dispatcher* and *ancillary services*. These are described in the following paragraphs.

Handlers. Handlers are the microservices that receive, translate and store the data that arrives from sensors and stations. Handlers are specialized for each type of sensor or station – rather than having a single service that deals with the heterogeneity of transmission protocols and message formats. Sensors and sensor stations may be remote, transmitting data via network, or they may be directly connected to the Edge Gateway. The handler's main tasks are to:

- establish and maintain communications with the sensor;
- receive and write data to the local InfluxDB database;
- translate the sensor message from the native to the cloud format;
- publish the translated messages to the local MQTT broker.

By publishing the data on the MQTT bus, the handlers make the data available to any other subscribed microservices on the Edge Gateway, making easy to insert additional functionality. Edge Gateways can easily support multiple stations (i.e., stations in different rooms or apartments in a building). They are data producers and MQTT publishers.

Dispatcher. The *dispatcher* forwards all messages passing through the MQTT broker to the data processing platform. It is a real-time consumer of all the data published on the MQTT bus – since it is subscribed to all the MQTT topics. The dispatcher is also a publisher to the MQTT broker on the data processing platform (Fig. 2).

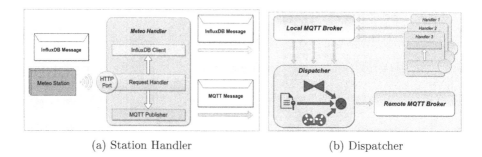

(a) Station Handler   (b) Dispatcher

Fig. 2. Data flow in TDM Edge Gateway micro-services.

Ancillary Services. A number of ancillary services run on the Edge Gateway
to provide supporting functionalities for application microservices and for user
interaction. The *Mosquitto*[2] Open Source lightweight MQTT broker provides
the internal publish/subscribe MQTT bus. Second, the Open Source time series
database *Influxdb*[3] is used to locally store data received from sensors and stations
connected to the Edge Gateway. The final ancillary service, the *Grafana*[4] Open
Source web-based dashboard, provides visualization of data stored in the local
Influxdb database.

2.1 Software Containers

Individual microservices are run on the Edge Gateway in separate Docker containers. Deploying these components as containers enables us to better leverage
the microservice architecture, allowing each one to be independently developed,
updated, or deployed while providing better protection against compromising the
functionality of other microservices and of the system as a whole. The adoption
of software containers for our use case does not impose any significant overhead in terms of computing resources [1,3], particularly since the services are
long-running. Using Docker container images does impose a slight storage overhead as compared to native software installation due to the write-only layered
image storage approach – which can easily result in some degree of file duplication – but that adverse effect is obviated by compiling the images carefully.
In addition to minimizing storage requirements, reducing container image sizes
also improves container download and start-up time [5]. In our Edge Gateway,
the container-based services are composed with the *Docker Compose* tool. It
creates and manages the entire deployment consisting of the container-based
microservices.

---

[2] https://mosquitto.org/.
[3] https://docs.influxdata.com/influxdb/v1.7/.
[4] https://grafana.com/.

3   Implementation

3.1   Edge Gateway Hardware and Operating System

Our Edge Gateway architecture has been implemented using the popular Raspberry Pi Version 3, Model B+ Single Board Computer, a board that has proven to have enough processing, memory and storage resources to be used as low-cost, energy-efficient computation nodes [2,8]. It runs *Arch Linux for Raspberry Pi 3* customized to simplify installation, configuration and maintenance by inexperienced users – e.g., high-school students, hobbyists. The resulting *image* is prepackaged with Edge Gateway's docker-compose definition file, all the Docker-related components required to run it, and a number of utility scripts to help manage the Edge Station. The Edge Gateway is programmed to automatically configure its internal WiFi device as an Access Point on the first boot to facilitate the configuration of the system by the user.

3.2   Handlers

The handler microservices in the Edge Gateway act as the interface between the myriad of possible sensors and the data processing platform. Our handlers on the Edge Gateway translate the various incoming message formats to a common FIWARE-compliant model. Once converted, the FIWARE messages are published on the Edge Gateway's internal MQTT bus. The handler microservices are implemented in *Python* and use few external libraries for communication and local storage.

The current Edge Gateway implementation includes the **SFDS handler**, the **IotaWatt handler** and the **Device handler** microservices.

SFDS Station Handler. The SFDS station handler microservice implements communications and data acquisition from the *Stuttgart Fine Dust Sensor*[5]. SFDS stations are equipped with a battery of sensors, including temperature, humidity, barometric pressure, wind and rain, and PM2.5 and PM10 particulate levels. These stations can be configured to HTTP POST data to an arbitrary InfluxDB database. We leverage this feature by implementing a compatible interface in the SFDS handler. Thus, the SFDS station is configured to send its data to the Edge Gateway as if the latter was an InfluxDB instance; the SFDS station handler running on the Edge Gateway accepts the POST requests in InfluxDB format, acquires the data and processes them.

IotaWatt Station Handler. The IotaWatt microservice handles interaction with the *IotaWatt Energy Monitor*[6]. This station can measure voltage and current, along with power and other derived electrical measures, on up to 14 different electrical channels. Since the IotaWatt station supports sending its data to an

---

[5] https://luftdaten.info/en/home-en/.
[6] https://iotawatt.com/.

InfluxDB instance, the data transmission mechanism between the station and the Edge Gateway is analogous to the one used for the SFDS station.

Device Handler. The Device handler generates messages with internal telemetry from the Edge Gateway system and handles sensors that are physically connected to our device. In the actual implementation, the handler reads data from a HTU21D temperature/humidity sensor that was physically attached to the Edge Gateway (through the I^2C electric bus). As with all handlers, the data is stored to the internal InfluxDB Database and published to the MQTT broker.

3.3 Dispatcher

As described in Sect. 2, the Dispatcher microservice relays the data acquired by the Edge Gateway to the data collection platform. The external transmission to the platform is authenticated by the remote MQTT broker and encrypted with SSL/TLS certificates. This microservice allows the overall platform to cope with temporary network outages and support widely differing uplink technologies – e.g., from LTE to ADSL or even GSM – even when using sensors with very simple transmission logic. Finally, the Dispatcher also adds Edge-Gateway-related metadata to the outgoing messages, like Edge Gateway ID, timestamp and position.

3.4 Dashboard

The Grafana ancillary service on the Edge Gateway is used to provide a user-accessible interface to the recorded data on the local InfluxDB instance. A convenient web dashboard that summarizes data collected from the standard handlers described in this Section is provided and preinstalled. Moreover, users can easily generate their own views of the data leveraging Grafana's functionality to plot graphs, charts and create gauge widgets that visualize collected data. In addition, the Grafana service can also be configured to send email alerts in the case of critical events.

3.5 Creating Small Docker Container Images

The size of software container images used in the Edge Gateway implementation directly affects the time to download and launch the images [5] – which entails effects on the time to first start the device and to deploy updates. To minimize their size we have chosen the Alpine Linux image for the ARM32 architecture as the base for all our container images (about 5 MB in size). The image grows quickly with the installation of the Python interpreter and external libraries. However, the layered storage approach used by Docker gives us the opportunity to contain the total size of all the images used by our system by ensuring they re-use the base layers – which are therefore downloaded and stored only once – while all the application-specific files are added at the top of the stack. Our overall layer stack is illustrated in Fig. 3.

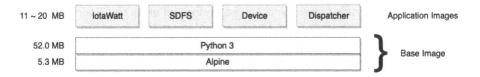

Fig. 3. Container layer stack.

To produce efficiently compact top layers for our images, a multi-stage Dockerfile is used. The building process is split in a *building* stage and a *final* stage. The first image contains all build-time dependencies like compilers, header files, and so on, while the latter includes only the resulting executables (copied from the build image) and the runtime dependencies.

Table 1 summarize the different layer sizes. Splitting handlers and dispatcher into simple microservices that only implement a single functionality results in code that is relatively short and readable, and facilitates debugging and correcting errors. By creating these microservices on images that share the same base layers, the storage required is reduced on average by 70%, thus avoiding the potential pitfall of multiplying the volume of images to transfer and store.

Table 1. Containers overview.

Container	Sensors	Lines	Layer size	Container size
sdfs	Weather/Air	402	20 MB	77.7 MB
iotawatt	Energy	354	20 MB	77.7 MB
device	Onboard	476	16 MB	73.9 MB
dispatcher	Data relaying	424	11 MB	68.9 MB
alpine-python		Base System and Python		58.0 MB

3.6 Deployment

A number of Edge Gateways were deployed and tested, first in a laboratory setting and later in offices and private homes. Fig. 4 depicts the overall architecture of the project TDM infrastructure spanning from sensors to the cloud-based data processing platform. The Edge Gateways collect and relay to the processing platform the data generated by sensors and stations. The TDM platform also integrates data from other sources, like satellite images, weather radar images, and various other geo-referenced data. Data are archived and indexed by a system that combines different storing technologies (i.e., *HDFS*, *SQL* and *NOSQL* databases). Various means are provided to access and process the collected data. *Jupyter*[7] notebooks are available for ad hoc queries and analyses. Event-driven

---

[7] https://jupyter.org/.

and periodic unattended operations can be performed using the *Apache Airflow* workflow engine or through *Grid Engine* batch computing jobs. Finally, aggregated and processed data are published as Open Data on the TDM *CKAN*[8] portal from where they can be downloaded.

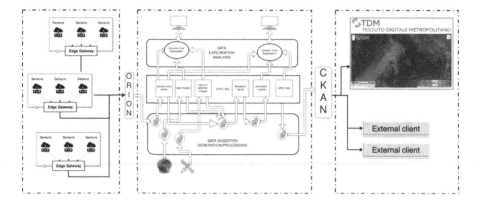

Fig. 4. TDM Cloud architecture.

Two Open Source Open Hardware sensor and measurement stations platforms were used as a starting sensor set: the SFDS weather and air station and the IotaWatt Energy Monitor. To support the three different scenarios for weather and air measurements – *outdoor*, *indoor*, and *mobile* – and to make station construction accessible to low-skill users, we have designed and produced a single PCB board to distribute to a number of early joiner volunteers (Fig. 5).

4   Related Work

Edge Computing is a hot topic in BigData analysis driven by the desire to leverage IoT devices for the wealth of valuable data they can collect and the fact that scalability, network latency and resiliency concerns make it unviable to rely solely on centralized computing to collect the data generated.

Pace et al. [13] identified Edge Computing as a way to overcome the issues that affect Cloud computing in Healthcare applications. Large-scale patient services can burden the network and thus deteriorate latencies and break the real-time constraints of critical applications. Moreover, patient data cannot always be stored in the Cloud due to privacy and data security concerns. In addition, speed of data analysis and response can be crucial in autonomous and semi-autonomous decision systems. They propose the *BodyEdge* complete architecture for a mobile Edge Gateway for uses in the Healthcare industry. It is composed by two complementary components: a smartphone-hosted relay node for the Body Sensor

---

[8] https://ckan.org/.

(a) Indoor Station   (b) Edge Gateway

Fig. 5. TDM SFDS indoor station and edge gateway

Network devices and an Edge Gateway that actually provides the healthcare services and communications to the far Cloud. Unlike the architecture we propose, BodyEdge modules seem to be monolithic applications. Microservice-based design or containerization are not mentioned, and communication between the modules are described as client-server.

In comparison, the *AGILE* framework for IoT gateways is based on a microservices architecture [5] and its software components are delivered using Docker containers. Various IoT high-level functionalities are provided, such as device and protocol management, UI and SDK for IoT development. Similar to our architecture, protocol handlers are implemented in individual containers and communicate with each other using DBus. Differing from the TDM Edge Gateway, AGILE specializes handler microservices on sensor communication protocol, instead of sensors types. The primary motivation behind this different decision is the fact that the TDM station handlers are primarily designed to translate sensors data to a common FIWARE format. It is not specified if AGILE uses D-Bus publish/subscribe or in one-to-one request-response mode.

Another architecture for general purpose Edge Gateways, similar to our TDM Edge Gateway, is the *LEGIoT – Lightweight Edge Gateway for the Internet of Things* [12]. The architecture proposed is based on microservices running on Docker containers and implemented using low-cost Single Board Computers like *Odroid* (C1+, C2) and Rasbperry Pi (RPi2, RPi3). It has a modular and flexible design similar to TDM Edge Gateway. Modules are divided in *Northbound*, in charge of communication to the remote end, and *Southbound* that deals with the local sensors. Modules are *activated on-demand* to limit power usage. Received data are saved to a local database. Unlike in our TDM Edge Gateway, the internal data exchange is performed by a dedicated module using a custom API, while the TDM design relies on standard asynchronous and agnostic publish/subscribe mechanisms. A deeper difference between the two designs is that the TDM Edge Gateway continuously transmits the acquired data, while LEGIoT implements a "pull" strategy, whereby data are retrieved by the remote end upon activation of a suitable Northbound module acting as protocol server. Finally, LEGIoT supports multi-tenancy while TDM Edge Gateway is single-tenant by design, responding to specific demands of TDM research.

Finally, Kura [14] is an extensive IoT Edge Framework. Kura is largely configurable and expandable. The framework and API are written in Java and Java programming is needed to develop new functionality and drivers. Moreover, the custom API is very large and the architecture quite complex. Our TDM Edge, conversely, relies on standard publish/subscribe protocol for internal data exchange, with a set of topics and standard data models, and a lean internal architecture imposing no constraints on the programming language to use.

5   Conclusions and Future Work

This paper presents a flexible and scalable microservice-based Edge Gateway architecture that facilitates integrating heterogeneous sensors in complex IoT data acquisition applications. The architecture is particularly well suited to research applications, given the possibility to quickly and easily add or substitute its on-board software components. The testing and deployment phases confirm the advantages of the microservice architecture when combined with publish/subscribe data exchange protocols.

The implementation of dynamic throttling in the dispatcher, adjusting the transmission rate and policy based on the available network bandwidth, is currently undergoing. From the Edge Computing perspective, we are evaluating the modular integration of algorithms for the estimation and forecasting of power consumption as containerized applications – e.g., those by Massidda et al. [9,10].

References

1. Beserra, D., Moreno, E.D., Endo, P.T., Barreto, J., Sadok, D., Fernandes, S.: Performance analysis of LXC for HPC environments. In: 2015 Ninth International Conference on Complex, Intelligent, and Software Intensive Systems. pp. 358–363. IEEE, July 2015. https://doi.org/10.1109/CISIS.2015.53
2. Cloutier, M., Paradis, C., Weaver, V.: A Raspberry Pi cluster instrumented for fine-grained power measurement. Electronics 5(4), 61 (2016). https://doi.org/10.3390/electronics5040061. http://www.mdpi.com/2079-9292/5/4/61
3. Di Tommaso, P., Palumbo, E., Chatzou, M., Prieto, P., Heuer, M.L., Notredame, C.: The impact of docker containers on the performance of genomic pipelines. PeerJ 3, e1273 (2015). https://doi.org/10.7717/peerj.1273
4. Docker Inc: Docker Documentation. https://docs.docker.com/. Accessed 20 May 2019
5. Dolui, K., Kiraly, C.: Towards multi-container deployment on IoT gateways. In: 2018 IEEE Global Communications Conference (GLOBECOM), pp. 1–7. IEEE, Abu Dhabi, United Arab Emirates, December 2018. https://doi.org/10.1109/GLOCOM.2018.8647688. https://ieeexplore.ieee.org/document/8647688/

6. Dragoni, N., Giallorenzo, S., Lafuente, A.L., Mazzara, M., Montesi, F., Mustafin, R., Safina, L.: Microservices: Yesterday, Today, and Tomorrow. In: Mazzara, M., Meyer, B. (eds.) Present and Ulterior Software Engineering, pp. 195–216. Springer International Publishing, Cham (2017). https://doi.org/10.1007/978-3-319-67425-4_12. https://doi.org/10.1007/978-3-319-67425-4_12

7. Fiware Foundation: Home – FIWARE. https://www.fiware.org/. Accessed 14 May 2019

8. Hajji, W., Tso, F.: Understanding the performance of low power raspberry Pi cloud for big data. Electronics **5**(4), 29 (2016). https://doi.org/10.3390/electronics5020029. http://www.mdpi.com/2079-9292/5/2/29

9. Massidda, L., Marrocu, M.: Quantile regression post-processing of weather forecast for short-term solar power probabilistic forecasting. Energies **11**(7), 1763 (2018). https://doi.org/10.3390/en11071763. http://publications.crs4.it/pubdocs/2018/MM18a

10. Massidda, L., Marrocu, M.: Smart meter forecasting from one minute to one year horizons. Energies **11**(12), 3250 (2018). https://doi.org/10.3390/en11123520. http://publications.crs4.it/pubdocs/2018/MM18b

11. Merkel, D.: Docker: lightweight linux containers for consistent development and deployment. Linux Journal 2014 (2014)

12. Morabito, R., Petrolo, R., Loscrì, V., Mitton, N.: LEGIoT: a lightweight edge gateway for the Internet of Things. Fut. Generation Comput. Syst. **81**, 1–15 (2018). https://doi.org/10.1016/j.future.2017.10.011. https://linkinghub.elsevier.com/retrieve/pii/S0167739X17306593

13. Pace, P., Aloi, G., Gravina, R., Caliciuri, G., Fortino, G., Liotta, A.: An edge-based architecture to support efficient applications for healthcare industry 4.0. IEEE Trans. Ind. Inform. **15**(1), 481–489 (2019). https://doi.org/10.1109/TII.2018.2843169. https://ieeexplore.ieee.org/document/8370750/

14. The Eclipse Foundation: Eclipse Kura. https://www.eclipse.org/kura/. Accessed 01 July 2019

mF2C: The Evolution of Cloud Computing Towards an Open and Coordinated Ecosystem of Fogs and Clouds

Xavi Masip-Bruin[1], Eva Marín-Tordera[1], Ana Juan Ferrer[2],
Antonio Salis[3(✉)], John Kennedy[4], Jens Jensen[5], Admela Jukan[6],
Andrea Bartoli[7], Rosa M. Badia[8(✉)], Matija Cankar[9],
and Marc Elian Bégin[10]

[1] Universitat Politècnica de Catalunya, CRAAX-UPC,
Vilanova i la Geltrù, Spain
{xmasip,eva}@ac.upc.edu
[2] ATOS Research and Innovation, Barcelona, Spain
ana.juanf@atos.net
[3] Engineering Sardegna, Cagliari, Italy
antonio.salis@eng.it
[4] Intel Research and Development, Leixlip, Ireland
john.m.kennedy@intel.com
[5] UK Research and Innovation/STFC RAL, Didcot, UK
jens.jensen@stfc.ac.uk
[6] Technische Universität Braunschweig, Brunswick, Germany
a.jukan@tu-bs.de
[7] Worldsensing Limited, Cambridge, UK
a.bartoli@worldsensing.com
[8] Barcelona Supercomputing Center, Barcelona, Spain
rosa.m.badia@bsc.es
[9] XLAB d.o.o., Lubjiana, Slovenia
matija.cankar@xlab.si
[10] SIXSQ, Geneve, Switzerland
meb@sixsq.com

Abstract. Fog computing brings cloud computing capabilities closer to the end-devices and users, while enabling location-dependent resource allocation, low latency services, and extending significantly the IoT services portfolio as well as market and business opportunities in the cloud and IoT sectors. With the number of devices growing exponentially globally, new cloud and fog models are expected to emerge, paving the way for shared, collaborative, extensible mobile, volatile and dynamic compute, storage and network infrastructure. When put together, cloud and fog computing create a new stack of resources, which we refer to as Fog-to-Cloud (F2C), creating the need for a new, open and coordinated management ecosystem. The EU Horizon 2020 program has recently funded a new research initiative (mF2C) bringing together relevant industry and academic players in the cloud arena, aimed at designing an open, secure, decentralized, multistakeholder management framework for F2C computing, including novel programming models, privacy and security, data storage techniques, service creation, brokerage solutions, SLA policies, and resource

© Springer Nature Switzerland AG 2020
U. Schwardmann et al. (Eds.): Euro-Par 2019 Workshops, LNCS 11997, pp. 136–147, 2020.
https://doi.org/10.1007/978-3-030-48340-1_11

orchestration methods. This paper introduces the main mF2C concepts, illustrates the need for a coordinated management ecosystem, proposes a preliminary design of its foundational building blocks and presents results that show the benefits mF2C may have on three key real-world scenarios.

Keywords: Cloud computing · Fog computing · Fog-to-cloud · Management · Distributed systems · Security · IoT

1 Introduction: The F2C Concept

The emergence of IoT –the networked connection of people, process, data and things – is expected to significantly increase the number of connected devices worldwide, from billions of units we have today, to tens of billions of units expected to be deployed in the coming years. Some predictions [1] suggest that 26 billion edge devices are to be connected by 2020, collecting more than 1.6 zettabytes (1.6 trillion GB) of data. According to Cisco reports, it is expected to have more than 50 billion devices connected by 2020, paving the way to fog computing [2]. At the same time, cloud service providers (Amazon AWS, Google Compute Engine, Microsoft Azure) today enable customers to quickly deploy a myriad of private and corporate services at comparably lower prices than buying and maintaining their own infrastructure. When combined, fog and cloud computing are without doubt setting standards in flexibility, cost, economy of scale, but also innovation in new services, devices and applications. Indeed, the computing and processing capacities offered by cloud computing can perfectly complement the comparably lower processing, storage and networking capacities of the edge devices building a novel, coordinated scenario between edge devices and the cloud.

In the combined scenario of cloud computing and a myriad of edge devices, one can observe that while data, users and decisions are at the edge side, processing capacities are primarily at the cloud side. As a result, today's systems need to address the challenges of overloading the network and inducing latency to transfer data from the edge to the cloud. Thus, the traditional approach of leveraging the centralized processing in the cloud premises may require a new thinking based on these two observations. First, the high latency values required to reach to the cloud in the centralized approach are not suitable for real time services. Second, forwarding data, stored and collected at the edge to the cloud to be processed, is non-optimal in terms of network resources allocation, and doubly so when results are to be returned to the device that sent them. This has set the stage for the evolution of fog computing, that can leverage a distributed approach based on bringing cloud capabilities closer to, or into, the edge devices, also referred to as mini-clouds, cloudlets, or small-scale clouds. Figure 1 illustrates the pyramid of today's fog and cloud ecosystem integrating the typically centralized cloud infrastructure, with various levels (or layers) of dispersed elements starting with smaller scale clouds, over to fog computing with various degrees of decision making and data processing capabilities [3].

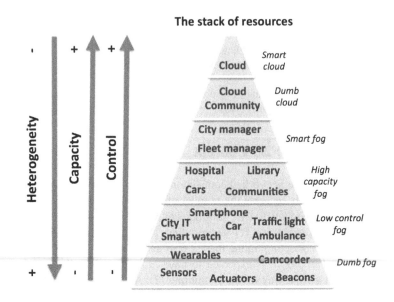

Fig. 1. Fog-to-cloud (F2C) layered structure: The stack of resources

In a combined Fog-to-Cloud (F2C) system, a critical question is how can a combined resource sharing and resource clustering approach efficiently extend the concept of a cloud provider to an unknown frontier, creating innovative resource-rich proximate infrastructures near to the user, while remaining profitable? To answer this question, we identified the need to provide a coordinated management of the combined F2C resources to ease and optimize the execution of existing and future services, through a myriad of new features including reduction of execution time, parallel execution, edge processing, fog security, locality, improved utilization of limited resources, improved energy efficiency ("green computing"), etc. To this end, a comprehensive control and management strategy is required, addressing efficient coordination and inter-operation of fog and clouds environments, as well as the innovative combined cloud/fog architecture.

This paper proposes a new research framework to achieve the same, which we refer to as mF2C focused at designing an open, secure, decentralized, multi-stakeholder management framework for F2C computing. An important feature of the system proposed is in its openness to integrating and supporting new functionalities and subsystems as they emerge, such as novel programming models, new privacy and security features, various data storage techniques, and brokerage solutions. This paper introduces the main idea behind the new mF2C concept, proposes a preliminary design of its foundational building blocks and presents results that show the benefits mF2C may have on three key real-world scenarios. This paper is structured as follows. Section 2 revisits the state of the art. Section 3 outlines main mF2C control and functionality, introducing the main architectural blocks as well as the main benefits expected from deploying mF2C in three real-world scenarios. Section 4 identifies main mF2C challenges and opportunities. Finally, Sect. 5 concludes the paper.

2   State of the Art

This section briefly revisits relevant contributions in four key F2C aspects (resource management, IoT management, programming models and security), emphasizing the need for designing innovative solutions to best match the computing demands of F2C.

2.1   Resource Management in Cloud and Fog Computing

Resource management in cloud computing has been subject to intense research with a myriad of important aspects, such as security, data privacy, data centers management, quality delivery, or energy consumption. Several cloud platforms are already available to manage cloud infrastructure, be it open source (CloudStack, Eucalyptus, OpenStack, and OpenNebula) or proprietary (Amazon EC2, Microsoft Azure, IBM Bluemix and Aneka). While there is no global consensus facilitating their seamless interaction in multi-cloud environment – no single, universal standard – standard APIs as well as libraries that abstract the cloud API have already been defined.

Recently significant efforts addressed "cloudification" of network functions under the umbrella of Network Function Virtualization Fig. 1. Fog-to-cloud (F2C) layered structure: The stack of resources (NFV), a software implementation of the network functions on "bare metal". However, their optimal placement and job scheduling especially in the cloud remains a hard problem, since network functions need to be managed in a dynamic fashion, and virtualized instances need to be able to migrate, grow, and shrink dynamically.

The combination of fog and cloud computing intensifies the resource management challenge. Several contributions exist aimed at managing how services are allocated into edge devices, or offloaded to execution, all based on meeting service level objectives, such as latency and VM setting capacity, see for instance [4]. However, fog computing as such is still in its infancy, lacking the standards and definitions of basic concepts. For instance, there is no a widely accepted definition for a fog node yet, mainly due to the diverse and heterogeneous set of edge devices. This diversity makes it very difficult to agree even on simple concepts, such as whether fog devices should be virtualized, and if so, whether the usage of the traditional VM concept, or containers is appropriate, etc. References can be found in the literature (see for example [5] and [6]) with divergent definitions of a fog node, defined to meet the needs of the specific application scenarios.

There are other contributions aimed at facilitating the management of IoT devices, ranging from pure data management to edge devices management. In the first area we can mention SENTILO [7] or IoT-LAB [8]. Both aim at easing the data collection from different IoT devices by putting all data together in a single repository for easy access. In device management, examples include the research projects FIWARE [9] and SOFIA [10], or in the commercial sector VORTEX [11]. Briefly, FIWARE consists of a catalogue of "enablers", i.e., enabling the development of applications and services in a cost-effective fashion. SOFIA's main goal is to ease systems interoperability aiming at promoting the development of new services and applications. The Vortex product contains different components to support different device data sharing configurations – Vortex Cloud for cloud data sharing, Vortex Fog for edge devices data sharing, etc.– aimed at data sharing and easing systems interoperability.

Overall, there is currently no coordination or integration strategy available which addresses the need for coordination among all cloud and fog resources.

2.2 Programming Models

Despite the plethora of programming models developed for the cloud (MapReduce, Aneka, Google app engine, etc.), applications to be executed in heterogeneous and distributed infrastructures – the ones considered in mF2C – cannot be supported directly. To the best of our knowledge, the only programming model that takes into account such an infrastructure is Mobile Fog [12]. However, the programming model proposed is very explicit with regard the infrastructure, and the availability of the system seems to be limited.

A particularly relevant programming framework for coordinated fog and cloud computing is COMPSs [13], a task based programming framework that enables the development of applications to be executed in distributed environments. COMPSs has two main aspects that may be used for mF2C deployment. First, it offers a simple programming interface and a set of tools that support the development of applications. Second, it comes with a powerful runtime environment able to build, at execution time, a workflow of the tasks comprising the application and execute them in a distributed environment. The runtime environment orchestrates the execution of the tasks in the workflow, and handles the required data transfers. The distributed computing platform can be composed of physical nodes or nodes in a cloud, and can include tasks deployed as web services.

2.3 Security Aspects

Security and privacy are well-known, widely addressed aspects, but remain greatly unsolved challenges in the cloud and fog areas, and are inherent to mF2C. Deploying fogs in fact exacerbates the traditional cloud security issues, since usually edge devices are located in non-controlled scenarios, and often misused by adversaries. This assessment is even extended when bringing together fog and cloud resources.

Information security in fog infrastructure currently builds on cloud, mobile, or network security. Many solutions are available when integrating with a single cloud provider, and several research initiatives have researched secure brokering of, and access to, multiple clouds. Mobile security is used by most of the apps, using either the user's telco account or their own app-specific security; in general, security is very application dependent and users have little control over it: the applications today either get all permissions they ask for, or nothing. Data confidentiality in-flight uses X.509 certificates or provider-specific symmetric keys; confidentiality at-rest is often via non-technical controls: contractual agreement – or trust. Authorization decisions are usually implicit – users who can access the service are authorized – or based on simple identity mappings or roles (RBAC). Intrusion detection is done via monitoring IaaS networks (e.g. Azure, Amazon, HPE) in addition to "traditional" methods of virus checking, etc.

We may conclude both: i) recent contributions in the security field for fog computing are not solid enough to be widely adopted by mF2C, and; ii) contributions in the cloud arena are too far from the specific mF2C needs, in terms for example of resources dynamicity or volatility.

3 mF2C Management Functionalities

Recognizing the need for a novel management ecosystem for F2C, this section outlines the mF2C management architecture, and shows preliminary benefits of an mF2C deployment in three illustrative real-world scenarios.

3.1 mF2C Management Architecture

The mF2C management architecture is structured into three architectural entities (mF2C Controller, mF2C Gearbox and Interfaces, shown in Fig. 2), all coordinated to work together in order to provide the different expected control and management functionalities.

mF2C Controller
This architectural entity consists of three connected and coordinated blocks. The three blocks share security and privacy aspects as a transversal requirement.

- *mF2C Resource Controller:* This function includes three main components Semantic Adaptation, Resource Management, and Security and Privacy. In turn, these components include methods and mechanisms implemented to guarantee both accurate knowledge about the available resources for each device and accurate information about the resource availability, including resource attributes, such as virtual/real, static/mobile, sharing capacities, clustering capacities, business policies, etc. (i.e., Resources Monitoring, Discovering, Virtualization). This is rather complex in F2C systems, due to the dynamicity inherent to its resources, the heterogeneity foreseen for the devices and systems comprising mF2C as well as the business relationship to be established among resources providers. To this end, mF2C can be envisioned as an opportunistic resources.
- *mF2C Service Controller:* Once the service request is validated, the service is categorized according to a dynamic taxonomy, which is yet to be designed, (i.e., Service Categorization and Decomposition). When required, the service can be decomposed into sub-services, ultimately turning it into a set of atomic services (sub-services) some of which can be executed in parallel. The set of sub-services may be preconfigured and stored in a repository. Challenging issues in this area include: to find the appropriate place to locate the service decomposition, to minimize the computing load and/or data transfer while keeping fast reaction time, to define to what extent these functions must be associated to the aggregation points, to define the dependency graph rules, and finally to develop strategies for sub-services search.
- *mF2C User Side:* mF2C must benefit from the user-specific context information to tailor service execution to specific user demands. To that end, a comprehensive set of functionalities must be defined, including but not limited to authentication, privacy, location, profiling, agreement policies, etc. (i.e., User and Context Functions). All these functionalities must meet the business policies in a real mF2C deployment. For example, a user may be willing to connect his/her smart car as a resource which requires appropriate economic incentives. The user could restrict the car compute system to send only anonymised data by default, as well as relay

emergency messages, or offer additional services via social networks (location, camera images, additional processing). A service request should be "validated" on the user side (or in an upper control layer if the device does not embed that functionality), checking for authentication and checking attributes release according to the user profile and the context (i.e. User Authentication and Profiling). To that end, novel strategies must be defined to describe the different new roles users may play, e.g., including fog providers or the capacity and incentives to share resources.

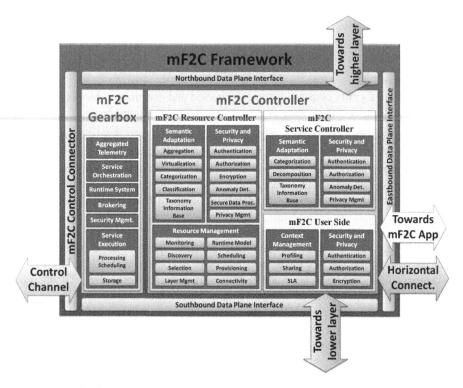

Fig. 2. Architectural blocks for the mF2C management framework

mF2C Gearbox

The set of preliminary components defined to build the Gearbox is:

- Aggregated telemetry: Rich, intelligent instrumentation and monitoring is required to inform decision making systems such as the service orchestration. For effective decision making and troubleshooting, this should cover the full-stack – from hardware up through operating system, middleware and hosted services be they deployed in containers or virtual machines. It should also be dynamically configurable, and support derived or aggregated metrics at the edge for maximum scalability of the overall solution.

- Service orchestration: This component is responsible for allocating services to the best available resources. The optimal allocation will depend on many factors. Considerations such as an analysis of historical invocations of the service, the precise nature and configuration of available resources in real time, and quality-of-service expectations and commitments could all have a bearing on where services, or elements of the service, are located. Effective abstractions and analytics will be required to ensure service orchestration systems are scalable at runtime.
- Runtime system: Different options may be considered for the runtime system in the F2C scenario, from traditional sequential execution to novel parallel execution. This component enables a transparent handling of the heterogeneous resources.
- Brokerage: Responsible for handling the dynamicity inherent to the edge devices while guaranteeing – or at least optimizing – that selected resources best match the services demands. Different resources registration policies may be considered depending on the context and the different devices.
- Service execution: Software execution and storage platform that unifies the model of all data (user, application and shared) into the potentially access controlled view seen by applications.

Interfaces

The *Interfaces* are key to the main feature of openness, modularity and extensibility of the mF2C framework and the platform. Since the mF2C is designed as an open layered framework for a customized usage by various devices and systems, the modules implemented by a specific F2C layer are connected with the overall system over these interfaces. Figure 3 illustrates the mF2C layered architecture (including agents and microagents to be deployed in edge devices with limited capacities) and the role of interfaces. The lowest layer represents the embedded devices, such as sensors with minimal processing capability, while the smart phone is in the middle layer (shown as a fog device), capable of processing an mF2C service on a small scale. Clouds are at the top layer, controlling the mF2C services at large scale. The control channels and data channels are separated. Data channels strictly follow the F2C layered hierarchy.

As it can be seen, multiple data channels connect to multiple child instances through the "Southbound" interface to lower layers. A single data channel connects to the (unique) parent instance through the "Northbound" interface. The "Eastbound" interface connects to the mF2C application as well as enables multi-cloud/fog communication within the same layer. All control channels (the "Westbound" interface) connect to the top layer instance that controls and manages the whole mF2C environment.

In addition to the three architectural entities mentioned above, security and privacy are cross-cutting concerns, transversal to the mF2C Controller and the mF2C Gearbox, meaning that all components in the overall mF2C management ecosystem must be designed, implemented, and operated to fulfill a common base set of security and privacy requirements and policies (these policies may of course depend on the device type or function). We expect that some security and privacy components will work in the same way, or at least in similar ways, for many mF2C components, including authorization decision that certain user data may be processed on a specific fog device. The basic functionalities for security and privacy for mF2C data are information classification, authentication, authorization, accounting, auditing, attack detection and finally secure data processing.

3.2   Applying mF2C to Real-World Scenarios

An mF2C coordinated resources management architecture is expected to help increasing revenues and product innovation to the businesses in various sectors. From a technology provider perspective this evolution (bottom-up) would boost the adoption of IoT devices and equipment in the various depicted scenarios (cities, buildings, etc.) and commercial development of value-added services.

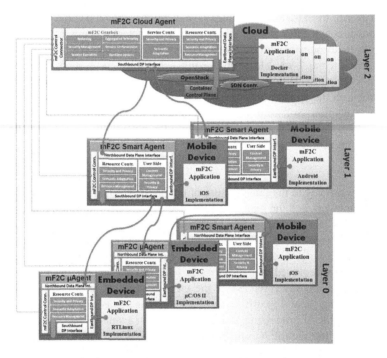

Fig. 3. Layered scenario with agents and interfaces

With the massive adoption of these devices, the revenues and requests for more sophisticated ones will increase as well. From a Service Provider perspective the availability of an extended platform (coming from the Cloud + Fog Providers) –with an elastic provisioning of resources that covers also the edge devices– offers them the opportunity to develop even more sophisticated services, like dependable e-health, or 3D real time navigation systems, thus widening the market scenario, extending their offering, and creating more value and revenues. Finally, from a Cloud provider perspective this evolution (top-down) creates ample opportunities for developing and extending the service chain offering, by adding one more ring (the Fog) in the provision of services, increasing the product/service portfolio and enabling new and challenging business models. In this way Cloud Providers could soon be renamed "Cloud + Fog Providers".

To illustrate the expected mF2C benefits and impact on these three different areas, we give examples of three real-world scenarios that can immediately deploy the systems akin to mF2C.

Scenario 1: Emergency Situation Management in Smart Cities (ESM): This application scenario is built upon real infrastructure developed in the city of Bogota, Colombia [14]. It consists of an implementation of distributed elements capturing signals and data, as well as a centralized traffic management system to integrate heterogeneous traffic-related information in a flexible and efficient cloud platform. A potential deployment of the mF2C management solution will enable cities to install fog computing infrastructure locally, for example in bus stops, and enable new real time services and push notifications without the need for tight connectivity infrastructure.

Scenario 2: Enriched Navigation Service (ENS): This scenario is based on the development and extension of the family of IoT devices and sensors that are oriented to operational support and monitoring in the marine sector, aiming at providing safer navigation even for less experienced sailors [15]. The example shows a relevant potential for making all the ship's sensors work together, processing and correlating the collected data in a combined fog and cloud computing system but also interacting with external data sources as well (e.g., other ships and marine vehicles, satellites). This achievement could lead to brand new added-value services of augmented reality in the marine sector. The mF2C management framework looks perfect for a technology like Sentinel [15], as the supporting technology for data processing orchestration and distribution, leveraging the access to open data databases and ontologies and the chance to develop new predictive models for forecast weather and travel related aspects, as part of new value-added services to support sailors' route planning. Currently the Sentinel devices work mainly individually but their crowd knowledge, which could be derived from combining and processing the data obtained from all distributed sensors, is not yet exploited.

Scenario 3: Smart Fog-Hub Service (SFHS): The third scenario is looking at the IoT evolution as a potential area where current cloud offering could be enriched and differentiated. Scenario 3 extends the concept of a "cloud hub" to a new concept of "fog hub", driven by real market needs. This scenario leverages the belief that value is generated at the business services level, particularly in spaces with recurring concentrations of people and objects that can communicate and interact. These scenarios are typical of airports, railway stations, seaports, shopping centers, hospitals, sports facilities, large parking areas, but also domestic scenarios with a communal clustering level. The scenario proposes to set up (Fog) Hubs in such scenarios to interact with all the objects within the scope of coverage, and to operate "in-proximity" marketing efforts, applying predictive algorithms to track (in an anonymized form) movements, choices and decisions of persons nearby, or even extend the hub with devices (e.g. beacons) capable of sending input (e.g. customized advertising) and determine the effectiveness of the specific campaign in terms of attention/visits rather than conversion (purchasing products/services). Potentially this model could be further extended by making different fogs, perhaps 5-15 km from each other, communicate, and by combining the results in terms of behavioral predictions in adjacent fogs.

4 Opportunities and Challenges in mF2C

There is no doubt that, to make the most out of the whole set of cloud and fog resources, that is for the overall F2C ecosystem to work, a new coordinated, open, secure, end-to-end management strategy must be developed to smartly orchestrate a large-scale, distributed, heterogeneous, open, dynamic and volatile set of resources in a decentralized, private, secure and trusted way, enabling open/multi–fog/cloud provider business models. But, this will not be enough. Users must endorse this computing strategy by sharing their resources (edge devices), thus enabling the collaborative model envisioned for F2C. User engagement should, in turn, incentivize the industrial sector to develop new business models and applications tailored to the F2C charac-teristics and the end users' engagement policies. We envision new cooperation modes to appear analogous to recent ideas in "sharing economy", such as Airbnb.

Cooperation can be fostered by shared interests and geographic proximity. For example, a group of cars in a parking lot may "decide" to "share" some of their resources to be offered to "other cars", hence becoming a local cloud or fog provider themselves (similar to the concept of micro data centers, small clouds or cloudlets) thus setting the stage for future business models. Already today models are emerging of negotiating and "selling" parking spaces, both on-demand use of vacant spaces outside homes as well as peer-to-peer selling between car owners in car parks.

5 Conclusions

This paper revisits the main cloud and fog computing concepts, envisioning their combination as next cloud evolution, making the best out of the set of distributed resources by combining cloud and fog computing. The paper introduces the need for a coordinated management of both systems and proposes a functional architecture of the management ecosystem able to intelligently manage the distributed set of resources, optimizing service execution according to resources availability and users' demands. The main functional blocks of the management architecture (referred to as mF2C) are proposed, along with an in-depth description of open challenges. We envision F2C as a key paradigm in the future as the next evolution in the cloud domain, and hence with a strong impact not only on the industrial sector but also on society and individuals. We believe in the prospect of collaborative computing model as foreseen for F2C, that can extend the well-known sharing economy model to edge devices owned by users.

Acknowledgments. This work was partially supported by the EU-funded mF2C project (Nr. 730929). Additionally, UPC authors are supported by the Spanish Ministry of Economy and Competitiveness and the European Regional Development Fund under contract RTI2018-094532-B-I00). BSC author is also supported by the Spanish Government (TIN2015-65316-P, SEV-2011-00067) and by the Generalitat de Catalunya (2014-SGR-1051).

References

1. Plummer, D.C., et al.: Top 10 Strategic Predictions for 2015 and Beyond: Digital Business is Driving "Big Change", Gartner Inc, October 2014. http://www.gartner.com/technology/home.jsp
2. Bonomi, F., et al.: Fog computing and its role in the Internet of Things. In: Proceedings of the First Edition of the MCC Workshop on Mobile Cloud Computing, Helsinki, Finland (2012)
3. Masip, X., et al.: Foggy clouds or cloudy fogs; a real need for a coordinated management of F2C computing systems. IEEE Wireless Communications Magazine, in press (preprint version at http://www.craax.upc.edu/images/Publications/journals/Fog-to-cloud_preprint.pdf). HP report at http://www8.hp.com/us/en/hp-news/press-release.html?id=1744676#.VqtAk8eC0hA De Filippi, P., McCarthy, S. "Cloud computing: Legal issues in centralized architectures. In: VII International Conference on Internet, Law and Politics (2011)
4. Barbosa, V., et al.: Handling service allocation in combined fog-cloud scenarios. IEEE ICC 2016, Malaysia, May 2016
5. Aazam, M., Huh, E.N.: Fog computing and smart gateway based communication for cloud of things. In: 2014 International Conference on Future Internet of Things and Cloud (FiCloud), Barcelona, Spain, August 2014
6. Cisco Fog Computing Solutions: Unleash the power of the Internet of Things. http://www.cisco.com/c/dam/en_us/solutions/trends/iot/docs/computing-solutions.pdf
7. Sentilo platform. http://www.sentilo.io
8. Future Internet-of-things Testbeds, IoT-LAB. https://www.iot-lab.info/
9. Fiware platform. http://www.fiware.org
10. Sofia platform. http://sofia2.com
11. VORTEX. www.prismtech.com/vortex
12. Hong, K., et al.: Mobile fog: a programming model for large–scale applications on the Internet of Things. In: Proceedings of the Second ACM SIGCOMM Workshop on Mobile Cloud Computing, MCC 2013, Hong Kong, July 2013
13. Rosa, M.B., et al.: COMP Superscalar, an interoperable programming framework, SoftwareX, vol. 3–4, December 2015, pp. 32–36. ISSN 2352-7110. http://dx.doi.org/10.1016/j.softx.2015.10.004
14. Smart city platform in Bogota. http://www.worldsensing.com/solutions/mobility/projects/worldsensing-iot-platform.html
15. Sentinel marine platform. http://www.sentinelmarine.net

FPDAPP - Workshop on Future Perspective of Decentralised Applications

International Workshop on Future Perspectives of Decentralized Applications (FPDAPP)

Workshop Description

Blockchain technologies (BCTs) make agreement among untrusted parties possible, without the need for certification authorities. Proposed frameworks have been put forward in sectors as diverse as finance, health-care, notary, intellectual property management, identity, provenance, international cooperation, social good, and security to cite but a few. Smart contracts, i.e. self-enforcing agreements in terms of executable software running on blockchains, have been developed in several contexts. Such an under-definition computational model introduces innovative aspects, such as the economics and trust of the decentralized computation relying on the shared contribution of peers and their decentralized consensus.

The second edition of the FPDAPP workshop aimed to foster the cross-fertilization between the blockchain and the distributed/parallel computing communities, which can strongly contribute to each other's development.

The FPDAPP workshop rigorously explored and evaluated the potentiality of such novel decentralized frameworks and applications. Of particular interest was the evaluation and comparison of killer applications that are showing evidence of how Distributed Ledger Technologies can revolutionize their domains or develop new application areas. Evaluation and comparisons are broadly understood, from technical aspects regarding the novel decentralized computer to the possible impact on society, business, and the public sector.

This year, we received nine articles for review. After a thorough peer-reviewing process focused on quality, innovative contribution, and applicability to real-world scenarios, we selected seven articles for presentation at the workshop. Each paper was revised by at least three independent reviewers, all members of the Program Committee. The final decision regarding paper acceptance was the result of the reviewers' discussion and agreement, leading to the high quality of selected articles, despite the acceptance ratio.

In addition to paper presentations, Prof. Fausto Spoto (University of Verona, Italy) gave a very interesting invited talk on a Java-based Smart Contracts implementation, while during the networking session all attendees (more than 30 throughout the day) had the opportunity to share their ideas and activities, as well as look for future collaborations. In the last session of the workshop we organized a panel, moderated by Nadia Fabrizio (Cefriel, Italy) on governance for the blockchain. Panelist also included Niklas Friese (Digilan, Bangladesh) and Imre Kocsis (Budapest University of Technology and Economics, Hungary).

Finally, we would like to thank all members of the FPDAPP Program Committee, the speakers, and the participants, as well as Euro-Par for hosting our new community and the workshop general chairs for the support provided.

Organization

Program Chairs

Andrea Bracciali	Stirling University, UK
Claudio Schifanella	University of Turin, Italy

Program Committee

Stefano Bistarelli	University of Perugia, Italy
Guido Boella	University of Turin, Italy
Maple Carsten	University of Warkwick, UK
Boris Düdder	University of Copenhagen, Denmark
Carlos Molina	University of Cambridge, UK
Paolo Mori	Consiglio Nazionale delle Ricerche, Italy
Federico Pintore	University of Oxford, UK
Massimiliano Sala	University of Trento, Italy
Aleš Zamuda	University of Maribor, Slovenia
Alberto Guffanti	University of Turin, Italy
Massimo Morini	Banca IMI, Italy
Nadia Fabrizio	Cefriel, Italy
Monika Di Angelo	Technische Universitat Wien, Austria
Yilei Wang	LuDong University, China
Santiago Zanella-Beguelin	Microsoft Research, UK
Luca Mazzola	Lucerne University of Applied Sciences and Arts

Academic Achievement Recognition and Verification Using Blockchain

Axel Curmi⬤ and Frankie Inguanez$^{(\boxtimes)}$⬤

Malta College of Arts, Science and Technology, Paola PLA9032, Malta
{axel.curmi.a100445,frankie.inguanez}@mcast.edu.mt
http://ict.mcast.edu.mt

Abstract. Falsification of certificates is a growing concern and the verification process can be a lengthy and challenging one. In this research, we are proposing a distributed ledger-based solution for the storage and verification of academic qualifications. An entity that would want to verify certificates can make use of our API service that would, in turn, scan a certificate, find the matching certificate template, extract the necessary data and verify it from a blockchain stored copy. In this research, we also propose an improved manner of verifying the ownership of a blockchain public address which also does not allow a user to present an address of a third party, this being one of the common security concerns of similar solutions. We also calculate the possible costs to adopt this system in all EU countries taking into consideration different gas prices, which is a determining factor to the transaction cost of a blockchain network. We conclude that a blockchain based certificate verification system addresses various issues related to document forgery and is a viable solution even with the current state of technology.

Keywords: Blockchain · Smart contracts · Certificates · User-access control · OCR

1 Introduction

Academic background and merit misinformation in CV have become a problem as people are more inclined to provide wrong information to seek advantage over the ever-growing competition. In addition, such information has become more difficult and bureaucratic to validate due to the ever-increasing security and privacy policies adopted by organisations. Falsification of such information not only sheds bad light on graduates, but also damages the reputation of the providing institution. Therefore, automated, easy and instant validation is required.

In this research, distributed ledger technology is used to publish academic achievement information on a peer-to-peer distributed network, known as the blockchain, such that this crucial information is protected thanks to advanced cryptographic techniques. Provided that both the academic institution and certificate holder have public blockchain addresses, a smart contract is used to

© Springer Nature Switzerland AG 2020
U. Schwardmann et al. (Eds.): Euro-Par 2019 Workshops, LNCS 11997, pp. 153–165, 2020.
https://doi.org/10.1007/978-3-030-48340-1_12

publish the recognition across parties, this equivalent to the graduation ceremony. Thus, the purpose of storing the certificate information on the blockchain is purely to serve any verification requests in a fully automated and instant manner, and not as a datastore to support such a system, so a mix of off-chain and on-chain data is needed. When a 3rd party receives a certificate and needs to verify its authenticity they can use our proposed API through which they can send a scanned image of the physical certificate together with the public blockchain address of the certificate holder. OCR and regular expression patterns make it ever more possible to extract the necessary information from existing documents, thus, further automating and improving the process flow. The extracted information would include the institution, for which the public blockchain address would have been previously registered. If the extracted data matches what is found on the blockchain then the certificate is verified instantly. One of the common challenges in having a blockchain based system is the verification of ownership for a blockchain public address, which is mostly of a concern in this scenario with regards to a certificate holder should an individual want to impersonate another to claim ownership of their achievements. We propose an adaptation of other research to solve this problem, which will be addressed further in Sect. 3. We also study the financial viability of our solution by identifying the low cost for registering the smart contract and evaluating our solution with the total number of tertiary qualifications in Europe. Given that there is no real rush to have certificates published instantly, these can be staged over a prolonged period in order to reduce the gas price and thus the actual financial cost for publishing certificates. The verification of academic achievement is technically free, in terms of blockchain transaction costs, yet computational power is needed for the extraction of data from scanned certificates as well as for bandwidth so to offer a good quality of service.

This paper is structured as follows, in Sect. 2, we present the Literature Review. The proposed solution is showcased in Sect. 3, the Research Methodology. In Sect. 4 the results are presented and discussed in detail, with concluding arguments and recommendations in Sect. 5.

2   Literature Review

2.1   Problems of Printed Certificates

Even though printed certificates are still preferred and seen as the most secure form of certificates, paper documents have a few notable disadvantages to keep in mind such as [5]: 1) Not being immune to forgery; 2) Awarding bodies are the single point of failure, meaning that certificates can still be valid, however the ability to validate them would be lost; 3) Secure certificates are costly (passports, routinely cost between €20 and €150); 4) No way to revoke the certificate without having the owner relinquish control; 5) Verification process is time consuming.

2.2   The Blockchain

A blockchain can be used to minimise the authority an intermediary has within a centralised service, such as validation of academic certificates [8]. For the purpose of this research, we shall be limiting the scope to public blockchain networks. By using a public blockchain, the data is not stored in a centralised location, instead, it is distributed between all participants in the network. By using this design, data is accessible to any participant in the network and secure at the same time, which means that the participants do not need to trust each other, including the owner of the data. This is because every participant in the network holds a ledger which contains every transaction taken place since the genesis block, and each participant can contribute to the creation of new blocks. Adding new blocks to a blockchain is an irreversible operation, meaning that once a block has been added to the chain in a validated state, this block or the data contained within the block can never be removed, even by the original author of the data. This is done by the way the blockchain structure is built, as every block contains two hash values, one for the previous block and one for itself. Any attempts to tamper with a block would invalidate the entire chain due to mismatches in hash values. As [8] stated, a consensus algorithm is used to achieve mutual trust between every participant in the network, as the creation of new blocks on the chain has to follow a strict protocol. At the time of writing, the two most popular consensus algorithms are: proof-of-work, and proof-of-stake. Bitcoin and Ethereum currently both operate with proof-of-work, however proof-of-stake is being considered by Ethereum as it is more cost effective and wastes a lot less energy. The number of research publications is greatly increasing and spreading around the globe [14], a few notable researches will be reviewed next.

2.3   Blockchain in Education

[10] stated that an application for blockchain in education would be to store records of achievement and credit, which would be added by the awarding institutions and be later accessed by the students. Having certificates published on the blockchain provides solutions to the issues regarding paper certificates, by providing public information regarding whether a certificate has been truly awarded to a certificate holder. However, as [10] mentioned, the blockchain does not verify the honesty of either party. Hashing techniques can also be used on the document such that rather than publishing private information, a digest of the document could be uploaded to act as a signature of the document while preserving the privacy of the document itself [5].

Various solutions to store certificates on the blockchain have been applied to several educational institutions, and the majority are built on the Bitcoin blockchain [11]. In Malta, the Blockcerts platform which was developed by MITs Media Lab and Learning Machine has been launched and will be used to issue and verify credentials using the Bitcoin network [7], and is currently the only open standard for issuing and verifying records using the blockchain [5]. In [11] the researchers have presented a proof of concept prototype, implemented on the open-source ARK blockchain platform, which grants academic credits to students, according to the European Credit Transfer and Accumulation System (ECTS), after they have successfully completed a course. This prototype is built on a consortium based distributed ledger, which will allow 3rd parties to easily validate a student's credits, after being granted access permission.

A solution for mitigating falsification of certificate documents has been presented by [13], in which the prototype is built by using a central server acting as a database, such that institutions publishing certificates communicate with this server to obtain a QR code, and 3rd parties communicate with this server to validate a certificate by simply scanning the QR code found on the document. The authors also mention that after validation testing, problems with treating user credentials were identified and later rectified from the system to avoid other major issues. A method for confirming ownership of an address has been presented by [11], in which the untrusted entity is given a randomly generated number, via private channels, representing a value amount, such that if the number was 1234, the value amount would be 0.001234 ETH. Having received the randomly generated number, the untrusted entity has to issue a transaction to the known party with the correct value amount. The known party then checks the transaction, and if the transaction amount is equal to the randomly generated number, the entity is proven to be the true owner of the address. Even though this method works, it does not stop entities working together by sharing the randomly generated number to validate their addresses for each other. [9] explains the importance of having participants protect, store, and backup their private keys not only digitally, but also in the physical world due to identity fraud. One solution to this issue would be to implement digital private keys into physical keys, such as magnetic stripe cards, devices with embedded ROM chips, and smart cards. This would allow the participant to use the application without having to remember the secret key, and if compromised, the adversary would not be able to retrieve the private key. In the event of losing the private key, the owner could personally contact the awarding body and transfer the awards to a new blockchain address, provided his/her identity is successfully proven [11]. Splitting the private key into two halves, and storing each half in a different medium is a solution to this, should one get lost, the private key is not compromised and can be easily changed [9]. Another solution would be to implement multi-signature wallets where a group blockchain addresses could be combined into one. Therefore, if one of the addresses was lost and unrecoverable, a new address could be generated as a replacement by using signatures from other addresses. This also improves security in the event of having a compromised secret key, this is because if the adversary attempts to impersonate the original owner, he/she would require official signatures from the other addresses.

2.4   Image Processing and Hard-Copy Documents

A method for evaluating the quality of certificate and bill images, such that images with poor quality are filtered out, keeping only the high-quality ones was proposed by [6]. However, this research does not consider optical character recognition (OCR) accuracy, which is an important requirement for bills and certificate recognition systems. [1] and [3] have proposed similar solutions, which mitigate forgery in hard copy documents by means of OCR, cryptography and 2D bar-codes (QR codes). The proposed solutions are very similar and follow three important steps when creating secure physical documents, which are: 1) Retrieve textual data from the document; 2) Generate a QR code based on the data to be validated; 3) Affix QR code on original certificate for validation process. However, when generating the QR codes [3] uses the selected text to be validated, while [1] uses the digest of the specified region of interest, thus having less data to be put into a QR code. [1] stated that the main challenge in the proposed system was the accuracy of the OCR, and thus experiments regarding the accuracy in terms of error occurrence were performed. The researchers outline two major factors which affect the accuracy of OCR, which are: 1) The font used; 2) Character weight. Their results indicate that the font "Times New Roman" performed the best by showing minimum error and using bold characters in the specified region of interest gives maximum performance. Tesseract OCR was used by [3] and concluded that overall recognition with case insensitivity was considerably better than case sensitivity.

3   Research Methodology

This research focuses on the verification of physical certificates, which information has been published on a blockchain network by the rewarding academic institution via a smart contract to the certificate holder on the respective public blockchain address. This research has been staged into three phases: 1) Institution registration and setup; 2) Issue of certificates; 3) Automatic verification and validation of certificates. From previous research [2], it was noted that the structure of the system should be implemented in a way that would allow academic organisations to publish certificates on their own smart contracts rather than one centralised smart contract. With this design academic organisations have several benefits, such as: 1) Complete control over smart contract containing certificates; 2) Complete freedom in choosing which information to be published as validation material.

Every academic organisation deploys a smart contract, with which all information about academic achievements found on physical certificates are published as a transaction between the academic organisation, certificate holder and actual smart contract, the equivalent of the physical certificate. This research mostly focuses on the third stage, more specifically: 1) Extraction of textual information from the scanned certificate image; 2) Creation of data structure from textual information; 3) Validation and verification from academic certificates and certificate holder (via the corresponding public blockchain address on which the certificate is registered). It is thus the aim of this research to determine whether the proposed solution, will improve the verification and validation process needed by academic institutions and/or employers. To implement the prototype several questions had to be answered beforehand: 1) What machine learning techniques can allow the extraction of textual information from scanned certificates? 2) How will the system handle different document layouts? 3) How will the blockchain be used to verify and validate academic certificates and the award holders?

The first step is extraction of textual information from the scanned certificate image, and for this we have opted to use Tesseract OCR. This is because, several research, [1] and [3], have shown that OCR, more specifically Tesseract OCR, is able to extract textual data contained within images of documents at a good accuracy level of 84% with Times New Roman font. One major problem encountered was that whenever logos were present in the academic certificates, the Tesseract was producing very inaccurate results. Some academic certificates prove to be problematic, due to having objects being unrecognised as letters or symbols, or due to having very small lettering. To address this problem, we have opted to use the OpenCV library to perform multi-scale template matching in order to identify the locations of the logos such that they can be removed by setting the logo area to white.

For the solution to be scaleable, a repository holding a large number of logos is required, such that when any party starts the certificate verification process, the application performs a sequential pattern matching and logo removal process. We have given the OCR different academic certificates having different text, image quality, noise levels, designs and also used different devices for scanning, being mobile devices and dedicated scanners, such that we could qualitatively analyse and identify limitations when opting for such a system. After having obtained a clean version of the academic certificate and having performed OCR on the academic certificate, the next task was to extract key information and organise it into a data structure.

In order to extract important information from an OCR result, we have opted for regular expression patterns (RegEx). Every institution uploads their own template files, which must match the certificates they will be uploading. Since there will be no standard certificate layout, the system will not know which information is important and which information is redundant on its own, therefore tags were used. The tags are customisable by the institution, however special non-customisable tags exist such as institution_name, award_holder_name, day, month, and year. These tags are then converted into named group capture RegEx pattern strings, such that useful information can be extracted with these tags. During extraction, a value representing the similarity between the template and the text is measured by using the difflib python library, which makes use of the Gestalt pattern matching technique, such that, the output with highest similarity is selected to be the correct output. In order to test this feature we have created multiple templates files for different awarding organisations in order to analyse how rigid pattern matching is when combined with OCR.

After having a complete dictionary, the next task is to verify and validate the certificate holders public address and the information found within the scanned certificate. This is needed so that an individual A, does not impersonate an individual B and claim the latter's certificates as one's own, especially since we are dealing with a public blockchain network. The certificate holders public address has to be verified using the CertificateChain smart contract while an academic certificate requires the academic organisations smart contract for verification. In order to conduct this research, we have chosen to develop and deploy multiple smart contracts, using the Truffle framework and Ganache. The CertificateChain smart contract acts as the main smart contract for this solution, as awarding organisations and third parties both make extensive use of this smart contract for registration, verification and validation. Several other smart contracts have been developed to act as smart contracts deployed, by fictitious academic organisations, with the purpose of storing academic certificate information from the respective academic organisation.

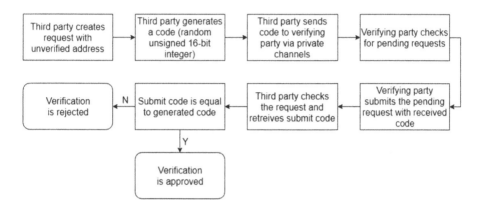

Fig. 1. Address verification process

In order to verify that the certificate holder truly owns a given address, we have adapted a solution similar to [3], which pipeline can be seen in Fig. 1, and involves the following steps: 1) 3rd party create a confirmation request on the CertificateChain smart contract; 2) 3rd party generates a random number between 1 and 65,535 and communicates this privately with the certificate holder; 3) the certificate holder logs-into the platform with his public key and proceeds to validate his/her pending request with the given randomly generated number; 4) 3rd party checks the status and code of the confirmation response and if the codes match, the certificate holder is trusted to be the true owner of the given address. The next step is to validate the certificate information from the previously created dictionary, however, some issues had to be evaluated beforehand: 1) The current version of Solidity, version 0.5.7, does not allow functions to return an array of structures; 2) Validation depends on the template keys chosen by the academic organisation. Since the template keys are different for every institution, every smart contract is required to expose a pure function which returns an array of strings representing the list of template keys, and also, since we are not able to get the list of certificates belonging to an address with one call, the smart contract is also required to expose a function which returns the number of certificates belonging to a specific address. The idea is that after validating the identity of the address received, the application gets the keys from the smart contract and gets the number of certificates owned by the address. Afterwards, the application starts to get the certificates owned by the address in a sequential manner and match the information stored on the blockchain with the information obtained by the OCR, giving every certificate a similarity score, very similar to how we choose a template. The certificate with the highest similarity, given that the highest similarity score is higher than a pre-determined threshold level, is shown on screen such that the third party can make some final checks before making their decision.

4   Results

4.1   Certificate Image Pre-processing and OCR

The removal of logos found within academic certificate images uses a multi-scale template matching approach. This is because OpenCV template matching requires the template to be very similar to a section within an image, therefore, if the size of the template does not match the size of the logo found within the image, the template matching operation could fail to operate as intended. Also, another limitation with template matching is that the operation will return a region in the image with highest similarity to the template, however, this does not always mean that the region is correct, which means that performing the operation with a template which is not found within the image still returns a region. The orientation of the certificate image must match the orientation of the logo for template matching and must be upright for the OCR to produce a valid result. Using different scanning devices, being dedicated scanners and mobile, made little difference in the result, as long as the certificate image result is clear for the OCR to process. Most certificates having a hand signature generated an invalid result when performing OCR due to two reasons being: 1) The signature overlapped some of the characters, thus the OCR could not identify properly the character; 2) The signature was being misread as a character to process.

When analysing the increase in time taken (in seconds), for the OCR to process certificates with different word counts, and having 300 dots per inch (dpi), a strong linear relationship can be observed, having correlation value of 0.95, thus, an increase in word count causes an increase in the time taken. Scalability is an issue with the proposed solution because each logo removal will take on average 4.32 s, thus, if each logo has to be stored in a repository, approximately every 830 logos stored will increase the time taken to automatically remove logos by one hour. A linear relationship is also present between the pixel count of the template and the time taken to perform logo removal, having correlation of 0.85. Possible solutions to such limitations shall be addressed in the final section.

4.2   Pattern Matching

To extract the useful information from the OCR result, we firstly need to identify the institution the certificate belongs to, which is done by performing a linear search for all registered institutions in the OCR result, thus scalability is also a problem in the event of having a large number of academic institutions registered. One major limitation with the proposed solution is that this stage depends on an API and database to retrieve the institutions and respective template files, therefore in the events of having the service go down, the validation process is halted until services are back online. The RegEx patterns in the template file had to be an almost perfect match, which means that in the event of having the OCR read an extra white space or spell something incorrectly, some of the information to be extracted could not be extracted. This problem can partially be solved by creating more elaborate RegEx patterns which caters for extra or missing white spaces.

4.3   Smart Contracts

To validate the certificates on the blockchain, the CertificateChain smart contract and our institution smart contracts were deployed which require money to pay for gas used by the Ethereum virtual machine (EVM). This solution has been developed solely on Ethereum not because there are technical limitations not met on other networks, but purely as a proof of concept, which can easily be migrated to other. The gas usage for CertificateChain is of 2,309,099 whilst for two local Universities renamed as A and B is of 1,853,264 and 1,658,387 respectively based on their respective certificate data. The costs are found in Table 1, this shows the low initial cost for deploying the smart contract on the blockchain.

Table 1. Costs in ETH and EUR for deploying prototype smart contracts

	ETH costs		
Gas price (Gwei)	CertificateChain	University A	University B
15	0.034636 (€4.95)	0.027799 (€3.97)	0.024876 (€3.56)
10	0.023091 (€3.30)	0.018533 (€2.65)	0.016584 (€2.37)
4	0.009236 (€1.32)	0.007413 (€1.06)	0.006634 (€0.95)
2	0.004618 (€0.66)	0.003707 (€0.53)	0.003317 (€0.47)

EVM gas consumption uses Gwei, in which 1 ETH is equal to 1,000,000,000 Gwei, and the exchange rates are dated 2nd of April 2019 16:00, in which 1 ETH is €142.93. Increasing the gas price will increase the speed of confirmation for the transaction, however, not all transactions should be created with a high gas price. In this case a lower gas price is ideal as both deployment of smart contract and publishing of academic certificates do not need to be done at instant speeds (Table 2).

When analysing gas fees for publishing 128-byte certificates according to number of graduates at University of Malta for the 2017–2018 scholastic year [12],

Table 2. Costs in ETH and EUR for publishing certificates with different sizes

	ETH costs		
Gas price (Gwei)	32 bytes/130,041 Gas	64 bytes/132,089 Gas	128 bytes/216,864 Gas
15	0.001951 (€0.28)	0.001981 (€0.28)	0.003253 (€0.46)
10	0.001300 (€0.19)	0.001321 (€0.19)	0.002169 (€0.31)
4	0.000520 (€0.07)	0.000528 (€0.08)	0.000867 (€0.12)
2	0.000260 (€0.04)	0.000264 (€0.04)	0.000434 (€0.06)

it was observed that the difference in price between 2 Gwei and 15 Gwei is €1,420.01. Gas fees for publishing 128-byte certificates is shown in Table 3 according to the number of tertiary education graduates per EU country in 2016 [4]. As can be seen in the results, the gas price makes a critical difference in the total costs. Case in point is the €2,297,168.14 difference between 2 Gwei and 15 Gwei. Having a high gas price is unnecessary for publication of certificates as these do not need to be available within seconds of graduation, thus, if a large number of certificates needs to be published, it is best to plan ahead of time and stage publishing with lower gas prices in order to avoid unnecessary costs.

4.4   Verification and Validation of Certificates and Addresses

To verify the owner of an address, a transaction must be made by both parties, therefore gas consumption must be paid to verify securely on the blockchain. The proposed solution uses 156,278 gas to create a request, which is 0.00067 ETH (€0.09), while 48,884 gas is used to confirm the request, which is 0.00021 ETH (€0.03) assuming the gas price is 4.3 Gwei and 1 ETH is €142.93. The speed of this process depends on the gas price of the transactions, if the verification party requires faster confirmation, a higher gas price such as 20 Gwei can be set and in return, higher transaction fees. The proposed solution has been adapted from [11], however, instead of using an inbuilt token, such as the EduCTX token, we are using a smart contract transaction and only pay for gas consumption. As the address verification process has very low gas consumption, the gas consumption fee is not refunded. To verify and validate an academic certificate, no transactions need to be created, this process is free and performed instantly without confirmation time. This process makes use of multiple function calls to the academic organisations smart contract due to limitations in the Solidity language. The academic certificates belonging to a certificate holder need to be fetched individually because the language does not support functions to return an array of structures, therefore, this process takes $O(n)$ time where n is the number of academic certificates belonging to a certificate holder stored in the academic organisations smart contract. Both verification and validation processes are not immune to malicious activity. In the case of owner verification, multiple users can work together by sharing the private key such that they would verify the address for each other. The proposed solution for academic certificate verification and validation crucially depends on the certificate data being published by the

Table 3. Gas fees for tertiary education certificates per EU country in 2016

		Gas price (Gwei) for 128 byte certificates			
	Total	2	4	10	15
EU-28	4,695.980	€291,116.68	€582,233.36	€1,455,583.41	€2,183,375.11
Belgium	119.141	€7,385.88	€14,771.75	€36,929.39	€55,394.08
Bulgaria	60.383	€3,743.31	€7,486.62	€18,716.54	€28,074.81
Czech Republic	90.725	€5,624.29	€11,248.58	€28,121.46	€42,182.19
Denmark	85.290	€5,287.36	€10,574.72	€26,436.81	€39,655.21
Germany	556.800	€34,517.56	€69,035.12	€172,587.80	€258,881.69
Estonia	10.262	€636.17	€1,272.34	€3,180.85	€4,771.27
Ireland	65.362	€4,051.97	€8,103.94	€20,259.85	€30,389.77
Greece	69.929	€4,335.09	€8,670.18	€21,675.45	€32,513.18
Spain	438.661	€27,193.80	€54,387.60	€135,968.99	€203,953.49
France	772.779	€47,906.69	€95,813.38	€239,533.45	€359,300.17
Croatia	34.028	€2,109.49	€4,218.98	€10,547.45	€15,821.17
Italy	373.775	€23,171.34	€46,342.68	€115,856.69	€173,785.03
Cyprus	8.420	€521.98	€1,043.96	€2,609.89	€3,914.84
Latvia	15.796	€979.24	€1,958.47	€4,896.19	€7,344.28
Lithuania	29.683	€1,840.13	€3,680.26	€9,200.65	€13,800.98
Luxembourg	1.682	€104.27	€208.54	€521.36	€782.04
Hungary	68.110	€4,222.33	€8,444.65	€21,111.63	€31,667.44
Malta	4.576	€283.68	€567.36	€1,418.39	€2,127.59
Netherlands	148.942	€9,233.32	€18,466.65	€46,166.62	€69,249.92
Austria	83.396	€5,169.95	€10,339.89	€25,849.73	€38,774.60
Poland	487.640	€30,230.14	€60,460.28	€151,150.71	€226,726.06
Portugal	73.086	€4,530.80	€9,061.60	€22,654.01	€33,981.01
Romania	121.788	€7,549.97	€15,099.94	€37,749.86	€56,624.79
Slovenia	30.967	€1,919.73	€3,839.46	€9,598.65	€14,397.97
Slovakia	56.280	€3,488.95	€6,977.90	€17,444.76	€26,167.14
Finland	56.066	€3,475.69	€6,951.37	€17,378.43	€26,067.64
Sweden	78.112	€4,842.38	€9,684.75	€24,211.89	€36,317.83
United Kingdom	754.301	€46,761.19	€93,522.38	€233,805.94	€350,708.91
Iceland	4.564	€282.93	€565.87	€1,414.67	€2,122.01
Liechtenstein	0.191	€11.84	€23.68	€59.20	€88.80
Norway	49.010	€3,038.26	€6,076.53	€15,191.32	€22,786.98
Switzerland	87.479	€5,423.06	€10,846.13	€27,115.32	€40,672.97
Macedonia	10.465	€648.75	€1,297.51	€3,243.77	€4,865.66
Serbia	50.326	€3,119.85	€6,239.69	€15,599.23	€23,398.85
Turkey	802.822	€49,769.14	€99,538.28	€248,845.69	€373,268.53
	5,700.837	**€353,410.52**	**€706,821.05**	**€1,767,052.62**	**€2,650,578.92**

academic organisations and cannot prevent such organisations from publishing false certificates in the first place, thus, if the academic organisation publishes false certificates, the proposed solution will identify it as a valid certificate.

5   Conclusion

We concluded that the proposed solution will improve the verification and validation process needed by academic institutions and/or employers. Using the proposed blockchain solution, academic institutions have the ability of having their academic certificates published on the blockchain network, having full freedom on the implementation of their smart contract. Institutions are required to pay gas fees in order to deploy their smart smart contracts, this fee depends on the size of the smart contract, however for our prototype the average cost for deploying smart contracts for the institutions was found to be €0.50 with gas price set to 2 Gwei. Gas fees also have to be paid when publishing new certificates onto the blockchain, and it was found to be €353,410.52 and €2,650,578.92 when publishing certificates to all 2016 tertiary education graduates in Europe when selecting 2 Gwei and 15 Gwei as gas prices respectively. In this case, transaction speed is not important, thus, low gas prices can be selected in order to cut a lot of extra costs. Since the proposed solution makes use of the blockchain network as the primary storage medium, the platform is immune to corruption and unauthorised alterations due to advanced cryptographic techniques. From these findings we have concluded that the proposed solution is very cost effective, when selecting lower gas prices, for the security benefits offered.

However, several scalability issues, discussed in the previous section, are found with the proposed solution, which need to be improved upon before implementing such a platform. The logo removal process takes approximately 4.32 s per logo, thus, approximately every 830 logos added to the logos repository will increase the time taken by one hour. From this finding we have concluded that template matching is not ideal as this requires us to store every logo as a template. One possible solution for this would be to train a neural network to identify the position of logos from the given image. The logo removal process also depends on the pixel count of the template image, such that the correlation between the linear relationship of the pixel count and time taken is 0.85. One possible solution for this issue would be to downscale the template and certificate images, such that the time taken is reduced.

References

1. Ambadiyil, S., Vibhath, V.B., Pillai, V.P.M.: On Paper digital signature (OPDS). In: Thampi, S., Bandyopadhyay, S., Krishnan, S., Li, K.C., Mosin, S., Ma, M. (eds.) Advances in Signal Processing and Intelligent Recognition Systems, pp. 547–558. Springer, Cham (2016). https://doi.org/10.1007/978-3-319-28658-7_46
2. Curmi, A., Inguanez, F.: BlockChain based certificate verification platform. In: Abramowicz, W., Paschke, A. (eds.) BIS 2018. LNBIP, vol. 339, pp. 211–216. Springer, Cham (2019). https://doi.org/10.1007/978-3-030-04849-5_18

3. Dlamini, N., Mthethwa, S., Barbour, G.: Mitigating the challenge of hardcopy document forgery. In: 2018 International Conference on Advances in Big Data, Computing and Data Communication Systems (icABCD), pp. 1–6. IEEE (2018)
4. Eurostat: Tertiary education statistics (2018)
5. Grech, A., Camilleri, A.F.: Blockchain in education (2017)
6. Jiang, F., Zhang, L.J., Chen, H.: Automated image quality assessment for certificates and bills. In: 2017 IEEE International Conference on Cognitive Computing (ICCC), pp. 1–8. IEEE (2017). https://doi.org/10.1109/IEEE.ICCC.2017.8
7. Learning Machine: The Republic of Malta: A better pathway (2017). https://www.learningmachine.com/customer-story-malta/
8. Puthal, D., Malik, N., Mohanty, S.P., Kougianos, E., Yang, C.: The blockchain as a decentralized security framework [future directions]. IEEE Consumer Electron. Magazine 7(2), 18–21 (2018). https://doi.org/10.1109/MCE.2017.2776459
9. Schneier, B.: Applied Cryptography: Protocols, Algorithms and Source Code in C, 20 anniversary edn. Wiley, New York (2015)
10. Sharples, M., Domingue, J.: The blockchain and kudos: a distributed system for educational record reputation and reward. In: Verbert, K., Sharples, M., Klobucar, T. (eds.) European Conference on Technology Enhanced Learning, pp. 490–496. Springer, Cham (2016). https://doi.org/10.1007/978-3-319-45153-4_48
11. Turkanović, M., Hölbl, M., Košič, K., Heričko, M., Kamišalić, A.: EduCTX: a blockchain-based higher education credit platform. IEEE Access 6, 5112–5127 (2018)
12. University of Malta: Number of students who completed awards (2017–2018) (2018)
13. Yahya, Z., et al.: A new academic certificate authentication using leading edge technology. In: Proceedings of the 2017 International Conference on E-commerce, E-Business and E-Government, pp. 82–85. ACM (2017)
14. Yli-Huumo, J., Ko, D., Choi, S., Park, S., Smolander, K.: Where is current research on blockchain technology? a systematic review. PLoS ONE 11(10), e0163477 (2016)

Crypto-Trading. Rechargeable Token-Based Smart Energy Market Enabled by Blockchain and IoT Technology

Michele Marchesi[1(✉)], Andrea Pinna[2], Francesco Pisu[1], and Roberto Tonelli[1]

[1] Department of Mathematics and Computer Science, University of Cagliari,
Via ospedale 72, Cagliari, Italy
marchesi@unica.it, f.pisu18@studenti.unica.it, roberto.tonelli@dsf.unica.it
[2] Department of Electrical and Electronic Engineering (DIEE),
University of Cagliari, Piazza D'Armi snc, 09123 Cagliari, Italy
a.pinna@diee.unica.it

Abstract. This paper presents the definition and the implementation of a decentralized system for the energy trading managed by blockchain technology. The system, called Crypto-Trading, is composed by three interacting subsystems: the trading platform, the blockchain, and the smart meters system. It is conceived to exploit the IoT technology of smart meters and the decentralization of smart contracts working inside the blockchain technology for managing exchange and trading of energy by means of specific tokens. The paper defines the system as a decentralized application, identifying system actors and describing user stories. Then provides the description of the use case concerning the rechargeable token, one of the main feature of our system, and its interaction with the other components of the system. Finally, the paper compares our implementation choice with other ongoing projects in the field of energy trading.

Keywords: Energy trading · Blockchain · Smart contracts · Smart grid · BOSE

1 Introduction

In the scenario of a growing proliferation of electricity production sites from renewable sources, the need of new forms of trading of self-produced energy emerges. More and more energy consumers are becoming prosumers, creating a distributed renewable energy supply. According to the Fraunhofer Institute for Solar Energy Systems, the global annual rate of new installed photo voltaic power was equal to 40% between the 2010 and 2017 [4]. The creation of free and decentralized markets could open to new change of profit for prosumers. The challenge is to create a trading system that captures the interest and answers

© Springer Nature Switzerland AG 2020
U. Schwardmann et al. (Eds.): Euro-Par 2019 Workshops, LNCS 11997, pp. 166–178, 2020.
https://doi.org/10.1007/978-3-030-48340-1_13

the needs of prosumers and also provides a data infrastructure that meet the necessity of electric service operators to govern the energy grid. The new business opportunity can help overcoming barriers that slow the growth of adoption of new technologies in the field of smart grids. We conceived Crypto-Trading to create a new typology of free and decentralized energy market, based on the blockchain technology. It is a blockchain oriented software system [13] compatible with the existent product of the Internet of Things (IoT) technologies and works in combination with the technology used in the energy sector by service operators, such as energy smart meters. The design of decentralized application can make use of recent design patterns of the software engineering, conceived for this typology of software system [7]. This paper follows the previous project presentation [6] and presents the definition of the system in terms of a decentralized application and provides a description of the implementation of the decentralized core of the system Crytpo-Trading. The following section provides a discussion about recent related works that frame our system in the sector of decentralized energy trading. Section 3 defines Crypto-Trading as a decentralized application, providing system description, actors and users stories. Section 4 describes the use case of energy production and consumption, which allow us to describe the role of the rechargeable energy token. Section 5 describes the implementation of the system as smart contract. Section 6 summarizes and concludes the paper.

2   Related Works

In the research area of the energy market, the last two years are characterized by the growing interest in development opportunities offered by the blockchain technology. This is well documented in a recently published systematic review on the use of blockchain technology in the energy sector by Andoni et al. [2]. They summarized the impact of blockchain technology in ten aspects of the business models of energy company operators such as billing, sale and management, trading and markets, automation, smart grid applications and data transfer, grid management, security and identity management, sharing of resources, competition, and transparency.

Decentralized energy trading is made possible thanks to the progress in energy smart grid deployment. Several works studied blockchain based systems able to govern smart grids to physically carry the energy from the seller to the buyer. Mengelkamp et al. [8] proposed an energy market based on several "micro-markets" extabilished in local "microgrids". Differently from Crypto-Trading, in this system each micromarket has its own rules and energy prices. The market is conceived as virtual layer of the system and is implemented on top of the physical layer (the energy smart grid). The smart grid will be programmed to make effective the energy transfer. Disadvantages of this approach are to be found in the technological complexity to create an efficient and reliable system [9,14]. To solve this problem, according to Pop et al. [12], blockchain can be used to govern smart grids. In particular, users' habits and global energy demand can be profiled in the decentralized ledger. Using these data, specific smart contracts are able to control smart grid units and to direct efficiently the energy supply.

Nehai et al. [10] described a scenario similar to ours, in which a transmission and distribution (T&D) service operator is present. Adopting decentralized energy markets, energy prosumers gains in possibility of choice that are self production or consume, production or consume in the decentralized market, or product and consume in the T&D network.

Studies on decentralized trading platform for the energy market describe the crucial role of Smart Contracts in the system development. Pee et al. [11] proposed a solution based on the Ethereum improvement ERC20 token. Yu et al. [16] described the layers of an energy auditing platform and describe the role of smart contract in the transactive mechanism. Castellanos et al. [3] put the attention on the origin of the energy, as required by the EU directive 2009/28/EC. They used Ethereum smart contracts to develop a system to trade the energy and register the origin and then examined price formation issues. Privacy issues in decentralized market have been studied by Aitzhan and Svetinovic [1] for what concerns the trading communication and by Guan et al. [5] for what concerns the use of blockchain as data layer to control smart grids.

Given this scenario, Crypto-Trading is a project which impacts especially in the first three sectors: "billing" concerns the use of smart contracts and smart metering to realize automated billing, "sales and marketing" concerns the combination with artificial intelligence to identify prosumer energy patterns, and finally, "Trading and Market" concerns the creation of distributed trading platforms for market management and commodity trading transactions.

3   System Definition

Crypto-Trading system is a system obtained as a result of the integration of three different subsystems. The main components are the blockchain subsystem, the smart metering subsystem and the trading platform subsystem. To these is added the energy transmission and distribution system, based on smart grids. Each subsystem has a specific role. The blockchain subsystem is in charge of the creation, the purchase and sale, and the circulation of tokens. The smart metering subsystem is an IoT system which acts both as a certified reference for monitoring the energy production and consumption, and as the physical interface between the first component of the Crypto-Trading system and the energy transmission grid, managed by the Transmission and Distribution system operators (T&DSO). The trading platform subsystem allows the trading of the Crypto-Trading tokens by means of artificial intelligence tools conceived for an easier and more profitable trading. Figure 1 represents the three subsystems and their interactions with Prosumers and with the physical layer of energy Smart Grid. Each subsystem can be described as a stand alone system, each with its own "actors", and in turn may be considered as an actor of one of the other subsystems. For instance, the smart metering subsystem must be considered as an actor of the blockchain subsystem. In this work we mainly focus and define the blockchain subsystem, which represents the decentralized core of the Crypto-Trading system.

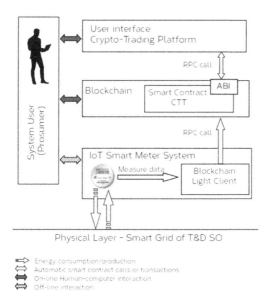

Fig. 1. Representation of the three subsystem of Crypto-Trading and their interactions.

3.1   Actors

The objective of the blockchain subsystem is to provide a decentralized infrastructure which creates and manages the Crypto-Tranding Energy Tokens. The main element of the blockchain subsystem is a smart contract we call *Crypto-Trading Token* (CTT) and we bound the blockchain subsystem to all its functions and responsibilities. The actors of this subsystem are all the entities who interact with the blockchain subsystem. The actors are: the *System Admin*, the *Prosumer*, the *Smart Meter*, and the *Trading Platform*.

- **System Admin**: he is the administrator of the CTT. He can set the parameters of the CTT contract. He is identified with an Ethereum address.
- **Prosumer**: he is the actor who can buy and sell CTT tokens. He has an associated list of Smart Meters which can interact with its token content. He is a person or a society responsible of consuming or producing electrical energy. He is identified with an Ethereum address.
- **Smart Meter**: it is an IoT device associated to a Prosumer. It measures the energy production and consumption, and send messages to the CTT whenever the production and the consumption reach a given threshold or whenever is triggered by the prosumer. It is identified by an Ethereum address and it knows the address of the Prosumer who owns it.
- **Trading Platform**: it is a decentralized application which provides a user interface to simplify the reading of the Prosumer account and provides tools for the trading of energy token.

3.2   User Stories

User stories describe how the actors act within the system. The User Stories of the blockchain subsystem are summarized in Table 1. The CTT is the Crypto-Trading Token, namely a smart contract which contains the Crypto-Trading Energy Tokens which can be sold, bought, consumed and recharged, by means of the interaction of the Prosumer and the Smart meter. Figure 2 shows the sequence diagram concerning the user stories which involve the Prosumer and the Smart Meter in the CTT. In this diagram the billing period is the reference period of time for the computation of a new energy bill.

Table 1. User stories of the Crypto-Trading blockchain subsystem.

User story	Name	Description
CRC	Create CTT	The system admin deploys the contract CTT in the blockchain and its address is registered as the admin in charge. Actor: System Admin
USA	Update System Admin	The System Admin in charge chooses a new System Admin, specifying its address. Actor: System Admin
STS	Set Tokens max Supply	The System Admin sets the maximum number of Crypto-Trading Energy tokens. Actor: System Admin
STC	Set Token Capability	The System Admin sets the max amount of kWh which can be recorded in one Energy token. Actor: System Admin
ST	Sell Token	The Prosumer puts a token on sale, establishing price of the token and the price of the quantity of energy. Actors: Prosumer
BT	Buy Token	The Prosumer chooses and buys a token for sale (or from another prosumer or from the CTT, if empty tokens still available). He uses the trading platform. The contract CTT records the buying. Actor: Prosumer, Trading Platform
ASM	Authorize Smart Meter	A Prosumer authorizes a Smart Meter to modify the energy amount of his Energy tokens and triggers the smart meter to execute the transaction to confirm the ownership. Actor: Prosumer, Smart Meter
CEA	Consume Energy Amount	The Smart Meter accesses and consumes the content of the Crypto-Trading Energy tokens associated with its owner (a Prosumer), according to the settings of its owner. Actors: Smart Meter, Prosumer
REA	Recharge Energy Amount	The Smart Meter accesses and increases the content of the Crypto-Trading Energy tokens associated with its owner (a Prosumer), according to the settings of its owner. Actors: Smart Meter, Prosumer

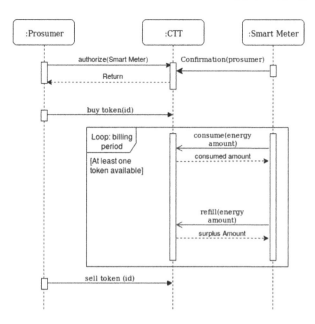

Fig. 2. Sequence diagram of the interaction between the actors Prosumer and Smart Meter through the CTT

4   Rechargeable Energy Token

First of all, our system relies on an external energy transmission and distribution system so that there exist already a physical network of electrical power distribution owned and managed by a public or private authority. The roles of such authority are: to distribute the energy through the network; to provide smart meters to prosumers or, alternatively, to check and asseverate that smart meters used by prosumers satisfy some basic requirements, so that the measured production of energy be reliable (the authority has the right of access to smart meters and can seal them in order to avoid cheating from prosumers); to measure from its own side the energy produced by each prosumer and injected into the power network; to measure energy consumption by each consumer (including prosumers); to request payments for energy consumption and for smart meter usage in case these are loaned to prosumers. Given these premises the exchange and trade of energy is managed by Ethereum tokens emitted by a Smart Contract (CTT), which could be owned by a specific system admin or by the same energy authority which controls the power distribution network.

For the sake of simplicity we chose to emit a large enough but limited number of tokens (user story STS in Table 1) which can be traded themselves and that are created empty. Tokens are sold into the energy market both by means the initial offering of empty tokens and by other prosumers, and prosumers must buy tokens and fill them with the energy they produce before selling them into the trading market. Consumers must buy filled tokens and consume the energy carried by them. The tokens will be then emptied and can be resold into the market, creating a trading parallel to the energy one (user stories BT, CT, CEA, REA in Table 1).

First we examine the energy production phase and the energy injection into the trading market. We set our system so that the tokens can be "charged" with discrete amounts of "energy" (but this choice is not restrictive) by the smart meters (SMs) through Ethereum transactions. Such discrete amounts can be released after the token is sold to a consumer and the corresponding energy consumed. As a consequence SMs must have associated an Etehreum address and some Ethers to pay transactions. Each prosumer decides when the energy produced can be injected into the tokens by activating the transaction governed by the SM using the usual public-private key pair associated to Ethereum addresses (to each SM). We set 1 kWh as the quantum, or the discrete amount of energy, that can be loaded into a token. When a SM produces more than N.M kWh of energy, where N is the integer part and M is the fractional, the prosumer can load N quantum into its tokens launching the opportune Ethereum transaction. Such amount of energy has been already injected into the power network, as measured by the SM, and is available to every consumer. The energy authority can easily acknowledge the injections by looking at its own measurements. At this point the prosumer holds a token with N quantum of energy (N kilowatt hours in our scheme) and sets a price for the ensemble token+energy. The tokens+energy on sale are exposed into a "web-shelf", or a reading table, where buyers can chose which token to buy at their own convenience. An intelligent robo-advisor ca be devised to optimize trading. The value carried by each token is the value of the energy at the price set by the prosumer plus the value of the token itself which has been bought by prosumers at the beginning and can be traded into the market like all Ethereum tokens even when it carries no energy.

The trading and exchange of tokens is managed by a ERC721 Ethereum Smart Contract. Prosumers can buy more than one token and, in order to be able to set an arbitrary number of quantum of energy in each token they hold, they can distribute the produced energy among all tokens they own. With this architecture one token is set for being charged by transactions activated by smart meters in discrete amounts. The tokens are then coloured by integer numbers (the kilowatt hours) and these amounts can be redistributed among the tokens owned by the same prosumer.

All the processes and events are recorded into the Ethereum blockchain and all the actors, (prosumers, consumers, and also the energy authority), can verify at any moment, in a transparent fashion, with publicly available data, that all tokens charged with energy correspond to actually produced energy and injected into the power network. Tokens are the containers, and have an associated value determined by the tokens trading market, and energy is the content, and has another associated value determined by the energy market.

Now we examine the energy consumption phase, assuming that a consumer bought some tokens with energy. Each consumer has a meter which is usually owned by the energy authority and which measures the total energy consumed by the consumer during a given period of time. The energy consumed, as measured by the meter, is composed by two parts, one associated to the quantum in the tokens and another which is simply energy consumed and never payed in the trading market. We here assume that the consumer has not enough quantum to cover all the energy consumption, which is the more complicated case.

Once a consumer has bought some tokens, the quantum into it must be consumed and tokens must be emptied. Consumers, the token's new owners, activate an Ethereum transaction to erase the quantum units carried by tokens (a partial consumption can be also set). To each energy kilowatt hour corresponds a deleted quantum and each quantum deletion is recorded permanently and is publicly available in the blockchain. The public authority has access to all the data and transactions and can easily associate the token ownership for consumed energy to the amount of consumed energy. The authority can produce a bill where the total of consumed energy is decreased by the amount of energy corresponding to the quantum erased from the tokens. In fact, such energy has not been produced by the energy authority but by the prosumers and has already been payed by consumers when they bought the corresponding tokens at a price determined by the market. The authority may eventually include a fee in the bill for transporting and delivering the energy through the physical infrastructure. If the energy consumed is all covered by the tokens then the due price is zero, since the consumer has already payed in Ether the energy to the prosumer who filled the tokens. A third implicit pattern, included in our approach, is the trading of filled tokens. Once an actor buy a token with some amount of energy, it can resell the token at any given price, inserting it once again into the "web-shelf" with a price set according to a best profit strategy. This operation can be done at any stage, even in the case where part of the energy originally carried by the token has been consumed, so that the token is resold with a lower energy content. Finally tokens emptied are re-sold into the market using the ERC721 contract, so that consumers do not waist money for the "energy containers" and to ensure tokens recycling into the market. In this way: there is no need to produce new tokens; the total number of circulating tokens can be set at the beginning; tokens have an intrinsic value determined by the market.

5   Implementation

In the following, the implementation of the blockchain subsystem of Crypto-Trading as a Smart Contract, and the Ethereum-compatible Tobalaba network is described.

Solidity Smart Contract. We implemented the Crypto-Trading blockchain subsystem by means of an Ethereum Smart Contract. We wrote the source code in Solidity language and we call *CTT* (abbreviation for Crypto-Trading Token) the main *contract* of the system. In short, CTT is the ERC721 compliant token of the Crypto-Trading platform. It implements the tracking and the management of an arbitrarily large number of non-fungible and rechargeable Energy tokens. Each CT token is characterized by a unique ID that allows the association between the given token and its owner. Token ownership is guaranteed by the ERC721 token. CTT is conceived to exploit the security level and features of standardized solidity frameworks of approved "Ethereum Improvement Proposal". In particular, CTT inherits the ERC721 implementation provided by the Openzeppelin framework[1] and uses the SafeMath library to protect form overflow and underflow.

Global variable *maxTokenSupply* records the Maximum number of Energy Tokens (MET), and *energyCapacity* records the Capacity of each Energy Token (CET) expressed in number of energy quantum (fixed equal to 1 kWh). Both variables can only be modified by the administrators of the Crypto-Trading system. The value of these two variables defines the total energy supply (TES) that can be traded in Crypto-Trading, as:

$$TES = MET * CET. \tag{1}$$

The inverted formula can be used to compute MET given TES and CET. For instance, considering CET equal to 10 kWh (order of magnitude of the average daily energy consumption of a family) and TES equal to 1 TWh (about the energy consumed in Italy in one day [15]), MET is equal to one hundred million tokens.

Two main data structures are implemented in the contract namely *Energy-Token* and *Prosumer*. The struct *EnergyToken* defines a specific token with the price of the token (TP), the price of one energy quantum (EP) and the energy amount (EA). A prosumer who owns a given token he wants to sell, can set the value of TP and EP of the token, according to his trading preferences. For each token we can compute the selling price (SP) as:

$$SP = TP + (EA * EP). \tag{2}$$

The struct *Prosumer* includes the address of the associated Smart Meter and the ID list of tokens he owns. We implemented User Stories described in 1 defining specific functions and appropriate solidity modifiers. Table 2 lists public and external function implemented in the smart contract. In the table, OSMP stands for *onlySmartMeterOfProsumer* which assert that the message sender is a smart meter associated to a given prosumer.

Network. We identified in Energy Web (EW)[2] the Ethereum platform that better fits the purposes of the project. EW is a project which aims to provide an "open-source, scalable blockchain platform specifically designed for the energy sector's regulatory, operational, and market needs". Tobalaba[3] is the testing

---

[1] https://github.com/OpenZeppelin.

[2] Energy Web Foundation https://energyweb.org/.

[3] On May 2019, Energy Web announced the release of a new testnet called Volta. https://energyweb.atlassian.net/wiki/spaces/EWF/pages/702677023/Chain+Volta.

Table 2. External and public functions implemented in CTT.

Function	Type	Parameters	Modifiers	User story - Action
setMaxTokenSuppy	Public	maxSupply:uint	onlyOwner	STS
setTokenCapability	Public	capability:uint	onlyOwner	STC
consume	External	MaxAmount: uint; prosumer: address	OSMP	CEA
refill/recharge	External	amount:uint; prosumer:address	OSMP	REA
register	Public	smartMeter: address		ASM
confirm	Public	prosumer:address	OSMP	ASM
buyEmptyToken	Public Payable			BT
setOnSale	Public	tokenID:uint		ST

blockchain in which blocks are mined in average every 3 s. This blockchain is ruled by the Aura (Authority Round)[4] Proof-of-Authority algorithm, already implemented in the Parity client. Special nodes called "authority" nodes can

Table 3. Comparison between Crypto-Trading and three other notable ongoing project of energy trading systems

Feature	Crypto-Trading	Enerchain	Exergy	Power ledger
Blockchain	Ethereum Tobalaba	Tenedermint Wormhole	Exergy	Ethereum
Consensum	Proof-of-Authority	Byzantine-fault tolerant	Proof-of-Ownership	Proof-of-Stake
Policy	Public	Permissioned	Private	Public and private
Token	EnergyToken (non-fungible ERC721 token)	EnerCoin	Exergy	Power (ERC20) and Sparks (ERC20)
Token aim	Marketable token and rechargeable energy account	Purchasable Euro based token for energy exchange	Function enabler purchasable token	Power: marketable token; Sparks: marketable energy quantum
Trading functions	AI aided energy and token trading	Openbazar based market	Transactive market and adaptive price formation	Double trading system (application host platform to trade starks)
Business model	Token selling	Transaction fees or subscription fee	Token Pre-selling	Token selling

---

[4] https://wiki.parity.io/Aura.

validate transactions and create new blocks. Only "affiliate" organizations that join EWF can run authority nodes entitled to validate and sign blocks. EW provides a network client suitable to smart meter systems to allow a direct connection with the blockchain.

Projects Comparison. We summarize in Table 3 some features of the Crypto-Trading system, in comparison with the features of three ongoing projects namely EnerChain[5] (by Ponton), Exergy[6] (by Lo3 Energy), and PowerLedger[7]. To the best of our knowledge, Crypto-Trading is the only one projects that incorporates in a single token both the enabler, energy accounting, and marketable token functionality.

6   Conclusion

This paper describes the implementation and the features of the Crypto-Trading system, a system designed to exploit the blockchain technology for supporting trading in the energy market. We identified system actors and their interaction with the different components as well as the main distinctive features of Crypto-Trading and its rechargeable energy token. In particular, we start from the hypothesis that an external actor, namely a Transmission and Distribution system operator, is the authority responsible of managing the energy grid and providing certificated smart meters. In Crypto-Trading, smart meters represent the subsystem which is connected to the internet and, periodically or on demand, sends data about energy production and consumption to the blockchain subsystem. The Crypto-Trading blockchain subsystem is based on newly designed energy token, which exploits and extends the Ethereum ERC721 token. In particular, each Crypto-Trading Token contains an energy amount that can be recharged by means a local energy production, or consumed to save money. A dedicated smart contract in the Ethereum blockchain accounts for tokens exchange, tokens energy refill and tokens energy consumption. The token owner can trade the token by setting the energy price and the token price and tokens can be traded in the trading platform subsystem. The blockchain subsystem is conceived to run on the Ethereum based Tobalaba blockchain platform, specifically designed for the energy sector. Crypto-Trading offers a new way to trade not only the energy but also the energy carriers (the tokens) and it is fully compatible with the existing technologies.

Acknowledgements. The work presented in this paper has been partially funded by Regione Autonoma della Sardegna, under project "Crypto-Trading" - Programmazione unitaria 2014–2020 POR FESR Sardegna 2014–2020.

---

[5] https://ponton.de/focus/blockchain/enerchain/.

[6] https://exergy.energy/.

[7] https://powerledger.io/.

References

1. Aitzhan, N.Z., Svetinovic, D.: Security and privacy in decentralized energy trading through multi-signatures, blockchain and anonymous messaging streams. IEEE Trans. Dependable Secure Comput. **15**(5), 840–852 (2018). https://doi.org/10.1109/TDSC.2016.2616861
2. Andoni, M., et al.: Blockchain technology in the energy sector: a systematic review of challenges and opportunities. Renew. Sustain. Energy Rev. **100**, 143–174 (2019). https://doi.org/10.1016/j.rser.2018.10.014
3. Castellanos, J.A.F., Coll-Mayor, D., Notholt, J.A.: Cryptocurrency as guarantees of origin: Simulating a green certificate market with the ethereum blockchain. In: 2017 IEEE International Conference on Smart Energy Grid Engineering (SEGE), August 2017, pp. 367–372 (2017). https://doi.org/10.1109/SEGE.2017.8052827
4. Fraunhofer Institute for Solar Energy Systems: Photovoltaics report (2018). https://www.ise.fraunhofer.de/content/dam/ise/de/documents/publications/studies/Photovoltaics-Report.pdf
5. Guan, Z., et al.: Privacy-preserving and efficient aggregation based on blockchain for power grid communications in smart communities. IEEE Commun. Mag. **56**(7), 82–88 (2018). https://doi.org/10.1109/MCOM.2018.1700401
6. Mannaro, K., Pinna, A., Marchesi, M.: Crypto-trading: Blockchain-oriented energy market. In: 2017 AEIT International Annual Conference, September 2017, pp. 1–5 (2017). https://doi.org/10.23919/AEIT.2017.8240547
7. Marchesi, M., Marchesi, L., Tonelli, R.: An agile software engineering method to design blockchain applications. In: Proceedings of the 14th Central and Eastern European Software Engineering Conference Russia, p. 3. ACM (2018)
8. Mengelkamp, E., Gärttner, J., Rock, K., Kessler, S., Orsini, L., Weinhardt, C.: Designing microgrid energy markets: a case study: the brooklyn microgrid. Appl. Energy **210**, 870–880 (2018). https://doi.org/10.1016/j.apenergy.2017.06.054
9. Mengelkamp, E., Notheisen, B., Beer, C., Dauer, D., Weinhardt, C.: A blockchain-based smart grid: towards sustainable local energy markets. Comput. Sci. Res. Dev. **33**, 207–214 (2017). https://doi.org/10.1007/s00450-017-0360-9
10. Nehaï, Z., Guerard, G.: Integration of the blockchain in a smart grid model. In: Proceedings of the 14th International Conference of Young Scientists on Energy Issues, CYSENI 2017, Kaunas, Lithuania, pp. 25–26 (2017)
11. Pee, S.J., Kang, E.S., Song, J.G., Jang, J.W.: Blockchain based smart energy trading platform using smart contract. In: 2019 International Conference on Artificial Intelligence in Information and Communication (ICAIIC), February 2019, pp. 322–325. https://doi.org/10.1109/ICAIIC.2019.8668978
12. Pop, C., Cioara, T., Antal, M., Anghel, I., Salomie, I., Bertoncini, M.: Blockchain based decentralized management of demand response programs in smart energy grids. Sensors **18**(1) (2018). https://doi.org/10.3390/s18010162
13. Porru, S., Pinna, A., Marchesi, M., Tonelli, R.: Blockchain-oriented software engineering: challenges and new directions. In: 2017 IEEE/ACM 39th International Conference on Software Engineering Companion (ICSE-C), pp. 169–171. IEEE (2017)
14. Richter, B., Mengelkamp, E., Weinhardt, C.: Maturity of blockchain technology in local electricity markets. In: 2018 15th International Conference on the European Energy Market (EEM), June 2018, pp. 1–6 (2018). https://doi.org/10.1109/EEM.2018.8469955

15. Terna - Rete Elettrica Nazionale S.p.A.: Dati generali (Italian) (2018). http://download.terna.it/terna/0000/1089/73.PDF
16. Yu, S., Yang, S., Li, Y., Geng, J.: Distributed energy transaction mechanism design based on smart contract. In: 2018 China International Conference on Electricity Distribution (CICED), September 2018, pp. 2790–2793 (2018). https://doi.org/10.1109/CICED.2018.8592130

Ethereum Transaction Performance Evaluation Using Test-Nets

Lin Zhang$^{(\boxtimes)}$, Brian Lee, Yuhang Ye, and Yuansong Qiao

Software Research Institute, Athlone Institute of Technology,
Dublin Road, Athlone, Co. Westmeath, Ireland
{lin.zhang,yye,ysqiao}@research.ait.ie, blee@ait.ie

Abstract. Blockchain technologies can safely and neutrally store and process transaction data (including smart contracts) on the chain. Based on smart contracts, a special type of applications can be deployed, known as Decentralized Applications (DApps). Within existing Blockchain platforms, Ethereum is the most popular one adopted for DApp developments. The performance constraints of Ethereum dramatical impact usability of DApp. In this paper, we experimentally evaluate the performances of Ethereum from 3 types of tests: 1) Account balance query latency 2) Block generation time and 3) End-to-end transaction acceptance latency. The results show that the end-to-end transaction time in Ethereum is unstable. Consequently, the applications with low latency constraints and high frequency transaction requirements are not ready to be deployed unless off-chain transaction methods are considered.

Keywords: Blockchain · Ethereum · Transaction · DApp · Performance

1 Introduction

Blockchain, a secure and trustless decentralised database, enables recording information using linked "blocks". Since the data structure used in Blockchain is naturally immune to tampering, the 1st-generation approaches rise up first in cryptocurrency applications, e.g. Bitcoin [1] is a decentralised ledger to record transactions, the characteristics are decentralisation, anonymous and transparent [2]. As a superset of ledgering, generic computations are supported by the 2nd-generation Blockchain. Ethereum [3] is a typical approach which supports Turing-complete computations through smart contracts [4] thus enabling Decentralised Applications (DApps) [5]. In other words, DApps are software that rely on smart contracts operating through Blockchain as backend services.

Comparing with Blockchain platforms that support DApps (E.g. EOS, Steem, POA and xDai), the majority of DApp approaches are developed and published for Ethereum (2486 DApps in Ethereum out of 2667 DApps in total till 21/May/2019[1]) which enables converging various aspects of life such as energy, healthcare, finance, entertainment and insurance. However, more than 21% of the DApps have been broken or abandoned on

---

[1] State of the DApps—DApp Statistics, DApp Statistics, 21-May-2019. [Online]. [Accessed: 21-May-2019].

U. Schwardmann et al. (Eds.): Euro-Par 2019 Workshops, LNCS 11997, pp. 179–190, 2020.
https://doi.org/10.1007/978-3-030-48340-1_14

the Ethereum platform. The high requirements and insufficient achieving ratio of DApps motivate us to further investigate the performances of Ethereum. The experimental results and learnt insights presented in this paper aims to guide DApp developers to better design their products.

In literatures, a few works evaluated the performances of Ethereum through private-nets. Specifically, Aldweesh et al. [7] tested the private chain using both Parity and Geth clients; Pongnumkul et al. [8] evaluated Hyperledger Fabric and Ethereum also through private-nets. Although existing works studied the performance of Ethereum using theoretical analysis without real-world generalizable experiments, to the best of the authors' knowledge, no works have tested the performance of Ethereum while considering practical use cases and constraints. To close this gap, we select Ethereum test-nets for comparative evaluations for the following reasons:

- Some test-nets, e.g. Ropsten, acts like main-nets, which use the same consensus scheme (Proof-of-Work, PoW).
- Kovan and Rinkeby use Proof of Authority (PoA) [9] consensus schemes, which are a potential direction of Ethereum evolutions.

In this paper, three test-nets (Ropsten, Kovan and Rinkeby) with popular consensus schemes are selected for evaluations. the experiments are designed, to measure:

- Account balance query latency: The access delay is obtained by inquiring account balances multiple times, which is the time interval between the point that an inquiry is sent out and the point that balance is received.
- Block generation time: The transaction confirmation speed through measuring the time duration of generation a block. To avoid rolling back of Ethereum Blockchain states, we continuously measure the time durations of generating 12 consecutive blocks.
- End-to-end transaction acceptance latency: Four levels of transactions (TXs) loads are considered: 1 single TX; 25 concurrent TXs; 50 concurrent TXs; 100 concurrent TXs.

The structure of the paper is as follows. Section 2 illustrates the related works about Ethereum. Evaluation methodology is developed and shown in Sect. 3. We present the experimental results in Sect. 4. Finally, Sect. 6 concludes this paper.

2   Related Work

2.1   Ethereum Overview

Ethereum [10] borrows heavily from the Bitcoin protocol and its Blockchain design, but tweaks it to support applications beyond money, in which Ethereum improves the concept of scripting and online meta-protocols.

From the perspective of ledgering transactions, different from the inefficient Unspent Transaction Output (UTXO) scheme [1] used in Bitcoin for estimating account balances, accounts are introduced in Ethereum, which formulate the states of the whole network. In addition, the state transitions are defined as the value transfers or data records between accounts (including smart contract).

The signed data package that stores a message to be sent from an account is defined as a transaction which contains the recipient, the sender's signature, the number of tokens and the data to send. In addition, Ethereum introduces gas which is to pay miners who execute transactions and smart contracts inside.

Both Ethereum and Bitcoin store the entire transaction histories in their respective networks. The difference is that Ethereum embeds smart contracts in the transactions in which contracts enable Turing-complete programming to support feature rich applications. These transactions are grouped 'block', every block being chained together with its previous blocks. But before the transaction can be added to the ledger, it needs to validate through a consensus algorithm, e.g. PoW or PoA.

In theory, the block gas limits in Ethereum is usually set to 7,999,992, where each transaction will cost 21,000 gas without smart contracts. This means Ethereum can store and execute around 380 pure transactions using each block. Because the block generation is around 14.37 s[2], this gives the transaction speed 25.346 TX/s approximately.

2.2 Ethereum Test Network (Test-Net)

Test networks [12] facilitates individual developers and companies to test their business logic by deploying smart contracts before delivering their products to the Ethereum main-net. The test-nets provides the exact same service without needs of exchanging monetary tokens. We'll be covering the most popular 3 test-nets, they are:

- Ropsten: The test-net in Ropsten, its Ether is mined following the same scheme as the main-net. Ropsten resemble the current main-net the most due to its PoW consensus algorithm which is the same to the real main-net.
- Kovan: Different from the main-net, Kovan supports the Parity[3] client only and uses PoA as the consensus algorithm. Thus, Kovan cannot be considered a very accurate simulation to the current main-net. Despite this, it is immune to spam attacks, reliable and stable, so it is convenient or public testing.
- Rinkeby: Rinkeby shares the advantages of Kovan, supporting the Geth[4] client only.

2.3 Distributed Consensus

PoW (Proof of Work) and PoA (Proof of Authority) are the main consensus algorithms using in Ethereum and test-nets. The details of PoW and PoA are listed below:

- **PoW:** In Bitcoin and Ethereum, PoW is employed to confirm transactions in the world and to prevent cyber-attacks on the network. The principle of PoW is to allocate the accounting rights and monetary rewards according to the computation

---

[2] Ethereum Network Status, Available: https://ethstats.net/. [Accessed: 24-May-2019]. Ethereum Network Status, Available: https://ethstats.net/. [Accessed: 24-May-2019].

[3] Blockchain Infrastructure for the Decentralised Web, Available: https://www.parity.io/.

[4] Go Ethereum, Available: https://geth.ethereum.org/.

power that is contributed by each node [14]. The workload as the safeguard in PoW. The new block will be connected to the previous block. If someone wants to tamper with the Blockchain that will difficult, all of nodes trust the longest chain and the cost can be less than gains from tampering. The PoW can protect the safety of the Blockchain.

- **PoA:** PoA consensus can be viewed an efficient deviation of Proof of Stake (PoS) where known validators will confirm transactions. It also includes a governance-based penalty system to punish malicious behavers. In practice, PoA can provide faster transaction rates than PoW without mining processes.

2.4   Existing Works of Performance Evaluation on Ethereum

According to the authors' study, only two paper experimentally evaluate the performance of Ethereum. Specifically, Aldweesh et al. [7] deploys private chains using both Parity and Geth clients with different consensus algorithms. The result demonstrates that Parity can handle concurrent transactions significantly better than Geth. Different from our work, Rouhani's work focuses on the intrinsic performance of Ethereum but does not study Ethereum which operates in the wild, i.e. with time-varying transaction burdens and numbers of users. In other words, its results cannot reflect the performance of the main-net. Pongnumkul et al. [8] comparatively evaluated Hyperledger Fabric and Ethereum by building private-nets, the experimental results indicate that Ethereum cannot achieve both higher throughput and lower latency but is able to handle more number of concurrent transactions. The paper lacks a discussion on why the performance of Ethereum is more unstable, and the test results captured from private-nets cannot reflect the performance of the main-net. Xu et al. [6] proposed a taxonomy method to compare blockchains and blockchain-based systems thus assisting the design and assessment of their impact on software architectures. Macdonald et al. [13] discussed how the blockchain can be used outside of Bitcoin, then presented a comparison of five general-purpose blockchain platforms which include Ethereum, IBM Open Blockchain, Intel Sawtooth Lake, BlockStream Sidechain Elements, Eris. Recently, Maple et al. [11] introduced a format for outlining a generic blockchain anatomy which ranges from permissions to consensus and can be referenced when assessing blockchain solutions architecture, to assist in the design and implementation of business logic.

In this paper, to capture the performance of Ethereum from a more reliable and generalisable manner, we select the test-nets that are popular and have strong links to the main-net. This experimental results targets to better understand Ethereum constraints and give advices on DApp development.

3   Evaluation Methodology

This section will discuss and present experimental design and testing results that are used for evaluating Ethereum through Ethereum test-nets (Ropsten, Kovan and Rinkeby). The performance of each test-net is evaluated through three aspects: 1) Account balance query latency 2) Block generation time and 3) End-to-end transaction acceptance latency. Each test is repeated 10 times to guarantee reliability.

Steps for Evaluating Transaction Acceptance Latency:

1 *User Operation:* A set of N (1, 25, 50 and 100) signed transactions, i.e. **TX** = {TX_0, TX_1, TX_2,... TX_{N-1}}, are created.

2 *User Operation:* The user node sends the created transactions to an Ethereum network and captures the current time point t.

3 *Ethereum Internal Process:* The Ethereum's P2P network distributes the transactions to miners. The mining process (e.g. PoW or PoA consensus algorithms) will confirm the valid transactions and broadcast them to all the nodes in Ethereum.

4 *User Operation:* The user node will continuously query the confirmation of each transaction through *Etherscan API* until all transactions in **TX** are confirmed. This is because Ethereum never returns the status of any transaction without queries.

5 *User Operation:* When a transaction $TX_n \in$ **TX** is confirmed, the user node captures the current time T_n then calculate and records the transaction time of TX_n, $\Delta t_n = T_n - t_n$.

6 *User Operation:* If no transactions are confirmed, *GOTO* Step 4.

Steps for Evaluating Ethereum Block Generation Time:

1 *User Operation:* The user node sends a query to check the block number N (i.e. the total number of confirmed blocks at the initial time) of the Ethereum network then record it with the current time point t_N.

2 *User Operation:* The user node continuously queries the block number n of the current time point t_n until the block number is increased by 12.

3 *User Operation:* If the change of block number is detected, e.g. $n = N + 1$, the user node calculates and records the time interval between generating two adjacent blocks, i.e. $\Delta t_n = t_n - t_N$. Then, it updates N using n and t_N using t_n, i.e. the block generation time is measured for each block.

4 *User Operation:* If no changes are detected, *GOTO* Step 2.

Steps for Evaluating Account Balance Query Latency:

1 *User Operation:* The user node sends a query to get the balance for its account and captures the current time point t.

2 *User Operation:* When the queried balance is received, the user node captures the current time point T, and then calculates and records the time interval $\Delta t = T - t$.

3 *User Operation:* The process is repeated 10 times to perform balance queries.

4 Experimental Results and Analysis

The experimental results first present the Blockchain's block generation time and transaction acceptance latency for each test-net separately. Then, the last sub-section will demonstrate the Blockchain's query latencies for the three test-nets.

Ropsten

Figure 1 shows that the time to produce blocks varies significantly (from 8.25 to 19.16 s for 12 blocks, and between 2 and 53 s per block) Fig. 2, 3, 4 and 5 present the transaction acceptance speeds with different loads (1, 25, 50 & 100 concurrent transactions), which show that the transaction time is between 21 and 418 s for 1 transaction, between 52 and 750 s for 25 transactions, between 31 and 463 s for 50 transactions, and between 4.79 and 186 s for 100 transactions.

In PoW, the averaged time interval between generating two hash values is predefined (15 s). However, due to the randomness of hitting a hash that meets the condition (to generate a block), the real time intervals between generating two blocks can be very different. The randomness of block generation speed potentially leads to longer transaction queues even when Blockchain is not congested [15]. This may be the culprit of fluctuations in transaction acceptance rates (Fig. 2, 3, 4 and 5). Furthermore, transaction acceptance rates depend on the transaction generation speed of the network and miners' policy for including a transaction in a block.

Kovan

Figure 6 shows that the total times for generating 12 blocks are similar (about 143 s), however, there is a large variation for each block (from 2 to 20 s, in Fig. 6 (a)). Figure 7, 8, 9 and 10 show the transaction acceptance latencies for different concurrent transactions (1, 25, 50, & 100). The transaction acceptance time is between 12 and 34 s for 1 transaction, between 5 and 29 s for 25 concurrent transactions, between 6.8 and 30 s for 50 concurrent transactions, and between 6.22 and 19.33 s for 100 concurrent transactions.

Figure 6 displays that the time of block generation is more stable than Ropsten. Kovan employs an authority round PoA algorithm (Aura) [9] instead of PoW. PoA is much more stable in block generation because the authority to generate a block is assigned to a node with more stable time intervals. The end-to-end transaction acceptance time is also more stable than that of Ropsten as shown in Fig. 7, 8, 9 and 10.

Rinkeby

Figure 11 displays that the time to produce 12 blocks is relatively stable (around 180 s for total 12 blocks, 13–16 s per block). Figure 12, 13, 14 and 15 show the transaction acceptance latencies for different transaction concurrencies (1, 25, 50, & 100). The time to accept the transactions is between 6 and 31 s for 1 transaction, between 11 s and 27 s for 25 concurrent transactions, and between 13.88 and 50 s for 50 transactions, and between 2.55 and 18 s for 100 transactions.

Like Kovan, Rinkeby uses PoA instead of PoW to prevent wasting of computational resources, which leads to stable transaction time. Notably, the consensus scheme used by Rinkeby is Clique PoA. According to Fig. 11 Rinkeby show better stabilities than Kovan which is using Aura PoA. However, it is observed that the time interval configuration of block generation is set to 15 s. This results the end-to-end transaction time, as shown Fig. 12, 13, 14 and 15, to be longer than those in Kovan.

EXP#	1	2	3	4	5	6	7	8	9	10
B#1	9	7	34	4	2	6	2	2	6	7
B#2	24	2	15	12	31	13	23	34	19	9
B#3	4	19	6	6	10	16	20	15	5	17
B#4	11	9	12	3	18	24	37	31	10	10
B#5	3	3	22	4	9	9	24	3	2	27
B#6	4	53	2	5	3	7	3	3	4	18
B#7	27	2	4	25	24	17	16	12	2	7
B#8	12	27	31	25	3	4	21	10	16	30
B#9	4	4	18	16	37	21	6	4	3	19
B#10	22	8	2	3	4	24	3	8	16	3
B#11	5	4	25	4	6	13	7	14	2	45
B#12	22	18	10	9	18	4	30	43	14	38

(a) **EXP**: Experiments; **B**: Block

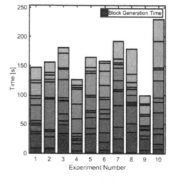

(b) Bar Plot

Fig. 1. Time of generating 12 blocks in Ropsten

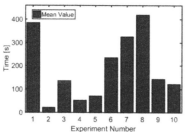

Fig. 2. Time of 1 transaction in Ropsten

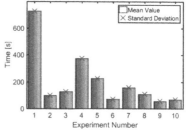

Fig. 3. Time of 25 concurrent transactions in Ropsten

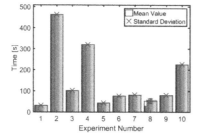

Fig. 4. Time of 50 concurrent transactions in Ropsten

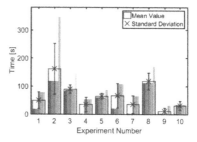

Fig. 5. Time of 100 concurrent transactions in Ropsten

186 L. Zhang et al.

EXP#	1	2	3	4	5	6	7	8	9	10
B#1	16	19	16	19	15	15	16	16	15	16
B#2	3	14	2	2	15	6	3	3	4	2
B#3	16	3	16	15	3	16	19	15	14	20
B#4	18	16	17	16	19	15	15	12	19	14
B#5	4	16	4	6	15	3	4	14	3	4
B#6	14	2	15	15	3	19	15	15	15	15
B#7	16	26	16	15	16	14	14	15	16	18
B#8	6	16	6	6	16	4	7	7	6	4
B#9	15	5	15	16	6	5	6	15	16	15
B#10	16	16	15	16	16	16	14	16	15	15
B#11	3	16	4	2	14	6	4	2	2	6
B#12	19	2	15	19	7	16	19	18	20	16

(a) **EXP**: Experiments; **B**: Block

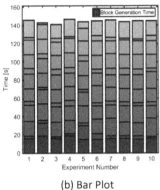

(b) Bar Plot

Fig. 6. Time of generating 12 blocks in Kovan

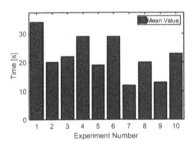

Fig. 7. Time of 1 transaction in Kovan

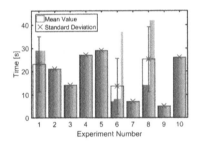

Fig. 8. Time of 25 concurrent transactions in Kovan

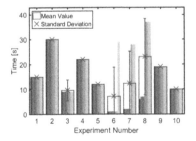

Fig. 9. Time of 50 concurrent transactions in Kovan

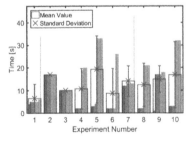

Fig. 10. Time of 100 concurrent transactions in Kovan

EXP#	1	2	3	4	5	6	7	8	9	10
B#1	15	16	15	15	16	16	15	15	16	13
B#2	16	12	16	16	16	15	16	15	15	14
B#3	14	15	14	15	15	12	15	13	15	15
B#4	16	16	16	15	14	16	15	15	15	16
B#5	15	15	15	16	16	14	16	15	16	16
B#6	15	14	15	15	16	15	15	16	12	15
B#7	15	16	16	16	14	16	12	15	15	14
B#8	15	15	16	12	16	15	16	15	16	16
B#9	16	16	14	16	15	15	14	16	15	15
B#10	15	16	13	14	16	16	16	14	16	16
B#11	14	14	15	15	14	15	15	16	14	14
B#12	16	15	16	16	13	16	16	15	15	16

(a) **EXP**: Experiments; **B**: Block

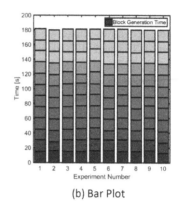

(b) Bar Plot

Fig. 11. Time of generating 12 blocks in Rinkeby

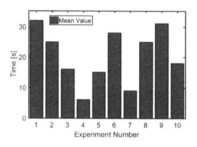

Fig. 12. Time of 1 transaction in Rinkeby

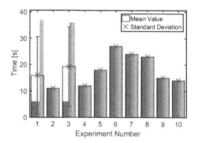

Fig. 13. Time of 25 concurrent transactions in Rinkeby

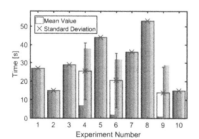

Fig. 14. Time of 50 concurrent transactions in Rinkeby

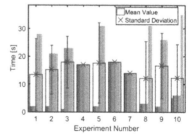

Fig. 15. Time of 100 concurrent transactions in Rinkeby

Balance Query Latency

Figure 16, 17 and 18 show the test results about the time of account balance query in Ropsten, Kovan & Rinkeby. The figures show that the time to check the balance is between 0.173 and 0.375 s in Ropsten, between 0.215 and 0.225 s in Kovan, and between 0.177 and 0.259 s in Rinkeby. The results show that the balance query latencies in all the test-nets are in the same order of magnitude with Kovan showing the least variations and Ropsten showing the largest variations.

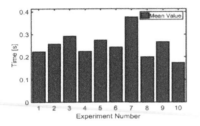

Fig. 16. Time of account balance query in Ropsten

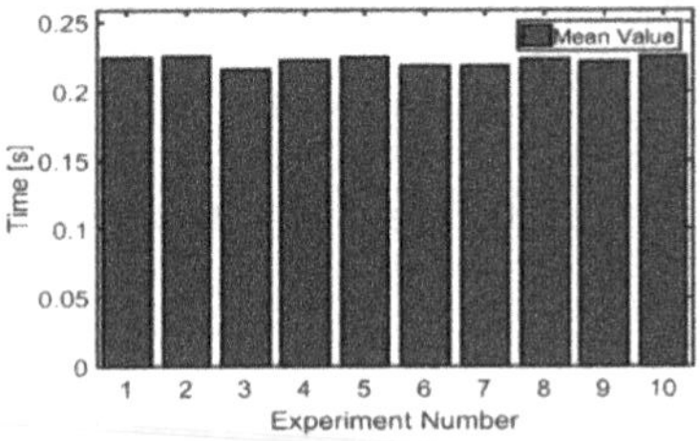

Fig. 17. Time of account balance query in Kovan

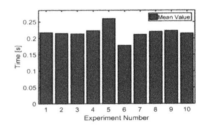

Fig. 18. Time of account balance query in Rinkeby

5   Discussion

The experimental results will quantize the impacts of consensus schemes on transaction performances such as throughputs and latencies. In consequence, we summaries the certainty and randomness of the Ethereum Blockchain. For PoW (Ropsten), although the average block generation time is around 15 s with high variances, the time duration from submitting a transaction to confirming it by miners can be more than 400 s, i.e. it is longer than generating 10 new blocks. For PoA (Kovan and Rinkeby), the stability of block generation time is dramatically improved, however the time cost of confirming a single transaction can be larger than the time of generating 3 new blocks (>45 s). As we can seem, for the experiments of 100 concurrent transactions for all the three test-net, the end-to-end latencies are slightly lower than the others. The reason is considered as the proportion of 100 transactions over the total transactions is higher than that of 1, 25, 50 transactions over the total transactions, thus it brings a higher probability to record more transactions in the most recent block and less in upcoming blocks, which reduces averaged latencies. However, the reduced latencies are trivial, which have little impacts on total latencies.

In short, the results demonstrate that the current Ethereum approaches with PoA and PoW consensus schemes suffer from long transaction time and instability issues. In other words, the existing on-chain consensus scheme can hardly support the applications (DApps) with frequent data submission requirements and low-latency constraints.

6   Conclusion and Future Work

In this paper, we present the performance evaluation results of Ethereum from different perspectives through three sets of experiments for Ropsten, Kovan and Rinkeby. The results show that the account balance query time is quite low and stable, which means that the time to access the latest Blockchain status and data is not the bottleneck. Nevertheless, for Ropsten, the transaction latencies fluctuate significantly in different experimental groups (with different transaction loads). This pattern also happens to the block generation time of Ropsten, i.e. the time to generate a new block is unstable. Note that Ropsten employs the same operating scheme (e.g. the PoW consensus algorithm) as Ethereum, which can be considered as the best approximation to the Ethereum main-net. In other words, the instability of Ropsten reflects the volatile performance of the current Ethereum.

As a conclusion, we consider that the current Ethereum approach is not powerful enough to support the applications (i.e. DApps) with low-latency constrains and high-frequency transaction submission requirements. For example, online games which requires a timely consensus on consistency among players cannot be supported by existing Ethereum approaches due to the inherent large time intervals (>10 s) of block generations. In the future work, we are going to investigate how off-chain transactions can tackle this problem, aiming at reducing transaction latencies and better supporting high-frequency transaction submission.

In future works, we plan to evaluate the performance of Ethereum for online game applications using real game datasets, especially focusing on consistency. In addition, we will extend the proposed experiments to the Ethereum main-net to capture more comprehensive results.

Acknowledgements. This paper has received financial support from the European Union Horizon 2020 research and innovation programme under grant agreement No. 700071 for the PROTECTIVE project and from Science Foundation Ireland (SFI) under Grant Number SFI 16/RC/3918, co-funded by the European Regional Development Fund.

References

1. Nakamoto, S.: Bitcoin: a peer-to-peer electronic cash system (2008)
2. Zhu, Y., Dickinson, D., Li, J.: Analysis on the influence factors of Bitcoin's price based on VEC model. Financ. Innov. **3**, 3 (2017)

3. Wood, G.: Ethereum: a secure decentralised generalised transaction ledger. Ethereum Proj. Yellow Pap. **151**, 1–32 (2014)
4. Scherer, M.: Performance and scalability of blockchain networks and smart contracts (2017)
5. Raval, S.: Decentralized Applications: Harnessing Bitcoin's Blockchain Technology. O'Reilly Media Inc, Sebastopol (2016)
6. Xu, X., et al.: A taxonomy of blockchain-based systems for architecture design. In: 2017 IEEE International Conference on Software Architecture (ICSA), pp. 243–252. IEEE (2017)
7. Aldweesh, A., Alharby, M., van Moorsel, A.: Performance benchmarking for Ethereum opcodes. In: 2018 IEEE/ACS 15th International Conference on Computer Systems and Applications (AICCSA), pp. 1–2. IEEE (2018)
8. Pongnumkul, S., Siripanpornchana, C., Thajchayapong, S.: Performance analysis of private blockchain platforms in varying workloads. In: 2017 26th International Conference on Computer Communication and Networks (ICCCN), pp. 1–6. IEEE (2017)
9. De Angelis, S., Aniello, L., Baldoni, R., Lombardi, F., Margheri, A., Sassone, V.: PBFT vs proof-of-authority: applying the CAP theorem to permissioned blockchain (2018)
10. Buterin, V.: A next-generation smart contract and decentralized application platform. White Pap. (2014)
11. Maple, C., Jackson, J.: Selecting effective blockchain solutions. In: Mencagli, G., Heras, D. B., et al. (eds.) Euro-Par 2018. LNCS, vol. 11339, pp. 392–403. Springer, Cham (2019). https://doi.org/10.1007/978-3-030-10549-5_31
12. Hu, Y.-C., Lee, T.-T., Chatzopoulos, D., Hui, P.: Hierarchical interactions between Ethereum smart contracts across testnets. In: Proceedings of the 1st Workshop on Cryptocurrencies and Blockchains for Distributed Systems, pp. 7–12. ACM (2018)
13. Macdonald, M., Liu-Thorrold, L., Julien, R.: The blockchain: a comparison of platforms and their uses beyond bitcoin. COMS4507-Adv Comput. Netw. Secur. (2017)
14. Mingxiao, D., Xiaofeng, M., Zhe, Z., Xiangwei, W., Qijun, C.: A review on consensus algorithm of blockchain. In: 2017 IEEE International Conference on Systems, Man, and Cybernetics (SMC), pp. 2567–2572. IEEE (2017)
15. Keshav, S.: Mathematical Foundations of Computer Networking. Addison-Wesley, Upper Saddle River (2012)

Blockchain-Based Trusted Cross-organizational Deliveries of Sensor-Equipped Parcels

Marcel Müller[(✉)] and Sandro Rodriguez Garzon

Server-centric Networking, Technische Universität Berlin, Berlin, Germany
{marcel.mueller,sandro.rodriguezgarzon}@tu-berlin.de
http://www.snet.tu-berlin.de

Abstract. Today's cross-organizational deliveries of high value and perishable goods are difficult to monitor in a reliable and trustful way. Every logistics organization operates its own track and trace system, usually in an isolated manner and with most being incompatible to each other. In order to provide better end-to-end insights and to speed-up conflict management processes, we propose to let all involved parties mutually confirm cross-organizational handovers of a parcel and to log the event immutably within a common distributed ledger. Smart sensors within or attached to parcels will in addition act as independent oracles to monitor environmental variables with respect to parcel-specific service level agreements. Violations of service level agreements will be trustfully detected and logged by the smart sensors directly on the distributed ledger, without potentially compromising legacy systems being involved. The proposed concept will serve as the base for future implementations and opens up new ways to analyze and optimize inter-organizational logistics.

Keywords: Distributed ledger · Blockchain · Supply chain · Peer-to-Peer logistics

1 Introduction

The delivery of a parcel across organizations or even beyond country borders requires a tight collaboration of multiple independent logistics organizations with commonly-coordinated business processes. Despite the existence of international standards with respect to the exchange of information related to cross-border parcel traffic, the tracking and tracing of parcels beyond organizations and country borders still remains an open issue. The risk of lost or significantly delayed parcels might be acceptable for goods of low value, but it poses a major hurdle for the transport of perishable high value goods such as medical products. To achieve a high customer intimacy, a trustable unified end-to-end tracking and tracing system is needed across organizations and beyond country borders as a first step towards improved coordinated cross-organizational business processes. This would make it possible to analyze the event log of cross-organizational deliveries in order to

© Springer Nature Switzerland AG 2020
U. Schwardmann et al. (Eds.): Euro-Par 2019 Workshops, LNCS 11997, pp. 191–202, 2020.
https://doi.org/10.1007/978-3-030-48340-1_15

optimize business process flows and to reduce costs. The need of such a system is underlined by the fact that globalization, visibility, customer intimacy, risk and cost containment pose the five key challenges most international supply chains face today [1]. Currently, most of these challenges are addressed by each participant in a logistics chain focusing on their own aims, independently of the others. Since subgranted partners and their subprocesses are hidden to a certain extent to the contradicting organizations, legal disputes due to damaged or lost parcels are difficult to resolve. But in case of incidents, logistics organizations need to justify and prove to their customers, who was responsible for what subprocess at what point in time. This is a complex and time-consuming task, since the single steps of a logistics chain are not visible from the outside and information is usually kept in silos. Data can even be tampered by one organization within the logistics chain in order to push responsibility to another.

Since the concept of a blockchain, as a specific distributed ledger technology, provides possibilities to share data in trusted and immutable way across organizations, logistics organizations started to leverage the advantages of this technology to improve cross-organizational business processes. While the first implementation of a blockchain provided possibilities to store data in a public, trusted and immutable way, newer developments opened up opportunities for new application scenarios. Especially for emerging smart contract platforms, where Turing-complete code can be executed, logistics is among the most attractive business applications. Further, the addition of sensor monitoring with Internet of Things devices provides a valuable benefit in measuring the environmental conditions under which freight is exposed to in real time. This makes it exactly traceable and comprehensible which damage was caused by which environmental condition or incident.

We propose a concept to support the operation of cross-organizational deliveries of sensor-equipped parcels with a domain-specific blockchain platform in order to provide a traceable and tamper-proof log of process steps and responsibilities. Within the proposed approach, smart sensors act as independent oracles, verifying previously defined service level agreements (SLAs) and logging their violation to the blockchain. Also tracking ownership and changes to it in a tamper-proof way is realized using the blockchain. The remainder of the paper is structured like the following: In Sect. 2, different approaches to supply chain management with sensors and logging with distributed ledgers, which have seen implementation in the past, are analyzed. In Sect. 3, our concept to execute trusted cross-organizational deliveries of sensor-equipped parcels backed by the blockchain technology, is presented and discussed with respect to privacy, organizational and transparency aspects in Sect. 4. Concluding remarks and an outlook are given in Sect. 5.

2   Related Work

The blockchain and other distributed ledger technologies are being used as a tool to maintain consensus on the state of a particular piece of information shared among a set of peers within a network. Such approaches have seen rapid evolution in recent years. Bitcoin [3] implemented a blockchain in the domain of digital money, addressing the core challenges of networks, where peers can potentially exhibit Byzantine behavior [4] to provide a way to securely exchange cryptocurrency in a decentralized manner. Platforms such as Ethereum [6], enabling users to deploy and execute arbitrary pieces of Turing-complete programming logic in a decentralized way, called Smart Contracts [5], have seen increasing adoption in different application domains. Permissioned blockchain approaches such as Hyperledger Fabric [8] provide different concepts to mitigate privacy and governance issues, caused by the openness of permissionless platforms. This makes them attractive to a new segment of business use cases.

A prime use case, which can largely benefit from the inherent properties a blockchain provides such as immutability, integrity, transparency, decentralization and accessibility, is *supply chain management* [9]. Within that context *logistics* is a subdomain of any supply chain dealing with the transport of physical goods. For such supply chains with logistics processes a permissioned blockchain enables data to be stored in a trusted and traceable way, while still maintaining privacy. This data can also serve as a base to optimize cross-organizational business processes on a large scale involved in supply chains. Past work has focused on modeling digital strategies for a blockchain based approach towards supply chain management [10], business process modeling [7] and its technical translation into smart contracts [15] in general. Thus, the blockchain can also be seen as an approach towards data integration [16], used as a many-to-many interface between different parties and different systems [17].

From an application point of view, concepts for e-commerce involving distributed ledger technologies in decentralized autonomous companies have been proposed [11]. Work in the domain of supply chain management using distributed ledger technologies have been proposed to model different roles throughout the whole supply chain process [18], to trace compound products back to their sources, employing token recipes to model manufacturing processes [19] as a next step to enhance general traceability and transparency in supply chains [17,20]. Focusing on the logistics part of supply chain management, previous work has been conducted, utilizing the linkage-mechanism provided by a blockchain in order to track ownership and responsibilities in an anti-counterfeiting way for high value goods, through the use of the RFID technology [12]. Such a trusted linkage, backed by sensors in the Internet of Things, can be a tremendous benefit for any high value item such as medicine [2] or for the post delivery chain in general [12].

Smart IoT devices can act as oracles in blockchain networks. An Oracle serves as the sources of information, which is present off-chain, but needs to be available on-chain in order to execute certain business processes. In many other application domains, the Internet of Things has been applied to act as such an interface towards the real-world, for instance in health care, communications and 5G, the automotive industry as well as in the energy domain [22]. In the supply chain domain empirical studies show that employees, working in the field see the biggest potential for a blockchain in operating the Internet of Things, easing paperwork, the identification of counterfeit products as well as origin tracking [2]. A general framework for the realization of supply chain quality management on the blockchain has been proposed in [13]. IBM started a pilot study on tracking a supply chain use case focusing on tracing the way of mangoes and pork from producer the to the consumer [21] using a blockchain. For monitoring of the items' current states, sensors within different transportation vehicles and warehouses have been utilized. As a different solution to the monitoring problem, the study of Gallay et al. [14] have utilized "talking containers" equipped with IoT sensors and a blockchain to log the results of the observation process. Both approaches provide ways to monitor freight throughout the majority of its journey, but leave gaps in the monitoring process. For example when the physical goods are brought out of the containers or when they are generally not in an tracked environment, fraudulent behavior could remain unnoticed.

This work goes a step further and proposes a concept where the sensors are directly attached to the smallest packaging of physical products, by putting them directly into the same primary package. It also presents a conceptual business process to track handovers between logistics organizations in an immutable way as well as a concept to operate smart IoT devices autonomously in order to monitor violations of independently registered SLAs. In the proposed approach, the placement of autonomously operated smart IoT sensors within parcels leads to a different governance and minimizes needed trust far beyond the capabilities of existing work. The blockchain acts hereby as a software connector between existing systems rather than as a replacement of traditional business structures by decentralized autonomous companies. Its utilization ensures data integrity between logistics companies regarding ownership and responsibility and, in addition, between end-customer and logistics company with respect to the adherence to predefined SLAs. This addresses end-customer intimacy and delivery transparency challenges of the logistics domain today.

3   Concept

We propose a blockchain-based cross-organizational delivery process where smart sensors are acting as independent oracles verifying service level agreements (SLAs) and their violations in a trusted way. Therefore, the blockchain tracks ownership changes, as emitted by handover events in the real world in an immutable manner. Mutual dependencies and smart contracts, enforcing logical process flows, prevent fraudulent behavior. The smart sensors are acting as independent but trusted oracles within the network. Through their time of use in the delivery process these smart sensors are monitoring violations of previously registered SLAs to the current state and log exceptions autonomously on the distributed ledger and reside in the same physical package as the goods.

3.1   Tamper-Proof Event Logging

A distributed ledger in the logistics domain can be utilized to track information such as ownership as well as violations of SLAs, in order to maintain data integrity and immutability of information in a network of different parties with different interests.

As a base for any execution of an inter-organizational business process, all involved parties need to agree on a certain state of particular pieces of information. In our context, the most important information regards the ownership of a parcel as well as the condition of a parcel and possible violations of SLAs. To store this information in a trusted way, we utilize a blockchain as a distributed linearly ordered event log. Hence, we interpret every parcel as a non-fungible asset, with properties for ownership, a list of delivery agreements, a list of agreement validations and a list of attached sensors creating persisting link between a parcel and a sensor. For modeling the blockchain we use an abstraction, which can be implemented in most real world blockchains with smart contract support. Essentially our abstraction consists of *assets*, which have a certain *state* at any given point in time and *transactions* executed by authorized *participants*, modifying properties of assets, hence transitioning to a new state. While this abstraction can be implemented in most smart contract platforms, the used terminology is aligned to Hyperledger Fabric's Composer modelling.

In the cross-organizational parcel delivery process, needed transactions are the registration of a new parcel `registerParcel`, which includes linking of smart sensors and SLAs. This enforces that later nobody can manipulate SLA status checks by adding a dummy smart sensor and neglecting the intended smart sensor. The `handoverFrom` and `handoverTo` transactions are utilized to track handover attempt and acknowledgment between different parties in the business network. Therefore, the ownership transfer can only be executed and persisted in the current state of the ledger when both the sender and the receiver during a particular handover acknowledge the handover event, preventing situation where a parcel is without an owner at any time. The logging of SLA violations is realized with the `logViolation` transaction. In the end it is needed to delete the parcel with a `deregisterParcel` transaction from the current state of the ledger after the deliver process has been finished.

For this concept we are assuming technical implementation with a permissioned solution with different *peers* and *clients*, where a peer's purpose is to validate transactions submitted by clients, as utilized with a BFT protocol in the implementation of Hyperledger Fabric. The validations include replaying the execution of the programming logic of the five transactions, encoded in smart contracts as well as ordering transactions linearly, so that consensus over the current global state can be reached. From a governance point of view, new validators are elected by the supervisory board of the network. There all logistic organizations are represented and each of them is maintaining at least one validator node, to ensure trust. Smart Sensors act as clients, submitting transactions. To ensure trust not only between logistics organizations, but also between consumers (sender/receivers) and the logistic organizations, these also have the possibility to become validators. It is envisioned that the supervisory board of logistics organizations also elects fully independent nodes outside the business processes to run validations and have the possibility to grant the rights to become validators also to major customers, with a large volume of transactions, to establish more trust in the smart contracts and the blockchain.

3.2   Smart Sensors as Autonomous Oracles

In order to make parcel condition monitoring more private, secure and trustful, we introduce smart sensors. These are packed into the parcel in the beginning of the delivery process to monitor the parcel conditions and log violations of previously defined SLAs autonomously to the blockchain, hence acting as trusted oracles. The packing of sensors *in* the packages rather than having sensors connecting to them dynamically, addresses problems in current solutions with gaps in the monitoring process.

Verifying the conditions of items within a parcel during a handover has two main issues: privacy and trust. If a shipper wants check if an item inside a parcel is not damaged, without the invocation of any sensor, it is necessary to open the parcel, assess the condition of the objects inside and close it again. This exposes all objects to the eyes of the post man, hence violating any privacy agreements. But this execution is also prone to manipulation, since the validation is done by "eyeballing". For a more private and less manipulable approach we equip every parcel with at least one smart sensor, which will stay there throughout the whole delivery process. We define a smart sensor as an IoT device, which can measure at least one value (e.g. temperature), store SLAs to measurable values, monitor the current values and log potential SLA violations to the blockchain using a light weight client. Therefore, the sensor also needs to be provided with some connectivity for example through cellular capabilities, narrow-band IoT connections or LTE.

In the beginning the sender is responsible for packing at least one smart sensor into the parcel and define SLAs to the sensor. The sensor checks if the desired agreements are not already violated, registers the SLAs afterwards and starts monitoring. This process needs to be repeated for all smart sensors and all desired SLA supervision tasks which can be measured by the respective sensors. In that way, a parcel might have a smart sensor measuring humidity and another smart sensor measuring temperature at the same time. Once the monitoring process is started, the smart sensor logs autonomously violations to the blockchain, immediately after a violation is detected. These violations are signed with the key of the sensor, in order to ensure integrity of the logging. In that way, later retrieval of this information provides the largest amount of trust, since the possibilities for fraudulent behavior or corruption are minimized.

During the handover process from a participant A to a participant B, A first checks if no SLA, monitored by any smart sensor inside the parcel has been violated since the last check by lookups on the blockchain. Then A attempts to handover to B. Participant B then also, checks the state of SLA violations. B again uses as only source of violation information the blockchain, scanning the log for violations. Based on that participant B can decide to accept or decline the parcel. With the invocation of the **handoverTo** transaction, reflection B's acceptance of the parcel, smart contract logic gets triggered, changing the ownership state of the parcel. The smart contract is also employed to enforce that ownership changes need to be mutually agreed, so that every parcel has always exactly one owner and ownership cannot be changed in case the receiver declines.

In this proposed concept smart sensors interact with the blockchain as a trusted oracle, autonomously logging violations of SLAs. Without that, another actor would have to log violations to the chain. Sender and receiver or middle man acting as intermediate senders and receivers have in certain cases incentives to log false information about the parcel condition to the blockchain. For example, in a Situation where an agent A wants to hand over a parcel to agent B, with both agents working for two different logistics organizations, A might want not log SLA violations, which occurred while being responsible for the parcel, even though they happened. Or in another case B might want to log a violation, which in fact never happened, if company B knows, that there will be a violation once B is responsible. In case B notices that the delivery truck is too hot to keep the parcel cool enough to not violate SLAs. In that situation B might want to blame A for the violation which is about to happen during B's time of responsibility. Therefore, we take these possibilities of fraud away from the biased actors to a smart sensor, operating independently.

From a governance point of view, the smart sensors are in the possession of the sender, which might have rented the device itself from an independent third party. This independent party might take care of maintenance of such devices such as (re-)charging or repairing defect devices but does not have an active role in the shipment process. Regarding trust, everyone relying on information originating from a sensor, needs to trust the autonomy of the sensor and the organization maintaining the sensors. It is beneficial to have several companies maintaining sensors, to make them as independent as possible and to incentivize them not to fake measured values. If one actor notices that a sensor is corrupted, due to bribe of the smart sensor's maintainer, the actor can refuse to participate in a process involving any sensor from a known to be corrupt maintainer. In that way maintainers are less likely to fake sensor measurements. With the established trust in the smart sensors, we are employing a blockchain to make transactions visible and traceable in case of disputes.

3.3 Conflict Resolution Based on Blockchain Logs

In a collaborative delivery chain across different companies any parcel can potentially be *lost, damaged* or *delayed*. By retrieving and examining blockchain logs, any of these situations can be analyzed and responsibility can clearly be allocated to the respective parties. In case of a lost parcel one can always trace back who is the current owner of a parcel, since the structure of our process enforces a parcel to always be in the possession of exactly one owner. Transactions can change the owner but never unset the owner through the time a parcel is registered in the current state of the ledger. The contents of a parcel can get damaged by a variety of different incidents. Smart sensors are utilized to manage these damages on a certain level, implemented by the verification of predefined SLAs. By the retrieval of violation logs from the blockchain it can be retraced in which time frame the damaging has occurred and who was the owner of the parcel at that point in time. Therefore, responsibility can be allocated for a conflict resolution process. However, the trusted detection of damage is limited to the monitoring capabilities of the used smart sensor and the borders provided within the SLAs. The fact that every transaction in a blockchain is timestamped and totally ordered, makes it traceable who in the delivery process caused the end delay to which extend. Therefore, only the handover event have to be observed in order to calculate how long a certain party in the network was responsible for time delays.

Transaction logs of the blockchain, originating from independent sensors and mutually accepted handover events can serve as an excellent base for any legally binding conflict resolution process as long as all provided entities acknowledge the blockchain as the trusted source of truth.

3.4   A Trusted Cross-organizational Delivery Process

The proposed trusted cross-organizational delivery process is in Fig. 1. A traditional BPMN 2.0 diagram is annotated with the addition of logging information, which must not be changed nor corrupted and which benefits from being open accessible to any participant in the case of disputes and sensor monitoring to validate parcel conditions. We introduce this small extension to BPMN by adding grey shaped boxes to symbolize logging to a distributed ledger.

The process starts with the sender packing the high value objects into a parcel and tagging it with information. At least one smart sensor needs to get packed into the parcel, SLAs need to get registered accordingly and the monitoring process needs to get started. The entire initialization process gets logged including the parcel id, attached smart sensors and their respective agreements with the `registerParcel` transaction to the blockchain. On the side of the smart sensor, the sensor is monitoring the registered SLAs and logs potential violations directly with the `logViolation` transaction to the blockchain. Once the first delivery agent is in the physical same location as the initial sender, the handover attempt takes place. This gets logged to the ledger with the `handoverFrom` transaction. The delivery agent then validates the state of SLAs by searching on the blockchain for logged SLA violations. Based on the validation of the SLA status the receiving delivery agent either rejects or accepts the incoming parcel. If no SLAs have been violated, the agent accepts the parcel, commits the ownership of the parcel with the `handoverTo` transaction and delivers it to the next point. There, the handover subprocess gets repeated until the parcel reached its final destination. After the last handover has been accepted and the process reached finality, the parcel gets deregistered from the blockchain with the `deregisterParcel` transaction. This process can also be executed without the inclusion of smart sensors, solely providing the trusted logging of ownership information, enforced by mutual handover acceptance.

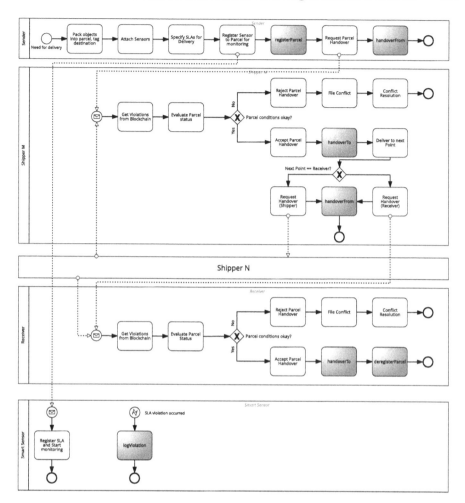

Fig. 1. The business process modeling the delivery of a high value item from a sender to a receiver using the BPMN 2.0 syntax, incorporating the proposed approach. The collapsed lane shipper N stands for an arbitrary amount of other shippers with the same business logic as shipper M, symbolizing business processes of an arbitrary amount of intermediate handovers between shippers. The gray shaded tasks stand of logging of a particular piece of information on the blockchain. A smart sensor is here monitoring parcel conditions and logging violations of registered SLAs onto the blockchain.

4   Discussion

Despite the advantages of a common cross-organizational ledger for the storage of parcel-related events, this concept carriers always the risk of revealing internal processes to a wider audience. Since in logistics, competitive organizations are obliged to collaborate according to international contracts of the Universal Post Union, it needs to be technically guaranteed that intra-organizational handovers, even if they are logged on a common distributed ledger, are not readable to a competitive organization. A distributed ledger for logistics and supply chain management must therefore provide ways to persist various kinds of events but to restrict its visibility only to those participants that in the future might get involved in a conflict in which the persisted events could potentially be used as evidence. In any case, the advantages of a higher level of transparency such as a more fine grain traceability and its related cost savings need to be traded off against the loss of the competitive advantage due to the possibility to infer internal business processes from the entries of a common distributed ledger.

So far, parcel-related incidents such as damaged goods due to shocks or temporary undercuts of minimum temperature are only detected by the recipient of a parcel. The introduction of a continuous end-to-end monitoring through the attachment of sensors to parcels enables the senders, the logistics organizations or the targeted recipients to react to critical incidents in an early stage. The end-to-end character of the proposed approach increases trust in comparison to previously proposed solutions where sensors are dynamically attached and detached and monitored by a dependent party, so gaps in the monitoring timeline could exist. In case goods are getting unusable due to critical incidents, parcels could be returned before they are forwarded to the recipient and with the proposed approach, it is evident that there existed no observation gaps in the monitoring process. Nevertheless, sensors need to be developed, reliably attached, detached, monitored and well maintained. Besides the need for new business processes for the provision, operation and redistribution of sensors, they need to be technically connected to the distributed ledger in trustworthy way because in contrast to the handover, transactions originating from the sensors are not mutually checked for correctness by two parties. For that, each smart sensor must act independently by monitoring sensor-specific SLAs and by logging each violation as an incident directly onto the ledger. Otherwise, SLA violations could be on purpose omitted by not publishing them onto the ledger by a middleman. But in practice, sensors cannot provision, maintain and redistribute themselves. At least one stakeholder, either a logistics organization or even an external independent sensor operator, owns and operates these sensors and will therefore break the chain of trust between the physical sensor readings and SLA violation entries in the ledger. The concept allows to add multiple sensors to a parcel originating from potentially different stakeholders for redundancy reasons in order to detect intentional misuse or sensor failures. Since attaching a single or multiple sensors to the parcel increases the costs of the shipment, an economically viable solution for an end-to-end monitored delivery between organizations is currently only possible for goods of high value.

5 Conclusion

This work presented an integrated concept for logistics delivery chains to make use of smart sensors to sense and distributed ledger technology to persist and share state-related information of parcels in a tamper-proof way. State changes of a parcel representation within the distributed ledger such as ownership change or parcel-specific SLA violations are thereby triggered by handovers as initiated by humans or by environmental incidents as detected by smart sensors. Handover-initiated state changes are mutually confirmed by at least two independent participants of the distributed ledger network while sensor-initiated state changes are caused by oracles, representing the independent sensors. Since both types of triggers do not depend on each other, it is also possible to support only one of them within a concrete implementation to immutable log either ownership changes or SLA violations. But to leverage the full power of the proposed concept, with handovers that confirm SLA violations, both types of state-changing events should be considered in a real world setup. The concept is not meant to replace legacy track and trace systems but to extend them with the functionality to enable end-to-end cross-organizational track and tracing of sensor-equipped parcels in a transparent and tamper-proof way. This opens up possibilities to provide the end-costumer a more fined-grained history of parcel-related events and the shippers the opportunity to detect weak points in the logistics chain and to resolve potential parcel-related conflicts between organizations on the basis of immutable and tamper-proof data within the common distributed ledger.

Acknowledgments. This work is partly being carried out within the GRAVITY project in collaboration with InnoTractor, Poste Italiane and Datacon, funded by the EIT Digital (European Institute of Technology) within the Innovation Focus Area Digital Industry.

References

1. Butner, K.: The smarter supply chain of the future. Strategy Leadersh. **38**, 22–31 (2010). https://doi.org/10.1108/10878571011009859
2. Hackius, N., Petersen, M.: Blockchain in logistics and supply chain: trick or treat? In: Proceedings of the Hamburg International Conference of Logistics (HICL), pp. 3–18 (2017). epubli
3. Nakamoto, S.: Bitcoin: a peer-to-peer electronic cash system (2008)
4. Lamport, L., Shostak, R., Pease, M.: The Byzantine generals problem. ACM Trans. Program. Lang. Syst. (TOPLAS) **4**(3), 382–401 (1982)
5. Szabo, N.: Smart contracts: building blocks for digital markets. EXTROPY J. Transhumanist Thought **16**, 18 (1996)
6. Wood, G.: Ethereum: a secure decentralised generalised transaction ledger. Ethereum project yellow paper **151**, 1–32 (2014)
7. Weber, I., Xu, X., Riveret, R., Governatori, G., Ponomarev, A., Mendling, J.: Untrusted business process monitoring and execution using blockchain. In: International Conference on Business Process Management, September 2016, pp. 329–347. Springer, Cham (2016). https://doi.org/10.1007/978-3-319-45348-4_19
8. Androulaki, E., et al.: Hyperledger fabric: a distributed operating system for permissioned blockchains. In: Proceedings of the Thirteenth EuroSys Conference, April 2018, p. 30. ACM (2018)
9. Mentzer, J.T., et al.: Defining supply chain management. Journal of Business logistics **22**(2), 1–25 (2001)

10. Perboli, G., Musso, S., Rosano, M.: Blockchain in logistics and supply chain: a lean approach for designing real-world use cases. IEEE Access **6**, 62018–62028 (2018)
11. Zhang, Y., Wen, J.: The IoT electric business model: using blockchain technology for the Internet of Things. Peer-to-Peer Netw. Appl. **10**(4), 983–994 (2016). https://doi.org/10.1007/s12083-016-0456-1
12. Toyoda, K., Mathiopoulos, P.T., Sasase, I., Ohtsuki, T.: A novel blockchain-based product ownership management system (POMS) for anti-counterfeits in the post supply chain. IEEE Access **5**, 17465–17477 (2017)
13. Chen, S., Shi, R., Ren, Z., Yan, J., Shi, Y., Zhang, J.: A blockchain-based supply chain quality management framework. In: 2017 IEEE 14th International Conference on e-Business Engineering (ICEBE), November 2017, pp. 172–176. IEEE (2017)
14. Gallay, O., Kari, K., Niemi, T., Nurminen, J.K.: A peer-to-peer platform for decentralized logistics. In: Proceedings of the Hamburg International Conference of Logistics (HICL), pp. 19–34 (2017). epubli
15. Lopez-Pintado, O., García-Bañuelos, L., Dumas, M., Weber, I.: Caterpillar: a Blockchain-based business process management system. In: BPM, September 2017. Demos
16. Xu, X., et al.: The blockchain as a software connector. In: 2016 13th Working IEEE/IFIP Conference on Software Architecture (WICSA), pp. 182–191. IEEE (2016)
17. Korpela, K., Hallikas, J., Dahlberg, T.: Digital supply chain transformation toward blockchain integration. In: Proceedings of the 50th Hawaii International Conference on System Sciences, January 2017
18. Abeyratne, S A., Monfared, R.P.: Blockchain ready manufacturing supply chain using distributed ledger (2016)
19. Westerkamp, M., Victor, F., Küpper, A.: Blockchain-based supply chain traceability: token recipes model manufacturing processes. arXiv preprint arXiv:1810.09843 (2018)
20. Kim, H.M., Laskowski, M.: Towards an ontology-driven Blockchain design for supply chain provenance. SSRN Electron. J. (2016)
21. Kamath, R.: Food traceability on blockchain: Walmart's pork and mango pilots with IBM. The JBBA **1**(1), 3712 (2018)
22. Ferrag, M.A., Derdour, M., Mukherjee, M., Derhab, A., Maglaras, L., Janicke, H.: Blockchain technologies for the internet of things: research issues and challenges. IEEE Internet of Things J. **6**(2), 2188–2204 (2018)

Towards a Trusted Support Platform
for the Job Placement Task

Alevtina Dubovitskaya(D), Luca Mazzola(✉)(D), and Alexander Denzler

HSLU-I, Hoschschule Luzern - Informatik,
Suurstoffi 41b, 6343 Risch-Rotkreuz, Switzerland
{alevtina.dubovitskaya,luca.mazzola,alexander.denzler}@hslu.ch

Abstract. HR tech is a new trend in the hiring process, still facing some inefficiencies and limits. This paper sketches a high level architecture of a trusted support platform for the job placement task. Our design is based on a multifaceted analysis of current practices and requirements from technical, legal, and social perspectives. Relying on the properties of intelligent data analysis approaches, blockchain technology, and distributed identity management, this solution will enable optimisation, compliance, and improvements of the candidate selection process for job openings. The outcomes of the current work will be further applied for the identification of data formats and specific technologies to be used for the implementation. Practical use-cases are currently under development with industry partners.

Keywords: HR tech · Job placement · Distributed ledger · Blockchain · Data validation · People analytics · Automatic matching · Self-sovereign identity

1 Introduction

In the today highly dynamical digital era, a curriculum vitae (CV) - written overview of someone's life's work including a complete career record, academic formation, publications, qualifications, etc. - can appear not anymore as an optimal and reliable source of information about a future employee. First, information can be falsified [4,13], and it is time-consuming, often impossible, to obtain reliable confirmation regarding the qualification of the applicant, due to, for instance, the original language of education certificate, or difficulty to reach out to a previous employer. Second, process of matching candidate's CV with the job description is performed by hiring company and can be very costly and not very efficient. One reason is limited capacities of HR personnel regarding the number of the applications they can analyse, combined with the attempts of some applicants to maximise their job opportunities by submitting many applications simultaneously. At the same time, an applicant with a perfectly matching profile may be just not aware of a job opening due to variety of the open positions currently available and the different platforms on which the openings can be listed.

© Springer Nature Switzerland AG 2020
U. Schwardmann et al. (Eds.): Euro-Par 2019 Workshops, LNCS 11997, pp. 203–215, 2020.
https://doi.org/10.1007/978-3-030-48340-1_16

Third, as, at the time being, HR tasks are usually conducted by personnel, any decision taken, especially at the selection and matching process, can be subjective and can introduce bias regarding gender, age, ethnicity, etc. Moreover, unintentional human-made mistakes can also take place. In our approach, these aspect are mainly considered for the pre-selection phase, in order to ensure a fair panel of candidates for the human task. All the above are currently affecting and making the job openings filling an ineffective and inefficient task.

This leads us to the question on how to structurally improve these inefficiencies by using approaches from distributed ledgers, from artificial intelligence and from data science. The main initial challenges identified are as follows: what other data sources can be of interest to the companies when looking for the new employees? Are there available technologies that can be used to optimise the candidates selection and matching their profile to the job description? Is it possible to remove the bias of a human decision-making, and if yes, what is the impact of such automatisation? How can a partially automated solution be integrated in the intrinsically human-based task of balancing soft and hard skills to, frequently unwritten or unsaid, job opening constraints and soft/organisational requirements?

Companies often use multiple third-party providers (e.g., Linkedin, Glassdoor) to advertise the information about open careers opportunities and attract the applicants. While being very helpful for the applicants to search for a job in specific areas, and even providing interfaces for data extraction from a CV ("Easy Apply" in Linkedin, CV upload in Glassdoor), the main benefit for the company lays in the increased visibility of an advertisement; nevertheless no proof of data-authenticity and accuracy can be provided, and even higher increase in received application load requires further matching effort and more manpower. Some partial solutions already exist in supporting the tasks of employee selection and management, e.g. people analytics, and in simplifying and promote the interaction with complex information, such as gamification. In fact, techniques used to mine consumer and industry data can help managers and executives to make decisions about their employees. By applying data science and machine learning techniques to large sets of talent data, people analytics can result in better decision-making. On the other hand, gamification approaches allowing data scientists to collect focused information, aim to build a picture of individual employees' personalities and cognitive skills [17]. However, use of such third-party service providers and people analytics, apart form bringing some functional benefits, can create serious threats from the perspective of individual's privacy. Additionally, no support for information validation and accuracy checking is provided by such solutions.

Using blockchain technology (BCT) has been recently proposed to ensure authenticity of human resource information, taking into account privacy concerns [16]. There also exist the approaches to employ blockchain technology for verifying authenticity of diplomas and certificates [4], and for setting up a global higher education credit platform [13]. Michaelides provides an interesting general discussion about how combining BCT with artificial intelligence (AI) techniques will enable more accurate approaches to hiring employees [10]. However, no specific solution or implementation of BCT-based system, that is able to address all the concerns mentioned above, has been proposed yet.

The use of BCT is here of paramount importance to enforce trust creation inside an otherwise untrusted network, composed by companies, universities, students and applicants. Even though BCT is not enough to guarantee truthfulness in the data, the trustfulness is one of its precondition. For its additional requirement, we point the reader to the paragraph about the *Oracle*, in the next Section. Building on the existing generic ideas, such as combining BCT and AI [5], current practices of HR analytics [17], and taking into account identified problems, this work envisions a blockchain-based solution for a trusted support platform for the job placement task.

We propose to employ matching algorithms over a subset of the verifiable data in the distributed settings, while preserving privacy of the applicants. In the next section, we analyse the need for efficient and trustworthy HR information management system, define its design goals, and present a potential solution sketch. Section 3 provides a short overview of the related work, whether Sect. 4 discusses the proposed architecture and considers some expected effects and some foreseeable issues by its application, from a technological, legal, and social perspectives. Finally, Sect. 5 concludes the paper by wrapping up the idea and the next steps of this work.

2   Requirements and Solution Sketch

In this section, we first formulate the problem statement and, based on them, define desirable design goals of the system. Second, we present the design of our proposed solution.

2.1   Problem Statement and Design Goals

The goal of this work is to address inefficiencies and limits in the current process of selecting and matching candidates for a job opening, from legal and economical perspectives. In particular, we focus on the following research questions (*RQ*s):

RQ-1: How to ensure trust to the data that are provided by the applicants?
RQ-2: How to optimise the process of selection of the candidates for the companies?
RQ3: How to facilitate the process of targeted dissemination of the information about the candidate, such as the skills, education, and previous work experience?
RQ-4: How to ensure candidate's privacy and the data security?
RQ-5: Is it possible to remove possible discrimination and bias of human-made decision? What would be possible consequences of such an automatisation?

In order to address the questions defined above, we formulate the properties that the system we intend to design should hold in a form of design goals (**DG**s). For each **DG**, we also specify which research question(s) the property is aiming to solve:

DG-1: Distributed architecture with direct involvement of the trustworthy data sources (**RQ-1**).

DG-2: Traceability and verifiability of the data - namely, each single atomic entry of a CV - provided by the applicants (**RQ-1, RQ-2**).

DG-3: Flexible and interoperable data-expressiveness layer for (I) the definition of the desired skills (singleton expressing expertises) on the company side and (II) the data model for management of the applicants' data (**RQ-3**).

DG-4: User-centric control over the data provided by the applicants, data privacy and security (**RQ-4**).

DG-5: Discrimination- and bias-free system that provides efficiency in selection of candidates and their matching to the corresponding job description (**RQ-2, RQ-5**).

2.2   Solution Sketch

Striving to ensure the desired properties, we propose to employ blockchain technology and artificial intelligence techniques to enhance how currently "HR tech" is approached.

Figure 1 presents the design of the proposed solution. Below, we depict each component and the step-by-step process flow. Then, we discuss possibilities (alternative approaches) for employing gamification, distributed matching algorithm and identity management, and distributed ledger technology/blockchain in our solution.

Applicant is a user that is looking for an employment. They register in the system and provide the data about themselves, which will be verified later on, and will be used to extract some structured information to be hashed and stored on the blockchain. All the entries composing the personal records are provided solely by the users; they are the only subjects entitled to create new information about themselves.

Company is another type of actor with the aim of finding/selecting employees. Additionally, the firm is also in charge of validation of the applicants data, whenever the working experience entry is related to a job position hosted by it. To build trustworthy data sources, a company can be a participant of the permissioned blockchain network (such as Hyperledger Fabric [1]), set up to provide a possibility to verify the information about the applicants, including work and education history, using the hashes generated from the structured anonymous data and stored on the blockchain. This actor also needs to provide a well suited description of the position offered, by means of a ranked and weighted set of skill. Universities and training institutions are specific types of *company*, and are also expected to provide validation of the parts of the applicant records related to education.

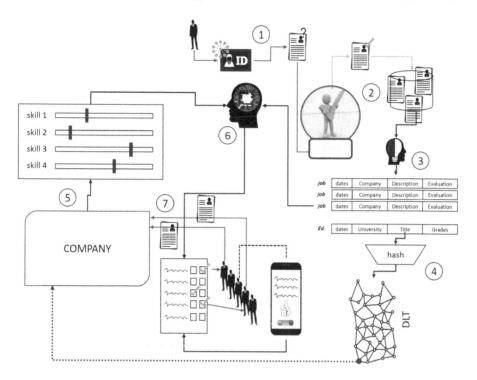

skill 1
skill 2
skill 3
skill 4

COMPANY

job	dates	Company	Description	Evaluation
job	dates	Company	Description	Evaluation
job	dates	Company	Description	Evaluation

| Ed. | dates | University | Title | Grades |

hash

DLT

Fig. 1. The design of the proposed solution towards a trusted support platform for the job placement task.

Oracle is a verification platform that can perform proofing tasks, to establish the truth. Different approaches for validation of the applicant provided data can be employed: (i) company, where applicant worked previously, validates data, (ii) validation is outsources to a third party, (iii) crowd-based method, where other actors in the system (peers) can support the applicant claim. Obviously, there are decreasing reputation levels connected with those types of validation: from a fully credible ones, when the confirmation of an experience entry and its evaluation is performed by the company itself, to intermediate trustworthiness, achieved through the use of third-party paid validation services, till a basic validation provided by majority voting amongst large enough group of peers. The latter is the faster approach and can provide a solution for the cold-start problem, even if it results in the lowest data authenticity level guarantee.

Matching algorithm is the application of AI techniques to provide ranked list of matches to the declared skillset of a job opening. Given the relative stability and low frequency in job posting, it is possible to pre-compute a suitable representation of all the available openings, to make the solution scalable. We expect to be able to compute the matching between the applicants data and jobs profiles in distributed settings. The matching algorithm will be based on natural language processing (NLP) and document semantic similarity estimation [9], and will benefit also from some AI-based concepts identification improvement for multi-grams [15]. This approach can support fairness by construction and bias-free results, at least from individual person prejudices.

Web-Interfaces. We define the following web-interfaces: (i) an interface for the applicant to register and input the information related to his education and employment history (after verification, these data will be used as an input to the matching algorithm); (ii) an interface for the company to define and adjust the desired profile of the future employee in terms of the skills and their importance (this information will also be used as an input to the matching algorithm), as well as for after-matching selection of the candidates; (iii) an interface for the oracle (i.e., crowd-based or for the previous employers/institutions) for the verification of the data provided by the applicant. Via these interfaces it will also be possible to query the information stored on the blockchain, to verify the authenticity of the applicant data. We will also leverage gamification techniques for the users, in order to simplify the initial matching process between applicants and companies (more details will be provided further in this section).

In the following step-by-step process description, we present our vision on the system behaviour:

1. *Applicant registration.* An applicant needs to be registered in the system in order to provide his education and employment history, and therefore to be able to release his data for potential job posting matching. At the registration phase, the verification, whether an applicant has already an account in the system, is performed. Also, companies need to be registered as well, in order to guarantee their unique identification and responsibility for the job posting provided. A Self Sovereign Identity (SSI) approach is a good candidate for this function, as it can naturally manage distribute data while helping to comply with the increased difficulties stemming from the full conformity to GDPR.

2. *Data authenticity verification.* In order to ensure that provided data are trustworthy, a verification platform (Oracle) is employed.

3. *Information extraction.* After the data verification, the factual structured data about the participants are being extracted. The sources of such data must be the companies and education institutions.

4. *Ledger updates.* The ledger then can be updated directly by the data sources ensuring authenticity for the data and for the source, using hash function and digital signature for each transaction.

5. *Job profile definition and adjustment.* To introduce a new job position availability, a registered company must define a job profile, by specifying the expected skills, and their importance.

6. *Matching algorithm.* The input to the algorithm is formed by the structured data, extracted from the verified information about the applicant and the job profile generated by a company. When a match happens, both sides should be notified, still without revealing personal information.

7. *Creation of the channel between the company and the applicant.* A channel can be created automatically, or initiated by the company/applicant based on

the top results of the output of the matching algorithm. Before this channel materialisation, the identity of the applicant is hidden from the company, yet the matching data authenticity is provided.

As already mentioned above, blockchain technology can be used to ensure authenticity and traceability of the HR information. However, choosing a technical solution that can effectively support the legal requirement in this domain is of paramount importance: a DTL (distributed ledger) should provide support for information revocation. Additionally, the economic aspect (cost of transactions) should be also considered, for a real scalability of the solution. Therefore, we propose to employ a permissioned blockchain technology, in order to create a network of peers, which will serve as a source of the trustworthy data related to the employment history of the candidate. Based on the properties of the permissioned blockchain technology, the access to the network and to the data stored on the ledger is governed by the membership service, thus, we can ensure that only legitimate companies can participate in the network. Moreover, we intend to store only hashes of the structured data about the candidates to enable verification and to ensure privacy (anonymity) of the candidates. Digital signature of every transaction submitting a hash as an update of the ledger will ensure authenticity of the data source. We envision to use Hyperledger Fabric - an implementation of the permissioned blockchain technology - to gain on the maturity of the framework, its flexibility in terms of the consensus protocol choice and the identity management approaches, and the built-in possibility to employ privacy-preserving mechanisms (channels, private collections, etc.) [1]. We will confirm our choice based on the business requirements of the use case.

Identity Management. To ensure that an applicant can create only one account in the system, identity verification and management mechanisms must be put in place. However, the account management has to be flexible to reflect multiple affiliations and guarantee the user's privacy. For this, one can employ distributed self-sovereign identity management approach (SSI). SSI systems combine distributed ledger and cryptographic primitives to create immutable identity records. The individual maintains a number of claims or attributes (that define the used identity) received from any number of organizations, including the state, in a networked ecosystem that is open to any organization to participate (e.g., to issue credentials) [12]. Each organization can decide whether to trust specific credentials based on which organization verified or attested them. Difference with other identity management approaches such as centralized or federated identity management solutions, is that once the claims are generated, a user is controlling what to reveal, and he can now be authorized without involving an intervening authority every time, and without being tied to a single provider. Anonymous credential systems [3], such as the ones that are based on zero-knowledge proofs (ZKP) [2], are already integrated in the suggested blockchain technology implementation [1] and can provide strong protection of user privacy.

Distributed Matching Algorithm. Task execution using centralized approach (i.e., executing a piece of code on a single machine) often introduces a single point of failure in a system and can represent a bottleneck for its scalability. Blockchain technology aims at addressing these issues by performing independent execution of a code/smart contract on multiple nodes. Performing computations on every node enables to ensure trustworthy and reliable execution of matching algorithm and elimination of a bias, but can be highly inefficient depending on the complexity of the task, data volume, and network structure. We, therefore, plan to leverage multi-agent systems approach to define an adaptive mechanism to choose a fraction of nodes that will do the computational task independently to avoid a single point of failure and to ensure certain task execution confidence level in an efficient manner.

Gamification. This approach can be used to foster the applicant engagement and promote his participation in the system. A very simple interface can support the applicant assessment of interest towards a good match with an opening, also for automatic channel settlement. The applicants can additionally be rewarded for providing trustworthy information, for example by having more possibilities for channel creation or for being allowed to explicitly initiate a channel with a company for an open position, even if there is not a perfect match.

3   State of the Art

Solutions that partially address the problems listed in the previous section are not entirely novel. HR tech already exists and aims at optimising the internal HR processes in the companies, as well as automatising the matching algorithms.

People analytics methods are application of procedure from big data to classify and better match skills hold by a, current or potential, employee with open positions and critical areas of development [7]. This approach is internal to the company, and it is currently seen as an extension of the competences of the HR department. Despite the added value of providing a series of advantages for the people management, meaning finding better applicants, supporting smarter hiring decisions, promoting employee performance and increasing expertise retention, it normally requires the companies to hire people well-trained in the domain; and the hiring department may lack some in-depth knowledge in the specific domains.

On another level, leveraging on the vast amount of data they own, platforms such as Glassdoor[1], and LinkedIn[2] propose an external one-stop solution for companies, by providing as a service an attempt to optimise HR processes and increase job openings reachability. They support matches between the skills defined in the job description and the skills of the candidate (defined based on his own input or the recommendations of his peers); while providing automatic data extraction from CV uploaded to the platform, feedback management system from the employees (Glassdoor), and an "Easy Apply" service, that enables to directly apply for a position using only the data already uploaded into the platform.

---

[1] https://de.glassdoor.ch/index.htm.

[2] https://www.linkedin.com/.

These concrete approaches, despite being already realities, allow to address only few of the research questions defined before. Such third parties store and process sensitive information of the individuals, therefore, they are required to be compliant with a number of international and local laws and regulations regarding personal data management. In addition, privacy of the individuals can be violated. For instance, LinkedIn proposes a service that allows to indicate that the candidate is in an active search for the new employment, while there is no guarantees, that this information will not be known by the current employer. In addition, from our point of view, one of the most important limitations is the lack of independent validation of the data, submitted by the user or his peers.

There exist already some propositions that aim at automatising and improving the process of validation of the education certificates, including some blockchain-based approaches [6]. To address the need of the employers to have manually verified all the diplomas that confirm the education history of the candidate by the corresponding issuer, Gresch et al. propose a blockchain based system for managing diplomas. The authors review existing initiatives and propose to use public Ethereum blockchain to store the hashes generated over the diplomas in PDF format, issued by the corresponding institutions. While using public permissionless blockchain network allows for the availability and automated verification of diplomas, the fundamental role of a verification mechanism for an institution eligibility to issue such certificates was only mentioned in the proposed solution, yet not addressed. Additionally, all the solutions existing in literature either aim at validating a single diploma or certificate or a full profile as an elementary unit of information (meaning an image or an encrypted PDF). Instead, we propose a different approach: (i) we consider each entry as a single experience stored in a raw textual format, as a part of the user record, (ii) hash is generated separately for each singly entry and stored for validation purposes on the distributed ledger. This enables more effective smart integration and usage of the matching algorithms.

EduCTX [13], a blockchain based higher education credit and grading platform, addressed aforementioned issue of validation of a new network node by requiring the members of the EduCTX distributed ledger network on receiving a registration (joining) request from a node (institution), to verify official information about this institution. Yet, there is no further details regarding the process of confirming the eligibility to issue the education certificates, and the number of the network members that must perform the verification.

BCDiploma[3] initiated the creation of a new global certification standard, with the first use case dedicated to diplomas certification. BlockFactory[4] proposes a solution for increasing diploma security using blockchain technology. However, no information about both of the aforementioned solutions can be found in scientific publications, therefore, a rigorous analysis of such platforms is missing.

---

[3] https://www.bcdiploma.com.
[4] https://www.blockfactory.com.

4 Discussion

Before the implementation and integration of a system design, presented in Sect. 2, multiple matters have to be considered from the technical, legal, and social points of view. In what follows, we highlight specific questions to be addressed.

HR Tech and Blockchain-Based Intelligent Data Management. Further developing HR tech, employing people analytics and using intelligent automatised approaches to filter potential candidates and execute matching tasks, - all these aim at ensuring optimization, fairness, and bias-free HR processes. Due to the fact that the algorithms are normally designed and reviewed by multiple actors, single bias tends to be limited, reducing the effect of bias in case of automatic matching compare to a single-view approach. However, the models and logic employed in these approaches are still developed and implemented by the humans, thus, it is not possible to ensure the absence of accidental mistake and malicious behaviour that can influence the desired fairness of the aforementioned approaches. The same considerations are also relevant for the blockchain technology, in particular for the smart contracts. Regardless the fact that they are deployed and executed on multiple nodes, it can be very challenging *to ensure that the implementation corresponds to the desired logic of the contract.*

It is challenging *to define the right format and granularity of the data,* such as evaluations provided by the previous employer, so that sufficient level of expressiveness and desired level of anonymity are ensured simultaneously. Additionally, currently during the evaluation of previous working experience, there is a need to employ de-fuzzification approaches, especially when comparison between candidates takes place. Having an access to appropriately formatted structured data will allow to avoid the need for de-fuzzyfication, often leading to introducing bias in the evaluation.

Compliance and Other Legal Aspects. The EU General Data Protection Regulation (GDPR) [11] aims at regulating the way personally identifying data are being gathered and consumed and to define the legal rights of people to the use of their data. The data related to the education and working history, especially including evaluation of the candidate's skills, fall into a category of personally identifiable data [8]. Therefore, *compliance with GDPR* is required. Management of sensitive data is expensive, as it requires dedicated infrastructure, security and compliance specialists, and in case of data breaches, a company's reputation can be damaged, which can result into additional money losses. Companies often look for outsourcing the data management, which is also expensive and can lead to even more challenges when trying to ensure practical compliance with the GDPR.

Employing blockchain technology can bring certain benefits such as keeping a complete history of all the actions performed over the data (the obligation to keep records of processing activities, Article 30). However, in case of blockchain technology, as well as the other types of machine data processing algorithms, including the use of artificial intelligence techniques, it is not an obvious task to ensure the right to erasure (Article 17) that states that the data controller (the entity in charge of processing personal data) must erase without undue delay the data, if requested by the data owner [14]. Mechanisms for data extraction, encryption and anonymisation are some measures required to ensure GDPR compliance, together with the adoption of SSI approach and the use of hash functions, to avoid storing raw data on the blockchain.

Social Implications. While attempting to attain fair and bias-free matching between candidates and job profiles and employing intelligent approaches for the data management, we do not aim to devalue and/or completely remove the social component of HR processes. The goal of a framework, such as the one proposed in this paper, is to optimise the process of matching and selection, thus enabling more quality time for the personal assessment of the chosen candidate, i.e., person-to-person interaction between the candidate and HR employee.

In order to benefit from an added value brought by such framework, it is important *to ensure wide adoption*, which is only possible if the easiness of usage is guaranteed. Thus, developing intuitive interfaces that allow to express requirements and provide required information in a simple way is of paramount importance. The algorithms may need to be adapted to ensure proper reachability and matching without overwhelming the candidates and the companies with too many job offers or applicants to consider, respectively.

Blockchain technology enables trustworthiness of the data regarding the evaluation of an employee by the company. However, it is important *to provide a possibility for the employee to express his opinion* about the company as well. The reviews provided by the employees can then be used in order to build the reputation of the companies and weight their validations. Providing such functionality, however, is one of the directions of our future work.

5   Conclusion

This paper proposes a high-level architecture of a framework providing trusted support for the job placement task. Relying on the properties of intelligent data analysis approaches, blockchain technology, and self-sovereign identity management, we aim at optimising and limiting bias in the process of candidate selection, while ensuring the candidate's data privacy. We aim at achieving *optimisation* by removing the need to search in multiple sources and making use of structured verified data and distribute matching algorithm; *fairness* and *privacy* by employing an SSI system and by relying on matching algorithm that enables reproducibility and bias-free execution (thus, ensuring objectivity of the algorithm, and therefore candidate selection). However, as discussed in the previous section, there is still a number of the open questions to be considered before such system can be implemented and widely adopted.

References

1. Androulaki, E., et al.: Hyperledger fabric: a distributed operating system for permissioned blockchains. In: Proceedings of the Thirteenth EuroSys Conference, p. 30. ACM (2018)
2. Blum, M., Feldman, P., Micali, S.: Non-interactive zero-knowledge and its applications. In: Proceedings of the Twentieth Annual ACM Symposium on Theory of Computing, STOC 1988, pp. 103–112. ACM, New York (1988). https://doi.org/10.1145/62212.62222
3. Camenisch, J., Van Herreweghen, E.: Design and implementation of the idemix anonymous credential system. In: Proceedings of the 9th ACM Conference on Computer and Communications Security, pp. 21–30. ACM (2002)
4. Cheng, J.C., Lee, N.Y., Chi, C., Chen, Y.H.: Blockchain and smart contract for digital certificate. In: 2018 IEEE International Conference on Applied System Invention (ICASI), pp. 1046–1051. IEEE (2018)
5. Dillenberger, D., et al.: Blockchain analytics and artificial intelligence. IBM J. Res. Dev. **63**, 5:1–5:14 (2019)
6. Gresch, J., Rodrigues, B., Scheid, E., Kanhere, S.S., Stiller, B.: The proposal of a blockchain-based architecture for transparent certificate handling. In: Abramowicz, W., Paschke, A. (eds.) BIS 2018. LNBIP, vol. 339, pp. 185–196. Springer, Cham (2019). https://doi.org/10.1007/978-3-030-04849-5_16
7. Isson, J.P., Harriott, J.S.: People Analytics in the Era of Big Data: Changing the Way You Attract, Acquire, Develop, and Retain Talent. Wiley, New York (2016)
8. Junge, N.: Between privacy protection and data progression-the GDPR in the context of people analytics. MaRBLe **4**, 1–16 (2018)
9. Mazzola, L., Siegfried, P., Waldis, A., Kaufmann, M., Denzler, A.: A domain specific ESA inspired approach for document semantic description. In: 9th IEEE International Conference on Intelligent Systems, IS 2018, Funchal, Madeira, Portugal, 25–27 September 2018, pp. 383–390 (2018). https://doi.org/10.1109/IS.2018.8710507
10. Michaelides, M.P.: The challenges of AI and blockchain on HR recruiting practices. Cyprus Rev. **30**(2), 185–197 (2018)
11. General Data Protection Regulation: Regulation (EU) 2016/679 of the European parliament and of the council of 27 April 2016 on the protection of natural persons with regard to the processing of personal data and on the free movement of such data, and repealing directive 95/46. Official J. Eur. Union (OJ) **59**(1–88), 294 (2016)
12. Tobin, A., Reed, D.: The inevitable rise of self-sovereign identity. The Sovrin Foundation 29 (2016)
13. Turkanović, M., Hölbl, M., Košič, K., Heričko, M., Kamišalić, A.: EduCTX: a blockchain-based higher education credit platform. IEEE Access **6**, 5112–5127 (2018)
14. Villaronga, E.F., Kieseberg, P., Li, T.: Humans forget, machines remember: artificial intelligence and the right to be forgotten. Comput. Law Secur. Rev. **34**(2), 304–313 (2018)
15. Waldis, A., Mazzola, L., Kaufmann, M.: Concept extraction with convolutional neural networks. In: Proceedings of the 7th International Conference on Data Science, Technology and Applications, DATA 2018, Porto, Portugal, 26–28 July 2018, pp. 118–129 (2018). https://doi.org/10.5220/0006901201180129

16. Wang, X., Feng, L., Zhang, H., Lyu, C., Wang, L., You, Y.: Human resource information management model based on blockchain technology. In: 2017 IEEE Symposium on Service-Oriented System Engineering (SOSE), pp. 168–173. IEEE (2017)
17. Wei, D., Varshney, K.R., Wagman, M.: Optigrow: People analytics for job transfers. In: IEEE International Congress on Big Data, pp. 535–542. IEEE (2015)

Blockchain Materialization as a General Purpose Technology: A Research Framework

Evgeniia Filippova[(⊠)]

AIT Austrian Institute of Technology, Center for Innovation Systems and Policy,
Vienna, Austria
evgeniia.filippova@ait.ac.at

Abstract. Blockchain, often treated as a next transforming general-purpose technology (GPT), might have the potential to revolutionize economic, political and social structures in the subsequent years. However, the actual impact of Blockchain will ultimately depend on the pace and direction of its diffusion process throughout the economy. Being currently in the nascent phase, the diffusion process of Blockchain remained largely neglected in the academic literature so far. The study at hand covers this research gap by investigating the forces affecting Blockchain diffusion leading to its materialization as a GPT. Identified from the broad literature on technological change, the various factors influencing diffusion patterns of GPTs are conceptualized in a framework of three interrelated groups: advancements in the GPT itself, advancements in its application sectors, and environmental factors. This conceptual framework is then applied to structure the current studies of Blockchain technology and reveal unexplored blind spots. In such a way, the present paper serves as a basis for further research on diffusion patterns of Blockchain and its materialization as a general-purpose technology.

Keywords: General purpose technologies · Blockchain · Diffusion

1 Introduction

Blockchain, widely known as an underlying technology of Bitcoin since 2008 [42], gained attention over the last years as a disruptive and game changing technology in several aspects. Its functional features, such as decentralization, immutability and transparency of record, reduce the cost of verification of transactions and cost of networking [13]. This cost saving potential makes Blockchain potentially beneficial for numerous industrial sectors. In fact, proofs of concept for Blockchain-based use cases exist, among others, in supply chain, healthcare, identity management, financial transactions, energy distribution, and other areas [46]. Along with its potential pervasiveness within the industry, Blockchain is expected to have disruptive impact on society. As an institutional technology, it enables decentralization of governance structures [4], thus provides an alternative for coordinating people and economic decision-making [17].

In a scientific debate regarding the economic nature of Blockchain, it is important to mention a recent empirical evidence of Blockchain as a general-purpose technology

© Springer Nature Switzerland AG 2020
U. Schwardmann et al. (Eds.): Euro-Par 2019 Workshops, LNCS 11997, pp. 216–227, 2020.
https://doi.org/10.1007/978-3-030-48340-1_17

in the making [19, 20]. As an emerging GPT, Blockchain is expected to have a long-term effect on macroeconomic dynamics [9], and to play an essential role in shaping economic, social and institutional structures in the next decades [35]. However, the actual impact of Blockchain, analogous to other GPTs over the history [26], will ultimately depend on the pace and direction of its diffusion throughout the economy [21, 26]. The current low diffusion rates of Blockchain, as acknowledged in various studies [6, 15] might be explained by its early stage [39]. To gain an understanding of the diffusion process at the beginning, an in-depth examination of the factors affecting Blockchain materialization as a transforming GPT is required.

Prominent scholars of technological change described various forces that hampered or accelerated materialization of historical GPTs [21, 35, 43, 45, 51], however, did not systematize them. Works of [45] and [26] represent the first important attempts to summarize ex-post the factors affecting technological diffusion in general based on numerous historical examples. The aim of the present study, which focuses on general-purpose technologies, is (1) to conceptualize ex-post identified factors that influence the materialization of general-purpose technologies from a broad literature on technological change, and (2) to map Blockchain-related papers based on the created conceptual framework to reveal the current focus areas and blind spots in Blockchain diffusion patterns and its materialization as a GPT. The results of the study, therefore, open up multiple research opportunities for economists and provide a structured overview about the known unknown for policy makers. Insights on forces affecting GPT diffusion might assist the comprehensive analysis of reasons, underlying Blockchain diffusion rates and, therefore, the materialization of its promises as a transforming GPT.

The next sections are structured as follows. (1) Derivation of a general conceptual framework to structure general literature about the materialization of technologies as a GPT: the identified factors affecting the materialization of GPTs are arranged in three focus areas. (2) Detailed comparison of the focus areas in the general conceptual framework with those of current Blockchain studies, including identification of the potential blind spots in Blockchain literature and recommendations for further research activities. (3) The study concludes with the summary of the findings.

2   Conceptual Framework

It is an intuitively clear and widely acknowledged fact, that the real value of GPTs can be captured only when they diffuse throughout the economy [9, 12, 47, 53]. The importance of the diffusion process in the realization of an impact from GPTs is due to the definition of the term 'general-purpose technology' itself. According to Bresnahan and Trajtenberg [9], who coined the term, GPTs have the following features: they are applied across numerous industries (pervasiveness), generate innovations in the downstream application sectors (innovation spawning effects), and provide solutions to complex problems that remained unsolved before with existing technologies (scope for improvement). The GPT literature focuses mainly on two research streams: (1) identification of GPTs (see, for example, [27] and [53] for quantitative GPT identification; and [35] for an overview of qualitative approaches to recognize GPTs); and (2) the modelling of GPT-induced economic growth (see [11] for an overview of various models). Though being not an explicit focus of the GPT literature (studies [9, 12, 26, 33, 50] are exceptions), various forces affecting GPT diffusion are featured in numerous studies of evolutionary paths of many important technologies throughout the history [26, 31, 35, 45]. Some of these ex-post identified factors are common to many technologies, while others are relevant only for a particular case [35]. Nonetheless, in order to enable analysis of technological change from multiple perspectives it is necessary to make an effort in creating a "conceptual apparatus", or, put differently, a sort of categorization of these factors [45]. Therefore, the next paragraphs are dedicated to the summary of the forces affecting materialization of GPTs from a broad literature in evolutionary economics, new growth theory, economic history, industrial organization, and structural change.

A so-called 'dual-inducement mechanism', a model developed by Bresnahan and Trajtenberg [9] in order to explain the diffusion mechanisms of GPTs, provides a good starting point for understanding how GPTs function. According to this model, the advancements in a GPT in terms of its quality and price trigger its diffusion across down-stream application sectors, while the advancements in these application sectors, such as, for example, formation of complementary assets and skills, foster the advancements in GPT itself. This mechanism is essential to explain why GPTs are different from other technologies, as the very existence of 'linked payoffs' between GPTs and application sectors generates a coordination game, subject to failure and externalities. Consistent with the evolutionary theory of technological change, the discovery of new GPT-using application domains also influences the investment levels in the emerging GPT [2, 47].

The later studies from the GPT literature built upon the dual-inducement mechanism model and extended it to some degree [12, 47]. [47] proposed a GPT reciprocal causality model, where advances in the GPT are "both a cause and a result" of advances in its application sectors and complementary technologies. [12] extended the original model of Bresnahan and Trajtenberg to a scenario where more than one GPT at a time struggle to gain pervasiveness in the economy.

In addition to improvements in a GPT and advancements in its application sectors [9], a range of other forces played an important role in shaping the evolutionary path of major technologies of the past [51]. Mentioned to some extent in the works of all major scholars of technological change, these forces include regulation [8, 26], public procurement [12, 18], social aspects [30, 51], and market structure [18, 28]. Consideration of the above listed factors is especially important when investigating the materialization of GPTs, since these technologies lead to paradigm shifts, and therefore, have important implications for economic, societal and institutional structures [35, 53]. In the conceptual framework of the present study, these factors are summarized in a focus area 'environmental factors'. The term 'environmental', used in the overview of diffusion of technologies in [26] indicates, that these forces affecting the materialization of GPTs do not directly relate neither to GPT itself, nor to its distinct downstream application sectors.

The three interrelated focus areas of the forces that affect the materialization of GPTs are graphically represented below in Fig. 1: (1) Environmental factors, (2) Improvements in the GPT, and (3) Advancements in its application sectors. Literature further shows that interaction effects can be found between these categories.

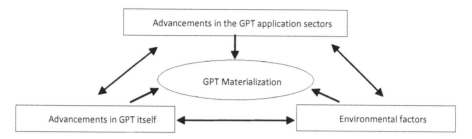

Fig. 1. Groups of factors affecting materialization of general-purpose technologies

3 Factors Affecting Materialization of Blockchain as a GPT

3.1 Advancements in the GPT Itself

The factors in this category reflect primarily the technological development of an emerging GPT, which in further consequence influences its economic success or failure. The historical observations point out that almost all technologies, especially radical innovations and GPTs, first appear in crude and primitive form, therefore, can often poorly compete with existing technologies [31, 45]. The capabilities of the telephone around 1880, productivity of computers in 1950s, the weight of the first IBM-invented hard-disk drive, or the 14-step process required to make one single copy with the early xerographic machine are just a few historical examples for a poor initial efficiency of new technologies [2, 14, 31]. Blockchain, being at the early stages of its technological maturity [39], is no exception in this regard. Current technical challenges of Blockchain, summarized by [48] and complemented by [54] include throughput, latency, size and bandwidth, security, usability, waste of resources, and privacy leakages. In fact, Blockchain does currently have issues with data malleability and data storage, needs a long time before a transaction is seen as committed, lacks of support for developers and end-users, and is characterized by high power consumption related to the proof-of-work consensus [48, 54].

The subsequent performance improvements, being an important factor affecting the diffusion rate of technology, are often subject to secondary innovations, representing essential improvements and modifications over the initial form of technology [26, 43]. Steam engine, an acknowledged example of a transforming GPT [35], gained its significance largely due to Watt's improvements, and its subsequent advancements embodied in the Corliss model are known fora "major re-organization process of industrial machinery" [45]. Blockchain does also undergo a continuous technological development. In addition to numerous literature, that suggests improvements in technology (see [49] for an overview), scholars examined potential solutions for the major technical challenges of Blockchain in the academic literature [52] and in patent applications [20].

The continuous improvements of a GPT itself lead to an increase in its relative advantages or benefits of the new technology over existing solutions [18]. Numerous scholars (for example, [41]), refers to general advantages of Blockchain technologies: they enable decentralization, can increase operational efficiency, reduce transaction costs and provide advanced security. Others investigate relative advantages of Blockchain within particular application scenarios (for example, [22]). Network effects that influence relative advantages, thus, diffusion rate of a GPT [26], are particularly relevant in case of Blockchain, since this technology is subject to network effects. Though conceptually mentioned by several authors [22], the empirical investigation is, to the best of my knowledge, currently limited only to network effects of cryptocurrencies (for example, [36]).

The relative advantages of an emerging GPT and their evolution over time deserve detailed investigation of scholars, since they represent one of the most important determinants for GPTs diffusion [9, 12]. Other determinants, related to the GPT downstream application sectors, are described in the next paragraph.

3.2 Advancements in the Application Sectors

The technological advancements alone are not able to determine the success of an emerging GPT. Gallium arsenide, a technology that could have replaced silicon in semiconductors in the 1980s due to the higher speed it enabled, never expanded beyond the initial application domain and, therefore, did not realize its GPT potential despite the superior technological features [2]. This and other examples of so-called 'failed GPTs' throughout the history [35] demonstrate, how important it is to shed light on the factors, which affect diffusion patterns of GPTs at the application level. As Dosi mentions in his work on technological paradigms, these factors, "acting as selectors, define more and more precisely the actual paths followed inside a much bigger set of possible ones" [18].

In the beginning a new GPT is most commonly applied to only one sector – the one that benefits most from distinctive functionality and accepts the initial technical imperfections [2], and thereafter gradually expanding to other application domains. This process of discovery of new applications for a GPT, often compared to a speciation event in the evolutionary theory [2, 12], presents an essential step toward technological maturity. Since considerable adaptation of a technology to each particular application sector is needed, the process, leading to an establishment of a pervasiveness of a GPT, is not costless [40]. Various scholars and practitioners, addressing Blockchain as "an innovative technology in search of use cases" [24], do have concerns regarding its applicability. The expansion of Blockchain from its initial application domain – Bitcoin – has already started [41]. This process can be supported by further research on the development of decision frameworks for Blockchain use cases ([32] provide an overview of current frameworks), and on the requirements for Blockchain-based solutions within various application areas (see [34] for an example of such an investigation within the e-agriculture domain).

Complementarities, or all the assets and capabilities needed to exploit the new technology, play an important role in shaping its diffusion patterns [26, 30, 43, 47]. The need of numerous complementarities and the long timeframe until they are set-up, often with periods of trial and error [18, 40], might explain the relatively slow diffusion of the electric dynamo, steam engine, information and communication technology, and other major technologies over the history [16]. The materialization of a GPT is especially subject to complementarities: these technologies foster advancements in the downstream application sectors (innovation spawning effects), which are, in turn, crucial for the successful implementation of a GPT itself. There are numerous examples, when complementary technologies are required for the successful implementation of Blockchain. In use cases, that involve the transaction of physical assets, internet-of-things technologies might be necessary to guarantee secure Blockchain-based transfers of not only ownership, but also possession of assets [1]. Mature identity solutions, multiple signature wallets, and other complementarities a required for land registry on Blockchain.

The implementation of a GPT requires not only the use of complementary technologies, but also other complementarities, such as business process redesign [39], investments into human capital, and transformations of business models [10]. Bringing this into the Blockchain context, two questions seem to be of relevance: (1) what complementarities are necessary for the successful Blockchain implementation within a certain use case; and (2) what specifics need to be considered in the Blockchain context to build them up? With an overall dearth of research on these topics, it is worth to mention several recent studies. Milani and Garcia-Banuelos conceptually explained the redesign of current business processes induced by Blockchain [39]. Clohessi et al. categorized the skills required by organizations to implement Blockchain [15]. Holotiuk et al. examined strategies of firms to build Blockchain-related technological knowledge [29]. These include the involvement in Blockchain consortia, external partnerships with start-ups, and engagements in open innovation activities [29]. Beck and Müller-Bloch conducted one of the first case studies within a bank to shed light on how financial organizations acquire capabilities to engage with Blockchain in different phases [7]. This line of research will probably grow in the subsequent years. Numerous literature on strategies employed by organizations to gain technological knowledge, their absorptive capacity, organizational readiness and their ability to adjust business models ([23, 26], and [47]) provide starting points for further Blockchain-related research about the set-up of complementarities.

3.3 Environmental Factors

In addition to technological improvements of GPTs and the necessary adjustments in their downstream application sectors, a large group of other socio-economic factors – addressed as ,environmental factors' in the present framework – play an important role in shaping the evolutionary path of GPTs in the making [26, 45]. Rosenberg pointed out that "any technology is never independent of its institutional context and therefore needs to be studied within that context" [45]. The similar conclusion is drawn in the works of Dosi [18] on technological trajectories and Perez [43] on techno-economic paradigms. Hall and Khan included environmental and institutional factors, in particular market structure and regulation, in their investigation of factors affecting diffusion of new technologies [26]. The investigation of the impact of socio-economic factors on technological development is further central to the sociological study of technology [51], more specifically to research on the social shaping of technology [38]. Numerous scholars of technical change acknowledge in their technology diffusion analyses the relevance of environmental factors, which can mainly be segmented into social factors, regulatory conditions, institutional factors, market structure [18, 26, 43, 45, 50].

The relationship between market structure and its influence on innovation incentives and technology diffusion has been widely discussed in the literature [18]. On the one side, big market players have a lot of capital embedded in the old technologies and complex bureaucratic structures that may slow the diffusion of an emerging technology [28]. On the other side, large firms under oligopolistic conditions are more likely to invest into new technologies due to the availability of funds, the possibility to spread the potential risks that cames along with a new technology, and the higher probability to benefit from innovation [18, 26]. Currently there is a lack in Blockchain research that focus on the investigation of market structures and its influence on Blockchain diffusion. The early stage of Blockchain might be an explanation for the current gap.

Governmental bodies and regulations play an essential role in the materialization of technologies [8, 26, 30]. Numerous empirical studies in healthcare, paper and pulp industries, nanotechnology [47], and others, confirm the power of regulations in fostering or hindering the diffusion process. Due to a radically different logic embedded in the new GPTs, these technologies require new regulation rules that, in turn, influence the evolutionary path of GPTs in a long term [43]. Blockchain regulation is a widely discussed topic in the last years (see [25] for an overview of legal challenges of Blockchain). However, it remains a certain "mismatch between technological promise and legal reality" [25], which represents one of the major hurdles for the adoption of Blockchain-based applications [49]. While efforts on Blockchain regulations are covered in the academic literature, the relationship between legal environment and Blockchain diffusion is still a nascent topic to pay attention to in further research.

Public procurement, in addition to regulation, is a powerful facilitator of GPTs in the pervasiveness gaining process [12]. In fact, a public demander might not only foster the design and development efforts around an emerging GPT [9] as happened, for example, with the synthetic chemistry and electronic industry in Germany [18], but also become provider of a GPT with network effects [26] and encourage the creation of complementary innovation in the application sectors [50]. Blockchain represents a promising technology for the public sector [5], and there already exist numerous examples of governmental support: Blockchain-based land registry in Sweden, monitoring of government expenditures in Canada, just to point out two among many others.

Consistent with the central idea behind social shaping of technology, the social factors, along with the other factors listed above, should be considered in detail in technological path forecasting [21, 51]. Freeman states, that "the realm of technically feasible is enormously wider than the realm of the economically profitable, and both are wider than the realm of the socially acceptable" [21] and [51] address innovation as a "garden of forking paths" [51], where the direction of technological development is inevitably shaped by society. Youtie et al. pointed out that the analysis of social factors accompanying the materialization of an emerging GPT is of especially importance due to paradigm shifts induced by this technology and the potentially transforming effects on society [53]. Blockchain might enable a paradigm shift from 'trusting humans' to 'trusting machines', as well as from 'centralized control' to 'decentralized control' [4]. The technology enables decentralization of governance structures, therefore, provides "institutional alternative for coordinating the economic actions of groups of people" [17]. The works of Allen [3] and Davidson [17] framed Blockchain as an institutional technology and suggested to consider this in future research. First analyses were made with the investigation of social perceptions of Blockchain through studies of technology's representation in news [20] and social media [37]. These studies represent an integral part of analyses of social factors affecting the technological diffusion [30]. However, they address only a part of the social context in which a GPT can evolve. More research on social trends and their impact on Blockchain diffusion, the perceptions of trust, and other social factors might emerge within the next years to fill this gap.

3.4 Interdependencies Affecting the Materialization of a GPT

All three categories – improvements in the GPT itself, advancements in its application sectors, and environmental factors – are influencing not only the materialization of GPTs directly but also indirectly through interdependencies between all three categories. As modelled by Bresnahan and Trajtenberg [9], technological improvements in the GPT lead to advancements in its application sectors, and vice-versa: the more adapted the application domains are to a new technology, the more investments flow into its further development. According to the studies [21] and [43], environmental factors, such as regulation, market structure, social acceptance and others, influence and, at the same time, are influenced by both the GPT advancements, and strategies of the application sectors.

The investigation of evolutionary path of Blockchain in the subsequent years cannot be limited to analysis of only one single particular category of factors but should also be aware of the interrelations between all the three categories. The conceptual framework and the identified main factors are graphically summarized below in Fig. 2.

The few current studies on Blockchain diffusion mainly focused on factors that affected the diffusion of Blockchain at the application level, and therefore, lead to a research gap in the examination of environmental factors and technological advancements of Blockchain. Batubara et al. [5] and Holotiuk and Moormann [29] focused on the diffusion of technology within certain domains – e-Government [5] and financial service sector [29]. Clohessy et al. [15] and Post et al. [44] summarized factors that influence Blockchain diffusion within organisations with the help of literature review and semi-structured interviews respectively. Perez [44] differentiated between strategic, tactical and operational factors important for the diffusion of Blockchain. Clohessy et al. represents one of the first Blockchain studies that consider, based on the TOE framework, various groups of factors, potentially affecting the Blockchain diffusion [15]. The used approach to examine factors from different categories supports the multi-perspective results of the conceptual framework at hand, however, still lacks in considering all GPT-relevant factors or interdependencies.

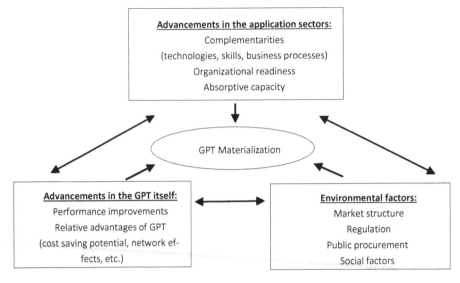

Fig. 2. Detailed conceptual framework with categories and main factors, that affect the materialization of Blockchain (as a general-purpose technology)

3.5 Summary

Table 1 below summarizes the current body of research on factors affecting Blockchain materialization as a GPT, based on the conceptual framework represented in the Fig. 2.

Table 1. Blockchain-related literature in line with studies on diffusion

Category	Factors	General literature	Blockchain literature
Advancements in GPT	Performance improvements	[26, 43, 45]	[20, 52]
	Relative advantages of GPT	[9, 12, 18, 26, 33, 50]	[22, 36, 41]
Advancements in application sectors	Complementarities s.l.	[10, 16, 18, 26, 30, 40, 43, 47]	[1, 15, 39]
	Organizational readiness	[10, 23, 47]	[7]
	Absorptive capacity	[10, 33]	[29]
Environmental factors	Market structure	[18, 26, 28]	No studies currently
	Regulation	[8, 30, 43]	[25]
	Public procurement	[9, 12, 50]	[5]
	Social factors	[18, 21, 51]	[17, 20, 37]
Interdependency of factors		[9, 12, 21, 43, 47]	[15]

As evident from the table, research on factors affecting diffusion patterns of Blockchain is currently in its nascent phase. Some of the factors, sketched within the previous sections, have not or only very rarely been investigated in the context of Blockchain, and therefore, might be very promising fields for future research directions.

4 Conclusion

The current low diffusion rates of Blockchain [6, 15] might be explained in a number of ways: the technology is in its early development stage [39]; not many purposeful application scenarios have been identified yet [24]; there exist serious technical issues to overcome [52]; there is a discrepancy between technological promise and regulatory environment [25]; and others. In the context of this scientific debate, the study at hand provides structured evidence of the factors, which, analogous to the other general-purpose technologies throughout the history, influence the materialization of Blockchain as a transforming GPT. Furthermore, it gives an overview about the fields already addressed in current studies and the blind spots that can be seen as a potential research agenda in the area.

References

1. Abadi, J., Brunnermeier, M.: Blockchain economics (No. w25407). National Bureau of Economic Research (2018)
2. Adner, R., Levinthal, D.: The emergence of emerging technologies. Calif. Manag. Rev. **45**(1), 50–66 (2002)
3. Allen, D.: Discovering and developing the blockchain cryptoeconomy. SSRN 2815255 (2017)
4. Aste, T., Tasca, P., Di Matteo, T.: Blockchain technologies: the foreseeable impact on society and industry. Computer **50**(9), 18–28 (2017)
5. Batubara, F., Ubacht, J., Janssen, M.: Challenges of blockchain technology adoption for e-government: a systematic literature review. In: Proceedings of the 19th Annual International Conference on Digital Government Research: Governance in the Data Age, p. 76. ACM (2018)
6. Beck, R., Avital, M., Rossi, M., Thatcher, J.B.: Blockchain technology in business and information systems research. Bus. Inf. Syst. Eng. **59**(6), 381–384 (2017). https://doi.org/10.1007/s12599-017-0505-1
7. Beck, R., Müller-Bloch, C.: Blockchain as radical innovation: a framework for engaging with distributed ledgers as incumbent organization (2017)
8. Beerepoot, M., Beerepoot, N.: Government regulation as an impetus for innovation: evidence from energy performance regulation in the Dutch residential building sector. Energy Policy **35**(10), 4812–4825 (2007)
9. Bresnahan, T., Trajtenberg, M.: General purpose technologies 'Engines of growth'? J. Econom. **65**(1), 83–108 (1995)
10. Brynjolfsson, E., Hitt, L.: Beyond computation: information technology, organizational transformation and business performance. J. Econ. Perspect. **14**(4), 23–48 (2000)

11. Cantner, U., Vannuccini, S.: A new view of general purpose technologies (No. 2012, 054). Jena Economic Research Papers (2012)
12. Cantner, U., Vannuccini, S.: Pervasive technologies and industrial linkages: modeling acquired purposes. Structural Change and Economic Dynamics (2017)
13. Catalini, C., Gans, J.: Some simple economics of the blockchain (No. w22952). National Bureau of Economic Research (2016)
14. Christensen, C.M.: The Innovator's Dilemma: When New Technologies Cause Great Firms to Fail. Harvard Business Review Press, Boston (2013)
15. Clohessy, T., Acton, T., Rogers, N.: Blockchain adoption: technological, organisational and environmental considerations. In: Treiblmaier, H., Beck, R. (eds.) Business Transformation through Blockchain, pp. 47–76. Springer, Cham (2019). https://doi.org/10.1007/978-3-319-98911-2_2
16. David, P.: The Dynamo and the computer: an historical perspective on the modern productivity paradox. Am. Econ. Rev. Pap. Proc. **80**, 355–361 (1990)
17. Davidson, S., De Filippi, P., Potts, J.: Economics of blockchain. SSRN 2744751 (2016)
18. Dosi, G.: Technological paradigms and technological trajectories: a suggested interpretation of the determinants and directions of technical change. Res. Policy **11**(3), 147–162 (1982)
19. Filippova, E.: Empirical evidence and economic implications of blockchain as a general purpose technology (2019, forthcoming)
20. Filippova, E., Scharl, A., Filippov, P.: Blockchain: an empirical investigation of its scope for improvement. In: Joshi, J., Nepal, S., Zhang, Q., Zhang, L.-J. (eds.) ICBC 2019. LNCS, vol. 11521, pp. 1–17. Springer, Cham (2019). https://doi.org/10.1007/978-3-030-23404-1_1
21. Freeman, C.: The Factory of the Future: The Productivity Paradox. Japanese Just-In-Time and Information Technology, PICT Policy Research Paper No. 3 (1988)
22. Francisco, K., Swanson, D.: The supply chain has no clothes: technology adoption of blockchain for supply chain transparency. Logistics **2**(1), 2 (2018)
23. Gambardella, A., McGahan, A.: Business-model innovation: general purpose technologies and their implications for industry structure. Long Range Plan. **43**(2–3), 262–271 (2010)
24. Glaser, F.: Pervasive decentralisation of digital infrastructures: a framework for blockchain enabled system and use case analysis (2017)
25. Hacker, P., Lianos, I., Dimitropoulos, G., Eich, S.: Regulating Blockchain: Techno-Social and Legal Challenges-An Introduction. Oxford University Press, Oxford (2019)
26. Hall, B., Khan, B.: Adoption of new technology (No. w9730). National Bureau of Economic Research (2003)
27. Hall, B., Trajtenberg, M.: Uncovering GPTs with patent data, No. w10901. National Bureau of Economic Research (2004)
28. Henderson, R., Clark, K.: Architectural innovation: The reconfiguration of existing product technologies and the failure of established firms. Adm. Sci. Q. **35**(1), 9–30 (1990)
29. Holotiuk, F., Moormann, J.: Organizational adoption of digital innovation: the case of blockchain technology. In: Proceedings of the European Conference on Information Systems (2018)
30. King, J., Gurbaxani, V., Kraemer, K., McFarlan, W., Raman, K., Yap, C.: Institutional factors in information technology innovation. Inf. Syst. Res. **5**(2), 139–169 (1994)
31. Kline, S., Rosenberg, N.: An overview of innovation. In: Studies on Science and the Innovation Process: Selected Works of Nathan Rosenberg, pp. 173–203 (2010)
32. Koens, T., Poll, E.: What blockchain alternative do you need? In: Garcia-Alfaro, J., Herrera-Joancomartí, J., Livraga, G., Rios, R. (eds.) DPM/CBT -2018. LNCS, vol. 11025, pp. 113–129. Springer, Cham (2018). https://doi.org/10.1007/978-3-030-00305-0_9
33. Korzinov, V., Savin, I.: General Purpose Technologies as an emergent property. Technol. Forecast. Soc. Chang. **129**, 88–104 (2018)

34. Lin, Y., Petway, J., Anthony, J., Mukhtar, H., Liao, S., Chou, C., Ho, Y.: Blockchain: the evolutionary next step for ICT e-agriculture. Environments **4**(3), 50 (2017)
35. Lipsey, G., Carlaw, I., Bekar, C.: Economic Transformations: General Purpose Technologies and Long-Term Economic Growth. OUP, Oxford (2005)
36. Luther, W.: Cryptocurrencies, network effects, and switching costs. Contemp. Econ. Policy **34**(3), 553–571 (2016)
37. Lynn, T., Rosati, P., Fox, G.: Legitimizing# Blockchain: an empirical analysis of firm level social media messaging on Twitter. In 26th European Conference on Information Systems (2018)
38. MacKenzie, D., Wajcman, J.: The Social Shaping of Technology. Open University Press, London (1999)
39. Milani, F., Garcia-Banuelos, L.: Blockchain and principles of business process re-engineering for process innovation. arXiv preprint arXiv:1806.03054 (2018)
40. Mokyr, J. (ed.): The Oxford Encyclopedia of Economic History, vol. 3. Oxford University Press on Demand, Oxford (2003)
41. Mougayar, W.: The Business Blockchain: Promise, Practice, and Application of the Next Internet Technology. Wiley, Hoboken (2016)
42. Nakamoto, S.: Bitcoin: A peer-to-peer electronic cash system (2008)
43. Perez, C.: Technological revolutions and techno-economic paradigms. Camb. J. Econ. **34**(1), 185–202 (2010)
44. Post, R., Smit, K., Zoet, M.: Identifying Factors Affecting Blockchain Technology Diffusion (2018)
45. Rosenberg, N.: Factors affecting the diffusion of technology. Explor. Econ. Hist. **10**(1), 3 (1972)
46. Salviotti, G., De Rossi, L., Abbatemarco, N.: A structured framework to assess the business application landscape of blockchain technologies. In: Proceedings of the 51st Hawaii International Conference on System Sciences (2018)
47. Shea, C.M.: Future management research directions in nanotechnology: a case study. J. Eng. Technol. Manage. **22**(3), 185–200 (2005)
48. Swan, M.: Blockchain: Blueprint for a New Economy. O'Reilly Media, Inc., Newton (2015)
49. Tasca, P., Widmann, S.: The challenges faced by blockchain technologies–Part 1. J. Digit. Bank. **2**(2), 132–147 (2017)
50. Thoma, G.: Striving for a large market: evidence from a general purpose technology in action. Ind. Corp. Change **18**(1), 107–138 (2008)
51. Williams, R., Edge, D.: The social shaping of technology. Res. Policy **25**(6), 865–899 (1996)
52. Yli-Huumo, J., Ko, D., Choi, S., Park, S., Smolander, K.: Where is current research on blockchain technology?—a systematic review. PLoS One **11**(10), e0163477 (2016)
53. Youtie, J., Iacopetta, M., Graham, S.: Assessing the nature of nanotechnology: can we uncover an emerging general purpose technology? J. Technol. Transfer **33**(3), 315–329 (2008). https://doi.org/10.1007/s10961-007-9030-6
54. Zheng, Z., Xie, S., Dai, H.N., Chen, X., Wang, H.: Blockchain challenges and opportunities: a survey. Int. J. Web Grid Serv. **14**(4), 352–375 (2018)

On Refining Design Patterns
for Smart Contracts

Marco Zecchini[1] (ID), Andrea Bracciali[2] (ID), Ioannis Chatzigiannakis[1] (ID),
and Andrea Vitaletti[1(✉)] (ID)

[1] Sapienza University of Rome, Rome, Italy
{zecchini,chatzigiannakis,vitaletti}@diag.uniroma1.it
[2] University of Stirling, Stirling, UK
abb@cs.stir.ac.uk

Abstract. The need for a Blockchain Oriented Software Engineering
(BOSE) has been recognized in several research papers. Design Patterns
are considered among the main and compelling areas to be developed in
BOSE. Anyway, design patterns need to be enhanced with some additional fields to better support the specific needs of Blockchain development. In this paper, we discuss the use of Solidity design patterns applied
to a water management use case and we introduce specific fields in their
description, aiming at offering to Blockchain developers more support in
the critical decisions to build efficient decentralized applications.

Keywords: Design patters · Blockchain Oriented Software
Engineering (BOSE) · Use case · Smart contracts · Solidity

1 Introduction

Since the release of Ethereum, there have been many cases in which the execution of Smart Contracts managing Ether coins has led to problems or conflicts.
Probably, the most well known example of such issues is "The DAO" [13,15].
The DAO, decentralized autonomous organization, was a concrete attempt to
implement a funding platform, similar to Kickstarter, running over Ethereum. It
went live in 2016 with between 10–20 thousand investors (estimation) providing
the equivalent of about US$ 250 million in funding and thus breaking all existing
crowdfunding records. However, after few months an unintended behavior of the
DAO's code was exploited draining the fund of millions of dollars' worth of ETH
tokens. The DAO experience makes clear the importance of suitable Blockchain
Software Engineering (BOSE) techniques, capable to reduce the risks connected
to "poorly" designed and implemented smart contracts. However, a discipline of
Smart Contract and Blockchain programming, with standardized best practices
is yet in its infancy and requires new approaches since smart contracts rely on a
non-standard software life-cycle; as an example, once deployed applications can
hardly be updated or bugs resolved by releasing a new version of the software.

© Springer Nature Switzerland AG 2020
U. Schwardmann et al. (Eds.): Euro-Par 2019 Workshops, LNCS 11997, pp. 228–239, 2020.
https://doi.org/10.1007/978-3-030-48340-1_18

In [12] the authors discuss the need for BOSE and propose three main areas for the initial development of this discipline: a) Best practices and development methodology, b) Design patterns and c) Testing.

Our work is focused on the use of Design Patterns for the development of Decentralized Applications (DApps) [25].

DApps are a new class of applications coded in programs running on the blockchain. DApps may provide a variety of services over the underlying P2P infrastructure that up to now have only been provided in the dominant Client/Server architectures. The Peer-to-Peer (P2P) nature of DApps and the lack of a central authority as in the Client/Server paradigm, is the key ingredient to implement infrastructures supporting new forms of democratic engagement of the users. A recent report by Fluence Labs [17] presents the state of the DApps ecosystem surviving 160 projects. The main findings can be summarized in the following points: a) DApps is a modern trend: 72% of the projects started in 2018, b) 87% of the projects run on Ethereum c) A quarter of the surveyed projects are gaming DApps. d) About half of the projects used a centralized tools to connect to the Ethereum blockchain. e) Transactional fees prevailed as the central monetization model for most projects. f) New user onboarding was mentioned by more than three quarters of the respondents as the major obstacle to adoption.

Problem Statement. Design Patterns are undoubtedly a useful tool to improve the development of DApps. Due to the nature of the Blockchain, more than in other contexts DApps are at risk of generating problems, which are hard to recover from. However, most of the available Design Patterns for Blockchain do not consider some useful information that can help the developer to implement correct and efficient solutions.

Contribution of the Paper. In this paper we analyse and evaluate best practices in the use of Design Patterns for a typical DApp. Moreover, we refine the format description of design pattern specific for blockchain with other fields, namely *Cost of execution* and *Decentralization level* and *On-chain/Off-chain components*, capable to help developers in trading-off between critical design and implementation choices. As a running example, we develop a DApp interacting with Internet Of Things devices to monitor and manage resource consumption, and encourage the democratic engagement and empowerment of citizens. In particular, our use case focuses on a DApp for the management of urban water resources. However, the Design Patterns employed in this specific use case are of general interest and can support a variety of other application scenarios.

2   Use Case: Decentralized Management of Urban Water Resources

The interactive statistics portal by the International Water Association (IWA) [8] provides data on water consumption, tariff structure and regulation of water services in 198 cities in 39 countries from all 5 continents. The IWA report stresses the importance of adopting modern emerging technologies and smart metering to improve the overall water management process in the city.

In nowadays cloud solutions, data on water consumption is collected by smart meters and delivered to a cloud service allowing live monitoring of the consumption and providing evidences on consumption patterns to the users in the hope that citizens will consequently act to reduce their water consumption.

It is worth noting that the overall success of such resource management strongly depends on the active and collective participation of citizens. The virtuous behaviour of an individual is commendable, but the risk is that it is literally "a drop in the ocean" if not accompanied by the joint action of the community.

Nowadays, the Client/Server paradigm dominates the cloud services market. However, decentralized applications (DApps), an emerging P2P framework, have the potential to revolutionize this market and democratize the whole process. The hope is that the empowerment of the citizen, guaranteed by this democratic process, will improve the participation and thus the overall chances of success of smart cities initiatives. As observed in [22], smart cities often do not optimally reach their objectives if the citizens are not suitably involved in their design.

We assume the availability of suitable Internet of Things (IoT) devices, i.e. smart water meters, capable to measure the performance of a target process, i.e. reducing water consumption. However, we want then to have citizens engaged in pursuing behavioural changes. It is well-known that behavioural changes are the effective way to better performances in resource management, e.g. closing the water while brushing teeth can save up to 20 L, and taking a shower can save up to four times the water necessary for a bath.

To support the active engagement and democratic participation of users, our proposed DApp will implement two main principles:

- Citizens propose smart contracts that encode measures of the effectiveness of water management policies. Typically, such smart contracts relies on IoT data to monitor the application of policies. Citizens also select a smart contract by a fair vote. Such smart contracts, capable of attracting the greater consensus from citizens, becomes currently operative. Selection may occur regularly, on demand, or on specific conditions.
- To further encourage the participation of citizens, the operative smart contract will also be in charge of distributing incentives to virtuous citizens, namely citizens that most actively contribute to fulfill policies, i.e. successfully reduce the water consumption.

2.1   Reference Architecture

The full implementation of the Proof of Concept (PoC) is available in the GitHub repository [2] and a simplified reference architecture is shown in Fig. 1.

Smart Contracts. The smart contracts have been developed in Solidity [11], the object-oriented, high-level language for implementing smart contracts on

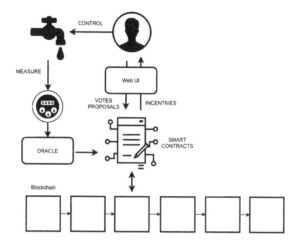

Fig. 1. A simplified picture of a DApp for water management. Contrary to central-ized architectures the back-end of this architecture is implemented on smart contracts running on the P2P decentralized blockchain infrastructure.

Ethereum, using Remix [4], the browser-based compiler and IDE that enables users to build Ethereum contracts and to debug transactions.

The *manager* smart contract, implemented in the *ManagerContract* class, is in charge to a) manage the interface with IoT sensors and safety of data, b) manage the voting process at each occurrence of it, and c) make operational the most voted proposal, which will monitor the application of policies and devolve incentives accordingly. Several variations to this general scheme are possible, of course, but for the sake of this paper such a general formulation will be adequate. In the next section we discuss the design patterns involved in the design of the proposed DApps for urban water management. The voting process code is inspired by the example on ballot available on Solidity documentation [5]. The vote starts and finishes, respectively, with the methods *startVote* and *winningProposal*. The latter, takes also care of counting the votes and electing the winner. The *addProposalContract* method allows users to propose a new contract, while the method *vote* allows user to vote for a proposal. Note that this method is *payable* because it has to collect the funding during the voting process and to transfer the accumulated funding to the winning proposal using the method *trasferToWinner*.

The *proposal* smart contract must essentially define a) how to measure the contribution by each citizen to the reduction of water consumption as measured by IoT sensors, and b) how to distribute incentives according to that contribu-tion. Citizens are free to present proposals, namely alternative solutions that are democratically voted by the citizens themselves. The class *ProposalContract* represents a proposal of a citizen. The *owner* variable maintains the owner of the contract (this is crucial for the implementation of the access restriction pat-tern, see Sect. 3). As already observed, the ManagerContract manages all the key phases of the process and consequently, before starting the voting phase, every participating contract should change its ownership to the ManagerContract calling *changeOwner* method.

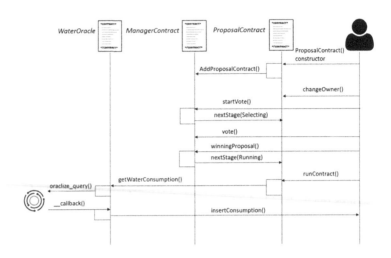

Fig. 2. Interaction with the smart contracts

Finally, the proposal that wins the election phase become runnable and the corresponding smart contract is executed invoking the method *runContract*. This results in a call to the smart contract in charge of collecting the data on water consumption interacting with the oracle. This data are stored in the Proposal-Contract by the *insertConsumption* method. Each citizen is allowed to access only its own consumption data. The hash table *consumers* maintains the association between the user credentials that are used by the oracle to access the data, and their address in the blockchain.

WaterOracle is the smart contract that collects the data on the water meters from a source of data external to the blockchain.

The whole process, summarized in Fig. 2, which allows the citizens to select the smart contract that will become operative can be divided in three phases: 1) the proposal phase, 2) the selection phase and 3) the running phase. During the proposal phase, proposal contracts are submitted by the community. In the selection phase, proposal contracts are voted by the community. For the sake of simplicity, we assume that citizen can access the vote only by providing a fee that is used to accumulate the incentives. More realistic fee policies are scope for future work. The voted contract becomes operative in the running phase, and will actually distribute the accumulated incentives according to its own policies.

Web UI. Users can access the functions of the system by *a web application* running on his/her premises that interacts with the blockchain. This app is developed in Nodejs and web3.js [6], which is a collection of libraries allowing to interact with a local or remote Ethereum node, through HTTP, WebSocket and IPC connection. While in principle citizens can make their proposals in the form of free smart contracts encoded in solidity, in this paper we focus on a template smart contract where the proposals are characterized by different parameters that users can freely select accessing the *Proposal* page of the Web UI. Examples of the parameters defining the smart contracts are: *What* will be monitored (e.g. apartment, building), the *Criteria* to distribute the incentive (e.g. ≤ a given threshold) and the *Interval* in which the monitoring activity is performed and incentives are distributed (e.g. semester).

Once a proposal has been formalized, it can be voted accessing the *Vote* page, showed in Fig. 3, where users can inspect the proposals and finally vote for the most liked one. After a suitable time interval, that allows each voter to express their preferences, the winner proposal is elected and starts the running phase.

In the *Run* page the user can finally allow the selected smart contract to access its data on water consumption. If the criteria defining a virtuous behaviour embodied in the smart contract are meet, the corresponding incentives are automatically sent to the user.

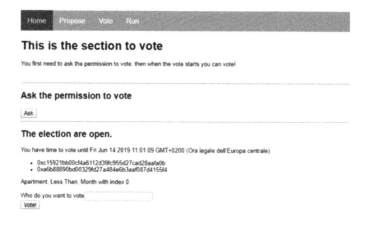

Fig. 3. The voting interface

3   Smart Contract Design Patterns

We used some of the Solidity design and programming patterns [9,24,25] collected by Franz Volland in his github repository [23]. The aim of this section is double: to discuss how these design patterns have been employed to implement the methods and the smart contracts in the proposed decentralized system for water management; to describe how a design pattern is expanded in the case of a blockchain design pattern (BDP).

The documentation for a design pattern describes the context in which the pattern is used, the forces within the context that the pattern seeks to resolve, and the suggested solution. A variety of different formats [14] have been used by different pattern authors. [23] uses one of these approaches. We intend to add two additional fields for describing a BDP:

- The first is *cost of execution - gas*, i.e. the unit to measure the amount of computational effort to execute certain operations. Its presence is fundamental and necessary for public blockchains such as Ethereum: this in fact avoids that an operation performs forever on the blockchain blocking the entire network.
- Secondly, there are the *blockchain specific features* which are a set of properties that highlights how BDP are related with peculiar characteristics of blockchains. We have identified decentralization and on-chain or off-chain properties.

For the sake of space we don't sketch the code of all patterns, the interested reader is referred to [2] and we do not report the formal description of the patterns already available at [23], but we focus our attention to the two additional descriptive fields presented above.

Ownership and Access Restriction Pattern. During the proposal phase, users make contract proposals. In order to participate to the next selection phase, users have to release contract ownership to the manager smart contract. This is done by implementing the *Access Restriction* pattern which allows the ownership of a contract to be changed. The proposer invokes the *changeOwner* function, providing as input the address of the manager that consequently becomes the owner. We stress here that at each instant in time there is only one owner for a contract and some functions can be invoked only by the owner because they are critical for the correct execution of the contract.

Cost of execution - gas	
changeOwner()	28595
Blockchain specific features	
Decentralization of the BDP	Decentralized BDP
On-chain or off-chain solution	The owner is stored into a variable of the smart contract, so it is an on-chain solution

State Machine Pattern. In each phase, a proposal contract can be in one of three possible states: proposal, selection and running. Only the owner of a contract can change the status of the contract.

The *State Machine* pattern [23] allows a contract to go through different states, with different functions enabled in the different states. A function modifier checks if the contract stage is equal to the required stage before executing the called function. Note that the manager, becoming the owner of the contracts, is the only one capable to change the state of a contract during the selection phase (see Access Restriction pattern: onlyBy(owner)).

Cost of execution - gas	
nextStage()	27632
Blockchain specific features	
Decentralization of the BDP	Decentralized BDP
On-chain or off-chain solution	It changes the internal state of a smart contract that lives on-chain

Oracle Pattern. Once in a running state, the winning smart contract needs to collect data from the smart meters to correctly dispense incentives to the users. This requires the communication with an Oracle, a centralization point, to gain access to data outside the blockchain. An Oracle is hence a trusted entity providing a unique view on a source of data considered credible.

Each node in the blockchain has to validate every computation performed in a smart contract. When this requires the interaction with off-chain sources of data, as in our case with smart meters, this becomes unpractical because, due to network issues (e.g. delays), there are not guarantee that all the node will access the same information as expected thus leading to a possible break in the consensus algorithm.

In our PoC, we use the oracle service provided by Oraclize [3], see Listing 1 (recently Oraclize changed its name to Provable).

Listing 1. The call of an Oracle to acquire the water meter readings and send them back to ProposalContract.

```
contract WaterOracle is usingOraclize {
    uint public water;

    function () public  payable {}
    function getWaterConsumption(string input_for_API)
    public {

        if (oraclize_getPrice("URL") > this.balance) {
            emit LogError("Put more ETH");
        }
        else {
            //call the oracle and save the request
        }
    }
    function __callback(bytes32 myid,
        string _result) public
    {
        //update consumption

    }
}
```

The function *getWaterConsumption* is invoked by the ProposalContract and performs the query to the oracle. The fallback function is necessary to support the necessary payments to the Oracle: only if the balance of the WaterOracle smart contract is sufficient, the query is delivered to the Oraclize contract that access the data interacting with the data source API. Once data are available a _callback function is called to store the values on the ProposalContract in the public variable *water*. The value of *water* is finally used to distribute the incentives.

Cost of execution - gas	
WaterOracle deployment	1362206
getWaterConsumtion()	144520
Blockchain specific features	
Decentralization of the BDP	Most oracles are points of centralization within the network. However projects on decentralized Oracles exists, such as ChainLink [1] which Provable, the new brand behind Oraclize, now supports
On-chain or off-chain solution	This pattern can be implemented either partly on-chain and off-chain (an oracle smart contract with external state injected by an off-chain injector) or totally off-chain (external server signing transactions) [25]

3.1 Discussion

Design Patterns are descriptions or templates to solve problems that can emerge in many different situations, and consequently are usually not a finished design that can be transformed directly into code [14]. However, in the Blockchain, the implementation details have direct consequences on the execution costs of a given pattern that are crucial to determine the feasibility and the success of a project. If the costs of running a system are higher than the expected benefits, users will possibly not participate in the initiative.

As far as concerns the level of decentralization this is crucial to support the democratization of an initiative and thus the active participation of the users, but can have a cost. Let's consider the oracle example. The simplest solution that relies on a single "centralised" oracle is likely the most cost effective. We can reduce the centralization requiring the same information to n independent oracles, but even assuming that we can get the exact same information (e.f. time and source) from all of them, this will result in a cost n-times higher.

The introduction of quantitative metrics (i.e. gas) to evaluate design patterns is not novel (see [7] and [10]) and necessarily require the implementation of the considered design patterns.

4 Related Work

The need for a blockchain-oriented software engineering (BOSE) is recognised in [19] where the authors suggest that ensuring effective testing activities, enhancing collaboration in large teams, and facilitating the development of smart contracts all appear as key factors in the future of blockchain-oriented software development. Compared to traditional Software Engineering, BOSE is not yet well developed and Smart Contracts rely on a non-standard software life-cycle. As an example, once delployed, they can be hardly updated and even simple bugs are difficult to fix. [12] suggests to focus on three main areas for the development of BOSE: a) Best practices and development methodology, b) Design patterns and c) Testing.

In [9] the authors quantify the usage of smart contracts on Bitcoin and Ethereum in relation to their application domain and analyse the most common programming patterns in Ethereum.

Due to the inherent nature of blockchain based contract execution, missing low level programming abstractions, and the constant evolution of platform features and security considerations, writing correct and secure smart contracts for Ethereum is a difficult task. In [24] the authors mined a number of design patterns providing design guidelines and showed that those patterns are widely used to address application requirements and common problems.

The literature on blockchain technologies in the smart cities has been recently reviewed in [21]. The paper analyses a number of sectors where the blockchain can contribute to build a smarter city, including water management. A privacy-friendly blockchain-based gaming platform aiming at engaging users in reducing water or energy consumption at their premises is proposed in [20], but this paper does not explicitly use smart contracts.

In [18] the authors stress that lack of transparency and trust on a centralized network infrastructure could be a key factor that hinders the true realization of the citizen participatory governance model. Our proposed DApp is an example of smart urban collaboration implemented over a P2P network thus overcoming most of the limits of traditional centralized networks and guaranteeing an unprecedented level of transparency and trust. In the blockchain, the trust shift from a single and centralized third party to the whole P2P infrastructure, that is decentralized in its nature.

Voting is considered among the most important application of the blockchain technology in the public sector [16]. In our proposed approach, voting is used to select which among the proposed contracts will become actually operative. A fully aware vote requires the understanding of smart contracts and their implications and we cannot expect this is within everyone's reach. The research on the methods to wider the audience capable of understanding smart contracts is out of the scope of this paper. In our implementation, we propose a smart contract template where users can simply and freely select some of the key parameters defining the contract.

5   Conclusion

In this paper we discussed the applicability of solidity design patterns to the development of decentralized application (DApp) for urban water management. The decentralized nature of DApp implements a democratic process that will hopefully encourage the active participation of the citizen to the actions necessary to reduce the water consumption. Design patterns are among the key ingredients that have been identified to develop a blockchain-oriented software engineering (BOSE) capable to reduce the risks connected to the unique life-cycle of smart contracts. The main contribution of the paper can be summarized in the following points:

- Moving from a centralized Client/Server architecture, typical of current implementations of smart city service, to DApps will remove the necessity of trusting central authorities, which is considered one of the most relevant factors that limit the true realization of citizen participatory governance [18].
- The code of the proposed DApp is available on the github repository [2].
- We propose an extension of the design patterns considering two additional fields, namely *cost of transaction* and *blockchain specific feature* that helps developers in implementing a more effective DApp.
- The proposed extension has been discussed in the implementation of the three design patterns [23] employed in the proposed DApp.

References

1. Chainlink web site (2019). https://chain.link/. Accessed May 2019
2. Dapp_water (2019). https://github.com/marcozecchini/Dapp_Water. Accessed June 2019
3. The provabletm blockchain oracle for modern DAPPS (2019). https://provable. xyz/. Accessed May 2019
4. Remix (2019). https://remix.ethereum.org. Accessed May 2019
5. Solidity documentation (2019). https://solidity.readthedocs.io/. Accessed May 2019
6. web3.js - Ethereum Javascript API (2019). https://web3js.readthedocs.io/en/1.0/. Accessed June 2019
7. Ampatzoglou, A., Chatzigeorgiou, A.: Evaluation of object-oriented design patterns in game development. Inf. Softw. Technol. **49**(5), 445–454 (2007)
8. International Water Association. Water statistics (2019). http://waterstatistics. iwa-network.org/. Accessed May 2019
9. Bartoletti, M., Pompianu, L.: An empirical analysis of smart contracts: platforms, applications, and design patterns. In: Brenner, M., et al. (eds.) FC 2017. LNCS, vol. 10323, pp. 494–509. Springer, Cham (2017). https://doi.org/10.1007/978-3-319-70278-0_31
10. Corsaro, A., Santoro, C.: The analysis and evaluation of design patterns for distributed real-time java software. In: 2005 IEEE Conference on Emerging Technologies and Factory Automation, vol. 1. IEEE (2005). 8-pp
11. Dannen, C.: Introducing Ethereum and Solidity: Foundations of Cryptocurrency and Blockchain Programming for Beginners, 1st edn. Apress, Berkely (2017)

12. Destefanis, G., Marchesi, M., Ortu, M., Tonelli, R., Bracciali, A., Hierons, R.: Smart contracts vulnerabilities: a call for blockchain software engineering? In: 2018 International Workshop on Blockchain Oriented Software Engineering (IWBOSE), pp. 19–25, March 2018

13. DuPont, Q.: Experiments in algorithmic governance a history and ethnography of "the dao", a failed decentralized autonomous organization. In: Campbell-Verduyn, M. (ed.) Bitcoin and Beyond: Cryptocurrencies, Blockchains, and Global Governance, Chap. 8, pp. 157–176. Routledge (2017)

14. Gamma, E.: Design Patterns: Elements of Reusable Object-Oriented Software. Pearson Education, New Delhi (1995)

15. Mehar, M.I., et al.: Understanding a revolutionary and flawed grand experiment in blockchain: the DAO attack. J. Cases Inf. Technol. (JCIT) 21(1), 19–32 (2019)

16. Kshetri, N., Voas, J.: Blockchain-enabled e-voting. IEEE Softw. 35, 95–99 (2018)

17. Fluence Labs: DAPP survey results (2019). https://medium.com/fluence-network/dapp-survey-results-2019-a04373db6452. Accessed May 2019

18. Meijer, A., Bolívar, M.P.R.: Governing the smart city: a review of the literature on smart urban governance. Int. Rev. Admin. Sci. 82(2), 392–408 (2016)

19. Porru, S., Pinna, A., Marchesi, M., Tonelli, R.: Blockchain-oriented software engineering: challenges and new directions. In: 2017 IEEE/ACM 39th International Conference on Software Engineering Companion (ICSE-C), pp. 169–171, May 2017

20. Rottondi, C., Verticale, G.: A privacy-friendly gaming framework in smart electricity and water grids. IEEE Access 5, 14221–14233 (2017)

21. Shen, C., Pena-Mora, F.: Blockchain for cities-a systematic literature review. IEEE Access 6, 76787–76819 (2018)

22. Simonofski, A., Asensio, E.S., Smedt, J.D., Snoeck, M.: Citizen participation in smart cities: evaluation framework proposal. In: 2017 IEEE 19th Conference on Business Informatics (CBI), vol. 01, pp. 227–236, July 2017

23. Volland, F.: Solidity patterns (2019). https://fravoll.github.io/solidity-patterns/. Accessed May 2019

24. Wohrer, M., Zdun, U.: Design patterns for smart contracts in the Ethereum ecosystem. In: 2018 IEEE International Conference on Internet of Things (iThings) and IEEE Green Computing and Communications (GreenCom) and IEEE Cyber, Physical and Social Computing (CPSCom) and IEEE Smart Data (SmartData), pp. 1513–1520 (2018)

25. Xu, X., Weber, I., Staples, M.: Architecture for Blockchain Applications, March 2019

HeteroPar - Workshop on Algorithms, Models and Tools for Parallel Computing on Heterogeneous Platforms

Workshop on Algorithms, Models and Tools for Parallel Computing on Heterogeneous Platforms (HeteroPar)

Workshop Description

HeteroPar is a forum for researchers working on algorithms, programming languages, tools, and theoretical models for efficiently solving complex problems on heterogeneous parallel platforms. Heterogeneity is emerging as one of the most profound and challenging characteristics of today's parallel environments. From the macro level, where heterogeneous networks interconnect distributed computers of diverse architectures, to the micro level, where ever deeper memory hierarchies and specialized accelerator architectures are increasingly common, the impact of heterogeneity on parallel processing is rapidly increasing. Traditional parallel algorithms, programming environments and tools designed for legacy homogeneous multiprocessors will at best achieve a small fraction of the efficiency and the performance expected from tomorrow's highly diverse parallel computing architectures. Therefore, efficiently using these new and multifarious parallel architectures requires innovative ideas, new models, novel algorithms, and other specialized or unified programming environments and tools.

The 17th International Workshop on Algorithms, Models and Tools for Parallel Computing on Heterogeneous Platforms (HeteroPar 2019) took place in Göttingen, Germany, organized for the 11th time in conjunction with the Euro-Par annual international conference. The format of the workshop included 2 keynote and 10 technical presentations. The workshop received good attendance of around 50 people on average throughout the day.

This year, the workshop received 18 paper submissions from 14 countries. After a thorough peer-reviewing process that included discussion and agreement among reviewers whenever necessary, the program chair selected 10 papers for presentation at the workshop. The review process focused on the quality of the papers, their innovation, and applicability to heterogeneous architectures. The quality and the relevance of the selected papers is high. The accepted papers represent an interesting mix of topics, addressing programming models, accelerators, software auto-tuning, benchmarking, performance prediction, code generation, scheduling, resource management, energy efficiency, language interoperability, workflows, serverless computing, and artificial intelligence-based methods oriented towards heterogeneous platforms, as the basis for the next generation exa-scale computers.

The program chair thanks all authors, the Program Committee, and the Steering Committee for their support in making the workshop a successful event. Special thanks are due to the Euro-Par organizers for hosting the HeteroPar community, and especially to the workshop chairs Dora Blanco Heras, Christian Boehme, and Ulrich Schwardmann for their help and support.

Organization

Steering Committee

Domingo Giménez	University of Murcia, Spain
Alexey Kalinov	Cadence Design Systems, Russia
Alexey Lastovetsky	University College Dublin, Ireland
Yves Robert	École Normale Supérieure de Lyon, France
Leonel Sousa	INESC-ID/IST, Universidade de Lisboa, Portugal
Denis Trystram	Université Grenoble Alpes, France

Program Chair

Radu Prodan	University of Klagenfurt, Austria

Program Committee

Hamid Arabnejad	Brunel University London, UK
Marcos Assunção	Inria, LIP, ENS Lyon, France
Jorge G. Barbosa	University of Porto, Portugal
Klavdiya Bochenina	ITMO University, Russia
George Bosilca	University of Tennessee, USA
Aurelien Bouteiller	University of Tennessee, USA
Louis-Claude Canon	Université de Franche-Comte, France
Juan J. Durillo	Leibniz Supercomputing Centre, Germany
Jorge Ejarque	Barcelona Supercomputing Center, Spain
Gabriel Falcão	University of Coimbra, Portugal
Jianbin Fang	National University of Defense Technology, China
Hamid Mohammadi Fard	Technical University Darmstadt, Germany
Edgar Gabriel	University of Houston, USA
Alexandru Iosup	University of Amsterdam, The Netherlands
Byunghyun Jang	University of Mississippi, USA
Helen Karatza	Aristotle University of Thessaloniki, Greece
Gabor Kecskemeti	Liverpool John Moores University, UK
Dragi Kimovski	University of Klagenfurt, Austria
Hatem Ltaief	King Abdullah University of Science and Technology, Saudi Arabia
Vincenzo de Maio	Vienna University of Technology, Austria
Pierre Manneback	University of Mons, Belgium

Ravi Reddy Manumachu	University College Dublin, Ireland
Loris Marchal	CNRS, France
Jing Gong	KTH Royal Institute of Technology, Sweden
Shuichi Ichikawa	Toyohashi University of Technology, Japan
Aleksandar Ilic	University of Lisbon, Portugal
Emmanuel Jeannot	Inria, France
Dana Petcu	West University of Timişoara, Romania
Florin Pop	University Politehnica of Bucharest, Romania
Alberto Proenca	University of Minho, Portugal
Enrique S. Quintana-Orti	Technical University of Valencia, Spain
Thomas Rauber	University of Bayreuth, Germany
Matei Ripeanu	The University of British Columbia, Canada
Sasko Ristov	University of Innsbruck, Austria
Rizos Sakellariou	The University of Manchester, UK
Thomas Scognand	Lawrence Livermore National Laboratory, USA
Frederic Suter	CC IN2P3, CNRS, France
Pedro Tomas	University of Lisbon, Portugal
Paolo Trunfio	University of Calabria, Italy

DataRaceOnAccelerator – A Micro-benchmark Suite for Evaluating Correctness Tools Targeting Accelerators

Adrian Schmitz[1]([✉]) [ID], Joachim Protze[1] [ID], Lechen Yu[2] [ID],
Simon Schwitanski[1] [ID], and Matthias S. Müller[1] [ID]

[1] IT Center, RWTH Aachen University, Aachen, Germany
{a.schmitz,protze,schwitanski,mueller}@itc.rwth-aachen.de
[2] Georgia Institute of Technology, Atlanta, USA
lechen.yu@gatech.edu

Abstract. The advent of hardware accelerators over the past decade has significantly increased the complexity of modern parallel applications. For correctness, applications must synchronize the host with accelerators properly to avoid defects. Considering concurrency defects on accelerators are hard to detect and debug, researchers have proposed several correctness tools. However, existing correctness tools targeting accelerators are not comprehensively and objectively evaluated since there exist few available micro-benchmarks that can test the functionality of a correctness tool.

In this paper, we propose DataRaceOnAccelerator (DRACC), a micro-benchmark suite designed for evaluating the capabilities of correctness tools for accelerators. DRACC provides micro-benchmarks for common error patterns in CUDA, OpenMP, and OpenACC programs. These micro-benchmarks can be used to measure the precision and recall of a correctness tool. We categorize all micro-benchmarks into different groups based on their error patterns, and analyze the necessary runtime information to capture each error pattern. To demonstrate the effectiveness of DRACC, we utilized it to evaluate four existing correctness tools: ThreadSanitizer, Archer, GPUVerify, and CUDA-MEMCHECK. The evaluation results demonstrate that DRACC is capable of revealing the strengths and weaknesses of a correctness tool.

Keywords: Micro-benchmark Suite · Error classification · Accelerator

1 Introduction

Hardware accelerators are becoming increasingly popular within high performance computing area since the last decade. On the Top500 list, six out of the top ten most powerful supercomputers are equipped with GPGPU or many-core co-processors[1]. To leverage accelerators when developing parallel applications,

---

[1] https://www.top500.org/.

© Springer Nature Switzerland AG 2020
U. Schwardmann et al. (Eds.): Euro-Par 2019 Workshops, LNCS 11997, pp. 245–257, 2020.
https://doi.org/10.1007/978-3-030-48340-1_19

programmers utilize parallel programming models such as CUDA, OpenACC, and OpenMP. Those programming models ease the access to accelerators by their built-in APIs and compiler directives, while exposing enough low-level details to help tuning parallel applications. Nevertheless, the increasing complexity of programs results in higher chances of concurrency defects caused by incorrect usage of underlying programming models. Due to the lack of suitable correctness tools considering accelerators, concurrency defects may remain undetected in well-tested parallel applications. As an example, our group just recently identified and reported a mapping bug in the SPEC ACCEL OMP benchmark application 503.postencil [8], which we condensed to the reproducer in Listing 1. The code mimics an iterative solver with a dynamic break condition and works on two arrays where the output of one iteration is the input for the next iteration. In this code, the swap in line 6 has no effect on the map clause and therefore for the map-from at the end of the target data region. The code always maps the array originally addressed by p1 back to the host; for odd numbers of iterations, p2 points to that array afterwards, while p1 points to the unmodified original p2 array. Because of the pointer swap, the code expects p1 to point to the result of this kernel.

Over the past years, a handful of correctness tools targeting concurrency defects on accelerators were presented, for example, GPUVerify [3], BAR-RACUDA [5], CUDA-MEMCHECK, and CURD [15]. Those correctness tools demonstrate the feasibility of detecting concurrency defects on accelerators. In this paper, we present *DataRaceOnAccelerator* (DRACC), a micro-benchmark suite designed to evaluate correctness tools objectively. DRACC focuses on possible concurrency defects in CUDA, OpenACC, and OpenMP programs. It covers common error patterns of concurrency defects incurred by conflicting memory accesses.

In summary, we make the following contributions:

- We present the micro-benchmark suite DRACC to evaluate correctness tools targeting accelerators;
- We thoroughly analyze the coverage of error patterns in DRACC by describing the mapping between micro-benchmarks to error pattern classifications proposed in previous work [11,14] and extending upon them by introducing mapping defects and a new categorization;

```
1  #pragma omp target data map(to:p2[0:N]) map(tofrom:p1[0:N])
2    { do {
3  #pragma omp target parallel for
4        for (int i = 0; i < N; i++)
5          p2[i] = 42 + p1[i];
6        std::swap(p1, p2); // executed on the host
7      } while (!done());
8    } // end of target data region: map(from:p1[0:N])
```

Listing 1. Mapping bug found in a SPEC ACCEL benchmark

- We introduce five levels of available information to understand the requirements and possibilities of analyzing each error pattern;
- We used DRACC to evaluate existing correctness tools: ThreadSanitizer [16, 17] and Archer [1], GPUVerify, and CUDA-MEMCHECK.

2   DataRaceOnAccelerator

Liao et al. [9,10] developed a benchmark suite, DataRaceBench, for data races in OpenMP. DataRaceBench is designed to test data race detectors for their capabilities of finding data races in OpenMP programs. This benchmark suite has been widely applied in the development and evaluation of OpenMP data race detectors [2,7].

Inspired by DataRaceBench, DRACC covers common memory driven defects on heterogeneous systems in CUDA, OpenMP, and OpenACC programs. DRACC provides a group of micro-benchmarks, developed upon following programming models and compilers: CUDA 9.1 with NVCC, OpenACC 2.6 with PGI compiler 18.4 and OpenMP 4.5 with Clang 7.0. The micro-benchmarks for DRACC are synthesized instances of the error patterns discussed in Sect. 3.

The complete micro-benchmark suite is available at Github[2] and can be compiled with the given Makefile for each programming model. All micro-benchmarks are designed based on specifications of abovementioned programming models. Thus, erroneous runtime implementations violating specifications may lead to unexpected results.

Listing 2 shows three kernels encountering an atomicity violation on the accelerator. Each of these kernels implements the same error pattern leading to an undefined value of the countervar variable. This failure is caused by the concurrent increment of the same variable countervar/d_countervar. For OpenMP and OpenACC the variable is globally accessible on the accelerator, causing a data race among the individual steps of the increment: read to a register, increment in a register, write to global memory. A further explanation of the error pattern is presented in Sect. 3.

The CUDA implementation in Listing 2 behaves differently from the OpenMP and OpenACC implementations. The device variable d_countervar is not explicitly defined as a global variable for CUDA, thus, each thread creates a thread-private copy of the variable, which is incremented accordingly. Due to CUDA's memory model, the result from each thread will then be copied back to the original variable. This results in a data race between the copy operations and a result of exactly d_countervar = 1 for each execution regardless of grid and block dimension. Similar to the OpenMP and OpenACC kernel, the CUDA kernel also implements an atomicity violation.

---

[2] https://github.com/RWTH-HPC/DRACC.

```
1  __global__ void count_kernel(int *d_countervar){
2      d_countervar[0]++;
3  }
4  void count(){//Launch CUDA Kernel
5      count_kernel<<<100,512>>>(d_count);}
```

```
1  void count(){//OpenACC Kernel
2      #pragma acc parallel copy(countervar) num_workers(256)
3      #pragma acc loop gang worker
4      for (int i=0; i<N; i++)
5          countervar++;}
```

```
1  void count(){//OpenMP Kernel
2      #pragma omp target map(tofrom:countervar) device(0)
3      #pragma omp teams distribute parallel for
4      for (int i=0; i<N; i++)
5          countervar++;}
```

Listing 2. Examples of an atomicity violation on the accelerator in CUDA, OpenACC and OpenMP.

3 Classification

To understand the coverage of micro-benchmarks in DRACC, in this section we introduce a defect classification for application errors on heterogeneous systems. The classification shown in Fig. 1 is based on the study of Shan Lu et al. on concurrency defects [11] and the error classification by Münchhalfen et al. [14]. The classification focuses on common application errors to provide a foundation for future tool support on accelerators. Additionally, to differentiate between cause and effect of an error, we utilize the notation by A. Zeller [19] that *failure* is the manifestation of an error, e.g., non-deterministic results or a blocking application; and *defect* is the source of an error, e.g., incorrect source code.

The classification is designed to cover defects for application-programming purposes, especially regarding CUDA, OpenACC, and OpenMP programs. Syntactic correctness of the code as well as the validation of the programming model implementation, i.e., compiler and runtime, are out of scope for this work.

3.1 Overview

Using parallel programming paradigms can introduce new kinds of defects which are finally observed as failures. These are either segmentation faults or non-deterministic results. In Fig. 1 an overview of the defect classification is presented. All accelerator application defects belong to one of the following categories:

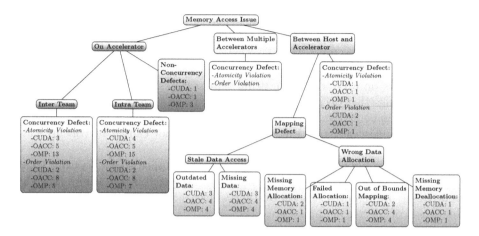

Fig. 1. A classification of common memory access defects in heterogenous computing. The number behind CUDA, OACC and OMP describes the number of micro-
benchmarks that expose the corresponding defect class for the given programming
model. Each micro-benchmark contains only a single defect.

1. *On Accelerator:* defects on the accelerator, independent of any other device.
2. *Between Host and Accelerator:* defects within the communication between
   host and device.
3. *Between Multiple Accelerators:* defects within the communication between
   multiple devices.

In this paper, we focus on the first two categories. Figure 1 provides an overview
of the number of micro-benchmarks for each defect pattern per programming
model. Since OpenMP allows the use of critical sections and locks on the device,
we find more different error patterns for OpenMP.

3.2 Concurrency Defects

Concurrency defects as defined in [11], classify defects caused by concurrency. A
non-deadlock concurrency defect can either be an *atomicity violation* or an *order
violation*. Atomicity violation means that the intended atomicity of a group of
memory accesses is not enforced. Order violation means that the intended order
of two groups of memory accesses is potentially inverted, i.e., the intended order
is not enforced. In this context memory accesses include memory reads, writes,
allocations, and deallocations.

3.3 On Accelerator

Accelerator programming models typically provide similar high-level abstractions for program execution. An application is executed by a number of threads
which are further divided into multiple *groups*. Threads belonging to the same

group can synchronize with each other, while threads from distinct groups execute independently. In this paper, we use the term *team* from OpenMP to refer to the notion of group (OpenMP *team*, OpenACC *gang*, and CUDA *thread block* express the same notion as group).

For defects on accelerators we define three classes: *Intra team concurrency defects* are bugs that occur within the same team of threads. In contrast, *inter team concurrency defects* are bugs between multiple teams of threads. Finally, *non-concurrency defects* are those defects that are not caused by concurrency, e.g., stack buffer overflows.

In general, defects occurring on CPUs may also happen on accelerators. Considering the overall architectures of hardware accelerators are vastly different from CPUs, we distinguish inter and intra team concurrency defects to clarify differences of corresponding failures.

3.4 Between Host and Accelerator

Defects between host and accelerator include order violations in the synchronization between host and accelerator, and atomicity violations for asynchronous kernels. In addition, for OpenMP atomicity violations may reside in synchronous kernels due to memory abstraction. The memory abstraction might hide the actual usage of unified or separate memory. Therefore an application relying on a specific implementation of OpenMP runtime may encounter atomicity violations.

Another defect class between host and accelerator are mapping defects. Mapping defects cover all defects related to data movement between host and accelerator. In different paradigms data movement is expressed by API functions or clauses for copy or mapping.

Some defects can be classified into both stale data access and wrong data allocation, for example, an asynchronous data movement conflicting with concurrent memory accesses. For those defects we treat it as concurrency defects.

Stale Data Access. Defects where data was not copied to or updated at the desired destination are defined as stale data access. Therefore, on host or accelerator data is missing. We distinguish *missing data*, where necessary data is not copied to the device; and *outdated data*, where data is changed on one device but not updated to the other device before accessing the data there. The example in Listing 1 shows the latter pattern, although it is not the root cause. Concurrent access to the same memory by both sides can be understood as outdated data in case of separate memory or concurrency defect in case of unified memory.

Wrong Data Allocation. Defects related to the allocation or deallocation of memory, that are not already covered by concurrency defects, are defined as wrong data allocation. We identified four different kinds of defects. When the application misses to check for a failed allocation and tries to use this memory afterwards we call this *failed allocation*. We find *out of bounds mapping*, when the memory allocation on either side is smaller than the requested size for the mapping or copy. On *missing memory deallocation*, allocated memory is not deallocated at the end of execution which results in memory leaks. We call it *missing memory allocation* if no memory is allocated for transferred data before the first access on the device.

4 Information Usage

To analyze and detect the various defects described in the previous section and exposed in the provided micro-benchmarks, more or less detailed information is necessary. In this section, we discuss different levels of information which can be observed by an analysis tool. Although this might be obvious to tool developers, we believe, the following might help tool users to better understand the possibilities, limitations, and runtime overhead of specific tools. The different levels of information come with different runtime overhead and different impact on the execution. Furthermore, we classify the previously introduced defects for their necessary levels of observable information.

4.1 Five Levels of Observable Information

The five levels of observable information are a classification of the information needed to detect the defined defect classes from the prior section. An overview of the levels is given in Fig. 2. Each level consists of information about events in a program, whereby an *event* can be any observed instruction during the execution of a program. The different levels build up a hierarchy, i.e., each higher level includes all information of the corresponding lower levels. The five levels cover the following information:

1. *Ordering:* Information on the causality of events is available such that a tool can derive a happened-before relation for the events of an execution.
2. *Memory Management:* Memory allocations and data movement are tracked; this includes source, destination, and size (if applicable).

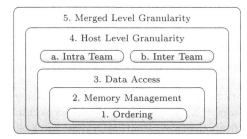

Tool	Level
CUDA-MEMCHECK	1 - 4a[a]
Archer	1 - 4
ThreadSanitizer	1 - 4
GPUVerify	None[b]

[a] shared memory only
[b] static tool

Fig. 2. The five levels of observable information and their dependencies on the left. Supported levels for all evaluated tools on the right.

3. *Data Access:* Memory location accesses are tracked on host and accelerator (read or write).
4. *Host Level Granularity:* In this level we distinguish *Intra Team Granularity*, when events within a group of threads (thread block/team/gang) can be attributed to the individual thread; and *Inter Team Granularity* when events within different groups of threads can be attributed to the group of threads.
5. *Merged Level Granularity:* The system is monitored as a whole allowing the differentiation between all threads on all devices when accessing the unified memory space.

4.2   Pattern Identification

In most cases, a tool will not be able to identify the concrete defect in the code, but in the best case pinpoint its location. The different defects result in different suspicious behavior which a tool is able to detect. This section presents for each level of information which of the previously discussed error patterns it can detect.

1. Ordering. Information on the causality of events enables a tool to detect simple order violations between host and device events. An example could be a program moving data from the host to device before any memory is allocated on the device. Since there is no further information on the address and size of the allocated memory regions, the detection capabilities of a tool with this restricted information are limited.

2. Memory Management. In case a tool tracks memory allocations and data movement in addition to just the ordering of events, it can detect all subclasses belonging to the *Wrong Data Allocation* class.

A tool can identify *Missing Memory Allocation* defects by testing if transferred memory at the destination has been allocated before the actual data movement. If the corresponding memory is only allocated afterwards, an order violation between host and accelerator could be diagnosed. *Missing Data Deallocation* defects can be detected by testing if the memory is released before the connection to the accelerator is closed. *Failed Allocation* defects can be detected by tracking if memory allocations result in errors. Subsequent null pointer access could be diagnosed as a potentially unhandled failed allocation. *Out of bounds mapping* defects can be detected by comparing the size of the data to be transferred, the size of allocated memory on source and destination, respectively.

3. Data Access. Tracking all memory accesses including their ordering on both host and device allows a tool to identify all patterns of the *Stale Data Access* class: *Missing data* defects can be diagnosed if data is read on the accelerator which is neither initialized nor copied from the host. If either is done after the access, an order violation is observed. *Outdated data* defects can be detected, when data is altered (write access) on one side but not updated to the other side before access. In both cases, information from the data access level is necessary to detect stale data access.

The data access level is also sufficient to detect *order violations* related to data mappings between host and accelerator, because no attribution to certain threads or groups of threads is required to identify this issue.

4. Host Level Granularity. In case of concurrency defects, namely *atomicity violations* and *order violations*, it is not enough to just track memory location accesses on the accelerator: A tool also has to attribute them to the originating thread within a group of threads (intra team) or to attribute them to the group of threads in case of multiple teams (inter team). If this information is available and additionally all kinds of possible synchronization constructs are tracked (e.g., exclusive accesses), then *atomicity violations* and *order violations* on the accelerator can be detected. If a concurrency defect within a group of threads should be detected, then *intra team* granularity is required. If a concurrency defect between groups of threads should be identified, then *inter team* granularity is required.

5. Merged Level Granularity. This granularity level is only required for atomicity violations and computation related order violations in case of unified memory between host and accelerator. Since any thread on any device can be synchronized to another thread on another device, differentiation of memory accesses and synchronization between all threads on all devices accessing the unified memory space must be possible.

5   Tool Evaluation

To understand the support level of correctness tools for accelerator programming, we used DRACC to evaluate a set of existing tools, namely: Thread-Sanitizer [16,17] delivered with LLVM 7.0, Archer [1] in a development version compatible with LLVM 7.0[3], GPUVerify [3] in version 2016-03-28[4], and CUDA-MEMCHECK[5] as delivered with CUDA 9.1. We carried out the experiments on Tesla P100 graphic cards on the CLAIX cluster at the RWTH Aachen University. Considering the supported programming models of these tools, we tested ThreadSanitizer and Archer with OpenMP micro-benchmarks, GPUVerify with CUDA micro-benchmarks, and CUDA-MEMCHECK with all three groups of micro-benchmarks. The supported levels of observable information for each tool are presented in Fig. 2.

Table 1 gives an overview of the evaluation results. It lists the counts of correct alerts (true positives, TP), false alerts (false positives, FP), error free

---

[3] https://github.com/PRUNERS/openmp/tree/archer_70 (303a691).

[4] http://multicore.doc.ic.ac.uk/tools/GPUVerify/download.php.

[5] https://docs.nvidia.com/cuda/cuda-memcheck/index.html.

(true negatives, TN), and omission (false negative, FN). Based on these counts, we calculated the metrics Precision ($P = \frac{TP}{TP+FP}$) and Recall ($R = \frac{TP}{TP+FN}$).

Since ThreadSanitizer and Archer do not support data race analysis on the accelerator, we force the OpenMP target regions in the OpenMP micro-benchmarks to be executed on the host. For both tools we compile the bench-mark with the flag *-fsanitize=thread*, and for Archer we additionally load the Archer runtime library during execution. 20 out of 50 OpenMP error patterns are detected by both Archer and ThreadSanitizer, and they identify the same group of error patterns. The LLVM OpenMP implementation decides to only run a single team for the teams construct, therefore no issues in the inter team concurrency micro-benchmarks can be observed. Mapping defects are not under-stood by the tools, but can lead to segmentation faults. No false alerts are reported by either tool. The error patterns detected by the tools are the kind of errors which would also be detected for host code, which could be derived by removing the target regions from these micro-benchmarks.

CUDA-MEMCHECK does not detect any defect in the CUDA version of DRACC, although some micro-benchmarks result in CUDA errors. Thus, 0 of the 26 CUDA pattern implementations are detected by this tool. According to the documentation this tool can detect data races in shared device memory. For the same reason, the tool cannot detect most data races in OpenMP or OpenACC micro-benchmarks of DRACC. However, for OpenMP tests CUDA-MEMCHECK detects a generic defect during the initialization of the target region, which is disregarded in Table 1. CUDA-MEMCHECK can detect out of bounds memory mapping from the device to the host in OpenMP and OpenACC.

Since GPUVerify supports two usage modes, *-findbugs* and *-verify*, we tested these two modes on DRACC irrespectively. In both two usage modes, GPUVerify correctly detected 7 out of 26 CUDA error patterns, reported one false alarm, and failed to tackle the remaining 18 CUDA error patterns. For intra team and inter team atomicity violations, GPUVerify pinpointed these concurrency defects and generated a counter example for each concurrency defect. When analyzing the micro-benchmark for stack overflow, GPUVerify reported a false alarm that the micro-benchmark may encounter null-pointer memory access. A possible explanation for this false alarm is that GPUVerify does not model memory accesses in recursive function invocations correctly. For the remaining 18 CUDA error patterns, GPUVerify reported internal errors when analyzing the corresponding micro-benchmarks. The reason for internal errors is these CUDA error patterns are related to stale data access and wrong data allocation, while GPUVerify currently only checks data races and barrier divergence. In addition, some micro-benchmarks use new atomic operations introduced in CUDA 8.0. Since the 2016-03-28 version of GPUVerify is released earlier than CUDA 8.0, GPUVerify cannot recognize these atomic operations, which leads to internal errors.

In summary, DRACC successfully evaluated the functionality of four correct-ness checking tools. The observed result matches our expectation based on the description in the documentation.

Table 1. Analysis results of DRACC on four different tools, values given for CUDA/OpenACC/OpenMP

Tool	TP	FP	TN	FN	P[%]	R[%]
ThreadSanitizer	-/-/26	-/-/0	-/-/7	-/-/23	-/-/100	-/-/53
Archer	-/-/26	-/-/0	-/-/7	-/-/23	-/-/100	-/-/53
GPUVerify	7/-/-	1/-/-	3/-/-	18/-/-	87.5/-/-	28/-/-
CUDA-MEMCHECK	0/2/3	0/1/0	3/9/7	26/31/46	0/67/100	0/6/6

6 Related Work

Münchhalfen et al. [14] published an error classification of OpenMP programs and solutions for the detection. The main focus of their work is OpenMP. Offloading with OpenMP is also considered in their classification, as part of data transfer errors and data races. The classification in our work covers offloading with OpenMP, OpenACC, and CUDA.

Friedline et al. [6] developed a test suite to validate OpenACC implementations and corresponding features in OpenACC 2.5. Their work provides a validation test suite for compiler architects and programmers. This validation test suite is designed for multiple hardware architectures to test the portability of OpenACC code between these architectures.

Similar test suites for OpenMP have been developed by Müller et al. for OpenMP 2.0 [12] and OpenMP 2.5 [13]. These two test suites aim to cover the complete standard and valid combinations of OpenMP constructs. Wang et al. [18] developed a validation test suite for OpenMP 3.1. For OpenMP 4.5 Diaz and Pophale et al. [4] provided a validation test suite. These two validation test suites can verify the correctness of runtime implementation according to the specification.

7 Conclusion and Future Work

This paper introduced DRACC, a micro-benchmark suite containing common concurrency defects in CUDA, OpenACC, and OpenMP programs. DRACC was designed as a test suite for correctness tools to evaluate their functionalities. To cover as many error patterns as possible, DRACC was developed based on error pattern classifications from previous studies on concurrency defects. The evaluation of existing correctness tools demonstrates that DRACC can reveal the strengths and limitations of a correctness tool being tested. The evaluation further shows that proper tools supporting different levels of observable information are required to detect the discussed error patterns in accelerator programming.

For future work, we plan to extend DRACC to other parallel programing models which also support accelerators, for example, Kokkos and OpenCL. Furthermore, we also plan to test correctness tools on other accelerators in addition to Nvidia GPUs to conduct a more comprehensive evaluation.

References

1. Atzeni, S., Gopalakrishnan, G., et al.: ARCHER: effectively spotting data races in large OpenMP applications. In: 2016 IEEE International Parallel and Distributed Processing Symposium, IPDPS, pp. 53–62 (2016)
2. Atzeni, S., Gopalakrishnan, G., et al.: SWORD: a bounded memory-overhead detector of OpenMP data races in production runs. In: 2018 IEEE International Parallel and Distributed Processing Symposium, IPDPS, pp. 845–854 (2018)
3. Betts, A., Chong, N., et al.: GPUVerify: a verifier for GPU kernels. ACM SIGPLAN Not. **47**, 113–132 (2012)
4. Diaz, J.M., Pophale, S., Hernandez, O., Bernholdt, D.E., Chandrasekaran, S.: OpenMP 4.5 validation and verification suite for device offload. In: de Supinski, B.R., Valero-Lara, P., Martorell, X., Mateo Bellido, S., Labarta, J. (eds.) IWOMP 2018. LNCS, vol. 11128, pp. 82–95. Springer, Cham (2018). https://doi.org/10.1007/978-3-319-98521-3_6
5. Eizenberg, A., Peng, Y., et al.: BARRACUDA: binary-level analysis of runtime RAces in CUDA programs. SIGPLAN Not. **52**(6), 126–140 (2017)
6. Friedline, K., Chandrasekaran, S., Lopez, M.G., Hernandez, O.: OpenACC 2.5 validation testsuite targeting multiple architectures. In: Kunkel, J.M., Yokota, R., Taufer, M., Shalf, J. (eds.) ISC High Performance 2017. LNCS, vol. 10524, pp. 557–575. Springer, Cham (2017). https://doi.org/10.1007/978-3-319-67630-2_39
7. Gu, Y., Mellor-Crummey, J.: Dynamic data race detection for OpenMP programs. In: Proceedings of the International Conference for High Performance Computing, Networking, Storage, and Analysis, SC 2018, pp. 61:1–61:12. IEEE (2018)
8. Juckeland, G., Grund, A., Nagel, W.E.: Performance portable applications for hardware accelerators: lessons learned from SPEC ACCEL. In: IEEE International Parallel and Distributed Processing Symposium Workshop (2015)
9. Liao, C., Lin, P.H., et al.: DataRaceBench: a benchmark suite for systematic evaluation of data race detection tools. In: Proceedings of the International Conference for High Performance Computing, Networking, Storage and Analysis, SC 2017. ACM (2017)
10. Liao, C., Lin, P., et al.: A semantics-driven approach to improving DataRaceBench's OpenMP standard coverage. In: Evolving OpenMP for Evolving Architectures (IWOMP 2018, Barcelona, Spain), pp. 189–202 (2018)
11. Lu, S., Park, S., et al.: Learning from mistakes - a comprehensive study on real world concurrency bug characteristics. ACM SIGOPS Oper. Syst. Rev. **42**(2), 329–339 (2008)
12. Müller, M., Neytchev, P.: An OpenMP validation suite. In: Fifth European Workshop on OpenMP, Aachen University, Germany (2003)
13. Müller, M.S., Niethammer, C., et al.: Validating OpenMP 2.5 for Fortran and C/C++. In: Sixth European Workshop on OpenMP (2004)
14. Münchhalfen, J.F., Hilbrich, T., Protze, J., Terboven, C., Müller, M.S.: Classification of common errors in OpenMP applications. In: DeRose, L., de Supinski, B.R., Olivier, S.L., Chapman, B.M., Müller, M.S. (eds.) IWOMP 2014. LNCS, vol. 8766, pp. 58–72. Springer, Cham (2014). https://doi.org/10.1007/978-3-319-11454-5_5
15. Peng, Y., Grover, V., et al.: CURD: a dynamic CUDA race detector. In: Proceedings of the 39th ACM SIGPLAN Conference on Programming Language Design and Implementation, pp. 390–403. ACM (2018)
16. Serebryany, K., Iskhodzhanov, T.: ThreadSanitizer: data race detection in practice. In: Proceedings of the Workshop on Binary Instrumentation and Applications, WBIA 2009, pp. 62–71. ACM (2009)

17. Serebryany, K., Potapenko, A., Iskhodzhanov, T., Vyukov, D.: Dynamic race detection with LLVM compiler. In: Khurshid, S., Sen, K. (eds.) RV 2011. LNCS, vol. 7186, pp. 110–114. Springer, Heidelberg (2012). https://doi.org/10.1007/978-3-642-29860-8_9

18. Wang, C., Chandrasekaran, S., Chapman, B.: An OpenMP 3.1 validation testsuite. In: Chapman, B.M., Massaioli, F., Müller, M.S., Rorro, M. (eds.) IWOMP 2012. LNCS, vol. 7312, pp. 237–249. Springer, Heidelberg (2012). https://doi.org/10.1007/978-3-642-30961-8_18

19. Zeller, A.: Why Programs Fail: A Guide to Systematic Debugging. Elsevier, Oxford (2009)

Application Topology Definition and Tasks Mapping for Efficient Use of Heterogeneous Resources

Kods Trabelsi$^{(\boxtimes)}$, Loïc Cudennec$^{(\boxtimes)}$, and Rihab Bennour$^{(\boxtimes)}$

Computing and Design Environment Laboratory, CEA, LIST,
91191 Gif-sur-Yvette, France
{kods.trabelsi,loic.cudennec,rihab.bennour}@cea.fr

Abstract. Nowadays, high-performance computing (HPC) not only faces challenges to reach computing performance, it also has to take in consideration the energy consumption. In this context, heterogeneous architectures are expected to tackle this challenge by proposing a mix of HPC and low-power nodes. There is a significant research effort to define methods for exploiting such computing platforms and find a trade-off between computing performance and energy consumption. To this purpose, the topology of the application and the mapping of tasks onto physical resources are of major importance. In this paper we propose an iterative approach based on the exploration of logical topologies and mappings. These solutions are executed onto the heterogeneous platform and evaluated. Based on these results a Pareto front is built, allowing users to select the most relevant configurations of the application according to the current goals and constraints. Experiments have been conducted on a heterogeneous micro-server using a video processing application running on top of a software-distributed shared memory and deployed over a mix of Intel i7 and Arm Cortex A15 processors. Results show that some counterintuitive solutions found by the exploration approach perform better than classical configurations.

Keywords: Heterogeneous architectures · Tasks mapping · Solutions space exploration

1 Introduction

Numerical simulation requires the efficient use of computing resources and leads to a growing demand in performance to provide more accurate results or to decrease the computing time. High-performance computing centers usually scale up to offer more computing power and, despite significant R&D efforts on the hardware side to limit the energy consumption, the power efficiency has become an important constraint in the design and management of such centers. Heterogeneous computing platforms combines high-performance and low-power computation nodes and are not only intended to be deployed in HPC but also in

© Springer Nature Switzerland AG 2020
U. Schwardmann et al. (Eds.): Euro-Par 2019 Workshops, LNCS 11997, pp. 258–269, 2020.
https://doi.org/10.1007/978-3-030-48340-1_20

embedded HPC as in autonomous vehicles, IoT and smart manufacturing. The efficient use of heterogeneous platforms is a complex task since it is the result of several intricated sub-problems including application sizing, task mapping and scheduling. The design of high-level tools to help users and platform managers has become an important field of research in the heterogeneous computing community.

One of the issues in such architectures is the deployment of distributed applications in respect of performance constraints and goals. Distributed applications can usually be configured prior to deployment by setting the number of tasks and the placement of tasks onto computing resources. The combination of application sizing and task mapping provides different computing performance (eg. computing time, latency, bandwidth..) and energy consumption (eg. instantaneous power in W or total consumption in kJ) for the same functionality. In this work we propose an exploratory approach to automatically evaluate different application configurations and relieves the user from manually configuring the deployment of applications. Configurations are evaluated on the heterogeneous platform when needed and a Pareto front is built according to constraints and objectives of interest. This representation is given as a decision tool for the user, from which it is possible to pick a particular configuration that meets at best the current requirements.

As a motivating example, we consider applications running on top of a software-distributed shared memory (S-DSM) and deployed over a heterogeneous computing platform. S-DSM is basically a runtime that aggregates distributed physical memories into a shared logical space. It is inherently a distributed system with different roles: S-DSM servers for managing data and metadata and application clients to run the user code. These roles can be instantiated, organized into topologies and mapped onto physical resources, hence leading to performance and energy consumption trade-off when deploying onto the heterogeneous platform. We use a video processing application on top of the S-DSM and evaluate the exploratory approach to build a Pareto front using an heterogeneous Christmann RECS|Box Antares Microserver as for testbed.

The paper is organized as follows: Sect. 2 describes the S-DSM model and deployment context. Section 3 introduces the S-DSM topology definition problem, the resolution approach and the results of the deployment on heterogeneous architectures. Section 4 defines the mapping problem, the developed strategies and the deployment on heterogeneous architectures results. Section 5 gives some references on previous works. Finally, Sect. 6 concludes this paper and gives new perspectives.

2   Topologies and Mappings for DSM

Shared memory is a convenient programming model in which a set of tasks can concurrently allocate and access data in a global memory space. While the implementation is quite straightforward in a single memory system, shared memory requires a tight design to be deployed on a complex architecture with physically distributed memories.

2.1   Distributed Shared Memory

The distributed shared memory (DSM) provides such a completely hardware-independent layer, at the price of hiding complexity into the runtime. The runtime is in charge of transparently managing local and remote data while minimizing the processing and communication costs. DSM have been studied since the late eighties with systems such as Ivy [9] and later adapted to new computation contexts such as clusters [1], grids [2] and many-core processors [11]. There is a price for offering hardware abstraction and code portability: most of DSM systems come with a significant overhead compared to distributed applications that use explicit communications. The contribution proposed in this paper, while based on a generic approach, is applied to the DSM context and aims at finding efficient configurations for the deployment of distributed shared memory applications.

2.2   Topology for DSM

In this work [3], a Software-DSM (S-DSM) is proposed to federate memories over heterogeneous architectures. The system can be seen as a regular distributed application with state machines to implement data coherence protocols. The S-DSM is organized as a semi-structured super-peer network as presented in Fig. 1. A set of clients are connected to a peer-to-peer network of servers, mixing both client-server and peer-to-peer topology types. Servers are in charge of the shared data and metadata management while clients stand as the interface between the application user code and the S-DSM API. Building constraints for topologies include: (1) a minimal topology is made of one server, (2) there is a fully connected graph between servers, (3) each client is connected to one and only one server and (4) connections are not allowed between clients.

2.3   Application Model and Description

Applications running on this S-DSM are defined as a set of roles. Roles can be instantiated into clients using a given implementation. For each role, the application description defines the following constraints: the minimum and maximum numbers of instances (clients) and the available implementations. A description example is given in Fig. 2. This application requires one client to decode the input video stream, at least one client to process the stream and one client to encode the output. From this description it is possible to build different functionally-equivalent S-DSM topologies by setting the number of S-DSM servers, the number of processing clients and the way it is connected.

In this paper we consider a video processing application as presented in Fig. 2. Video frames are decoded by the input role, assigned to one of the process role using an eager scheduling strategy and encoded by the output role. Frames are stored into shared buffers within the Distributed Shared Memory: one input buffer and one output buffer for each processing task. The processing task applies an edge detection algorithm (a convolution using a 3×3 kernel) and a line

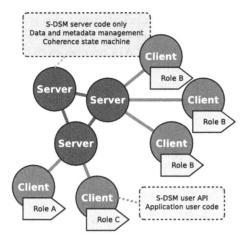

Fig. 1. S-DSM semi-structured super-peer topology.

ROLE	MIN	MAX	IMPLEM
sdsm_server	1	∞	C, Pthread
video_input	1	1	OpenCV
video_process	1	∞	C, Pthread, OpenMP
video_output	1	1	OpenCV

Fig. 2. Video processing application description.

detection algorithm (a Hough transform implemented in double precision). For technical reasons, the input and output roles are implemented using the OpenCV library and always deployed on the Core i7 processors. The processing role can be instantiated in C, Pthread (4 threads) and OpenMP. The input is a 1-min video file, with a total of 1730 frames and a resolution of 1280×720 pixels.

2.4 Heterogeneous Platform

Previous results in [3] have shown that building relevant topologies and mappings are of major importance when it comes to efficiently use computing resources. This is particularly true when considering heterogeneous resources. The platform used in [3] is close to the one that is used in this work. It is a Christmann RECS|Box micro-server with heterogeneous processing elements. This server is a 1U rack composed by a backplane that provides power supply and networking capabilities to a set of slots. Each slot can host a computing node such as high-performance processors, low-power processors, accelerators, GPGPUs and FPGAs. Processing elements are different in terms of computing power and energy consumption. In this configuration, and for our own applications, a Cortex A15 is nearly 4 times slower than a Core i7. Instantaneous power consumption is around 7W for A15 and 30W for i7 at full load. The network also presents disparities in terms of bandwidth and latency due to different mediums and network architectures. For example, the Ethernet over USB is common for embedded devices and the Cortex A15 processors that rely on this interface are loosely connected compared to the i7 processors. In this work, we limited resources to a subset of the computations nodes available on the RECS|Box Antares micro-server. Figure 3 gives details of the nodes used in this paper as well as the number of processing units and supported implementations.

Node	PU	IMPLEM
Intel I7	8	C, OpenMP, Pthread, OpenCV
Cortex A15	2	C, OpenMP, Pthread
Cortex A15	2	C, OpenMP, Pthread
Cortex A15	2	C, OpenMP, Pthread
Cortex A15	2	C, OpenMP, Pthread

Fig. 3. Computing nodes used in the experiments.

Consequences on Heterogeneous Resources. In Fig. 4, processing times are given for an image processing application with different topologies and mappings. S-DSM servers are represented with green cylinders, image input and output clients with orange arrows and processing clients with blue arrows. For each client, an horizontal segment indicates to which server it is connected. Topologies and mappings lead to very different results, even when comparing similar configurations. Even with a tight knowledge of the application, the S-DSM runtime and the hardware, it is difficult to find efficient hand-made solutions based on the sole expression of intuition.

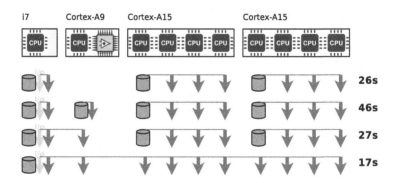

Fig. 4. S-DSM performance results for different topologies.

In this context, an automatic design space exploration should be used to build application configurations. This is particularly important when considering adversarial metrics such as computing time and power consumption, while

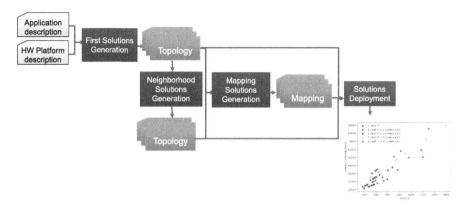

Fig. 5. Automatic design space exploration flow for efficient use of heterogeneous resources

targeting heterogeneous resources. In that case, the exploration system should propose different trade-off solutions and help the user to take an appropriate decision. Furthermore, this has to be done quite transparently for the application, without any code modification such as *pragmas*.

In this work, we propose to automatically explore application configurations and mappings over heterogeneous resources. Figure 5 illustrates the proposed design space exploration flow. Topologies and mappings are generated from given application and hardware descriptions. Solutions are evaluated by deploying and monitoring the application on the targeted computing hardware platform. The results are then used to build a Pareto front allowing a user to select relevant configurations corresponding to his objectives and constraints.

3   Space Exploration for Topologies

Generating all possible configurations is not acceptable because it is a time consuming operation. However, in order to generate a relevant set of topologies, we have been inspired by approximate methods. This class of methods, called also heuristics, gives a trade-off between the computation time and the quality of solutions. Neighborhood search (local search), is a meta-heuristic method for solving computationally hard optimization problems. This type of algorithms is widely applied to various computational problems in several fields. This algorithms move from a solution to another in the space of candidate solutions (the search space) by applying local changes, until a solution deemed as optimal is found or a time bound is elapsed.

In this work, we instrument a multi-starts local search to investigate the search space. This approach involves starting from several solutions and performing as much parallel local searches in order to generate a set of new solutions. The key point of this approach is the generation of starting solutions. The starting solutions have to be sufficiently scattered in the search space to explore it at best.

We chose to implement this approach among others because of its simplicity. Moreover, it can be a good starting point for building more sophisticated approaches such as simulated annealing algorithm. This method involves two steps. The first step is the generation of initial solutions. The second one corresponds to the neighborhood exploration. Initial solutions and those generated using local search were deployed on the RECS|Box Antares micro-server for evaluating their execution times and their energetic costs. For the rest of the document, "solution" designates a topology.

3.1   Initial Solutions Generation

Initial solutions are built using a greedy approach. To build a solution we have to set the number of servers, the number of tasks for each role and the connections between servers and clients. To obtain various starting solutions, we varied the number of servers and the number of tasks for each role. The server number has been varied from one to the number of nodes available on the targeted computing platform (5 in our example), to obtain a set of partial solutions. Then for each partial solution, we varied the number of the processing role instances to obtain a new set of partial solutions. Once the number of servers and the number of tasks for each role are set, a function is in charge of randomly establishing connections between servers and tasks preserving the uniqueness constraint. This last step leads to the completion of all the solutions. The generated topologies are not necessarily valid solutions: at this stage we can not guarantee that each topology will have at least one possible mapping on the target computing platform.

Deployment of Initial Solutions on Heterogeneous Platform

Figure 3 gives details on the resources used while the application is described on Fig. 2. Figure 6 shows the performance and energetic costs of initial solutions. First, the energy consumption increases according to the number of nodes. Second, the execution time does not necessarily decrease if we use more computing nodes, hence falling beyond speedup. Figure 7 gives details of the solutions used to build the Pareto front (Solutions A and B). Solution B takes less time to complete its execution thanks to the extra processing task and the load distribution between the two S-DSM servers. However this has an additional cost for energy consumption and solution B is not as efficient as solution A when comparing frames per second per KJ (FPS/KJ).

Solution A' (Fig. 7) is obtained by adding to solution A a processing instance mapped on the Intel processor. Adding this processing task should intuitively decrease the application execution time, but that is not what happens. The Open MPI runtime implementation is intended to be deployed on HPC systems. In order to be as responsive as possible, the receive function busy-waits and continuously polls for new messages, the latter being CPU-demanding. When deploying several MPI processes on the same CPU, the local OS scheduler has to cope with legitimate MPI processes running user code and falsely busy MPI processes waiting for messages, the first being slowed down by the second.

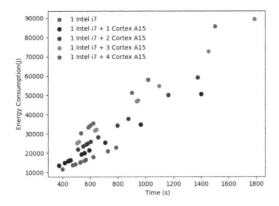

Fig. 6. Initial topologies

Solutions	Nodes	nb_s	nb tasks	Time (s)	FPS	KJ	FPS/KJ
solution A	1 Intel	1	4	398	4.3	11.5	0.38
solution B	1 Intel + 1 Cortex A15	2	5	375	4.6	13.5	0.34
solution A'	1 Intel	1	5	375	4.6	13.5	0.34

Fig. 7. Solutions of the initial Pareto front (A and B) and solution A' obtained by adding a processing task onto the Intel node. nb_s stands for the number of S-DSM servers. Frames per second (FPS). Energy is given in KJ.

3.2   Neighborhoods Description

A neighborhood is obtained by applying a given number of modifications such as sub-topology swapping to the original solution. This generates several new solutions. In our context, several modifications are used such as adding or deleting S-DSM servers, adding or deleting a role instance (in respect with the min and max constraints), deleting a connection between a task and a server and establishing a connection with a new server. A first neighborhood is obtained by moving a client from the clients's list of a server to a clients's list of another server. The second neighborhood is obtained by merging all servers clients's lists into a single list, shuffling the clients, splitting the list according to the initial number of servers, and finally randomly assigning new lists to servers.

Deployment of Local Solutions on the Heterogeneous Platform

In Fig. 8a the performance and the energy consumption of the initial solutions are compared with the solutions generated by the local search. For these experiments we have discarded solutions that overrun 16 minutes of execution time. This figure reveals that the local search allowed to conquer empty spaces in which solutions are of better quality in terms of both energy cost and execution time, compared to those generated initially. The best solution found using the neighborhood exploration regarding the performance metric is 16% better than the best solution of the initial set. Figure 9 gives details about the solutions used to build the Pareto front with local search.

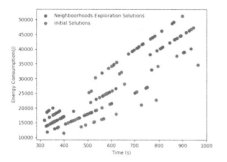 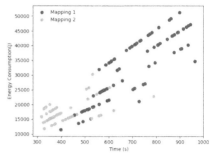

(a) Initial vs. neighborhoods topologies   (b) 'mapping 1' vs. 'mapping 2' strategies

Fig. 8. Topologies and mapping solutions spaces exploration.

Solutions	Nodes	nb_s	Time (s)	FPS	KJ	FPS/KJ
solution C	1 Intel + 3 Cortex A15	4	316	5.4	15.8	0.35
solution D	1 Intel + 2 Cortex A15	3	324	5.3	13.9	0.38
solution E	1 Intel + 1 Cortex A15	2	328	5.3	11.8	0.45

Fig. 9. Solutions building the Pareto front using local search.

Solution C takes less time to complete its execution thanks to an efficient load distribution between 4 S-DSM servers. The Pareto front solutions have the following pattern: a server, the I/O clients and the processing tasks are mapped onto the Intel i7 node and additional servers are mapped on the Cortex A15 nodes. The more servers we have, the lower the processing time is. This rule stops being true for solutions having 5 and more servers. Increasing the number of S-DSM servers balances the load of access requests from the clients, and avoids the centralized bottleneck server issue. However, after reaching a given number, the benefit vanishes because of the increasing probability for a server to forward the request to another one, leading to additional communication delays (multi-hop). Using more Cortex A15 to manage shared data increases the energy consumption and solution C is not efficient considering FPS/KJ.

4   Mapping Problem

In this section, we evaluate the impact of the mapping step on the execution time and energy consumption of the generated topologies. The mapping step consists in assigning servers and tasks instances to computing resources, taking into consideration the heterogeneous aspect of the platform and the available implementations (a role can provide different implementations, eg. pthread, OpenMP, OpenCL). A complete mathematical formulation of tasks mapping on heterogeneous system problem is available in [13]. In this work, two straightforward mapping strategies were developed for the experiments. The first strategy mapping 1 attempts to co-localize the clients with their corresponding servers in order to benefit from data locality. The second mapping strategy `mapping` 2 randomly assigns servers and clients to computing nodes. For both strategies we limit the exploration to one server per node at most. Figure 8b shows the impact of the two mapping strategies on performance and energy consumption. Blue dots in the Pareto indicates solutions with the `mapping` 1 strategy while the yellow dots are for solutions with `mapping` 2. This figure reveals that the solutions coming from `mapping` 2 are better in both execution time and energy consumption. Intuitively, collocating processing tasks together with their attached S-DSM servers sounds to be an efficient strategy to benefit from data locality. This does not appear to be an efficient strategy: processing tasks that are mapped onto Cortex A15 severely slow down the entire computation as this kind of processor is not suited for executing high performance tasks. Conversely, Cortex A15 are better used to host S-DSM servers only, as application helpers, which is quite counterintuitive at first given the poor network communication capabilities. In conclusion, as applications and heterogeneous computing platforms become more complex, the automatic exploration of configurations appear to be a steady approach towards an efficient use of resources.

5   Related Works

The idea of using the most suitable hardware resource for a specific application is not new and has been explored in previous works. However, the two different subjects of exploring the application topology and the task mapping are usually addressed separately. Some works have targeted regular MapReduce-based applications. For instance, the TARA [8] system uses a description of the application to allocate the resources. However, this work is tailored for a very specific class of applications and does not address hardware details. In [6] the authors introduce a new topology-aware resource selection algorithm to determine the best choice among the available processing units of the platform, based on their position within the network and taking into account the applications communication matrix. However this work does not study the methodology impact on energy consumption. In mARGOt [5] the authors propose a design space exploration method leading to the building of a Pareto front. Their method requires code transformations and code variants called *software knobs*. In this work, there is no need to modify the application. The tasks mapping problem has been extensively studied in the last decade and numerous methods have been reported in the literature under various assumptions and objectives. In [4] the authors aim at finding a trade-off between energy consumption and execution time using genetic algorithm heuristic to build a Pareto front. In [12] the authors resolve task assignment problem on heterogeneous platform attempting to minimize the total execution time and the communication cost. In [10] an iterative algorithm is proposed for the mapping problem on heterogeneous computing platforms with load balancing as a goal. In [13] the authors model both task scheduling and mapping in a heterogeneous system as a bi-objective optimization problem between energy consumption and system performance.

Previous works have not established a relationship between the application sizing, the application topology building and the task mapping problems, and their impact on both performance and energy consumption. In our work we propose to combine these problems and explore different configurations without relying on user hints, code modifications, pragmas or a specific dataflow programming model. We evaluate the solutions on the heterogeneous platform and build a Pareto front allowing users to select the most relevant configuration as in a decision system. In the early 2000, a definition of autonomic computing has been introduced by IBM [7] including self-managing attributes. This work contributes to the self-configuring and self-optimizing attributes.

6   Conclusion

The new great challenge for today's high-performance computing stands in the energy savings. Innovative heterogeneous computing platforms such as the Christmann RECS|Box offers several computing units with different specifications in order to offer to the users the possibility to optimize the execution of their applications in terms of performance and energy consumption. However, the efficient use of these platforms remains an open topic for both the academic and the industrial worlds. In this work we have presented some experiments using a video processing application on heterogeneous computing machine to analyze the impact of the S-DSM topology definition and mapping steps on the execution time and energetic cost. To achieve this, we have proposed a local search method to generate several topologies that have been evaluated in order to build a Pareto front. This Pareto allows users to choose the solution that matches at best their current goals and constraints in terms of execution time and energy consumption. Thanks to this approach we were able to find counterintuitive solutions that perform surprisingly well for both performance and energy. Future work will include a model for energy and performance estimation to evaluate topology and mapping solutions at a higher level and avoid as much as possible the deployment of the generated solutions onto the hardware.

Acknowledgement. This work received support from the H2020-ICT-2015 European Project M2DC under Grant Agreement number 688201.

References

1. Amza, C., et al.: TreadMarks: shared memory computing on networks of workstations. IEEE Comput. **29**(2), 18–28 (1996)
2. Antoniu, G., Bougé, L., Jan, M.: JuxMem: an adaptive supportive platform for data-sharing on the grid. Scalable Comput. Pract. Exper. (SCPE) **6**(3), 45–55 (2005)
3. Cudennec, L.: Software-distributed shared memory over heterogeneous micro-server architecture. In: Heras, D.B., Bougé, L. (eds.) Euro-Par 2017. LNCS, vol. 10659, pp. 366–377. Springer, Cham (2018). https://doi.org/10.1007/978-3-319-75178-8_30

4. Friese, R., et al.: An analysis framework for investigating the trade-offs between system performance and energy consumption in a heterogeneous computing environment (2013)
5. Gadioli, D., Palermo, G., Silvano, C.: Application autotuning to support runtime adaptivity in multicore architectures. In: 2015 International Conference on Embedded Computer Systems: Architectures, Modeling, and Simulation (SAMOS), pp. 173–180, July 2015
6. Georgiou, Y., Jeannot, E., Mercier, G., Villiermet, A.: Topology-aware resource management for HPC applications. In: Proceedings of the 18th International Conference on Distributed Computing and Networking, ICDCN 2017, pp. 17:1–17:10. ACM, New York (2017). https://doi.org/10.1145/3007748.3007768
7. Horn, P.: Autonomic computing: IBM's perspective on the state of information technology 2007, October 2001
8. Lee, G., Tolia, N., Ranganathan, P., Katz, R.H.: Topology-aware resource allocation for data-intensive workloads. SIGCOMM Comput. Commun. Rev. **41**(1), 120–124 (2011). https://doi.org/10.1145/1925861.1925881
9. Li, K.: IVY: a shared virtual memory system for parallel computing. In: Proceedings of the 1988 International Conference on Parallel Processing, pp. 94–101. University Park, August 1988
10. Renard, H., Vivien, F., Legrand, A., Robert, Y.: Mapping and load-balancing iterative computations. IEEE Trans. Parallel and Distrib. Syst. **15**, 546–558 (2004). https://doi.org/10.1109/TPDS.2004.10
11. Ross, J.A., Richie, D.A.: Implementing OpenSHMEM for the adapteva epiphany RISC array processor. Procedia Comput. Sci. **80**, 2353–2356 (2016). International Conference on Computational Science 2016, ICCS 2016, 6-8 June 2016, San Diego, California, USA
12. Ucar, B., Aykanat, C., Kaya, K., Ikinci, M.: Task assignment in heterogeneous computing systems. J. Parallel Distrib. Comput. **66**(1), 32–46 (2006). https://doi.org/10.1016/j.jpdc.2005.06.014
13. Zaourar, L., Aba, M.A., Briand, D., Philippe, J.M.: Modeling of applications and hardware to explore task mapping and scheduling strategies on a heterogeneous micro-server system. In: IEEE International Parallel and Distributed Processing Symposium Workshops (IPDPSW) (2017). http://doi.ieeecomputersociety.org/10.1109/IPDPSW.2017.123

Toward Heterogeneous MPI+MPI Programming: Comparison of OpenMP and MPI Shared Memory Models

Lukasz Szustak[✉], Roman Wyrzykowski, Kamil Halbiniak, and Pawel Bratek

Czestochowa University of Technology, Dabrowskiego 69, 42-201 Czestochowa, Poland
{lszustak,roman,khalbiniak,pbratek}@icis.pcz.pl

Abstract. This paper introduces our research on investigating the possibility of using heterogeneous all-MPI programming for the efficient parallelization of real-world scientific applications on clusters of multicore SMP/ccNUMA nodes. The investigation is based on verifying the efficiency of parallelizing a CFD application known as MPDATA, which contains a set of stencil kernels with heterogeneous patterns. As the first step of the research, we consider the level of SMP nodes, and compare the performance achieved by the MPI Shared Memory model of MPI-3 versus the OpenMP approach. In contrast to other works, this paper aims to evaluate these two programming models in conjunction with the parallelization methodology recently proposed [1] for performance portable programming across multicore SMP/ccNUMA platforms. We show that the shared memory extension of MPI delivers portable means for implementing all steps of this methodology efficiently, to take advantages of emerging multicore ccNUMA architectures.

Keywords: MPI shared memory · Multicore SMP/ccNUMA · MPDATA

1 Introduction

The Message Passing Interface (MPI) [2] is a dominant parallel programming model for distributed memory systems, including large clusters with tightly coupled SMP nodes. In the recent past, applications written with nothing except MPI were able to deliver an acceptable and portable performance, as well as scalability. However, as the number of cores per node has increased, programmers have increasingly took advantage of the hybrid (heterogeneous) parallel programming with MPI for internode communications in conjunction with shared memory programming systems, such as OpenMP, to manage intranode parallelism [3]. While this hybrid model, known as MPI+X [4], provides a lot of flexibility and performance potential, it burdens programmers with the complexity of using two parallel programming systems in the same application [5]. Apart from problems with a proper work of interface between two systems, there are other open issues, e.g., who manages the cores and how is that negotiated?

© Springer Nature Switzerland AG 2020
U. Schwardmann et al. (Eds.): Euro-Par 2019 Workshops, LNCS 11997, pp. 270–281, 2020.
https://doi.org/10.1007/978-3-030-48340-1_21

Version 3.0 of the MPI standard introduces another option for hybrid programming that uses the new MPI Shared Memory (SHM) model [6] to build MPI-everywhere codes for clusters with SMP nodes. In this MPI+MPI model, the MPI SHM extension enables programmers to create regions of shared memory that are directly accessible by MPI processes within the same shared memory domain. Also, several functions were added that enable MPI ranks within a shared memory region to allocate shared memory for direct load/store access. The ability to directly access a region of memory shared between ranks can improve performance in comparison with the pure MPI option, by reducing memory motion and footprint [3,5].

This paper introduces our research on investigating the possibility of using heterogeneous all-MPI programming for the efficient parallelization of real-world scientific applications on clusters of multicore SMP/ccNUMA nodes. The investigation is based on verifying the efficiency of parallelizing a CFD application known as MPDATA (Multidimensional Positive Definite Advection Transport Algorithm) [7]. It contains a set of stencil kernels with heterogeneous patterns.

As the first step of our research, we consider the level of SMP nodes, and compare the performance achieved by the MPI SHM model versus the OpenMP approach. The latter has become [4] a dominant choice for parallel programming of modern shared memory systems used as cluster nodes. The capabilities of such systems are constantly growing as a result of quick progress in multicore technology. It is quite easy to build SMP nodes with 112 or even 224 cores (2×56 cores with Intel Xeon Platinum 9282 or 8×28 with Intel Xeon Platinum 8280, see https://ark.intel.com). Thus, efficient harnessing of multicore SMP nodes with high degree of parallelism becomes of vital importance for the total performance of applications.

This paper is organized as follows. Section 2 discusses related works, while Sect. 3 presents a brief comparison of MPI SHM and OpenMP models. The MPDATA application is introduced in Sect. 4, which presents also the parallelization methodology for shared memory multi- and manycore architectures. Mapping MPDATA decomposition onto OpenMP and MPI Shared Memory is revealed in Sect. 5, while results of experimental evaluation of these two options are presented and discussed in Sect. 6. The paper is concluded in Sect. 7.

2   Related Work

The MPDATA code has been recently re-written and optimized for execution on HPC platforms with multicore CPUs and Intel MIC accelerators. The new C++ implementation proposed in [8] allows a more efficient distribution of computations across the available resources. It makes use of the (3+1)D decomposition strategy for heterogeneous stencils, that transfers the data traffic from the main memory to the cache hierarchy by reusing caches properly. Also, to improve the efficiency of computations, the algorithm groups the cores/threads into independent work teams in order to reduce inter-cache communication overheads due to transfers between neighbor cores.

Next, to harness the heterogeneous nature of communications in shared memory systems with ccNUMA architecture, the islands-of-cores approach was proposed in [9]. It allows a flexible management of the trade-off between computation and communication costs in accordance with features of multicore ccNUMA architectures. Finally, to reduce the synchronization overheads, an innovative strategy for the data-flow synchronization in shared memory systems was developed in [10]. As all designed codes were implemented with OpenMP, their direct extension on clusters with multicore SMP nodes requires utilizing the hybrid MPI+OpenMP approach.

This approach has already been applied quite successfully to real scientific applications [11,12]. For the CFD simulation considered in [11], the hybrid code can outperform a pure MPI version by up to 20%, while pure MPI still outperforms hybrid MPI+OpenMP in modeling of granular materials [12]. Recent scientific works enlighten the complexity of many aspects of the hybrid model that affect the overall performance and development costs of hybrid programs [2,3,5]. Thus, choosing a right option for parallel programming of real-world applications on clusters requires further research. In particular, there are surprisingly few works on performance comparison between MPI+MPI and MPI+OpenMP approaches. An example is work [13] on a performance evaluation of the MPI SHM model compared to OpenMP, using two relatively simple case studies: the matrix-matrix multiplication and Conway's game of life. The latter is an example of an 8-point stencil application. In contrast to this work, our research aims at evaluating these two programming models in conjunction with the parallelization methodology proposed recently [1] for performance portable programming across multicore SMP/ccNUMA systems. What is important, this methodology is not tailored to a particular programming approach.

3   MPI Shared Memory Model Compared to OpenMP

By default MPI codes are executed under the distributed memory model that assumes the private data allocation for each MPI process. In consequence, all processes have to communicate with each other using calls to MPI functions that typically moves data explicitly or perform some collective operations [14]. In this memory model, data are not shared automatically across MPI processes.

The MPI-3 RMA (Remote Memory Access) interface extends the default memory model with a new unified model [3] that is exposed through the MPI window. An MPI window object can be used to allocate shared memory regions [14] using the collective MPI routine `MPI_Win_allocate_shared`. It enables also the non-contiguous shared memory allocation by specifying the key info parameter `alloc_shared_noncontig` in order to fully utilize ccNUMA architectures. In addition, the function `MPI_Win_shared_query` is provided to query pointers to the memory allocated on MPI processes, that enable them immediate load/store operations with automatically propagated updates of data. As a result, data are automatically shared between MPI processes in a similar fashion as for OpenMP codes, where all OpenMP threads access data in parallel and coherent way [15].

MPI requires the explicit control of data parallelism. It is responsibility of programmers to formulate explicitly the workload distribution strategy. Nevertheless, the richness of the MPI library makes this shortage relatively easy to overcome. In contrast, OpenMP offers a straightforward mechanism for data parallelism that can automatically split the workload across available threads. However, as shown in [1], the parallel efficiency of an application can be significantly improved by replacing the standard solution for data parallelism, such as `#pragma omp for`, by a custom strategy for workload distribution adapted to the application, as well as to a target architecture. As a result, the data or loop parallelism with threads often requires a specific parallelisation strategy which in fact is similar to that of MPI, especially for shared memory programming.

4 Overview of MPDATA Parallelization

4.1 Introduction to MPDATA Application

The MPDATA application implements a general approach to modeling a wide range of complex geophysical flows on micro-to-planetary scales [7]. MPDATA belongs to the class of methods for the numerical simulation of fluid flows that are based on the sign-preserving properties of upstream differencing. It is mainly used to solve the advection problems on moving grids for a sequence of time steps, that classifies MPDATA into the group of forward-in-time algorithms. In this paper, we consider solving 3D problems. The MPDATA numerical scheme is described in detail in [7].

MPDATA is typically used for long simulations that run thousands of time steps. A single step operates on five input matrices (arrays), and returns a single output array that is used in the next step. Each MPDATA step performs a collection of 17 kernels that depend on each other (the outcomes of prior kernels typically are inputs for the subsequent ones). Each kernel is a stencil code that updates elements of its 3D output array, according to a specific pattern.

4.2 Parallelization Methodology for Shared Memory Systems

In the basic version of MPDATA (Listing 4.1) all kernels are executed sequentially, one by one, with each kernel processed in parallel using OpenMP. This version exploits data parallelism across i-dimension, based on distributing data across available resources by `#pragma omp for` directive, and then incorporates vectorization along k-dimension using `#pragma vector` directive [16].

The operational intensity of each MPDATA kernel is not high enough [1,17] to utilize computing resources of modern processors efficiently. Since the code is not optimized for cache reusing, the performance of this MPDATA version is limited by the main memory bandwidth. To alleviate these constraints, we developed [1,8–10] a parallelization methodology for MPDATA heterogeneous stencil computations. It contributes to ease the memory and communication bounds, and to better exploit resources of multicore ccNUMA/SMP systems.

This methodology consists of the following parametric optimization steps:

Listing 4.1. Part of 3D MPDATA basic version, corresponding to the 4-th kernel

```
/*...*/
//Kernel 4
#pragma omp for
for( ... ) // i - dimension
 for( ... ) // j - dimension
  #pragma vector
  for( ... ) // k - dimension
   x[i,j,k]=XIn[i,j,k]-(((F1[i+1,j,k]-F1[i,j,k])+(F2[i,j+1,k]
           -F2[i,j,k])+(F3[i,j,k+1]-F3[i,j,k]))/H[i,j,k]);
/*...*/
```

- *(3+1)D decomposition of MPDATA* [8] – the prime goal of is to take advantage of cache reusing by transferring the data traffic between kernels from the main memory to the cache hierarchy. For this aim, a combination of loop tiling and loop fusion optimization techniques is used, that allows reducing the main memory traffic at the cost of additional computations.
- *Data-flow strategy of synchronization* [10] – the main purpose is to synchronize only interdependent threads instead of using the barrier approach that typically synchronize all threads. This strategy reduces the cost of synchronization. Implementing this strategy for MPDATA needs to reveal the scheme of inter-thread data traffic during execution of MPDATA kernels.
- *Partitioning cores into independent work teams* [9] – this strategy delivers two scenarios for executing MPDATA kernels: the first one performs less computations but requires more data traffic, while the second scenario allows us to replace the implicit data traffic by replicating some of computations. As a result, the second scenario is successfully used to reduce inter-processor communications between caches in ccNUMA systems, while the first scenario is applied inside each processor.
- *Vectorization* – the last step is responsible for ensuring the performance portability of vectorizing MPDATA computations. In paper [1], we proposed the 7-step procedure for the MPDATA code transformation to allow the compiler to perform the vectorization automatically.

Figure 1 illustrates the hierarchical decomposition of MPDATA according to the proposed methodology. In general, the MPDATA domain is partitioned into p sub-domains that are processed by p processors of a given ccNUMA platform (Fig. 1a). Now each processor embraces a work team of cores, where each work team processes a sub-domain following the (3+1)D decomposition (Fig. 1b). Furthermore, each sub-domain is decomposed into blocks of size that enables keeping all the required data in the cache memory. The successive blocks are processed sequentially, one by one, where a given block exploits data parallelism across i- and j-dimensions (Fig. 1c) to distribute workload across available cores/threads. Each core of a given work team executes computations corresponding to all MPDATA kernels, that are performed on appropriate chunks of data arrays.

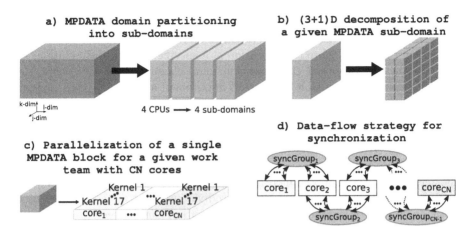

Fig. 1. Decomposition of MPDATA: a) domain partitioning into sub-domains, b) sub-domain decomposition into blocks of size adjusted to cache capacity, c) parallel execution of kernels within a single block by a given work team, and d) synchronization

Finally, the data layout used for storing arrays enforces performing the vectorization along k-dimension.

Because of data dependencies between the kernels, two synchronization levels have to be considered: inside every work team (first level), and between all work teams (second one). The parallelization of every block requires providing five synchronization points inside every work team. To improve the efficiency for the first level, only interdependent threads are synchronized according to data dependencies of kernels (Fig. 1d). Additionally, all work teams have to be synchronized after each time steps to ensure the correctness of simulation.

In order to implement the parallelization methodology automatically, we proposed [1] the parameterized transformation of the MPDATA code to achieve the high sustained and scalable performance for ccNUMA shared memory systems. As a result, the adaptive MPDATA code follows along with parameters of hardware components such as memory hierarchy, multi-/manycore, threading, vectorization, and their interaction with MPDATA computations.

5 Mapping MPDATA Decomposition onto Shared Memory Programming

5.1 Data Parallelism

The complexity of the proposed hierarchical decomposition (see Fig. 1) makes it impossible to efficiently implement parallelization across available cores using general approaches for data parallelism, such as `#pragma omp for` construct of OpenMP. Instead, based on the four-step procedure for MPDATA code customization [1], we developed a dedicated scheduler that is responsible for the management of workload distribution and data parallelism. The main assumption is to calibrate the developed hierarchical domain decomposition for a given computing platform, before the execution of a specific numerical simulation.

Following the proposed customization, our scheduler explicitly define the scope of work for all available computing resources of a given ccNUMA system. As a result, each physical core is assigned to a given work team that process all MPDATA blocks from its sub-domain, and then is linked to appropriately selected pieces of distributed data for all MPDATA kernels within every block. This is achieved by providing a suitable loop-level management of loop iterations distributed across computing resources. A simplified structure of loop-level management for the proposed hierarchical decomposition is shown in Listing 5.1.

Since the scope of work for each core is individually determined, the proposed methodology can be successfully implemented for any shared memory model that supports data parallelism. To map efficiently the proposed decomposition onto shared memory programming systems, such as OpenMP and MPI SHM, each OpenMP thread or MPI process has to be associated with the workload defined for a given physical core, using its ID (OpenMP thread ID or MPI rank). A part of this issue is selecting a correct policy for binding OpenMP threads or MPI processes to physical cores that can guarantee optimality of both data parallelism and inter-core communication paths. Both Intel MPI and Intel OpenMP offer a flexible interface to control thread/process affinity [14,16].

5.2 Memory Allocation and Data Sharing

The MPDATA code distinguishes two groups of data: (i) a large set of 3D arrays (matrices) of floating-point type processed during MPDATA computation, and relatively small packages of data of various types required for the loop-level management with the proposed scheduler. For performance reasons, it is of vital importance to allocate the first group of data *closest* to a physical core on which a given OpenMP thread or MPI process is executed. For the OpenMP version, achieving this goal is based on utilizing the first-touch policy with parallel initialization. For the MPI version, specifying the `alloc_shared_noncontig` info key enables to allocate the first group of data in noncontiguous memory regions, and as a result allow eliminating negative ccNUMA effects.

The noncontiguous memory allocation strategy also permits us to avoid replications of data of the first group between MPI processes. In contrast, we propose replicating the read-only data of the second group to expose their copies individually to each MPI process. Because of heterogeneity and fine-grain nature of these data, this replication data strategy definitely simplifies the structure of code at the negligible cost of extra memory consumption.

5.3 Synchronization

Besides solving issues of data parallelism, memory allocation and data sharing, the new version of MPDATA requires also providing an efficient synchronization mechanism. We solved [10] this issue for the OpenMP code by developing the

Listing 5.1. Structure of loop-level management of new 3D MPDATA implementation

```
for(...)  // i-dim for sub-domains
  for(...)  // j-dim for sub-domains
    for(...)  // i-dim for MPDATA blocks
      for(...)  // j-dim for MPDATA blocks
        for(...)  // k-dim for MPDATA blocks
        {
        //Parallelization across cores
        for(...)  // i-dim for sub-blocks of 1st kernel
          for(...)  // j-dim for sub-blocks of 1st kernel
            //Vectorization
            for( ..)  // k-dim for sub-blocks of 1st kernel
              /*.... Kernel 1 ...*/
        /*... Synchronization Points  ...*/
        /*... and other MPDATA kernels ...*/
        }
```

custom mechanism for our data-flow strategy. This mechanism uses low-level compiler intrinsincs such as `fetch-and-add` instruction. This solution negatively affects the code portability across emerging compilers and CPU architectures, due to the need for validation of the correctness of code before its real use.

In contrast, the MPI-3 version delivers programming solutions that allow the portable implementation of the proposed synchronization strategy. This implementation is based on the non-blocking barrier `MPI_ibarrier` and corresponding `MPI_Waitall` routine used for the subsequent completion. Following the scheme of inter-core data traffic in the MPDATA application outlined in [10], the execution of computations by a given core depends on outcomes generated by two neighbor cores placed on its right and left sides (see also Fig. 1d). As a result, the data-flow strategy can be successfully implemented by starting the non-blocking synchronization for the left neighbor of every core, next for its right neighbor, and afterward waiting until all of the cooperated cores complete the synchronization operations identified by MPI requests (Listing 5.2).

The MPI SHM interface assumes also an explicit use of synchronization to ensure memory consistency, as well as the visible of changes in memory to the other processes [14]. In consequence, we select the passive target synchronization model, defined by the pair of `MPI_Win_lock_all` and `MPI_Win_unlock_all` functions. These functions specify the time interval, called an RMA access epoch,

Listing 5.2. A code snippet for MPI version of data flow strategy

```
MPI_Win_sync(MPDATA_Win_to_Sync);
MPI_Ibarrier(MPDATA_LEFT_MEMBERS_COMMUNICATOR, MPIreq+0);
MPI_Ibarrier(MPDATA_RIGHT_MEMBERS_COMMUNICATOR, MPIreq+1);
MPI_Waitall(2, MPIreq);
```

when memory operations are allowed to occur. Afterward, the `MPI_Win_sync` function has to be used to ensure completion of memory updates before using the `MPI_ibarrier` that synchronize all processes in time [14].

6   Benchmarking MPDATA Codes

We benchmark four versions of MPDATA: (**A**) basic, non-optimized implementation; (**B**) code with (3+1)D decomposition of MPDATA domain; (**C**) version B with data-flow synchronization; (**D**) version C with partitioning cores into independent work teams. All versions are implemented using both MPI and OpenMP shared memory programming. A series of experiments is performed on three shared memory ccNUMA platforms (Table 1). Among them are 2-socket servers with either Cascade Lake-SP (CLX-SP) or Skylake-SP (SKL-SP) Intel Xeon CPUs, and 4-socket server with Broadwell (BDW-EX) Intel Xeon CPUs. The MPDATA codes provide vector-friendly data structures that enable us to easy switch between AVX 2.0 and AVX-512, by setting a properly chosen compiler arguments [1]. All experiments are compiled using Intel compiler version 18.0.5 with the optimization flag -O3 and properly chosen compiler arguments for enabling auto-vectorization. The MPI codes are developed with Intel MPI Library 2018 Update 4. All tests are repeated 10 times, and average execution times are used to obtain statistically sound results, with the relative standard deviation (RSD) less than 1%.

Figure 2 depicts comparison of execution times (in seconds) for OpenMP and MPI codes of all MPDATA versions, achieved on three computing platforms outlined in Table 1 for the domain of size $2048 \times 1024 \times 64$. In addition, both OpenMP and MPI implementations of all MPDATA versions are compared for different sizes of domain. An example of such comparison is illustrated in Fig. 3.

Table 1. Specification of computing platforms (https://ark.intel.com)

Computing resources		2× Intel Xeon Platinum 8280L (CLX-SP)	2× Intel Xeon Platinum 8168 (SKL-SP)	4× Intel Xeon E7-8890v4 (BDW-EX)
Scalar/SIMD Turbo freq. [GHz]		3.3/2.4	3.4/2.5	2.6
Sockets		2	2	4
Cores/Threads		56/112	48/96	96/192
SIMD		AVX-512	AVX-512	AVX2 (256 bits)
Main memory		2 × 6 × 16 GB DDR4-2933	2 × 6 × 16 GB DDR4-2666	4 × 4 × 16 GB DDR4-2400
Memory bandwidth [MB/s]		281.5	255.9	204.8
Peak performance* [Gflop/s]	Scalar	369.6	326.4	499.2
	SIMD	2150.4	1920.0	1996.8

*Refers to multiplication instructions performed with Turbo frequency

The presented performance results correspond to the double precision floating point format, and 5000 time steps.

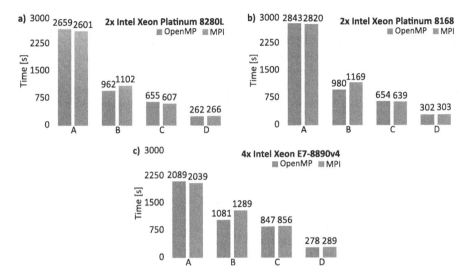

Fig. 2. Comparison of execution times of different MPDATA versions (A, B, C and D) achieved for both OpenMP and MPI, assuming the domain of size $2048 \times 1024 \times 64$, while using various computing platforms: a) $2\times$ CLX-SP, b) $2\times$ SKL-SP, and c) $4\times$ BDW-EX

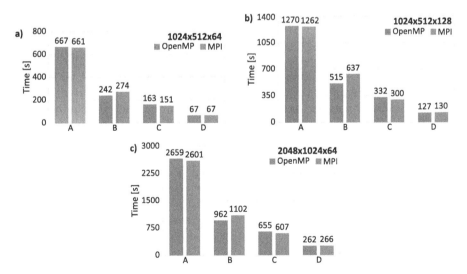

Fig. 3. Comparison of execution times of different MPDATA versions obtained for both OpenMP and MPI with various problem sizes on the platform equipped with two Intel Xeon Cascade Lake-SP CPUs ($2\times$ CLX-SP)

The benchmark results achieved for the first version ((**A**)) confirm a slightly high performance of the MPI code against the OpenMP implementation. This is an effect of overheads introduced by OpenMP runtime scheduling, while the MPI implementation from the beginning uses our scheduler that performs the loop distribution before computations.

In contrast, the OpenMP implementation of the version **B** returns better performance results for all performed tests. In fact, this benchmark reveals a negative impact of large number of synchronization points required by the (3+1)D decomposition of MPDATA [9] on the overall performance, with the MPI barrier resulting in greater performance losses than the OpenMP barrier.

The version **C** allows us to solve the synchronization issue for both MPI and OpenMP. As a result, the achieved performance is kept on a similar level for both programming models, with some advantage of MPI on the platforms with two CPUs. Finally, MPI and OpenMP implementations of the resulting version **D** feature practically the same performance, since the differences in the execution time between OpenMP and MPI models do not exceed 4% in favour of OpenMP.

7   Conclusions and Future Works

This paper demonstrates that the shared memory extension added in MPI-3 is efficient enough to take advantages of emerging multicore ccNUMA architectures. An example of such architectures is the newest Cascade Lake Intel Xeon Platinum 9282 processor, which packs two whole processors in a single socket offering 56 cores totally. Another remarkable example is the second generation of AMD EPYC processors, known as Rome. Using the multi-chip design with 4 modules interconnected via AMD Infinity Fabric, these emerging architecture is expected to deliver up to 64 cores per CPU.

The presented benchmarks show very similar performance results for both OpenMP and MPI shared memory implementations of the MPDATA CFD application on ccNUMA platforms with 2 and 4 CPUs. What is important is that MPI SHM delivers portable means to implement efficiently all steps of the parallelization methodology recently proposed for performance portable programming across multicore SMP/ccNUMA platforms. As a result, the resulting MPI code allows us to accelerate the MPDATA application more than 9 times as compared to the original version, achieving the sustained performance of 583 Glop/s for the server with two Cascade Lake Intel Xeon processors (each with 28 cores).

The aim of our future paper is to extend these results on the cluster level, in order to verify if heterogeneous MPI+MPI programming is able to successfully replace the common MPI+OpenMP hybrid programming model, providing portable application programming across forthcoming HPC platforms.

Acknowledgments. This research was supported by the National Science Centre (Poland) under grant no.UMO-2017/26/D/ST6/00687 and by the project financed within the program of the Polish Minister of Science and Higher Education under the name "Regional Initiative of Excellence" in the years 2019–2022 (project no.

020/RID/2018/19, the amount of financing 12 000 000 PLN). The authors are grateful to Intel Technology Poland for granting access to HPC platforms.

References

1. Szustak, L., Bratek, P.: Performance portable parallel programming of heterogeneous stencils across shared-memory platforms with modern Intel processors. Int. J. High Perform. Comput. Appl. **33**(3), 507–526 (2019)
2. Rabenseifner, R., Hager, G., Jost, G.: Hybrid MPI/OpenMP parallel programming on clusters of multi-core SMP nodes. In: Proceedings of the 17th Euromicro International Conference on Parallel, Distributed and Network-Based Processing, PDP 2009, pp. 427–436 (2009)
3. Hoefler, T., et al.: MPI+MPI: a new hybrid approach to parallel programming with MPI plus shared memory. Computing **95**(12), 1121–1136 (2013). https://doi.org/10.1007/s00607-013-0324-2
4. Rabenseifner, R., Hager, G., Blaas-Schenner, C., Reichl, R.: MPI+X—Introduction to Hybrid Programming in HPC (2019). https://moodle.rrze.uni-erlangen.de/course/view.php?id=388
5. Gropp, W.: MPI+MPI: Using MPI-3 Shared Memory As a Multicore Programming System. https://www.caam.rice.edu/mk51/presentations/SIAMPP2016_4.pdf
6. Brinskiy, M., Lubin, M., Dinan, J.: MPI-3 shared memory programming introduction. In: High Performance Parallelism Pearls: Multicore and Many-core Programming Approaches, vol. 2, pp. 305–318. Morgan Kaufmann (2015)
7. Smolarkiewicz, P.K.: Multidimensional positive definite advection transport algorithm: an overview. Int. J. Numer. Methods Fluids **50**(10), 1123–1144 (2006)
8. Szustak, L., Rojek, K., Olas, T., Kuczynski, L., Halbiniak, K., Gepner, P.: Adaptation of MPDATA heterogeneous stencil computation to Intel Xeon Phi coprocessor. Sci. Program. **2015**, Article ID 642705, 14 p. (2015). https://doi.org/10.1155/2015/642705
9. Szustak, L., Halbiniak, K., Wyrzykowski, R., Jakl, O.: Unleashing the performance of ccNUMA multiprocessor architectures in heterogeneous stencil computations. J. Supercomput. **75**(12), 7765–7777 (2018). https://doi.org/10.1007/s11227-018-2460-0
10. Szustak, L.: Strategy for data-flow synchronizations in stencil parallel computations on multi-/manycore systems. J. Supercomput. **74**(4), 1534–1546 (2018)
11. Ouro, P., Fraga, B., Lopez-Novoa, U., Stoesser, T.: Scalability of an Eulerian-Lagrangian large-eddy simulation solver with hybrid MPI/OpenMP parallelism. Comput. Fluids **179**(3), 123–136 (2019)
12. Yan, B., Regueiro, R.A.: Comparison between pure MPI and hybrid MPI-OpenMP parallelism for Discrete Element Method (DEM) of ellipsoidal and poly-ellipsoidal particles. Computat. Particle Mech. **6**(2), 271–295 (2018). https://doi.org/10.1007/s40571-018-0213-8
13. Karlbom, D.: A performance evaluation of MPI shared memory programming. Master's thesis, KTH, Sweden (2016)
14. Intel MPI Library Developer Guide for Linux OS, March 2019
15. OpenMP Application Programming Interface Version 5.0, November 2018
16. Intel C++ Compiler 19.0 Developer Guide and Reference, March 2019
17. Stengel, H., Treibig, J., Hager, G., Wellein, G.: Quantifying performance bottlenecks of stencil computations using the execution-cache-memory model. In: Proceedings of the 29th ACM International Conference on Supercomputing, pp. 207–216 (2015)

Multicore Performance Prediction – Comparing Three Recent Approaches in a Case Study

Matthias Lüders[✉], Oliver Jakob Arndt, and Holger Blume

Institute of Microelectronic Systems, Leibniz University Hannover, Hanover, Germany
{lueders,arndt,blume}@ims.uni-hannover.de
http://www.ims.uni-hannover.de

Abstract. Even though parallel programs, written in high-level languages, are portable across different architectures, their parallelism does not necessarily scale after migration. Predicting a multicore-application's performance on the target platform in an early development phase can prevent developers from unpromising optimizations and thus significantly reduce development time. However, the vast diversity and heterogeneity of system-design decisions of processor types from HPC and desktop PCs to embedded MPSoCs complicate the modeling due to varying capabilities. Concurrency effects (caching, locks, or bandwidth bottlenecks) influence parallel runtime behavior as well. Complex performance prediction approaches emerged, which can be grouped into: *virtual prototyping, analytical models*, and *statistical methods*. In this work, we predict the performance of two algorithms from the field of advanced driver-assistance systems in a case study. With the following three methods, we provide a comparative overview of state-of-the-art predictions: GEM5 (virtual prototype), IBM Exabounds (analytical model), and an in-house developed statistical method. We first describe the theoretical background, describe the experimental- and model-setup, and give a detailed evaluation of the prediction. In addition, we discuss the applicability of all three methods for predicting parallel and heterogeneous systems.

Keywords: Performance prediction · Virtual prototyping · Parallelization · Advanced driver-assistance systems · Scalability · MPSoC

1 Introduction

Due to the gap between theoretically provided and practically gathered performance of parallel systems, the development of multicore applications requires proper hardware-software co-design. In order to prevent developers from implementation errors and to reduce development time and costs, an early estimation of an application's performance and bottlenecks is necessary. Performance prediction enables software optimization even in early development phases. Modern architectures have superscalar out-of-order instruction pipelines, feature speculative execution, and are influenced by concurrency effects (e.g., caching effects)

© Springer Nature Switzerland AG 2020
U. Schwardmann et al. (Eds.): Euro-Par 2019 Workshops, LNCS 11997, pp. 282–294, 2020.
https://doi.org/10.1007/978-3-030-48340-1_22

due to parallelism. Therefore, modeling a modern processor's performance, especially for heterogeneous systems, became a complex task. Parallel software, written in high-level languages, aims to be portable across different processor types. In fact, a parallel program, developed on system A, does not necessarily scale on system B that may exhibit a different microarchitecture, component compilation, and resulting capabilities. Because of this diversity in hardware design decisions and heterogeneity of used components, it is key to have a generic prediction method that is able to deal with all platform types.

This paper addresses the prediction of characteristics and scalability of parallel programs on unavailable target platforms. Because of the complexity of comparing varying platform types, many approaches focus on certain architecture types (e.g., GPGPUs). In contrast, the prediction methods compared in this work cover multicore platforms of varying instruction-set architectures ranging from embedded- over desktop- to HPC-processors. Thereby, some approaches require detailed knowledge about processor internals, while others only use abstract parameters (see Fig. 1). While differing in their models, simulation time, and accuracy, prediction methods can be grouped into three categories:

1. **Virtual prototyping:** full functioning software-simulator of the hardware. To predicted the runtime, software is executed on the emulated hardware.
2. **Analytical models:** use characteristics of the target platform and the software as input and calculate the performance with mathematical models.
3. **Statistical methods:** train machine learning or regression from datasets of independent hardware and software characteristics to obtain a model.

Virtual prototyping fully simulates each processor operation in software and is the most precise but also the slowest method. An analytical model, realized with a mechanistic processor model, uses higher abstractions in parameterization of the hardware (e.g., pipeline depth) and software (e.g., branch-miss rate). Statistical prediction methods use the most abstract mathematical models, which are not specialized to simulate processor behavior. But, through the use of large databases, a higher complexity of the model is achieved (e.g., machine learning).

In this work, we present a comparative performance prediction of two real-world algorithms from the field of advanced driver-assistance systems: *Semi-Global Matching* (SGM) for stereo-vision and *Histograms of Oriented Gradients* (HOG) for pedestrian detection. Predicting these algorithms is particulary relevant because they represent examples for algorithms with real-time requirements,

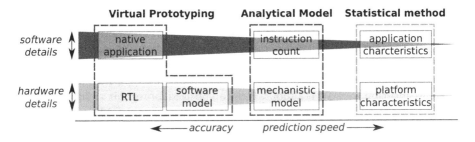

Fig. 1. Different abstraction levels of modeling hardware and software independently.

and high computational demands. This even more complicates architecture mapping on heterogeneous platforms. We make use of three prediction methods, each as a representative of one of the above mentioned approaches: *GEM5* (virtual prototype), *IBM Exabounds* (analytical model), and an in-house developed statistical method [6]. As prediction target platform, we use the ARM Cortex-A53 cores of the heterogeneous Zynq Ultrascale+ MPSoC. This work presents:

- Description of the model setup for all three prediction methods
- Evaluation of differences in simulation speed and accuracy
- Discussion on the applicability of different prediction methods

Section 2 introduces the different prediction approaches. Section 3 describes the concrete prediction setups and modeling processes. Section 4 evaluates the results of our competitive case study and Sect. 5 concludes the paper.

2   Prediction Methods

Traditional performance prediction is the task of estimating the runtime characteristics of a given software on an unavailable target platform. Prediction approaches differ in the abstraction level of the models as well as simulation speed, modeling effort, and prediction accuracy. Virtual prototypes can offer a high precision with the disadvantage of a long simulation time. Analytical models are fast, but offer less accurate results. Statistical methods fill the gap between virtual prototypes and analytical models in terms of speed and accuracy.

2.1   Virtual Prototyping

A virtual prototype is a full functioning software model of a specific hardware system. It can cover the whole range from singlecore microcomputers over complex homogeneous and heterogeneous MPSoCs up to high performance computers. In order to predict the performance of an application, a simulator fully emulates the behavior of a system on instruction level. On a virtual prototype, the application can run in *system emulation mode* directly on the system, or in *full system mode* with an underlying operating system (e.g., Linux or Android). Further, approaches vary in their level of hardware details from *function accurate* up to *cycle accurate*. Function accuracy enables the user to evaluate, whether their applications execute correctly. Cycle accuracy enables a very precise prediction of runtime parameters and provides a comprehensive view into internals like status of pipeline-stages and caches, at the cost of time consuming simulation.

To create a virtual prototype, domain specific high-level language like SystemC (for system components) and TLM (for component connections) are often used. Figure 2 shows a prediction workflow using a virtual prototype with a qualitative time classification. QEMU is a tool, which can be used for regular virtualization or for full-system and user-mode emulation of a specific architecture. The full-system mode can emulate whole MPSoCs like Xilinx Ultrascale+ EG. To execute applications, QEMU uses function accurate dynamic translation of instructions. QEMU

Table 1. Overview of different frameworks for virtual prototyping.

Framework	Accuracy	Processor architectures
QEMU [7]	Function	ARM, x86, microblaze, ...
ARM FVP [2]	Function	ARM
Imperas OVP [13]	Instruction	ARM, MIPS, POWERPC, RISCV, ...
GEM5 [8]	Function to cycle	ARM, MIPS, x86, ...
Cadence VSP [9]	Function to instruction	ARM, MIPS, Renesas, PowerPC

can be extended by SystemC models and TLM and so enables small timing support. GEM5 is an open source event driven simulator, which consists of the full-system simulator M5 and the memory centric simulator GEMS [8]. GEM5 uses C++ for creating system components and Python for assembling all components to a final system. GEM5 offers the options to simulate homogeneous and heterogeneous multicore systems with the possibility to run a fast function accurate up to a slow cycle accurate simulation. Power et al. [18] present the GEM5-gpu simulator, which offers the possibility to simulate heterogeneous platforms with CPUs and GPUs by adding GPU simulators. GEM5 comes with a set of ready-to-use models and system parts but also offers the possibility to be extended it with new modules written in SystemsC or TLM. Therefore, Menard et al. [16] present how GEM5 can be extended by SystemC and TLM to cover a larger design space without loosing much performance. In Table 1, we present a short overview of some virtual prototyping frameworks.

2.2 Analytical Models

Analytical models describe the architectural behavior by mathematical equations using hardware parameters and software characteristics. A generalized approach is to express the performance of an application on a specific hardware as cycles per instruction (CPI) or its reciprocal instructions per cycle (IPC). The CPI or IPC is effected by events like cache misses, branch misses and pipeline stalls. Thereby, in analytical models the CPI can be expressed in a function of processor internal design features and software characteristics:

$$CPI = f(L1dCacheMisses, L1iCacheMisses, branchMisses, ILP...). \quad (1)$$

Each of these effects is described either with hardware independent software description models, or software independent architecture properties. These

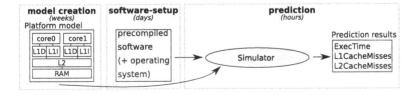

Fig. 2. Virtual prototyping using a platform model and precompiled software.

models use architectural parameters like cache size, pipeline configuration, or count of floating point units, and software properties like parallelization calls, count of floating point operations, or count of vector operations (Fig. 3).

Eyerman et al. [11] describe a mechanistic model to predict the performance of a superscalar out-of-order singlecore. For predicting the performance of a multithread application, Pestel et al. [10] extended the singlecore model of Van de Steen et al. [19]. Combining different analytical models, Jongerius et al. [15] present the prediction framework IBM Exabounds. IBM Exabounds can predict in-order and out-of order multicore processor systems with the restriction of a fixed processor structure. To characterize the software, IBM Exabounds uses the LLVM based IBM PISA toolchain, which produces a microarchitecture-independent profile of the software. IBM PISA support parallelization with OpenMP and MPI. The processor structure in IBM Exabounds is a hierarchical architecture with a core-model (pipeline with functional units, L1 and L2 cache), processor model (core-model and L3 cache), and compute-node (processor-model and main memory) and can be parameterized in a JSON file. Figure 3 shows the three steps with a qualitative time specification. IBM Exabounds predict the singlecore performance of a Xeon E5-2697 v3 and an ARM Cortex A15 with an average error of 59% and the influence of multicore performance with a maximum of 11% [14]. The Silexica toolchain not only supports the development and optimization of parallel programs, but also offers a prediction of the runtime of sequential software on a target architecture as well as the potential speedup of automatically parallelized sections in the software code. Next to automatic parallelization, it can also offload software sections to accelerators like GPUs.

2.3 Statistical Methods

Statistical prediction approaches use separate, ideally independent, characteristics of hardware and software as descriptive features to train machine learning or regression models from a database of features to predict the performance. Therefore, statistical predictions rely on the quality of extracted features to gain good prediction accuracy. But, the extraction of independent characteristics is complex as runtime parameters mostly interfere between hardware and software. Also, many parameters like performance counters lack of interpretability because of variations between architectures, such that many prediction approaches focus on specific architecture families like GPUs. Ardalani et al. [1] use microarchitecture-independent characteristics [12] as software features of CPU code to predict the corresponding GPU-kernel performance using ensemble

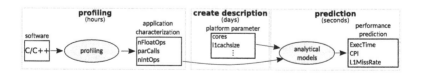

Fig. 3. Analytical prediction using a software profile and platform parameter.

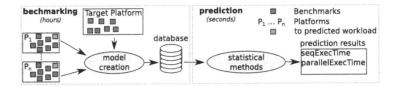

Fig. 4. The in-house developed statistical prediction using scalability characteristics.

techniques with an error of 27% (Maxwell) and 36% (Keppler). Another app-roach uses skeletons from CPU code to predict the according performance on a GPU [17]. Using two common CPU benchmarks, deep neural networks as well as linear regression was used to predict singlecore execution times on new core configurations with an average error of 5% (SPEC) and 11% (Geekbench).

In our in-house developed statistical prediction method [6] used in this case study (see Fig. 4), scalability metrics are used to form descriptive feature vec-tors. The scalability of a parallel program describes its capability of distributing work over increasing numbers of cores n and the tendency of simultaneously involving parallelization overhead, finally resulting in an individual paralleliza-tion speedup. In fact, we split the parallel runtime behavior that is extracted from profiles into the following parameters, which are observed over increasing numbers of cores:

- *Redundancy:* Percentage increase of the summed execution time of all parallel tasks $\sum_i t_i(n)$ due to memory bottlenecks/caching effects (t_{lock} excluded).
- *Synchronization:* Percentage of the time $t_{lock}(n)$ that a task spends on waiting for a lock in relation to the available CPU time.
- *Work imbalance:* Percentage of the available CPU time, which can not be used for effective task execution due to improper work split (idle time).
- *Scheduling overhead:* Fraction of the available CPU time, which was needed to manage tasks: creation, distribution, switch, and synchronization (join).

A simple mathematical curve is fitted into the scaling parameters' trends to receive quantitative numbers, which characterize the entire scalability. The final feature vector is concatenated of scaling parameters and performance counters. These features include interfering characteristics that are not separable between hardware and software effects. Therefore, a regular machine learning is not fea-sible. Instead, we directly predict new performance numbers from related candi-dates from database, which we determine using distance metrics. The prediction of the sequential execution and the scalability (parallelization speedup) is sepa-rated, but uses the same methodology, which is structured into three steps:

1. **Distance estimation:** Normalized geometric distance metrics are used to estimate distances between prediction candidates.
2. **Candidate selection:** One or more prediction candidates with low distances to the target get selected for prediction.
3. **Target reconstruction:** In an interpolating transformation, the target scal-ability vector (and the scalability trend and speedup) is reconstructed.

3   Prediction Setup

The modeling procedure and required effort varies between prediction methods. In the following, we show the established workflows to build a virtual prototype with GEM5, to setup an analytical processor model with IBM Exabounds, and to create a comprehensive database for our statistical prediction approach.

3.1   Target Platform and Algorithms

We use the four ARM Cortex-A53 cores of the Xilinx Zynq Ultrascale+ EG SoC as target platform, which run at 1.2 GHz. Each core has its private L1 cache. The SoC features 1MB shared L2 cache and 4 GB DDR4 RAM (Fig. 5). Nevertheless, to this static platform parameters virtual prototypes as well as analytic models require more detailed internals (*dynamic* information) like pipeline structure and cache latencies. According to our experience, a high precision of dynamic information is key for good prediction accuracy, but can be hard to achieve. For some architectures, vendors provide precise details in datasheets, other platforms' parameters need to be extracted from micro-benchmarks.

We use parallel implementations of stereo vision (*SGM*) and pedestrian detection (*HOG*) algorithms from the field of advanced driver-assistant systems. Both implementations consist of a series of consecutive algorithm-stages, each with its own parallelization that splits the work by domain decomposition [3,5]. We consider each stage as an individual workload, since they potential exhibit varying execution characteristics. To enable an automated profiling, they are parallelized using the MPAL abstraction layer [4], which measures the execution time of all individual parallel sections without including measurement overhead.

3.2   Virtual Prototyping

Representing a common and widely used state-of-the-art framework, we use the cycle-accurate simulation of GEM5 as exemplary virtual prototyping approach. The preparation and prediction with GEM5 covers the following three steps:

Create the Virtual Architecture: Given the beforehand mentioned target platform, we make use of a generic ARMv8 in-order processor model (GEM5

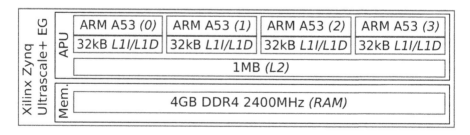

Fig. 5. Platform overview of the Xilinx Zynq Ultrascale+ EG ARM Cortex-A53 SoC.

internal HPI-model) and configure it with core specifications and cache parameters. The selection of suitable simulators for system components not only requires deep knowledge of the target architecture, but insights of the simulator's internal structures as well. We use standard components of GEM5 for RAM, RTC, serial console, etc. The interconnect between system components (AXI-Bus) is realized using the TLM-like, abstract, and message-event driven bus-system of GEM5. The component composition and high-level parameterization (e.g., clock frequency and memory size) is configured in Python.

Software Environment: As we simulate in full system mode, a regular Linux Kernel is used, which we customized to be compatible to the simulated platform. Therefore, an adapted headless Ubuntu 16.04 is used as root-filesystem. Using the QEMU user emulation mode (*chroot*), the same root-filesystem could be used to compile software (no cross compilation) and to test and modify the environment directly on the host-PC. Through the use of MPAL even inside the virtual prototype, the execution of individual stages could be easily profiled without modifying the code.

Prediction Toolchain: To avoid a long startup procedure the simulator is booted with *function accuracy* and the simulation changes to *cycle accuracy* when executing relevant workload. The cycle accurate simulation is very time consuming and lasts up to 10 h for both algorithms, while the execution on the physical target-platform takes 550 ms. Unfortunately, even parallel components (e.g., parallel CPU cores) are simulated in a single sequential process. In this case study, the simulation of parallelized algorithms (four cores) takes 20% longer than the simulation sequential workloads.

3.3   Analytical Model

In order to evaluate a recent analytical model, we use IBM Exabounds (Jongerius et al. [15]). The prediction process of IBM Exabounds includes the following steps:

Processor Parameterization: The fixed analytical processor model is configured to an in-order-pipelined core with multiple floatingpoint, integer, and vector functional units. We also configured parameters like individual latencies for pipeline stages and bandwidth of the memory. The only restriction is the differing L2 Cache, which is private in the analytical model but shared in our target platform. Therefore, we set the size and latencies of the L2 cache to zero and used the shared L3 cache of the model to substitute the shared L2 cache.

Software Profiling: As described in Sect. 2.2, we extract software characteristics with IBM PISA. To predict each algorithmic stage, a time consuming profiling of each stage needs to be performed with manual changes in the software code (separation of code sections). Presupposed that the algorithm is parallized with OpenMP or MPI the profiling can be executed on parallel cores. The profiling time linear scales with the runtime of the algorithms.

Prediction Calculation: The performance prediction is performed in a Wolfram Mathematica Notebook. Thus, we load the hardware description, a pre-configured memory model, and the profile in the Notebook. The prediction is performed in a few seconds per workload (algorithm stage) and the results like predicted runtime, system statistics (e.g., cache misses and used bandwidth), and power consumption is shown in textual and graphical form.

3.4   Statistical Method

Because the statistical prediction is based on the existence of a database of profiling measures of scalability characteristics, we assume to have a sufficient set of benchmarks available [6].

Setup the Database: The requirement of the statistical method is a database that contains profiles of several platforms and workloads. We use a prepared and ready-to use benchmarkset of 18 workloads, each with an individual parallelization strategy and characteristics. Therewith, we profile six x86-servers, three x86 desktop pcs, and two ARM platforms. The benchmarks show a varying execution behavior on different platforms. Because we also spent much effort on tuning parameters of the virtual prototype and the analytical description, we added profiles of an Amlogic S905 SoC to the database, which contains a similar quadcore ARM Cortex-A53 processors at 1.5 GHz and 2 GB DDR3 RAM. In addition, the target platform has to be characterized by profiling the benchmarks as references. The process of extracting scaling parameters and adding descriptive features to the database is fully automated.

Perform the Prediction: The statistical prediction is implemented in a python script. The prediction is called by passing the database that contains the new profiles of the target platform respectively the target algorithm. The prediction always returns the entire predicted scalability curves, all scaling parameters (i.e., locks, work-imbalance, redundancy, etc.), and the predicted runtime.

4   Evaluation

In the previous sections, we described the background and modeling setup for all three prediction methods. To now evaluate the prediction accuracy and

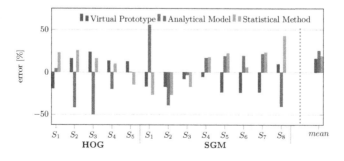

Fig. 6. Errors of the statistical method, virtual prototype, and analytical model.

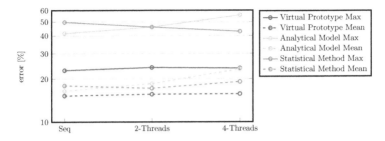

Fig. 7. Max and mean prediction errors related to the number of used processor cores.

applicability of the methods to be used for parallel systems, we predict the runtime behavior of all parallelized algorithmic stages of SGM and HOG (S_n – each representing a separate workload with individual characteristics and parallelization strategies) and compare the results with the profiled data from the physical architecture. Figure 6 shows the percentage prediction error at the use of all four cores. On average, the virtual prototype achieves the highest accuracy of 16.1% error. This results from the combination of the cycle accurate simulator GEM5, the detailed processor model, as well as the identical software environment running on the simulator and target platform. The statistical method predicts the performance with an average error of 19%, which can be reached because of the comprehensive database with varying workloads profiled on different parallel architectures. The parameterized analytical model predicts with the highest error of 23% on average, due to missing influences of the OS, the differing cache model (L2 configured as L3 cache), and the mismatch of the number of instructions between the profiling system (x86) and the target platform (ARM). To verify the accuracy, we also determine the standard deviation, which is 6% for the virtual prototype, 10% for the statistical method, and 18% for the analytical model.

In addition, we investigate the trend of the prediction error from sequential to full parallelized execution to analyze the capability of the methods to predict parallelization influences. Figure 7 emphasizes the trend of mean and maximum error (over all stages S_n) in a logarithmic scale over the discrete number of used cores. The rising mean and maximum error of IBM Exabounds can be attributed to the differing L2/L3 cache configuration that caused a mispredicted behavior especially for inter-core communication (also described in [14]). Whereas, the low deviation of the virtual prototype is due to the relative exact replication of the reference platform. This can be verified by using micro-benchmarks, which stress caches and interconnects on the virtual prototype. Results of the micro-benchmarks show a good correlation with low deviations by about 15%. Because the statistical method is focused on the prediction of parallel workloads with a database of various optimized implementations with varying parallelization strategies, it also shows a low variability for varying numbers of cores. For further evaluations of the prediction methods, it is planned to extend our benchmark-set with parallel benchmarks from e.g., SPEC or NPB.

Table 2. Summary of the comparative case study.

	Flexibility	Accuracy	Prediction time	Modeling effort	Single core	Multi core	Physical platform	Heterogeneity
GEM5	++	+	--(10 h)	--(32 days)	√	√	X	√
IBM Exabounds	--	o	++(few sec.)	-(10 days)	√	√	X	X
Statistical method	o	+	++(few sec.)	+(few hours)	√	√	√	X

As we verified in this case study, virtual prototypes perform detailed predictions a the cost of a high modeling effort (here 32 days) and long simulation times (here 10 h). Thereby, virtual prototypes are not limited to multicore or multiprocessor systems, but can also be extended to large and heterogeneous systems equipped with accelerators like GPUs or DSPs. Analytical models can perform a fast prediction with the restriction of a slow profiling. The profiling time in this case study was about 6 h, because every algorithmic stage has to be profiled separately by contrast the prediction is performed in a few seconds. Consequently, analytical models can be used for a fast exploration of a multitude of platforms for a single workload in an early development step. Statistical methods can be used to predict varying workloads on multiple platforms with the requirement of benchmark-profiles of a physically existing platform, which are included in the database. Table 2 summarizes the results of the case study.

5   Conclusion

This paper presents a comparative case study, consisting of exemplary predictions of two parallelized real-world algorithms from advanced driver-assistance systems using a virtual prototype, an analytical model, and a statistical method. Based on the initial qualitative classification that differentiates the methods by their accuracy and prediction speed, we introduced backgrounds and discussed particularities to show the individual eligibility on predicting the design-space of parallel heterogeneous processors. Further, we gave a detailed illustration on the setup for each prediction approach (GEM5, IBM Exabounds, and our in-house developed statistical method). The evaluation shows that the virtual prototype has the smallest mean error of 16.1%, followed by our statistical method with a mean error of 19%, and the analytical model with a mean error of 25.3%. We also evaluated the accuracy of the prediction of the scaling behavior, which results in an identical order of the accuracy. Analytical models offer the possibility to predict the behavior of an application on a large set of processors. Statistical methods can perform a fast prediction with a good precision without user input, but only with profiling information. Virtual Prototypes can predict the behavior of an application with high precision and enables a deep view into system internals. Additionally, they can predict the performance of heterogeneous multicore platforms, and accelerators like GPUs or DSPs. Table 2 lists the results of this case study and important properties of the different prediction methods.

Thereby, this paper shows, that all prediction methods are capable to predict the runtime of parallel algorithms for varying multicore platforms and architectures.

References

1. Ardalani, N., Lestourgeon, C., Sankaralingam, K., Zhu, X.: Cross-architecture performance prediction (XAPP) using CPU code to predict GPU performance. In: International Symposium on Microarchitecture. ACM (2015)
2. ARM: ARM Fast Models. https://developer.arm.com/tools-and-software/simulation-models/fast-models. Accessed 17 May 2019
3. Arndt, O.J., Becker, D., Banz, C., Blume, H.: Parallel implementation of real-time semi-global matching on embedded multi-core architectures. In: International Conference on Embedded Computer Systems: Architectures, Modeling, and Simulation (SAMOS). IEEE (2013)
4. Arndt, O.J., Lefherz, T., Blume, H.: Abstracting parallel programming and its analysis towards framework independent development. In: International Symposium on Embedded Multicore/Many-Core Systems-on-Chip (MCSoC). IEEE (2015)
5. Arndt, O.J., Linde, T., Blume, H.: Implementation and analysis of the histograms of oriented gradients algorithm on a heterogeneous multicore CPU/GPU architecture. In: Global Conference on Signal and Information Processing (GlobalSIP). IEEE (2015)
6. Arndt, O.J., Lüders, M., Blume, H.: Statistical performance prediction for multicore applications based on scalability characteristics. In: International Conference on Application-specific Systems, Architectures and Processors (ASAP). IEEE (2019)
7. Bellard, F.: QEMU, a fast and portable dynamic translator. In: Annual Technical Conference. USENIX Association (2005)
8. Binkert, N., Beckmann, B., Black, G., Reinhardt, S.K., Saidi, A., Basu, E.A.: The Gem5 simulator. ACM Comput. Archit. News 39(2), 1–7 (2011)
9. Cadence: Cadence Virtual System Platform. https://www.cadence.com/content/dam/cadence-www/global/en_US/documents/Archive/virtual_system_platform_ds.pdf. Accessed 17 May 2019
10. De Pestel, S., Van den Steen, S., Akram, S., Eeckhout, L.: RPPM: rapid performance prediction of multithreaded applications on multicore hardware. IEEE Comput. Archit. Lett. **17**, 183–186 (2018)
11. Eyerman, S., Eeckhout, L., Karkhanis, T., Smith, J.E.: A mechanistic performance model for superscalar out-of-order processors. ACM Trans. Comput. Syst. **27**(2), 3:1–3:37 (2009)
12. Hoste, K., Eeckhout, L.: Microarchitecture-independent workload characterization. Micro **27**, 63–72 (2007)
13. Imperas: Open Virtual Platforms. http://ovpworld.org/. Accessed 17 May 2019
14. Jongerius, R., Anghel, A., Dittmann, G., Mariani, G., Vermij, E., Corporaal, H.: Analytic multi-core processor model for fast design-space exploration. IEEE Trans. Comput. **67**, 755–770 (2018)
15. Jongerius, R., Mariani, G., Anghel, A., Dittmann, G., Vermij, E., Corporaal, H.: Analytic processor model for fast design-space exploration. In: International Conference on Computer Design (ICCD). IEEE (2015)

16. Menard, C., Castrillón, J., Jung, M., Wehn, N.: System simulation with gem5 and SystemC: the keystone for full interoperability. In: International Conference on Embedded Computer Systems: Architectures, Modeling, and Simulation (SAMOS). IEEE (2017)
17. Meng, J., Morozov, V.A., Kumaran, K., Vishwanath, V., Uram, T.D.: GROPHECY: GPU performance projection from CPU code skeletons. In: International Conference on High Performance Computing, Networking, Storage and Analysis. ACM (2011)
18. Power, J., Hestness, J., Orr, M.S., Hill, M.D., Wood, D.A.: gem5-gpu: a heterogeneous CPU-GPU simulator. IEEE Comput. Archit. Lett. **14**(1), 34–36 (2015)
19. Van den Steen, S., De Pestel, S., Mechri, M., Eyerman, S., Carlson, T., Black-Schaffer, D., et al.: Micro-architecture independent analytical processor performance and power modeling. In: International Symposium on Performance Analysis of Systems and Software (ISPASS). IEEE (2015)

Exploiting Historical Data: Pruning Autotuning Spaces and Estimating the Number of Tuning Steps

Jaroslav Oľha[1,2]([envelope]), Jana Hozzová[1], Jan Fousek[1], and Jiří Filipovič[1]

[1] Institute of Computer Science, Masaryk University, Brno, Czech Republic
{olha,hozzova}@ics.muni.cz, {izaak,fila}@mail.muni.cz
[2] Faculty of Informatics, Masaryk University, Brno, Czech Republic

Abstract. Autotuning, the practice of automatic tuning of code to provide performance portability, has received increased attention in the research community, especially in high performance computing. Ensuring high performance on a variety of hardware usually means modifications to the code, often via different values of a selected set of parameters, such as tiling size, loop unrolling factor or data layout. However, the search space of all possible combinations of these parameters can be enormous. Traditional search methods often fail to find a well-performing set of parameter values quickly.

We have found that certain properties of tuning spaces do not vary much when hardware is changed. In this paper, we demonstrate that it is possible to use historical data to reliably predict the number of tuning steps that is necessary to find a well-performing configuration, and to reduce the size of the tuning space. We evaluate our hypotheses on a number of GPU-accelerated benchmarks written in CUDA and OpenCL.

Keywords: Autotuning · Prediction of tuning cost · Tuning space pruning · Sensitivity analysis

1 Introduction

With ever-changing hardware architectures, it is difficult and costly to keep applications performing well on a wide range of hardware – in order to retain high performance, the implementation needs to be modified to adapt to a new execution environment. In a well-written code, it is often sufficient to change the values of a few pre-selected parameters, such as block size or loop unrolling factor. Since the manual search for the right combination of parameter values can be tedious and error-prone, an automatic method, called *autotuning*, has been developed to search the space of possible implementations and find the best one (a comprehensive survey of autotuning can be found in [2]). This search can be performed before the application is launched (offline tuning), or at runtime, switching implementations on-the-fly whenever a faster configuration is found

© Springer Nature Switzerland AG 2020
U. Schwardmann et al. (Eds.): Euro-Par 2019 Workshops, LNCS 11997, pp. 295–307, 2020.
https://doi.org/10.1007/978-3-030-48340-1_23

(dynamic tuning) [2] – the latter approach being particularly useful in cases where changing the characteristics of the input affects optimization choices.

However, the tuning spaces of many problems are difficult to navigate [1,9,15] – discrete values of parameters influence each other in a non-linear way, and the tuning spaces have low locality (two similar configurations can perform very differently). Therefore, traditional search methods usually perform similarly to random search [7,9,13].

In this paper, we analyze the spaces of tuning parameters and search for properties which do not change significantly across different hardware devices. We show two ways this information can be used to improve autotuning.

Firstly, we can estimate how many tuning iterations are needed to achieve reasonable performance. Such information is essential if we need to decide whether tuning time can be amortized. We demonstrate that the portion of a tuning space composed of well-performing configurations remains stable for a given problem across different hardware for a majority of cases.

Secondly, we can prune the tuning space, helping an autotuner to find a well-performing implementation more quickly. We propose that certain tuning parameters are more significant than others when it comes to performance, depending on the application, and their significance is portable across hardware. As a result, we are able to remove insignificant parameters and thus reduce the dimensionality of the tuning space without losing well-performing configurations.

Our methods are evaluated on ten GPU kernels and five generations of GPU accelerators. We believe that the method can also be used for different hardware devices, such as CPUs.

We are using the following terminology in the paper. A *tuning parameter* is a variable which affects the code in a user-defined way (e.g. determines loop unroll factor). The *tuning space* is a space composed of all the possible values of all tuning variables. *Configuration* is a single point in the tuning space, which fully determines one possible implementation of the tuned code.

The rest of the paper is organized as follows. The overview of the benchmark set and used hardware is given in Sect. 2. Our methods are described and evaluated in Sect. 3 (prediction of the portion of tuning space which needs to be searched) and Sect. 4 (pruning the tuning space). The comparison with related work is given in Sect. 5. We conclude and outline future research in Sect. 6.

2   Benchmark Set

To show that our proposed hypotheses are not problem- or application-specific, we have developed a rather wide set of benchmark problems implemented in a way that enables autotuning. In this section, we introduce the benchmarks and hardware that we have used for evaluation.

2.1   Benchmarks

An overview of the benchmarks, including the size and dimensionality of their tuning spaces, is given in Table 1. To produce as many diverse benchmarks as

Table 1. A list of the benchmarks, and the size and the dimensionality of their tuning spaces.

Benchmark name	Configurations	Dimensions
BiCG	5 122	11
2D convolution	3 928	10
3D Coulomb sum	1 260	8
GEMM	241 600	15
GEMM batched	424	11
Hotspot	480	6
Matrix transpose	5 916	9
N-body	9 408	8
Reduction	175	5
3D Fourier reconstruction	430	7

possible, we have collected autotuned computation kernels which are either publicly available or developed by ourselves in several previous projects. We believe that the benchmark set is representative for HPC problems, and its assembly requires less manual effort than re-implementation of an entire existing benchmark set such as Rodinia [4] for autotuning. The benchmarks are composed of important computational kernels spanning across multiple application domains: 3D Fourier reconstruction [14] and 2D convolution (adopted from [9]) are image processing kernels, BiCG, GEMM (adopted from [9]), GEMM batched, Matrix transpose and Reduction [6] are linear algebra kernels, Direct Coulomb summation [6] is a computational chemistry kernel, N-body (autotuned version of NVIDIA CUDA SDK sample) and Hotspot (based on implementation from Rodinia benchmark [4]) are differential equation solvers. These benchmarks autotune a variety of tuning parameters, changing implementation properties such as work-group size, cache blocking, thread coarsening, explicit caching in local memory, loop unrolling, explicit vectorization or data layout optimization (i.e. array of structures vs. structure of arrays). These tuning parameters were determined by the programmer during development – we did not add or remove any tuning parameters afterwards, e.g. after the analysis of parameters' importance.

All the benchmarks have been evaluated on sufficiently large inputs, so that the available parallelism of a GPU was utilized. The 3D Fourier benchmark processes a large number of small images and its performance is highly sensitive to the size of the images. Therefore, we have autotuned 3D Fourier Reconstruction for multiple image sizes: 32×32, 64×64 and 128×128, referred to as Fourier (32), Fourier (64) and Fourier (128) in the following text. The GEMM Batched benchmark performs batched matrix multiplication of small matrices – we have measured the performance on 16×16 matrices. All benchmarks use single-precision arithmetic.

The 3D Fourier reconstruction [14] is available in Xmipp software[1], the rest of the benchmarks are available in Kernel Tuning Toolkit as examples installed with the tuner[2]. The Kernel Tuning Toolkit [6] has been used to obtain the results for this paper.

2.2 Hardware

We have evaluated all of the benchmarks on five GPUs of different architectures and performance, see Table 2.

Table 2. A list of the GPUs used in our tests.

GPU	Architecture	SP performance	Bandwidth	Released
AMD Radeon RX Vega 56	GCN 5	8,286 GFlops	410 GB/s	2017
NVIDIA Tesla K20	Kepler	3,524 GFlops	208 GB/s	2012
NVIDIA GeForce GTX 750	Maxwell	1,044 GFlops	80 GB/s	2014
NVIDIA GeForce GTX 1070	Pascal	5,783 GFlops	256 GB/s	2016
NVIDIA GeForce RTX 2080Ti	Turing	11,750 GFlops	616 GB/s	2018

3   Estimating the Number of Tuning Steps

In theory, autotuning makes a program faster when it is executed on new hardware or with changed input characteristics. However, to achieve that, the performance improvement must outweigh the time it takes to find a well-performing configuration – the tuning process needs to be amortized. Whereas in some scenarios the tuning time is amortized in almost any case (e.g. long execution on supercomputers), in other scenarios the tuning time matters (e.g. when an application is not supposed to use many CPU hours, or tuning decisions are sensitive to input data, which are changing). Therefore, knowing how long it will take to find such a configuration is vital in order to decide if autotuning is worthwhile.

To predict the tuning time, we need to know the number of tuning steps and the average time of a tuning step. Additionally, the amortization of tuning time is determined by how many times we need to execute the tuned kernel and how much speedup will be achieved by tuning. In this paper, we target the first question: predicting the number of steps required to search a tuning space.

3.1 Prediction Method

Application parameter autotuning allows tuning parameters to be translated into virtually any property of the source code, from changing loop unrolling factor to selecting an entirely different algorithm. Therefore, tuning spaces can

---

[1] https://github.com/I2PC/xmipp.

[2] https://github.com/Fillo7/KTT/tree/master/examples.

vary in their size and also in the effect of each tuning parameter. Whereas some tuning spaces may contain a high number of configurations with near-optimal performance [7], other tuning spaces may contain only a few well-performing configurations [9,15]. The performance distribution among all various configurations on our benchmark set is shown in Fig. 1. Here, the benchmarks' tuning spaces are shown using violin plots – histograms of computation times are plotted on the y-axis (the wider the graph, the more configurations fall within the given performance range), with the better-performing configurations at the bottom. The histograms vary significantly for different computational problems – for example, many implementations of the Batched GEMM benchmark have very good performance, whereas the Hotspot benchmark only has a few fast implementations. Therefore, an estimation of the number of tuning steps required to reach sufficient performance is not straightforward.

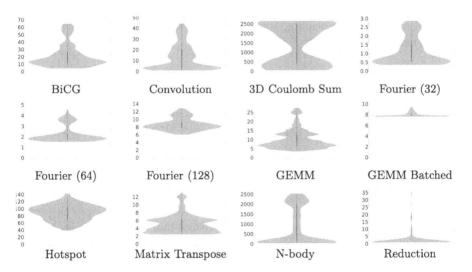

Fig. 1. Violin plots of computation times for various benchmarks, measured on GeForce GTX 1070. X-axis shows the amount of configurations, Y-axis shows computation time (in ms).

We hypothesize that the number of well-performing configurations remains similar for a computation problem across different hardware devices. The intuition behind this hypothesis is as follows. For a given processor, autotuning needs to balance many tuning variables. Some of them are very critical and must be set to an optimal value, while others may have a wider interval of well-performing values. When we change the processor, the optimal values may be shifted (e.g. by adding more cache, the optimal cache blocking factor may change), but the required precision of selection will be similar. Of course, hardware development may change the number of well-performing values – for example, adding more registers to the processor may lead to a wider range of efficient loop unrolling factors. However, those changes are not expected to be drastic, as hardware development is limited by the manufacturing process. In contrast, changes of tuning parameters may have a much higher impact on the shape of the tuning space and hence the relative amount of well-performing configurations. Therefore, the amount of well-performing configurations should be more stable with respect to the changing hardware than to the changing computational problems.

If the portion of well-performing configurations remains stable across different hardware – and therefore it can be predicted using historical data – we can use this to estimate the number of configurations we need to evaluate in order to find a good one. When random search is used, we can easily infer Formula 1 – let p_b be the portion of the tuning space that is well-performing, and p_s be the desired probability of finding a well-performing configuration. Then the relationship between them is defined as $(1 - p_s) = (1 - p_b)^{n_{conf}}$, where n_{conf} is the number of random attempts needed to reach a certain probability of finding a good-enough configuration. Therefore, to determine the number of attempts (i.e. the number of autotuning steps) required, we only need to calculate the corresponding logarithm:

$$n_{conf} = log_{(1-p_b)}(1 - p_s) \tag{1}$$

For example, if historical data show us that well-performing configurations comprise 1% of the tuning space, then in order to have a 90% chance of reaching a good solution, we need to explore $log_{(1-0.01)}(1 - 0.9) \approx 230$ configurations.

3.2 Evaluation

To support our hypothesis, we have prepared the following experiment. We consider a configuration well-performing if it achieves at least 90% of the performance of the best configuration. We have executed an exhaustive search on all benchmarks using all GPUs. The result is shown in Table 3. For each combination of GPU and benchmark, the table shows the portion of the tuning space comprised of well-performing configurations (e.g. 0.05 means that 5% of all configurations are well-performing)[3].

It can be seen in Table 3 that the variation of well-performing configurations is usually not high across GPU architectures – they are not in orders of magnitude, excepting some outliers (GEMM on 2080Ti, Matrix transpose on 1070 and Reduction on Vega56). Therefore, when the portion of tuning space containing well-performing implementations is known for at least one hardware device, we can use it to predict the number of tuning steps on other devices. Note that

---

[3] Note that some numbers are missing in the table: the 3D Fourier Reconstruction is implemented in CUDA and is therefore not measured on Radeon Vega56. It is also not measured on Nvidia Tesla K20, because we were unable to install Xmipp on the system. Some benchmarks have been executed with a smaller tuning space on Radeon Vega56, because AMD ROCm driver crashed with some tuning configurations (mainly using vectors of size 16 and higher loop unrolling factors). Therefore, we have omitted those benchmarks as their tuning spaces differ significantly.

Table 3. The portion of each tuning space consisting of well-performing configurations (i.e. reaching 90% of the best performance). The average portion with standard deviation for each problem is shown in the last column.

	Vega56	K20	750	1070	2080Ti	Avg ± Std dev
BiCG	0.00459	0.00527	0.00332	0.0168	0.0181	0.00962 ± 0.0072
Convolution	0.00280	0.00321	0.00117	0.00204	0.00175	0.00274 ± 0.00082
3D Coulomb sum	N/A	0.06032	0.0405	0.0389	0.0476	0.0468 ± 0.0098
Fourier (32)	N/A	N/A	0.0190	0.0286	0.0357	0.0278 ± 0.0084
Fourier (64)	N/A	N/A	0.0595	0.119	0.0357	0.0714 ± 0.043
Fourier (128)	N/A	N/A	0.0167	0.0571	0.0119	0.0286 ± 0.025
GEMM	N/A	0.000791	0.00107	0.00231	0.00793	0.00302 ± 0.0033
GEMM batched	0.120	0.0943	0.151	0.818	0.642	0.365 ± 0.34
Hotspot	0.0169	0.00743	0.00495	0.00495	0.0149	0.00983 ± 0.0057
Matrix transpose	0.0210	0.0461	0.0413	0.150	0.0101	0.0492 ± 0.052
N-body	N/A	0.0207	0.0576	0.0277	0.0492	0.0388 ± 0.017
Reduction	0.0775	0.3272727	0.463	0.715	0.368	0.390 ± 0.23

even if there may be several-fold misprediction, the method still provides valuable information – without the prediction, we would have absolutely no idea how difficult the search process is. For example, if we try to guess the number of well-performing configurations on a GPU using data from different benchmarks on the same architecture, the difference in the portion of tuning space containing well-performing configurations can reach two orders of magnitude.

4   Tuning Space Pruning

Autotuning of a computational kernel can take a long time if the tuning space is large and full of low-performing configurations. Pruning of the tuning space can accelerate the search. In [12], authors proposed a method based on the assumption that biasing search towards configurations which perform well on one processor can speed up the search on another processor. The method works well if the relative performance of the tuned codes correlates across different hardware (at least for the well-performing configurations). Often, this seems to be the correct assumption. However, we have found cases where the correlation is not good – this is demonstrated in Fig. 2, where well-performing configurations have high correlation for Matrix transposition, but low correlation for the Fourier (128) benchmark.

4.1   Proposed Pruning Method

Here, we propose an alternative method of tuning space pruning, which is based on the importance of tuning parameters. Even though the optimal *values* for

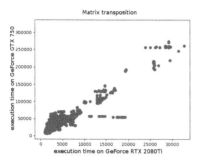
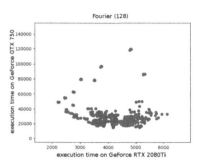

Fig. 2. The correlation between kernel runtime on GeForce GTX 750 and GeForce RTX 2080Ti for the Matrix transposition benchmark (left) and the Fourier (128) benchmark (right) in milliseconds. Each dot represents a configuration.

parameters change from hardware to hardware, we hypothesize that the *significance* of parameters (how much they influence the resulting performance) remains more stable. For example, if a problem is cache-sensitive on one GPU, it will probably remain cache-sensitive on any other GPU, even though the exact value of optimal cache blocking size will change.

When the tuning space is known for a hardware device, we can compute mutual information[4] between tuning variables and runtime. We propose to prune the less significant parameters (i.e. those with low mutual information with runtime) from the tuning space by fixing their values on a median and not changing them during the search. The pruning of insignificant parameters will lower the dimensionality of the tuning space, while keeping the well-performing configurations. It should be noted that our pruning approach is not designed as a brand new search method – rather, it can be used to improve the performance of already existing search algorithms.

4.2   Evaluation

To evaluate the proposed pruning method, we first computed mutual information for data measured on GPU-1070[5]. Then, we pruned the tuning space by fixing dimensions with mutual information lower than 20% of the highest mutual information value.

Table 4 shows state space reduction (SSR), the number of pruned parameters, and performance retention (PR) in all the benchmarks after the less significant parameters have been pruned (e.g. SSR of 16 means that the state space has been reduced 16-fold, and PR of 0.92 means that the best configuration in the pruned tuning space performs at 92% of the best performance reachable from the original tuning space).

---

[4] A sensitivity analysis metric which measures the dependency between variables – higher values mean higher dependency.

[5] Analyzing data from that GPU mimics the situation when the developer has knowledge of tuning space on that GPU only.

Table 4. State space reduction (SSR), the number of pruned/all parameters (PP) and performance retention for all tested hardware/benchmark combinations, after pruning all the parameters with low mutual information.

	SSR	PP	Vega56	K20	750	1070	2080Ti
BiCG	16.34	5/11	0.92	0.99	0.97	0.99	1.0
Convolution	285.33	4/10	1.0	0.51	0.50	0.59	0.55
3D Coulomb sum	10.0	4/8	0.99	1.0	0.97	0.97	0.97
Fourier (32)	4.0	3/7	N/A	N/A	1.0	0.98	0.99
Fourier (64)	4.0	3/7	N/A	N/A	1.0	0.98	1.0
Fourier (128)	4.0	3/7	N/A	N/A	1.0	0.99	0.99
GEMM	47.19	6/15	0.97	0.92	0.90	1.0	0.97
GEMM batched	22.32	8/11	0.96	0.92	0.99	1.0	0.99
Hotspot	6.97	2/6	0.83	0.98	1.0	1.0	0.99
Matrix transpose	6.0	2/9	1.0	1.0	1.0	1.0	1.0
N-body	2.22	2/8	1.0	1.0	1.0	0.98	1.0
Reduction	1.0	0/5	1.0	1.0	1.0	1.0	1.0

As we can see in Table 4, our method is able to significantly reduce the size of the state space, while sacrificing only a few percent of performance in most cases. For example, we can reduce the tuning space of BiCG more than 16× with 0–8% performance loss. The only example where performance loss is significant is Convolution, where the reduction of state space is enormous, but reachable performance is within 50% of the optimum only. Note, however, that the reachable performance is also low on GPU-1070, which has been used to select the parameters to be pruned. This suggests that the performance loss was not caused by low correlation of parameter significance across hardware, but rather by poor choice of parameters – in this case, a more sophisticated selection of pruned dimensions would be needed.

The pruned space can be used in two scenarios. Firstly, we can execute exhaustive search on it, reducing the number of tuning iterations by a factor of SSR (see Table 4). Excluding the Convolution example, we can reach good performance with a lower number of tuning iterations. Secondly, we can search iteratively within the pruned space. We elaborate on the second use case in the rest of this section.

We expect the search method to converge faster to a well-performing configuration on the pruned space with lower dimensionality, but to be outperformed by a search on the full space after the majority of the pruned space has been searched (because the pruned space may not include the optimal configuration).

To confirm this, we have prepared the following experiment. We have executed autotuning with random search on both the full and the pruned space

$1000\times$ to get statistically significant results[6]. To get results on the complete problem set, we have measured how quickly the tuning process converges to 90% of the best performance for all combinations of GPUs and problems. The results are given in Table 5. Although the pruned space contains well-performing configurations for Radeon Vega56 in most cases, the search method performs better on the full space. We suppose this is due to significant differences in the AMD architecture. For NVIDIA GPUs, the random search is usually faster when working on the pruned space (in 27 out of 37 cases).

The drawback of our method is that it prunes dimensions of low significance, so the relative amount of well-performing configurations is not increased in the pruned space. Since random search is known to perform well on spaces containing dimensions of low significance [3], we hypothesize that the pruning method can bring better speedups for more sophisticated search methods.

Table 5. The number of tuning steps required (on average) to reach 90% of the best performance. The full and the pruned spaces are compared. The Convolution benchmark is omitted (no well-performing configurations are available in the pruned space), as is the Reduction benchmark (no dimensions have been pruned).

	Vega56		K20		750		1070		2080Ti	
	Full	Pruned	Full	Pruned	Full	Pruned	Full	Pruned	Full	Pruned
BiCG	200	142	113	47	204	92	49	29	71	52
3D Coulomb sum	2	2	23	21	33	26	31	24	28	51
Fourier (32)	N/A	N/A	N/A	N/A	39	22	25	15	23	16
Fourier (64)	N/A	N/A	N/A	N/A	17	11	5	5	20	13
Fourier (128)	N/A	N/A	N/A	N/A	35	17	13	17	47	39
GEMM	200	302	2108	911	761	N/A	303	153	89	84
GEMM batched	10	12	9	11	6	3	1	1	2	2
Hotspot	88	N/A	126	33	108	22	131	31	74	24
Matrix transpose	255	267	35	30	51	57	18	16	160	98
N-body	9	6	37	37	18	16	32	25	19	33

5   Related Work

Numerous autotuning frameworks allow for the tuning of implementation parameters for heterogeneous computing [1,6,9,11,15]. All of these tuners are able to autotune OpenCL or CUDA code by altering their implementations, but the papers evaluate tuning spaces on rather limited benchmark sets.

---

[6] We have used the rapid testing of the search method implemented in Kernel Tuning Toolkit – first, all of the configurations are executed and their performance data are gathered, then during searcher testing the autotuner reads measured times instead of performing empirical tuning. This allows for performing many experiments in reasonable time.

To the best of our knowledge, there is no previous work attempting to predict the number of tuning search steps. Therefore, we limit the comparison of our work to methods improving tuning space search.

Search methods can be *model-based* or *model-free*. Considering model-free methods, most autotuning papers show that random search performs similarly to more sophisticated search methods, such as simulated annealing or particle swarm optimization [7,9,13]. A promising improvement of model-free search has been introduced recently in [15], outperforming other local and global search methods in most cases. Tuning space pruning introduced in this paper can be combined with any model-free search method.

Model-based methods attempt to take advantage of existing knowledge of the tuned system to predict the performance of a given implementation. Analytical solutions, which construct a mathematical model of performance, are specialized to a particular problem domain. A more scalable approach is to leverage empirical data, either from previous tuning runs or from concurrent profiling, to guide the tuning process.

Methods based on machine learning use historical data to build a performance model. In [10], authors built regression trees from an already explored part of the tuning space to steer a search method towards exploring more promising configurations. However, no historical data from previous tuning runs have been used. Data from previous runs are used for learning in [8] and [5]. Those papers focus on dynamic selection from a very limited number of code variants [8], or optimization of a single tuning parameter at compilation time [5]. We are focusing on the usage of historical data in more complex tuning spaces.

Probably the closest method to our work uses historical data to prune tuning space or bias search towards a configuration which performs better on another hardware device [12]. The method is based on the assumption that configurations which perform well on one device also perform well on another (see Sect. 4 for a deeper discussion). In contrast, our method assumes that tuning space dimensions which have a low impact on performance on one device will also have a low impact on another.

6   Conclusion and Future Work

In this paper, we have introduced methods using historical data gained from previous tuning of the same problem on different hardware, allowing us to:

- predict the number of search steps necessary for tuning;
- accelerate the tuning by pruning the tuning space.

We have prepared a set of ten benchmarks and demonstrated the usability of the proposed methods. The benchmark set is available to the community together with the Kernel Tuning Toolkit.

In the future, we plan to further analyze the tuning spaces. We plan to categorize tuning parameters and study their importance for particular types of hardware, as well as their interactions. We also plan to test more search methods and more advanced pruning (e.g. using profiling counters) in order to speed up the tuning process.

Another possible research direction would be to use the historical data from benchmarks to build a machine learning model which might actually *predict* the correct optimizations for a new set of hardware, or at least to guide the search of the configuration space instead of using random search.

Acknowledgements. The work was supported from European Regional Development Fund-Project "CERIT Scientific Cloud" (No. CZ.02.1.01/0.0/0.0/16_013/0001802). Access to the CERIT-SC computing and storage facilities provided by the CERIT-SC Center, provided under the programme "Projects of Large Research, Development, and Innovations Infrastructures" (CERIT Scientific Cloud LM2015085), is greatly appreciated.

References

1. Ansel, J., et al.: OpenTuner: an extensible framework for program autotuning. In: Proceedings of the 23rd International Conference on Parallel Architectures and Compilation, PACT 2014, pp. 303–316 (2014)
2. Balaprakash, P., et al.: Autotuning in high-performance computing applications. Proc. IEEE **106**(11), 2068–2083 (2018)
3. Bergstra, J., Bengio, Y.: Random search for hyper-parameter optimization. J. Mach. Learn. Res. **13**(1), 281–305 (2012)
4. Che, S., et al.: Rodinia: a benchmark suite for heterogeneous computing. In: IEEE International Symposium on Workload Characterization (IISWC) (2009)
5. Cummins, C., Petoumenos, P., Wang, Z., Leather, H.: End-to-end deep learning of optimization heuristics. In: 2017 26th International Conference on Parallel Architectures and Compilation Techniques (PACT), pp. 219–232 (2017)
6. Filipovič, J., Petrovič, F., Benkner, S.: Autotuning of OpenCL kernels with global optimizations. In: Proceedings of the 1st Workshop on Autotuning and Adaptivity Approaches for Energy Efficient HPC Systems (ANDARE 2017) (2017)
7. Kisuki, T., Knijnenburg, P.M.W., O'Boyle, M.F.P.: Combined selection of tile sizes and unroll factors using iterative compilation. In: Proceedings 2000 International Conference on Parallel Architectures and Compilation Techniques (PACT 2000) (2000)
8. Muralidharan, S., Roy, A., Hall, M., Garland, M., Rai, P.: Architecture-adaptive code variant tuning. SIGARCH Comput. Architect. News **44**(2), 325–338 (2016)
9. Nugteren, C., Codreanu, V.: CLTune: a generic auto-tuner for OpenCL kernels. In: Proceedings of the IEEE 9th International Symposium on Embedded Multicore/Many-Core Systems-on-Chip (MCSoC) (2015)
10. Price, J., McIntosh-Smith, S.: Improving auto-tuning convergence times with dynamically generated predictive performance models. In: 2015 IEEE 9th International Symposium on Embedded Multicore/Many-Core Systems-on-Chip (2015)
11. Rasch, A., Gorlatch, S.: ATF: a generic directive-based auto-tuning framework. Concurr. Comput. Pract. Exp. **31**(5), e4423 (2018)
12. Roy, A., Balaprakash, P., Hovland, P.D., Wild, S.M.: Exploiting performance portability in search algorithms for autotuning. In: 2016 IEEE International Parallel and Distributed Processing Symposium Workshops (IPDPSW) (2016)

13. Seymour, K., You, H., Dongarra, J.: A comparison of search heuristics for empirical code optimization. In: 2008 IEEE International Conference on Cluster Computing (2008)
14. Střelák, D., Sorzano, C.O.S., Carazo, J.M., Filipovič, J.: A GPU acceleration of 3D Fourier reconstruction in Cryo-EM. Int. J. High Perform. Comput. Appl. **33**, 948–959 (2019)
15. van Werkhoven, B.: Kernel tuner: a search-optimizing gpu code auto-tuner. Futur. Gener. Comput. Syst. **90**, 347–358 (2019)

Advancing Automatic Code Generation for Agent-Based Simulations on Heterogeneous Hardware

Jiajian Xiao[1,2]([⊠]), Philipp Andelfinger[1,3], Wentong Cai[3], Paul Richmond[4], Alois Knoll[2,3], and David Eckhoff[1,2]

[1] TUMCREATE, Singapore, Singapore
{jiajian.xiao,philipp.andelfinger,david.eckhoff}@tum-create.edu.sg
[2] Technische Universität München, Munich, Germany
knoll@in.tum.de
[3] Nanyang Technological University, Singapore, Singapore
aswtcai@ntu.edu.sg
[4] University of Sheffield, Sheffield, UK
p.richmond@sheffield.ac.uk

Abstract. The performance of agent-based simulations has been shown to benefit immensely from execution on hardware accelerator devices such as graphics processing units (GPUs). Given the increasingly heterogeneous hardware platforms available to researchers, it is important to enable modellers to target multiple devices using a single model specification, and to avoid the need for in-depth knowledge of the hardware. Further, key modelling steps such as the definition of the simulation space and the specification of rules to resolve conflicts among agents should be supported in a simple and generic manner, while generating efficient code. To achieve these goals, we extend the OpenABL modelling language and code generation framework by three aspects: firstly, a new OpenCL backend enables the co-execution of arbitrary agent-based models on heterogeneous hardware. Secondly, the OpenABL language is extended to support graph-based simulation spaces. Thirdly, we specify a generic interface for specifying conflict resolution rules. In a performance comparison to the existing OpenABL backends, we show that depending on the simulation model, the opportunity for CPU-GPU co-execution enables a speedup of up to 2.0 over purely GPU-based simulation.

Keywords: Agent-based simulation · Parallel and distributed simulation · Heterogeneous hardware · OpenABL · OpenCL

1 Introduction

Agent-based simulation (ABS) is widely used for system analysis and the answering of what-if questions in domains such as transport, computer networks, biology, and social sciences [17]. Each agent, e.g., a vehicle or a pedestrian, is an autonomous entity that makes decisions based on its environment, other agents,

© Springer Nature Switzerland AG 2020
U. Schwardmann et al. (Eds.): Euro-Par 2019 Workshops, LNCS 11997, pp. 308–319, 2020.
https://doi.org/10.1007/978-3-030-48340-1_24

and a number of behavioural models. Due to increasingly complex models and large numbers of agents, large-scale ABS often suffer from long execution times.

There exists an ample body of methods to speed up agent-based simulation to meet increasing performance needs, commonly based on parallel and distributed simulation techniques. In the last decade, the increasing prevalence of heterogeneous hardware composed of CPUs and *accelerators* such as GPUs or FPGAs opens up new possibilities to accelerate ABSs [28]. For instance, computationally intensive segments can be offloaded to run on an accelerator where they can be executed faster or ran in parallel to other parts being executed on the CPU.

However, placing the burden of tailoring the simulation to the target hardware platform on the simulationist degrades the maintainability of the simulation code as well as the portability to other hardware platforms. To avoid these issues, the modelling language OpenABL [6] has been proposed to enable code generation from high-level model and scenario specifications using a C-like syntax. A number of *backends* are provided to generate parallelised code targeting CPUs, GPUs, clusters, or cloud environments.

Previous to the work presented in this paper, each backend supported by OpenABL targeted one specific type of hardware platform, i.e., co-execution on combinations of CPUs, GPUs, FPGAs was not possible. This leaves a large range of computational resources untapped, even though previous work has demonstrated high hardware utilisation using co-execution [2]. Further, the simulation environment was limited to continuous 2D or 3D spaces, which excludes graph-based simulation spaces as commonly used in domains such as road traffic and social sciences. Lastly, OpenABL did not provide a mechanism for conflict resolution, requiring modellers to manually provide code to detect and resolve conflicts in situations where multiple agents request the same resources.

We address these limitations and contribute to the state of the art as follows:

- We extend OpenABL by an OpenCL backend to support automatic code generation for heterogeneous hardware.
- We provide new syntactic elements to support graph-based simulation spaces.
- We define an interface that enables conflict resolution code to be generated from user-specified rules.

Our extensions are open-source and available online[1]. The remainder of the paper is organised as follows: In Sect. 2, we introduce OpenABL as well as OpenCL and give an overview of related work in the field. In Sect. 3, we describe our extensions to OpenABL. We evaluate the performance of the extended OpenABL in Sect. 4. Section 5 summarises our work and concludes the paper.

2   Related Work and Background

The acceleration of ABS through parallelisation has received wide attention from the research community. A number of frameworks simplify the process of developing ABSs, e.g. MASON [15], Repast [19], Swarm [18], or FLAME [11]. Simulator variants that exploit CPU-based parallelisation or distributed execution

---

[1] https://github.com/xjjex1990/OpenABL_Extension.

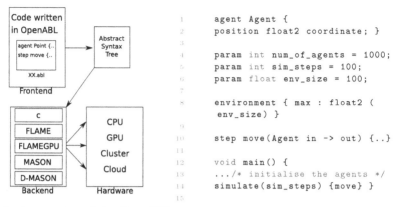

Fig. 1. An overview of the OpenABL.

Listing 1. Example OpenABL code.

include D-MASON [5] and Repast-HPC [4]. Making full use of those frameworks requires modellers to be knowledgeable in parallel or distributed computing.

A comprehensive review of existing techniques to overcome the challenges of ABS on hardware accelerators is found in [28]. One important method is to abstract from hardware specifics to simplify porting to hardware accelerators. FLAME GPU [23] is an extension to FLAME that provides a template-driven framework for agent-based modelling targeting GPUs based on a state machine model called X-machine. The Many-Core Multi-Agent System (MCMAS) [12] provides a Java-based tool-kit that supports a set of pre-defined data structures and functions called plugins to abstract from native OpenCL code. Agent models can be implemented using these data structures or plugins. In contrast to our work, MCMAS and FLAME GPU target GPUs only. Several previous works focus on the generation of performance-portable code targeting heterogeneous hardware by pattern-matching parallelisable C snippets [9], relying on code templates [13], or using domain-specific languages [24]. Some works perform pattern-matching procedures on intermediate representations instead of high-level code [25,26]. Unlike OpenABL, which can exploit the parallelisable structure shared by most ABS, the above works focus on automatically detecting parallelisable computations such as nested loops with predictable control flows.

In parallel ABS, conflicting actions may occur, e.g., when two agents move to the same position at the same point in time. Approaches proposed to detect and resolve such conflicts typically rely either on the use of atomic operations during the parallel agents updates [16] or on enumerating the agents involved in conflicts once an update cycle has completed [22]. In both cases, the winner of each conflict is determined according to a tie-breaking policy, which may be stochastic or rely on model-specific tie-breaking rules. A taxonomy and performance evaluation of the conflict resolution methods from the literature is given by Yang et al. [29]. In the present work, we provide a generic interface to define a conflict search radius and a tie-breaking policy from which low-level code is generated automatically.

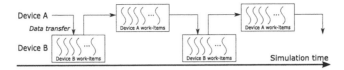

Fig. 2. Co-execution on devices A and B. Each work-item of device A processes the step functions assigned to A. After that, the data is transferred to Device B (via host) for processing the step functions assigned to B.

2.1 OpenABL

OpenABL is a domain-specific language to describe the behaviour of agent-based simulation and a framework to generate code targeting multiple execution platforms. It acts as an intermediate layer to generate parallel or distributed time-stepped ABS, given sequential simulation code written in the C-like Open-ABL language. An overview of the OpenABL framework is depicted in Fig. 1. The framework consists of a *frontend* and a *backend*. Listing 1 shows an example of frontend OpenABL code, where users can define agents with a mandatory position attribute (keyword `agent`, L.1-2), constants (keyword `param`, L.4-6), simulation environments (keyword `environment`, L.8), step functions (keyword `step`, L.10), and a main function (keyword `main()`, L.12-14).

The OpenABL compiler parses OpenABL code and compiles it to an Intermediate Representation (IR) called Abstract Syntax Tree (AST). The AST IR is then further relayed to one of the available backends. The backend reconstructs simulation code from the AST IR and parallelises the step functions targeted for CPUs, GPUs, clusters or cloud environments. OpenABL supports the following backends: C, FLAME [11], FLAME GPU [23], MASON [15], and D-MASON [5].

2.2 OpenCL

The Open Computing Language (OpenCL) is a framework that allows users to write parallel programs in a C-like syntax without considering low-level hardware specifics. An OpenCL execution environment is comprised of a host (usually CPUs) and one or multiple devices (e.g., CPUs, GPUs). A host program initialises the environment, control, memory, and computational resources for the devices. A device program consists mainly of so-called kernels that implement the computational tasks. Threads that process the tasks are referred to as work-items. Parallelism is achieved by processing many work-items in parallel. OpenCL is supported by a wide range of hardware including CPUs, GPUs, APUs, and FPGAs, allowing it to target heterogeneous hardware environments.

3   Extending OpenABL

In this section, we propose extensions to the OpenABL language and framework to support a wider range of simulation models as well as additional types of

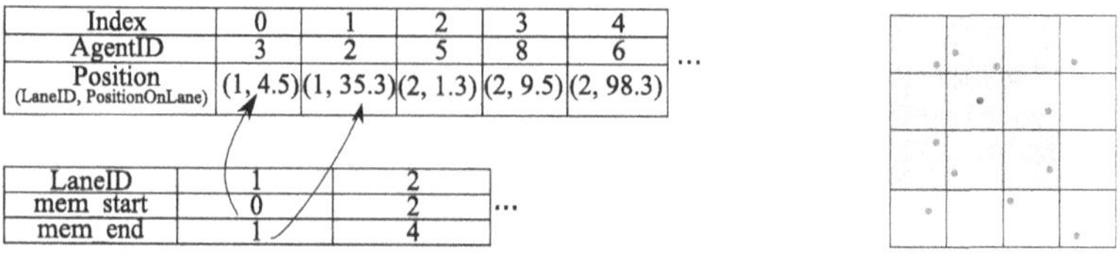

(a) Agents are sorted by their `position` (e.g. `EdgeID` and `PositionOnEdge`). Each element in the environment array keeps a `mem_start` and a `mem_end` pointer to its agents in global memory.

(b) In a grid with cell width at least the search radius, the neighbour search of the red agent loads itself and adjacent cells.

Fig. 3. Coalesced memory access in the generated OpenCL code.

hardware. We first provide an OpenCL backend to support code generation targeting heterogeneous hardware environments, enabling the execution on a variety of devices as well as a multi-device co-execution, e.g., combining a CPU and an FPGA. Further, we extend the OpenABL language to allow for the definition of graph-based simulation spaces. Finally, we introduce a mechanism for automated resolution of inter-agent conflicts based on user-defined rules.

3.1   Code Generation for Heterogeneous Hardware

OpenABL enables the addition of new backends without modifying the frontend, which allows us to target heterogeneous hardware by adding an OpenCL backend. The existing backends only allow for the execution on a single platform, e.g., a GPU. In contrast, OpenCL enables *co-execution* across multiple devices of different types. Our aim is to allow modellers to fully utilise the available hardware without specifying simulation code for each device manually.

The OpenCL backend takes as input the AST IR generated by the OpenABL frontend. The output of the OpenCL backend consists of a host program and a device program for each available device. Agents, the environment, constant declarations and all auxiliary functions are duplicated in both the host and device programs, as they may be referenced on either side.

The generated host program initialises the devices, allocates the required memory, and initialises the agent state variables as well as the environment. In a co-execution setting, the host program also orchestrates the data exchange between devices. After each simulation iteration, data processed by different devices is transferred back to the host. In the `simulate` statement, each step function is annotated with the identifier of the OpenCL device on which the step function should execute, e.g.: `simulate(sim_steps) {stepFunc1(0)`, `stepFunc2(1)}`.

One `compute_kernel` function is created in the device program for each device, where the designated step functions are called in sequence. On each device, the work-items execute in parallel with each one processing one step function.

The main loop of the simulation calls the `compute_kernel` of each device iteratively until the step count defined in the parameter of `simulation()` has been reached. As shown in Fig. 2, the execution of subsequent `compute_kernels` across devices is serialised to guarantee that data dependencies across kernels are respected. In the future, additional merging steps based on the model-specific dependencies could allow kernels to execute in parallel across devices.

3.2   User-Specified Environments

The original OpenABL limits the simulation environment to continuous 2D or 3D spaces, parametrised by the `max`, `min`, and `granularity` attributes in the `environment` declaration. Furthermore, user-defined types can only be used within agents, and not in function bodies or the environment, complicating the model specification. We extend the OpenABL syntax and frontend to lift these limitations. User-defined types for arbitrary variables in function bodies as well as in the definition of the simulation environment can be specified as follows:

```
Lane {
    int laneId;
    float length;
    int nextLaneIds[MAX_LANE_CONNECTIVITY]; }
environment { env : Lane lanes[env_size] }
```

The keyword `env` inside the environment declaration defines the simulation environment. It accepts an environment array of all native types supported by the original OpenABL as well as user-defined types. In this example, the environment is defined as an array of the user-defined type `Lane`. The `Lane` type encapsulates a lane's identifier, its length, and its connections to other lanes.

Accelerators typically employ a memory hierarchy composed of *global memory* accessible to all work-items and one or more types of memory accessible to groups or individual work-items. Due to the high latency of global memory accesses, data locality is an important consideration in ABS development [6]: accesses of adjacent work-items to adjacent memory addresses can frequently be coalesced, i.e., translated to a single memory transaction, allowing for peak memory performance on OpenCL devices such as GPUs. In common ABS models, agents tend to interact only with agents within a certain radius or on the same edge in a graph environment. To achieve data locality during execution, we implemented the efficient neighbour search method by [14]. Spatial locality is exploited by partitioning the simulation space into a grid of cells. Each cell's side length equals the largest search radius that appears in the model. In the original OpenABL, data locality is achieved in 2D or 3D space by specifying a radius using the following neighbour search query:

```
for (AgentType neighbours : near (currentAgent, radius))
```

We extend the language to allow for a similar neighbour search query for graph-based models: `for (AgentType neighbours : on (env))`

In the example of a traffic simulation with graph edges representing road lanes, the following query retrieves all agents on a lane:

```
for (Vehicles neighbours : on (lanes[currentVehicle.currentLane]))
```

Coalesced memory access is achieved by always keeping the array of agents in the global memory sorted according to the individual dimensions of the `position` attributes. Each element in the environment array keeps track of its start and end address in global memory. As illustrated in Fig. 3a, two attributes `mem_start` and `mem_end` record the start and end address of each single lane in the global array of agents. The two attributes are updated after all step functions have terminated. When the neighbour search query is called, instead of iterating through global memory, only a chunk of memory is loaded. In a graph-based setting, the chunk of memory is indicated by `env.mem_start` and `env.mem_end`. For 2D or 3D simulation spaces, we load chunks of memory holding the agents in current partition and all the neighbouring partitions (cf. Fig. 3b).

3.3   Conflict Resolution

In parallel ABS, simultaneous updates of multiple agents can result in multiple agents being assigned the same resource at the same time, e.g., a position on a road or consumables [7]. Unlike desired spatial collisions, e.g., in particle collision models, conflicts introduced purely by the parallel execution must be resolved to achieve results consistent with a sequential execution.

Conceptually, conflict resolution involves two steps: First, *conflict detection* determines pairs of conflicting agents, and second, *tie-breaking* determines the agent that acquires the resource. The loser of a conflict can be rolled back to its previous state. Since roll-backs may introduce additional conflicts, the process repeats until no further conflicts occur. A number of approaches for conflict resolution on parallel hardware have been proposed in [29]. Here, we propose a generic interface to specify a spatial range for conflict detection and a policy for tie-breaking, from which low-level implementations are generated.

The conflict resolution is specified as follows:
`conflict_resolution(env, search_radius, tie_breaking)`
All pairs of agents residing on the same element in the `env` array are checked for conflicts based on the agents' state variables. When considering 2D and 3D environments, the environment array is comprised of the internally generated partitions of the simulation space, with `search_radius` specifying the search radius. `tie_breaking` is a binary predicate that, given two agents A and B as arguments, returns `true` if A should be rolled back. If the agents are not in conflict or agent B should be rolled back, `tie_breaking` returns `false`.

As an example, in a traffic simulation scenario, the `env` is the environment array `roads[]`. Assuming the desired position of an agent is indicated by the state variables (`LaneID`, `PositionOnLane`), the `tie_breaking` function can be defined so that the agent with larger `PositionOnLane` wins the conflict. The position and velocity of the other agent involved in the conflict are reverted to their previous values. The generated conflict resolution code is executed once all step functions have been executed. The conflict detection relies on the neighbour search methods introduced in Sect. 3.2. As the step functions may change the agents' positions, the environment array is sorted and the `mem_start` and `mem_end` pointers are updated after each iteration (cf. Sect. 3.2). Currently, the

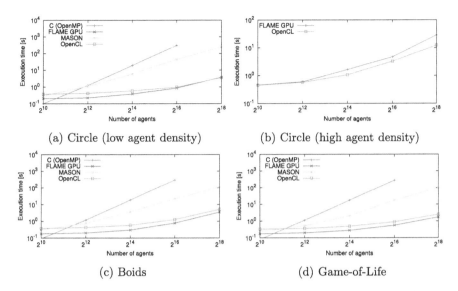

Fig. 4. Performance of the C, FLAME GPU, MASON and OpenCL code.

conflict resolution code is based on a user-specified tie-breaking rule. Our future work includes the automatic generation of model-agnostic resolution code [29].

4 Experiments

We evaluate the extended OpenABL on a system equipped with a 4-core Intel Core i7-4770 CPU, 16 GB of RAM and an NVIDIA GTX 1060 graphics card with 6 GB of RAM. We rely on GCC version 5.4, OpenCL version 1.2, and NVIDIA CUDA 10.0.292. We compare the performance of the OpenCL backend and the other backends: C with OpenMP, FLAME GPU, MASON. We consider three existing models: Circle, a benchmark for accessing neighbours within a certain radius provided in [3]; Conway's Game of Life [8]; and Boids [21], which simulates the flocking behaviour of birds. We based our implementation on the code provided in the OpenABL repository[2]. During preliminary experiments, we observed that FLAME GPU's performance is severely affected by file system I/O to store simulation statistics, which we disabled in our measurements. We run the simulations in two scenarios: "low agent density" generates agents evenly throughout the simulation space, whereas "high agent density" generates agents only in the upper left quadrant. We run all simulations for 100 time steps to allow for comparison with the existing results in [6].

As illustrated by Fig. 4a, 4c, 4d, the C variant is slow in all cases. This is because it iterates through all agents to search neighbours while the other backends rely on grid-based approaches to limit the search space. The performance of

---

[2] https://github.com/OpenABL/OpenABL.

Table 1. Breakdown of simulation runtime [s] for Circle (2^{16} agents)

Backend	Agent updates	Neighb. search	Other	Total
C	308.5 (100.0%)		0.00 (0.0%)	308.5
OpenCL	0.32 (33.3%)	0.61 (63.5%)	0.03 (3.2%)	0.96
FLAME GPU	0.24 (28.9%)	0.17 (20.5%)	0.42 (50.6%)	0.83
MASON	45.00 (100.0%)	0.00 (0.0%)	0.08 (0.0%)	45.08
OpenCL, high density	2.64 (81.2%)	0.58 (17.8%)	0.03 (1.0%)	3.25
FLAME GPU, high density	2.52 (54.1%)	1.74 (37.3%)	0.40 (8.6%)	4.66

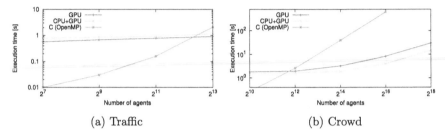

(a) Traffic   (b) Crowd

Fig. 5. Performance of the CPU-GPU co-execution.

the OpenCL backend is on par with the FLAME GPU backend and outperforms the other backends for low agent densities. As shown in the first four rows of Table 1, this is mainly owing to the massive parallelism on the GPU and the efficient neighbour search implemented by both backends. Despite the relatively long initialisation time as shown in Table 1 (the 'Other' column), FLAME GPU performs the best in low agent density scenarios. This is owing to FLAME GPU's message passing mechanism that generates one message per agent in the current cell. However, the performance is sensitive to the agent density. In contrast, the OpenCL backend sorts all agents in global memory after each simulation iteration to ensure their correct assignment to cells. The performance of sorting is barely affected by the density of agents. Thus, with high agent density, the OpenCL backend outperforms FLAME GPU in all cases, as depicted in Fig. 4b and the last two rows of Table 1. The other two models follow the same trend.

Our extensions to the OpenABL enable modellers to generate graph-based ABSs. As a proof of concept, we developed a traffic simulation akin to a previous manual implementation [27]. The agent behaviour is governed by two models: the Intelligent Driver Model determines the agents' longitudinal movement, whereas Ahmed's lane-changing model [1] determines the lateral movement. The generation of the conflict resolution code is enabled, the winner of each conflict being the agent further ahead on the same lane. We evaluate two execution schemes: executing purely on a GPU as well as CPU-GPU co-execution. In the co-execution scheme, the car-following model is offloaded to the CPU, while the lane-changing model and conflict resolution remain on the GPU. In all tested cases, the time spent on conflict resolution occupies less than 0.1% of the overall runtime with on average 0.86 rollbacks per agent in 100 simulation steps. As shown in Fig. 5a, with a small number of agents, the C variant outperforms the others due to the conflict resolution overhead and the data transfers between the CPU and the GPU in the co-execution case. As the number of agents increases, the GPU and co-execution variants produce better results than the C variant. The absolute runtime of the pure GPU and co-execution variants is similar. The co-execution achieves a maximum speedup of 1.78x over the C variant while the purely GPU-based execution achieves a maximum speedup of 2.29x. To further demonstrate the benefit of co-execution, we developed a crowd simulation based on the building evacuation behaviour described in [20]. Agents are divided into two groups based on their high-level behaviour: *Leaders*, which are assumed to have a floor plan of the building, conduct path finding to search for the exits. *Followers* flock to the nearest leader and follow the leader's movement. If there is no leader within a defined radius, the followers move in a random direction. All agents follow the Social Force Model [10] as their low-level behaviour. In the co-execution scheme, the memory-intensive path finding based on Dijkstra's algorithm is executed on the CPU, while the computationally intensive Social Force Model is executed on the GPU. Similar to the traffic simulation, with a small number of agents, the C backend variant outperforms the others, as illustrated in Fig. 5b. As the number of agents increases, the co-execution variant outperforms the other variants. A maximum speedup of 3.5x over the C variant and 2.03x over pure GPU is achieved through co-execution.

Finally, the OpenCL backend also opens up the possibility of executing on OpenCL-enabled FPGA devices. For instance, Intel offers an SDK to compile OpenCL code for FPGAs[3]. While in preliminary experiments, the considered models exceeded the hardware resources of a Terasic DE10-Standard, we plan to explore the area of FPGA-based acceleration in future work.

5 Conclusion and Future Work

In this paper, we presented our work towards automatic code-generation of agent-based simulations for heterogeneous hardware environments. We extended the OpenABL framework to overcome limitations in terms of the supported hardware platforms and the representation of the simulation space to support portable high-performance ABS for various model types. Our extensions are fully open-source and available online. Furthermore, we presented a semi-automated conflict resolution mechanism required to maintain the correctness of the parallelised simulation. Our addition of an OpenCL backend to the OpenABL framework not only enables the execution on CPUs and accelerators such as GPUs and FPGAs, but also opens up new possibilities such as multi-device co-execution.

We evaluated the performance of the OpenCL backend using three existing simulation models. It was observed that on a GPU, our approach outperformed the existing C and MASON backends, mainly due to a more efficient neighbour

---

[3] http://fpgasoftware.intel.com/opencl/.

search method. In a high agent density scenario, our backend also delivers better performance than the FLAME GPU backend. In addition, we demonstrated our approach by developing two proof-of-concept traffic and crowd simulations, showing the performance benefits of a CPU-GPU co-execution.

Our future work will focus on the automated assignment of computational tasks to the available hardware devices.

Acknowledgement. This work was financially supported by the Singapore National Research Foundation under its Campus for Research Excellence And Technological Enterprise (CREATE) programme.

References

1. Ahmed, K.I.: Modeling drivers' acceleration and lane changing behavior. Ph.D. thesis, Massachusetts Institute of Technology (1999)
2. Belviranli, M.E., Bhuyan, L.N., Gupta, R.: A dynamic self-scheduling scheme for heterogeneous multiprocessor architectures. ACM Trans. Archit. Code Optim. **9**(4), 57 (2013)
3. Chisholm, R., Richmond, P., Maddock, S.: A standardised benchmark for assessing the performance of fixed radius near neighbours. In: Desprez, F., et al. (eds.) Euro-Par 2016. LNCS, vol. 10104, pp. 311–321. Springer, Cham (2017). https://doi.org/10.1007/978-3-319-58943-5_25
4. Collier, N., North, M.: Repast HPC: a platform for large-scale agent-based modeling (2011)
5. Cordasco, G., De Chiara, R., Mancuso, A., Mazzeo, D., Scarano, V., Spagnuolo, C.: A framework for distributing agent-based simulations. In: Alexander, M., et al. (eds.) Euro-Par 2011. LNCS, vol. 7155, pp. 460–470. Springer, Heidelberg (2012). https://doi.org/10.1007/978-3-642-29737-3_51
6. Cosenza, B., et al.: OpenABL: a domain-specific language for parallel and distributed agent-based simulations. In: Aldinucci, M., Padovani, L., Torquati, M. (eds.) Euro-Par 2018. LNCS, vol. 11014, pp. 505–518. Springer, Cham (2018). https://doi.org/10.1007/978-3-319-96983-1_36
7. Epstein, J.M., Axtell, R.: Growing Artificial Societies: Social Science from the Bottom Up. Brookings Institution Press, Washington, D.C. (1996)
8. Gardner, M.: Mathematical games: the fantastic combinations of John Conway's new solitaire game "life". Sci. Am. **223**(4), 120–123 (1970)
9. Grewe, D., Wang, Z., O'Boyle, M.F.: Portable mapping of data parallel programs to OpenCL for heterogeneous systems. In: Proceedings of the International Symposium on Code Generation and Optimization, pp. 1–10. IEEE (2013)
10. Helbing, D., Molnar, P.: Social force model for pedestrian dynamics. Phys. Rev. E **51**(5), 4282 (1995)
11. Kiran, M., Richmond, P., Holcombe, M., Chin, L.S., Worth, D., Greenough, C.: FLAME: simulating large populations of agents on parallel hardware architectures. In: Proceedings of the International Conference on Autonomous Agents and Multiagent Systems, pp. 1633–1636. IFAAMAS (2010)
12. Laville, G., Mazouzi, K., Lang, C., Marilleau, N., Herrmann, B., Philippe, L.: MCMAS: a toolkit to benefit from many-core architecure in agent-based simulation. In: an Mey, D., et al. (eds.) Euro-Par 2013. LNCS, vol. 8374, pp. 544–554. Springer, Heidelberg (2014). https://doi.org/10.1007/978-3-642-54420-0_53

13. Li, P., Brunet, E., Trahay, F., Parrot, C., Thomas, G., Namyst, R.: Automatic OpenCL code generation for multi-device heterogeneous architectures. In: Proceedings of the International Conference on Parallel Processing, pp. 959–968. IEEE (2015)
14. Li, X., Cai, W., Turner, S.J.: Efficient neighbor searching for agent-based simulation on GPU. In: Proceedings of the International Symposium on Distributed Simulation and Real Time Applications, pp. 87–96. IEEE (2014)
15. Luke, S., Cioffi-Revilla, C., Panait, L., Sullivan, K., Balan, G.: MASON: a multi-agent simulation environment. Simulation **81**(7), 517–527 (2005)
16. Lysenko, M., D'Souza, R.M., et al.: A framework for megascale agent based model simulations on graphics processing units. J. Artif. Soc. Soc. Simul. **11**(4), 10 (2008)
17. Macal, C.M., North, M.J.: Tutorial on agent-based modelling and simulation. In: Proceedings of the Winter Simulation Conference, pp. 2–15. IEEE (2005)
18. Minar, N., Burkhart, R., Langton, C., Askenazi, M., et al.: The swarm simulation system: a toolkit for building multi-agent simulations. Technical report (1996)
19. North, M.J., Collier, N.T., Vos, J.R.: Experiences creating three implementations of the repast agent modeling toolkit. ACM Trans. Model. Comput. Simul. **16**(1), 1–25 (2006)
20. Pelechano, N., Badler, N.I.: Modeling crowd and trained leader behavior during building evacuation. IEEE Comput. Graphics Appl. **26**(6), 80–86 (2006)
21. Reynolds, C.W.: Flocks, herds, and schools: a distributed behavioral model. In: Proceedings of the ACM SIGGRAPH, pp. 25–34. ACM (1987)
22. Richmond, P.: Resolving conflicts between multiple competing agents in parallel simulations. In: Lopes, L., et al. (eds.) Euro-Par 2014. LNCS, vol. 8805, pp. 383–394. Springer, Cham (2014). https://doi.org/10.1007/978-3-319-14325-5_33
23. Richmond, P., Walker, D., Coakley, S., Romano, D.: High performance cellular level agent-based simulation with FLAME for the GPU. Briefings Bioinf. **11**(3), 334–347 (2010)
24. Steuwer, M., Fensch, C., Lindley, S., Dubach, C.: Generating performance portable code using rewrite rules: from high-level functional expressions to high-performance OpenCL code. ACM SIGPLAN Not. **50**(9), 205–217 (2015)
25. Steuwer, M., Remmelg, T., Dubach, C.: LIFT: A functional data-parallel IR for high-performance GPU Code generation. In: Proceedings of the International Symposium on Code Generation and Optimization, pp. 74–85. IEEE (2017)
26. Sujeeth, A.K., et al.: Delite: a compiler architecture for performance-oriented embedded domain-specific languages. ACM Trans. Embedded Comput. Syst. **13**(4s), 134 (2014)
27. Xiao, J., Andelfinger, P., Eckhoff, D., Cai, W., Knoll, A.: Exploring execution schemes for agent-based traffic simulation on heterogeneous hardware. In: Proceedings of the International Symposium on Distributed Simulation and Real Time Applications, pp. 1–10. IEEE (2018)
28. Xiao, J., Andelfinger, P., Eckhoff, D., Cai, W., Knoll, A.: A survey on agent-based simulation using hardware accelerators. ACM Comput. Surv. **51**(6), 131:1–131:35 (2019)
29. Yang, M., Andelfinger, P., Cai, W., Knoll, A.: Evaluation of conflict resolution methods for agent-based simulations on the GPU. In: Proceedings of the Conference on Principles of Advanced Discrete Simulation, pp. 129–132. ACM (2018)

Optimization of Data-Parallel Applications on Heterogeneous HPC Platforms for Dynamic Energy Through Workload Distribution

Hamidreza Khaleghzadeh$^{(\boxtimes)}$ ⓘ, Muhammad Fahad ⓘ,
Ravi Reddy Manumachu ⓘ, and Alexey Lastovetsky ⓘ

School of Computer Science, University College Dublin, Belfield, Dublin 4, Ireland
{hamidreza.khaleghzadeh,ravi.manumachu,alexey.lastovetsky}@ucd.ie,
muhammad.fahad@ucdconnect.ie

Abstract. Energy is one of the most important objectives for optimization on modern heterogeneous high performance computing (HPC) platforms. The tight integration of multicore CPUs with accelerators in these platforms present several challenges to optimization of multithreaded data-parallel applications for dynamic energy.

In this work, we formulate the optimization problem of data-parallel applications on heterogeneous HPC platforms for dynamic energy through *workload distribution*. We propose a solution method to solve the problem. It consists of a data-partitioning algorithm that employs load imbalancing technique to determine the workload distribution minimizing the dynamic energy consumption of the parallel execution of an application. The inputs to the algorithm are discrete dynamic energy profiles of individual computing devices.

We experimentally analyse the proposed algorithm using two multithreaded data-parallel applications, matrix multiplication and 2D fast Fourier transform. The load-imbalanced solutions provided by the algorithm achieve significant dynamic energy reductions (on the average 130% and 44%) compared to the load-balanced ones for the applications.

Keywords: High performance computing · Heterogeneous platforms · Energy of computation · Multicore CPU · GPU · Xeon Phi

1 Introduction

Energy consumption is one of the main challenges hindering high performance computing (HPC) community from breaking the exascale barrier [9].

Supported by Science Foundation Ireland (SFI) under Grant Number 14/IA/2474.

Electronic supplementary material The online version of this chapter (https://doi.org/10.1007/978-3-030-48340-1_25) contains supplementary material, which is available to authorized users.

© Springer Nature Switzerland AG 2020
U. Schwardmann et al. (Eds.): Euro-Par 2019 Workshops, LNCS 11997, pp. 320–332, 2020.
https://doi.org/10.1007/978-3-030-48340-1_25

Energy optimization in HPC context is studied briefly in connection with bi-objective optimization for performance and energy. State-of-the-art solution methods for bi-objective optimization problem can be broadly classified into *system-level* and *application-level* categories. System-level solution methods aim to optimize performance and energy of the environment where the applications are executed. The methods employ application-agnostic models and hardware parameters as decision variables. The dominant decision variable in this category is Dynamic Voltage and Frequency Scaling (DVFS). Majority of the works in this category optimize for performance with energy budget as a constraint. Application-level solution methods proposed in [2,12–14] use application-level parameters as decision variables and application-level models for predicting the performance and energy consumption of applications. The application-level parameters include the number of threads, number of processors, loop tile size, workload distribution, etc. Chakraborti et al. [2] consider the effect of heterogeneous workload distribution on bi-objective optimization of data analytics applications by simulating heterogeneity on homogeneous clusters. The performance is represented by a linear function of problem size and the total energy is predicted using historical data tables. Research works [13,14] demonstrate by executing real-life data-parallel applications on modern multicore CPUs that the functional relationships between performance and workload distribution and between energy and workload distribution have complex (non-linear) properties. They target homogeneous HPC platforms.

Modern heterogeneous HPC platforms feature tight integration of multicore CPUs with accelerators such as graphical processing units (GPUs) and Xeon Phi coprocessors to provide cutting-edge computational power and increased energy efficiency. This has resulted in inherent complexities such as severe resource contention for shared on-chip resources (Last Level Cache, Interconnect) and Non-Uniform Memory Access (NUMA). One visible manifestation of these complexities is a complex functional relationship between energy consumption and workload size of applications executing on these platforms where the shape of energy profiles may be highly non-linear and non-convex with drastic variations. This, however, provides an opportunity for application-level energy optimization through workload distribution as a decision variable.

Consider the dynamic energy profiles of multithreaded matrix-matrix multiplication (DGEMM) and 2D fast Fourier transform (2D-FFT) application executed on two connected heterogeneous multi-accelerator NUMA nodes, HCLServer1 (Table 1) and HCLServer2 (Table 2). The multicore CPU in HCLServer1 is integrated with one Nvidia K40c GPU and one Intel Xeon Phi 3120P. The multicore CPU in HCLServer2 is integrated with one Nvidia P100 GPU. DGEMM computes the matrix product, $C = \alpha \times A \times B + \beta \times C$, where A, B, and C are respectively dense matrices of size $m \times n$, $n \times n$, and $m \times n$ and α and β are constant floating-point numbers. 2D-FFT computes the Fourier transform of a complex matrix of size $m \times n$.

A data-parallel application executing on this heterogeneous platform, consists of a number of kernels (generally speaking, multithreaded), running in parallel on

Table 1. HCLServer1 specifications.

Intel Haswell E5-2670V3		Nvidia K40c		Intel Xeon Phi 3120P	
Socket(s), Cores per socket	2, 12	No. of processor cores	2880	No. of processor cores	57
Main memory	64 GB	Total board memory	12 GB	Total main memory	6 GB
Idle Power (W)	60	Idle Power (W)	68	Idle Power (W)	91

Table 2. HCLServer2 specifications.

Intel Xeon Gold 6152		Nvidia P100 PCIe	
Socket(s), Cores per socket	1, 22	No. of processor cores	3584
Main memory	96 GB	Total board memory	12 GB
Idle Power (W)	60	Idle Power (W)	30

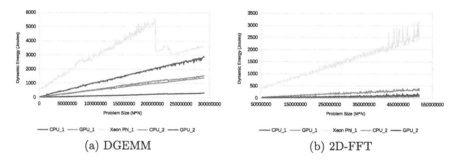

(a) DGEMM   (b) 2D-FFT

Fig. 1. Dynamic energy functions for the five abstract processors on HCLServer1 and HCLServer2. (a) DGEMM, and (b) 2D-FFT.

different computing devices of the platform. In order to apply our optimization algorithms, each group of cores executing an individual kernel of the application is modelled as an abstract processor [21] so that the executing platform is represented as a set of abstract processors. HCLServer1 is modelled by three abstract processors, CPU_1, GPU_1, and PHI_1. CPU_1 represents 22 (out of total 24) CPU cores. GPU_1 involves the Nvidia K40c GPU and a host CPU core connected to this GPU via a dedicated PCI-E link. PHI_1 is made up of one Xeon Phi 3120P and its host CPU core connected via a dedicated PCI-E link. In the same manner, HCLServer2 is modelled by two abstract processors, CPU_2 and GPU_2. Since there should be a one-to-one mapping between the abstract processors and computational kernels, any hybrid application executing on the servers should consist of five kernels, one kernel per computational device.

The dynamic energy profiles for the applications are shown in the Fig. 1. Each profile presents the dynamic energy consumption of a given processor versus workload size executed on the processor. In the figure for 2D-FFT, the dynamic energy profile for Phi_1 is ignored since it consumes 10 times more energy and dominates the other profiles. The dynamic energy consumptions are measured using Watts Up Pro power meter. We will elaborate the practical methodology to construct the discrete dynamic energy profiles in a following section.

Consider the execution of DGEMM for the workload size 2496×10112 employing all the five abstract processors, {CPU_1,CPU_2,GPU_1,GPU_2, PHI_1}. The solution determined by load-balanced algorithm is {64,320,64, 2048,0} and its dynamic energy consumption is 84 J. The optimal workload distribution assigns the whole workload to GPU_2 resulting in dynamic energy consumption of 24 J and thereby providing 150% reduction in energy. Consider the execution of 2D-FFT for the workload size 9120×51200 (2D signal) employing all the five abstract processors. The solution (workload distribution) determined by load-balanced algorithm is {1200,5376,1024,1472,0} and its dynamic energy consumption is 82 J. The load-balancing algorithm employs horizontal decomposition of the rows of the 2D signal. The optimal workload distribution assigns the whole workload to CPU_2 resulting in dynamic energy consumption of 40 J and thereby providing 105% reduction in energy. Our proposed solution finds these optimal workload distributions.

In this work, we propose a novel data-partitioning algorithm, *HEOPTA*, that determines optimal workload distribution minimizing the dynamic energy consumption of data-parallel applications executing on heterogeneous platforms for the most general shapes of dynamic energy profiles of the participating processors. To model the performance of a parallel application and build its speed functions, the execution time of any computational kernel can be measured accurately using high precision processor clocks. There is however no such effective equivalent for measuring the energy consumption. Physical measurements using power meters are accurate but they do not provide a fine-grained decomposition of the energy consumption during the application run in a hybrid platform. We propose a practical methodology to determine this decomposition, which employs only system-level energy measurements using power meters. The methodology allows us to build discrete dynamic energy functions of abstract processors with sufficient accuracy for the application of HEOPTA.

We experimentally analyse the accuracy of our energy modelling methodology and the performance of HEOPTA using two data-parallel applications, DGEMM and 2D-FFT, on a cluster of two heterogeneous nodes. We show that the load-imbalanced solutions provided by the algorithm achieve significant dynamic energy reductions compared to the load balanced solutions.

Our main contribution of this work is a novel data-partitioning algorithm that determines optimal workload distribution minimizing the dynamic energy consumption of data-parallel applications executing on heterogeneous platforms for the most general shapes of dynamic energy profiles of the processors.

The paper is organized as follows. Section 2 presents related work. Section 3 presents the formulation of the heterogeneous dynamic energy optimization problem. Section 4 describes our algorithm solving the problem. In Sect. 5, the device-level approach for dynamic energy modelling is illustrated. Section 6 presents the experimental results. Finally, Sect. 7 concludes the paper.

2 Related Work

In this section, we will cover research works on bi-objective optimization for performance and energy and notable works model the energy of computation.

Analytical studies of bi-objective optimization for performance and energy are presented in [3,5,15]. Choi et al. [3] extend the energy roofline model by adding an extra parameter, power cap, to their execution time model. Drozdowski et al. [5] use iso-energy map, which are points of equal energy consumption in a multi-dimensional space of system and application parameters, to study performance-energy trade-offs. Marszalkowski et al. [15] analyze the impact of memory hierarchies on time-energy trade-off in parallel computations, which are represented as divisible loads. The works reviewed do not consider workload distribution as a decision variable.

Basmadjian et al. [1] constructs a power model of a server using the summation of power models of its components: the processor (CPU), memory (RAM), fans, and disk (HDD). A model representing the energy consumption of a multi-core CPU by a non-linear function of workload size is developed in [13]. Nagasaka et al. [16] propose PMC-based statistical power consumption modelling technique for GPUs that run CUDA applications. Song et al. [20] present power and energy prediction models based on machine learning algorithms such as back-propagation in artificial neural networks (ANNs). Shao et al. [19] develop an instruction-level energy consumption model for a Xeon Phi processor.

3 Formulation of Heterogeneous Dynamic Energy Optimization Problem

Consider a workload size n executing on p processors with dynamic energy functions, $E = \{e_0(x), ..., e_{p-1}(x)\}$ where $e_i(x)$, $i \in \{0, 1, \cdots, p-1\}$, is a discrete dynamic energy function of processor P_i with a cardinality of m. The heterogeneous dynamic energy optimization problem can be formulated as follows:

Heterogeneous Dynamic Energy Optimization Problem, $HEOPT(n,$ p, m, E, X_{opt}, e_{opt}): The problem is to find a workload distribution, $X_{opt} = \{x_0, ..., x_{p-1}\}$, for the workload n executing on p heterogeneous processors so that the solution minimizes dynamic energy consumption during the parallel execution of n. The parameters (n, p, m, E) are the inputs to the problem. The outputs are X_{opt}, which is the optimal solution (workload distribution), and e_{opt}, which represents the dynamic energy consumption of the optimal solution. The formulation below is a integer non-linear programming (INLP) problem.

$$e_{opt} = \min_{X} \sum_{i=0}^{p-1} e_i(x_i) \qquad \text{Subject to} \quad \sum_{i=0}^{p-1} x_i = n,$$

$$\text{where} \quad p, m, n \in \mathbb{Z}_{>0} \quad \text{and} \quad x_i \in \mathbb{Z}_{\geq 0} \quad \text{and} \quad e_i(x) \in \mathbb{R}_{>0} \tag{1}$$

The objective function in Eq. 1 is a function of workload distribution X, $X = \{x_0, ..., x_{p-1}\}$, for a given workload n executing on the p processors. The number of active processors (processors that are assigned non-zero workload size) in the optimal solution (X_{opt}) may be less than p.

4 HEOPTA: Algorithm Solving HEOPT Problem

In this section, we will introduce HEOPTA, a branch-and-bound algorithm solving HEOPT. The bounding criteria in HEOPTA are *energy threshold* and *size threshold*, which are explained below.

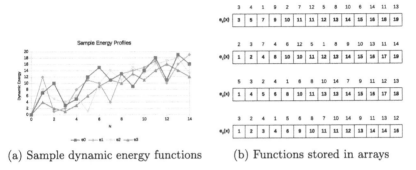

(a) Sample dynamic energy functions   (b) Functions stored in arrays

Fig. 2. (a) Dynamic energy functions of a sample application executing on four heterogeneous processors. (b) The same functions stored in arrays.

First, the algorithm is informally explained using a simple example. Consider a workload $n = 12$ executing on a given platform consisting of four heterogeneous processors $(p = 4)$. Figure 2 (a) shows the discrete dynamic energy functions, $E = \{e_0(x), \cdots, e_3(x)\}$, with a cardinality of 14 $(m = 14)$, as inputs to HEOPTA. Figure 2 (b) shows the discrete dynamic energy functions which are stored as arrays in non-decreasing order of energy consumption.

To solve the HEOPT problem and find the optimal workload distribution, a straightforward approach is to explore a full solution tree in order to build all combinations and finally select a workload distribution that its dynamic energy consumption is minimum. The tree explored by such a naive approach is shown in Fig. 3 which contains all the combinations for $n = 12$ and $p = 4$. Due to the lack of space, the tree is shown partially.

The naive algorithm starts tree exploration from the root at the level L_0 of the tree. The root node is labelled by 12 which represents the whole workload to be distributed between 4 processors $\{P_0, P_1, P_2, P_3\}$. Then, fifteen $(= m + 1)$ problem sizes, including a zero problem size along with all problem sizes in the dynamic energy function $e_0(x)$, are assigned to the processor P_0 one at a time. Therefore, the root is expanded into 15 children. The value, which labels an

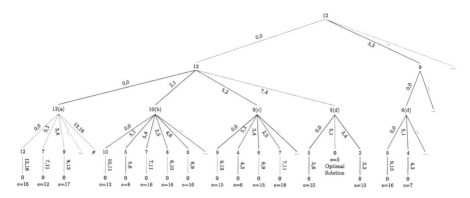

Fig. 3. Applying naive approach to examine all combinations and select a workload distribution with the minimum dynamic energy consumption.

internal node at level L_1 (root's children), determines the remaining workload to be distributed between processors $\{P_1, P_2, P_3\}$.

Similarly, each child of the root in the next level L_1 turns into a root of a sub-tree, which is a solution tree to solve HEOPT for the remaining workload between three processors $\{P_1, P_2, P_3\}$. Each edge, which connects the root and its child, is labelled by the problem size assigned to P_0 and its energy consumption.

In Fig. 3, the leaf node at level L_1 labelled by 0 represents a solution leaf. Generally, any leaf node labelled by 0 illustrates one of the possible solutions, where its dynamic energy consumption is calculated as the summation of the consumed energies labelling the edges in the path connecting the root and the solution leaf. *No-solution* leaves are labelled by $\varnothing$.

In this example, the distribution $\{(0,0), (7,4), (5,1), (0,0)\}$, highlighted in blue, with the consumed dynamic energy of 5, represents the optimal solution.

The cost of this naive algorithm is exponential. HEOPTA utilizes two bounding criteria, *energy threshold* and *size threshold*, and saving the intermediate solutions to find optimal solutions in a polynomial complexity of $O(m^3 \times p^3)$.

The *energy threshold*, represented by ε, is the dynamic energy consumption of load-equal distribution, allocating each processor the same workload of size $\frac{n}{p}$ (assuming n is divisible by p). HEOPTA will not examine data points with the dynamic energy consumption greater than or equal to the energy threshold.

The *size threshold* assigns each level of the tree a threshold, $\sigma_i, i \in \{0, \ldots, p-1\}$, which represents the maximum workload that can be executed in parallel on processors $\{P_i, \cdots, P_{p-1}\}$ so that the dynamic energy consumption by every processor $\{P_i, \cdots, P_{p-1}\}$ is less than ε.

HEOPTA explores solution trees in the left-to-right depth-first order as shown in Fig. 3. Before exploring a branch, the branch is checked against two upper estimated bounds, *energy threshold* and *size threshold*, and is discarded if it cannot result in a better solution than the best one found so far. All subtrees, not explored by applying the bounding criteria, are highlighted in red in Fig. 3. We call this key optimization operation *Cut*.

When a solution is found, the following operations are performed: (i) The energy threshold ε is updated, (ii) If ε decreases, the vector σ of size thresholds is updated, and (iii) The solution is saved in the memory. Green nodes in the tree highlight ones whose solutions are saved. We call this key operation, *Save*. Before exploring a node, HEOPTA read the memory to retrieve its solution (if it have already been saved). This key operation is called READMEMORY. The solution of the orange node in the tree is retrieved from the memory.

In summary, HEOPTA uses three key operations, *Cut*, *Save*, and READMEMORY, to find the optimal solutions. In supplemental available online in [11], we elucidate using an example how these key operations reduce the search space of solutions. The pseudocode of HEOPTA, its correctness and complexity proofs are also presented in the supplemental in [11].

5 Device-Level Dynamic Energy Decomposition in Heterogeneous Hybrid Platforms

We describe our practical approach here to construct the discrete dynamic energy profiles of the abstract processors in a hybrid heterogeneous server. The method is based purely on system level measurements. The approach comprises of two main steps. The first step is the identification or grouping of the computing elements satisfying properties that allow measurement of their energy consumptions to sufficient accuracy. We call these groups as *abstract processors*. The second step is the construction of the dynamic energy models of the abstract processors where the principal goal apart from minimizing the time taken for model construction is to maximize the accuracy of measurements.

5.1 Grouping of Computing Elements

We group individual computing elements executing an application together in such a way that we can accurately measure the energy consumption of the group. We call these groups *abstract processors*. We consider two properties essential to composing the groups:

- *Completeness:* An abstract processor must contain only those computing elements which execute the given application kernel.
- *Loose coupling:* Abstract processors do not interfere with each other during the application. That is, the dynamic energy consumption of one abstract processor is not affected by the activities of other abstract processor.

Based on this grouping approach, we hypothesize that the total dynamic energy consumption during an application execution will equal the sum of energies consumed by all the abstract processors. So, if E_T is the total dynamic energy consumption of the system incorporating p abstract processors $\{AP_1, \cdots, AP_p\}$, then $E_T = \sum_{i=1}^{p} E_T(AP_i)$, where $E_T(AP_i)$ is the dynamic energy consumption of the abstract processor AP_i. We call this our *additive* hypothesis.

5.2   Energy Models of Abstract Processors

We describe here the second main step of our approach, which is to build the dynamic energy models of the p abstract processors. We represent the dynamic energy model of an abstract processor by a discrete function composed of a set of points of cardinality m. The total number of experiments available to build the dynamic energy models is $(2^p - 1) \times m$. Consider, for example, three abstract processors {A,B,C}. {A,B,C, {AB,C}, {A,BC}, {AC,B}, ABC}. The category {AB,C} represents parallel execution of application kernels on A and B followed by application kernel execution on C. For each workload size, the total dynamic energy consumption is obtained from the system-level measurement for this combined execution of kernels. The categories {AB,C} and {BA,C} are considered indistinguishable. There are m experiments in each category. The goal is to construct the dynamic energy models of the three abstract processors {A,B,C} from the experimental points to sufficient accuracy. We reduce the number of experiments to $p \times m$ by employing our additive hypothesis.

6   Experimental Results

We employ two connected heterogeneous multi-accelerator NUMA nodes, HCLServer1 (Table 1) and HCLServer2 (Table 2). HCLServer1 is modelled by three abstract processors, CPU_1, GPU_1 and PHI_1, as described earlier. HCLServer2 is modelled by two abstract processors, CPU_2 and GPU_2.

   We employ two popular data-parallel applications, matrix-matrix multiplication (DGEMM) and 2D fast Fourier transform (2D-FFT). Each application executing on the servers in parallel consists of five kernels, one kernel per computational device. Figure 1 shows discrete dynamic energy functions for the five abstract processors for DGEMM and 2D-FFT. For the DGEMM application, workload sizes range from 64×10112 to 28800×10112 with a step size of 64 for the first dimension m. For the 2D-FFT application, workload sizes range from 1024×51200 to 10000×51200 with a step size of 16 for the first dimension m.

   For measuring dynamic energy consumption, each node is facilitated with one WattsUp Pro power meter which sits between the wall A/C outlets and the input power sockets of the node. Each power meter captures the total power consumption of one node. We use *HCLWattsUp* API [8], which gathers the readings from the power meter to determine the dynamic energy consumption during the execution of an application. HCLWattsUp has no extra overhead and therefore does not influence the energy consumption of the application execution. Fans are significant contributors to energy consumption. To rule out the contribution of fans in dynamic energy consumption, we set the fans at full speed before executing an application.

   For each data point in the functions, the experiments are repeated until sample means of all the five kernels executing on the abstract processors fall in the confidence interval of 95%, and a precision of 0.1 (10%) is achieved.

   Our approach on how to instrument computational kernels in a hybrid application and measure their execution times and dynamic energies is explained in detail in [11]. We also present our analysis of the accuracy of the additive approach to constructing discrete dynamic energy profiles in [11].

While the proposed method is rather expensive and requires significant time to build the energy profiles, the alternative approaches, namely, on-chip power sensors, such as Intel RAPL [7], Nvidia NVML [17], or AMD APM [4], and software models using performance counters as predictor variables, are still too inaccurate for the use in application-level optimization for energy [6,18].

6.1 Analysing HEOPTA

HEOPTA is analysed using two sets of experiments. For the first set, we compare the dynamic energy consumption of solutions determined by HEOPTA with the dynamic energy of load-balanced solutions. Load-balanced solutions are workload distributions with equal execution times for each abstract processor. The number of active processors in a solution (those assigned non-zero workload size) may be less than the total number of available processors. The dynamic energy saving against load-balancing algorithm is obtained as follows: $Energy\_Saving_{balance}(\%) = \frac{e_{balance} - e_{heopta}}{e_{heopta}} \times 100$, where $e_{balance}$ and e_{heopta} are the dynamic energy consumptions of solutions determined by load-balancing and HEOPTA algorithms.

For the second set, we examine the interplay between dynamic energy optimization and performance optimization using the workload distribution determined by HPOPTA. HPOPTA [10] is a data-partitioning algorithm for optimization of data-parallel applications on heterogeneous HPC platforms for performance. The energy saving of HEOPTA against HPOPTA is obtained as follows: $Energy\_Saving_{hpopta}(\%) = \frac{e_{hpopta} - e_{heopta}}{e_{heopta}} \times 100$, where e_{hpopta} represents the dynamic energy consumption of the solution determined by HPOPTA. The inputs to HPOPTA are discrete speed (or performance) functions.

The experimental dataset for DGEMM contains the workload sizes, $\{64 \times 10112, 128 \times 10112, \cdots, 57600 \times 10112\}$. The minimum, average, and maximum reductions in the dynamic energy consumption of HEOPTA against load-balancing algorithm, $Energy\_Saving_{balance}$, are 0%, 130%, and 257%. Zero percentage improvement represents the same workload distribution is determined by HEOPTA and load-balancing algorithm. These values for $Energy\_Saving_{hpopta}$ are 0%, 145%, and 314%. Figure 4 compares HEOPTA against the dynamic energy consumption of solutions determined by load-balancing and HPOPTA. Performance optimization increases dynamic energy consumption by an average of 145%.

The experimental data set for 2D-FFT includes workload sizes, $\{1024 \times 51200, 1040 \times 51200, \cdots, 20000 \times 51200\}$. The minimum, average, and maximum dynamic energy reductions of HEOPTA against load-balancing algorithm, $Energy\_Saving_{balance}$, are 0%, 44%, and 105%. The minimum, average, and maximum of $Energy\_Saving_{HPOPTA}$ are 0%, 32%, and 77%. Figure 5 compares HEOPTA against the dynamic energy consumption of solutions determined by load-balancing and HPOPTA. Optimization for performance increases dynamic energy consumption by an average of 32%.

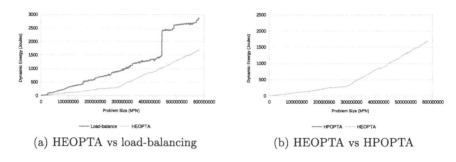

(a) HEOPTA vs load-balancing   (b) HEOPTA vs HPOPTA

Fig. 4. Dynamic energy consumption of DGEMM executed using HEOPTA in comparison with (a) Load-balanced solutions (b) HPOPTA.

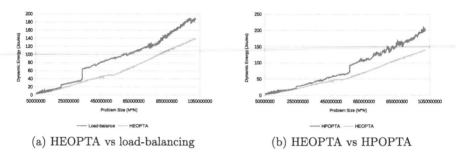

(a) HEOPTA vs load-balancing   (b) HEOPTA vs HPOPTA

Fig. 5. Dynamic energy consumption of the 2D-FFT application executed using HEOPTA in comparison with (a) Load-balanced solutions, (b) HPOPTA.

We conclude that HEOPTA demonstrates considerable improvements in average and maximum dynamic energy consumptions for the two applications in comparison with the load-balancing and HPOPTA algorithms. Performance optimization also increases dynamic energy consumption for both applications.

7 Conclusion

Modern heterogeneous HPC platforms feature tight integration of multicore CPUs with accelerators, which resulted in inherent complexities. One visible manifestation of these complexities is a complex functional relationship between energy consumption and workload size of applications executing on these platforms thereby providing an opportunity for application-level energy optimization through workload distribution as a decision variable.

We proposed HEOPTA that determines optimal workload distributions minimizing the dynamic energy consumption of data-parallel applications running on heterogeneous HPC platforms. We showed that the load-imbalanced solutions provided by the algorithm achieve significant dynamic energy reductions compared to the load balanced solutions. As future work, we will study the impact of dynamic energy optimization on performance.

The software implementation for HEOPTA is available at [11].

References

1. Basmadjian, R., Ali, N., Niedermeier, F., de Meer, H., Giuliani, G.: A methodology to predict the power consumption of servers in data centres. In: 2nd International Conference on Energy-Efficient Computing and Networking. ACM (2011)
2. Chakrabarti, A., Parthasarathy, S., Stewart, C.: A pareto framework for data analytics on heterogeneous systems: implications for green energy usage and performance. In: 46th International Conference on Parallel Processing (ICPP), pp. 533–542. IEEE (2017)
3. Choi, J., Dukhan, M., Liu, X., Vuduc, R.: Algorithmic time, energy, and power on candidate HPC compute building blocks. In: IEEE 28th International Parallel and Distributed Processing Symposium, pp. 447–457. IEEE (2014)
4. Devices, A.M.: Bios and kernel developer's guide (BKDG) for AMD family 15h models 00h–0Fh processors (2012). https://www.amd.com/system/files/TechDocs/42301_15h_Mod_00h-0Fh_BKDG.pdf
5. Drozdowski, M., Marszalkowski, J.M., Marszalkowski, J.: Energy trade-offs analysis using equal-energy maps. Future Gener. Comput. Syst. **36**, 311–321 (2014)
6. Fahad, M., Shahid, A., Manumachu, R.R., Lastovetsky, A.: A comparative study of methods for measurement of energy of computing. Energies **12**(11), 2204 (2019)
7. Gough, C., Steiner, I., Saunders, W.: Energy Efficient Servers: Blueprints for Data Center Optimization. Apress, New York (2015)
8. HCL: HCLWattsUp: API for power and energy measurements using WattsUp Pro Meter (2016). https://csgitlab.ucd.ie/ucd-hcl/hclwattsup
9. Hsu, J.: Three paths to exascale supercomputing. IEEE Spectr. **53**(1), 14–15 (2016)
10. Khaleghzadeh, H., Manumachu, R.R., Lastovetsky, A.: A novel data-partitioning algorithm for performance optimization of data-parallel applications on heterogeneous HPC platforms. IEEE Trans. Parallel Distrib. Syst. **29**(10), 2176–2190 (2018)
11. Khaleghzadeh, H., Reddy, R., Lastovetsky, A.: HEOPTA: heterogeneous model-based data partitioning algorithm for optimization of data-parallel applications for dynamic energy (2019). https://csgitlab.ucd.ie/HKhaleghzadeh/heopt
12. Lang, J., Rünger, G.: An execution time and energy model for an energy-aware execution of a conjugate gradient method with CPU/GPU collaboration. J. Parallel Distrib. Comput. **74**(9), 2884–2897 (2014)
13. Lastovetsky, A., Reddy, R.: New model-based methods and algorithms for performance and energy optimization of data parallel applications on homogeneous multicore clusters. IEEE Trans. Parallel Distrib. Syst. **28**(4), 1119–1133 (2017)
14. Manumachu, R.R., Lastovetsky, A.: Bi-objective optimization of data-parallel applications on homogeneous multicore clusters for performance and energy. IEEE Trans. Comput. **67**(2), 160–177 (2018)
15. Marszałkowski, J.M., Drozdowski, M., Marszałkowski, J.: Time and energy performance of parallel systems with hierarchical memory. J. Grid Comput. **14**(1), 153–170 (2015). https://doi.org/10.1007/s10723-015-9345-8
16. Nagasaka, H., Maruyama, N., Nukada, A., Endo, T., Matsuoka, S.: Statistical power modeling of GPU kernels using performance counters. In: International Green Computing Conference and Workshops (IGCC). IEEE (2010)
17. Nvidia: Nvidia management library: NVML reference manual, October 2018. https://docs.nvidia.com/pdf/NVML_API_Reference_Guide.pdf
18. O'Brien, K., Pietri, I., Reddy, R., Lastovetsky, A., Sakellariou, R.: A survey of power and energy predictive models in HPC systems and applications. ACM Comput. Surv. **50**(3), 37 (2017)

19. Shao, Y.S., Brooks, D.: Energy characterization and instruction-level energy model of Intel's Xeon Phi processor. In: Proceedings of the 2013 International Symposium on Low Power Electronics and Design, ISLPED 2013. IEEE Press (2013)
20. Song, S., Su, C., Rountree, B., Cameron, K.W.: A simplified and accurate model of power-performance efficiency on emergent GPU architectures. In: 27th IEEE International Parallel and Distributed Processing Symposium (IPDPS), pp. 673–686. IEEE Computer Society (2013)
21. Zhong, Z., Rychkov, V., Lastovetsky, A.: Data partitioning on multicore and multi-GPU platforms using functional performance models. IEEE Trans. Comput. 64(9), 2506–2518 (2015)

Search-Based Scheduling for Parallel Tasks on Heterogeneous Platforms

Robert Dietze$^{(\boxtimes)}$ and Gudula Rünger

Department of Computer Science, Chemnitz University of Technology, Chemnitz,
Germany
{dirob,ruenger}@cs.tu-chemnitz.de

Abstract. Scheduling is a widely used method in parallel computing, which assigns tasks to several compute resources of the parallel environments. In this article, we consider parallel tasks as the basic entities to be scheduled onto a heterogeneous execution platform consisting of multicores of different architecture. A parallel task has an internal potential parallelism which allows a parallel execution for example on multicore processors of different type. The assignment of tasks to different multicores of a heterogeneous execution platform may lead to different execution times for the same parallel tasks. Thus, the scheduling of parallel tasks onto a heterogeneous platform is more complex and provides more choices for the assignment and for finding the most efficient schedule. Search-based methods seem to be a promising approach to solve such complex scheduling problems. In this article, we propose a new task scheduling method HP* to solve the problem of scheduling parallel tasks onto heterogeneous platforms. Furthermore, we propose a cost function that reduces the search space of the algorithm. In performance measurements, the scheduling results of HP* are compared to several existing scheduling methods. Performance results with different benchmark tasks are shown to demonstrate the improvements achieved by HP*.

Keywords: Search-based scheduling · Heterogeneous platforms · Parallel tasks

1 Introduction

The execution time of compute-intensive applications depends strongly on the efficient utilization of compute resources. Task-based applications are partitioned into a set of tasks each of which can be assigned to different execution units. Independent tasks can be executed concurrently on the execution units which may lead to a significant reduction of the execution time of the application. For such a reduction of the execution time an efficient utilization of all execution units is needed. A common approach to determine such an assignment of tasks to compute resources is the use of task scheduling methods.

U. Schwardmann et al. (Eds.): Euro-Par 2019 Workshops, LNCS 11997, pp. 333–344, 2020.
https://doi.org/10.1007/978-3-030-48340-1_26

Parallel computing environments within or across institutions are often composed of nodes with different capabilities. Achieving a high efficiency when executing parallel applications on such a heterogeneous system strongly depends on the methods used to schedule the tasks of a parallel application. The heterogeneous compute resources considered in this article consist of several multicore nodes. Each node may have a different architecture which leads to differences in the performance. For the scheduling of parallel tasks two properties of the compute nodes are particularly important, the number of processor cores and the computational speed of each node.

Many proposed task scheduling methods focus on sequential tasks that are assigned to exactly one processor of a compute node. Large applications that are based on parallel programming models may be decomposed into a set of parallel tasks. The term *parallel task* describes a task that can be executed on a single compute node using an arbitrary number of processor cores. Since the tasks are independent from each other, a flexible execution order and a concurrent execution on one compute node are possible. The parallel execution time of each parallel task depends on the number of cores utilized. Thus, for the assignment of parallel tasks to heterogeneous platforms, the particular compute node and the number of processor cores to be used on this node have to be determined for each task. The resulting scheduling problem becomes increasingly complex due to the increasing number of options for placing tasks. Consequently dedicated scheduling methods are required.

Since task scheduling is a NP-complete problem, many of the proposed scheduling methods are based on heuristics [1,2,4,12,18]. Heuristic scheduling methods may find solutions that are acceptable for a specific use case but finding an optimal solution is not guaranteed. In certain scenarios the optimal solution of a scheduling problem is needed, e.g. for evaluating the quality of heuristic scheduling methods. In the worst case, a search of the entire solution space is required to find such an optimal solution. For the proposed scheduling problem, the search space contains all possible assignments of tasks to compute nodes. Additionally, for each node, all possible combinations for assigning tasks to a number of processor cores have to be considered. Since the computation time required to find an optimal solution can be extremely long, informed search-based algorithms which prune the search space are advantageous. It has been shown that informed search algorithms, such as the A* search algorithm [8], find an optimal solution if an admissible and consistent cost function is used [5].

In this article, we propose a new task scheduling method HP* for assigning parallel tasks to heterogeneous platforms which is based on the A* search algorithm. The goal of HP* is to find an assignment that provides a total execution time that is as low as possible. Furthermore, a cost function is proposed that is able to reduce the solution space searched by HP*. Experiments with programs from the SPLASH-3 benchmark suite [14] used as parallel tasks are performed on a heterogeneous compute cluster and show the competitive behavior of HP*.

The rest of the article is organized as follows: Section 2 defines a scheduling problem for parallel tasks and describes the modeling of the task execution times. Section 3 proposes a the new search-based scheduling algorithm HP* for parallel tasks and the cost function used. Section 4 presents experimental results. Section 5 discusses related work and Section 6 concludes the article.

2 Scheduling of Parallel Tasks on Heterogeneous Platforms

In the following, the considered scheduling problem for the execution of parallel tasks on heterogeneous platforms is described. Furthermore, a cost model for parallel tasks with unknown program structure is presented.

2.1 Scheduling Problem

The scheduling problem considered in this article comprises of n_T parallel tasks T_i, $i = 1, \ldots, n_T$ that are independent from each other. A parallel task can be executed on a single compute node utilizing an arbitrary number of processor cores. The number of cores used by each task is fixed during the task execution. The tasks are non-preemptive, i.e. their execution can not be interrupted. For each task $T_i, i \in \{1, \ldots, n_T\}$, its parallel execution time using p cores of compute node $N_j, j \in \{1, \ldots, n_N\}$ is denoted by $t_{i,j}(p)$.

The considered heterogeneous platform consists of n_N multicore compute nodes $N_1, \ldots, N_{n_N}$. The heterogeneity of the platform results from the different architectures of each node. Thus, each compute node N_j, $j \in \{1, \ldots, n_N\}$ might have a different computational speed and a different number of processor cores p_j. It is also stated that each processor core can execute only one task at a time. Thus, each parallel task might be executed on 1 to p_j cores of a node N_j, $j \in \{1, \ldots, n_N\}$. However, several tasks can be executed on a node at the same time depending on the number of cores utilized on a compute node.

A solution for the scheduling problem described above is an assignment of the tasks T_i, $i = 1, \ldots, n_T$ to the compute nodes N_j, $j = 1, \ldots, n_N$. For each task $T_i, i \in \{1, \ldots, n_T\}$, the resulting schedule S provides the following information:

- the compute node and the number of cores to be utilized,
- the calculated start time s_i and finish time e_i.

The total execution time $T(S)$ of a schedule S is the difference between the earliest start time and latest finish time of all tasks. We assume that the execution of the first task starts at time 0, thus, the total execution time is identical to the latest finish time of all tasks. This can be expressed as $T(S) = \max\limits_{i=1,\ldots,n_T} e_i$.

The goal is to determine a schedule S such that the total execution time $T(S)$ is minimized.

2.2 Cost Model for Parallel Tasks

The decisions made by scheduling methods are usually based on predictions of the execution times of single tasks. These predictions can be completely determined by benchmark measurements or can be calculated using a specific cost model. Since the program structures of the parallel tasks are unknown, existing cost models for parallel programming, such as PRAM [7], BSP [16], or LogP [3], can not be used for the considered scheduling problem. Thus, we use the following runtime formula to model the execution time $t_{i,j}$ of each task $T_i, i = 1, \ldots, n_T$ on a compute node $N_j, j = 1, \ldots, n_N$ depending on the number of utilized processor cores p:

$$t_{i,j}(p) = f_j \cdot (a_i/p + b_i + c_i \cdot \log p) \tag{1}$$

The parameter f_j denotes the performance factor of node N_j that describes the computational speed of the compute node N_j. It is defined as the ratio between the sequential execution time of a task on a reference node N_r and the compute node N_j. The remaining part of Eq. (1) represents the execution time of task T_i on the reference node N_r. The structure of this part was chosen to cover the runtime behavior of typical parallel tasks. It consists of a parallel computation time a_i that decreases linearly with the number of cores p, a constant sequential computation time b_i and a parallelization overhead c_i that increases logarithmically with the number of cores p (e.g. for synchronization or communication). To determine the parameters a_i, b_i and c_i of a task T_i, first, the execution times are measured on the reference node with different numbers of cores. Then the concrete values of the parameters are calculated based on a least squares fit of these execution times. Table 1 summarizes the notations used to describe the scheduling problem.

Table 1. Notation of the scheduling problem

Notation	Meaning
n_T	Number of parallel tasks
$T_1, \ldots T_{n_T}$	Independent shared memory tasks
n_N	Number of compute nodes in the heterogeneous cluster
$N_1, \ldots N_{n_N}$	Compute nodes of the cluster
p_j	Number of processor cores of compute node N_j, $j = 1, ..n_N$
f_j	Performance factor of compute node N_j
$t_{i,j}(p)$	Parallel execution time of task T_i on p cores of node N_j
$T(S)$	Total execution time of schedule S

3 Search-Based Scheduling Algorithm

In this section, we propose a new task scheduling method HP* for assigning parallel tasks to heterogeneous platforms, which is based on the A* search algorithm. First, a short description of the A* search algorithm is given.

Algorithm 1: A* search algorithm.

---

1 Mark s 'open' and calculate $f(s)$
2 Select the open node n with the smallest value $f(n)$
3 **if** $(n \in T)$ **then** Mark n 'closed' and terminate the algorithm
4 **else**
5   Mark n 'closed'
6   **for** (each successor u of n) **do**
7   Calculate $f(u)$
8   **if** (u is not marked 'closed') **then** Mark u 'open'
9   **else if** (the current value of $f(u)$ is lower as when u was 'closed') **then**
10   Mark u 'open'
11   **end if**
12   **end for**
13   Proceed with line 2
14 **end if**

3.1 The A* Search Algorithm

The A* search algorithm is commonly used to find the shortest path in a directed graph with positive edge weights. The goal of the algorithm is to find the shortest path in a graph G from a start node s to a nonempty set of goal nodes T. For its search, the algorithm uses a function $f(n)$ representing the cost of a path from s to a goal node via node n. The function $f(n)$ consists of two parts: the actual cost $g(n)$ from s to n and the estimated cost $h(n)$ from n to a goal node. The cost function $f(n) = g(n) + h(n)$ is called admissible if the heuristic function $h(n)$ underestimates the exact cost $h^*(n)$ for each node n, i.e. $h(n) \leq h^*(n)$. For any pair of adjacent nodes x and y with edge weight $d(x, y)$, $f(n)$ is called consistent if the following holds:

$$h(x) \leq d(x, y) + h(y) \tag{2}$$

In [5], it was shown that using an admissible and consistent function $f(n)$ the A* search algorithm is guaranteed to find an optimal solution.

Algorithm 1 shows the pseudocode of the A* search algorithm presented in [8]. First, the start node s is marked 'open' and the cost function $f(s)$ is evaluated. Then, the 'open' node n with the smallest cost $f(n)$ is selected and marked 'closed'. Each unmarked successor u of n is marked 'open' and $f(u)$ is calculated. Nodes u that are 'closed' are marked 'open' if the current cost $f(u)$ is lower than the cost when they were marked 'closed'. The algorithm continues selecting the next node n with the smallest cost $f(n)$ (line 2) until a goal node is reached.

3.2 Scheduling Parallel Tasks with HP*

For the scheduling of parallel tasks onto heterogeneous platforms, we propose a new scheduling method HP* (HETEROGENEOUS PARALLEL TASK SCHEDULING

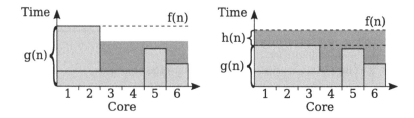

Fig. 1. Illustration of the calculation of the cost function $f(n)$ with scheduled tasks (gray) and remaining workload (blue) that is lower (left) or greater (right) than the computational capacity.

BASED ON A*) based on the A* search algorithm. As in the A* search algorithm, a directed graph with positive edge weights is used as an input for HP*. Therefore, the considered scheduling problem described in Sect. 2.1 is transformed into such a graph where each node n represents a partial schedule S_n. The initial node s is an empty schedule, i.e. where no tasks have been scheduled yet. The successors of a node are created by adding all possible assignments of a task to the respective schedule. The weight $d(n, u)$ of the edge between a node n and its successor u is the difference between the total execution times of the corresponding schedules S_n and S_u, i.e. $d(n, u) = T(S_u) - T(S_n)$. Each complete schedule is a goal node in terms of the A* search algorithm. A schedule is called complete if all tasks are assigned to compute nodes.

According to the A* search algorithm the cost function $f(n) = g(n) + h(n)$ consists of two parts:

- $g(n)$ which is the total execution time $T(S_n)$ of the schedule S_n corresponding to node n,
- $h(n)$ which is a heuristic for the total execution time of the remaining tasks.

For the calculation of the function $h(n)$ it is assumed that the remaining tasks can be distributed 'optimally' to all cores. It is also assumed that in a node n the tasks $T_x, ..., T_{n_T} | x \in \{1, ..., n_T\}$ have not been scheduled yet. The remaining sequential workload W_s is then calculated as

$$W_s = \sum_{i=x}^{n_T} t_{i,r}(1) \tag{3}$$

using Eq. (1) considering the reference node N_r. The computational capacity available on all cores of the compute nodes regarding to a schedule S_n is defined as

$$K(S_n) = \sum_{j=1}^{n_N} \sum_{k=1}^{p_j} (T(S_n) - \max_{T_i \in C_{j,k}} e_i). \tag{4}$$

Algorithm 2: Pseudocode of the HP* method.

---

 1 Let L_{open} and L_{closed} be empty lists
 2 Let s_{init} be a node with an empty schedule
 3 Add s_{init} to L_{open} and calculate $f(s_{init})$
 4 **while** (L_{open} is not empty) **do**
 5   Let s_{cur} be the node in L_{open} with the smallest value $f(s_{cur})$
 6   Remove s_{cur} from L_{open}
 7   **if** (s_{cur} is a complete schedule) **then** Terminate the algorithm
 8   **if** ($s_{cur} \notin L_{closed}$) **then**
 9   Select an unscheduled task T
10   Add s_{cur} to L_{closed}
11   **for** ($j = 1, \ldots, n_N$ and $p = 1, \ldots, p_j$) **do**
12   **for** (each assignment of task T to p cores of compute node N_j) **do**
13   Create a new node s as a copy of s_{cur}
14   Add the assignment to s and calculate $f(s)$
15   Add s to L_{open}
16   **end for**
17   **end for**
18   **end if**
19 **end while**

For a compute node N_j, $j = 1, \ldots, n_N$, the set $C_{j,k}$ denotes all tasks that have been assigned to core k of this node. For each node n, the function $h(n)$ can be computed as follows:

$$
h(n) = \begin{cases} (W_s - K(S_n)) / \sum_{j=1}^{n_N} (p_j \cdot f_j), & \text{if } W_s > K(S_n) \\ 0, & \text{otherwise} \end{cases} \tag{5}
$$

If the remaining workload is bigger than the available computational capacity, then $h(n)$ is set to the difference divided by the total compute power, i.e. the sum of $p_j \cdot f_j$ over all nodes N_j, $j = 1, \ldots, n_N$. Otherwise, there is enough computational capacity available for the remaining workload which leads to $h(n) = 0$. Figure 1 shows an illustration of the calculation of the proposed cost function $f(n) = g(n) + h(n)$ with tasks scheduled already (gray) and the remaining workload (blue). In this example, the remaining workload is either lower (left) or greater (right) than the computational capacity.

In Algorithm 2 the pseudocode of the HP* method is shown. HP* maintains two lists, L_{open} and L_{closed}. L_{open} contains all nodes that have been created but not visited yet. The list L_{closed} is used to avoid that nodes are revisited. At the beginning, both lists are empty and the initial node s_{init} represents an empty schedule. $f(s_{init})$ is calculated and the node is added to L_{open}. In each step of the main loop (lines 4–19), the node s_{cur} with the smallest value $f(s_{cur})$ is selected and removed from L_{open}. If s_{cur} represents a complete schedule, the solution is found and the algorithm terminates. If s_{cur} is already part of

L_{closed}, s_{cur} is skipped and the algorithm continues with the next node. Otherwise, s_{cur} is added to L_{closed} and a task T is selected that has not been scheduled in s_{cur} yet. For each possible assignment of task T, a new node s is created. This is done by an iteration over all compute nodes N_j, $j = 1, \ldots, n_N$ and all numbers of cores p from 1 to p_j. In each step of this iteration, all possible assignments of task T to p cores of node N_j are generated. Each assignment is added to the schedule used in s_{cur} and the resulting schedule is represented by a new node s. Then value $f(s)$ of this new node s is calculated and s is added to L_{open}.

4   Experimental Results with Parallel Tasks on a Heterogeneous Compute Cluster

In the following, we present experimental results of the scheduling method for the execution of parallel tasks on a heterogeneous compute cluster.

4.1   Experimental Setup

The heterogeneous compute cluster used consists of 3 nodes with a total of 16 processor cores. Table 2 lists the properties of these compute nodes. The compute node sb1 is used as reference node for the determination of the parameters described in Sect. 2.2. The scheduling method described in Sect. 3.2 is implemented in C++ using the gcc compiler with optimization level 2. Additionally, we have implemented three existing heuristic scheduling methods which are suitable for the scheduling of parallel tasks on heterogeneous platforms:

HCPA: The HETEROGENEOUS CRITICAL PATH AND ALLOCATION method [11] transforms a heterogeneous compute cluster with individual computational speeds of the processors into a "virtual" homogeneous cluster with equal speed. Then, an existing method for homogeneous compute clusters (i.e., CPA [13]) is used for the scheduling.

Δ **-CTS:** The Δ-CRITICAL TASK SETmethod [17] is an extension of an existing scheduling method for sequential tasks on heterogeneous compute clusters (i.e., HEFT [19]) to parallel tasks. In each step, the method selects a set of tasks with similar sequential execution time. For each of these particular tasks, the compute node and number of cores are determined separately such that the earliest finish time of the task is minimized. The maximum number of cores to be used by each task depends on the number of selected tasks.

WLS: The WATER-LEVEL-SEARCH method [6] combines list scheduling with a search based approach. The method uses a limit for the predicted total execution time that must not be exceeded by the finish time of any task. First, a list scheduling approach is applied several times while the limit is increased until all tasks are scheduled. All computed finish times of all tasks are collected in a set of limits. Then a binary search on this list is performed to find the smallest limit where all tasks can be scheduled.

Table 2. List of nodes of the utilized heterogeneous compute cluster.

Nodes	Processors	Number of cores	Total RAM	GHz
skylake1	Intel i7-6700	4	16 GB	3.40
hw1	Intel i7-4770K	4	16 GB	3.50
sb1	Intel Xeon E5-2650	8	32 GB	2.00

A separate front-end node of the compute cluster is responsible for the scheduling and for starting the task execution using SSH connections to the compute nodes. The tasks are executed according to the determined schedule and the total execution time is measured. The measurements are performed five times and the average result is shown.

As parallel tasks two application tasks and two kernel tasks from the SPLASH-3 benchmark suite [14] are used. Unless otherwise stated, the default parameters or the provided "parsec-simlarge" parameter sets are used for the different benchmark tasks. The following application and kernel tasks were selected:

- **BARNES (application):** Simulation of a particle system using the Barnes-Hut algorithm. The number of particles is set to 2^{18}.
- **FMM (application):** Simulation of a particle system using the Fast Multipole Method. The number of particles is set to 2^{19}.
- **CHOLESKY (kernel):** Cholesky factorization of a sparse matrix. The input matrix "tk29.O" of size $13\,992 \times 13\,992$ is used.
- **LU (kernel):** LU factorization of a dense matrix. The size of the input matrix is set to 4096×4096.

4.2 Performance Results with Benchmark Tasks

In the following, the search-based scheduling method (HP*) proposed in Sect. 3.2 and the scheduling methods (HCPA, Δ-CTS, WLS) described in the previous subsection are investigated in several measurements. These methods are used to determine schedules for the execution of the SPLASH-3 benchmark tasks on a heterogeneous cluster. The heterogeneous cluster used for the following measurements consists of all compute nodes listed in Table 2.

Figure 2 (top) shows the measured total execution times of the BARNES application tasks (left) and FMM application tasks (right) of the SPLASH-3 benchmark depending on the number of tasks. For both types of application tasks the measured times using the HP* method are lower or equal than the results of the three heuristic scheduling methods (HCPA, Δ-CTS, WLS). The results of WLS and HP* show a more steady increase compared to HCPAand Δ-CTS. Especially for Δ-CTS, a strong increase of the execution times for 7 and 13 tasks can be observed. This behavior might be caused by the heuristics used by Δ-CTS. Using HP* leads to slightly lower or equal measured execution times compared to WLS, except for 7 and 8 tasks where HP* achieves up to 23% lower execution times.

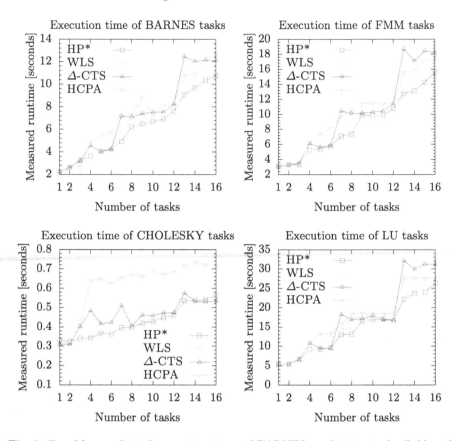

Fig. 2. Top: Measured total execution times of BARNES application tasks (left) and FMM application tasks (right) depending on the number of tasks using all compute nodes of Table 2. Bottom: Measured total execution times of CHOLESKY kernel tasks (left) and LU kernel tasks (right) depending on the number of tasks using all compute nodes of Table 2.

Figure 2 (bottom) shows the measured total execution times of CHOLESKY kernel tasks (left) and LU kernel tasks (right) depending on the number of tasks using all compute nodes of Table 2. For the CHOLESKY tasks, the execution times using HCPA are up to 87% higher than the best results. A reason for these significant differences might be that HCPA favors a parallel task execution that uses many cores for each task. However, the execution times of the CHOLESKY tasks are too small to achieve a proper reduction of the parallel execution time for increasing numbers of cores. The other methods achieved very similar results, except for task numbers between 3 and 7 where Δ-CTS leads to execution times that are up to 42% higher. For the LU tasks, the differences between the results of the methods used are smaller. The execution times using HCPA and Δ-CTS are slightly higher than for WLS and HP* with large increases for 7 and 13 tasks. As for the application tasks, the execution times for 7 and 8 tasks are up to 11% lower using HP* compared to WLS. All in all, HP* leads to lower or equal execution times with a more steady increase compared to the other methods.

5 Related Work

Search-based approaches have been applied to many task scheduling problems. A comparison of search-based and heuristic approaches for scheduling independent tasks onto heterogeneous systems can be found in [2]. An experimental comparison of several scheduling algorithms including A*, genetic algorithms, simulated annealing, tabu search as well as popular list scheduling heuristics is given in [9]. The work considers the problem of mapping sequential tasks with dependencies onto a homogeneous cluster. A few algorithms for solving the task scheduling problem based on the A* search algorithm have been reported in the literature. Kwok and Ahmad [10] proposed a scheduling algorithm for the assignment of sequential tasks to homogeneous platforms based on the A* search algorithm. A number of pruning techniques to reduce the search space as well as a parallelization of the algorithm are presented. Sinnen [15] proposed a scheduling algorithm based on the A* search algorithm using an improved cost function along with several pruning techniques to reduce the search space. In contrast to these works, we consider the scheduling of parallel tasks to heterogeneous platforms.

6 Conclusion

In this article, we have proposed a task scheduling method HP* for assigning parallel tasks to heterogeneous platforms, which is based on the A* search algorithm. In addition, a cost function has been proposed that is able to reduce the search space of our algorithm. Measurements with benchmark tasks have been performed and the scheduling results of HP* have been compared to several existing scheduling methods. Our performance results demonstrate that the use of HP* can lead to a reduction of the total execution times of the resulting schedules in comparison with known algorithms.

Acknowledgments. This work was supported by the German Ministry of Science and Education (BMBF) project "SeASiTe", Grant No. 01IH16012A/B and the German Research Foundation (DFG), Federal Cluster of Excellence EXC 1075 "MERGE".

References

1. Arabnejad, H., Barbosa, J.G.: List scheduling algorithm for heterogeneous systems by an optimistic cost table. IEEE Trans. Parallel Distrib. Syst. **25**(3), 682–694 (2014)
2. Braun, T.D., et al.: A comparison of eleven static heuristics for mapping a class of independent tasks onto heterogeneous distributed computing systems. J. Parallel Distrib. Comput. **61**(6), 810–837 (2001)

3. Culler, D., et al.: LogP: Towards a realistic model of parallel computation. In: Proceedings of the 4th ACM SIGPLAN Symposium on Principles and Practice of Parallel Programming, PPOPP 1993, pp. 1–12. ACM (1993)
4. Daoud, M.I., Kharma, N.: A high performance algorithm for static task scheduling in heterogeneous distributed computing systems. J. Parallel Distrib. Comput. **68**(4), 399–409 (2008)
5. Dechter, R., Pearl, J.: Generalized best-first search strategies and the optimality of A*. J. ACM **32**(3), 505–536 (1985)
6. Dietze, R., Hofmann, M., Rünger, G.: Water-level scheduling for parallel tasks in compute-intensive application components. J. Supercomputing **72**, 1–22 (2016). https://doi.org/10.1007/s11227-016-1711-1
7. Fortune, S., Wyllie, J.: Parallelism in random access machines. In: Proceedings of the 10th Annual ACM Symposium on Theory of Computing, pp. 114–118. ACM (1978)
8. Hart, P.E., Nilsson, N.J., Raphael, B.: A formal basis for the heuristic determination of minimum cost paths. IEEE Trans. Syst. Sci. Cybern. **4**(2), 100–107 (1968)
9. Jin, S., Schiavone, G., Turgut, D.: A performance study of multiprocessor task scheduling algorithms. J. Supercomput. **43**(1), 77–97 (2008)
10. Kwok, Y.K., Ahmad, I.: On multiprocessor task scheduling using efficient state space search approaches. J. Parallel Distrib. Comput. **65**(12), 1515–1532 (2005)
11. N'Takpé, T., Suter, F.: Critical path and area based scheduling of parallel task graphs on heterogeneous platforms. In: Proceedings of the 12th International Conference on Parallel and Distributed Systems, ICPADS 2006, vol. 1, pp. 3–10. IEEE (2006)
12. Radulescu, A., van Gemund, A.J.C.: Low-cost task scheduling for distributed-memory machines. IEEE Trans. Parallel Distrib. Syst. **13**(6), 648–658 (2002)
13. Radulescu, A., Van Gemund, A.: A low-cost approach towards mixed task and data parallel scheduling. In: Proceedings of the International Conference on Parallel Processing, pp. 69–76. IEEE (2001)
14. Sakalis, C., Leonardsson, C., Kaxiras, S., Ros, A.: Splash-3: A properly synchronized benchmark suite for contemporary research. In: Proceedings of the IEEE International Symposium on Performance Analysis of Systems and Software, ISPASS 2016, pp. 101–111. IEEE (2016)
15. Sinnen, O.: Reducing the solution space of optimal task scheduling. Comput. Oper. Res. **43**, 201–214 (2014)
16. Skillicorn, D.B., Hill, J., McColl, W.: Questions and answers about BSP. Sci. Prog. **6**(3), 249–274 (1997)
17. Suter, F.: Scheduling δ-critical tasks in mixed-parallel applications on a national grid. In: Proceedings of the 8th IEEE/ACM International Conference on Grid Computing, pp. 2–9. IEEE (2007)
18. Topcuoglu, H., Hariri, S.: Performance-effective and low-complexity task scheduling for heterogeneous computing. IEEE Trans. Parallel Distrib. Syst. **13**(3), 260–274 (2002)
19. Topcuoglu, H., Hariri, S., Wu, M.Y.: Task scheduling algorithms for heterogeneous processors. In: Proceedings of the 8th Heterogeneous Computing Workshop, HCW 1999, pp. 3–14. IEEE (1999)

Adaptation of Workflow Application Scheduling Algorithm to Serverless Infrastructure

Maciej Pawlik$^{(\boxtimes)}$, Pawel Banach, and Maciej Malawski

AGH University of Science and Technology, Krakow, Poland
m.pawlik@cyfronet.pl, pbanach@student.agh.edu.pl, malawski@agh.edu.pl

Abstract. Function-as-a-Service is a novel type of cloud service used for creating distributed applications and utilizing computing resources. Application developer supplies source code of cloud functions, which are small applications or application components, while the service provider is responsible for provisioning the infrastructure, scaling and exposing a REST style API. This environment seems to be adequate for running scientific workflows, which in recent years, have become an established paradigm for implementing and preserving complex scientific processes. In this paper, we present work done on adaptation of a scheduling algorithm to FaaS infrastructure. The result of this work is a static heuristic capable of planning workflow execution based on defined function pricing, deadline and budget. The SDBCS algorithm is designed to determine the quality of assignment of particular task to specific function configuration. Each task is analyzed for execution time and cost characteristics, while keeping track of parameters of complete workflow execution. The algorithm is validated through means of experiment with a set of synthetic workflows and a real life infrastructure case study performed on AWS Lambda. The results confirm the utility of the algorithm and lead us to propose areas of further study, which include more detailed analysis of infrastructure features affecting scheduling.

Keywords: Serverless · Cloud functions · Workflow scheduling · Infrastructure testing

1 Introduction

Scientific workflows are an established paradigm of implementing and preserving a scientific process. Workflows allow for modeling complex scientific procedures with help of abstractions over infrastructure or implementation details. Workflows are usually represented by an Directed Acyclic Graph (DAG) which enables to analyze them and determine the relations and dependencies between individual tasks. This allows for parallelization and execution planning.

In most cases, scientific workflows are executed by a Scientific Workflow Management System [5], which provides features required to execute the process.

© Springer Nature Switzerland AG 2020
U. Schwardmann et al. (Eds.): Euro-Par 2019 Workshops, LNCS 11997, pp. 345–356, 2020.
https://doi.org/10.1007/978-3-030-48340-1_27

Additionally, management systems usually provide features aimed at automating and streamlining the process, like basic infrastructure management and some fault tolerance. In order to execute the workflow we need two additional components, data to operate on and a computing infrastructure. The data is usually provided by the scientist or is an artifact produced by or directly included in the workflow. The infrastructure can be a personal computer, a HPC computing cluster or the cloud. Due to the features like: availability, pricing models and possibility to dynamically adapt to the workloads, cloud infrastructure seems to be a natural choice. One of the newest additions in cloud service provider's portfolios is the Function-as-a-Service. FaaS infrastructures provide computing power while taking the responsibility for on-demand provisioning of execution environments. Additionally FaaS offers an attractive pricing model where user is billed only for the actual time spent on computing, usually with 100 ms granularity. In case of such infrastructure, a developer is responsible only for supplying the application code and declaring memory requirements. Applications destined to run of FaaS are called *Serverless Applications* in order to emphasize the lack of operating on traditional servers or virtual machines, during the deployment and operation of the application. In contrast to Platform-as-a-Service a serverless application doesn't directly manage scaling and provides a limited run time for individual tasks. While those characteristics are a limitation, they allow the provider to supply a significantly greater scaling potential and speed of infrastructure provisioning.

Due to the unique features of FaaS we need to revisit some of the aspects of workflow execution and scheduling, as explained in [11]. One of such topics is the preparation of an execution plan. FaaS provides a highly elastic infrastructure, with unique performance characteristics, where CPU cycles are tied to the declared amount of memory and user is billed per 100 ms of execution time. Furthermore functions don't have a persistent local storage, so each task needs to explicitly manage its inputs and outputs. This combination of features justifies the need for a dedicated scheduling algorithm. In this paper, we propose a Serverless Deadline-Budget Constrained Scheduling (SDBCS) algorithm, a heuristic which aims to prepare an execution plan satisfying budget and time constraints, while not introducing a high cost of plan preparation. SDBCS was implemented with help of HyperFlow [3], a proven and extensible workflow execution engine, written in JavaScript.

This paper is structured as follows. Section 2 elaborates on current body of knowledge related to scheduling workflow applications in FaaS infrastructures. Described references include analysis of the infrastructure, applications and possible scheduling algorithms. Section 3 describes in detail the used procedure of scheduling a workflow for FaaS. The environment, tooling and solution architecture is presented. The proposed scheduling algorithm is shown in Sect. 4. Scheduling problem is formally stated and methods for obtaining a plan are described in detail. Section 5 contains experiment results based on synthetic test package and a real life experiment involving usage of AWS Lambda functions. The paper concludes with Sect. 6 which give a summary of the paper and provide outlook for future work.

2 Related Work

FaaS was originally designed to host event-based asynchronous applications, coming from Web or mobile usage scenarios. However, there is an ongoing work on finding other alternative use cases for FaaS, as shown in [2], which include event processing, API composition and various flow control schemes.

There are efforts which aim to implement frameworks, like pywren [7], which allow performing general purpose computing on FaaS clouds. One of the main features would be to enable dynamic transformation of applications to FaaS model while simultaneously providing deployment services, which would allow for seamless migration to cloud functions. The result would be a workflow application consisting of tasks which represent parts of the original application.

FaaS infrastructures, as a novelty, are subject to rapid changes. Work done in [10] describes the current details of FaaS provider offerings, service types, limitations and costs. The performance of cloud functions was further studied in [6] and [13]. Included results allow to construct the model the available performance and infrastructure provisioning characteristics like efficiency and limits.

In our earlier work [12] we proposed means to adapt scientific workflows to FaaS, using HyperFlow[1]. In [9] we proposed and validated a FaaS specific scheduling algorithm, which is used as a reference point for validating algorithm presented in this paper.

There is a plethora of workflow scheduling algorithms available for clouds based on virtual machines. Those algorithms can be adapted to FaaS, which would allow to benefit from the available body of knowledge. We chose the Deadline-Budget Constrained Scheduling algorithm [1] as a suitable for adaptation, due to its low complexity and good performance.

Workflow applications are a well studied field. In the case of this paper we evaluated the proposed algorithm with the help of available workflow test data set for Pegasus system, which is described in more detail in [8].

3 Serverless Workflow Execution

3.1 Scheduling the Workflow

As presented in [9], executing workflows on FaaS is significantly different from execution on virtual machines. From the application's point of view, we need to distribute individual tasks across functions, so that the whole process can be executed with the imposed per task time limit. While the cloud provider is responsible for provisioning of the infrastructure, we need to declare suitable function configurations, so that the deadline and budget requirements are met. In case of the proposed algorithm, the output of the planning process is the assignment of tasks to function configurations. Each configuration is characterized by an amount of memory, which is proportional to available computing cycles per second, which in turn determines the execution time of tasks. If the

---

[1] HyperFlow repository: https://github.com/hyperflow-wms/hyperflow.

cost of running the application is lower than the budget, and the makespan is shorter than the deadline, the scheduling is considered successful.

3.2   The Environment, Tools and Solution Architecture

In the course of our studies of FaaS infrastructures, we tested and evaluated multiple FaaS providers [6]. For the scope of this work we chose to work on Amazon infrastructure. We used AWS Lambda for running cloud functions and AWS S3 for cloud storage. The tight integration of both services, namely support for credential delegation greatly simplifies the deployment process, as cloud functions can hold delegated credentials required to access storage. At the time of writing this paper AWS Lambda imposes several limits on cloud functions. Functions are limited by time to 900 s, the amount of declared and used memory must be in the range of 128 MB to 3008 MB, which translates to available computing performance. Local storage available within a function environment is limited to 512 MB, and deployment package (function code and auxiliary applications) need to fit in a 250 MB package. Concurrent function executions are limited to 1000 instances. Table 1 includes function configurations used during the evaluation of the proposed algorithm. For the sake of simplicity of the application model some features of FaaS, like cold starts, are not directly addressed.

Table 1. Function configurations and prices. Note that memory size affects available CPU time (computing performance).

Memory size	Cost per 100 ms of execution
256 MB	$0.000000417
512 MB	$0.000000834
1024 MB	$0.000001667
1536 MB	$0.000002501
2048 MB	$0.000003334
2560 MB	$0.000004168
3008 MB	$0.000004897

HyperFlow served as a workflow execution engine. Workflows are represented as JSON structures containing a DAG. HyperFlow keeps track of the state of the application and is responsible for transforming tasks to function calls. Function calls are implemented as simple REST Calls, where REST APIs are exposed by the FaaS deployment. The deployment consists of prepared functions (part of HyperFlow package) which handle incoming calls and execute bundled components of the application.

The scheduler was implemented as a set of components, which include tools used to perform application test runs to gather performance characteristics of the tasks and the main scheduler module. The scheduler parses performance data, pricing, user defined constrains: deadline and budget, the output is an execution plan in form of a decorated workflow. The output workflow is a HyperFlow compatible DAG, which includes mapping of each task to a target function type. Scheduler module is open source and its repository is publicly available[2].

Figure 1 presents the architecture used during the development and evaluation of the proposed algorithm. The whole process can be described as follows. Workflow application, in form of a JSON DAG, is supplied to the scheduler, which is responsible for producing an execution plan. The plan, a decorated DAG, is supplied to HyperFlow, which executes the application according to plan. Workflow manipulation, planning and execution management are performed outside of FaaS, on a dedicated machine. The execution of application's tasks is performed by calling a function with proper arguments. Each task is executed inside of individual function instance. Tasks share a common storage, which is available remotely, through a S3 protocol.

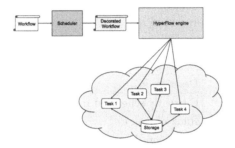

Fig. 1. Deployment diagram of workflow execution system

4   The Scheduling Algorithm

As mentioned in Sect. 1, there is a variety of available scheduling algorithms for workflow applications. We chose the Deadline-Budget Constrained Scheduling algorithm [1] as suitable for adapting to serverless infrastructures. The algorithm is a list scheduling algorithm applicable to cloud environments and operates on heterogeneous resources. The adaptation consisted of reimplementing the algorithm with the notion of functions instead of virtual machine oriented processors. This removed the need for part of algorithm responsible for selecting an available processor. Required functions are supplied by the FaaS provider in an on demand manner. Additionally calculation of storage and transfer costs were removed, as those basic functions are supplied and not directly contributing to costs.

4.1   Serverless Deadline-Budget Constrained Scheduling Algorithm (SDBCS)

The problem of scheduling can be defined as assigning individual tasks of workflow application to resources available from a heterogeneous environment. In this

---

[2] https://github.com/PawelBanach/CloudFunctionOptimizer.

case resources are represented by cloud functions, available function configurations are listed in Table 1, where the number of functions in limited only by concurrency constraint. User supplies the application in form of a Directed Acyclic Graph (DAG), which can be represented by a tuple $G = \langle T, E, Data \rangle$ where $T = t_1, t_2, ..., t_n$ represents a set of tasks of workflow, and E represents edges connecting tasks, which model dependencies and control flow between tasks. Data represents input and intermediate information needed to run the application. Scheduling problem becomes a matter of finding a map $G : T \rightarrow F$, where F denotes the mentioned set of functions. The algorithm is a single step heuristic which meets the budget constrain and may or may not achieve the required deadline. Successful scheduling is achieved when all constraints are meet. The core functionality of the algorithm is based on sorting tasks according to upward rank, calculating sub-deadlines and quality score for each task on each resource. Sub deadline is inferred from user supplied makespan deadline. Quality is calculated based on task execution time on a given resource. Description of the algorithm uses notation presented in Table 2.

Table 2. Symbols and notation used for algorithm description.

Symbol	Description
t_{curr}	Currently scheduled task
$rank_u(t)$	Rank of task t
$ET(t)$	Execution time of task t
$succ(t)$	Successors of task t
$FT(t, r)$	Finish time of task t on resource r
$FT_{min}(t, r)$	Minimum finish time of task t on resource r
$FT_{max}(t, r)$	Maximum finish time of task t on resource r
$Cost(t, r)$	Cost of executing task t on resource r
$Cost_{min}(t)$	Minimum cost of executing task t
$Cost_{max}(t)$	Maximum cost of executing task t
$Cost_{best}(t)$	Cost of fastest execution of task t
$Cost_{cheapest}$	Minimum cost of executing all tasks
$AC(t)$	Assigned cost of running task t
Δ_{Cost}	Spare budget

Specific elements of the algorithm operate base on the following rules. The spare budget is calculated with the formula:

$$\Delta_{Cost} = \Delta_{Cost} - [AC(t_{curr}) - Cost_{min}(t_{curr})] \tag{1}$$

where the spare budget is the difference between available budget and the cheapest assignment for unscheduled tasks. The initial spare budget is expressed as:

$$\Delta_{Cost} = BUDGET_{user} - Cost_{cheapest} \tag{2}$$

and

$$Cost_{cheapest} = \sum_{t_i \in T} Cost_{min}(t_i) \tag{3}$$

Task selection and priority is based on a computed rank of tasks. The rank represents the length of longest path from task to the exit node with addition of average execution time of task:

$$rank_u(t_i) = \overline{ET}(t_i) + max_{t_{child} \in succ(t_i)}\{rank_u(t_{child})\} \tag{4}$$

Where $\overline{ET}(t_i)$ represents the average execution time of task over available resources and the latter part of equation represents the maximum of ranks of all immediate successors of task t_i.

The budget available for task execution is expressed as:

$$CL(t_{curr}) = Cost_{min}(t_{curr}) + \Delta_{Cost} \tag{5}$$

which represents the minimum execution cost with addition of spare budget. The sub-deadline is defined for each task as:

$$DL(t_{curr}) = min_{t_{child} \in succ(t_{curr})}[DL(t_{child}) - ET_{min}(t_{child})] \tag{6}$$

where tasks' individual deadline is calculated as the minimum of difference between subsequent tasks' deadline and minimum execution time of current task.

The $Time_Q$ and $Cost_Q$ represent time and cost quality of assigning task to resource, quality measures are expressed as:

$$Time_Q(t_{curr}, r) = \frac{\Omega * DL(t_{curr}) - FT(t_{curr}, r)}{FT_{max}(t_{curr}) - FT_{min}(t_{curr})} \tag{7}$$

$$Cost_Q(t_{curr}, r) = \frac{Cost_{best}(t_{curr}) - Cost(t_{curr}, r)}{Cost_{max}(t_{cur}) - Cost_{min}(t_{cur})} * \Omega \tag{8}$$

and:

$$\Omega = \begin{cases} 1 \text{ if } FT(t_{curr}, r) < DL(t_{curr}) \\ 0 \text{ otherwise} \end{cases} \tag{9}$$

Time and Cost qualities aim to represent the distance of studied solution in the range between *best* and *worst* case scenarios. In case of time, the range of values spans between the sub-deadline and minimum execution time, while in case of cost boundaries are set at the minimum and maximum execution costs. The Ω parameter is responsible for complying with the deadline set for current task.

The final quality measure is expressed as:

$$Q(t_{curr}, r) = Time_Q(t_{curr}, r) + Cost_Q(t_{curr}, r) * \frac{Cost_{cheapest}}{Budget_{Unconsumed}} \tag{10}$$

the equation combines both quality measures with addition of weighting the $Cost_Q$ with the ratio of cheapest execution cost to unconsumed budget.

SDBCS is presented as Algorithm 1. The process included in algorithm can be described as follows. Initialization of the algorithm requires user to supply a workflow graph, a deadline and available budget. If the budget is less than the lowest possible cost of executing the workflow the algorithm indicates it is impossible to create an appropriate plan. Next step (lines 3–4) determines if the supplied budget is more than the highest possible cost of execution, in that case each task is scheduled to execute on the fastest resource. Line 6. is responsible for assigning the initial value of spare budget, next step is to calculate ranks and task priority. Lines 8–15 contain the main scheduling loop, which iterates over task in order of priority. Quality measure is computed for currently scheduled task against all available resources, based on that the best resource is selected. The final part of the loop is the update of spare budget which is calculated according to Eq. 1.

Algorithm 1. Serverless Deadline-Budget Constrained Scheduling algorithm

---

Require: DAG, time (D_{user}), budget (B_{user})
1: **if** $B_{user} < Cost_{min}(DAG)$ **then**
2:     **return** no possible schedule
3: **else if** $B_{user} > Cost_{max}(DAG)$ **then**
4:     **return** schedule map on the most expensive resource
5: **end if**
6: $\Delta_{Cost} \Leftarrow BUDGET_{user} - Cost_{cheapest}$
7: Compute upward rank $(rank_u)$ and sub-deadline for each task
8: **while** there is unscheduled task **do**
9:     $t_{curr} \Leftarrow t$ next ready task with highest rank
10:     **for** $r \in$ resources **do**
11:         Calculate quality measure $Q(t_{curr}, r)$
12:     **end for**
13:     $r_{selected} \Leftarrow r$ with highest quality value
14:     assign t_{curr} to $r_{selected}$
15:     $\Delta_{Cost} \Leftarrow \Delta_{Cost} - [AC(t_{curr}) - Cost_{min}(t_{curr})]$
16: **end while**
17: **return** schedule map

---

5   Evaluation and Results

5.1   Scheduling Performance

The proposed algorithm was evaluated in a series of experiments. Experiments are meant to test the scheduling success rate for a set of test workflow applications in multiple input parameters. Tests were designed with the use of Montage, which in recent years became an established benchmark application for workflow scheduling systems. Montage is a astronomical mosaic application, which combines an array of smaller images into larger mosaics. The application is composed of several steps and contains many tasks executed in parallel, thus it is suitable to validate scheduling performance. Testing workflows were obtained from the workflow repository available at Pegasus system homepage[3], described in more detail in [4] and [8]. It is important to note that Montage was chosen as a utility to verify algorithm's performance and not as an ideal application to run in FaaS environment. Test package contains 220 workflows, with task counts ranging from 50 to 1000. Workflows were converted to HyperFlow format and task run time for each resource was estimated. The estimation was made based on package-supplied synthetic run time and function performance metrics from our earlier work [6]. Synthetic run time was treated as time taken by task execution on slowest cloud function. Other run times, for faster function configurations, were obtained by simply scaling it by expected function performance. In a real world use case, one would be required to supply run time of each task on each function configuration.

The experiments were conducted for Serverless Deadline-Budget Constrained Scheduling (SDBCS) and Serverless Deadline-Budget Workflow Scheduling (SDBWS) algorithm. SDBWS is described in more detail in [9]. The main difference of SDBWS is that it operates on tasks grouped in levels, which are assigned a global sub-deadline, whereas SDBCS treats each task as a separate entity. Additionally SDBWS utilizes different formulas to calculate quality. SDBCS can be treated as a more general derivative of SDBWS and is expected to provide better performance. Due to the focus of this paper, experiments were narrowed to test only two mentioned algorithms.

The set of deadline and budget parameters were generated based on minimal and maximal possible values. Specific values at $0.3, 0.5$ and 0.7 points of range were chosen. The final values of deadline and budget were calculated for each workflow with the following equations:

$$Deadline_{user} = Deadline_{min} + a_D * (Deadline_{max} - Deadline_{min}) \quad (11)$$

$$Budget_{user} = Budget_{min} + a_B * (Budget_{max} - Budget_{min}) \quad (12)$$

The results of scheduling experiments are presented in Figs. 2, 3 and 4. Each figure contains results for a specified value of budget parameter, whereas the X axis spans across multiple values of a_D parameter. Results show that SDBCS overall performance is better than SDBWS, with exception of smaller value of deadline, where both algorithms presented low success rate. In case of $a_D = 0.5$ SDBCS clearly delivers better performance and for $a_D = 0.7$ SDBCS advantage over SDBWS is present but not as significant. The case of $a_D = 0.7$ and $a_B = 0.7$ results in both algorithms succeeding at scheduling all test workflows.

---

[3] https://download.pegasus.isi.edu/misc/SyntheticWorkflows.tar.gz.

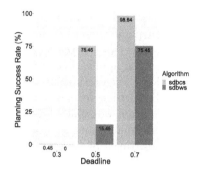

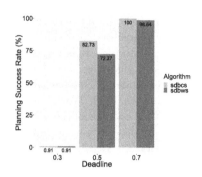

Fig. 2. Scheduling success rate with budget $a_B = 0.3$ and deadline $a_D \in \{0.3, 0.5, 07\}$

Fig. 3. Scheduling success rate with budget $a_B = 0.5$ and deadline $a_D \in \{0.3, 0.5, 07\}$

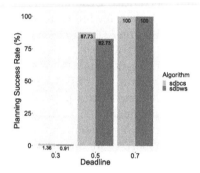

Fig. 4. Scheduling success rate with budget $a_B = 0.7$ and deadline $a_D \in \{0.3, 0.5, 07\}$

5.2   Tests on Physical Infrastructure

As part of validation of the proposed algorithm, we performed a real life experiment. The test used physical infrastructure in order to prove the applicability of the solution. Procedure included scheduling a sample workflow, namely Montage application containing 43 tasks. The next step was to run the application on setup described in Sect. 3.2, where tasks were executed on AWS Lambda. Figure 5 contains a Gantt chart depicting the *trace* of execution, X axis represents time, each bar represents run time of a single task. Task types are distinguished by color, distinction between types allows to determine dependencies between tasks. Transparent bars represent planned execution while opaque are executions measured in real life. The chart allows to visually inspect the accuracy of planning. In the presented case, plan closely matched the real life execution, and only with 4 tasks, the execution was started slightly after the planed time.

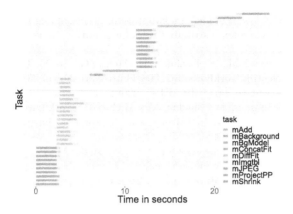

Fig. 5. Gantt chart depicting a trace of Montage execution. Execution of each task is represented by a opaque bar, while a transparent bar represents scheduled execution.

6 Conclusions and Future Work

Presented adaptation of scheduling algorithm was made after careful analysis of target infrastructure and provided insight into characteristics of running workflows on FaaS infrastructures. Obtained results confirm, that the presented Serverless Deadline-Budget Constrained Scheduling algorithm is capable of producing valid execution plans according to supplied parameters. Experiments with scheduling a Montage workflow proven that SDBCS achieves better results than the previously studied SDBWS algorithm. Real life infrastructure tests also illustrate, that the generated execution plan is valid in practical applications.

Future work includes further study of workflow scheduling algorithms and exploring new methods of adapting them to FaaS infrastructures. Additionally, our work on studying commercially available infrastructures, led us to conclusion that the behaviour of FaaS is still not completely explored. Functions tend to experience phenomena like execution throttling or delays, which have an impact on workflow execution and could be accounted for in scheduling algorithms.

Acknowledgements. This work was supported by the National Science Centre, Poland, grant 2016/21/B/ST6/01497.

References

1. Arabnejad, H., Barbosa, J.G., Prodan, R.: Low-time complexity budget-deadline constrained workflow scheduling on heterogeneous resources. Future Gener. Comput. Syst. **55**, 29–40 (2016)
2. Baldini, I., et al.: Serverless computing: current trends and open problems. In: Chaudhary, S., Somani, G., Buyya, R. (eds.) Research Advances in Cloud Computing, pp. 1–20. Springer, Singapore (2017). https://doi.org/10.1007/978-981-10-5026-8_1

3. Balis, B.: HyperFlow: a model of computation, programming approach and enact-ment engine for complex distributed workflows. Future Gener. Comput. Syst. **55**, 147–162 (2016)
4. Bharathi, S., Chervenak, A., Deelman, E., Mehta, G., Su, M.H., Vahi, K.: Charac-terization of scientific workflows. In: 2008 Third Workshop on Workflows in Support of Large-Scale Science, pp. 1–10. IEEE (2008)
5. Deelman, E., Gannon, D., Shields, M., Taylor, I.: Workflows and e-science: an overview of workflow system features and capabilities. Future Gener. Comput. Syst. **25**(5), 528–540 (2009)
6. Figiela, K., Gajek, A., Zima, A., Obrok, B., Malawski, M.: Performance evaluation of heterogeneous cloud functions. Concurr. Comput. Pract. Exp. (2017, accepted)
7. Jonas, E., Pu, Q., Venkataraman, S., Stoica, I., Recht, B.: Occupy the cloud: distributed computing for the 99%. In: Proceedings of the 2017 Symposium on Cloud Computing, pp. 445–451. ACM (2017)
8. Juve, G., Chervenak, A., Deelman, E., Bharathi, S., Mehta, G., Vahi, K.: Char-acterizing and profiling scientific workflows. Future Gener. Comput. Syst. **29**(3), 682–692 (2013)
9. Kijak, J., Martyna, P., Pawlik, M., Balis, B., Malawski, M.: Challenges for schedul-ing scientific workflows on cloud functions. In: 2018 IEEE 11th International Con-ference on Cloud Computing (CLOUD), pp. 460–467. IEEE (2018)
10. Lee, H., Satyam, K., Fox, G.C.: Evaluation of production serverless computing environments. In: Proceedings of the 3rd International Workshop on Serverless Computing. ACM (in print)
11. Malawski, M.: Towards serverless execution of scientific workflows-hyperflow case study. In: WORKS SC, pp. 25–33 (2016)
12. Malawski, M., Gajek, A., Zima, A., Balis, B., Figiela, K.: Serverless execution of scientific workflows: experiments with HyperFlow, AWS Lambda and Google Cloud Functions. Future Gener. Comput. Syst. (2017). https://doi.org/10.1016/j.future. 2017.10.029. http://linkinghub.elsevier.com/retrieve/pii/S0167739X1730047X
13. Pawlik, M., Figiela, K., Malawski, M.: Performance evaluation of parallel cloud functions. Poster Presented at ICPP 2018: International Conference on Parallel Processing, Eugene, Oregon, USA (2018)

CCAMP: OpenMP and OpenACC Interoperable Framework

Jacob Lambert[1]([⊠]), Seyong Lee[2], Allen Malony[1], and Jeffrey S. Vetter[2]

[1] University of Oregon, Eugene, USA
{jlambert,malony}@cs.uoregon.ed
[2] Oak Ridge National Laboratory, Oak Ridge, USA
{lees2,vetter}@ornl.gov

Abstract. Heterogeneous systems have become a staple of the HPC environment. Several directive-based solutions, such as OpenMP and OpenACC, have been developed to alleviate the challenges of programming heterogeneous systems, and these standards strive to provide a single portable programming solution across heterogeneous environments. However, in many ways this goal has yet to be realized due to device-specific implementations and different levels of language support across compilers. In this framework we aim to analyze and address the different levels of optimization and compatibility between OpenACC and OpenMP programs and device compilers. We introduce the **CCAMP** framework, built on the OpenARC compiler, which implements language translation between Open**ACC** and Open**MP**, with the goal of exploiting the maturity of different device-specific compilers to maximize performance for a given architecture. We show that CCAMP allows us to generate code for a specific device-compiler combination given a device-agnostic OpenMP or OpenACC program, allowing compilation and execution of programs with specific directives on otherwise incompatible devices. CCAMP also provides a starting point for a more advanced interoperable framework that can effectively provide directive translation and device, compiler, and application specific optimizations.

Keywords: OpenMP · OpenACC · Directive-based programming · Heterogeneous computing · CCAMP

1 Introduction

Coincident with the breakdown of Dennard Scaling and the slowing of Moore's law, heterogeneous programming has emerged as an alternative to traditional homogeneous computation [11]. The explosion in popularity of GPGPU programming, and now other devices like many-core processors and FPGAs, has led to the development of several new low-level programming approaches in order to map computations to these specific devices. Low-level heterogeneous programming approaches like CUDA and OpenCL grant knowledgeable programmers the

© Springer Nature Switzerland AG 2020
U. Schwardmann et al. (Eds.): Euro-Par 2019 Workshops, LNCS 11997, pp. 357–369, 2020.
https://doi.org/10.1007/978-3-030-48340-1_28

ability to write applications catered specifically to unique devices in an attempt to maximize performance.

However, these low-level device-specific programming approaches sacrifice the functional and performance portability enjoyed by more traditional homogeneous implementations. Rewriting and maintaining different versions of the same applications for different devices can be unsustainable and error-prone. Furthermore, the low-level device-specific approaches are intimidating and inaccessible to less experienced programmers.

Several higher-level, directive-based, device-agnostic programming standards have emerged to address the issues with device-specific implementations. These standards aim to enable programmers to annotate a general, sequential application with simple instructions for parallelism, transferring much of the low-level specifics to the compiler. However, as we discuss in Sect. 2, these directive-based approaches come with their own set of issues as well, and the ideal performance and portability proposed by the standards do not match the current reality.

CCAMP, an OpenACC and OpenMP interoperability framework, exists to bridge the gap between the current realities of performance and portability within existing standard implementations, and initial goals and intentions of these directive-based standards. CCAMP also provides programmers who only have experience with one directive-based programming model an easy alternative to learning another model by providing a translation framework.

2   Background

A primary goal of the CCAMP framework is to allow programmers to fully utilize the OpenMP and OpenACC directive-based programming standards, which have become a popular option for high-level heterogeneous programming.

OpenMP [3] has been an essential tool in the general parallel programming environment for decades. With the introduction of directives in the 4.X+ standards, OpenMP has also become a viable tool for heterogeneous programming, offering a high-level, offload programming model alternative to languages like CUDA and OpenCL.

OpenACC [12] is a newer directive-based standard, originally developed as a high-level alternative to CUDA for GPU computing. While OpenACC differs from OpenMP with regard to high-level design principles, they share a common goal of providing programmers with a high-level approach to heterogeneous programming.

While both OpenMP 4.X+ and OpenACC directives provide a method for high-level heterogeneous programming, there exist several important issues and setbacks to using these standards.

A primary issue in the directive-based heterogeneous programming space is the lack of portability between programming models. Although the goal of both OpenMP and OpenACC is to provide a portable, high-performance, cross-platform solution, they are often at the mercy of vendor-specific compiler implementations. Many devices achieve high performance when using the vendor-compiler tied to that device, which often supports only one of OpenACC and

OpenMP. Typically, GPU-centric and CPU-centric ecosystems prefer OpenACC and OpenMP, respectively. However, even among compilers preferring a specific directive-based standard, the level of support and implementation strategies for the standard can vary greatly.

As a result of these issues, both OpenACC and OpenMP 4.X+ fail to achieve the goal of being portable solutions for heterogeneous systems. One way to address this gap would involve the development of an optimization that takes a device-agnostic input code in either OpenACC and OpenMP, and automatically generates device-optimized code specific to a target device and compiler combination. The CCAMP framework, with its baseline translation capabilities, is an initial effort to realize such an optimization framework.

The main contributions of this work are as follows:

- We introduce a novel baseline directive-translation framework, allowing programmers to automatically flow between standards to utilize the maturity of single-standard compilers on different devices (Sect. 3).
- We provide a commentary on the current status of the popular OpenACC and OpenMP compilers and their levels of support for the directive-based standards across an array of devices (Sect. 4).
- We evaluate the effectiveness of CCAMP's baseline translation using an array of different heterogeneous ecosystems. We demonstrate how our compiler-translated code can perform similarly or even better than hand-written code, and how CCAMP can allow programmers to execute translated code in ecosystems that may not support the original source language (Sect. 5).
- We discuss the future of CCAMP and the extensions needed to develop a fully-fledged framework capable of providing true interoperability between OpenACC and OpenMP (Sect. 6).

3   CCAMP Framework

In it's current state, the CCAMP framework consists of three baseline translations, built on top of the OpenARC [9] compiler framework:

- OpenMP 4.X+ to OpenACC
- OpenACC to OpenMP 4.X+
- OpenACC to OpenMP 3.0

As previous researchers have noted [1,13,14], many directives in OpenMP and OpenACC have a straightforward, one-to-one directive mapping. These include data movement, allocation, and update directives, entries to parallel regions, and general clauses like *if, collapse, reduction*. Similarly, many of the relevant API calls have analogous counterparts in both directive sets.

However, despite their surface-level similarities, fundamental differences in the core of the language designs lead to some challenges in the language translation process, especially when deciding how to map parallelism to a specified device.

3.1 OpenARC

CCAMP is built on top of the existing OpenARC [9] framework. OpenARC is a research-focused OpenACC compiler for heterogeneous systems, and already contains some language-translation features to generate device-specific code like OpenCL and CUDA, and OpenMP directive parsing capabilities, inherited from the base Cetus compiler infrastructure [4].

One of the primary strengths of OpenARC lies in its capabilities to allow quick prototyping of code transformations, which proved crucial when developing the transformations and optimizations for CCAMP. Essentially, CCAMP exists as a translation and optimization layer that follows OpenARC's initial lexical analysis and AST generation.

3.2 OpenMP 4.X+ to OpenACC Translation

By design, OpenMP is implemented as a prescriptive set of directives, explicitly specifying how parallelism in a program should be mapped to CPU threads or GPU cores. This prescriptive nature simplifies the OpenMP 4.X+ to OpenACC translation pass, as the burden of specifying parallelism is placed on the programmer instead of the compiler. Because of this, the prescriptive OpenMP parallelism clauses can be directly translated to descriptive OpenACC counterparts without additional compiler analysis.

However, there are still several OpenMP language constructs that don't allow for a direct translation or mapping, including OpenMP critical regions and tasking. These non-trivial translations require some additional compiler analysis for correct translation.

By design, the OpenACC standard does not contain a directive analogous to the OpenMP critical region. GPUs represented the main target architecture during the design of OpenACC, and synchronization constructs like critical regions typically lead to poor performance on GPUs. To prevent programmers from experiencing this pitfall, critical regions were intentionally omitted. However, one use of OpenMP critical regions can be efficiently mapped to GPUs: array-reductions.

Currently when encountering OpenMP critical regions in the OpenMP to OpenACC translation, CCAMP emits an error and terminates translation. However, CCAMP is designed to detect if an OpenMP critical region is used to encapsulate an array reduction, and can appropriately translate the reduction using OpenACC reduction clauses.

Another OpenMP construct that does not directly translate to OpenACC is the recently introduced task construct. OpenMP task translation is not currently supported by CCAMP, but will likely be a focus of future extensions.

3.3 OpenACC to OpenMP 4.X+ Translation

Unlike OpenMP, OpenACC is designed with a descriptive outlook. The core principle of OpenACC is that the directives allow a programmer to expose or describe parallelism within a program, and shift the burden of mapping parallelism to hardware from the programmer to the compiler. OpenACC also contains prescriptive directives and clauses to allow the programmer explicitly specify the mapping of parallelism, but these directives are not mandatory.

This difference in fundamental design complicates the OpenACC to OpenMP 4.X+ translation, as we're required to generate a prescriptive output from a descriptive input. In CCAMP, we tackle this issue by applying a compiler analysis to automatically annotate ambiguous OpenACC directives with specific parallelism clauses. Using an optimizing-loop-directive-prepossessing pass, we can automatically assign OpenACC *gang* and *worker* clauses to un-annotated loops.

More specifically, CCAMP utilizes OpenARC's auto-parallelization pass to mark kernel inner loops as independent when possible, exploiting available parallelism. Marked loops are then annotated with OpenACC parallelization clauses before the direct substitution translations to OpenMP occur.

In addition to the differences in requirements for descriptive detail, CCAMP also addresses several low-level syntactical differences when translating OpenACC to OpenMP. For example, the requirements on the location of *reduction* clauses differ between the standards, and so CCAMP performs a reduction directive migration pass. Similarly, the requirements on the OpenMP *num_threads* and *simdlen* clauses require migration of the corresponding *num_workers* and *vector_length* OpenACC clauses during translation.

Interestingly, OpenMP lacks a clause analogous to the OpenACC *present* clause. To mimic the behavior of the OpenACC *present* clause, we use an *assert()* function call along with the OpenMP *omp_target_is_present()* API call.

3.4   OpenACC to OpenMP 3.0

Although OpenMP 4.X+ exists as a super-set of OpenMP 3.0-only directives, in some cases programmers may wish to restrict the translated output to only employ OpenMP 3.0 directives. On systems without offload capabilities, or without more modern compilers that support newer OpenMP directives and OpenACC, this translation pass allows execution of previously unsupported applications. Also, because OpenMP 3.0 directive sets are much older and more pervasive across compilers, even compilers that do support OpenMP 4.X+ directives may perform better using the older directives when targeting CPU devices.

CCAMP's OpenACC to OpenMP 3.0 translation pass is a straight-forward stripped-down alternative to the OpenACC to OpenMP 4.X+ pass. OpenACC parallel regions are mapped to OpenMP parallel regions, and outermost OpenACC loop parallelization clauses are mapped to OpenMP *parallel for* clauses. The innermost OpenACC parallelization clause is mapped to OpenMP *simd* clauses. Intermediate OpenACC parallelization clauses are ignored.

In general, this translation can be useful any time a programmer is targeting a CPU device with a compiler that may struggle with the OpenMP 4.X+ directives, which is far from rare. The converse of this translation, OpenMP 3.0 to OpenACC, is not currently included in CCAMP, as this would require automatic generation of data movement directives, and more complicated analysis of multi-tier parallelism.

4 Experimental Setting

4.1 Benchmarks

We chose to evaluate the CCAMP framework using the SPEC Accel Benchmark Suite [7] for several reasons. Most importantly, SPEC Accel already contains hand-optimized OpenACC and OpenMP implementations of the same set of applications. This provided an ideal baseline against which to compare our code translated by CCAMP. Additionally, SPEC Accel is well-supported, well-documented, and representative of a wide array of common scientific programming applications. While SPEC Accel contains both C and Fortran applications, we only target the C applications, as CCAMP does not currently support Fortran OpenACC and OpenMP codes.

We used the following SPEC Accel applications in our evaluations:

- X03 ostencil, (303 for OpenACC, and 503 for OpenMP) a thermodynamics stencil kernel
- X14 omriq, an application widely used in the medical field
- X52 ep, an embarrassingly parallel application
- X54 cg, a conjugate gradient kernel
- X57 csp, a scalar penta-diagonal solver, and
- X70 bt, a block tri-diagonal solver for 3D PDEs

The X52, X54, X57, and X70 benchmarks are adapted from the NAS Parallel Benchmark Suite [2], a benchmark set widely used for evaluating performance on heterogeneous systems. We also initially explored evaluating CCAMP using the Rodinia benchmark suite. Like SPEC Accel, Rodinia contains both hand-optimized OpenACC and OpenMP implementations. However, the OpenMP offloading implementations in Rodinia are optimized specifically for Xeon Phi devices, and perform poorly on GPU devices. This shortcoming further motivates the necessity of a framework like CCAMP, which can be used to generate device-agnostic OpenMP code from the existing Rodinia OpenACC implementations.

4.2 Devices

We evaluated CCAMP using a wide array of the most commonly used CPU and GPU devices in heterogeneous programming. The different devices are each coupled with vendor-specific compilers, which typically exhibit a preference between OpenMP and OpenACC. This further motivates a fluid way to translate between directive sets.

We evaluated CCAMP using three CPU systems:

- Xeon CPU: Intel(R) Xeon(R) CPU E5-2683 v4 @ 2.10 GHz, 32 CPUs, 1 thread per core, 16 cores per socket, 2 sockets
- Xeon Phi: Intel(R) Xeon Phi(TM) CPU 7250 @ 1.40 GHz, 272 CPUs, 4 threads per core, 68 cores per socket, 1 socket
- Power9: IBM POWER9, altivec supported, 176 CPUs, 4 threads per core, 22 cores per socket, 2 sockets

We also evaluated CCAMP using two GPU systems:

- P100: Nvidia Tesla P100-PCIE-12 GB (Pascal), Xeon CPU host (as mentioned above)
- V100: Nvidia Tesla V100 SXM2 16 GB (Volta), Power9 host (as mentioned above)[1]

4.3 Compilers

Across different devices, vendor-supplied compiler frameworks often achieve the best performance on a specific device. In the context of directive-based approaches, these vendor-supplied compilers may only support one of OpenACC and OpenMP, or may strongly prefer one over the other. One of the primary goals of CCAMP is to allow programmers to exploit this compatibility between devices and vendor-compilers regardless of the chosen directive-based approach (using language translation).

To evaluate the effectiveness of CCAMP, we employed a breadth of compilers, some tied to specific devices (IBM xlc, Intel icc) and others multi-platform (Clang clang, PGI pgcc).

IBM's *xlc* C/C++ compiler is restricted to the Power9 and attached V100 devices. Currently, this compiler only supports OpenMP, although it does support both OpenMP host and OpenMP offload computation models. We use IBM XL C/C++ for Linux, V16.1.1. For evaluations on the Power9 device, we use the flags "-O3 -qsmp=noauto:omp -qnooffload", and for the V100 device we use the flags "-O3 -qsmp=noauto:omp -qoffload".

Intel's *icc* C/C++ compiler currently only supports OpenMP, with support for both host Xeon CPU devices, and Xeon Phi devices through OpenMP offloading. For CCAMP evaluations on the Xeon Phi, we use icc version 19.0.1.144 (gcc version 4.8.5 compatibility), and the following flags: "-O3 -xMIC-AVX512 -qopenmp -qopenmp-offload=host".

The open-source LLVM-based C/C++ compiler *clang* is not tied to a specific device. While clang doesn't currently support OpenACC, it fully supports the OpenMP host computation model, and there are ongoing efforts to develop full support for the OpenMP offloading model. For evaluations using clang on the Xeon CPU, we use release version 8.0.0 (git tag llvmorg-8.0.0-rc5). Support for correct handling of math functions in clang's OpenMP offload model has only

---

[1] The Power9+V100 configuration is very similar that of the Summit supercomputer nodes.

recently been added. For this reason, we installed clang directly from the master branch (git hash 431dd94) for evaluations using clang and the P100 device. When targeting the Xeon CPU, we use the flags "-Ofast -fopenmp -fopenmp-targets=x86_64", and for the P100 device we use "-Ofast -fopenmp -fopenmp-targets=nvptx64".

Although PGI's *pgcc* C/C++ compiler is now tied to Nvidia, pgcc supports all of the devices used in this work. However, to limit the project scope we only evaluate CCAMP using pgcc on the Xeon CPU, P100, and V100 devices. The pgcc compiler is the only compiler used in the evaluations that currently supports OpenACC. PGI's pgcc supports OpenMP 3.0 and a subset of OpenMP 4.X+ directives, although they do not yet support data transfer directives, limiting the OpenMP evaluations to host CPU devices. On the Xeon CPU and P100 devices we use version 18.10-0 64-bit (Community Edition). On the V100 device, we use the slightly older 18.4 edition. On the Xeon CPU we use the flags "-V18.10 -fast -Mnouniform -acc -ta=multicore" for OpenACC programs, and "-V18.10 -fast -Mnouniform -mp -Mllvm" for OpenMP programs. On the P100 and V100 devices, which are only supported via OpenACC, we use the flags "-V18.10 -fast -Mfprelaxed -acc -ta=tesla:cc60" and "-V18.4 -fast -Mnouniform -acc -ta=tesla:cc70" respectively.

Ideally for a more fair evaluation we would have no variations in compiler versions across different devices. However, this became a challenge due to the different levels of access and privileges across ecosystems, and the goal of using the most recent compiler releases. In future extensions to CCAMP, we plan to rectify these inconsistencies.

While a complete list of the most commonly used compilers in heterogeneous programming would include the GNU C/C++ Compiler *gcc*, we chose to exclude it from this work in progress due to difficulties with installation for OpenMP and OpenACC offloading, and to limit the scope of the project. We fully intend to include gcc on future works extending CCAMP.

5   Evaluation Results

We evaluated the effectiveness of the CCAMP framework using an exhaustive approach, compiling and testing as many different applications with as many different device+compiler combinations as possible. This required a significant effort, including installing software across different devices, and wading through the different levels of support for the multiple compilers.

5.1   OpenACC to OpenMP 4.X+ Baseline Evaluation

To evaluate the effectiveness of CCAMP's OpenACC to OpenMP 4.X+ baseline translation pass, we first evaluated the hand-coded OpenMP 4.X+ applications in the SPEC Accel benchmark suite without applying any transformations or optimizations. We used the resulting execution times as a baseline by which to compare the execution times of our translated (from OpenACC) OpenMP 4.X+ code.

In Fig. 1, we see the results of this comparison. Each bar represents the average (across all benchmarks) ratio of the translated runtime divided by the hand-coded runtime. Values below 1 represent cases where the translated code performed better, while values above 1 represent cases where further improvements need to be made to the translation pass to match the hand-coded performance. While the translation pass still has room for improvement on some device+compiler combinations, it performs acceptably well for many of the other combinations.

Averaging results across different benchmarks certainly results in loss of information. However the very large number of experimental results across devices, compilers, and benchmarks required a heavy amount of aggregation for a simplistic overarching view of the relative performances between the original and translated codes. We aim to provide more detailed evaluations focused on specific applications in future works, including profiling analysis and investigations into differences in performance.

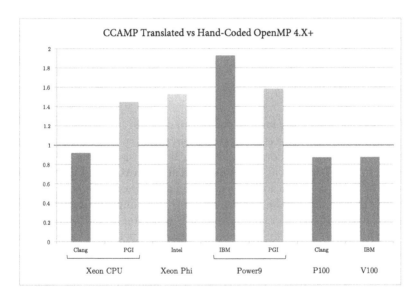

Fig. 1. Run-time comparison of translated OpenMP 4.X+ with hand-coded OpenMP 4.X+

5.2 OpenMP 4.X+ to OpenACC Baseline Evaluation

Similarly to the previous translation, to evaluate CCAMP's OpenMP 4.X+ to OpenACC translation pass we compare hand-coded OpenACC execution times with translated code times.

In Table 1, we list runtimes (in seconds) on the devices we used to evaluate this translation pass. Because the PGI compiler is the only compiler evaluated

that currently supports OpenACC (in this case translated from OpenMP 4.X+),
PGI is used for all of the compilations in the figure.

We see that in most cases the translated code performs very similarly to
the hand-coded counterparts. The dashed values represent cases where we failed
to correctly execute the application, primarily due to unsupported features or
errors pending correction in CCAMP.

Table 1. Run-time comparison of translated OpenACC with hand-coded OpenACC.
Time in seconds.

Device	Translation	X03	X14	X52	X54	X57	X70
Xeon CPU	None	82.06	670.03	184.84	82.06	102.73	153.02
Xeon CPU	Baseline	81.39	670.15	184.58	182.17	88.18	-
P100	None	26.45	146.22	76.09	61.66	45.17	19.31
P100	Baseline	26.67	146.37	65.57	51.48	-	42.802
V100	None	12.33	38.84	47.71	33.04	20.19	9.14
V100	Baseline	13.95	33.35	52.91	31.42	-	25.03

6   Related Work

Several previous works explore the performance and portability of directive-
based approaches across heterogeneous systems. In [8], Vergara et al. evaluate
OpenMP applications on Power8 and Tesla devices using the IBM and clang
compilers. In [10], Lopez et al. experiment with OpenACC and OpenMP implementations of core computational kernels, including Daxpy, Dgemv, Jacobi, and
HACCmk. They evaluate the performance of these implementations using the
Cray, Intel, and PGI compilers on Nvidia GPU and Intel Xeon Phi devices. In [6],
Gayatri et al. implement a single material science kernel, and evaluate OpenMP
3.0, OpenMP 4.0, OpenACC, and CUDA implementations on Xeon CPUs, Xeon
Phis, Nvidia P100s, and Nvidia V100s. This closely resembles the languages
and devices evaluated in our work, although we evaluate multiple applications.
Gayatri et al. also discuss their experiences with different compilers, including
the PGI, Intel, IBM, and GCC compilers, and the then-current status of their
directive-based language support. These works all highlight the high variability in performance of directive-based approaches across different compiler and
device combinations, which helps to motivate the utility of a framework like
CCAMP.

There are also several previous works that research the potential of an OpenACC and OpenMP translation framework. In [14], Wolfe explores this idea and
discusses some obvious and some more-subtle challenges that would arise when
implementing such a framework. He also discusses motivations and significance of
developing such a framework, which are in line with the motivations we present

here. In [1], Sultana et al. present a prototype OpenACC to OpenMP translation scheme, which consists of a combination of automated directive translation performed using the Eclipse user interface and manual user-performed code restructuring. This work represents a promising first attempt to develop an automated translation framework, although they only evaluate a single benchmark and support only a subset of the OpenACC standard. In [13], Pino et al. describe a mapping between the most common directives of OpenACC and OpenMP, and compare the performance between the two different sets of directives on several SHOC and NAS benchmarks, but do not propose any automated scheme or framework to perform the actual translation. In [5], Denny et al. present an ongoing work to develop an OpenACC to OpenMP 4.5 translator (Clacc) within the clang compiler, as a means to allow clang to support OpenACC. Clacc represents a rigorous effort to develop a translation scheme supporting the full OpenACC standard, which accomplishes the goal of our OpenACC to OpenMP 4.5 baseline translation, but is constrained by the clang compiler, preventing it from utilizing the maturity of device-specific back-end compilers.

In contrast to previous works, that either represent only a conceptualization of a translation scheme, or in the case of Clacc [5] are tied to a specific device-level compilers, CCAMP presents an actual implementation of directive translation that is applicable across different device ecosystems and integrated with several different back-end compilers.

7   Conclusion

As systems become more exotic and specialized, the HPC community has experienced an increased demand for high-level, portable, programming solutions. While directive-based standards and approaches aim to provide a solution, they fail to realize this goal due to competition between vendor compilers, and inconsistent levels of standard support.

In this work, we present the CCAMP framework, with the goal of allowing programmers to seamlessly flow between different directive sets, enabling programmers to execute directive-based code on previously incompatible devices. We introduce two primary translation passes, and show that these passes can generate output code in a different directive context that performs similarly to hand-coded programs. We also provide a commentary on the current status of the different devices and compilers commonly used in heterogeneous programming.

In the future, we plan to develop and extend CCAMP in several ways. A primary goal is to develop an optimized translation pass that can generate not only generalized directive sets in different languages, but also directive sets specifically catered toward an indented target device. We also plan to incorporate other compilers (GCC, Clacc), and other devices (FPGAs). Finally we would like to expand our evaluations to include other benchmarks besides SPEC Accel.

Acknowledgements. This research was supported in part by the Exascale Computing Project (17-SC-20-SC), a collaborative effort of the U.S. Department of Energy Office of Science and the National Nuclear Security Administration.

This manuscript has been co-authored by UT-Battelle, LLC under Contract No. DE-AC05-00OR22725 with the U.S. Department of Energy. The United States Government retains and the publisher, by accepting the article for publication, acknowledges that the United States Government retains a non-exclusive, paid-up, irrevocable, worldwide license to publish or reproduce the published form of this manuscript, or allow others to do so, for United States Government purposes. The Department of Energy will provide public access to these results of federally sponsored research in accordance with the DOE Public Access Plan.

References

1. Arnold, G., Calvert, A., Overbey, J., Sultana, N.: From OpenACC to OpenMP 4: toward automatic translation. In: XCEDE 2016, Miami, FL (2016)
2. Bailey, D., Harris, T., Saphir, W., Van Der Wijngaart, R., Woo, A., Yarrow, M.: The NAS parallel benchmarks 2.0. Technical report, Technical Report NAS-95-020, NASA Ames Research Center (1995)
3. Dagum, L., Menon, R.: OpenMP: an industry-standard API for shared-memory programming. Comput. Sci. Eng. **1**, 46–55 (1998)
4. Dave, C., Bae, H., Min, S.J., Lee, S., Eigenmann, R., Midkiff, S.: Cetus: a source-to-source compiler infrastructure for multicores. IEEE Comput. **42**(12), 36–42 (2009). http://www.ecn.purdue.edu/ParaMount/publications/ieeecomputer-Cetus-09.pdf
5. Denny, J.E., Lee, S., Vetter, J.S.: CLACC: Translating OpenACC to OpenMP in clang. In: IEEE/ACM 5th Workshop on the LLVM Compiler Infrastructure in HPC (LLVM-HPC), pp. 18–29. IEEE (2018)
6. Gayatri, R., Yang, C., Kurth, T., Deslippe, J.: A case study for performance portability using OpenMP 4.5. In: Chandrasekaran, S., Juckeland, G., Wienke, S. (eds.) WACCPD 2018. LNCS, vol. 11381, pp. 75–95. Springer, Cham (2019). https://doi.org/10.1007/978-3-030-12274-4_4
7. Juckeland, G., et al.: SPEC ACCEL: a standard application suite for measuring hardware accelerator performance. In: Jarvis, S.A., Wright, S.A., Hammond, S.D. (eds.) PMBS 2014. LNCS, vol. 8966, pp. 46–67. Springer, Cham (2015). https://doi.org/10.1007/978-3-319-17248-4_3
8. Larrea, V.V., Joubert, W., Lopez, M.G., Hernandez, O.: Early experiences writing performance portable OpenMP 4 codes. In: Proceedings of the Cray User Group Meeting, London, England (2016)
9. Lee, S., Vetter, J.: OpenARC: open accelerator research compiler for directive-based, efficient heterogeneous computing. In: Proceedings of the ACM Symposium on High-Performance Parallel and Distributed Computing, HPDC 2014, Short Paper, June 2014
10. Lopez, M.G., et al.: Towards achieving performance portability using directives for accelerators. In: 2016 Third Workshop on Accelerator Programming Using Directives (WACCPD), pp. 13–24. IEEE (2016)
11. Mittal, S., Vetter, J.S.: A survey of CPU-GPU heterogeneous computing techniques. ACM Comput. Surv. (CSUR) **47**(4), 69 (2015)
12. OpenACC: OpenACC: directives for accelerators (2011). http://www.openacc.org

13. Pino, S., Pollock, L., Chandrasekaran, S.: Exploring translation of OpenMP to OpenACC 2.5: lessons learned. In: IEEE International Parallel and Distributed Processing Symposium Workshops (IPDPSW), pp. 673–682. IEEE (2017)
14. Wolfe, M.: Compilers and more: OpenACC to OpenMP (and back again), June 2016. https://www.hpcwire.com/. Accessed 29 June 2016

HPCN - High Performance Computing and Networking in Aerospace

Workshop on High Performance Computing and Networking in Aerospace (HPCN)

Workshop Description

The HPCN workshop has a long history at the German Aerospace Center (DLR) where it was initiated and organized by T-Systems since 1999. The two drivers for its introduction were the information of HPC-users in DLR about the latest developments and trends in HPC hard- and software on the one hand, and, showing the applications and usage of HPC at DLR to familiarize technology-providers with DLRs' needs in the field, on the other hand. Organizing this workshop for the first time as a Euro-Par workshop offered an excellent opportunity to enhance the visibility of the aerospace-related HPC-activities within the HPC-community and the Euro-Par conference within the aerospace community.

The focus of the workshop was on High Performance Computing as a key enabler for numerical simulation of aerodynamics of air- and spacecraft and their components. The essential need of tailored HPC-systems in aerospace requires a close cooperation with providers of these systems. Thus the workshop was comprised of contributions from aerospace research and from HPC-hard- and software providers. The presentations from (aerospace) research were on larger-scale applications employing HPC and emphasizing specific requirements, achievements, and limitations related to HPC. The keynotes given by the providers covered current and future developments in HPC-hardware and software.

Compared to former DLR-internal HPCN workshops, only a small number of contributions was submitted to the Euro-Par workshop, partly due to the different community and partly due to an Euro-Par-conformal review process involving the submission of full papers for the review instead of abstracts only. From the five papers submitted, two were from DLR-institutes and three from universities, one from outside Germany, namely Sweden. The review process focused on the quality of the papers and their relevance to High Performance Computing, avoiding any conflicts of interest when selecting the reviewers. Only three papers were of suitable quality regarding the workshop subjects and thus accepted.

As planned from the beginning, the number of accepted scientific papers was then matched against an equal number of invited talks (no paper) from companies providing HPC-hard- and software. The six talks were then organized as a half-day workshop. The workshop was very successful from the PC point of view as many participants from the Euro-Par community (45 in total) were drawn to the lecture hall.

Last, but not least, the HPCN workshop chairs would like to thank the members of the HPCN Program Committee as well as all invited speakers, who made the workshop possible. We would also like to thank Euro-Par for hosting the event, and the general workshops chairs (Euro-Par 2019) Dora Blanco Heras, Christian Boehme, and Ulrich Schwardmann for their help and support.

Organization

Program Committee

Alfred Geiger	T-Systems, Germany
Thomas Gerhold	DLR Dresden, Germany
Cornelia Grabe	DLR Göttingen, Germany
Wolfgang Hafemann	T-Systems, Germany
Ewald Krämer	University of Stuttgart, Germany
Norbert Kroll	DLR Braunschweig, Germany
Edmund Kügeler	DLR Köln, Germany
Dieter Schwamborn	DLR Göttingen, Germany
Misha Strelets	Peter the Great St.Petersburg, Russia

HPC Requirements of High-Fidelity Flow Simulations for Aerodynamic Applications

Axel Probst[1(✉)], Tobias Knopp[1], Cornelia Grabe[1], and Jens Jägersküpper[2]

[1] German Aerospace Center (DLR), Institute of Aerodynamics and Flow Technology,
37073 Göttingen, Germany
`axel.probst@dlr.de`
[2] German Aerospace Center (DLR), Institute of Aerodynamics and Flow Technology,
38108 Braunschweig, Germany

Abstract. This paper relates the computational demand of turbulence-resolving flow simulations for aircraft aerodynamics to the parallel scalability of the DLR flow solvers TAU and THETA, as well as the new CODA solver optimized for many-core HPC systems. Based on existing lower-fidelity simulations, the computational requirements for wall-resolved LES are first estimated for single aircraft components at wind-tunnel scale. It is shown that such simulations at reduced Reynolds numbers would be realizable within days to weeks with the current methods, if the largest available HPC clusters with more than 100,000 cores were used. However, an extrapolation to the HPC requirements of LES for a full 3D wing of an aircraft at flight Reynolds numbers highlights the urgent need for larger HPC resources and adapted parallel code designs, as well as more efficient numerical algorithms and physical models.

Keywords: High-Performance Computing · Large-Eddy Simulation · Aircraft aerodynamics · TAU · THETA · CODA

1 Introduction

Today's aerodynamic design, optimization and analysis of modern transport aircraft relies on a combination of flight test, wind tunnel testing and numerical simulation. Depending on the aircraft operation mode the contribution of numerical simulation, i.e. Computational Fluid Dynamics (CFD) to these disciplines varies within the flight envelope: while current CFD methods exhibit high maturity in cruise flight close to the design point of the aircraft, less confidence exists for low-speed take-off and landing configurations as well as for certain high-speed operation conditions [10]. State-of-the-art CFD codes employ a Finite Volume discretization of the Navier-Stokes equations. At present, turbulent flow is usually modelled with a Reynolds-Averaged Navier-Stokes (RANS) ansatz through additional transport equations. These RANS turbulence models were derived

© Springer Nature Switzerland AG 2020
U. Schwardmann et al. (Eds.): Euro-Par 2019 Workshops, LNCS 11997, pp. 375–387, 2020.
https://doi.org/10.1007/978-3-030-48340-1_29

and calibrated mainly for attached and steady flow conditions, as appear in cruise flight. During low-speed take-off and landing, the turbulent flow near the aircraft's surface experiences strong adverse pressure gradients, leading to flow separation. In these situations standard RANS turbulence models fail to predict the flow with sufficient accuracy [7]. For high-speed operation, the flow around the aircraft is susceptible to the buffet phenomenon, an unsteady periodic shock wave oscillation involving shock-induced separation. The accurate prediction of buffet is of significant importance, as the latter marks the limit of operation before structural damage of the aircraft may occur. Solutions obtained using RANS turbulence models to predict these flow conditions are strongly dependent on simulation parameters and grid resolution [3] and suitability or correct application of these models are still under investigation [10].

Recently, NASA published the *CFD Vision 2030 Study* [9] to highlight the current status of CFD in aerodynamics and to set up a roadmap for meeting present and future requirements in the field. The *Vision* emphasizes the shortcomings of current RANS turbulence models for certain flow phenomena and identifies the need for developing suitable turbulence resolving methods, e.g. Large Eddy Simulation (LES) methods, in which turbulence is partly modelled and partly resolved. To underline the importance of this development goal, the first of a total of four Grand Challenges that were proposed in the Vision is the LES of a powered aircraft configuration across the entire flight envelope. However, while the application of LES promises accurate predictions at the border of the flight envelope, it also requires large High Performance Computing (HPC) resources and significantly increases the computational effort compared to RANS turbulence models.

This paper gives an overview of the different turbulence modelling approaches applied at DLR to perform computations on industrially relevant aerodynamic configurations. The basics of these methods are introduced, as well as DLR's CFD codes and their respective HPC concepts. The HPC requirements for the simulation of flows around two aircraft components are assessed depending on the employed turbulence modelling approach. This assessment is used for estimating the computational effort of wall-resolved LES applied to a full 3D aircraft wing, both on wind-tunnel scale and for the real aircraft in different flight conditions. The paper concludes with required improvements and developments to achieve these simulations with acceptable computational cost.

2   Aerodynamic Flow Simulation

The computational effort of a flow simulation is governed by the resolution requirement of the spatial and temporal discretization of the partial differential equations to be solved. One key factor is the treatment of turbulence, i.e. small quasi-random unsteady fluctuations which emerge above a certain Reynolds number (defined as $Re = U_\infty l_{ref}/\nu$) and which strongly affect the aerodynamic performance of air vehicles (e.g. drag force, stall behaviour).

While all relevant physics of turbulence can be captured by a *Direct Numerical Simulation* (DNS) based on the Navier-Stokes equations, the requirement to fully resolve the turbulent fluctuations in both space and time yields extremely large number of grid points (i.e. small mesh-cell sizes) and small physical time steps. Moreover, DNS resolution increases dramatically with the Reynolds number, i.e. the number of grid points N scales with $\sim Re^{37/14}$ in wall-bounded flow [1]. At relevant (flight) Re-numbers of aircraft ($Re = 10^7 - 10^8$) DNS will therefore remain beyond available computing capacities in the foreseeable future, see Fig. 1. This encouraged the development of less demanding methods to compute turbulent flow, which are briefly outlined in the following.

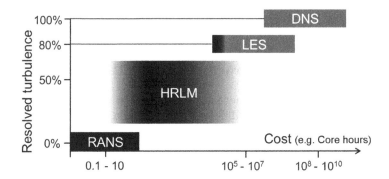

Fig. 1. Schematic relation of turbulence resolution level and computational cost in different flow simulation approaches.

RANS Modelling. The *Reynolds-averaged Navier-Stokes* (RANS) approach applies a temporal averaging to the Navier-Stokes equations which converts the unsteady turbulent fluctuations into mean statistical quantities, i.e. the Reynolds stresses. These stresses describe the effect of turbulence on the (steady) mean flow and need to be modelled by additional physical closure assumptions, called turbulence models. Such models usually consist of partial differential equations which pose no particular resolution requirements compared to the steady RANS equations. However, they often lack accuracy in complex turbulent flows, e.g. near the border of the flight envelope of aircraft.

Large-Eddy Simulation. In *Large-Eddy Simulations* (LES) the Navier-Stokes equations are formally filtered (often using a top-hat filter based on the local mesh-cell size) so that turbulence is decomposed into an unsteady resolved part and a smaller modelled part, the latter being usually provided by algebraic sub-grid scale models. LES requires high temporal and spatial resolution of the resolved turbulent fluctuations to meet the commonly accepted criterion [5] of at least 80% resolved turbulent kinetic energy (see Fig. 1). For wall-bounded flow, this leads to the number of grid points scaling roughly as $N \sim Re^{13/7}$ [1]. However, due to the reduced empirical modelling, the mean-flow predictions of LES often approach DNS accuracy.

Hybrid RANS/LES. *Hybrid RANS/LES Methods* (HRLM) combine the specific benefits of both methods by locally adapting the applied modelling to the flow topology and available grid resolution. For instance, the well-known *Detached-Eddy Simulation* aims to apply RANS modelling, where usually sufficient (i.e. attached near-wall flow) and LES, where needed (i.e. separated flow). More elaborate variants of DES offer wall-modelled LES capabilities [8] by applying RANS close to the wall and consistent transition to LES in the outer boundary layer, thus reducing the Re-number-dependency to $N \sim Re$ [1]. Note that the physical time step is not easily adapted to the local modelling, i.e. the time resolution in the local LES regions dictates the global time step. Due to the flexible localization of RANS and LES regions, HRLM covers a wide intermediate regime of turbulence resolution and effort, as depicted in Fig. 1.

3   Parallel Scaling Characteristics of DLR Flow Solvers

Numerical simulation tools for aeronautical flows classically rely on the finite-volume approach. At DLR two different finite-volume solvers for unstructured meshes have been developed: the TAU code for compressible flow and the THETA code for incompressible flow. Although both codes are written in C and share common data structures as well as similar implementations of the modelling approaches described in Sect. 2, the specific solution algorithms for flows with variable and constant density lead to different parallel scalability characteristics.

3.1   Parallel Scalability of Present Codes TAU and THETA

For decades, MPI-based domain decomposition has been the dominating parallelization paradigm for mesh-based CFD to make use of HPC resources for flow simulation. The computational domain is statically split into a number of parts, called domains. Each domain maps one-to-one with an MPI process. The domain-local calculations are often stencil-based, for instance the flux balance for each finite (control) volume. As a consequence, data from neighboring domains are needed for control volumes touching a domain boundary. These data are often called the domain's halo. Halo data allow for a complete stencil for each domain-local control volume. As the simulation proceeds, halo data need to be frequently updated. TAU as well as THETA use a lock-step approach: before each stencil loop, halo data gets communicated using point-to-point communication. Namely, each process (domain) posts an `MPI_Irecv` for each neighboring domain, followed by an `MPI_Isend` to each neighbor, and finalized by an `MPI_Waitall` on all these immediate MPI calls. The number of neighbors of a domain can be considered limited, say around the order of 10, independent of the number of domains used (given the mesh is large). The smaller the domains, the fewer halo data is contained in a message, resulting in halo communication becoming latency and/or message-rate bound. In contrast to point-to-point communication for the halo update, global reduce operations result in a communication time growing logarithmically in the number of processes involved. And what is more (actually worse), load imbalances accumulate at such process-synchronization points. In particular for THETA, which makes use of full implicit time-integration schemes in combination with multi-grid acceleration, global reductions limit the parallel scalability. Due to the different time-integration schemes used for the compressible equations, TAU's scalability is less affected in this regard.

The scalability of both TAU and THETA is examined in exemplary LES computations of the periodic turbulent channel flow at $Re_\tau = 395$ on the same mesh. The goal of this study was to determine the lowest achievable wall-clock time for one physical time step on currently installed HPC hardware at DLR (Intel Xeon@2.8GHz, Ivy Bridge EP, Infiniband Connect). Due to its more efficient solution algorithm for this incompressible flow, THETA needs more than a magnitude less time to compute one time step on a given domain decomposition (number of grid points per CPU core) than TAU, see Fig. 2 (left).[1] With increasing parallelization, i.e. fewer points per core, both codes initially yield a linear reduction in wall-clock time before gradually departing from the ideal scalability curve. With minimum values of about 2 s for TAU and 0.15 s for THETA at 4800 points/core, TAU slightly reduces the initial (relative) wall-time margin thanks to its somewhat better scalability. This is also reflected in the relative parallel efficiency (reciprocal of wall-clock time × number of CPU cores) of both codes, as depicted in Fig. 2 (left).

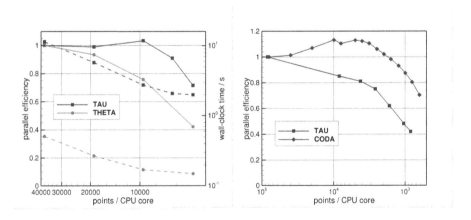

Fig. 2. *Left:* Parallel efficiency (solid lines) and wall-clock time per simulated time step (dashed lines) from LES of a channel flow with DLR-codes TAU and THETA. *Right:* Parallel efficiency of TAU and CODA in a generic (non-LES) benchmark case.

---

[1] Note on the other hand, that incompressible solvers are not generally applicable to aeronautical flows.

3.2   Potential of New CODA Solver

In 2014, DLR started from scratch a new flexible unstructured CFD solver ("Flucs") [4], which has by now become the basis for a common CFD capability for/of Onera (the French Aerospace Lab), DLR, and Airbus ("CODA"). Just as TAU/THETA, also CODA uses domain decomposition to make use of distributed-memory parallelism. In contrast to TAU/THETA, however, CODA features overlapping halo-data communication with computation to hide network latencies and, thus, improve scalability. As an alternative to MPI, the GASPI implementation GPI-2 can be used for halo communication. This Partitioned Global Address Space (PGAS) library features highly efficient one-sided communication, minimizing network traffic as well as latencies. Moreover, CODA features sub-domain decomposition, i.e., each domain can again be partitioned into subdomains to make use of shared-memory parallelism. Each subdomain is processed by a dedicated software thread that is mapped one-to-one to a hardware thread, maximizing data locality. In contrast to the 1st level decomposition, this 2nd level (sub)decomposition does not use halo data (but makes use of shared memory). Just as on process level, also for the thread level, the SPMD paradigm is applied, trying to reduce thread synchronization to a minimum. For CODA, running one process per multicore chip has turned out best practice. If a chip features multiple (Non-)Uniform Memory Access ((N)UMA) domains, however, depending on the performance of the cache-coherence logic, running one process per UMA domain may be beneficial. For each process, as many threads (subdomains) are run as hardware threads are available. CODA's 2-level domain decomposition just described in combination with communication/computation overlap allows for a significantly improved parallel efficiency and scalability, see Fig. 2 (right). Note that a parallel efficiency of more than 100% corresponds to a super-linear speed-up. This effect, in particular observed for CODA in Fig. 2 (right), is due to the distributed simulation fitting into the total L3 cache memory of the HPC-cluster nodes utilized. Also note that a wall-clock time analysis of LES with CODA as in Fig. 2 (left) has not yet been conducted.

4   HPC Requirements of LES for Aircraft - Case Studies

As discussed in Sect. 1, the increasing demand for accurate border-of-envelope simulations has stimulated an interest in LES of full aircraft configurations. To approach the question of feasibility, we first consider two exemplary aircraft components in wind-tunnel conditions and estimate the respective computational effort for LES. Then we discuss possible extrapolations to a full 3D wing of an aircraft in different regimes of the flight envelope (low-/high-speed borders).

4.1   Delta Wing

The nacelle strake is an important component for the aircraft performance at high-lift. We consider a delta wing as a generic generator of a longitudinal vortex with similar properties as for a strake vortex.

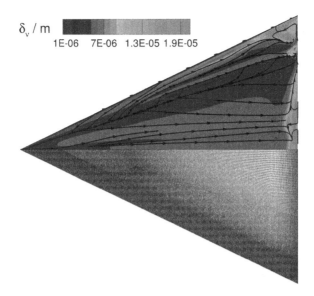

δ_v / m

1E-06   7E-06   1.3E-05 1.9E-05

Fig. 3. Top view on the delta wing: Distribution of the viscous length scale and surface streamtraces (top); surface mesh for the RANS computation (bottom).

For a large-eddy simulation, the largest computational costs arise for the resolution of the smallest vortices in the boundary layers of the delta wing. Their size is of the order of the viscous length scale $\delta_\nu = \nu/u_\tau$, which is computed from the kinematic viscosity ν and the local friction velocity u_τ. The surface flow pattern together with the viscous length scale computed with RANS are shown in Fig. 3. The aim is to use an anisotropic surface mesh in the region of attached flow in the inner part of the wing and an isotropic surface mesh in the region of the separated flow in the outer part of the wing. To estimate a spatial resolution sufficient to resolve the near-wall vortices, the grid spacings Δx_i are expressed in wall units, i.e. $\Delta x_i^+ = \Delta x_i/\delta_\nu$. Based on commonly accepted criteria for wall-resolved LES [5] the estimated normalized grid spacings in streamwise direction Δx^+, wall-normal direction Δy^+ and spanwise direction Δz^+ as well as the associated number of mesh points N_x, N_y, and N_z are given in Table 1. The estimate is based on a chord length $c = 0.3$ m, onflow velocity $U_\infty = 55.5$ m/s and an average viscous length scale of $\delta_\nu = 5 \times 10^{-6}$ m. The total number of mesh points in the boundary layers on both sides of the delta wing is $N_{pnt} = 6.75 \times 10^8$.

For the temporal resolution, we assume a total simulation time of 25 CTUs (convective time units) with CTU $= c/U_\infty$. For the resolution of the boundary layers we adopt a normalized time step size of $\Delta t^+ = 0.4$ as suggested in [2], leading to $\Delta t = \Delta t^+ \nu u_\tau^{-2} = 1.6 \times 10^{-7}$ s. The number of physical time steps becomes $N_t = 8 \times 10^5$.

To estimate the HPC requirements and wall-clock times for such a simulation with TAU and THETA[2], we consider the LES of a channel flow from Sect. 3 and assume that the parallel efficiency and wall-clock times per physical time step from Fig. 2 (left) apply to any LES with these flow solvers. For appropriate HPC usage, we further demand $\geq$90% parallel efficiency, which allows distributing 6,500 points/core with TAU, and 20,000 points/core with THETA. The resulting wall-clock times and total core usage for an LES of the delta wing would be 19.3 days on 104,000 cores with TAU, and 2.3 days on 34,000 cores with THETA.

Table 1. Estimated spatial resolution for LES of a delta wing (upper and lower side).

Grid region	Mesh type	Δx^+	Δy^+	Δz^+	N_x	N_y	N_z	N_{pnt} in 10^6
Inner wing	Anisotropic	40	1	20	1500	100	1500	225
Outer wing	Isotropic	20	1	20	3000	100	1500	450

4.2 High-Lift Wing Section

Due to the low speed of an aircraft during take-off and landing, the lift of the wings needs to be increased by deploying slats at the leading edge and flaps at the trailing edge. Simulating the flow around such a wing in high-lift configuration is a crucial but challenging task, since complex interactions of turbulent boundary layers, co-fluent shear layers and flow separation may occur. In this case study, we consider a section of the 3-element DLR-F15 airfoil [12] at wind-tunnel conditions ($Re = 2.1 \cdot 10^6$ and $M = 0.15$), which is inclined with an angle of attack of $\alpha = 6°$.

Requirements of RANS and Hybrid RANS/LES. Present experience on this case comprises TAU simulations using the RANS approach with different turbulence models as well as hybrid RANS/LES with Improved Delayed DES (IDDES) applying wall-modelled LES in the attached boundary layers.

For an unswept wing section (airfoil), the RANS approach can be applied on a two-dimensional mesh in the xy-plane, yielding just about 0.2×10^6 grid points in the given case. Moreover, the simulation can be conducted in steady mode, i.e. omitting temporal resolution of the RANS equations. For illustration, Fig. 4 (top-left) shows the normalized vorticity and the streamlines from the RANS simulation in the vicinity of the deployed flap.

In contrast, the IDDES requires adequate spanwise resolution of the resolved three-dimensional turbulence and a sufficient spanwise domain extent in order not to restrict the resolved structures, visible in Fig. 4 (bottom-left). The largest occurring structures can be estimated by the maximum boundary layer thickness (including displacement due to separation), leading in this case to a minimum span of 8% of airfoil chord in combination with periodic boundary conditions.

---

[2] With an onflow Mach number of $M = 0.16$, the flow is mostly incompressible.

The spatial discretization for wall-modelled LES using IDDES requires full wall-normal resolution down to the wall, i.e. $\Delta y^+ \approx 1$, whereas the tangential (stream- and spanwise) spacing scales with the boundary layer thickness. Figure 4 (right) shows the resulting distribution of the wall-tangential (stream- and spanwise) spacings normalized in wall units for a block-structured grid used in [6] on all three airfoil elements. This adequate (yet not highly-resolved) IDDES grid contains $N_{xy} = 0.27 \times 10^6$ grid points in the xy-plane and $N_z = 100$ equidistant spanwise layers in z-direction, yielding $N_{pnt} = 27 \times 10^6$ points in total, cf. Table 2.

The physical time step was chosen as 5000 steps per CTU ($=c/U_\infty$) which yields a mean normalized timestep in wall-units of about $\Delta t^+ = 0.55$, but with maxima up to 1.6 near the leading edges. Due to the rather small-scale flow phenomena (boundary layers with local separations), which bear only limited impact on the global flow field, an overall simulation time of about 10 CTU is considered sufficient, corresponding to $N_t = 5 \times 10^4$ physical time steps.

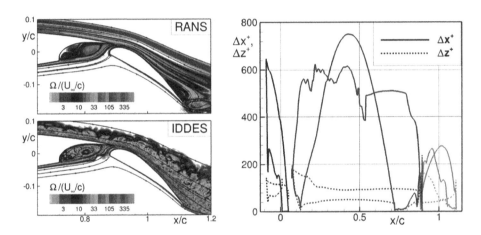

Fig. 4. DLR-F15 airfoil. *Left:* Snapshot of normalized vorticity and time-averaged streamlines around the flap from different modelling approaches. *Right:* Wall-tangential grid spacing in wall-units in the IDDES grid (colors indicate different airfoil elements). (Color figure online)

Extrapolation to LES. For a wall-resolved LES, the domain size and the overall simulation time can be kept as for IDDES. However, the wall-tangential spacing needs to be refined to meet common LES requirements for wall-bounded flow, i.e. $\Delta x^+ \approx 40$ and $\Delta z^+ \approx 20$. Considering Fig. 4 (right), this (roughly) leads to a 10× refinement in stream-, and a 5× refinement in spanwise direction, yielding $N_{pnt} = 1.35 \times 10^9$ total grid points for the same block-structured topology. To ensure a sufficient temporal resolution of $\Delta t^+ \leq 0.4$ in the all flow regions [2], the time step should be divided by 4 compared to IDDES, resulting in $N_t = 2 \times 10^5$ time steps for 10 CTU, cf. Table 2.

With these data and demanding $\geq 90\%$ parallel efficiency according to Sect. 3.1, a total number of around 210,000 cores could be used efficiently with TAU, and the simulation would take 4.9 days. For THETA, with a lower (efficient) core number of around 70,000 the simulation would take 0.6 days (if the local compressibility effects at this Mach number are neglected).

Table 2. Spatial and temporal resolution of different simulation approaches for the DLR-F15 airfoil.

Modelling	Δx^+	Δy^+	Δz^+	N_{xy} in 10^6	N_z	N_{pnt} in 10^6	$\Delta t/(c/U_\infty)$	N_t in 10^3
RANS	"∞"	1	"∞"	0.2	1	0.2	–	(steady)
HRLM	500	1	100	0.27	100	27	2×10^{-4}	50
LES	40	1	20	2.7	500	1350	5×10^{-5}	200

4.3 3D Wing of Aircraft in Flight

The previous sections show the enormous computational cost associated with wall-resolved LES of the flow around aircraft components at wind-tunnel scale. In this section we extrapolate the computational cost for the main aerodynamic device of a full aircraft in flight conditions, i.e. the wing. Details strongly depend on the operating point of the aircraft, e.g. low-speed take-off and landing or high-speed operation. Note that such a range of flow conditions can only be handled with compressible flow solvers like TAU (or CODA in the future).

First we extrapolate the above estimate for the three-element wing-section of 8% span for the small wind-tunnel Reynolds number of $Re = 2.1 \times 10^6$ to a full wing. For modern transport aircraft, the aspect ratio of wing half span to mean aerodynamic chord is around 4.5 to 5. Using the former, the number of nodes in spanwise direction on a single wing side increases by a factor of 56 compared to the 8%-span wing-section, leading to a total number of 7.6×10^{10} mesh points. Using the same number of time steps ($N_t = 2 \times 10^5$) and cores (210,000) as given in the previous section, the simulation time with TAU can be linearly extrapolated (i.e., assuming perfect weak scaling) to 250 days.

In the second step we include the Reynolds number effects. We assume a take-off speed of 77 m/s and a mean aerodynamic chord length of $c_{MAC} = 5.8$ m, close to the values for an A350, together with $\nu = 1.5 \times 10^{-5}$ m^2/s. The Reynolds number is thus $Re_{c,MAC} = 30 \times 10^6$. Then the viscous length scale $\delta_\nu = \nu/u_\tau$ is decreasing according to $\delta_{\nu,high}/\delta_{\nu,low} \sim \sqrt{c_{f,high}/c_{f,low}}\, Re_{high}/Re_{low}$. For the Re-dependence of c_f we use the Coles-Fernholz correlation with $c_{f,low}/c_{f,high} \approx 1.5$ and together with $Re_{high}/Re_{low} = 15$ we obtain $\delta_{\nu,high}/\delta_{\nu,low} \approx 1./12.2$. This leads to an increase of the number of grid points by a factor of $(\delta_{\nu,low}/\delta_{\nu,high})^2 = 150$ for $N_x \times N_z$, and we neglect a possible small increase of N_y. This leads to a total number of 1.1×10^{13} grid points for a single wing. Note that this estimate agrees well with the Re-based extrapolation according to [1], see Sect. 2.

For temporal discretization, the condition $\Delta t^+ = 0.4$ [2] implies that the physical time step needs to be decreased by a factor of $(\delta_{\nu,\text{low}}/\delta_{\nu,\text{high}})^2 \approx 150$. Then the number of time steps becomes $N_t = 3 \times 10^7$ and the wall-clock time would rise by a factor of 150^2 compared to the low-Reynolds-number case, yielding more than 15 thousand years on 210,000 cores. But even with exclusive access to the largest existing cluster of Xeon-CPUs comparable to DLR's, i.e. "Tianhe-2A" with almost 5 million cores [13], such a TAU simulation would take around 650 years, when extrapolated linearly. As a final remark, for a full aircraft a simulation time of 10 CTUs may not be sufficient. Following [11], the trailing-vortex system needs to be resolved over 50 c_{MAC} downstream of the wing, increasing the simulation time by another factor of 5.

High-speed buffet occurs at even higher Reynolds numbers. The oscillating shock wave and the involved shock-induced flow separation not only requires highly robust numerical algorithms but extensive LES regions to resolve turbulence for the complete buffet region. For an estimate of the flow conditions representative for the boundary of the flight envelope in the high-speed regime, we assume $Ma_\infty = 0.9$ and that the local flow speed can reach $U_\infty = 400\,\text{m/s}$ in the supersonic flow regions above the wing. On the other hand, at 10 km altitude, the small density of air of around $0.41\,\text{kg/m}^3$ leads to larger values of the kinematic viscosity of $\nu \approx 3.5 \times 10^{-5}\,\text{m}^2/\text{s}$. Therefore $Re_{c,\text{MAC}} \approx 66 \times 10^6$ is increased by a factor of approximately 2 compared to low-speed high-lift conditions. Therefore the mesh resolution is increased roughly by a factor of 2^2, and the physical time step needs to be decreased by a factor of 2^2.

5   Conclusion

Various aspects affecting the feasibility and HPC requirements of high-fidelity flow simulations around aircraft at the border of the flight envelope were discussed. Due to the large resolution requirements of wall-resolved LES at high Reynolds numbers, even the flow around isolated aircraft components at wind-tunnel scale, e.g. narrow wing sections or nacelle strakes, were shown to yield grid-point numbers in the order of 10^9. Even though the present DLR codes with MPI-based inter-process communication could theoretically make use of up to $\sim 200,000$ CPU cores[3] for such problem sizes (assuming perfect weak scaling), the time integration over sufficiently long simulation intervals still leads to wall-clock times in the order of days to weeks.

The subsequent extrapolation to a full 3D wing of an aircraft in take-off conditions (but still at wind-tunnel scale) adds a factor of >50 to either the core number or the wall-clock time, both being infeasible for nowadays industrial use. Finally, with wall-clock times of more than 600 years using one of the largest existing HPC clusters exclusively, the extrapolation to flight Reynolds numbers clearly reveals the inability of present methodologies to resolve all relevant turbulent scales with LES around aircraft flying at the border of the envelope.

---

[3] Consuming more than half of Germany's top-ranked HPC cluster 'SuperMUC-NG' with 305,856 cores [13].

Based on these estimates the following complementary requirements for future turbulence-resolving simulations of aircraft can be formulated:

- Further expansion of available HPC resources, allowing the regular use of >100,000 computing cores in a single flow simulation.
- Modern parallel code designs beyond classical MPI (as the new CODA solver) to further increase parallel efficiency on many-core HPC hardware.
- More efficient and yet robust numerical algorithms to reduce the wall-clock time for one physical time step in a given distributed simulation.
- Finally, despite the appeal of minimized turbulence modelling, the local use of classical RANS in regions with less complex flow physics appears inevitable for industrial use. This leads to hybrid RANS/LES methods with wall modelling in resolved flow regions, possibly supplemented by model-based efficiency improvements like locally-embedded LES regions (using synthetic turbulence injection) or wall functions to bridge the near-wall region.

References

1. Choi, H., Moin, P.: Grid-point requirements for large eddy simulation chapman's estimates revisited. Center for Turbulence Research, Annual Research Briefs 2011, pp. 31–36 (2011)
2. Choi, H., Moin, P.: Effects of the computational time step on numerical solutions of turbulent flow. J. Comput. Phys. **113**(1), 1–4 (1994)
3. Illi, S., Lutz, T., Krämer, E.: On the capability of unsteady RANS to predict transonic buffet. In: Third Symposium Simulation of Wing and Nacelle Stall, 21–22 June, Braunschweig, Germany, pp. 1–13 (2012)
4. Leicht, T., et al.: DLR-project digital-X: next generation CFD solver 'Flucs', Deutscher Luft- und Raumfahrtkongress 2016, Deutsche Gesellschaft für Luft- und Raumfahrt (2017). http://www.dglr.de/publikationen/2017/420027.pdf
5. Pope, S.B.: Turbulent Flows. Cambridge University Press, New York (2000)
6. Probst, A., Löwe, J., Reuss, S., Knopp, T., Kessler, R.: Scale-resolving simulations with a low-dissipation low-dispersion second-order scheme for unstructured flow solvers. AIAA J. **54**(10), 2972–2987 (2016)
7. Rumsey, C.L., Slotnick, J.P., Sclafani, A.J.: Overview and Summary of the Third AIAA High Lift Prediction Workshop, AIAA-2018-1258, AIAA Aerospace Sciences Meeting, Kissimmee, Florida, 8–12 January 2018
8. Shur, M.L., Spalart, P.R., Strelets, M.K., Travin, A.K.: A hybrid RANS-LES approach with delayed-DES and wall-modelled LES capabilities. Int. J. Heat Fluid Flow **29**(6), 406–417 (2008)
9. Slotnick, J.P., et al.: CFD vision 2030 study: a path to revolutionary computational aerosciences, NASA/CR–2014-218178, March 2014
10. Slotnick, J.P., Heller, G.: Emerging opportunities for predictive CFD for off-design commercial airplane flight characteristics. In: 54th 3AF International Conference on Applied Aerodynamics, Paris, 25–27 March 2019
11. Spalart, P.R., Jou, W.H., Strelets, M., Allmaras, S.R.: Comments on the feasibility of LES for wings, and on a hybrid RANS/LES approach. In: Liu, C., Liu, Z. (eds.) Advances in DNS/LES First AFOSR International Conference on DNS/LES, Ruston, LA, 4–8 August 1997, Greyden, Columbus, OH, 1997 (1997)

12. Wild, J., Pott-Pollenske, M., Nagel, B.: An integrated design approach for low noise exposing high-lift devices. In: 3rd AIAA Flow Control Conference (2006)
13. TOP500 List: June 2019. https://www.top500.org/lists/2019/06/. Accessed 16 Sept 2019

Data-Adapted Parallel Merge Sort

Johannes Holke$^{(\boxtimes)}$, Alexander Rüttgers, Margrit Klitz, and Achim Basermann

Institue for Software Technology, Department High-Performance Computing, German Aerospace Center (DLR), Linder Höhe, 51147 Cologne, Germany
{johannes.holke,alexander.ruettgers,margrit.klitz,achim.basermann}@dlr.de

Abstract. In the aerospace sciences we produce huge amounts of data. This data must be arranged in a meaningful order, so that we can analyze or visualize it. In this paper we focus on data that is distributed among computer processes and then needs to be sorted by a single root process for further analysis. We assume that the memory on the root process is too small to hold all sorted data at once, so that we have to perform the sorting and processing of data chunk-wise. We prove the efficiency of our approach in weak scaling tests, where we achieve a near constant bandwidth. Additionally, we obtain a considerable speed up compared to the standard parallel external sort. We also demonstrate the usefulness of our algorithm in a real-life aviation application.

Keywords: Parallel sorting · High-performance computing · Merge sort · Data analysis · Aerospace sciences

1 Introduction

In the German Aerospace Center (DLR - Deutsches Zentrum für Luft- und Raumfahrt) huge amounts of data arise day by day. On the one hand this data is produced by scientific and engineering simulations, e.g. from the full numerical simulation of an aircraft. On the other hand, lots of data is collected for Earth observation or the exploration of other planets.

Very often the accumulated data needs to be sorted to become useful. In this work, we focus on data that is at first distributed among different processes of a supercomputer but then needs to be processed in a sorted order by a single root process. Furthermore, we assume that the memory on the root process is too small to hold all sorted data at once, so that we have to perform the sorting and processing of data chunk-wise.

The contribution of this paper is as follows: We present a new parallel merge sort algorithm that can skillfully handle arbitrary unsorted data sets that are distributed on a large number of processes. We dynamically adjust the size of the buffer for each process depending on the distribution of data. Compared to a fixed buffer size, we reduce the number of necessary messages and can use the dynamic buffer very efficiently. In particular we optimize the routine to account for pre-sorted parts of the data and for imbalanced loads. In a benchmark

© Springer Nature Switzerland AG 2020
U. Schwardmann et al. (Eds.): Euro-Par 2019 Workshops, LNCS 11997, pp. 388–399, 2020.
https://doi.org/10.1007/978-3-030-48340-1_30

study on the JUWELS supercomputer at FZ Jülich [4] we test our algorithm on up to 768 MPI ranks sorting up to 240 GiB of data. In weak scaling tests, we achieve a near constant bandwidth. Compared to the well-known parallel external sort [1,3] we demonstrate an up to 2 times speed-up on randomized data sets and up to 4.6 times on partly sorted data. In the latter case, we reduce the number of MPI messages to a constant that does not depend on the number of processes anymore.

Furthermore, on the DLR internal $C^2A^2S^2E$-2 cluster [2], we show that introducing our new algorithm in the DLR application code CODA [9] reduces the runtime of the complete mesh output operation by a factor of over 4 in the average case and by a factor of 100 in the (previous) worst case.

The remainder of this paper is organized as follows: In Sect. 2 we introduce the details of our data-adapted merge algorithm and point out the difference to the parallel external merge algorithm. Section 3 presents benchmark results with different sorting scenarios computed on JUWELS at FZ Jülich [4]. In addition, we focus on a specific case CFD application for which the algorithm was developed. For the scenario of a complete HDF5 export, we also show scaling results. We conclude our paper in Sect. 4 with a summary and suggestions for further research.

2   Data-Adapted Merge Algorithm

Let $I = \{\,id_0, \ldots, id_{N-1}\,\} \subseteq \mathbb{N}_0$ be a set of $N = |I|$ so called Ids (or keys) and $D = \{\,d_0, \ldots, d_{N-1}\,\}$ be a set of N data items. We say that id_j is the Id of item d_j, writing $id_j = Id(d_j)$. The sets I and D are distributed across P processes $\{\,p_0, \ldots, p_{P-1}\,\}$ in an arbitrary order. Thus, for each $0 \leq p < P$ we have a set $I_p \subseteq I$, such that

$$\bigcup_p I_p = I, \text{ and} \tag{1}$$

$$I_p \cap I_q = \emptyset, \text{ for } p \neq q, \tag{2}$$

and each process p holds the index set I_p and the corresponding data set $D_p = \{\,d_j \in D \mid id_j \in I_p\,\}$. We denote the number of items on process p by N_p.

In this paper we are concerned with the following task:

Task 1. *A single designated process r, which we call the* root *process, needs to access all data items in D once in ascending order of their Ids. Thus, first d_0, then d_1, and so on. Furthermore, we assume that due to limited memory resources the number of Ids and data items that r can store simultaneously is bounded and significantly smaller than N.*

Our particular application is in the context of computational fluid dynamics. Here, the Ids correspond to the elements of a computational mesh and the data represents the state of the simulation. The j-th data item is associated with the j-th mesh element and can for example store coordinates, fluid velocities, concentrations, or other relevant data[1]. We then want to output this simulation state to a file, for example to visualize the simulation or to have a checkpoint to restart the simulation in the future. In order to have this output independent of the partition, we want to store our data in order, sorted by the Ids. Furthermore, in some situations we are limited to using serial file I/O through a single process r. Therefore, we are in the setting described by the task above.

Of the different approaches to solve these kinds of sorting problems, we aim for one similar to a parallel merge sort, where the data is sorted locally on the processes and then merged to sorted data on the root[2].

From now on we assume that the processes' local sets D_p and I_p are sorted.

2.1   The Parallel External Merge Sort

The parallel external merge sort algorithm is a common method [3,7,10] that proceeds as follows. Given a chunk size C (divisible by P), the root process allocates memory for C many data items and assigns each process a portion of C/P many items. Each process then sends its next C/P items to the root. In a P-way merge step, the root process merges the data from the P buffers into a sorted array of size C, the *output chunk*. As soon as the root has merged all data items from process p a new communication is requested and process p sends its next C/P data items to the root. If the output chunk is full, this chunk of data can be passed on for further processing (serial data analysis, file I/O, etc.) and the root clears the output chunk to sort the next C items; see Fig. 1.

We observe two drawbacks of this method.

First, the number of messages that each process sends to the root is always the same, regardless of the distribution of the data. We can calculate this number for a process p as the amount of data on p divided by the size of p's buffer on the root, C/P:

$$|\{\,\text{Messages from } p \text{ to } r\,\}| = \frac{N_p P}{C}. \tag{3}$$

In particular, this number increases with the number of processes P.

However, if large portions of the data on a process p are contiguous, we could use much fewer messages. In the extreme case the data is already sorted on the processes. In this situation the optimal strategy is to send packs of C data items from process 0 to the root until all items on process 0 are processed, then continue with packs of C many items from process 1, and so on. Each process then sends $\frac{N_p}{C}$ messages, a reduction by a factor of P.

The second issue arises during the algorithm if a process p has sent all its elements to the root, but other processes still have data left. In this situation

---

[1] Data may also reside on a subset of the mesh elements, in which case gaps in the Ids I occur.

[2] A related problem is the so called external sort problem. Here the data resides unsorted on a hard drive and has to be written back to the hard drive in sorted order, while only a limited amount of data can fit into the memory of the calculating process [10].

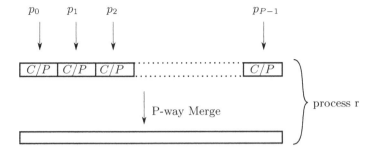

Fig. 1. In the classical external merge sort, the root allocates a buffer of size C/P for each process and receives the current portion of data from each process into this buffer. These buffers are then merged into the sorted output chunk. As soon as all C/P items from one process are merged, this process sends its next C/P items to the buffer.

the segment of the root's buffer associated to p is not used in the remaining part of the algorithm, having the same effect as shrinking the buffer size and thus increasing the effective runtime of the algorithm. This effect is of particular interest when the data is not distributed evenly among the processes or, in the extreme case, when some processes do not have any data at all.

2.2   The Data-Adapted Parallel Merge

We propose a new data-adapted parallel merge algorithm to overcome these issues. Instead of assigning a fixed buffer on the root for each process we dynamically adjust its size depending on the distribution of the data. Thus, we ensure that the buffer on the root is utilized more efficiently and that fewer messages have to be send for sorted parts of the data.

For a thorough understanding of our approach, we provide pseudo-code in Algorithms 2.1, 2.2, and 2.3: In a setup step 'InitNextID' each process sends the smallest element of I_p to the root, where these Ids are stored in an array NextIDs. During the algorithm NextIDs[p] will be updated to always contain the smallest Id on process p for which no data was sent to the root yet.

The algorithm then enters its main loop. In each iteration the root collects data from the other processes to fill the output chunk with the next C many data items. To achieve this, we proceed in three steps.

UpdateDataRange (see Algorithm 2.2): The root determines the Ids of the data items that will be processed in this iteration. This range starts at the smallest non-processed Id $m := \min \text{NextIDs}$ and ends at $m + C$. This range is then broadcasted across all processes.

GatherData (see Algorithm 2.3): In this step, the root collects the data from the processes. Each process whose next Id is within the data range, sends all data in the data range to root. Thus, process p sends d_j if and only if $m \le id_j < m + C$. In particular, processes with no data in the data range do not send

---

Algorithm 2.1: data_adapted_parallel_merge (ID_Array I_p, Data_Array D_p, Chunk_size C, root r)

---

1 pos ← 0   /* Current position in I_p and D_p */
2 **if** $p == r$ **then**
3 | Allocate Id and data buffer to hold C items respectively.
4 | Allocate Output chunk to hold C data items.
5 InitNextID()
6 **while** *Data left on any process* **do**
7 | UpdateDataRange()
8 | GatherData()
9 | MergeData()
            /* Application on r processes data in ouput chunk */

---

messages to the root. If a process sends data to the root it additionally sends its next unprocessed Id to the root or, if no data is left, an End of data flag.

Algorithm 2.2: UpdateDataRange()

---

1 **if** $p == r$ **then**   /* This process is root */
2 | minId ← min { NextIDs }   /* Smallest next Id */
3 | data_range[0] ← minId
4 | data_range[1] ← minId + C
5 | Broadcast **data_range** to all other ranks
6 **else**
7 | Receive data_range from root

At the end of this routine the root process determines from which processes it receives messages using the information in NextIDs and the data range, and then receives the data into its receive buffer. For these processes the root also updates the NextIDs array. If the sending process is the root itself ($p == r$), we do not need to send an MPI message here, but instead copy the data locally.

MergeData: In GatherData, the root received $k \leq P$ messages of sorted data. These are now merged in a k-way merge step into the output chunk.

After the MergeData step the output chunk represents the next sorted portion of the complete data set and can be processed by the calling application.

In Fig. 2 we depict the first two loop iterations of a small example with three processes p_0, p_1, and p_2. The first items of the sets I_p are given as

$$I_0 = \{ 0, 3, 100, \dots \}, \ I_1 = \{ 1, 4, 7, 101, \dots \}, \ I_2 = \{ 5, 6, 110, \dots \}, \quad (4)$$

and the sets D_p contain the corresponding data items. As chunk size we choose $C = 4$ (Certainly, C would be much larger in realistic applications; see Sect. 3). We show the Ids and data of each process on the left hand side and the data

---

Algorithm 2.3: GatherData()

---

1   **if** $I_p[pos] \geq data\_range[1]$ **then**
2 | return   /* This process does not send data */
3   Find j, such that $I_p[pos + j] < data\_range[1] \leq I_p[pos + j + 1]$
4   $S_p^0 \leftarrow \{ I_p[pos], I_p[pos + 1], \ldots, I_p[pos + j] \}$
5   $S_p^1 \leftarrow \{ D_p[pos], D_p[pos + 1], \ldots, D_p[pos + j] \}$
6   $pos \leftarrow pos + j + 1$ /* Update position in I_p */
7   $NextID_p \leftarrow I_p[pos]$ /* The next unused Id */
8   Send S_p^0, S_p^1 and $NextID_p$ to the root process.
9   **if** $p == r$ **then**   /* This process is root */
10 | **for** $q \in \{ \hat{q} \mid NextID[\hat{q}] < data\_range[1] \}$ **do**
11 | | Receive S_q^0 and S_q^1 and store into Id- and Data-Chunk.
12 | | Receive $NextID_q$
13 | | $NextIDs[q] = NextID_q$

---

on the root on the right hand side of Fig. 2. The initial `InitNextID` step is not depicted and was already performed.

We observe that only the processes that hold data of the current requested chunk send data to the root and that additionally the size of the messages may differ. The root receives all data for the current chunk in one go and does not need to wait for multiple sends from the same process.

By determining the minimum of the next Ids, gaps in the Id array can be skipped. Observe that from step 2 to step 3 the requested data range jumps from [4,8) to [100, 104), since the root knows that there are no Ids in between 8 and 100. However, gaps in the Id range within the currently requested data range lead to less than C items received on the root. We observe this in step 1 where one slot in the chunk remains unused. Nevertheless, this drawback has only minor influence on the runtime of our algorithm as we demonstrate in Sect. 3.1.

Remark 1. In our description of Task 1 we explicitly assume that different data items have different Ids. We use this in the algorithm when we determine the next data range. It is possible to adapt the algorithm to cope with duplicated Ids if we know a bound $\hat{n}$ on the number of usages of the same Id beforehand. In this case, `UpdateDataRange` may request a range from m to $m + \frac{C}{\hat{n}}$ instead.

3   Results and Discussion

3.1   Data-Adapted Parallel Merge

In this section we test our algorithm for four scenarios. The first is a random distribution of Ids, in the second the Ids are sorted, in the third blocks of 10,000 contiguous Ids are randomly distributed, and in the fourth the data is not distributed evenly among the processes and has large gaps (half the processes have twice as much data as the others). The random distributions are generated by

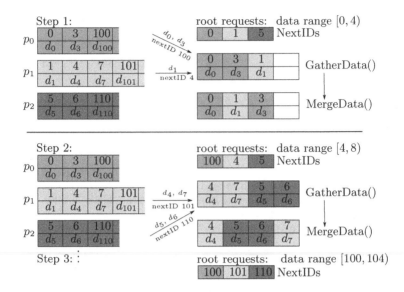

Fig. 2. Graphical description of our proposed data-adapted parallel merge algorithm. We show the first two loop iterations of an example with three processes and chunk size $C = 4$. On the left hand side we depict the Ids and data sets I_p and D_p of the processes. On the right hand side, we show how the root process receives and stores the different messages. Note that the root process will be one of p_0, p_1, p_2.

using the random number generator from [8]. For the results in Table 1 and Fig. 3 we have 8.388.608 Ids per process, 4 `double` entries ($4 \times 8 = 32$ Byte) per Id and a chunk size of $C = 32.768$ on the root process. Since we keep the problem size per process constant while increasing the number of processes, this can be seen as a weak scaling study. In a further step, we compare our algorithm with a reference implementation of the external parallel merge sort.

Our results were obtained on JUWELS at FZ Jülich [4]. Each node consists of a Dual Intel Xeon Platinum 8168 with $2 \times 24 = 48$ cores at 2.7 GHz each and $12 \times 8 = 96$ GB of RAM.

Table 1 lists the results of our new data adapted parallel merge algorithm with 48 to 768 processes on JUWELS for the first three scenarios. Since the problem size per process is kept constant, the total amount of data to be merged in GiB increases with the number of processes. In particular, we have a 15 GiB per compute node throughout our tests.

If we compare the number of messages per process between our algorithm and the external sorting algorithm in the second column of Table 2, we see that the number of messages per process is distinctly lower for our algorithm than for the external sorting algorithm in the scenarios *Sorted* and *Contiguous*. We achieve this advantage by the dynamic chunk size in our algorithm. In the scenario *Random*, the numbers of messages sent per process are exactly the same for our algorithm and the classical external sorting algorithm. Here, the number of messages is given by Eq. (3). For this scenario, the advantage of a dynamic chunk size in our algorithm can not be exploited. In most application use cases, however, we do not expect a totally random distribution of IDs.

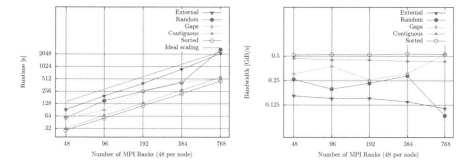

Fig. 3. Runtime (left) and bandwidth (right) for our four test scenarios compared with the parallel external merge.

Figure 3 compares runtimes and bandwidths achieved for all four scenarios between our algorithm and the external sorting algorithm for 48 to 768 processes on JUWELS. In the scenarios *Sorted* and *Contiguous* the runtimes of our algorithm are significantly shorter than the runtimes of the external sorting algorithm. The main reason is the distinctly reduced number of messages per process by exploiting a dynamic chunk size in our algorithm. In addition the number of messages in our algorithm stays nearly constant with increasing process number, cf. Table 2. In the sorted case, we even have an exactly constant number of messages, 256.

Table 1. Scaling results for our four test cases *Random, Sorted, Contiguous*, and *Gaps* compared with the original parallel external sort. We show the runtimes (left) and bandwidth (right) for our experiments for $P = 48$ up to $P = 768$ processes on JUWELS.

		Runtime [s]					Bandwidth [GiB/s]				
# ranks	GiB	External	Random	Sorted	Contiguous	Gaps	External	Random	Sorted	Contiguous	Gaps
48	15	92.3	58.0	29.1	31.9	55.8	0.16	0.26	0.52	0.47	0.30
96	30	198.8	152.3	57.3	66.5	90.3	0.15	0.20	0.52	0.45	0.37
192	60	399.7	258.0	115.6	133.6	264.8	0.15	0.23	0.52	0.45	0.25
384	120	873.8	417.9	225.0	275.8	440.5	0.14	0.29	0.53	0.44	0.31
768	240	2,118.0	2,604.3	457.6	561.7	511.6	0.11	0.09	0.52	0.43	0.53

Note that we expect a linear increase in the total runtime for both algorithms since the total amount of data rises and all data has to be processed on the root process. This linear increase is indicated by the 'Ideal scaling' line in Fig. 3. We also observe a clear advantage of our algorithm in the case of not

Table 2. Left: Number of messages per process for the external sorting algorithms and our algorithms for the first three scenarios (*Random, Sorted, Contiguous*). Right: Runtimes for different chunk sizes with 768 MPI ranks of the external sorting algorithms and our proposed algorithm for the *Random* scenario.

# ranks	External	Random	Sorted	Contiguous
48	12,288	12,288	256	1,060.85
96	24,576	24,576	256	1,078.35
192	49,152	49,152	256	1,086.90
384	98,304	98,304	256	1,089.76
768	196,608	196,608	256	1,093.00

Chunk size	External sort	Data-adapted
32,768	2,118.0	2,601.0
131,072	1,909.6	1,572.8
262,144	1,866.9	1,358.0

evenly distributed data, scenario *Gaps*. Here, the dynamic chunk size is of particular advantage, since with increasing process number more and more processes become idle after some iterations due to the load imbalance in this scenario. For the scenario *Random*, our algorithm still shows superior runtime behavior compared with the external sorting algorithm except for 768 processes. In the latter case the overhead of managing the parallel messages is a possible explanation for the slower runtimes. However, if we increase the chunk size as in Table 2, we can also for 768 processes achieve distinctly shorter runtimes with our algorithm than with external sorting algorithm. Larger chunk sizes improve the computation to communication ratio and are advantageous for both algorithms, but can be more efficiently exploited in our data-adapted parallel merge implementation.

Figure 3 displays the bandwidth behavior of our algorithm in comparison to the external sorting algorithm. We observe that with increasing processor numbers the bandwidth stays more or less constant for our algorithm in the scenarios *Sorted* and *Contiguous*, while the bandwidth of the external sorting algorithm decreases. Moreover, the bandwidth of our algorithm is distinctly higher than that of the external sorting algorithm, in the best case by a factor of about 5. The only exception is again scenario *Random* with 768 processes, but as for the runtime this can be changed by adapting the chunk size according to Table 2.

3.2 Application: File I/O with FlowSimulator

One of DLR's ongoing goals in aviation is the virtual design of an aircraft. A key element in the aerodynamic design process is the numerical flow simulation for which the DLR develops its next-generation CFD (computational fluid dynamics) software code CODA [9].

CODA is developed as part of the FlowSimulator (FS), which is an HPC platform for the integration of multiple parallel components into a process chain. All components ("plug-ins") are integrated via a Python interface so that the whole simulation process chain can be controlled by a Python script; see Fig. 4, left. For a detailed description of FS, we refer to [11] and [12].

The storage and the parallel management of data in FS is performed by an HPC-library called FlowSimulator Data Manager (FSDM). FSDM stores data in a collection of C++ container classes that are all wrapped to Python. It has a

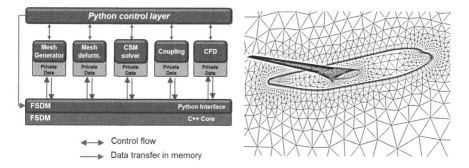

Fig. 4. Left: Basic architecture of the FlowSimulator framework. Right: Illustration of an unstructured grid that is used for a CFD simulation around an airplane. (Color figure online)

wide range of import and export filters for the most common file formats such as HDF5, CGNS, NetCDF and Tecplot. After the import, FSDM decomposes the data and distributes it over the different MPI domains. Here, FSDM makes use of popular partitioning algorithms such as ParMETIS or RGB (Recursive Graph Bisection) [5,6]. Other ingredients of FSDM include geometry operations, mesh deformation and interpolation to only name a few.

Due to the various export formats that are supported by FSDM, we often encounter a situation as described in Task 1 in the case that the export filter only supports sequential file I/O. In the following, we benchmark the file I/O of a CFD simulation into an HDF5 file using FSDM. Note that we are aware of the fact that the HDF5 library [13] supports parallel file I/O. However, the current HDF5 export is performed by the root process only.

In the following, we consider an unstructured mesh that models an airplane as illustrated in Fig. 4 and that contains various simulation datasets, e.g. the velocity and the pressure field. The mesh is adaptively refined at the region of interest close to the airplane's wing and consists of nodes, surface elements (triangles, quadrangles) and volume elements (tetrahedrons, hexahedrons). Each mesh element is identified by a unique Id integer number. As an example, the color of the mesh elements in Fig. 4 represent their associated Id number. Here, on the one hand the mesh elements that model the airplane have low Ids (colored in blue) and on the other hand the mesh elements of the far field have high Ids (colored in red).

Table 3 shows the results of the HDF5 file export in FS on the DLR $C^2A^2S^2E$-2 [2] cluster. Each cluster node consists of two Intel Xeon E5-2695v2 processors with $2 \times 12 = 24$ cores, 2.4 GHz per core and $8 \times 16 = 128$ GiB of RAM. The exported dataset has a size of 7.2 GiB and consists of a mesh with 17 CFD subdatasets that are exported one after another. The table compares the runtime of the original file I/O implementation in FSDM with the proposed new algorithm described in Sect. 2. In this case, the chunk size of the new algorithm is $C = 10^6$. We explicitly note that file I/O is performed by the root process r in all cases so that the increase in runtime with larger processor numbers is to be expected.

Table 3. Runtime comparison of the original HDF5 file export with the proposed algorithm in FlowSimulator.

#ranks	Old export	Runtime [s] Old export + Ids invert.	New export
24	742	19,536	182
48	1,104	32,907	278
96	1,575	34,602	356
192	2,126	–	534
384	2,995	–	803
768	4,524	–	1,052

In the old export routine, r performs the data exchange with one process after another and then writes a contiguous block of m data elements $\{d_j, d_{j+1}, \ldots, d_{j+m}\}$ with m as large as possible to file. Since the dataset D_p on each process p has been sorted locally, we usually obtain contiguous block sizes m in the order of several thousand elements. The runtime results for this case are listed in the second column of Table 3. The third column considers the situation that the local order on each process has been destroyed since we deliberately invert the list of local Ids. This reduces the number of elements m that can be written in one operation by r and increases the total runtime by a factor of 20–30. Due to the enormous increase in runtime, we have only computed the results up to four nodes on $C^2A^2S^2E$-2. Finally, the last column states the results with our proposed new algorithm. In this case, there is always a local sort on each process so that the runtime results do not depend on the initial local order. We observe that the new implementation reduces the runtime compared to the old export (second column) by a factor of four. This underlines the usefulness of the algorithm for sequential file I/O on moderate processor numbers.

4   Conclusion

In this paper we introduce a new algorithm to solve a parallel sorting problem, where data resides on distributed processes and needs to be accessed by a single root process in sorted order. Due to limited memory resources the root can only access this data chunk-wise. We optimize our network communication to automatically adapt to the data distribution among the processes. Compared to the common parallel external sort approach, we obtain speed-ups of factors 2 to 4. With our method we are able to exploit pre-sorted parts of the data and can handle unbalanced loads.

Additionally to our results in benchmark studies, we applied our approach to sequential file I/O in the DLR FlowSimulator environment. Here, we demonstrated speed-ups of the complete I/O routine of a factor of 4 in the general case and up to 100 in our previous worst case. We are certain that many more applications can benefit from our work, especially in the areas of data-analysis and visualization, and in situations where parts of a tool-chain are serial. Future work on the techniques presented in this paper may include improved handling of duplicated keys and a generalization of the algorithm to multiple root processes. The latter could be promising on clusters with many compute nodes and a limited number of I/O nodes.

Acknowledgments. This research was carried out under the project *Virtual Aircraft Technology Integration Platform* (VicToria) by the German Aerospace Center (DLR).

The authors gratefully acknowledge the Gauss Centre for Supercomputing e.V. (www.gauss-centre.eu) for funding this project by providing computing time through the John von Neumann Institute for Computing (NIC) on the GCS Supercomputer JUWELS at Jülich Supercomputing Centre (JSC).

References

1. Bitton, D., DeWitt, D.J., Hsiao, D.K., Menon, J.: A taxonomy of parallel sorting. Technical report, Cornell University (1984)
2. CASE-2: SGI ICE X, Intel Xeon E5–2695v2 12C 2.4 GHz, Inifiniband, FDR. https://www.top500.org/system/178196. Accessed 16 Apr 2019
3. Friedland, D.B.: Design, analysis, and implementation of parallel external sorting algorithms. Ph.D. thesis (1981). aAI8206830
4. JUWELS: http://www.fz-juelich.de/ias/jsc/EN/Expertise/Supercomputers/ JUWELS/JUWELS_node.html. Accessed 15 Apr 2019
5. Karypis, G., Schoegel, K., Kumar, V.: ParMETIS - parallel graph partitioning and sparse matrix ordering library, version 3.1 (2013)
6. Kernighan, B.W., Lin, S.: An efficient heuristic procedure for partitioning graphs. Bell Syst. Tech. J. **49**(2), 291–307 (1970)
7. Knuth, D.E.: The Art of Computer Programming: Sorting and Searching, vol. 3. Pearson Education, London (1997)
8. Langr, D., Tvrdík, P., Dytrych, T., Draayer, J.P.: Algorithm 947: Paraperm-parallel generation of random permutations with MPI. ACM Trans. Math. Softw. **41**(1), 51–526 (2014). https://doi.org/10.1145/2669372. http://doi.acm.org/10.1145/2669372
9. Leicht, T., et al.: DLR-Project Digital-X - Next generation CFD solver 'Flucs'. Deutscher Luft- und Raumfahrtkongress 2016, February 2016. https://elib.dlr.de/ 111205/
10. Leu, F.C., Tsai, Y.T., Tang, C.Y.: An efficient external sorting algorithm. Inf. Proces. Lett. **75**(4), 159–163 (2000)
11. Meinel, M., Einarsson, G.O.: The FlowSimulator framework for massively parallel CFD applications. In: PARA 2010 Conference: State of the Art in Scientific and Parallel Computing. Citeseer (2010)
12. Reimer, L.: The FlowSimulator–a software framework for CFD-related multidisciplinary simulations. In: European NAFEMS Conference Computational Fluid Dynamics (CFD) - Beyond the Solve, December 2015. https://elib.dlr.de/100536/
13. The HDF Group: Hierarchical Data Format, version 5 (1997-NNNN). http://www. hdfgroup.org/HDF5/

In Situ Visualization of Performance-Related Data in Parallel CFD Applications

Rigel F. C. Alves$^{(\boxtimes)}$ and Andreas Knüpfer

Center for Information Services and High Performance Computing (ZIH),
Technische Universität Dresden, 01062 Dresden, Germany
rigel.alves@tu-dresden.de
https://tu-dresden.de/zih/

Abstract. This paper aims at investigating the feasibility of using ParaView as visualization software for the analysis and optimization of parallel CFD codes' performance. The currently available software tools for reading profiling data do not match the generated measurements to the simulation's original mesh and somehow aggregate them (rather than showing them on a time-step basis). A plugin for the open-source performance tool Score-P has been developed, which intercept an arbitrary number of manually selected code regions (mostly functions) and send their respective measurements – amount of executions and cumulative time spent – to ParaView (through its in situ library, Catalyst), as if they were any other flow-related variable. Results show that (i) the impact of mesh partition algorithms on code performance and (ii) the load imbalances (and their eventual relationship to mesh size/simulation physics) become easier to investigate.

Keywords: Parallel computing · Performance analysis · In situ processing

1 Introduction

Many tools for analyzing the performance of parallel applications exist; one example of them is *Score-P*[1]1 [11], whose development the University of Dresden participates in. It acts as a wrapper which encapsulates the original code, thus can be easily turned on or off by the user at compilation stage. This is illustrated in Fig. 1 below.

The original version of this chapter was revised: The two videos were added. The correction to this chapter is available at https://doi.org/10.1007/978-3-030-48340-1_64

---

[1] *Scalable Performance Measurement Infrastructure for Parallel Codes* – an open-source "highly scalable and easy-to-use tool suite for profiling, event tracing, and online analysis of HPC applications": https://www.vi-hps.org/projects/score-p/.

Electronic supplementary material The online version of this chapter (https://doi.org/10.1007/978-3-030-48340-1_31) contains supplementary material, which is available to authorized users.

© The Author(s) 2020, corrected publication 2020
U. Schwardmann et al. (Eds.): Euro-Par 2019 Workshops, LNCS 11997, pp. 400–412, 2020.
https://doi.org/10.1007/978-3-030-48340-1_31

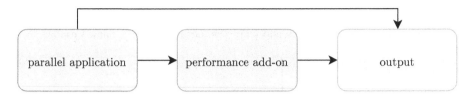

Fig. 1. Schematic of software components for performance analysis tools.

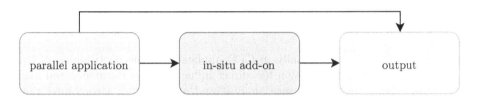

Fig. 2. Schematic of software components for in situ visualization.

As a separate category of add-ons, tools for enabling *in situ visualization* [5] of applications' output data (like *temperature* or *pressure* in a CFD simulation) already exist too; one example is *Catalyst*[2] [3]. It also works as an optional add-on to the original code and can be activated upon request, by means of preprocessor directives at compilation stage (Fig. 2).

This paper's goals are two-fold. First, unify the overlapping functionalities of both kinds of tools insofar as they augment a parallel application with additional functionality which is not strictly required for the application to work in the first place. Both collect or "steal" data from the parallel application and transfer it out via a side channel. Second, make use of the advanced visualization function-alities of dedicated visualization software tools for the purpose of performance analysis. With this we propose to map parallel performance properties to the simulation geometry as it is already done for flow-related properties. Figure 3 illustrates the idea.

The high-performance computing (HPC) performance tools usually output either *performance profiles* or *event traces*. In the case of Score-P, they are:

- performance profiles in the Cube4 format to be visualized at *Cube*[3] [14];
- parallel event traces in the OTF2 format to be visualized at *Vampir*[4] [10].

But neither of them, nor the other currently available performance tools (to be explained in Sect. 2), match their measurements to the original simulation's geometry; what makes the proposal novel. On the other hand, the proposal is

---

[2] An open-source "in situ use case library, with an adaptable application program-ming interface (API), that orchestrates the delicate alliance between simulation and analysis and/or visualization tasks": https://www.paraview.org/in-situ/.

[3] A free, but copyrighted "generic tool for displaying a multi-dimensional performance space consisting of the dimensions (i) performance metric, (ii) call path, and (iii) system resource": http://www.scalasca.org/software/cube-4.x/download.html.

[4] An "easy-to-use framework that enables developers to quickly display and analyze arbitrary program behavior at any level of detail": https://vampir.eu/.

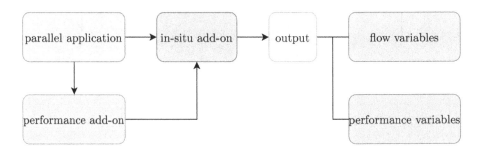

Fig. 3. Schematic of the software components for a combined add-on.

deemed also useful as, especially in CFD applications, the partitioning of the compute mesh for parallelization has direct influence on performance and load balancing. Hence for performance analysis and optimization a combined view into simulation properties and performance properties is helpful.

A design requirement is that the combined solution must be able to be integrated into a parallel code easily, yet without becoming a permanently required component. Instead, it needs to be easy to switch on and off on demand, as it is for each of its constitutive parts. As evaluation case, the Rolls-Royce in-house CFD code (*Hydra*) [12] will be used.

2   Related Work

Apart from Score-P → Cube and Score-P → Vampir (mentioned above), other workflows – with graphical support – used for performance analysis include:

- *HPCToolkit*[5] [1], whose outputs are visualized through *hpcviewer* (profiling) and *hpctraceviewer* (tracing);
- *Periscope*[6] [7], whose outputs are visualized through *Pathway* (an Eclipse-based graphical user-interface);
- *Tau*[7] [18], whose outputs are visualized through *ParaProf* [6] (profiling) and Vampir (tracing), among others;
- *Paraver*[8] [13] and *Dimemas*[9] [4], with integrated visualization capabilities;

---

[5] An open-source "integrated suite of tools for measurement and analysis of program performance on computers": http://hpctoolkit.org/.

[6] A free "suite of tools designed to assist the HPC application developer in the optimization of their application": https://periscope.in.tum.de/.

[7] A "portable profiling and tracing toolkit for performance analysis of parallel programs written in Fortran, C, C++, UPC, Java, Python": http://www.cs.uoregon.edu/research/tau/home.php.

[8] A "very powerful performance visualization and analysis tool based on traces that can be used to analyse any information that is expressed on its input trace format": https://tools.bsc.es/paraver.

[9] A "simulation tool for the parametric analysis of the behaviour of message-passing applications on a configurable parallel platform": https://tools.bsc.es/dimemas.

– *SLOG-2*, a drawable logging format visualized through *Jumpshot*[10] [8];
– *Scalasca*[11] [9] as an optional add-on to either Score-P or Tau;
– *READEX*[12] [17], with a bunch of visualization options.

None of them, however, currently match the generated data back to the simulation's geometry. Furthermore, displaying profiling results on a time-step basis is not straightforward. This paper would like to address those issues.

3 Prerequisites

The goal aimed by this research depends on the combination of two basic, scientifically established methods: *performance measurement* and *in situ processing*.

3.1 Performance Measurement

When applied to a source file's compilation, Score-P automatically inserts probes between each code "region" (mostly function calls, but also constructors, destructors etc.), which will at run-time measure:

– the *number of times* that region was executed, and;
– the total *time* spent in those executions.

By each rank/thread within the simulation. Its application is done by simply prepending the word *scorep* into the compilation command, e.g.: `scorep mpicc foo.c`. The tool is also equipped with an API, which allows the user to extend its functionalities through plugins [15]. The combined solution proposed by this paper takes the form of such a plugin.

3.2 In Situ Processing

In order for Catalyst to interface with the simulation code, an adapter needs to be built, which is responsible for exposing the native data structures (mesh and flow properties) to the *coprocessor* component. Its interaction with the simulation code happens through three function calls, illustrated in Fig. 4.

Once implemented, the adapter allows the generation of post-mortem files (by means of the *VTK*[13] [16] library) and/or the live visualization of the simulation, both through *ParaView*[14] [2].

---

[10] A "Java-based visualization tool for doing postmortem performance analysis": https://www.mcs.anl.gov/research/projects/perfvis/.

[11] A "a software tool that supports the performance optimization of parallel programs by measuring and analyzing their runtime behavior": http://www.scalasca.org/.

[12] A tool suite that "supports users to improve the energy-efficiency of their HPC applications": https://www.readex.eu/.

[13] An open-source "software for manipulating and displaying scientific data": https://www.vtk.org/.

[14] An open-source "multi-platform data analysis and visualization application": https://www.paraview.org/.

Fig. 4. Illustrative example of changes needed in a simulation code due to Catalyst.

4   Combining Both Tools

A Score-P plugin has been developed, which allows performance measurements for an arbitrary number of manually selected code regions to be pipelined to the simulation's Catalyst adapter. It must be activated at run-time through an environment variable (`export SCOREP_SUBSTRATE_PLUGINS=Catalyst`), but works independently of Score-P's profiling mode being actually on or off. Figure 5 illustrates the modifications needed in the source.

Apart from the three basic calls (*initialize*, *"run"* and *finalize*; like with the Catalyst adapter), a call must be placed immediately before each function to be pipelined; e.g.:

```
#ifdef CATALYST_SCOREP
    ! add this region to the list of plugin variables
    CALL cat_sco_pipeline_me()
#endif

CALL desired_function(argument_1, argument_2...)
```

The above layout ensures that the desired function will be captured when executed at that specific moment and not in others (if the same routine is called multiple times – with different inputs – throughout the code, as it is usual for CFD simulations). The selected functions may or not be nested.

Finally, the user needs to add a small piece of code into the Catalyst adapter's source, in order for the plugin-generated variables to be pipelined (together with the traditional simulation variables), as shown in Fig. 6. It contains two vectors

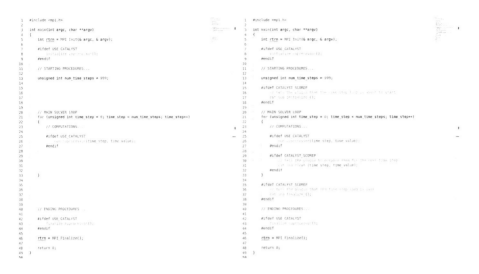

Fig. 5. Illustrative example of further changes needed in the code due to the plugin.

because for each selected region inside the simulation's code, the plugin will generate two variables (which correspond to the two basic measurements made by Score-P; see above).

5 Early Evaluation

5.1 Settings

Hydra is Rolls-Royce's in-house CFD code [12]. Figure 9 shows the test case selected for this paper: it represents a generic Q3D idealized model for a turbine stage. Preliminary analyses with Score-P → Cube revealed two code functions to be especially time-consuming: *iflux_edge* and *vflux_edge* (both mesh-related); they were selected for pipelining.

All simulations were done using an entire node in Dresden University's HPC cluster (Taurus), with 12 ranks (i.e. pure MPI, no OpenMP), one per core, each with the entire core memory (3875 MB) available. One full engine's shaft rotation was simulated, comprised of 100 time-steps (i.e. one per 3,6°), each internally converged through 40 iteration steps. Catalyst was generating post-mortem output files every fifth time-step (i.e. every 18°), what led to 20 "stage pictures" by the end of the simulation. Finally, version 4.0 of Score-P was used in association with release 2018a of Intel® compilers.

5.2 Results

Hydra supports multiple mesh partition algorithms, selectable at run-time. We compared them with our newly proposed approach. Figure 7 shows the time spent

```
// Score-P plugin variables
#ifdef CATALYST_SCOREP
    std::vector < vtkNew < vtkIntArray    > > scorep_tick(cat_sco::get_number_variables() );
    std::vector < vtkNew < vtkDoubleArray > > scorep_time(cat_sco::get_number_variables() );

    for (std::size_t i = 0; i < cat_sco::get_number_variables(); ++i)
    {
        scorep_tick[i] -> SetName( (cat_sco::get_variable_name(i) + " : tick").c_str() );
        scorep_time[i] -> SetName( (cat_sco::get_variable_name(i) + " : time").c_str() );

        scorep_tick[i] -> SetNumberOfComponents(1);
        scorep_time[i] -> SetNumberOfComponents(1);

        scorep_tick[i] -> SetNumberOfTuples(n_local_points);
        scorep_time[i] -> SetNumberOfTuples(n_local_points);

        scorep_tick[i] -> FillTypedComponent(0, cat_sco::get_variable_counter(i) );
        scorep_time[i] -> FillTypedComponent(0, cat_sco::get_variable_time   (i) );

        pointSet -> GetPointData() -> AddArray(scorep_tick[i].GetPointer() );
        pointSet -> GetPointData() -> AddArray(scorep_time[i].GetPointer() );
    }
#endif
```

Fig. 6. Addition needed in the Catalyst adapter's code due to the plugin.

inside the two chosen functions in two different grid partitions: the upper images refer to geometric mesh partitioning and the lower ones were produced using ParMETIS;[15] the left-hand side pictures refer to function *iflux_edge*, whereas the right-hand side to *vflux_edge*. Here only one time-step is represented, but – as opposed to the traditional way of visualizing profiling results (which aggregate multiple time-steps into one single measurement) – in ParaView it is possible to see each time-step individually and even play them (as frames of a video). Finally, the minimum and maximum thresholds in each of the four pictures' scales are adjusted to comprise all time-steps.

The analysis of the results reveals that, when compared against the geometric mesh partition, using ParMETIS brings slight benefits to the selected functions' performance: the overall maximum execution time (per time-step) drops in both of them, the overall minimum in *vflux_edge*; and the max/min ratio of the execution time (per time-step) for both of them is also decreased.

Playing the saved time-steps in ParaView reveals a trend in all four layouts: the slowest/fastest rank to execute each function is always the same. This means there are still load imbalances when using ParMETIS; otherwise, the slowest/fastest rank should randomly change each time-step (due to stochastic phenomena at hardware-level during run-time). See the respective video.

Figure 8 compares the results when profiling is activated (below) or not (above). They let clear that doing simultaneous code profiling significantly slows each region's execution time, but the max/min ratio remains roughly the same:

---

[15] An open source "MPI-based parallel library that implements a variety of algorithms for partitioning unstructured graphs, meshes, and for computing fill-reducing orderings of sparse matrices": http://glaros.dtc.umn.edu/gkhome/metis/parmetis/overview.

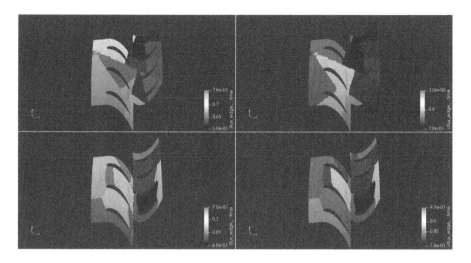

Fig. 7. Comparison between two code functions in two mesh partitions.

– from $0.57/0.46 \approx 1.24$ to $0.75/0.60 = 1.25$ in *iflux_edge*;
– from $0.85/0.69 \approx 1.23$ to $0.97/0.78 \approx 1.24$ in *vflux_edge*.

This means the overhead associated with each feature (Score-P's profiling and/or the plugin) is linear, hence the results are valid from a comparative point of view. Indeed, playing the respective video reveals the same trend (slowest/fastest rank) as in the previous comparison.

Finally, the generated performance variables are accessible also live (interactively) in ParaView. In Fig. 9, notice the "catalyst" icon on the *Pipeline Browser*, as well as the presence of the selected code regions' measurements among the *Data Arrays*.

5.3 Overhead

Table 1 analyses the impact of the proposed plugin on the code's performance. ParMETIS was used for mesh partitioning.

Memory. The "memory" row in Table 1 refers to the *peak* memory consumption per rank, reached somewhen during the simulation. From the numbers it is clear that the memory overhead introduced by Score-P is negligible (less than 10%); and that the memory overhead introduced by the plugin is also negligible. It may even require less memory than doing the traditional profiling (depending upon the number of code regions being pipelined) and, in our case, was below the statistical margin of oscillation (given *profiling + plugin* took less memory than *profiling only*). Indeed, in order to pipeline the two code functions shown above, it was not necessary to increase the default amount of memory (16 MB) that Score-P reserves for itself.

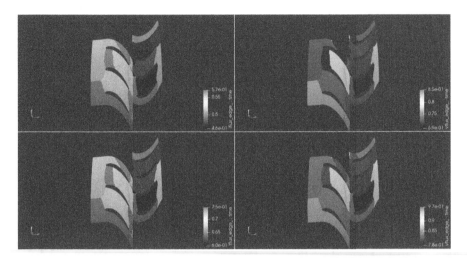

Fig. 8. Comparison between two code functions when profiling is activated (below) or not (above).

Table 1. Analysis of time and memory overhead of the plugin.

	Profiling + plugin	Profiling only	Plugin only	Without Score-P
Memory (kB)	290432 (6%)	294120 (7%)	284440 (4%)	273956 (-)
Run-time lightweight	4 m 18 s (8%)	4 m 10 s (5%)	4 m 06 s (3%)	3 m 58 s (-)
Run-time heavyweight	8 m 30 s (114%)	7 m 05 s (79%)	6 m 48 s (71%)	3 m 58 s (-)

Time. The run-time overhead is more critical and is shown in Table 1 with two cases. The light-weight instrumentation case shows the overhead of the presented approach with a sensible set of instrumented subroutines as it may have been achieved with carefully selecting the most interesting subroutines for the performance analysis process. This is the suggested way according to the Score-P documentation. In that case, the plugin produces a run-time overhead of 3%. This is less than Score-P in profiling mode with 5%. If both are used together, the overhead adds up. This is a sensible overhead and suitable for practical performance analysis. The second case with heavy-weight instrumentation reflects the worst-case scenario where some short subroutines are called very frequently (several billion times in this example). In that case, the overhead can dominate the entire run-time and the performance analysis insights are not reflecting the pristine parallel performance behavior. However, this scenario in Table 1 shows that our plugin behaves similar to Score-P in profiling mode; actually even slightly better with 71% overhead compared to 79%.

Fig. 9. Geometry used in the simulations.

6   Conclusions and Future Work

Visualization techniques are usually not the specialization field of researches working with code performance: it is more reasonable to take advantage of the currently available graphic programs (like ParaView) than attempting – from scratch – to equip the existing profiling tools with their own GUIs. In this threshold, the developed plugin adds to the currently available spectrum of performance optimization resources the capacity to:

- match performance-related measurements against the simulation's mesh, what makes the impact of grid partition algorithms on code performance easier to investigate;
- analyze performance-related measurements on a time-step basis, what makes the load imbalances (and their eventual relationship to mesh size/flow physics) easier to diagnose.

We plan to extend this work in multiple directions:

More Extensive Evaluation Cases. To run the plugin in bigger test cases, as the difficulty in matching each parallel region's id number with its respective grid part (hence the benefit of matching performance data back to the simulation's mesh) increases with scaling. Concomitantly, to run the plugin in test cases which comprise regions with distinct flow physics, when the computational load becomes less dependent on the number of points/cells per domain and more dependent on the flow features themselves (given their non-uniform occurrence): chemical reactions in the combustion chamber, shock waves in the inlet/outlet (at the supersonic flow regime), air dissociation in the free-stream/inlet (at the hypersonic flow regime) etc.

Improve and Further Integrate Tool's Runtime Components. To automatize the selection of code regions to be pipelined, what currently needs to be manually done by the user at compile time (as shown in Sect. 4).

Develop New Visualization Schemes for Performance Data. To take advantage of the multiple filters available in ParaView for the benefit of the performance optimization branch, e.g. by recreating in it the statistical analysis – display of *average* and *standard deviation* between the threads/ranks' measurements – already available in other tools.

Acknowledgments. The authors would like to thank: Rolls-Royce Germany (Especially Marcus Meyer, Axel Gerstenberger, Jan Suhrmann & Paolo Adami.), for providing both the CFD code and the test case for this paper, what has been done in the context of BMWi research project *Prestige* (FKZ 20T1716A); Kitware (especially Mathieu Westphal & Nicolas Vuaille), also part of Prestige, for the support with Catalyst; and the Score-P support and development team (Especially Bert Wesarg.), for the assistance with the plugin API.

References

1. Adhianto, L., et al.: HPCTOOLKIT: tools for performance analysis of optimized parallel programs. Concurrency Comput. Pract. Exp. **22**(6), 685–701 (2010). https://doi.org/10.1002/cpe.1553
2. Ahrens, J., Geveci, B., Law, C.: ParaView: An End-User Tool for Large Data Visualization. The Visualization Handbook, vol. 717. Academic Press, Cambridge (2005)
3. Ayachit, U., et al.: ParaView catalyst: enabling in situ data analysis and visualization. In: Proceedings of the First Workshop on In Situ Infrastructures for Enabling Extreme-Scale Analysis and Visualization, ISAV 2015. pp. 25–29. ACM, New York (2015). https://doi.org/10.1145/2828612.2828624
4. Badia, R.M., Labarta, J., Gimenez, J., Escale, F.: DIMEMAS: predicting MPI applications behavior in grid environments. In: Workshop on Grid Applications and Programming Tools (GGF8), vol. 86, pp. 52–62 (2003)
5. Bauer, A.C., et al.: In situ methods, infrastructures, and applications on high performance computing platforms. Comput. Graph. Forum **35**(3), 577–597 (2016). https://doi.org/10.1111/cgf.12930
6. Bell, R., Malony, A.D., Shende, S.: *ParaProf*: a portable, extensible, and scalable tool for parallel performance profile analysis. In: Kosch, H., Böszörményi, L., Hellwagner, H. (eds.) Euro-Par 2003. LNCS, vol. 2790, pp. 17–26. Springer, Heidelberg (2003). https://doi.org/10.1007/978-3-540-45209-6_7
7. Benedict, S., Petkov, V., Gerndt, M.: PERISCOPE: an online-based distributed performance analysis tool. In: Müller, M.S., Resch, M.M., Schulz, A., Nagel, W.E. (eds.) Tools for High Performance Computing 2009, pp. 1–16. Springer, Heidelberg (2010). https://doi.org/10.1007/978-3-642-11261-4_1

8. Chan, A., Gropp, W., Lusk, E.: An efficient format for nearly constant-time access to arbitrary time intervals in large trace files. Sci. Program. **16**, 155–165 (2008). https://doi.org/10.3233/SPR-2008-0252. https://www.hindawi.com/journals/sp/2008/749874/cta/

9. Geimer, M., Wolf, F., Wylie, B.J.N., Ábrahám, E., Becker, D., Mohr, B.: The scalasca performance toolset architecture. Concurrency Comput. Pract. Exp. **22**(6), 702–719 (2010). https://doi.org/10.1002/cpe.1556

10. Knüpfer, A., et al.: The Vampir performance analysis tool-set. In: Resch, M., Keller, R., Himmler, V., Krammer, B., Schulz, A. (eds.) Tools for High Performance Computing, pp. 139–155. Springer, Heidelberg (2008). https://doi.org/10.1007/978-3-540-68564-7_9

11. Knüpfer, A., et al.: Score-P: a joint performance measurement run-time infrastructure for periscope, Scalasca, TAU, and Vampir. In: Brunst, H., Müller, M.S., Nagel, W.E., Resch, M.M. (eds.) Tools for High Performance Computing 2011, pp. 79–91. Springer, Heidelberg (2012). https://doi.org/10.1007/978-3-642-31476-6_7

12. Lapworth, L.: HYDRA-CFD: a framework for collaborative CFD development. In: International Conference on Scientific and Engineering Computation (ICSEC), Singapore, June, vol. 30 (2004). https://www.researchgate.net/publication/316171819_HYDRA-CFD_A_Framework_for_Collaborative_CFD_Development

13. Pillet, V., Labarta, J., Cortes, T., Girona, S.: PARAVER: a tool to visualize and analyze parallel code. In: Proceedings of WoTUG-18: Transputer and OCCAM Developments, vol. 44, pp. 17–31. IOS Press (1995). https://citeseerx.ist.psu.edu/viewdoc/download?doi=10.1.1.46.1277&rep=rep1&type=pdf

14. Saviankou, P., Knobloch, M., Visser, A., Mohr, B.: Cube v4: from performance report explorer to performance analysis tool. Procedia Comput. Sci. **51**, 1343–1352 (2015). https://doi.org/10.1016/j.procs.2015.05.320. International Conference On Computational Science, ICCS 2015

15. Schöne, R., Tschüter, R., Ilsche, T., Schuchart, J., Hackenberg, D., Nagel, W.E.: Extending the functionality of Score-P through plugins: interfaces and use cases. In: Niethammer, C., et al. (eds.) Tools for High Performance Computing 2016, pp. 59–82. Springer, Cham (2017). https://doi.org/10.1007/978-3-319-56702-0_4

16. Schroeder, W.J., Martin, K.M., Lorensen, W.E.: The design and implementation of an object-oriented toolkit for 3D graphics and visualization. In: Proceedings of Seventh Annual IEEE Visualization 1996, San Francisco, CA, USA, pp. 93–100. IEEE, October 1996. https://doi.org/10.1109/VISUAL.1996.567752

17. Schuchart, J., et al.: The READEX formalism for automatic tuning for energy efficiency. Computing **99**(8), 727–745 (2017). https://doi.org/10.1007/s00607-016-0532-7

18. Shende, S.S., Malony, A.D.: The tau parallel performance system. Int. J. High Perform. Comput. Appl. **20**(2), 287–311 (2006). https://doi.org/10.1177/1094342006064482

LSDVE - Workshop on Large Scale Distributed Virtual Environments

Workshop on Large Scale Distributed Virtual Environments (LSDVE)

Workshop Description

The 7th International Workshop on Large Scale Distributed Virtual Environments (LSDVE 2019) was held in Gottingen, Germany, in August 2019. For the seventh time, this workshop was organized in conjunction with the Euro-Par annual series of international conferences.

The main focus of the workshop has always been on large scale networked applications: distributed social networks, cryptocurrencies, blockchain technology, collaborative work, and so on. The workshop welcomes contributions both in the area of applications, and in that of the infrastructures, like peer-to-peer, fog, IoT, and so on. This year, the workshop was a venue for researchers to present and discuss important aspects of large scale networked collaborative applications and of international projects related to these topics. In particular, several contributions were presented in the area of blockchain technology which has recently been applied to different areas, like IoT, e-health, financial services, etc. In this area, important challenges are, for instance, exploitation of the classical blockchain technology to support collaborative applications, discussion on alternative distributed consensus algorithms, as well as privacy and security issues.

This year, the workshop has provided two sessions. In the first session, the paper "Bitcoin price variation: an analysis of the correlations" presents a methodological framework for the analysis of the bitcoin transaction graph which shows interesting dynamics of the bitcoin price in short time periods. The last two papers "A novel Data-Centric Programming Model for Large-Scale Parallel Systems" and "Auto-Scaling for a Streaming Architecture with Fuzzy Deep Reinforcement Learning" present some preliminary results obtained in the ASPIDE European Project. The first one shows the main features and the programming constructs of a new programming model designed for the implementation of data-centric large-scale parallel applications on Exascale computing platforms. The second one presents a streaming architecture for processing and storing data in real-time or nearly real-time for Big Data analytics and IoT.

The second section includes papers presenting contributions from the ARTICONF H2020 project. The paper "ARTICONF: towards a Smart Social Media Ecosystem in a Blockchain Federated Environment" summarizes the initial architecture of the ARTICONF ecosystem and the industrial pilot use cases for validating it. The second paper "Co-located and Orchestrated Network Fabric (CONF): An Automated Cloud Virtual Infrastructure for Social Network Applications" introduces an automated cloud virtual infrastructure solution for social network applications, while the third paper "A Semantic Model for Self-Adaptive and Autonomous Relevant Technology for Social Media Applications" describes an adaptive microservice-based design capable of finding relevant communities by extracting semantic information and applying role-stage model while preserving anonymity.

We wish to thank all who helped make this 7th edition of the workshop a sucess: authors submitting papers, colleagues who refereed the submitted papers, the numerous colleagues who attended the sessions, and finally the Euro-Par 2019 organizers whose invaluable support greatly helped in the organization of the workshop.

Organization

Program Chairs

Laura Ricci	University of Pisa, Italy
Barbara Guidi	University of Pisa, Italy
Radu Prodan	University of Klagenfurt, Austria

Program Committee

Emanuele Carlini	ISTI, CNR, Italy
Barbara Guidi	University of Pisa, Italy
Damiano Di Francesco Maesa	University of Cambridge, UK
Ombretta Gaggi	University of Padova, Italy
Dragi Kimovski	University of Klagenfurt, Austria
Kevin Koidl	Trinity College Dublin, Ireland
Paolo Mori	IIT, CNR, Italy
Claudio Palazzi	University of Padova, Italy
Symeon Papadopoulos	CERTH, Greece
Dana Pectu	University of Timisoara, Romania
Radu Prodan	University of Klagenfurt, Austria

ARTICONF: Towards a Smart Social Media Ecosystem in a Blockchain Federated Environment

Radu Prodan[1(✉)], Nishant Saurabh[1(✉)], Zhiming Zhao[2], Kate Orton-Johnson[3], Antorweep Chakravorty[4], Aleksandar Karadimce[5], and Alexandre Ulisses[6]

[1] Institute of Information Technology, University of Klagenfurt, Klagenfurt, Austria
{radu,nishant}@itec.aau.at
[2] Informatics Institute, University of Amsterdam, Amsterdam, The Netherlands
[3] School of Social and Political Science, University of Edinburgh, Edinburgh, UK
[4] Department of Electrical Engineering and Computer Science,
University of Stavanger, Stavanger, Norway
[5] University of Information Science and Technology,
Ohrid, Republic of North Macedonia
[6] MOG Technologies, Maia, Portugal

Abstract. The ARTICONF project funded by the European Horizon 2020 program addresses issues of trust, time-criticality and democratisation for a new generation of federated infrastructure, to fulfil the privacy, robustness, and autonomy related promises critical in proprietary social media platforms. It aims to: (1) simplify the creation of open and agile social media ecosystem with trusted participation using a two stage permissioned blockchain; (2) automatically detect interest groups and communities using graph anonymization techniques for decentralised and tokenized decision-making and reasoning; (3) elastically autoscale time-critical social media applications through an adaptive orchestrated Cloud edge-based infrastructure meeting application runtime requirements; and (4) enhance monetary inclusion in collaborative models through cognition and knowledge supply chains. We summarize the initial envisaged architecture of the ARTICONF ecosystem, the industrial pilot use cases for validating it, and the planned innovations compared to related other European research projects.

Keywords: Decentralized social media · Privacy · Trust · Blockchain · Semantic network · Auto-scaling · Cloud and edge computing

1 Introduction

Social media platforms are key technologies for next generation connectivity with the potential to shape and mobilise patterns of communication, practices of exchange and business, creation, learning and knowledge acquisition. Typically, social media platforms are centralised with a single proprietary organisation

---

ARTICONF receives funding from the European Union's Horizon 2020 research and innovation program under grant agreement number 825134.

U. Schwardmann et al. (Eds.): Euro-Par 2019 Workshops, LNCS 11997, pp. 417–428, 2020.
https://doi.org/10.1007/978-3-030-48340-1_32

controlling the network. This poses critical issues of trust and governance over created and propagated content. This is particularly problematic when data breaches, at the hands of centralised intermediaries, are a regular phenomenon. In order to facilitate global reach, improved trust, and decentralised control and ownership, innovative solutions at the user level (i.e. consumers, prosumers, businesses) and the underlying social media environment level are required.

The ARTICONF project funded by the Horizon 2020 programme of the European Union researches and develops a novel set of trustworthy, resilient, and globally sustainable decentralised social media services. ARTICONF addresses issues of trust, time-criticality and democratisation for a new generation of federated infrastructure, to fulfil the privacy, robustness, and autonomy related promises that proprietary social media platforms have failed to deliver.

Objective 1: Transparent and Decentralised Infrastructure Creation and Control. The ultimate aim is to simplify transparency in the creation, integration and federation of agile decentralised social media platforms. We achieve this by creating a novel permissioned blockchain with anonymized identities with two benefits. First, it improves users control with a secure, permanent and unbreakable link to their data and controls content ownership shared further down the network through an adaptive state transition modelling. Second, it allows users content be secured from any central authority, third parties or unauthorised individuals.

Objective 2: Improved and Trusted Participation. ARTICONF will deliver technologies to improve trust and eliminate malicious actors in participatory exchanges throughout the collaboration lifecycle. It will research heuristics coupled with blockchain to ensure verifiable and traceable content ownership, while preserving anonymity. It will provide abstractions to characterise diverse sets of anonymised participants and to maintain their traceability and ownership activity down the network. Through these heuristics, ARTICONF will not only be able to identify bad actors, but will also improve collaboration and trust in the environment without violating users privacy. Moreover, it will simplify and optimise maintenance costs and identify users with fake profiles to prevent the spread of malicious content.

Objective 3: Democratic and Tokenized Decision-Making. To improve democratic participatory exchanges and collaborative decision making in social media through its collective human-agent decentralised reasoning approach, ARTICONF will research heuristics to enable crowd-cooperative applications and engage with the correct audience in an anonymised ecosystem. It will also employ role-stage programming techniques and semantic abstractions to conceptualise and map the diverse geographically distributed characteristic entities. This will bring three key benefits. First, it will improve the quality of content using a collective problem solving approach with the correct subset of users. Second, it will optimise the costs of finding interest groups and communities through smart matching with precise targeting without violating users privacy and anonymity. Finally, it will provide incentivisation to the users participating in decision-making.

Objective 4: Elastic Resource Provisioning. To improve efficiency for customising, provisioning and controlling distributed peer-to-peer and Cloud virtual infrastructures required by time-critical social media applications, ARTICONF aims to deliver technologies providing a self-adaptive and self-monitored infrastructure over orchestrated networked services bringing two benefits. First, it will optimise QoS performance metrics (e.g. distribution time, latency) with proximity-based geo-profiling through seamless provisioning of a customised infrastructure across multiple geographical locations. Second, it will ensure fast recovery in the presence of faults or performance drops through rapid deployment and/or migration of application resources close to problem areas.

Objective 5: Cognitive Analytics for Improved Collaborative Economy. ARTICONF develops tools to improve efficiency and inject intelligent insights into operational and mission-critical social media businesses, achieved through guided analytics with social and predictive models for consumers, prosumers and business markets. The tools will enable contextualised socially aware and spatial-temporal data aggregation, knowledge extraction, cognitive learning about users behaviour, and risk quantification for business markets. This is seamlessly coupled with distributed blockchain-based services for early alert, real-time tracking and updated data triggers for reach and engagement analysis of events. This will allow users to analyse, control and track their return-on-investment to enhance monetary inclusion in collaborative social media.

2   Architectural Design

Given these requirements, ARTICONF researches and validates a ubiquitous social media ecosystem and platform around four important services, displayed in Fig. 1. Trust and Integration Controller (TIC), Co-located and Orchestrated Network Fabric (CONF), Semantic Model with self-adaptive and Autonomous Relevant Technology (SMART), and Tools for Analytics and Cognition (TAC).

2.1   Trust and Integration Controller (TIC)

TIC provides support for creating a decentralised social media interface around three modules. First, a federated consortium blockchain which provides a set of third party authentication providers for verification of each new user with a unique identity joining the network. Second, a relationship system, which is a Turing-complete programmable unit, features the transaction states between actors and allows users define conditions on data-sharing through smart contracts. Third, personal certificate authority which is a client software and manages user groups, securely shares the keys with their members, keeps records of shared keys, and encrypts shared data before broadcasting and storing it on the blockchain and the Cloud. By design, TIC provides agreement in nearly real-time between actors by applying byzantine fault tolerant consensus mechanism.

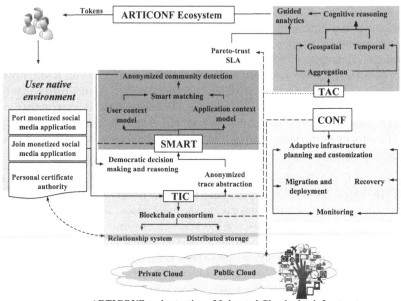

ARTICONF orchestration of federated Cloud-edge infrastructure

Fig. 1. ARTICONF architecture.

Permissioned consortium blockchain is the fundamental service of TIC for developing consistency, accountability and traceability of shared data. A set of third party authentication providers needs to be integrated for verification of each new user who joins the network for a given use case, providing them with a unique identity. Additionally, TIC designs and evaluates mechanisms for byzantine fault tolerant consensus algorithms able to provide agreement in nearly real-time between the different organisations, part of the permissioned blockchain network. To maintain the same federated truth for the users and improve upon the trusted collaboration, consortia of distinct organisations will equally own and maintain the blockchain seamlessly coupled with trust-based heuristics (e.g. game theoretic), and validate the transaction history for all users.

Cloud-based Big Data storage allows distributed storage of shared large data items, stored in a distributed manner with efficient indexing and traversals. This is important, as all participating nodes in the network must maintain a copy of the blockchain ensuring availability of the same version of truth. To reduce replication and network throughput, the blockchain only contains transactions logs referring to the fingerprints of the data items stored in the Cloud.

Relationship system is a Turing-complete programmable unit of the blockchain that features loops, internal states, and makes transactions with other actors. The computation executes on every participating node in the network to verify the validity of the shared transactions. This allows users define conditions on data sharing and use rights through smart contracts, and enable them complete control over their content. Although the blockchain removes the need for centralised authorities by entrusting the network and its peers with validation and maintenance of social interactions as transactions, it still requires mechanisms for validating user-defined conditions and successful transactions.

Certificate authority is a client software that manages user groups, securely shares the keys with their members, keeps records of shared keys, and encrypts shared data before broadcasting and storing it on the blockchain and the Cloud. It allows creation of a separate communication channel for exchange of encrypted keys between data owners and individuals with whom they share their content. It also provides identity management for users participating in the network, and ensures anonymised recording of all transactions in the blockchain, with the ability to couple them back with the original identities within local environment.

2.2   Co-located and Orchestrated Network Fabric (CONF)

CONF provides adaptive infrastructure provisioning for social media applications over an orchestrated network. It seamlessly integrates with the Cloud edge infrastructure, able to intelligently provision services based on abstract application service requirements, operational conditions at infrastructure level, and time-critical event triggering. The distribution of the networked infrastructure provisioned by CONF receives information from the intelligent community analytics of SMART and TAC services, and improves the infrastructure planning and customization of time-critical applications through predictive deployment, migration and failure-recovery. CONF extends the work developed in the SWITCH project [19] with support for blockchain [20] and social network business services.

Adaptive Infrastructure Planning Driven by Application-Level Requirements and Time-Critical Events. CONF plans an infrastructure based on social media application requirements and adapts it in response to changing conditions, ensuring a continued and sustained satisfaction of QoS requirements.

Seamless Provisioning of Customised Infrastructure Across Multiple Sites. CONF provisions services and resources based on performance and reliability, taking into account locality of data sources to minimise transfers and delays, while ensuring a smooth operation of the distributed application.

Rapid Deployment, Migration and Recovery of Application Services. Given a distributed multi-site social media infrastructure, CONF ensures efficient deployment of application services on resources close to the active infrastructure, for fast recovery in the presence of faults or performance drops.

Self-Monitoring and Self-Adaptation Based on Internal and External Stimuli. The infrastructure provisioned by CONF monitors its own state, taking timely adaptation responses to failures, performance losses or other trigger conditions. CONF also provides interfaces required by application managers for manual adaptation, and learns how to best respond to various events based on historical data and machine learning.

2.3 Semantic Model with Self-Adaptive Autonomous Relevant Technology (SMART)

SMART service provide the semantic link network (SLN) abstraction model for contextualizing diverse social media actors and applications by exploiting anonymized activity traces recorded by TIC. Moreover, SMART utilizes semantic links in SLN through graph anonymisation [9] heuristics capable of detecting relevant interest group and communities without violating users privacy and anonymity. The autonomously evolving SLN model provisions SMART adaptively respond to the changing requirements, and provide inputs to CONF. SMART also researches decentralised decision making and reputation mechanisms together with TIC for solving disputes in collaborative models. To preserve the trustful environment, SMART formalizes Pareto-trust metric as a part of SLA which quantifies the quality of implicit and explicit trust-based collaboration considering various conflicting parameters, such as content accuracy, timeliness, low latency ownership verification, and high anonymity preservation.

Semantic Framework for Federated Social Media Abstraction. SMART develops a conceptual model for federated social media involving large-scale entities with three abstraction levels, exploiting decentralised reasoning and relevant communities with interest groups: concrete perception of users and of associated smart objects in a global domain, structure of the perceived relationships, and communication among entities. SMART provides abstractions in representing diverse sets of participants over an anonymised social media through descriptions of classes of self-sovereign networked entities.

Autonomous and Adaptive User-Centric Model. SMART utilises and researches role-stage programming techniques integrating various facets of social media for the design and development of a flexible, adaptive, user-centric ecosystem, involving three essential building blocks called stages, roles and agents. For this, it develops a human-agent collective-based model describing, reasoning and conceptualising consumer, prosumer and business processes at model description and at runtime. Together with TIC, SMART researches novel and efficient algorithms to preserve the autonomous interaction between diverse agents and entities with varying roles, so that one entity can rely on the others' actions.

Anonymised Trace Abstraction. SMART develops a framework to exploit the experiential anonymised activities embedded in blockchain. Henceforth, it provides effective and quick comparison and retrieve activity traces represented at different abstraction levels, interfaced to the TAC analytic operational support.

Smart Matching with Community Detection. SMART researches graph anonymization techniques for social media businesses to engage with the correct set of audience and relevant communities based on semantic abstraction and application requirements, interfaced to the CONF immersive networking support service. It also provides techniques to shift through a large number of entities, focussing on the appropriate ones through a selection of relevant, reachable and credible channels with optimised business costs.

Decentralised Decision Making and Reputation Mechanism. Through its decentralised reasoning, SMART provides opportunities for each entity irrespective of its role to be a part of decision-making process for enhancing the efficiency of collaborative business and prosumer models. Henceforth, it provisions subjectively viewed quality and immersive content creation by eradicating disputes and dissatisfaction between entities through decentralised participation. Moreover, it provides incentivisation opportunities for all social media participants for participating in such a decentralised process through its unique ripples-based reputation mechanisms, defined through evolutionary semantics abstraction and changing entity roles at varying stages during the collaborative lifecycle.

2.4   Tools for Analytics and Cognition (TAC)

TAC provides guided analytics by coupling with inputs from TIC to social media consumer, prosumers and businesses, aggregating contextualised data over spatial-temporal boundaries based on socio-cultural abstraction and extracting knowledge. Its goal is to provide automated cognitive learning to predict user engagement with inputs from TIC, CONF and SMART, and evaluate the risk quantification for all participants to enable, track and control the return-of-investment for each participant.

Geospatial, Social-Contextual and Temporal Data Aggregation. Aggregation and visualisation of geographical and socially diverse data are an important part of digital platforms data mining, adaptive infrastructure modelling, and management. TAC develops and integrates aggregation and data-synthesis tools using state-of-the-art technologies exploiting qualitative mapping and specification of geospatial and temporal data built upon a cross-contextualised socially aware model both internal and external to ARTICONF ecosystem.

Augmented Cognition and Reasoning Model. TAC develops robust tools for monitoring and reasoning social and cognitive states and integrate them with the ARTICONF ecosystem providing social media consumers with enhanced cognitive abilities, especially under complex collaborative participation scenarios using active and automated learning methods. Through this intelligent process, TAC reduces uncertainty, double-checks validity of information and their sources in a hostile environment, and models cross-check analytical inferences in a complex and rapidly changing social media network, requiring increased collaboration and communication. This improves collaboration amongst intelligently defined communities elaborating over the shared knowledge acquisition and learning, reduces biases, and gains additional benefits by drawing on the unique set of expertise and knowledge of each participant in a non-intuitive scenario.

Guided Analytics for Collaborative Economy. TAC develops an interactive interface to assist the social media consumers, prosumers and businesses inject intelligent insights in data aggregation and cognition. This guided analytics approach goes beyond a simple review of trends in sales figures by identifying techniques for increasing revenue and predicting future outcomes for an improved collaborative economy. Moreover, it provides real-time tracking of mentions, engagements, true reach and ROI. TAC is a fundamental part of ARTICONF enhancing productivity by tracking updated data triggers. TAC also allows users analyse and control their ROI through real-time cost per engagement analysis.

3   Pilot Use Cases

ARTICONF gathered four complementary social media use cases to pilot and validate its technology.

Crowd journalism with news verification is an application providing opportunities to independent journalists and news broadcasting industry to create content outside mainstream media by gathering crowdsourced news with public participation. Two of the main challenges faced by application providers are to validate the crowdsourced news with a requirement to find precise and trustworthy participation avoiding fake news, and to provision time-critical infrastructure resources closer to news location.

Car sharing is a form of person-to-person lending or collaborative consumption, part of the sharing economy, whereby car owners rent their vehicles to other people for short periods of time. Two challenges faced by this application are low public awareness on shared mobility, and geographical constraints with precise route, types offering precise planning, reliability and optimised business costs.

Co-creation of financial value with video is a collaborative platform for publishing and subscribing to online videos, allowing non-professional users to record videos, share them on platforms and earn rewards when their video gets watched. Two challenges faced by this application are the contextualised and thematic search of audio-visual metadata in a large video library, and the security and privacy of a scalable business model that rewards users for their interactions, including but not limited to content generation.

Smart energy uses a peer-to-peer monetised utility platform to reduce the energy bill of the prosumers by stimulating energy sharing and demand response, such that with the increasing installation of distributed generation at the demand side, more consumers become prosumers and can both generate and consume energy. Such human-agent models face two challenges: lack of intelligent techniques to identify the behavioural convergence of the prosumer decisions over a specific smart appliance, and lack of efficient data management plan to keep track of the amount of energy produced by each user for efficient rewards allocation.

4   Social Media Application Development and Integration

The TIC, CONF, SMART and TAC services are integrated part of a single coherent ARTICONF social media development platform, depicted in detail in Fig. 1. Each service encapsulates part of the overall functionality of the platform, ensuring a high-level of modularity. We aim to define a high-level abstract and generic application-programming interface between each service to ensure portability and sustainability, so that new implementations works with the rest as the technology evolves. The application development occurs in three phases, each phase consisting of seven steps.

Collaborative application porting has seven steps:

1. Social media application providers begin by porting their application using TIC, configuring their suitability and integration to the underlying permissioned blockchain;
2. Providers define application and event scenarios, scale, goals and trust requirements for performance and crowd-cooperative participation.
3. SMART service exploits specific requirements to contextualize application's trust and time-critical constraints and map them onto self-organized semantic link network (SLN) data model allowing the ecosystem to link applications with similar characteristics;
4. SMART interacts with turing-complete programmable unit of TIC to obtain the logged transactional activities of anonymised users and map them onto SLN model of the ecosystem;
5. SMART triggers the CONF's network orchestrator with the virtual infrastructure hosting the application by providing inputs with regards to precise targeting of users and communities with customised geo-profiling;
6. SMART configures TAC by providing inputs to aggregation, cognition and learning modules that analyse the behaviour and engagement of the application and social media actors, diagnose performance risks, and provide guided analytics to consumer prosumers and application providers to improve collaboration and return of investment (ROI);
7. SMART provide a decision making and reasoning model integrated to TIC's consensus mechanism based on the automatically evolving SLN based contextualization model, provided constraints, exploiting diverse cognitive states of all social objects and their characteristics generated within the SMART environment, throughout the ARTICONF ecosystem lifecycle.

Collaborative elastic provisioning has three steps:

1. CONF receives application specification inputs from the SMART distributed knowledge base and customises a microservices-based virtual infrastructure based on the applications requirements;
2. CONF interacts with SMART and TIC to obtain information about the available and trusted Cloud edge resources obtained from subscribed infrastructure providers or users in the permissioned consortium, and creates a customised infrastructure that best meets the application needs;
3. CONF provisions the planned virtual infrastructure on selected edge providers closest to the event location, deploys all applications in cooperation with SMART, and finally schedules the execution of the application.

Table 1. ARTICONF innovations.

Obj.	EU project	State-of-the-art	Innovation
1	BLOOMEN [1]	Monetized content creation and sharing with distributed database	Novel time-to-transform metric Decentralised and anonymised ecosystem
	V4Design [16]	Personalized data retrieval	Two-stage configurable permissioned consortium blockchain with relationship system and PCA
2	InVID [8]	Verified and rights-cleared video content	Pareto-trust metric (tradeoffs - accuracy, timeliness, low latency ownership verification high anonymity preservation)
	SHARE4RARE [14]	Unverified data co-creation	
	FuturePulse [6]	Social media discussions	
3	REVEAL [12]	Community detection	Decentralized decision making and regulation mechanisms for improved collaboration
	X5gon [18]	Homogeneous network, learning and knowledge aquisition	
	SAUCE [13]	Contextualization, semantic labelling	
	CrowdRec [4]	Crowd engagement	
	SAM	Content syndication	Smart matching and community detection without de-anonymization
	FINE [5]	Tools for professional media producers	
4	IcoSOLE [7]	Content extraction from heterogeneous sources	Co-located and orchestrated networked infrastructure, planning, configuration and adaptation
	SWITCH [15]	Time-critical applications	
	NUBOMEDIA [10]	Time-critical Cloud applications	
	Grassroot Wavelength [17]	Scalability	Resilient and elastic provisioning with focus on time-critical social media applications
	CPN [3]	Inelastic platform	
5	ReTV	Data collection and retrieval; semantic knowledge	Novel ROC metric (operational, productivity, strategic)
	PTwist [11]	Plastic reuse application centric; circular economy	Improved monetary inclusion in a collaborative economy through smart aggregation, cognition and guided analytics
	COMPACT [2]	Improving skills guidelines in participatory model	

Application execution has two steps:

1. Through its byzantine consensus approach to maintain truth, TIC monitors the trusted behaviour of actors transaction over execution of the runtime system. It provides dynamic information to SMART and TAC, and activates the analytics and learning components in TAC for cognition and knowledge extraction via its deployed services and diagnose the runtime status when events related to cooperation, performance and security occur;
2. TIC in cooperation with SMART decides when the system is in danger of trust violations, drops in performance, or failures of the application or host

infrastructure. It then invokes the infrastructure control interface provided by CONF to adapt the infrastructure accordingly. TIC records the control and adaptation solutions of CONF and SMART, further used by TAC for analysis and guided analytics.

5 Innovation

ARTICONF innovative solutions to problems not yet covered in sufficient depth by EU-funded projects, as summarised in Table 1.

6 Conclusions

We presented the ARTICONF project and its envisioned architecture, researching and developing a novel social media ecosystem and development platform focusing on achieving a major breakthrough in transparent, decentralised infrastructure creation for social media networks; with anonymous trusted participation and democratic decision-making with underlying permissioned blockchain, peer-to-peer, and elastic Cloud edge-based technologies. The project plans to validate its results on a carefully selected set of industrial applications targeting crowd journalism with news verifications, car sharing, co-creation of financial value with videos, and smart energy sharing. The project started in January 2019 and expects to achieve its first prototype results by 2020.

References

1. BLOOMEN: Blockchain for creative work. http://bloomen.io/
2. COMPACT: Bridging western and eastern Europe for better social media and mainstream media convergence. http://compact-media.eu/
3. CPN: Content personalisation network. https://www.projectcpn.eu/
4. CrowdRec: Crowd-powered recommendation for continuous digital media. http://www.crowdrec.eu/
5. FINE: Freeview immersive networked experience. http://www.projectfine.eu/
6. FuturePulse. http://www.futurepulse.eu/
7. ICoSOLE: Immersive coverage of spatially outspread live events. http://icosole.eu/
8. InVID: In video veritas! https://www.invid-project.eu/
9. Nguyen, H.: Social Graph Anonymization. Theses, Université de Lorraine, November 2016. https://hal.inria.fr/tel-01403474
10. NUBOMEDIA: The open source cloud for real-time multimedia communications. http://www.nubomedia.eu/
11. PTwist: An open platform for plastics lifecycle awareness, monetization, and sustainable innovation. http://capssi.eu/caps-projects/ptwist/
12. REVEAL: Realising education through virtual environments and augmented locations. https://revealvr.eu/
13. SAUCE: Smart asset re-use in creative environments. https://www.sauceproject.eu/

14. Share4Rare: Social media platform dedicated to rare diseases, using collective intelligence for the generation of awareness and advanced knowledge on this large group of diseases. http://capssi.eu/caps-projects/share4rare/

15. SWITCH: Software workbench for interactive, time critical and highly self-adaptive cloud applications. http://www.switchproject.eu/

16. V4Design: Visual and textual content re-purposing for architecture, design and virtual reality games. https://v4design.eu/

17. Grassroot Wavelengths: Highly networked grassroots community radio through a scalable digital platform. https://capssi.eu/caps-projects/grassroots-wavelengths/

18. X5GON: Cross modal, cross cultural, cross lingual, cross domain, and cross site global OER network artificial intelligence and open educational resources. https://www.x5gon.org/

19. Zhao, Z., et al.: A software workbench for interactive, time critical and highly self-adaptive cloud applications (SWITCH). In: 2015 15th IEEE/ACM International Symposium on Cluster, Cloud and Grid Computing. IEEE, May 2015. https://doi.org/10.1109/ccgrid.2015.73

20. Zhou, H., de Laat, C., Zhao, Z.: Trustworthy cloud service level agreement enforcement with blockchain based smart contract. In: 2018 IEEE International Conference on Cloud Computing Technology and Science, CloudCom. IEEE, December 2018. https://doi.org/10.1109/cloudcom2018.2018.00057

Bitcoin Price Variation: An Analysis of the Correlations

Barbara Guidi[ID] and Andrea Michienzi[(✉)][ID]

Department of Computer Science, University of Pisa,
Largo B. Pontecorvo, 56127 Pisa, Italy
{guidi,andrea.michienzi}@di.unipi.it

Abstract. The Bitcoin system is attracting a huge community both from specialists and common people, who see in it a great opportunity of investment. Thanks to the fact that the Bitcoin blockchain in publicly available, and considering that it shows properties of a real economy, Bitcoin is becoming more and more often subject of a number of studies. One of the hardest task in this field, yet interesting also from a non specialist point of view, is the bitcoin price correlation and prediction. In this paper we present a methodological framework for the bitcoin exchange graph analysis which helps in focusing only on restricted time spans that show interesting dynamics of the bitcoin price. We also present our study on three separate time spans and show that empirical correlations can be found between the bitcoin price and some bitcoin exchange graph measures. Lastly, with our framework we are also able to detect some unexpected behaviour from particular users which tend to pile up big amounts of bitcoin over the selected time spans.

Keywords: Bitcoin · Blockchain · Graph analysis · Cryptocurrency

1 Introduction

During the last decades we witnessed to the birth of numerous cryptocurrencies, which had a huge impact on the economic systems. Contrary to the well known currencies, a cryptocurrency is not issued by a bank or government, but instead rely on a set of cryptographic tools and distributed consensus protocols used by the users. Therefore, there is no more a central entity, usually a bank, which checks that a payment is valid, but instead all the users of the system have to cooperate such that only valid payments are accepted. Up to date, the most famous cryptocurrency is Bitcoin [17], which is based on the blockchain technology. For the sake of clarity, we use the term *Bitcoin*, with capital *B*, to refer to the whole distributed system, and we use the term *bitcoin*, with lower case *b*, to refer to the currency unit. Bitcoin came out in early January 2009 as the first functioning cryptocurrency, and over time attracted a lot of interest, both from specialists, coming mainly from computer science and economics fields, and also common people. This widespread interest gathered a very big community, which

U. Schwardmann et al. (Eds.): Euro-Par 2019 Workshops, LNCS 11997, pp. 429–441, 2020.
https://doi.org/10.1007/978-3-030-48340-1_33

resulted in the first example of worldwide cryptocurrency economy, thus making it worth to be studied. Contrary to what one may think, the whole history of transactions of Bitcoin is public, meaning that one can read all the transactions issued without even being a Bitcoin user. This attracted a lot of interest in studying the properties of the system from a usage point of view. In fact, we find several studies in literature that try to characterise the system from a purely economic point of view [4,6,10]. From computer scientists a lot of effort was put in the study of the transaction graph for various purposes [9,12,13,18]. The most studied topic on Bitcoin is the bitcoin price prediction, which was proven to be a very difficult task. Despite the fact that this problem was tackled with the most various techniques [1,7,8,14], the prediction accuracy is very limited.

In this paper we present a different kind of study, in which we try to find correlations between the bitcoin price and some relevant measures of the transaction graph. Our contribution consists of:

- A methodological framework for studying the transaction graph in terms of users and the transactions among them;
- A study of the transaction graph using some efficient techniques in order to determine possible correlation between the bitcoin price and the bitcoin exchanges among users;
- The detection of particular users, which follow an irregular pattern of acquisition of bitcoin.

With respect to similar studies [2,10,19], we make our framework self-contained, meaning that it does not need information coming from outside the Bitcoin blockchain, and focused on very specific time spans which show particular characteristics. Restricting the study on specific time spans, rather than on the whole blockchain, helps in having a focused view, which buries out previously undetected correlations and users with unexpected behaviours.

The rest of this paper is organised as follows: Sect. 2 presents the state of the art regarding the main studies on the Bitcoin transaction and bitcoin price. Section 3 contains the proposed framework from the information stored on the Bitcoin blockchain to the results, while Sect. 4 presents and discusses the obtained results. Concludes the paper Sect. 5 pointing out some possible future works.

2   State of the Art

Blockchain based systems, and Bitcoin in particular, attracted a lot of interest from researchers, especially computer scientists and economists. The Bitcoin blockchain has been studied for the sake of a number of different purposes, including P2P network analysis and the de-anonymization [11,18], anomaly detection [13], or quantitative analysis [9,12]. Yet, the most interesting aspects to be studied, from a multidisciplinar point of view, are the ones related to the bitcoin price, that is the amount of dollars one has to pay to buy a bitcoin. In particular bitcoin price prediction has attracted a lot of interest, with techniques coming machine learning [14], time series analysis [1] or theory of signals [7]. We also find studies about bitcoin price volatility [8], and studies that try to determine the factors that drives the bitcoin price, such as supply and demand [4], attractiveness [10], or a combination of them [6]. Some interesting studies also find good correlations between bitcoin price and *Google Trends* or *Wikipedia* queries [10], or attempts in speculative trading [2].

However studies in which author try to correlate the bitcoin price with measures from the transaction graph are lacking. In [19] authors study the whole blockchain, up to block at height 317,000 (October 2014), with the aim of trying to find correlations between the Bitcoin graph of transaction and the bitcoin price. In particular, they studied the α value of the power-law distribution of the transactions, the number of nodes and edges of the transaction graph, the size of the blocks, and lastly the bitcoin gains distribution. The findings show a positive correlation between bitcoin price and number of edges, and number of nodes of the transaction graph, and a similar result for the block size. Instead authors observe no correlation with the α values of the power laws, and a negative correlation with the bitcoin gains.

3 Bitcoin Rate Study: Methodology

The aim in this paper is to analyse the evolution over time of the bitcoin exchange rate, possibly showing a correlation with other properties of the Bitcoin system. As a major novelty introduced in this paper, we will only focus on some specific time spans. The idea of focusing the study on short time spans comes from the fact that analysing the whole blockchain may not show specific behaviours happening during particular events. Restricting the study to very short time spans will help us in having a more detailed view. Before venturing forward in the description of the methodology used, we introduce some basic concepts to help the reader understand the process.

3.1 Transaction Graph and User Graph

In order to analyse the Bitcoin price variation and the correlation with other characteristics, we need to model the activity of Bitcoin. Within the Bitcoin blockchain, payments are stored in transactions which can have multiple inputs and multiple outputs. Therefore, the most natural modelling tool to model the set of all transactions is an hypergraph. An hypergraph $H = (X, E)$ is a generalization of a graph in which edges, or hyperedges, have as source and destination sets of nodes. With this model, we can easily model transactions as hyper-edges: the set of input addresses makes the source of the edge, and the set of output addresses makes the destination of the edge. In this way we are able to build the so called Transaction graph. It is important to point out that in the Transaction graph the set X of nodes is made of the Bitcoin addresses of the users, not the users themselves. In fact, users are also encouraged to create more addresses so that their privacy is protected. Analysing the Transaction graph is not trivial for the following reasons:

- The Transaction graph is an hypergraph, and therefore the well known measures and algorithms must be adapted;
- The two ends of the edges are Bitcoin addresses, not Bitcoin users, so when we perform the analysis we also must take into account this fact.

It is important for us not to consider the transactions of the Bitcoin system, but actually how users of the Bitcoin system exchange bitcoins. We introduce a different model, called the User graph $G = (V, E)$ as a multigraph in which the set of vertices V is used to model the users of Bitcoin and the set of edges E is used to model the bitcoin exchanged by the users. In this model, each user $v \in V$ is associated with one or more addresses and each transaction is associated with one or more edge $e \in E$ if the User graph.

3.2   From the Transaction to the User Graph

Switching from the Transaction graph to the User graph is not an easy task. The biggest challenges are strictly related to the process used to determine which addresses belong to the same user. In literature there are several heuristics to cluster addresses belonging to the same user based on change analysis [15,20], on temporal information [16], or other features [5]. The most well known heuristic is the *common-input-ownership heuristic* [17], formulated by Satoshi Nakamoto himself. This heuristic states that all the inputs of a transaction are likely to belong to the same user. This is because Bitcoin expects that each input of a transaction is signed by the respective owner, and since a private key is needed to sing inputs, it is unlikely that inputs of the same transaction belong to different users. The common-input-ownership is just an heuristic, meaning that even if it makes sense to consider the addresses appearing as input of a transaction belonging to the same user, we have no certainty that this process exactly associates users to their addresses. On the other hand, new techniques are rising, such as CoinJoin, Mixcoin [3], and Blindcoin [21], based on mixing different payments in the same Bitcoin transaction, which cause these heuristics to produce a lot of false positives. However, for what concern this work, we stick to the application of the plain common-input-ownership heuristic [17], as it shows good results while remaining very simple and intuitive.

If we apply recursively the common-input-ownership heuristic to the Transaction graph we observe two effects:

- The resulting nodes of the hypergraph are the users of Bitcoin;
- The resulting hyper-edges have a single node as source of the edge.

At this point, it is enough to split the hyper-edges in simple edges to obtain a multigraph where nodes model the users and edges model the bitcoin exchange between the users, or, in other words, the User graph.

3.3   Study of the User Graph

In this paper we are interesting in the study of the User graph, with the particular intent of finding correlation between the bitcoin exchange rate and measures of

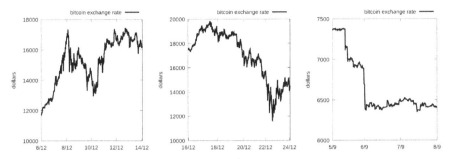

(a) Bitcoin exchange rate **(b)** Bitcoin exchange rate **(c)** Bitcoin exchange rate between the 7th and 13th of between the 16th and 23rd between the 5th and 7th of December 2017   of December 2017   September 2018

Fig. 1. Bitcoin exchange rate in the three considered time spans

the graph. For bitcoin exchange rate we mean the number of dollars needed to buy one bitcoin from a reference exchanger. To carry on this study, we firstly detected interesting time spans where the bitcoin exchange rate is extremely volatile. At this point, we built the Transaction graph limited to that time span, and then we created the User graph derived from it.

Before venturing forward in presenting the analyses performed and the intuition behind them, we briefly present and motivate the three time spans chosen. The three spans have two main characteristics:

– They show high fluctuation of the bitcoin exchange rate;
– They are shorter than 7 days.

The request of having an high fluctuation of the bitcoin exchange rate during the time span comes from the fact that we expect to detect unusual behaviours in these cases, rather than when the bitcoin exchange rate is stable. Having spans shorter than 7 days help us to concentrate our efforts in time proximity of such events, so that a causality relation between the fluctuation of the bitcon exchange rate and possible unexpected behaviour can be established.

The first analysed time span starts on the 7th and ends on the 13th of December 2017. As we can see from Fig. 1a, the fluctuation of the bitcoin exchange rate is quite high during all the week. The rate starts just below 13,000$ per bitcoin on the 7th, then raises to 17,000$ in just one day. In the following three days we observe the rate continuously rise and fall, often by over 1,000$ per bitcoin, reaching 13,500$ per bitcoin on the 10th. In the last few days the bitcoin exchange rate increases once again, reaching the time span maximum of almost 17,500$ per bitcoin on the last day.

The second time span considered starts on the 16th and ends on the 23rd of December 2017, just a few days later than the first one. Figure 1a shows the bitcoin exchange rate in this time span. At the beginning of the time span, a bitcoin is exchanged for 18,000$, and the rate has a steep increase at the beginning of the 17th, reaching the all-time high of 19,783.06\$ per bitcoin at the end of the same day. Then we observe a gradual decrease of the bitcoin exchange rate, with two big drops on the 20th, from 19,000\$ to 16,000\$ per bitcoin, and on the 22nd, from 17,000\$ to 12,000\$ per bitcoin.

The last time span analysed starts on the 5th and ends on the 7rd of September 2018. This last time span is several months further in time, with respect to the first two, and it is shorter, lasting only three days, but contains a very steep drop, which was of relevant interest for our particular study. The bitcoin exchange rate of this time span is shown in Fig. 1c. As we observe, the exchange rate is much more stable in this time span, except for the two sharp drops. The first one happens on the 5th, around midday, and consist of the drop from 7,400\$ to 7,000\$ per bitcoin, while the second one happens on the 6th, around 1 AM, and consist of the drop from 7,000\$ to 6,400\$ per bitcoin. After this steep two-step drop, we observe that the bitcoin exchange rate remains stable around 6,400\$ per bitcoin for the rest of the time span considered. We decided to keep also this two days long tail to possibly observe users acquiring a big amount of bitcoin after the drop of the day before.

4   Bitcoin Exchange Rate Correlation Studies

In this section we present the results of our study in which we try to find correlation between the bitcoin exchange rate and some properties of the User graph. It is important to point out that in this paper we will only focus on empirical correlation found in the various plots we produced.

4.1   Number of Bitcoin Exchanged

Our first idea is to study the correlation between the bitcoin exchange rate and the number of bitcoin exchanged over the same time span. The results we present are aggregated every six hours. Figures 2a, b, and c show the bitcoin exchange rate (black) and the number of bitcoin exchanged (grey) during the three time spans considered. Due to different orders of magnitudes, the bitcoin exchange rate is plotted using the left scale, while the number of bitcoin exchanged is plotted using the right scale. In all three cases we see that the number of bitcoins exchanged follows a periodic pattern of 24 h, which suggests us that this is highly correlated with human life. With respect to the rate, instead, we observe that there is some positive correlation, especially in the two December spans. In detail, in the first December span (Fig. 2a), we see that when the bitcoin exchange rate is high, also the number of exchanged bitcoin is high and vice versa. This correlation is much more clear in the second half of the time span. Also in the second December span (Fig. 2b) we can see this correlation: when the exchange rate is high, the number of bitcoin exchanged ranges between 50,000 and 85,000, while when the exchange rate is low, the number of bitcoin exchanged ranges

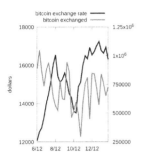 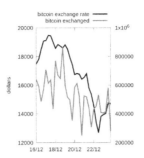 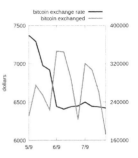

(a) Correlation graph be-
tween the bitcoin exchange
rate and the number of bitcoin exchanged from the 7th
to the 13th of December
2017

(b) Correlation graph be-
tween the bitcoin exchange
rate and the number of bitcoin exchanged from the
16th to the 23rd of December 2017

(c) Correlation graph be-
tween the bitcoin exchange
rate and the number of bitcoin exchanged from the 5th
to the 7th of September
2018

Fig. 2. Correlation graph between the bitcoin exchange rate and the number of bitcoin exchanged in the three considered time spans

between 20,000 and 50,000. In the last time span (Fig. 2c), due to its low length, there seems to be not a clear correlation, however we can see that, one day after the steep drop of the bitcoin exchange rate, also the number of bitcoin exchanged seem to drop accordingly.

4.2 Number of Transactions and Number of Users

Having seen that there is a certain degree of correlation between the bitcoin exchange rate and the number of bitcoin exchanged, we analyse the User graph to check if there is a similar correlation found in Sect. 4.1, but this time with the number of nodes and edges in the user graph. Nodes and edges in the User graph correspond to the number of users involved in at least one transaction (nodes) and to the number of transactions (edges). Figures 3a, b, and c show the bitcoin exchange rate (black), and the number of nodes and edges in the User graph (grey) during the three time spans considered. Due to different orders of magnitudes, the bitcoin exchange rate is plotted using the left scale, while the number of nodes and edges are plotted using the right scale. Also the number of nodes and edges in the User graph seem to follow a 24 h recurring pattern, lust like the bitcoin exchange rate, confirming that the Bitcoin ecosystem is highly related to human activities. Concerning possible correlations, what we expected was to find a good degree of correlation, also according to similar studies present in literature. However, what we can see from the three plots is that there is no clear correlation as in all cases the number of nodes and edges in the graph tend to remain much more stable in time. In any case, we observe that during the first two spans, when the bitcoin exchange rate is always higher than 13,000$ per bitcoin, the number of nodes and edges in the User graph fluctuates around

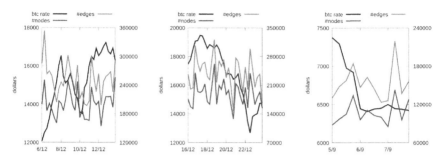

(a) Correlation graph be-
tween the bitcoin exchange
rate and the number of
nodes and edges in the User
graph from the 7th to the
13th of December 2017

(b) Correlation graph be-
tween the bitcoin exchange
rate and the number of
nodes and edges in the User
graph from the 16th to the
23rd of December 2017

(c) Correlation graph be-
tween the bitcoin exchange
rate and the number of
nodes and edges in the User
graph from the 5th to the
7th of September 2018

Fig. 3. Correlation graph between the bitcoin exchange rate and the number of nodes
and edges in the User graph in the three considered time spans

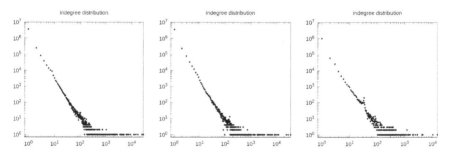

(a) Indegree distribution of
the User graph from the
7th to the 13th of December
2017

(b) Indegree distribution of
the User graph from the
16th to the 23rd of December 2017

(c) Indegree distribution of
the User graph from the
5th to the 7th of September
2018

Fig. 4. Indegree distribution of the User graph in the three considered time spans

20,000, while in the last span, when the exchange rate is halved, the number of
nodes and edges in the User graph is also lower. Finally, we also notice that the
number of nodes is similar to the number of edges in the User graph, suggesting
us that the degree distribution may be a power law.

This expectation was fully met, as we can see from the distribution of in
degree, Fig. 4, and out degree, Fig. 5, for the three time spans in log-log plots. It
is also interesting to see that the distribution of both degrees of the September
time span, Fig. 4c for the indegree and Fig. 5c for the outdegree, present some
possible outliers which are worth to be investigated.

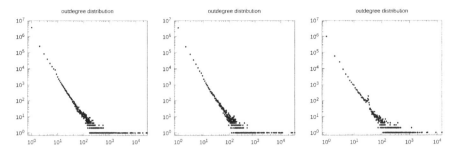

(a) Outdegree distribution of the User graph from the 7th to the 13th of December 2017

(b) Outdegree distribution of the User graph from the 16th to the 23rd of December 2017

(c) Outdegree distribution of the User graph from the 5th to the 7th of September 2018

Fig. 5. Outdegree distribution of the User graph in the three considered time spans

4.3 Bitcoin Gain Distribution

After having detected some possible anomalies in the out degree distribution of the User graph, we tried to further concentrate our effort in discovering the source of this effect. In particular, we study the bitcoin gain distribution, that is the number of bitcoin gained by the users. It is important to point out that the gain distribution has nothing to do with the exchange rate, as we are not measuring how many dollars each user gained. Measuring the gain distribution sums up to count, for each user separately, the number of bitcoin on the incoming edges and subtracting the number of bitcoin on the outgoing edges, and then plotting the distribution of the obtained values. The distribution of the bitcoin gain, during the three time spans considered, are presented in Figs. 6a, b, and c. Also in this case, the y axis has a logarithmic scale while the x axis has a

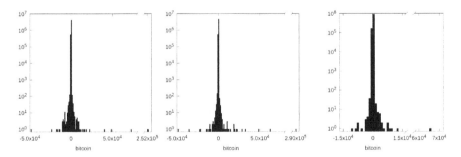

(a) Bitcoin gain distribution from the 7th to the 13th of December 2017

(b) Bitcoin gain distribution from the 16th to the 23rd of December 2017

(c) Bitcoin gain distribution from the 5th to the 7th of September 2018

Fig. 6. Bitcoin gain distribution in the three considered time spans

linear scale. Moreover, for readability reasons, we skipped some values on the x axis because they were empty, and we grouped the distribution values in bins of 1,000 bitcoin each. The three distributions follow a Gaussian law centered on 0 with not much variance, showing us that the vast majority of the users does not gain any bitcoin. Considering how we built the User graph, almost all users that acquire bitcoin usually spend them within one week or less. While in this case we see no clear correlation between the bitcoin exchange rate and the bitcoin gain distribution, as the three plots do not show any particular difference, we observe that in all the cases we have an outlier. The outlier is located in all three cases on the right side of the distribution, meaning that he gained bitcoin, rather than giving them away. The address of the outlier is different in each case, meaning that it is not the same user. Moreover, we observe that the amount of bitcoin gained is sensibly higher compared to all the other users: more than 250,000 bitcoin in the two December spans, and 65,000 in the September span.

4.4   Gain Outliers

As final step of this analysis, we study the bitcoin gain outliers. The aim is to see if they adopt a particular pattern to acquire bitcoin, and if the pattern is correlated in some way to the bitcoin exchange rate. Figures 7a, b, and c show the bitcoin exchange rate (black), and the number of bitcoin gained by the outlier (grey) during the three time spans considered. Each plot shows only the outlier found in the same time span, considering the outliers as different users. Due to different orders of magnitudes, the bitcoin exchange rate is plotted using the left scale, while the number of bitcoin gained by the outlier is plotted using the right scale. From these plots we observe that the outliers tend to acquire most of the bitcoin in a very short time span. In fact, in the first December span, Fig. 7a, 70,000 bitcoins, roughly 22% of the total amount of bitcoin acquired by the outlier in the whole time span, are acquired between 6 AM and midday on the

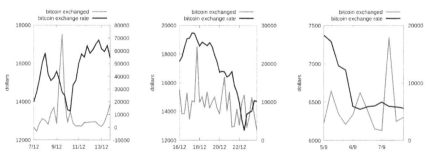

(a)   Bitcoin   outlier   gain   (b)   Bitcoin   outlier   gain   (c)   Bitcoin   outlier   gain from the 7th to the 13th of   from the 16th to the 23rd of   from the 5th to the 7th of December 2017   December 2017   September 2018

Fig. 7. Bitcoin outlier gain in the three considered time spans

9th of December. We have a similar situation, although less highlighted, in the second December span, Fig. 7b, with 25,000 bitcoin in six hours, out of almost 300,000 acquired in the whole span. Also in the third span, Fig. 7c, we observe that the outlier gathered almost 28% of the total amount of bitcoin in just six hours. Anyway, while there is a clear pattern with which the outliers acquire bitcoin, there seems to be not a clear strategy. In fact, in the first and third spans we observe that the peak is very close to the lowest point of the bitcoin exchange rate. This is not true in the second time span, in which the peak is instead close to the highest point of the bitcoin exchange rate. However, in the second case, the bitcoin acquired by the outlier are more evenly distributed over time, which, joint to the fact that the exchanged rate reached its all time high value, makes us think that there was high uncertainty whether the exchange rate would grow even further or not.

5   Conclusion and Future Works

In this paper we tackled the problem of finding correlations between the bitcoin exchange rate and measures on the User graph. We proposed a methodological framework that, starting from the transactions stored on the Bitcoin blockchain, let us study the User graph in a temporal way, focusing only on specific time spans. In detail, the framework consist of starting from the Transaction graph, an hypergraph where nodes are sets of Bitcoin addresses and edges are the Bitcoin transactions. On the Transaction graph, the common-input-ownership [17] heuristic is applied so that in the resulting graph nodes can be identified with the users of Bitcoin. The resulting graph, called User graph, is a multigraph where each node correspond to a Bitcoin user, and each edge models a bitcoin exchange. We studied several topological measures of the User graph built on limited time spans, which let us identify previously undetected correlations which may also help in the price prediction task. We, moreover, detected some users with unusual behaviour which stockpile bitcoin with unusual patterns.

As future works, we plan to deepen our studies in three directions. At first, we want to replicate our studies on more time spans, possibly characterising them in few categories based on the bitcoin exchange rate, such as "big increase", "big decrease", "stability", or "high volatility". A second direction to follow is the one of analysing the User graph in more detail, studying more measures, using more advanced techniques or at a finer granularity, but also different heuristics used to detect the users of Bitcoin. One last direction to follow is to study more in depth the outliers and, in particular, use some advanced de-anonymization technique to discover if the user corresponds to a person or an entity, or find out more of the piling up of bitcoin by these users.

References

1. Amjad, M., Shah, D.: Trading bitcoin and online time series prediction. In: NIPS 2016 Time Series Workshop, pp. 1–15 (2017)
2. Blau, B.M.: Price dynamics and speculative trading in bitcoin. Res. Int. Bus. Finan. **41**, 493–499 (2017)
3. Bonneau, J., Narayanan, A., Miller, A., Clark, J., Kroll, J.A., Felten, E.W.: Mixcoin: anonymity for bitcoin with accountable mixes. In: Christin, N., Safavi-Naini, R. (eds.) FC 2014. LNCS, vol. 8437, pp. 486–504. Springer, Heidelberg (2014). https://doi.org/10.1007/978-3-662-45472-5_31
4. Buchholz, M., Delaney, J., Warren, J., Parker, J.: Bits and bets, information, price volatility, and demand for bitcoin. Economics **312**, 2–48 (2012)
5. Remy, C., Rym, B., Matthieu, L.: Tracking bitcoin users activity using community detection on a network of weak signals. In: Cherifi, C., Cherifi, H., Karsai, M., Musolesi, M. (eds.) COMPLEX NETWORKS 2017. SCI, vol. 689, pp. 166–177. Springer, Cham (2018). https://doi.org/10.1007/978-3-319-72150-7_14
6. Ciaian, P., Rajcaniova, M., Kancs, D.: The economics of bitcoin price formation. Appl. Econ. **48**(19), 1799–1815 (2016)
7. Delfin-Vidal, R., Romero-Meléndez, G.: The fractal nature of bitcoin: evidence from wavelet power spectra. In: Pinto, A.A., Accinelli Gamba, E., Yannacopoulos, A.N., Hervés-Beloso, C. (eds.) Trends in Mathematical Economics, pp. 73–98. Springer, Cham (2016). https://doi.org/10.1007/978-3-319-32543-9_5
8. Dyhrberg, A.H.: Bitcoin, gold and the dollar-a garch volatility analysis. Finan. Res. Lett. **16**, 85–92 (2016)
9. Kondor, D., Pósfai, M., Csabai, I., Vattay, G.: Do the rich get richer? An empirical analysis of the bitcoin transaction network. PloS one **9**(2), e86197 (2014)
10. Kristoufek, L.: Bitcoin meets google trends and wikipedia: quantifying the relationship between phenomena of the internet era. Sci. Rep. **3**, 3415 (2013)
11. Maesa, D.D.F., Franceschi, M., Guidi, B., Ricci, L.: Bitker: a p2p kernel client for bitcoin. In: 2018 International Conference on High Performance Computing & Simulation (HPCS), pp. 130–137 (2018)
12. Maesa, D.D.F., Marino, A., Ricci, L.: Uncovering the bitcoin blockchain: an analysis of the full users graph. In: 2016 IEEE DSAA, pp. 537–546 (2016)
13. Maesa, D.D.F., Marino, A., Ricci, L.: Detecting artificial behaviours in the bitcoin users graph. Online Soc. Netw. Media **3–4**, 63–74 (2017)
14. McNally, S., Roche, J., Caton, S.: Predicting the price of bitcoin using machine learning. In: 2018 26th Euromicro PDP, pp. 339–343 (2018)
15. Meiklejohn, S., et al.: A fistful of bitcoins: characterizing payments among men with no names. In: Proceedings of the 2013 Conference on Internet Measurement Conference, pp. 127–140 (2013)
16. Monaco, J.V.: Identifying bitcoin users by transaction behavior. In: Biometric and Surveillance Technology for Human and Activity Identification XII, vol. 9457, p. 945704. International Society for Optics and Photonics (2015)
17. Nakamoto, S.: Bitcoin: A peer-to-peer electronic cash system (2008)
18. Reid, F., Harrigan, M.: An analysis of anonymity in the bitcoin system. In: Altshuler, Y., Elovici, Y., Cremers, A., Aharony, N., Pentland, A. (eds.) Security and privacy in social networks, pp. 197–223. Springer, New YorK (2013). https://doi.org/10.1007/978-1-4614-4139-7_10
19. Sorgente, M., Cibils, C.: The reaction of a network: exploring the relationship between the bitcoin network structure and the bitcoin price (2014)

20. Spagnuolo, M., Maggi, F., Zanero, S.: BitIodine: extracting intelligence from the bitcoin network. In: Christin, N., Safavi-Naini, R. (eds.) FC 2014. LNCS, vol. 8437, pp. 457–468. Springer, Heidelberg (2014). https://doi.org/10.1007/978-3-662-45472-5_29

21. Valenta, L., Rowan, B.: Blindcoin: blinded, accountable mixes for bitcoin. In: Brenner, M., Christin, N., Johnson, B., Rohloff, K. (eds.) FC 2015. LNCS, vol. 8976, pp. 112–126. Springer, Heidelberg (2015). https://doi.org/10.1007/978-3-662-48051-9_9

A Semantic Model with Self-adaptive and Autonomous Relevant Technology for Social Media Applications

Zahra Najafabadi Samani$^{(\boxtimes)}$, Alexander Lercher, Nishant Saurabh, and Radu Prodan

Institute of Information Technology, University of Klagenfurt, Klagenfurt, Austria
{zahra,alexander,nishant,radu}@itec.aau.at

Abstract. With the rapidly increasing popularity of social media applications, decentralized control and ownership is taking more attention to preserve user's privacy. However, the lack of central control in the decentralized social network poses new issues of collaborative decision making and trust to this permission-less environment. To tackle these problems and fulfill the requirements of social media services, there is a need for intelligent mechanisms integrated to the decentralized social media that consider trust in various aspects according to the requirement of services. In this paper, we describe an adaptive microservice-based design capable of finding relevant communities and accurate decision making by extracting semantic information and applying role-stage model while preserving anonymity. We apply this information along with exploiting Pareto solutions to estimate the trust in accordance with the quality of service and various conflicting parameters, such as accuracy, timeliness, and latency.

Keywords: Semantic information · Community detection · Pareto-trust · Decentralized social media · Role-stage model

1 Introduction

Recently, decentralized social media applications (e.g. crowd journalism, car sharing, collaborative video creation) is gaining traction. Such systems with underlying decentralized social media orchestrate diverse actors into a permission-less peer-to-peer network with threefold benefits. First, it improves users control with a secure, permanent and unbreakable link to their data. Second, it allows users' content to be secured from any central authority, third parties or unauthorized individuals through a smart contract. Third and foremost, it provides a democratic environment where a user can join or leave the network at any time (based on peer-to-peer principle) with the same right for decision making and voting for a consensus. This will facilitate global availability and decentralized control and ownership. Although such systems truly democratize the technical world of social media, yet they pose some serious challenges [3,8].

© Springer Nature Switzerland AG 2020
U. Schwardmann et al. (Eds.): Euro-Par 2019 Workshops, LNCS 11997, pp. 442–451, 2020.
https://doi.org/10.1007/978-3-030-48340-1_34

Essentially, decentralized social media is often described as a trust-less system. While inherently they do not actually eliminate trust, they instead minimize the amount of trust required from any single actor in the system. Primarily, such permission-less based social media hinder the process to tackle prominent issues such as fake news, cultural barriers, biased propaganda, trolling, identifying malicious content, and bad social media actors. To mitigate such challenges, there is a need to research for intelligent design addressing trust based on various social media requirements [18]. By contrast, in most previous works trust does not address all the service requirements [2]. Hence, we propose a Semantic Model with self-adaptive and Autonomous Relevant Technology (SMART) architectural framework applying trust through various parameters according to quality of service (QoS) metrics such as accuracy, timeliness, and latency. SMART exploits Pareto solutions and game-theory based optimization approach to find the right and trustworthy subset of users participating in consensus process and social media applications.

However, integrating trust in a permission-less network requires utilizing the contextualized activity traces over the time [8,11]. More precisely, if activity traces are semantically linked at contextual levels, this would (i) significantly improve detection of the correct set of audience, interested groups and relevant communities, (ii) provide adaptive infrastructure provisioning for time-critical events (e.g. corresponding to an accident via news) across the right subset of user's geo-location, and (iii) inject intelligent insights across different communities, groups, and users into pattern prediction, recommendation and decision making. Finally, it will significantly improve trusted participation in collaborative social media applications.

Several studies were proposed to analyze decentralized network and identify network construction. To the best of our knowledge, those methods mostly focus on link analysis without content analysis to infer activity traces [9,13,17], while network topology alone can not precisely reveal peers behavior pattern in the network. Hence, SMART adopts a novel community detection approach based on a role-stage model to precisely identify implicit and explicit behaviors and interactions of participants in the network by dynamically extracting semantic information along with network topology while preserving peers privacy and anonymity. In order to give better control over the design, implementation and evolution of the system, we design SMART based on microservices [5].

The paper is organized as follows. Initially, we survey in Sect. 2 the research background related to our work. Section 3 outlines the architecture of the proposed model, further discussed in Sect. 4 and followed by possible future directions and open issues. We conclude the paper in Sect. 5.

2   Related Work

In this section we introduce the state of the art barriers existing in the social networks with relation to our research.

Decentralized Social Media. Centralized social media creates critical issues of trust and privacy [3,6,8]. Towards this issue, decentralized social media have been proposed to provide more control over private data. While decentralized social media is widely documented to demonstrate availability, democratic decision making, and ownership in the social media, they face their own problems and challenges such as identifying malicious content and bad social media actors, tracking peers behavior pattern and network analyses, and Trust in social media platforms [3,8,11]. Here, we briefly review some recent proposed solutions to address these problems.

Identification of Malicious Actors. The anonymization of identities across self sovereign identity in decentralized network make them vulnerable to misbehaviour in the network for illegal interests. Therefore, several studies were proposed to analyse decentralized network for identifying malicious actors. Maesa et al. [14] inferred unusual behavior of outliers by analyzing the Bitcoin users graph. The authors illustrated that these behaviours are a consequence of unusual chains of transactions, which indicated the existence of outliers in the in-degree of frequency distribution and the high diameter of the users graph. To identify attacks, Meiklejohn et al. [15] grouped Bitcoin users by adopting a heuristic based on changed addresses to cluster addresses belonging to the same user. However, this approach considered static network which is in conflict with the reality.

Tracking Peers Behavior Pattern and Network Analyses. To provide appropriate services, it is crucial to have a clear understanding of evolving relationships among data and predict their future trend. However, tracking users behavior in an anonymized heterogeneous environment is very challenging as illustrated by several decentralized network studies. Most of them extracted the user link graph to track users behavior, while transaction graph alone does not declare all of the relationships in the network. The authors in [9,17] introduced a method for tracing users behavior in decentralized network based on the similarity of sequences extracted from the transactions over the time.

The authors in [17] clustered nodes by exploiting a behavior pattern clustering algorithm after measuring the sequences similarity, while in [9] they adopted an end-to-end neural network to classify peers. The work in [13] provided analyses of the user link graph in Bitcoin to trace users behavior and derived the user graph from the transaction graph by a clustering process. The research in [7] provided a community detection approach (SONIC-MAN) within ego-network of the users to track peers behavior pattern in distributed online social networks. SONIC-MAN is based on a Temporal Trade-off approach adopting a set of superpeers, chosen from the nodes in the ego networks, to the manage communities over time.

Trust in Social Media Platforms. Trust plays an important role in decision making, recommendations and consensus reached between multiple users [18]. Therefore, there have been several researches that introduced trust based on different value to offer more relevant services. Azadjalal et al. [2] proposed a method to identify the most trustworthy users for the recommendation process by exploiting a reliability measure and Pareto solution. The authors calculated the unknown rating values to identify trust relationships, however, they did not take into account QoS factors to identify trustworthy users. Alhanahnah et al. [1] provided a trust framework considering factors according to both service characteristics and user perspective in making recommendation, however, they did not assumed dynamic nature of the network, while trust in such dynamic network is a dynamic concept which changes over the time and requires continuous updates [11].

3 SMART Architecture Design

We propose a framework underlying decentralized social media called SMART, capable of finding relevant interest communities without violating users' privacy and anonymity. Its objective is to improve trust and eliminate malicious actors in participatory exchanges and collaborative decision making. To fulfill this goal, we adopt a role-stage model inspired by [12] integrating various facets of social media to define users based on social information and content attributes. We apply this information to estimate trust using game theoretic approaches in accordance with various QoS conflicting parameters, such as accuracy, timeliness, latency, and anonymity preservation. The output of the SMART architecture enables social media applications engage with the correct subset of users based on their QoS requirements. The architecture also improves democratic decision making by choosing trustworthy agents to vote for consensus and reduce cost and latency by analyzing previous voting outcomes and preferences.

Coping with the heterogeneous and dynamic social media infrastructure requires continuous updates and integration of new features without interrupting system operation [5]. To achieve this goal and overcome the limits of a monolithic architecture, we designed the SMART architecture shown in Fig. 1 using sixteen different sets of microservices: two for input transactions hub, nine for evolutionary semantic contextual data hub as the main part of architecture, and five for smart results in SMART transaction hub (out). The API gateway takes all the requests and routes them to the message broker for transparent transaction management and communication through message validation, transformation, routing and guaranteed delivery.

3.1 SMART Transaction Hub (In)

SMART transaction hub provides an input interface to schedule and manage input queries and information to SMART framework consisting of trace retrieval and network metrics retrieval microservices.

Trace Retrieval Microservice provides an input interface to extract the experiential anonymized activity traces required by SMART framework.

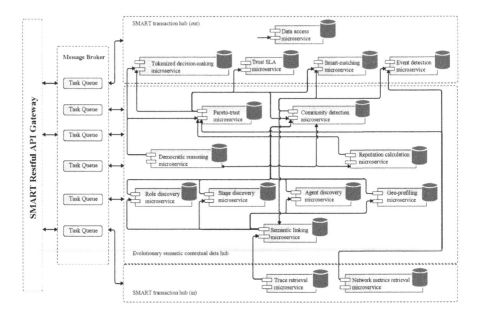

Fig. 1. SMART architecture proposal.

Network Metrics Retrieval Microservice provides an interface for the network-related QoS and quality of experience metrics and runtime information, including their physical network distribution to calculate the Pareto trust. Additionally it will help the event detection service by assigning geo-locations to events.

3.2   Evolutionary Semantic Contextual Data Hub

This hub represents as the main part of the SMART architecture offering intelligent heuristic outputs for crowd-cooperative applications through nine following microservices.

Semantic Linking Microservice explores complex and evolving relationships among data to have a clear understanding of the network and predict their trend in the future. We formulate the problem to extract semantic data combining event and link analysis for representing peer behaviors in decentralized social media considering dynamic network. Several sequences are usually extracted as the roles and stages for each user over the time to gain valid and valuable insights and information from user patterns, while guaranteeing for preserving users anonymity and privacy when releasing aggregate statistical personal information of individuals. This microservice improves community detection and reveals network properties and role of users in social media by defining implicit and explicit behaviors and interactions of participants in the network.

Agent Discovery Microservice defines the concept of agents as users and participants in decentralized social networks, where they usually have equal rights in querying, sending transactions, and participating in decision making. We apply this microservice for identifying users to understand the network more deeply and assigning tasks to them in accordance with their roles in the social network.

Role Discovery Microservice aims to precisely discover communities by specifying agents according to their roles in the social network. The concept of roles improves the conceptualization and community detection in social media since roles can reveal semantic information and interaction between agents. Therefore, we define roles as properties and behaviors assumed by agents over time and place. In this microservice, we characterize agents by multiple roles as also taken by people in the real world [10]. For example, a person usually belongs to several social groups such as family, friends, and colleagues.

Stage Discovery Microservice detects the interaction between different roles in the social media represented as sequences of stages, where each stage contains the details of the role's actions. Detection of these stages can be beneficial for discovering communities and agents based on their role in the social media.

Community Detection Microservice helps in deeper network understanding and reveals interesting properties shared by the members [7,8]. Detection of these communities can be beneficial for numerous topics such as recommendation systems, link prediction, anomaly detection, information spreading, and finding of like minded marketing users [10]. Existing studies on community detection mainly focus on link analysis or topological network structure that ignores content analysis for community finding. The drawback is that each community identified by these methods can only reflect the strength of the connections, while in reality a social network community is a group of users not only sharing common events and friends, but also having similar interests [16]. Moreover, the amount of covert information extracted from a network is very limited. On the other hand, most of these studies assume that every node belongs to exactly one non-overlapping community, while people in a real social network naturally belong to multiple community. Thus, it is more reasonable to cluster users into overlapping communities [10]. We propose a novel approach that combines event clustering and link analysis to detect communities along with clustering users into overlapping communities via agent, role, stage discovery microservices.

Reputation Calculation Microservice that increases trust is an essential factor of a successful social network [18]. Generally, the security provided by decentralized social media is better than by a centralized data management, however, there are still trust issues as attacks are inevitably growing by exploiting decentralized ownership vulnerabilities. The reputation measures the amount of community trust achieved based on previous interactions.

Nevertheless, integrating trust in complex and dynamic scenarios where users are heterogeneous and anonymous is very difficult. Moreover, trust is a dynamic concept which changes over the time [11]. Hence, we provide a model for trust computing in accordance with the temporal factor of user's interactions. Reputation systems on decentralized social media have different goals, from choosing reliable resources to the quality of content of a shared file [18]. Therefore, the reputation needs to be addressed in many different ways according to the various services over time. For example, in crowdsourced journalism reporting on recent events, (in contrast to other informational content shared online), news is valued much more in terms of timeliness, accuracy, geo-location. Therefore, we propose efficient trust based heuristics using a game theoretic approach and community detection to estimate devices' trustworthiness considering various conflicting parameters, such as accuracy, timeliness, latency, and high anonymity preservation.

Pareto Trust Microservice considers trust through various parameters according to domain of services and QoS performance metrics such as accuracy, timeliness, and latency. However, these conflicting trust-based factors need to be simultaneously optimized to achieve an optimal solution.

To solve this multi-objective optimization problem where there is a trade-off between trust-based elements, we adopt cooperative game-theory based optimization algorithm to obtain the true Pareto-optimal frontier. Cooperative game theory is a mathematical model providing multi-objective optimization where multiple decision makers are involved in decision-making exploiting learning approaches to find an elitist spread of solutions [4].

Democratic Reasoning Microservice serves as a central knowledge-based component providing all facts and rules for other microservices. Hence, other microservices follow this rules for evaluation and execution.

Geo-profiling Microservice provides a mapping of agents location in the network over the time. This microservice will help classify agents depending on their locations to improve community detection and enable social media applications engage with smart devices closest in proximity to the event locations.

3.3   SMART Transaction Hub (Out)

This hub offers outputs and elicit solutions for various social media applications taking advantage of evolutionary semantic contextual data hub as an input to facilitate and improve trustworthiness and democratic decision-making.

Tokenized Decision-making Microservice is essential in public decentralized social media, where everyone is open to join or leave and all entities have the same power. Therefore, in a trustless environment, nodes need to run a consensus protocol to ensure that they all agree on the transactions. A consensus algorithm helps deciding the validity of the transactions and avoid the forking problem in decentralized social media. However, decision-making to reach consensus in such anonymized environments without any centralized authorities is a challenge and current algorithms still have many shortages. To address this issue, we provide heuristic decision-making algorithm for the decentralized social media consortium that predicts future results and helps the decentralized social media reduce costs and latency by analyzing previous voting outcomes and preferences.

Trust SLA Microservice needs to take optimized decisions according to conflicting objectives to suggest relevant communities for various services over the time, in order to improve the recommendation quality and eliminate malicious actors in participatory exchanges. Service level agreements (SLAs) are contracts between agents in social media to guarantee expected quality levels of services via elitist solutions [1]. Therefore, we offer SLA trust microservice adopting Pareto solution to negotiate trustworthy agents with precise targeting in decentralized social media. This microservices enabling social media applications engage with the right subset of users based on system requirements and QoS over the time.

Smart-matching Microservice preserves security in this distributed environment through decentralized consensus based on voting among the recommended list of reputable agents to express their acceptance of valid transaction [3,18]. However, finding such nodes is another challenge in decentralized social media. Towards this issue, we apply Pareto-trust microservice as an input and introduce appropriate agents for voting in consensus through a selection of relevant, reachable and credible ones.

Event Detection Microservice publishes information about events to its subscribers. If new communities are detected, for instance if the geo-profiling algorithm assigns a group of users to a physical location, this event of forming a physical group is broadcast to consumer services.

Data Access Microservice offers the heuristics and data from SMART to enable other components apply evaluation and cognition for different use-cases.

4   Discussion

Centralized social media do not offer a sufficient level of privacy due to singular data management. This leads to critical trust and privacy concerns across the large scale social media user-base. Decentralized social media can keep privacy over the network [3,8], however, data distribution among peers in the decentralized network poses new issues. To preserve system security, the nodes need to run a consensus protocol to ensure that they all agree on the transactions. However, finding trustworthy nodes to vote for the valid transactions makes a challenging issue in decentralized environment. In addition, in such anonymized system without any central authority, malicious actors have more freedom to spread fake information over the network. Thus, decentralized social media needs to consider trust as an important factor to ease users interactions. As different applications may have different requirements in social media, trust needs to be addressed in different ways according to the requirement of services [18], while in most previous works trust does not address all the service requirements [2]. To tackle with this problem, we apply a Pareto-trust microservice enabling consensus process and social media applications engage with the right subset of users. Our model applies trust through various parameters according to domain of services and QoS performance metrics such as accuracy, timeliness, and latency.

Nevertheless, integrating trust in complex social networks scenarios with uncertain knowledge is not achievable without having a clear understanding of the network. Therefore, a system needs to extract the users behavior to discover the networks more deeply. Discovering community structures can help us reveal network properties, role of users, and their interactions. The existent studies on community detection mainly focus on one non-overlapping community for each node and only link analysis without content analysis [9,13,17], while these can not reflect whole information of the network. To do so, we propose a novel approach clustering users into overlapping communities which combines event clustering and link analysis to detect communities precisely through role-stage model considering various aspect of social media. Our proposed model improves community detection in social media by defining implicit and explicit behaviors and interactions of participants in the network without disclosing individual's information.

5   Conclusion

Nowadays, decentralized social media attract many attention to maintain users privacy. However, in the absence of a central authority, it is difficult to identify malicious actors and reach a consensus agreement. In this paper, we proposed an adaptive framework to improve trust and group decision making in decentralized social media through applying multi-objective trust model. To do so, we applied different microservices enabling social media applications engage with relevant and most trustworthy users based on services requirements. We provided a role-stage model to precisely infer network construction and communities based on semantic information, users roles, and their transactions while preserving users privacy and anonymity.

Acknowledgments. This work was accomplished as a part of project *"ARTICONF"* (http://www.articonf.eu/), funded by the European Union's Horizon 2020 research and innovation program under grant agreement No 644179. The authors would also like to thank anonymous reviewers for their valuable comments.

References

1. Alhanahnah, M., Bertok, P., Tari, Z., Alouneh, S.: Context-aware multifaceted trust framework for evaluating trustworthiness of cloud providers. Future Gener. Comput. Syst. **79**, 488–499 (2018)
2. Azadjalal, M.M., Moradi, P., Abdollahpouri, A., Jalili, M.: A trust-aware recommendation method based on pareto dominance and confidence concepts. Knowl.-Based Syst. **116**, 130–143 (2017)
3. Bahri, L., Carminati, B., Ferrari, E.: Decentralized privacy preserving services for online social networks. Online Soc. Netw. Media **6**, 18–25 (2018)
4. Curiel, I.: Cooperative Game Theory and Applications: Cooperative Games Arising from Combinatorial Optimization Problems, vol. 16. Springer, Boston (1997). https://doi.org/10.1007/978-1-4757-4871-0

5. Dragoni, N., et al.: Microservices: yesterday, today, and tomorrow. In: Mazzara, M., Meyer, B. (eds.) Present and Ulterior Software Engineering, pp. 195–216. Springer, Cham (2017). https://doi.org/10.1007/978-3-319-67425-4_12

6. Guidi, B., Amft, T., De Salve, A., Graffi, K., Ricci, L.: DiDuSoNet: a P2P architecture for distributed dunbar-based social networks. Peer-to-Peer Network. Appl. **9**(6), 1177–1194 (2016)

7. Guidi, B., Michienzi, A., Ricci, L.: SONIC-MAN: a distributed protocol for dynamic community detection and management. In: Bonomi, S., Rivière, E. (eds.) DAIS 2018. LNCS, vol. 10853, pp. 93–109. Springer, Cham (2018). https://doi.org/10.1007/978-3-319-93767-0_7

8. Guidi, B., Michienzi, A., Rossetti, G.: Towards the dynamic community discovery in decentralized online social networks. J. Grid Comput. **17**(1), 23–44 (2019)

9. Huang, B., Liu, Z., Chen, J., Liu, A., Liu, Q., He, Q.: Behavior pattern clustering in blockchain networks. Multimedia Tools Appl. **76**(19), 20099–20110 (2017). https://doi.org/10.1007/s11042-017-4396-4

10. Jonnalagadda, A., Kuppusamy, L.: A survey on game theoretic models for community detection in social networks. Soc. Netw. Anal. Min. **6**(1), 1–24 (2016). https://doi.org/10.1007/s13278-016-0386-1

11. Kalaï, A., Zayani, C.A., Amous, I., Abdelghani, W., Sèdes, F.: Social collaborative service recommendation approach based on user's trust and domain-specific expertise. Future Gener. Comput. Syst. **80**, 355–367 (2018)

12. Kathambari, V., Sasaki, A.: Role-stage model for design and implementation of user-centric business applications. In: 2014 International Conference on Computational Science and Computational Intelligence, vol. 1, pp. 235–240. IEEE (2014)

13. Maesa, D.D.F., Marino, A., Ricci, L.: Uncovering the bitcoin blockchain: an analysis of the full users graph. In: 2016 IEEE International Conference on Data Science and Advanced Analytics (DSAA), pp. 537–546. IEEE (2016)

14. Maesa, D.D.F., Marino, A., Ricci, L.: Detecting artificial behaviours in the bitcoin users graph. Online Soc. Netw. Media **3**, 63–74 (2017)

15. Meiklejohn, S., et al.: A fistful of bitcoins: characterizing payments among men with no names. In: Proceedings of the 2013 Conference on Internet Measurement Conference, pp. 127–140. ACM (2013)

16. Qin, M., Jin, D., Lei, K., Gabrys, B., Musial-Gabrys, K.: Adaptive community detection incorporating topology and content in social networks. Knowl.-Based Syst. **161**, 342–356 (2018)

17. Tang, H., Jiao, Y., Huang, B., Lin, C., Goyal, S., Wang, B.: Learning to classify blockchain peers according to their behavior sequences. IEEE Access **6**, 71208–71215 (2018)

18. Urena, R., Kou, G., Dong, Y., Chiclana, F., Herrera-Viedma, E.: A review on trust propagation and opinion dynamics in social networks and group decision making frameworks. Inf. Sci. **478**, 461–475 (2019)

A Novel Data-Centric Programming Model for Large-Scale Parallel Systems

Domenico Talia[1]([✉]), Paolo Trunfio[1], Fabrizio Marozzo[1], Loris Belcastro[1],
Javier Garcia-Blas[2], David del Rio[2], Philippe Couvée[3], Gael Goret[3],
Lionel Vincent[3], Alberto Fernández-Pena[4], Daniel Martín de Blas[4],
Mirko Nardi[5], Teresa Pizzuti[5], Adrian Spătaru[6], and Marek Justyna[7]

[1] University of Calabria, Rende, Italy
talia@dimes.unical.it
[2] University Carlos III of Madrid, Madrid, Spain
[3] Atos BDS R&D Data Management, Échirolles, France
[4] Instituto de Investigación Sanitaria Gregorio Marañón, Madrid, Spain
[5] INTEGRIS, Rome, Italy
[6] Institute e-Austria Timişoara, Timişoara, Romania
[7] PSNC, Poznan, Poland

Abstract. This paper presents the main features and the programming constructs of the *DCEx* programming model designed for the implementation of data-centric large-scale parallel applications on Exascale computing platforms. To support scalable parallelism, the *DCEx* programming model employs private data structures and limits the amount of shared data among parallel threads. The basic idea of *DCEx* is structuring programs into data-parallel blocks to be managed by a large number of parallel threads. Parallel blocks are the units of shared- and distributed-memory parallel computation, communication, and migration in the memory/storage hierarchy. Threads execute close to data using near-data synchronization according to the PGAS model. A use case is also discussed showing the *DCEx* features for Exascale programming.

Keywords: Large-scale parallelism · Exascale systems · Data-centric applications

1 Introduction

High-level parallel programming models assist designers accessing and exploiting high-performance computing (HPC) resources abstracted from physical entities such as storage, memory, and cores. Their main goal is facilitating the programming task, increasing programmer productivity, achieving scalability, and improving software portability. Exascale systems refers to highly parallel computing systems capable of at least one exaFLOPS. Therefore, their implementation represents a big research and technology challenge. The design and development of Exascale systems is currently under investigation with the goal of

U. Schwardmann et al. (Eds.): Euro-Par 2019 Workshops, LNCS 11997, pp. 452–463, 2020.
https://doi.org/10.1007/978-3-030-48340-1_35

building by 2020 high-performance computers composed of a very large number of multi-core processors expected to deliver a performance of 10^{18} operations per second. Programming paradigms traditionally used in HPC systems (e.g., MPI, OpenMP, OpenCL, Map-Reduce, and HPF) are not sufficient/appropriate for programming software designed to run on systems composed of a very large set of computing elements [1]. To reach Exascale size, it is required to define new programming models and languages that combine abstraction with both scalability and performance. Hybrid models (shared/distributed memory) and communication mechanisms based on locality and grouping are currently investigated as promising approaches. Parallel applications running on Exascale systems will require to control millions of threads running on a very large set of cores. Such applications will need to avoid or limit synchronization, use less communication and remote memory, and handle with software and hardware faults that could occur. Nowadays, no available programming languages provide solutions to these issues, specially when data-intensive applications are targeted. In this scenario, the EU funded Horizon 2020 project *ASPIDE* is studying models for extreme data processing on Exascale systems, starting from the idea that parallel programming paradigms must be conceived in a data-driven style especially for supporting for Big Data analysis on HPC systems.

This paper introduces the main features and the programming constructs of the *DCEx* programming model designed in the *ASPIDE* project. *DCEx* is based upon data-aware basic operations for data-intensive applications supporting the scalable use of a massive number of processing elements. The *DCEx* model uses private data structures and limits the amount of shared data among parallel threads. The basic idea of *DCEx* is structuring programs into data-parallel blocks, which are the units of shared- and distributed-memory parallel computation, communication, and migration in the memory/storage hierarchy. Computation threads execute close to data, using near-data synchronization based on the *Partitioned Global Address Space* (PGAS) model, which assumes the memory is partitioned into a global shared address space and a portion that is local to each process [3]. In the *DCEx* model, three main types of parallelism are exploited: data parallelism, task parallelism, and *Single Program Multiple Data* (SPMD) parallelism. A prototype API based on that model will be implemented.

The rest of the paper is structured as follows. Section 2 presents principles and features of the data model used in *DCEx*. The data block concept is presented and data access and management operations are discussed. Section 3 introduces the principles and the kinds of parallelism exploited in *DCEx*. Section 4 presents a use case designed using the programming mechanisms of *DCEx*. Finally, Sect. 5 outlines related parallel models and languages recently proposed for scalable applications on Exascale systems.

2   The DCEx Data Model

The role of data management and processing is central in the *DCEx* programming model. The data model used in the *DCEx* is based on the *data parallel block*

(DPB) abstraction. DPBs are the units of shared- and distributed-memory parallel computation, communication, and migration. Blocks and their message queues are mapped onto processes and placed in memory/storage by the ASPIDE runtime. Decomposing a problem in terms of block-parallelism (instead of process-parallelism) enables migrating blocks during the program execution between different locations in the hardware. This is the main idea that lets us integrate in- and out-of-core programming in the same model and change modes without modifying the source code.

A DPB is used for managing a data element in the main memory of one or multiple computing nodes. In particular, a DPB d can be composed of multiple partitions:

```
d = [ part 0 ][ part 1 ][ part 2 ][ part 3 ]...[ part n-1 ]
```

where each partition is assigned to a specific computing node.

Notation $d[i]$ refers to the i-th partition of DPB d. However, when a DPB is simply referred by its name (e.g., d) in a computing node (e.g., the k-th node), it is intended as a reference to the locally available partition (e.g. $d[k]$).

A DPB can be created using the *data.get* operation, which loads into main memory some existing data from secondary storage. This operation is specified by the following syntax:

```
d = data.get(source, [format], [part|repl], ...) at [Cnode|Carea];
```

where:

- **d**: is the DPB created to manage in main memory the data element read from secondary storage;
- **source**: specifies the location of data in secondary storage (e.g., an URL);
- **format**: is an optional parameter specifying the format of data;
- **part|repl**: is an optional parameter, which should be specified only if the optional *Carea* directive is included (see below). If *part* is used, d must be partitioned across all the computing nodes in *Carea*. If *repl* is used, d must be replicated in all the computing nodes of the *Carea*;
- the ellipsis indicate further parameters to be defined;
- **Cnode|Carea**: is an optional directive to specify how d should be mapped on a single computing node or on an area of computing nodes. In particular, if a *Cnode* is specified, d is loaded in the main memory of that specific computing node; if a *Carea* is specified, d is partitioned (if the *part* flag is used) or replicated (if the *repl* flag is used) in the main memory of the computing nodes included in that area.

In addition to *data.get*, it is also possible to use the *data.declare* operation, which declares a DPB that will come into existence in the future, as a result of a task execution. Here is an example of DPB declaration:

```
d = data.declare();
```

The use of *data.declare* in association with task operations allows to store the output of a task.

A DPB can be written in secondary storage using the *data.set* operation, which is defined as follows:

```
data.set(d, dest, [format]);
```
where:

- d: is the DPB to be stored in secondary storage;
- dest: specifies where of data must be written in secondary storage (e.g., an URL);
- format: is an optional parameter specifying the format of data.

3   The DCEx Parallelism Model

In the *DCEx* model, data are the fundamental artifact and they are processed in parallel. In particular, *DCEx* exploits three main types of parallelism for managing the data parallel blocks: data parallelism, data-driven task parallelism, and SPMD parallelism.

To simplify the development of applications in heterogeneous distributed memory environments, large-scale data- and task-parallelism techniques can be developed on top of the data-parallel block abstractions divided into partitions. Different partitions are placed on different cores/nodes where tasks will work in parallel on data partitions. This approach allows computing nodes to process in parallel the data partitions at each core/node using a set of statements/library calls that hide the complexity of the underlying operations. Data dependency in this scenario limits scalability, thus it should be avoided or limited to a local scale.

Some proposals for Exascale programming are based on the adaptation of traditional parallel programming languages and on hybrid solutions. This incremental approach is conservative and often results in very complex codes that may limit the scalability of programs on many thousands or millions of cores. Approaches based on a partitioned global address space (PGAS) memory model appear to be more suited to meeting the Exascale challenge [5]. PGAS is a parallel programming model that assumes a global memory address space that is logically partitioned. A portion of the address space is local to each task, thread, or processing element. In PGAS the partitions of the shared memory space can have an affinity for a particular task, in this way data locality is implemented. For these reasons PGAS approaches have been analyzed and adopted in the *DCEx* model for partitioning of the address space using locality to limit data access overhead.

3.1   Basic Features

As mentioned before, the *DCEx* model for managing a very large amount of parallelism exploits three main types of parallelism: Data parallelism, task parallelism, and SPMD parallelism. Those forms of parallelism are integrated with PGAS features taking into account computing areas and other data and computing locality features.

Data parallelism is achieved when the same code is executed in parallel on different data blocks. In exploiting data parallelism, no communication is needed, therefore this type of parallelism allows for the independent execution of code processing in parallel different partitions of data without suffering of communication or synchronization overhead.

Task parallelism is exploited when different tasks that compose an application run in parallel. The task parallelism in *DCEx* is data driven since data dependencies are used to decide when tasks can be spawn in parallel. As input data of a task are ready its code can be executed. Such parallelism can be defined in two manners: *i*) explicit, when a programmer defines dependencies among tasks through explicit instructions; *ii*) implicit, when the system analyses the input/output of tasks to understand dependencies among them.

SPMD parallelism is achieved when a set of tasks execute in parallel the same code on different partitions of a data set (in our case parallel data blocks); however, differently from data parallelism, processes cooperate to exchange partial results during execution. Communication occurs among the processors when data must be exchanged between tasks that compose an SPMD computation. Tasks may execute different statements by taking different branches in the program and it is occasionally necessary for processors to synchronize, however processors do not have to operate in locksteps as in SIMD computations.

In *DCEx*, these three basic forms of parallelism can be combined to express complex parallel applications. This can be done by programming Exascale applications in a *Directed Acyclic Graph* (DAG) style that corresponds to workflow programming, where a parallel program is designed as a graph of tasks. As data-intensive scientific computing systems become more widespread, it is necessary to simplify the development, deployment, and execution of complex data analysis applications. The workflow model is a general and widely used approach for designing and executing data-intensive applications over high performance systems or distributed computing infrastructures. Data-intensive workflows consist of interdependent data processing tasks, often connected in a DAG style, which communicate through intermediate storage abstractions. This paradigm in the *DCEx* model can be exploited to program applications on massively parallel systems like Exascale platforms.

The combination of the three basic types of parallelism allows developers to express other parallel execution mechanisms such as pipeline parallelism, which is obtained when data is processed in parallel at different stages. Pipeline parallelism is in particular appropriate for processing data streams as their stages manage the flow of data in parallel [6]. As mentioned before, the types of parallelism discussed here are combined in *DCEx* with the features of the PGAS model that support the definition of several execution contexts based on separate address spaces. For any given task, this allows for the exploitation of memory affinity and data locality that provides programmers with a clear way to distinguish between private and shared memory blocks, and determine the association to processing nodes of shared data locations [7]. In fact, in the PGAS model, the computing nodes have an attached local memory space and portions of this local storage can be declared private by the programming model, making them not visible to other nodes. A portion of each node's storage can be also shared with others nodes. Each shared memory location has an affinity, which is a computing node on which the location is local, with the effect that data access rate is higher for code running on that node. Therefore, through data affinity mechanisms a programmer can implement parallel applications taking into account local data access and communication overhead facilitating high performance and scalability.

3.2   Programming Constructs

This section introduces the main programming concepts and constructs designed in the *DCEx* model. The description is focused on the two main components of the model: *i*) computing nodes and areas that identify single processing elements or regions of processors of an Exascale machine where to store data and run tasks; *ii*) tasks and task pools that represent the units of parallelism.

Computing Nodes and Computing Areas. The *DCEx* model defines two basic constructs to refer to computing nodes and computing areas:

- Cnode representing a single computing node, and
- Carea representing a region (or area) including a set of computing nodes.

In general, Cnodes and Careas are used to implement data and task locality by specifying a mapping between data loading operations and (the main memory of) computing nodes, and task execution operations and (the processors of) computing nodes.

A Cnode variable may be used to specify in a data loading operation the computing node that should be used to store (in its main memory) a given data element read from secondary storage. It can be used also in a task execution operation to specify the computing node on which a task should be executed.

A Carea variable may be used to specify in a data loading operation the set of computing nodes that should be used to store (in their main memory) a given data element read from secondary storage, by partitioning data on all the nodes. In a task execution operation a Carea is used to specify the computing nodes on which a pool of tasks should be executed. A Cnode is declared as follows:

```
node = Cnode;
```

where **node** is a variable used to refer to the computing node.
Through this declaration, the runtime chooses which computing node will be assigned to variable **node**. Alternatively, it may be specified by annotations to help the runtime in choosing the computing node, e.g.:

```
node = Cnode({hardware annotation parameters})
```

A Carea can be defined as an array of computing nodes. For instance, the example below defines nodes as an array of 1000 computing nodes:

```
nodes1 = Carea(1000);
```

Similarly, the following examples defines a two-dimensional array of 100 × 100 computing nodes:

```
nodes2 = Carea(100,100);
```

Referring to the last example, the following notation:

```
nodes2[10][50]
```

identifies the computing node at row 10 and column 50 in the nodes Carea. It is also possible to create a Carea as a view of a larger Carea:

```
nodes3 = Carea(nodes2,10,10);
```

which extracts a 10 × 10 matrix of computing nodes from the Carea defined by nodes2.

Tasks and Task Pools. In *DCEx*, tasks are the basic elements for implementing concurrent activities. To manage the parallel execution of multiple tasks, a task data dependency graph is generated at runtime. Each time a new task is executed, its data dependencies are matched against those of the other tasks. If a data dependency is found, the task becomes a successor of the corresponding tasks. Tasks are scheduled for execution as soon as all their predecessors in the graph have produced data they need as input. The programming model allows to express parallelism using two concepts: *task* and *task_pool*.

A task can be defined according to the following syntax:

```
t = Task(f_name,f_param_1,...,f_param_n) [at Cnode|Carea] [on failure ignore
    |retry|...];
```

where:

- t: is a numeric identifier to the task being created;
- f_name: is the name of the function to be executed;
- f_param_i: the i-th parameter required by the function identified by f_name;
- at Cnode|Carea: is an optional directive that allows to specify on which given computing node the *task* should be executed (if a *Cnode* is specified), or to execute the task on any computing node from a set of computing nodes (if a *Carea* is specified).
- on failure: is an optional directive that allows to specify the action (for instance, *ignore* or *retry* with it) to be performed in case of task failure.

According to the basic assumptions about concurrent task execution mentioned above, the *Task* keyword allows to concurrently execute a method in the future, as soon as its data dependencies are resolved (i.e., its input data are ready to be used). Moreover, the *at* directive that specifies the execution of a task on a given *Cnode* is intended as request/suggestion to runtime that can be satisfied or not, depending on available hardware resources, their status and load, and the runtime execution optimization strategy.

As an example, let assume we defined the following function:

```
partitioner(in:dataset, out:trainset, out:testset);
```

that takes as input a *dataset* and returns (by reference) a *trainset* and a *testset* extracted from the dataset. The following code shows how that function may be executed:

```
dsURL = ''some url''; trainURL = ''some url''; testURL ''some url'';
node = Cnode; ds = data.get(dsURL) at node;
train = data.declare(); test = data.declare();
t = Task(partitioner, ds, train, test);
data.set(train, trainURL); data.set(test, testURL);
```

Tasks can be used in a *for* loop to exploit data-driven task parallelism. For example, a set of tasks can be executed in parallel in such a way:

```
N = 10; vec = [];
for (i=0; i<N; i++) {
  if (cond)
    vec[i] = Task(f1, f1_par_1, ..., f1_par_n);
  else
    vec[i] = Task(f2, f2_par_1, ..., f2_par_n);
}
```

In this code example we assume functions $f1$ and $f2$ have been already defined.

To implement SPMD parallelism in *DCEx*, the *Task_Pool* abstraction is defined to represent a set of tasks. In fact, tasks in a pool are activated to execute the same function that implements the algorithm executed by the *Task_Pool* in an SPMD parallel style. The basic syntax for declaring a pool of tasks is as follows:

```
tp = Task_Pool([size]);
```

where:

- `tp`: is an identifier of the task pool being defined, it can be also used with an index to identify a single task of the pool; and
- `size`: is an optional parameter specifying the number of tasks in the pool.

The statement above declares a task pool but does not spawn its execution. Each task in the pool must be activated explicitly using a *for* loop as in the following example:

```
N = 10; nodes = Carea(N);
for (i=0; i<N; i++) {
  f_param_1 = ...; f_param_n = ...;
  tp[i] = Task(f_name, f_param_1, ..., f_param_n) at nodes[i];
}
```

If there are no dependencies among the tasks initialized in the loop, they execute concurrently. On the other hand, if a task works on some data that is not yet available, it waits until that data becomes available, according to the execution model outlined before. On a *Task_Pool tp* some operations such as the following listed here can be defined:

- `size(tp)` to access the number of tasks in a pool.
- `structure(tp)` to know how the tasks in a pool are structured (e.g., in a vector, a two-dimensional matrix, a tree).
- `zone(tp)` to know in which *Carea* the tasks of a pool are mapped.

4   Use Case

To show through a real data-intensive application how the *DCEx* constructs can be used, in the following is described a trajectory data analysis application coded in DCEx. The workflow shown in Fig. 1 represents the main steps of the applications (some of them are optional):

A. *Crawling*: multiple crawlers are instantiated and run in parallel for gathering data from social media. If data have already been downloaded and stored in files, a specific crawler (FileCrawler) is used to load the data.
B. *Filtering*: filtering functions are run in parallel to verify if social media items meet or not some conditions.
C. *Automatic keywords extraction and data grouping*: the keywords that identify the places of interests are extracted; these keywords will be used to group social media items according to the places they refer to.
D. *RoIs extraction*: a data parallel clustering algorithm is used to extract Regions-of-Interest (RoIs) from social media data grouped by keywords [2]. RoIs represent a way to partition the space into meaningful areas; they are the boundaries of points-of-interest (e.g., square of a city).
E. *Trajectory mining*: This step is executed to discover behaviour and mobility patterns of people by analyzing geotagged social media items. Highly parallel versions of the FP-Growth (frequent itemset analysis) and Prefix-Span (sequential pattern mining) algorithms are used here.

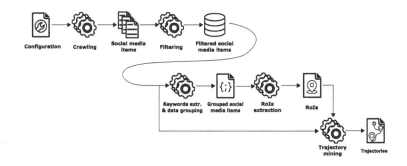

Fig. 1. Workflow of the urban computing use-case.

Listing 1.1 shows the *DCEx* pseudo-code for the trajectory data analysis use case introduced above. Initially the dataset "FullFlickrData.json" is loaded (line 2), a *Carea* of 16,000 nodes is defined (lines 3–4), then the dataset is split into 16,000 partitions and mapped onto the computing nodes (line 5). After that, filtering tasks are executed in parallel on the partitions to filter out Flickr posts that are not geotagged or do not refer to the city of Rome (lines 6–12). Filtering data is processed in parallel to extract keywords in each cell (lines 13–19). Then, such keywords are aggregated to find the top keywords in the area (lines 20–30). Afterward, filtering data have been used again and aggregated based on top keywords (lines 31–39). Finally, the RoI extraction (lines 40–48) and trajectory mining tasks (49–51) are executed concurrently.

Listing 1.1. DCEx code for the urban computing use-case.

```
1   //Crawling
2   source="/home/UNICAL/FullFlickrData.json";
3   numNodes = 16000;
4   nodes = Carea(numNodes);
5   dd = data.get(source, FILE, part) at nodes;

6   //Filtering
7   filterTasks = Task_Pool(nodes.size);
8   ddfilt = []; f_param_0 = "IsGeotagged"; f_param_1 = "IsInRome";
9   for(i=0; i<nodes.size; i++){
10    ddfilt[i] = data.declare();
11    filterTasks[i] = Task(filteringFunc, dd[i], ddfilt[i], f_param_0, f_param_1) at nodes[i];
12  }

13  //Keywords extraction
14  keywordsInCellTasks = Task_Pool(nodes.size);
15  keywordsInCellParts = []; cell_width = "500m";
16  for(i=0; i<nodes.size; i++){
17    keywordsInCellParts[i] = data.declare();
18    keywordsInCellTasks[i] = Task(findKeywordsInCell, ddfilt[i], keywordsInCellParts[i],
          cell_width) at nodes[i];
19  }
20  keywordsInCell = groupByKey(keywordsInCellParts);
21  numCells = keywordsInCell.size;
22  topKeywordsInCellTasks = Task_Pool(numCells);
23  nodes = Carea(numCells);
24  topKeywordsInCell = []; numTopKeywords = 5;
25  for(j=0; j<numCells; j++){
26    topKeywordsInCell[j] = data.declare();
27    topKeywordsInCellTasks[j] = Task(findTopKeywords, keywordsInCell[j], topKeywordsInCell[j],
          numTopKeywords) at nodes[j];
28  }
29  topKeywords = data.declare();
30  aggregateKeysTask = Task(aggregateKeywords, topKeywordsInCell, topKeywords);

31  //Data grouping
32  splitDataPerKeywordsTasks = Task_Pool(numNodes);
33  nodes = Carea(numNodes);
34  dataPerKeywordsParts=[];
35  for(i=0; i<numNodes; i++){
36    dataPerKeywordsParts[i] = data.declare();
37    splitDataPerKeywordsTasks[i] = Task(assignDataToKeywords, ddfilt[i], dataPerKeywordsParts[i],
          topKeywords) at nodes[i]);
38  }
39  dataPerKeywords = groupByKey(dataPerKeywordsParts);

40  //RoIs extraction
41  numRoIs = dataPerKeywords.size;
42  roiTasks = Task_Pool(numRoIs);
43  nodes = Carea(numRoIs);
44  rois=[]; eps = 50; minPts=150; splits = 32;
45  for(k=0; k<numRoIs; k++){
46    rois[k] = data.declare();
47    roiTasks[k] = Task(findRoI, dataPerKeywords[k], rois[k], eps, minPts, splits) at nodes[i];
48  }

49  //Trajectory mining
50  trajectories = data.declare();
51  trajectoryTask = Task(trajectoryMining, ddfilt, trajectories, rois);
```

5 Related Work

This section discusses a few parallel programming models and languages that have been proposed for the implementation of scalable applications on Exascale machines [9]. The approach and the main features of those models and languages are briefly discussed. To manage programming issues of data-intensive applications, different scalable programming models have been proposed [4]. Several parallel programming models, languages and libraries are currently under development for providing high-level programming interfaces and tools for implementing high-performance applications on future Exascale computers. Here we introduce the most significant proposals and outline their main features.

The programming models for Exascale systems can be classified according to four categories: distributed memory, shared memory, partitioned memory, and hybrid models. Since Exascale systems can be composed of millions of processing nodes using large distributed memory, message passing programming systems, such as MPI, are candidate tools for programming applications for such class of systems. However, traditional MPI all-to-all communication does not scale well in Exascale environments. Hence to solve this issue new MPI releases (like MPI+X) have been proposed to support neighbor collectives for providing sparse "all-to-some" communication patterns that limit the data exchange on limited regions of processors [5]. Other distributed-memory languages for Exascale are Legion[1] and Charm++[2]. On the other side, the shared-memory paradigm offers a simple parallel programming model although it does not provide mechanisms to explicitly map and control data distribution and it includes non-scalable synchronization operations that are making very challenging its implementation on massively parallel systems.

As a trade-off between distributed and shared memory organizations, PGAS model [8] has been designed for implementing a global memory address space that is logically partitioned and portions of it are local to single processes. The main goal of the PGAS model is to limit data exchange and isolate failures in very large-scale systems. DASH[3] offers distributed data structures and parallel standard template library algorithms via a PGAS approach. A variant of the PGAS model, *Asynchronous PGAS (APGAS)* [7] that has been adopted by some programming languages, such as X10[4] and Chapel[5], supports both local and remote asynchronous task creation. Differently for the PGAS model, the APGAS model does not require that all processes run on similar hardware and supports dynamically spawning of multiple tasks. In fact, multiple threads be active simultaneously in a *place*, using either local or remote data. In addition, it does not require that all the places in a computation must be homogeneous [10]. PGAS-based languages proposed recently are X10, Chapel and UPC[6]. They share some concepts with *DCEx*, although they are not specifically designed for data-centric applications. In fact, in exploiting the PGAS approach, *DCEx* integrates PGAS with local communication mechanisms and data parallel blocks.

---

[1] https://legion.stanford.edu/.

[2] https://charmplusplus.org/.

[3] https://www.dash-project.org/.

[4] https://x10-lang.org/.

[5] https://chapel-lang.org/.

[6] https://upc-lang.org/.

6   Conclusions

Traditional parallel programming paradigms are not appropriate for programming scalable software designed to run on systems composed of a very large set of computing nodes. Therefore, to reach Exascale size it is required to define new programming models, languages and APIs that combine abstraction with scalability and performance. Hybrid models (shared/distributed memory) and locality-based communication mechanisms are currently investigated as promising approaches. The main goal of the ASPIDE project is the design and development of a new Exascale programming model for extreme data applications. The designed *DCEx* programming model includes data parallel blocks and data-driven parallelism for the implementation of scalable algorithms and applications on top of Exascale computing systems with a special emphasis on the support of massive data analysis applications. We presented here the language features and a use case. The implementation of the *DCEx* language is an ongoing activity.

Acknowledgments. This work has been partially funded by the ASPIDE Project funded by the European Union's Horizon 2020 Research and Innovation Programme under grant agreement No 801091.

References

1. Belcastro, L., Marozzo, F., Talia, D.: Programming models and systems for big data analysis. Int. J. Parallel Emergent Distrib. Syst. **34**(6), 632–652 (2019)
2. Belcastro, L., Marozzo, F., Talia, D., Trunfio, P.: G-Roi: automatic region-of-interest detection driven by geotagged social media data. ACM Trans. Knowl. Discov. Data **12**(3), 27:1–27:22 (2018)
3. Culler, D.E., et al.: Parallel programming in Split-C. In: Proceedings of the 1993 ACM/IEEE Conference on Supercomputing, pp. 262–273, November 1993
4. Diaz, J., Munoz-Caro, C., Nino, A.: A survey of parallel programming models and tools in the multi and many-core era. IEEE Trans. Parallel Distrib. Syst. **23**(8), 1369–1386 (2012)
5. Gropp, W., Snir, M.: Programming for exascale computers. Comput. Sci. Eng. **15**(6), 27–35 (2013)
6. del Rio Astorga, D., Dolz, M.F., Fernández, J., García, J.D.: A generic parallel pattern interface for stream and data processing. Concurrency Comput. Pract. Exp. **29**(24), e4175 (2017)
7. Saraswat, V., et al.: The asynchronous partitioned global address space model. In: The 1st Workshop on Advances in Message Passing, pp. 1–8 (2010)
8. Stitt, T.: An introduction to the partitioned global address space programming model (2010). CNX.org
9. Talia, D.: A view of programming scalable data analysis: from clouds to exascale. J. Cloud Comput. **8**(1), 1–16 (2019). https://doi.org/10.1186/s13677-019-0127-x
10. Tardieu, O., et al.: X10 and APGAS at petascale. In: ACM SIGPLAN Notices, vol. 49, pp. 53–66. ACM (2014)

Co-located and Orchestrated Network Fabric (CONF): An Automated Cloud Virtual Infrastructure for Social Network Applications

Zeshun Shi[1], Huan Zhou[1], Yang Hu[1], Spiros Koulouzis[1], Carlos Rubia[2], and Zhiming Zhao[1(✉)] [iD]

[1] Informatics Institute, University of Amsterdam, Amsterdam, Netherlands
{z.shi2,h.zhou,y.hu,s.koulouzis,z.zhao}@uva.nl
[2] Agilia Center (AGI), Sevilla, Spain
carlos.rubia@agiliacenter.com

Abstract. Cloud environments can provide virtualized, elastic, controllable and high-quality on-demand infrastructure services for supporting complex distributed applications. However, existing IaaS (Infrastructure-as-a-Service) solutions mainly focus on the automated integration or deployment of generic applications; they lack flexible infrastructure planning and provisioning solutions and do not have rich support for the high service quality and trustworthiness required by social network applications. This paper introduces an automated cloud virtual infrastructure solution for social network applications, called Co-located and Orchestrated Network Fabric (CONF), which was conducted in a recently funded EU H2020 project ARTICONF. CONF aims to improve the existing infrastructure support in the DevOps lifecycle of social network applications to optimize QoS performance metrics as well as ensure fast recovery in the presence of faults or performance drops.

Keywords: Cloud · Virtual infrastructure · Social network applications

1 Introduction

With the wide deployment of smart objects, mobile devices and increased connectivity, many applications nowadays operate on an ever-growing scale with high rates of churn and unpredicted peak demand. In this environment, social network applications allow for cooperative interactions among many participants, whether via mass public engagement (e.g., in crowdsourcing content creation) or as part of a persistent online community (e.g., car sharing services). Those applications have critical time constraints and strict trust requirements and therefore require a dynamic, adaptable infrastructure for hosting system components and supporting application users.

© Springer Nature Switzerland AG 2020
U. Schwardmann et al. (Eds.): Euro-Par 2019 Workshops, LNCS 11997, pp. 464–475, 2020.
https://doi.org/10.1007/978-3-030-48340-1_36

By providing elastic capacity and flexible pay-as-you-go business model, the virtualized infrastructure offered by cloud environments can significantly reduce the operational cost for resource-intensive applications like big data, deep learning and the Internet of Things (IoT). To effectively deploy social network applications in the cloud, the capacity of planning, provisioning, monitoring and adaptation of the application's virtual infrastructure needs to be automated and seamlessly integrated into the whole process of the development and operation (DevOps) lifecycle. Moreover, such a virtual infrastructure solution has to effectively address the increased demand for Quality of Service (QoS) and Quality of Experience (QoE). However, existing cloud infrastructure services, e.g., provided by the DevOps environment of public providers, mainly focus on the automated integration or deployment of the generic applications; they have minimal support for the high performance and quality requirements of social network applications.

In this paper, we present an automated cloud virtual infrastructure solution for social network applications, called Co-located and Orchestrated Network Fabric (CONF). The work is conducted in a recently funded EU H2020 project ARTICONF. We will first analyze the requirements for the infrastructure automated solutions and then review the state of the art. After identifying the gaps, we will present the architecture design of the CONF system, and demonstrate the functional components of the system using a car sharing use case.

2   State of the Art

In this section, we will first introduce the problem context of social network applications for infrastructure services and then review the related work as well as opportunities and challenges for future research.

2.1   Problem Context

Cloud and edge/fog platforms provide a virtualized infrastructure solution that can significantly optimize application usages and reduce operational costs of social network application [2]. However, in a large-scale heterogeneous and fragmented social network with smart objects spanning geographical boundaries, resource exploitation is challenging with respect to time-critical constraints, failovers, and QoS requirements. More specifically, current social network applications and PaaS (Platform as a Service) platforms lack flexible infrastructure planning and provisioning solutions. For example, if an application or platform needs to be deployed on the cloud and scale vertically or horizontally, current infrastructure services have the problem of vendor lock-in and cannot provide efficient resources to meet QoS requirements in an economical way. Moreover, existing social media cloud services lack of pervasive monitoring services to QoS metrics, as well as a self-adaptive mechanism to recover quickly from sudden failures. Monitoring QoS related metrics is necessary to improve efficiency for customizing, provisioning and controlling heterogeneous virtual infrastructures required by time-critical social network applications. An effective self-adaptive mechanism specifically to ensure fast recovery in the presence of faults or performance drops is also needed for quality-critical social network applications.

2.2 Related Work

In the DevOps lifecycle of cloud applications, infrastructure solutions are required in the whole process of infrastructure planning, provisioning, deployment, and monitoring [2]. Based on this idea, we identified the following four research topics to review the current related work.

Infrastructure Planning. Deploying the same application on different cloud infrastructures with the same specification may lead to entirely different results [11]. Therefore, developing an infrastructure planner that is bound to a specific budget without sacrificing performance is quite essential. A good cloud infrastructure planner should generate an optimal infrastructure strategy that not only meets the QoS requirements of the application but also achieves additional objectives such as minimizing monetary cost and power consumption, low latency, etc. For this reason, cloud infrastructure planning is often more challenging than scheduling application workflows onto fixed infrastructure [18]. Existing solutions about planning infrastructures for time-constrained applications typically have a global deadline. For example, IaaS Cloud Partial Critical Paths (IC-PCP) and Critical Path-based Iterative (CPI) are two typical algorithms that calculate the critical paths for VM services. To address the problem of multiple time constraints when responding to new events, Wang et al. [13] proposed a Multi-dEadline workflow Planning Algorithm (MEPA) to plan the most cost-effective virtual infrastructure for an application workflow.

Infrastructure Provisioning. Most IaaS clouds provide dedicated virtual infrastructure resources to applications with limited programmability and controllability, which enlarges the management gap between infrastructures and applications [17,19]. To bridge this gap, there have been substantial academic research as well as commercial tools. Zhou et al. [19] designed *CloudsStorm*, which is an application-driven DevOps framework that allows cloud users to program and control the cloud infrastructure directly. *SWITCH* is a software workbench for interactive time-critical and highly self-adaptive cloud applications. It also provides a programming model and toolkit to help programmers specify the QoS and QoE metrics of their distributed applications [19]. *Cloud-Perfect* [9] is another toolkit-based architecture for optimizing cloud infrastructure management, evaluating performance, and providing selection processes. The trustworthiness of the service quality is crucial to guarantee the run-time performance of the virtual infrastructure; smart contracts and blockchains have been used to enforce the SLA between providers and infrastructure users as well [20].

Software Deployment for Social Network Applications. Typically, social networks are centralized platforms with a single proprietary organization controlling the network. This poses critical issues of trust and governance over created and propagated content. To solve this problem, some scholars put the idea of deploying social network applications and platforms on distributed cloud systems [6]. In this respect, Tan and Su [12] first proposed a new architecture for the media cloud and made some suggestions on how to build a media cloud in the future. Kim and Lee [7] presented their Social Media Cloud Computing (SMCC) model, which aims to provide flexible computing resources for processing large social media data and platforms. Wu et al. [14] proposed some algorithms for dynamic, optimal scaling of a social network application in geo-distributed clouds. Moreover, Chakravorty and Rong [3] put the idea of blockchain-based social network applications. Their platform, called *Ushare*, can support decentralization, anonymity, and traceability properties for future social network networks.

Infrastructure Monitoring and Self-adaptation. Due to the dynamic nature of the cloud, continuous monitoring of QoS attributes is necessary to optimize cloud infrastructure operations or data transfer [8]. In this respect, Bleikertz et al. [1] established an automated security system called *Cloud Radar*, which could continuously monitor virtualized infrastructures for changes. Based on these changes, *Cloud Radar* updates a graph model representation of the infrastructure and maintains a dynamic information flow graph to determine isolation properties. Yuriyama and Kushida [16] proposed a new infrastructure model called *Sensor-Cloud Infrastructure* which can manage physical sensors on IT infrastructures. Yang et al. [15] proposed and validated an extensible SDN and NFV-enabled network traffic monitoring system. Mohammed et al. [10] developed a monitor and failure prediction model with Auto-Regressive Moving Average (ARMA) which focused on high-performance cloud data center infrastructure.

When some data centers are not accessible or some part of the computing resources crashed, the adaptability of infrastructure is therefore essential for these applications to recover quickly from sudden failures. Evans et al. [4] presented an approach to application reconfiguration scenarios of a distributed real-time social network application, called *Sentinel*. Zhou et al. [19] proposed a co-provisioning mechanism to improve the automatic recovery capability of the cloud infrastructure. More recently, Gill et al. [5] introduced their *CHOPPER* model, which offers self-configuration of applications and self-optimization for maximum resource utilization.

2.3 Challenges and Opportunities

In conclusion, during the DevOps lifecycle of social network cloud applications, application developers and managers need to plan and provide virtual infrastructures based on application requirements, deploy software platforms and application components on the virtual infrastructure, schedule and monitor the application execution, and adapt the infrastructure when performance declines. However, current infrastructure supporting mechanisms for social network applications are inefficient. Existing cloud infrastructure services, e.g., provided by the DevOps environment of public providers, mainly focus on generic applications, or the automated integration or deployment; they have minimal support for the high performance and quality requirements of social network applications. Besides, they lack techniques to provision resources geographically closer to a specific event, which can lead to failovers such as service failures or performance drops, as the number of streaming users varies together with the processing needs corresponding to an event trigger. Therefore, there is an urgent need to design a complete set of infrastructure framework to provide resources support for the lifecycle of DevOps of social network applications.

3   Architecture and Prototype

The CONF component of ARTICONF project provides a suite of micro-services that collectively perform the planning, provisioning, monitoring, and adaptation of customized virtual infrastructures for federated time and quality critical social network applications. It seamlessly integrates with the cloud/edge infrastructure, able to intelligently provision services based on abstract application service requirements, operational conditions at the infrastructure level, and time-critical event triggering. In this section, we will first introduce the system architecture and then discuss the development and implementation plan of the CONF system.

3.1   System Architecture

Based on the current technical requirements for social network applications, we designed our CONF framework, which is shown in Fig. 1. In general, CONF will adopt a microservice architecture and will be composed of the following components:

- *Manager*. This component is implemented as a REST web service that allows CONF functions to be invoked by external clients. Each request is directed to the appropriate component by the *manager*, which is responsible for coordinating the individual components. Although the service of a single component can be called directly, it is common to perform all operations through the *manager* to simplify the interaction between sub components.
- *Message broker*. This component facilitates communications between the manager and the different components. The message brokering is an architectural pattern for message validation, transformation, and routing. It can help compose asynchronous, loosely coupled applications by providing transparent communications to independent components.

– *Application Specifications.* Each social media application will store and modify its specifications in a social network. Here we need to define QoS/QoE attributes for social network applications to check if they are satisfied for the given scenarios and if there have some potential bottlenecks.
– *Metrics Database.* This component is used by application and infrastructure agents to store predefined metrics. Here we plan to use time series databases (e.g., Cassandra and InfluxDB) because they are capable of collecting large amounts of data and are easy to provide monitoring services.
– *Planner.* This component encapsulates the infrastructure planning functionality. It will use several state-of-the-art scheduling and planning algorithms to produce efficient infrastructure topologies based on application retirements and constraints and will select optimal cost-effective virtual machines.
– *Provisioner.* This component will automate the provisioning of infrastructure plans provided by the *planner* onto underlying infrastructure services. The *provisioner* can decompose the infrastructure description and provision it across multiple clouds, edge or fog infrastructure with transparent network configuration.
– *Deployer.* This component deploys application components onto provisioned cloud/edge infrastructures. The *deployer* is able to schedule based on network bottlenecks and maximize the satisfaction of deployment deadlines. It is also responsible for deploying blockchain applications and a monitor system required to monitor the application as well as its underlying infrastructure autonomously.
– *Controller.* This component will swiftly take measures to control and change the infrastructure solutions based on the QoS metrics of social network applications and their infrastructures. These decisions shall be executed via the whole process of planning, provisioning, and deployment when some actions are needed to ensure system self-adaptability.

3.2   Development and Implementation

For CONF development and implementation, we will follow DevOps practices. Contentious testing and integration tools (e.g., Travis CI) will be leveraged for each development stage. We will define the external APIs with their documentations at first. For example, the *planner* API returns a concrete plan with resources (e.g., the number and size of VMs) based on the abstract plan for the applications. Similarly, given a concrete application plan, the *provisioner* API returns a document with provisioned resources and their specifications (IP addresses, etc.). Moreover, the *deployer* API returns a list of application components that need to be deployed based on the application specification documents produced by *provisioner*. And, given a deployed application, the *controller* API sets rules that will scale any part of the application (software components, VMs, etc.).

Next, we will define some tests for the APIs together with a suitable test environment. For each of the API endpoint, we will define tests to ensure the

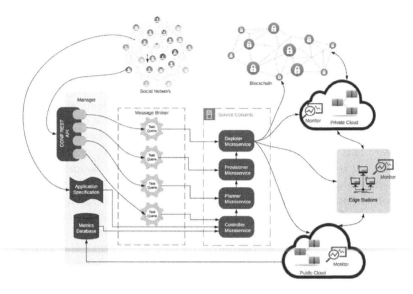

Fig. 1. The system architecture of CONF.

correct functionality of the API. Besides, it is necessary to define a simple representative application with well defined behavior to make sure the REST API performs as expected. And, a communication model should be defined between the components and the *manager*. This communication model should include action messages and status messages, in which the action messages are requests from the manager to the components while the status messages are responses about an action to the manager and will be available to users via the API.

Finally, we will implement each component of CONF one by one. More specifically, *Message Broker* will configure and define message queues that satisfy the communication model. *Manager* will implement the REST APIs and implement message queue dispatchers for each service according to the internal message model. *Planner* will implement parser to extract requirements from an abstract application specification and implement algorithms to achieve the optimal infrastructure plan. *Provisioner* will define abstract API that encapsulates the functionality of clouds (e.g. start, stop, delete and scale VMs) and implement drivers for specific cloud providers (ExoGENI, Amazon, etc.). *Deployer* will implement orchestration engine capable of configuring and installing any kind of social network applications onto VMs or other provisioned resources. *Controller* will implement error measuring and scaling decision making for changing the number and type of resources to achieve self-adaptation.

4   Case Study

Car sharing is a new collaborative model providing an alternative solution to private car ownership. This model allows customers to temporarily use a vehicle (on-demand) at a variable fee, charged depending on the distance traveled or time used. This sharing economy example, which can be business-to-consumer (B2C) or consumer-to-consumer (C2C), intends to satisfy transportation demand in a sustainable way by lowering emissions per city (due to fewer vehicles) and per vehicle (encouraging the use of electric or hybrid cars) and reducing traffic and parking congestion. In this section, we will leverage car sharing as a use case to show how our CONF solution meet the requirements for social network applications.

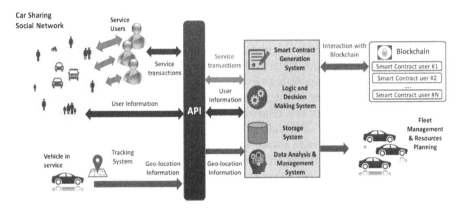

Fig. 2. The car sharing application scenario of AGI.

4.1   Application Scenario

The car sharing use case scenario of AGI (Agilia Center) is shown in Fig. 2. AGI is currently designing a new platform based on the blockchain and smart contracts to face this recent market and meet the appropriate requirements of the service. For this purpose, AGI deploys a social network platform for each city, used by customers to interact, plan (where and when a vehicle is available), hire a service, or share contents like photos and short videos. The platform allows the deployment of smart contracts in blockchain and verifies their compliance. A secondary system tracks the vehicle in service (by user) through a geo-location monitoring system that verifies the time and location in real-time, and the clauses of the contract. This business model suits car-renting companies too, as they use social networks to manage their vehicle fleet according to information provided by customers (e.g. for cleaning, repair, maintenance services). Moreover, the customer service obtains valuable information through data analysis to improve the offered service, forecast budgets, and procurement, design new services, or manage issues with unsatisfied customers. A problem is the unpredictability of the service that often leads to inefficient provisioning of resources. City events or bad weather conditions are examples that involve unexpected service demand peaks and high resource consumption, currently solved by over provisioning to maintain a time-critical response.

4.2   CONF Solutions and Benefits

The car sharing use case evaluates and takes advantage of the CONF impact in the following steps, which is shown in Fig. 3: The owners of vehicles and potential renting users together build a car sharing social network, in which the owners can post their rental advertisements while the users can interact with owners to find available vehicles. New users need to authenticate their identities to enter this social network. At the same time, the car owners need to authorise AGI to manage and track the real-time locations of vehicles. Next, the car sharing social network collects and submits the user information, the geographical location information of vehicles, and the application description data of the car rental behaviour (e.g. renting time, the departure place and the destination) to CONF. Based on these data, CONF calculates the optimal infrastructure support solution through planning algorithms and then triggers public/private cloud service providers to launch corresponding virtualized infrastructures. Besides, some edge resource stations that close to the geographical locations of the problem areas will also be triggered to ensure fast recovery in the presence of faults or performance drops. In this process, CONF has sufficient programmability and controllability to provide flexible infrastructure solutions, and it also avoids vendor lock-in problem for cloud providers in this process.

Then, CONF deploys car sharing blockchain applications on the cloud/edge virtual resource to provide real-time Blockchain-as-a-Service. The blockchain-based platform also supports penalties for contract breaches implemented in the smart contract. Moreover, when new transactions occur, CONF will continuously monitor the real-time status of cloud/edge computing resources and return the results to a metrics database. In this way, CONF can automatically control and adjust the computing resources when some unexpected happened. For example, when there are too much car rental transactions at a certain time and the existing computing resources cannot satisfy the car sharing blockchain applications, CONF will automatically start new cloud/edge infrastructures to meet the needs. Finally, CONF returns data from the cloud and blockchain to the social network so that all historical records of previous car rental transactions can provide a reference for new transactions. In conclusion, the benefits of CONF can be summarized as the following three:

Agile Infrastructure Planning and Provisioning. CONF provides optimized planning and seamless provisioning of customized infrastructure across multiple cloud providers while ensuring a smooth horizontal and vertical scaling of the car sharing social network applications. More specifically, CONF optimize infrastructures solutions for car sharing social network applications in cloud/edge environments through the following actions: 1) Develop new algorithms for planning virtual infrastructure for a given social network application based on constraints on security, performance, locality and budget. 2) Develop an automated infrastructure provisioning engine able to deploy car sharing applications on a federated cloud infrastructure (over multiple sites if necessary). 3) Provide a secure API for the other services to invoke and query the provisioning engine.

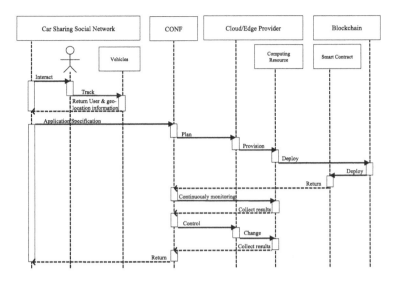

Fig. 3. The sequence diagram of the CONF solutions in car sharing use case.

Pervasive Monitoring of Applications and Infrastructures. The monitoring services offered by CONF allowing systematic collection of information about the runtime status of the car sharing applications and of their underlying infrastructure and network. CONF also provide the analytic necessary to process the monitoring information in real-time and to identify indicators of reduced performance or faults through the following actions: 1) Provide an API for application integration and monitoring of key quality attributes. 2) Develop tools for monitoring the runtime state of the virtual infrastructure hosting an application. 3) Deploy a monitoring database service alongside applications with full integration.

Self-learning Autonomous Infrastructure Adaptation. CONF will implement an infrastructure control model for time and trust-critical car sharing applications that captures the dependencies between infrastructure programmability and the applications performance. This autonomously adapts the infrastructure in response to the threats identified via the CONF's monitoring framework, or to changes in requirements triggered by the other services through the following actions: 1) Research of performance models for time and trust-critical federated social network applications. 2) Development of a control model for adapting the virtual infrastructure based on the interplay between the requirements and the metrics provided via monitoring. 3) Provision of an agent-based service for autonomous adaptation of the CONF-deployed infrastructure.

5   Conclusion and Future Work

In conclusion, to improve the efficiency for customising, provisioning and controlling distributed cloud virtual infrastructures required by time-critical social network applications, CONF aims to deliver technologies providing a self-adaptive and self-monitored infrastructure over orchestrated networked services bringing two benefits. First, it will optimize QoS performance metrics (e.g. distribution time, latency) with proximity-based geo-profiling through seamless provisioning of a customised infrastructure across multiple geographical locations. Second, it will ensure fast recovery in the presence of faults or performance drops through rapid deployment and/or migration of application resources close to problem areas. As we mentioned before, the CONF solution is implemented in the ARTI-CONF project. Currently, some features of CONF are still under development. CONF will work with other components such as the Semantic Model with self-adaptive and Autonomous Relevant Technology (SMART), Trust and Integration Controller (TIC), and Tools for Analytics and Cognition (TAC) to provide integrated services of ARTICONF. For the future work, we will focus on continue to optimize the service components of CONF and design better algorithms to provide better infrastructure services for social network applications.

Acknowledgement. This work was supported by the European Union's Horizon 2020 research and innovation programme under grant agreements 825134 (ARTICONF project).

References

1. Bleikertz, S., Vogel, C., Groß, T.: Cloud radar: near real-time detection of security failures in dynamic virtualized infrastructures. In: Proceedings of the 30th Annual Computer Security Applications Conference, pp. 26–35. ACM (2014)
2. Casale, G., et al.: Current and future challenges of software engineering for services and applications. Procedia Comput. Sci. **97**, 34–42 (2016)
3. Chakravorty, A., Rong, C.: Ushare: user controlled social media based on blockchain. In: Proceedings of the 11th International Conference on Ubiquitous Information Management and Communication, p. 99. ACM (2017)
4. Evans, K., et al.: Dynamically reconfigurable workflows for time-critical applications. In: Proceedings of the 10th Workshop on Workflows in Support of Large-Scale Science, p. 7. ACM (2015)
5. Gill, S.S., Chana, I., Singh, M., Buyya, R.: CHOPPER: an intelligent qos-aware autonomic resource management approach for cloud computing. Cluster Comput. **21**(2), 1203–1241 (2018). https://doi.org/10.1007/s10586-017-1040-z
6. Hu, Y., Zhou, H., de Laat, C., Zhao, Z.: ECSched: efficient container scheduling on heterogeneous clusters. In: Aldinucci, M., Padovani, L., Torquati, M. (eds.) Euro-Par 2018. LNCS, vol. 11014, pp. 365–377. Springer, Cham (2018). https://doi.org/10.1007/978-3-319-96983-1_26
7. Kim, M., Lee, H.: SMCC: social media cloud computing model for developing SNS based on social media. In: Lee, G., Howard, D., Ślęzak, D. (eds.) ICHIT 2011. CCIS, vol. 206, pp. 259–266. Springer, Heidelberg (2011). https://doi.org/10.1007/978-3-642-24106-2_34

8. Koulouzis, S., Belloum, A.S., Bubak, M.T., Zhao, Z., Živković, M., de Laat, C.T.: SDN-aware federation of distributed data. Future Gener. Comput. Syst. **56**, 64–76 (2016)
9. Kousiouris, G., et al.: A toolkit based architecture for optimizing cloud management, performance evaluation and provider selection processes. In: 2017 International Conference on High Performance Computing & Simulation (HPCS), pp. 224–232. IEEE (2017)
10. Mohammed, B., Modu, B., Maiyama, K.M., Ugail, H., Awan, I., Kiran, M.: Failure analysis modelling in an infrastructure as a service (Iaas) environment. Electron. Notes Theor. Comput. Sci. **340**, 41–54 (2018)
11. Sun, Y., White, J., Eade, S.: A model-based system to automate cloud resource allocation and optimization. In: Dingel, J., Schulte, W., Ramos, I., Abrahão, S., Insfran, E. (eds.) MODELS 2014. LNCS, vol. 8767, pp. 18–34. Springer, Cham (2014). https://doi.org/10.1007/978-3-319-11653-2_2
12. Tan, M., Su, X.: Media cloud: when media revolution meets rise of cloud computing. In: Proceedings of 2011 IEEE 6th International Symposium on Service Oriented System (SOSE), pp. 251–261. IEEE (2011)
13. Wang, J., et al.: Planning virtual infrastructures for time critical applications with multiple deadline constraints. Future Gener. Comput. Syst. **75**, 365–375 (2017)
14. Wu, Y., Wu, C., Li, B., Zhang, L., Li, Z., Lau, F.: Scaling social media applications into geo-distributed clouds. IEEE/ACM Trans. Netw. (TON) **23**(3), 689–702 (2015)
15. Yang, C.T., Chen, S.T., Liu, J.C., Yang, Y.Y., Mitra, K., Ranjan, R.: Implementation of a real-time network traffic monitoring service with network functions virtualization. Future Gener. Comput. Syst. **93**, 687–701 (2019)
16. Yuriyama, M., Kushida, T.: Sensor-cloud infrastructure-physical sensor management with virtualized sensors on cloud computing. In: NBiS, vol. 10, pp. 1–8 (2010)
17. Zhao, Z., van Albada, D., Sloot, P.: Agent-based flow control for HLA components. SIMULATION **81**(7), 487–501 (2005)
18. Zhao, Z., Belloum, A., De Laat, C., Adriaans, P., Hertzberger, B.: Using Jade agent framework to prototype an e-Science workflow bus. In: Seventh IEEE International Symposium on Cluster Computing and the Grid, CCGrid 2007, pp. 655–660. IEEE, Rio de Janeiro, May 2007
19. Zhou, H., et al.: CloudsStorm: a framework for seamlessly programming and controlling virtual infrastructure functions during the DevOps lifecycle of cloud applications. Softw. Pract. Experience **49**(10), 1421–1447 (2019)
20. Zhou, H., Ouyang, X., Su, J., Laat, C., Zhao, Z.: Enforcing trustworthy cloud SLA with witnesses: A game theorybased model using smart contracts. Concurrency Comput. Pract. Experience (2019)

Auto-scaling for a Streaming Architecture with Fuzzy Deep Reinforcement Learning

Dong Nguyen Doan[1(✉)], Daniela Zaharie[1], and Dana Petcu[1,2]

[1] Computer Science Department, West University of Timişoara, Timişoara, Romania
{dong.nguyen10,daniela.zaharie,dana.petcu}@e-uvt.ro
[2] Institute e-Austria Timişoara, Timişoara, Romania

Abstract. A streaming architecture is aiming to transport, process and store data and acts on real-time or nearly real-time for Big Data analytics and Internet of Things (IoT). The main requirement for such architecture to achieve its aim is the elasticity. Cloud computing is an excellent solution to satisfy the elasticity requirement. Its auto-scaling processes are allowing to automatically acquire or release resources according to the arriving workload. However, the fluctuation in scaling up and down resources is still not fully solved. We propose a novel approach called Fuzzy Deep Reinforcement Learning to scale the resources effectively and efficiently. The experimental results show that our proposed approach outperforms the existing approach based on Fuzzy Q-Learning.

Keywords: Cloud computing · Auto-scaling · Fuzzy Logic · Reinforcement Learning

1 Introduction

The rise of social media, IoT and multimedia have yielded an enormous data flow in term of volume and data types [17]. With the growth rate in the volume of data, an appropriate platform for data storage and analysis the data is needed.

The streaming architecture is widely used for Big Data analytics and IoT. The data is transported from data sources for processing, filtering, enriching and storing. The elasticity is a strong requirement for such architecture.

Cloud computing is a computing paradigm offering services to users on demand [27]. It is a promising solution to facilitate Big Data storage and provide the requested processing capacity [21]. One of the key features in Cloud Computing is the elasticity allowing the resources to be acquired and released dynamically. However, deciding on the appropriate amount of resources to be provisioned/de-provisioned is still problematic. An auto-scaling process is able to scale the amount of resources automatically in response to the change of workload to fulfill the Quality of Service (QoS) parameters namely, minimizing response time or cost for availability. In this work, we refer to the resources as being Virtual Machines (VMs) and the workload is referred as inputs for a given system [11].

U. Schwardmann et al. (Eds.): Euro-Par 2019 Workshops, LNCS 11997, pp. 476–488, 2020.
https://doi.org/10.1007/978-3-030-48340-1_37

There have been many approaches proposed recently for auto-scaling. Their methodologies are related to Threshold-based rules, Time series analysis, Queuing Theory, Control Theory, and Reinforcement Learning (RL). Unfortunately, the threshold-based rules can lead to instability with the high variation in workload. The time series analysis is utilized by predicting workload or resources but the uncertainty of predictions is a major obstacle. Queuing theory can be used as a reactive or proactive approach, but a deep understanding of systems is required, and its assumption is unrealistic. Control theory is appropriate for workload with low variation, but it will fail in case of a sudden burst in workload.

RL is a solution for auto-scaling problem in the case when the various types of workload are involved. RL can be combined with Fuzzy Logic Control in the self-adaptive mechanism: RL can tune the conclusions of Fuzzy Inference System (FIS) and Fuzzy Logic can generalize the state space in RL. Fuzzy Q-Learning (FQL) approaches have been applied successfully in capacity control [25] and auto-scaling problem [6] on clouds. However, the fluctuation in provisioning resources with the high variation in workload is still not fully solved.

The aim of this study is to investigate the auto-scaling efficiency of the FQL approach for a streaming architecture based on Cloud and propose and investigate the benefits of another approach using Fuzzy Logic and Deep RL[1].

The rest of this paper is organized as follows. The next section discusses the related work. Section 3 discusses the Big Data streaming architecture, FIS, and RL. The FQL and the proposed approach for auto-scaling are introduced in Sect. 4. Section 5 is about experimental setup and simulations. Finally, the conclusions are in Sect. 6.

2   Related Work

The auto-scaling approaches can be classified according to criteria such as architectures, policies, and techniques.

The architectures can be centralized or decentralized [2]. Most of the researches and business solutions focus on the centralized architecture. In centralized architectures, there is only one controller in charge of provisioning and de-provisioning the resources. Whereas, decentralized architecture has many controllers, as in [10,12]. The auto-scaling action policies can be grouped into two classes: reactive and proactive [23]. The reactive one uses the last value obtained from the environments for the system to react. The proactive systems take the predicted demands to make the decisions. In term of the techniques, the approaches are divided into five groups: Threshold-based rules, Time series analysis, Control theory, Queuing theory, and RL [2,23].

The threshold-based rules are popularly used by cloud providers namely Amazon EC2 or RightScale. This technique can be seen as a reactive approach. The rules contain conditions defined based on several metrics namely request rates, CPU loads, and average response time. This approach is very intuitive

---

[1] https://github.com/doandongnguyen/autoscaling.

and simple but it requires a good knowledge of systems to be setup. The work in [15] uses threshold-based rules and RL for horizontal scaling. The authors also propose a method to prevent oscillations by using the cool-down time.

In auto-scaling, time series analysis is used to detect the patterns in workloads and forecast future values. The authors of [28] used an Auto-Regressive model to predict workload. An optimization algorithm uses the response time estimated by the predicted workload to compute the best resource allocations. The algorithm considers the SLA violation, configuration and leasing resources. In [18], a sliding window of history values is used as inputs of a Neural Network (NN) to predict future values to decrease the SLA violations by initializing the VMs boot in advance for the demand in resources. The main drawback of time series analysis is the reduced accuracy of predictions that is highly dependent on the workload pattern, and history windows [23].

Queuing theory is a mathematical study for queues or waiting lines. The metrics used in queuing are arrival rate, waiting time or service rate. The Queuing Network is used in [31] to model applications. Based on the predicted workload, the number of servers for each layer can be calculated. In [4], a queuing model is developed for a Cloud-hosted application to estimate the resource based on the parameters such as a given workload and the mean response time. The queuing theory-based approaches are invalid for complex and real systems because they usually do not satisfy the stationarity assumption [5]. Besides, it requires a good knowledge of systems to be modelled [13].

Control theory enables the dynamic systems to maintain the output or controlled variable close to the desired value by adjusting the input or manipulated variable. The manipulated variable can be the number of VMs, and the controlled variable can be the SLA value, CPU load and so on. Control theory is used as a reactive approach, but it can be proactive if it is combined with a predictive model. In [3] a hybrid controller is proposed for adaptive control to scale up and down, in which the workload is estimated by using a queuing model. In [9], an adaptive controller is combined with a statistical model to predict the performance of systems and minimize the number of resources. The use of control theory as the reactive approaches are suitable in case of the slow change in workload. For proactive approaches, finding a reliable predictive model is still a challenge [23].

RL is a type of machine learning where an agent is learning by interacting with an environment to maximize its rewards. In the context of auto-scaling, an agent is considered as an auto-scaler. The agent makes a decision to scale based on the current state that can be the workload or the current number of VMs. The popularly used approaches are Q-Learning algorithm and SARSA. In [30], a SARSA approach is used for resource allocation, in which the workload and the number of allocated VMs are considered as the states. The authors of [6] propose an approach for horizontal scaling in Openstack where Q-Learning tunes FIS conclusions. The used workloads in experiments are bursting, variation and fast growth patterns. The paper [24] reports the use of Deep RL to learn how to allocate and schedule computer resources to waiting jobs in order to minimize

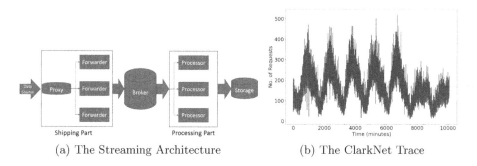

(a) The Streaming Architecture   (b) The ClarkNet Trace

Fig. 1. The streaming architecture and the workload evolution

the average job slowdown. The difficulties in RL approach are time-consuming in training and the exploration-exploitation trade-off.

The fluctuations in provisioning (or oscillations) comes from scaling the resources up/down too frequently. That would lead to a negative impact on the systems. The main reason is due to the high variation in workload. Most of the work focused on the effectiveness of auto-scaling to ensure the QoS parameters namely minimizing the response time or cost. In this paper, we propose a novel approach aiming to tackle these difficulties of RL and the fluctuations of auto-scaling with the high variation of workload.

3   Theoretical Background

3.1   Big Data Streaming Architecture

A streaming architecture is an architecture that has a capability of ingesting the incoming data [7]. The architecture is illustrated as in Fig. 1a. The data are transported from Data Source by a Shipping part to a message broker or buffer layer. The roles of the buffer layer are decoupling the architecture between the shipping part and the processing part and ensuring that the data will not be lost. The processing part has several roles such as transforming, validating and enriching data. The ELK architecture (ElasticSearch, Logstash and Kibana) is an example of a streaming architecture which is used in our monitoring platform [14].

There are some existing obstacles in the streaming architecture. On one hand, a problem is the system degradation and the loss of incoming data due to the bottleneck at the broker. The processing part usually requires a lot of computing resources and is time-consuming. This might lead to the explosion for the buffer due to accumulating data over time when the incoming data exceeds the processing capacity of the system. On the other hand, if the incoming data is low, it requires few processors to consume the data. Hence, there is a need for a mechanism to acquire and release automatically the computation resources according to the change in incoming data.

3.2   Fuzzy Inference Systems

In the context of RL, Fuzzy Logic can be used as an approach to cope with continuous spaces of states and actions. On the other hand, in the context of Fuzzy Logic, machine learning can be used to tune fuzzy controllers [20].

Let x be the input variable, $x = (x^1, x^2, \ldots, x^M)$, and o the output variable $o = (o^1, o^2, \ldots, o^K)$. A rule R_j, $j \in J$ in a FIS has the following form:

$$R_j : \textbf{IF} \quad (x^1 \text{ is } L_j^1) \ldots \textbf{AND} \quad (x^i \text{ is } L_j^i) \ldots \textbf{AND} \quad (x^M \text{ is } L_j^M) \quad \textbf{THEN} \quad a = o_j$$

where R_j is the j-th rule in the rule base, L_j^i is a fuzzy label (linguistic term) of the input variable x^i and o_j is a vectorial output variable.

The first step in a FIS is to map the input variables into fuzzy sets by the membership functions $\mu_{L_j^i}(x)$. The fuzzy set values are computed corresponding to the fuzzy labels. After that, the degree of truth values for a given input vector x is calculated as in Eq. 1. Finally, based on the degree of truth values, the output will be calculated and tuned by using RL (described in Sect. 4.1).

$$\alpha_j(x) = \prod_{i=1}^{M} \mu_{L_j^i}(x^i) \tag{1}$$

In our proposed approach, we use Fuzzy Logic as a data representation for the input variables. Therefore, we are interested in the degree of truth values.

3.3   Reinforcement Learning

RL [29] is based on a trial-and-error process. At the time step t, an agent observes a state s_t, then it chooses an action a_t to interact with the environment to get the next state s_{t+1} and a reward r_{t+1}. The objective of the agent is to find a policy which the optimal action (a) is mapped to the state (s_t) in order to maximize the expected cumulative discounted reward: $\sum_{k=0}^{\infty} \gamma^k r_{t+k+1}$, where $\gamma \in [0, 1]$ is a discount factor that determines the relative importance of future rewards.

The policy is based on the function $Q(s_t, a)$, a so-called Q-value function, that represents the goodness of an action a taken in state s_t. The most used approach to construct the Q-value function is the Q-Learning algorithm.

4   Algorithms for Auto-scaling

4.1   Fuzzy Q-Learning

Fuzzy Q-Learning (FQL) [20] is a method in which the conclusions of FIS are tuned by using RL. FQL has been successfully applied to auto-scaling problems [6]. Therefore, we use FQL as a baseline. The algorithm is described in Algorithm 1.

The RL formulations are defined as follow:

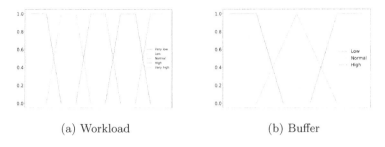

(a) Workload   (b) Buffer

Fig. 2. Membership functions for Workload and Buffer

State Space. Fuzzy Inference maps the set of inputs to a set of outputs through fuzzy rules [6]. In our case, the input is $x = (w, b)$, where (w) is the workload and (b) is the occupied buffer percentage. The membership functions will partition the state space of each input variable into fuzzy sets. The linguistic terms for workload (w) are {*very low, low, normal, high, very high*}, and for the occupied buffer (b) are {*low, normal, high*}. The membership functions are triangular and trapezoidal as in Fig. 2 and they have been selected by fine-tuning and by using prior knowledge on the data. Consequently, there are 15 states by fully combining membership functions of the variables w and b.

Action Space. An action specifies a change in the number of VM instances and the possible values are in $\{-2, -1, 0, 1, 2\}$ corresponding to decrease/increase (1 or 2 VMs) or keep the number unchanged. An example of a rule is:

IF w is high AND b is high THEN a = 2

where a is the control signal.

Reward. We consider two criteria to design the reward function r_t. Firstly, it is the occupied buffer percentage violations. The purpose is to keep this percentage in a safe zone which can be in a range $[low\_threshold, high\_threshold]$ such as $[30, 70]$ or $[40, 60]$. Another criterion is to minimize the number of resources. Thus, following [6], the reward function can be defined by combining these criteria as in Eq. 2:

$$r_t = w_1 \cdot BU_t + w_2 \cdot \left(1 - \frac{vm_t}{vm_{max}}\right) \qquad (2)$$

where BU_t is estimated using Eq. 3, vm_t is the current number of VMs and vm_{max} is the maximum number of VMs. w_1, w_2 are weights to indicate the relative importance of each term in the reward function. Their values are in $[0, 1]$ and $w_1 + w_2 = 1$.

$$BU_t = \begin{cases} -(b(t) - hi\_thres)/(b_{max} - hi\_thres) & \text{if } b(t) > hi\_thres \\ -2(b(t) - hi\_thres)/(hi\_thres - lo\_thres) & \text{if } b(t) \in [mid\_thres, hi\_thres] \\ (b(t) - lo\_thres)/lo\_thres & \text{if } b(t) < lo\_thres \\ 2(b(t) - lo\_thres)/(hi\_thres - lo\_thres) & \text{if } b(t) \in [lo\_thre, mid\_thres] \end{cases}$$

$$\qquad (3)$$

Algorithm 1. FQL Algorithm

Require: Discount factor γ and learning rate η
1: Initialize q-values table, $q[i, k]$.
2: Observe the current state, s_t.
3: Choose an action,a_i for each rule for state s_t based on $\epsilon - greedy$ policy
  $a_i = \underset{k}{\operatorname{argmax}}\, q[i, k]$ with probability 1 - ϵ
  $a_i = random(\{1, 2, \ldots, K\})$ with probability ϵ
4: Select the rule i^* for which $\alpha_{i^*}(s_t)$ (in Eq.1) is maximal and set the action a to a_{i^*}
5: Approximate the Q function using:
  $Q(s_t, a) = \sum\limits_{i \in J} (\alpha_i(s_t) \cdot q[i, a_i])$
6: Execute action a and observe the reward, r_{t+1}, and the new state s_{t+1}. The value of the new state s_{t+1} is calculated by:
  $V(s_{t+1}) = \sum\limits_{i \in J} \alpha_i(s_{t+1}) \cdot \max\limits_{k}(q[i, k])$
7: The error signal is calculated as following formula:
  $\Delta Q = r_{t+1} + \gamma \cdot V(s_{t+1}) - Q(s_t, a)$
8: Update the q-values:
  $q[i, a_i] \leftarrow q[i, a_i] + \eta \cdot \Delta Q \cdot \alpha_i(s_t)$
9: Set the state s_t to the new state s_{t+1}
10: Repeat from step 3 until converged

---

where $b(t)$ is the current value for the buffer, b_{max} is the maximum value (100), lo_thres, hi_thres is the *low threshold* and *high threshold* to be controlled. In our experiments, we chose the range $[30, 70]$. The *mid_threshold* value is 50. The computation of BU_t is a refined version of that proposed in [6].

4.2   Deep Q-Network

The drawback of Q-Learning method is that it cannot cope with a large number of states. To overcome this problem, there are some methods to approximate the Q-value function such as Support Vector Machines and NNs. The Deep Q-Network (DQN) [26] is one of the most widely-used methods. Recently, there have been many new variants aiming to improve the DQN performance.

For the basic DQN, the Q-values tend to be overestimated. In the Double DQN [32], a target network is used to calculate the $Q(s_{t+1}, a)$ and then updated with the trained network after a given step. The $\epsilon - greedy$ policy is the most used method for exploration-exploitation in RL. The ϵ value is decreased over time from 1.0 to a small value such as 0.1 or 0.05. This method is efficient for a simple environment, but it is still hard to control in the learning process. In [16], a method is proposed for exploration-exploitation. The idea is to put noise into the fully connected layers of the NN and then adjust the network weights and biases using back-propagation during training. In dueling DQN [33], the $Q(s_t, a)$ is divided into two quantities: the state value $V(s_t)$ and the advantage of the action $A(s_t, a)$. Therefore, dueling DQN takes the features and process them in two paths: one path is to predict $V(s_t)$ and the other is to predict individual advantage value $A(s_t, a)$. Then, $Q(s_t, a)$ is the sum of $V(s_t)$ and $A(s_t, a)$ [22]. Another improvement of DQN performance is obtained by using the Distributional DQN [8]. The Q-values are replaced with a probability distribution.

4.3 Fuzzy Deep Reinforcement Learning

In this subsection, we describe our Fuzzy Deep RL method which is based on using Fuzzy Logic to generate features from data and on using the recent techniques mentioned previously to improve performance.

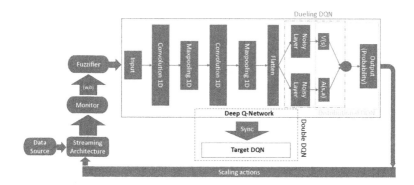

Fig. 3. Fuzzy deep RL framework

The framework of the proposed approach for auto-scaling in a streaming architecture is depicted as in Fig. 3. The monitor part is to collect the metrics including the current workload, percentage of occupied buffer values and the number of VMs, from the streaming architecture. The fuzzifier is responsible with the transformation of the crisp values (w, b) into degree of truth values based on the predefined membership functions. The DQN will take the transformed values as an input and then, make decisions. The RL elements are defined as follow:

State Space. The workload and occupied buffer values can be considered as the time series data. Using a sliding window of history values is a common technique to process time series data for forecasting and classifying. Therefore, instead of taking a single value for each input variable as in FQL algorithm, we use N recent past values as the sliding window for both workload w and buffer occupied percentage b. These values will be fuzzified, thus the result is a $L \times N$ matrix containing the degrees of truth values (Eq. 1), where L denotes the total number of rules. Using Fuzzy Logic to generate meaningful features also can be applied for time series classification and prediction.

Action Space. We also consider five actions $\{-2, -1, 0, 1, 2\}$ as in Sect. 4.1.

Reward. The reward function is designed as in Sect. 4.1.

DQN Model. We use a Deep NN as in Fig. 3 with several Convolution 1D and MaxPooling 1D layers to extract features from the generated states. These layers are used popularly for time series forecasting and Natural Language Processing. We also use the Noisy layers, Double, Dueling and Distributional DQN in our model. The combination of the variants in DQN has been proved to improve significantly the performance [22].

5   Experiment Settings and Results

5.1   Experiment Settings

Simulation Tool. The workload used in the experiment is the Clarknet Trace [1] as in Fig. 1b that describes the number of HTTP requests to the servers. This workload is highly varying in time.

Our simulation tool for the streaming architecture contains three parts. The first part is the generator which is responsible to generate the workload and ingest to the buffer. The generator is considered as the shipping part in the streaming architecture. The buffer or message broker collects the incoming data. The last part is the processor which will take data from the buffer and process it.

The amount of processed requests follows a Beta distribution with parameters $a = 20$ and $b = 2$ [19]. The maximum number of VMs in the simulation is 5.

The simulation tool also considers the latency for scaling up decisions. Typically, it takes $5 - 10$ minutes to turn on a VM; therefore, after 10 iterations (one iteration corresponds to one minute), a new instance will be brought up. In addition, the cool-down time is set to 10 for each scaling decision.

A monitoring part is used to record the data when conducting experiments. The recorded data includes the workload, occupied buffer percentage and current number of VMs. The models will take these data from the monitor to learn but the taken workload data will be smoothed by a sliding window with a size of 5.

Parameter Settings for Algorithms. For FQL algorithm settings, we set the discount factor $\gamma = 0.99$ to take into account on future rewards and the learning rate $\eta = 0.1$ to have less impact on the recent one. For the $\epsilon - greedy$ policy, we set the maximum value for ϵ to 1.0 and decrease to the minimum value of 0.1 since we consider less fluctuations in provisioning VMs. The learning process will be stopped when the changing in Q-values table is small or after enough iterations (the maximum iteration value is 280 was used).

For the Fuzzy DQN settings, the discount factor γ is chosen to be 0.99. We set the window size for the number of recent series values, N, to 10. In the DQN architecture, we used two Convolution 1D layers with 32 filters (the kernel size of 2 for the first layer and 3 for the second), two MaxPooling 1D layers with the kernel size of 3 and stride size of 2 and Noisy layers with the size of 128 for exploration. Also, we utilize the Double, Dueling and Distributional DQN. The learning process also will be stopped when the mean reward is high enough (the threshold value of 140 was used) or after enough epochs. The used parameters have obtained by fine-tuning during conducting experiments.

We choose the values for the weights $w_1 = 0.8$ and $w_2 = 0.2$ in Eq. 2 to put more importance on the buffer percentage term.

5.2 Experimental Results

Figure 4 and 5 show the behaviors of the proposed approach and of the FQL model after training with the Clarknet set and the mean of 50 recent cumulative rewards after training, respectively. It is clear that the Fuzzy DQN outperforms the FQL model in term of scaling behavior (Fig. 4a and 5a) and training time as the Fuzzy DQN converges much faster than the FQL (Fig. 4b and 5b). Furthermore, the mean rewards during FQL model training have fluctuations while in the case of Fuzzy DQN, they are much smoother.

Although the occupied buffer percentage is in the control range, the resources are scaled frequently in the FQL approach due to the high variations of workloads and the dynamic of systems namely, the delay in scaling VMs, in which the monitor does not record the metrics during turning on VMs. Therefore, the time axis in Fig. 5a is less than the one in Fig. 4a. Furthermore, Fuzzy Logic is to divide the input values into parts, so it can be seen as a smoothing approach to make the workload less fluctuated, but it seems to be insufficient for FQL approach. The results on FQL model, reported in [6], have been obtained for data with much less frequent changes in the workload which might be unrealistic.

On the contrary, by taking series of workloads and buffer values, the Convolution filters used in the Fuzzy DQN model are able to extract appropriate features to allow the DQN to learn well the particularities of the data. Therefore, the scaling behavior of Fuzzy DQN approach is more stable than FQL approach.

In a real world context, we can use the original workload to train the model without changing or tweaking it; so the setup and training time can be reduced with respect to those corresponding to the case when the model in [6] is used.

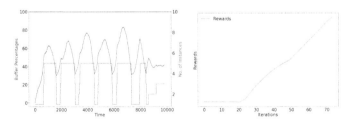

(a) Fuzzy DQN scaling behavior (b) Mean rewards vs. Iterations

Fig. 4. Fuzzy DQN results

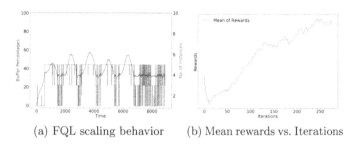

(a) FQL scaling behavior   (b) Mean rewards vs. Iterations

Fig. 5. FQL results

6   Conclusions and Future Work

In this paper, we propose a novel approach applied in auto-scaling for a streaming architecture. The results show that our approach outperforms the existing one with respect to the training time, setup cost and scaling behavior. As in the common case of RL, finding optimal configurations and convergence thresholds is still a challenge also in the proposed approach. The hyper-parameters involved in the DQN need to be tuned carefully. Also, designing the reward functions is nontrivial because the parameters used in the rewards functions also need to be tuned. However, we believe that the proposed approach is a promising solution not only for auto-scaling but also for scheduling problems.

Acknowledgement. The work of the third author has received funds from H2020 ASPIDE action (Agreement 801091 with European Commission).

References

1. ClarkNet HTTP Trace (From the Internet Traffic Archive). ftp://ita.ee.lbl.gov/traces/. Accessed 20 May 2019
2. Al-Dhuraibi, Y., Paraiso, F., Djarallah, N., Merle, P.: Elasticity in cloud computing: state of the art and research challenges. IEEE Trans. Serv. Comput. **11**(2), 430–447 (2018)
3. Ali-Eldin, A., Kihl, M., Tordsson, J., Elmroth, E.: Efficient provisioning of bursty scientific workloads on the cloud using adaptive elasticity control. In: Proceedings of the 3rd workshop on Scientific Cloud Computing, pp. 31–40. ACM (2012)
4. Ali-Eldin, A., Tordsson, J., Elmroth, E.: An adaptive hybrid elasticity controller for cloud infrastructures. In: 2012 IEEE Network Operations and Management Symposium, pp. 204–212. IEEE (2012)
5. Allspaw, J.: The Art of Capacity Planning: Scaling Web Resources. O'Reilly Media Inc., Sebastopol (2008)
6. Arabnejad, H., Jamshidi, P., Estrada, G., El Ioini, N., Pahl, C.: An auto-scaling cloud controller using fuzzy Q-learning - implementation in OpenStack. In: Aiello, M., Johnsen, E.B., Dustdar, S., Georgievski, I. (eds.) ESOCC 2016. LNCS, vol. 9846, pp. 152–167. Springer, Cham (2016). https://doi.org/10.1007/978-3-319-44482-6_10

7. Azarmi, B.: Scalable Big Data Architecture. Apress, Berkeley (2016). https://doi.org/10.1007/978-1-4842-1326-1

8. Bellemare, M.G., Dabney, W., Munos, R.: A distributional perspective on reinforcement learning. In: Proceedings of the 34th International Conference on Machine Learning-Volume 70, pp. 449–458 (2017). JMLR.org

9. Bodík, P., Griffith, R., Sutton, C.A., Fox, A., Jordan, M.I., Patterson, D.A.: Statistical machine learning makes automatic control practical for internet datacenters. HotCloud **9**, 12 (2009)

10. Calcavecchia, N.M., Caprarescu, B.A., Di Nitto, E., Dubois, D.J., Petcu, D.: DEPAS: a decentralized probabilistic algorithm for auto-scaling. Computing **94**(8–10), 701–730 (2012)

11. Calzarossa, M.C., Massari, L., Tessera, D.: Workload characterization: a survey revisited. ACM Comput. Surv. **48**(3), 48:1–48:43 (2016)

12. Chieu, T.C., Chan, H.: Dynamic resource allocation via distributed decisions in cloud environment. In: 2011 IEEE 8th International Conference on e-Business Engineering, pp. 125–130. IEEE (2011)

13. Das, R., Tesauro, G., Walsh, W.E.: Model-based and model-free approaches to autonomic resource allocation. IBM Ressearch report, RC 23802 (2005)

14. Doan, D.N., Iuhasz, G.: Tuning Logstash garbage collection for high throughput in a monitoring platform. In: 2016 18th International Symposium on Symbolic and Numeric Algorithms for Scientific Computing (SYNASC), pp. 359–365. IEEE (2016)

15. Dutreilh, X., Moreau, A., Malenfant, J., Rivierre, N., Truck, I.: From data center resource allocation to control theory and back. In: 2010 IEEE 3rd International Conference on Cloud Computing, pp. 410–417. IEEE (2010)

16. Fortunato, M., et al.: Noisy networks for exploration. arXiv preprint arXiv:1706.10295 (2017)

17. Hashem, I.A.T., Yaqoob, I., Anuar, N.B., Mokhtar, S., Gani, A., Khan, S.U.: The rise of "big data" on cloud computing: Review and open research issues. Inf. Syst. **47**, 98–115 (2015)

18. Islam, S., Keung, J., Lee, K., Liu, A.: Empirical prediction models for adaptive resource provisioning in the cloud. Future Gener. Comput. Syst. **28**(1), 155–162 (2012)

19. Janert, P.K.: Feedback Control for Computer Systems: Introducing Control Theory to Enterprise Programmers. O'Reilly Media Inc., Sebastopol (2013)

20. Jouffe, L.: Fuzzy inference system learning by reinforcement methods. IEEE Trans. Syst. Man Cybern. Part C (Appl. Rev.) **28**(3), 338–355 (1998)

21. Khan, Z., Anjum, A., Kiani, S.L.: Cloud based big data analytics for smart future cities. In: 2013 IEEE/ACM 6th International Conference on Utility and Cloud Computing, pp. 381–386. IEEE (2013)

22. Lapan, M.: Deep Reinforcement Learning Hands-On: Apply Modern RL Methods, with Deep Q-Networks, Value Iteration, Policy Gradients, TRPO, AlphaGo Zero and More. Packt Publishing Ltd., Birmingham (2018)

23. Lorido-Botran, T., Miguel-Alonso, J., Lozano, J.A.: A review of auto-scaling techniques for elastic applications in cloud environments. J. Grid Comput. **12**(4), 559–592 (2014)

24. Mao, H., Alizadeh, M., Menache, I., Kandula, S.: Resource management with deep reinforcement learning. In: Proceedings of the 15th ACM Workshop on Hot Topics in Networks, pp. 50–56. ACM (2016)

25. Masoumzadeh, S.S., Hlavacs, H., Tomás, L.: A self-adaptive performance-aware capacity controller in overbooked datacenters. In: 2016 International Conference on Cloud and Autonomic Computing (ICCAC), pp. 12–23. IEEE (2016)

26. Mnih, V., et al.: Playing Atari with deep reinforcement learning. arXiv preprint arXiv:1312.5602 (2013)

27. Peter, M., Timothy, G.: The nist definition of cloud computing. NIST Spec. Publ. **800**, 800–814 (2011)

28. Roy, N., Dubey, A., Gokhale, A.: Efficient autoscaling in the cloud using predictive models for workload forecasting. In: 2011 IEEE 4th International Conference on Cloud Computing, pp. 500–507, July 2011

29. Sutton, R.S., Barto, A.G.: Reinforcement Learning: An Introduction. MIT Press, Cambridge (2018)

30. Tesauro, G., Jong, N.K., Das, R., Bennani, M.N.: A hybrid reinforcement learning approach to autonomic resource allocation. In: 2006 IEEE International Conference on Autonomic Computing, pp. 65–73. IEEE (2006)

31. Urgaonkar, B., Shenoy, P., Chandra, A., Goyal, P., Wood, T.: Agile dynamic provisioning of multi-tier internet applications. ACM Trans. Auton. Adapt. Syst. (TAAS) **3**(1), 1 (2008)

32. Van Hasselt, H., Guez, A., Silver, D.: Deep reinforcement learning with double q-learning. In: Thirtieth AAAI Conference on Artificial Intelligence (2016)

33. Wang, Z., Schaul, T., Hessel, M., Van Hasselt, H., Lanctot, M., De Freitas, N.: Dueling network architectures for deep reinforcement learning. arXiv preprint arXiv:1511.06581 (2015)

ParaMo - International Workshop on Parallel Programming

Workshop on Parallel Programming Models in HP Cloud (ParaMo)

Workshop Description

ParaMo is a forum for researchers working on programming models, networkings, managements, and runtimes for solving the problems on parallel computing in HP cloud. The notion of cloud computing has changed the way we utilize computing resources. Since High-Performance Computing (HPC) has long suffered from under- or over-utilization of resources, many HPC researchers are trying to adapt HPC applications to the cloud environment. With proper adaptation, HPC applications are able to enhance their resource utilization ratio and scalability by using virtualized and on-demand resources on clouds. While we discuss HPC on clouds, we should include the topics of parallel programming models as well. Various parallel programming models and their frameworks (e.g., MPI, OpenMP, OpenCL, CUDA, and MapReduce) have been proposed for parallel computing. For example, the MapReduce programming model has been used for various big data processing applications since it helps to reduce the complexity of problem parallelization such as decomposition, communication, and scheduling. However, a parallel programming model should be carefully selected for HPC applications to achieve high-performance and efficient resource usage because their target hardware architectures (e.g., many-core, GPU, Infiniband, etc.) are different as well as the abstraction levels. In addition, since traditional parallel programming models, such as MPI, are implemented for a single tenant cluster environment, applying these models to HPC applications on the cloud is challenging in terms of resource management.

The First International Workshop on Parallel Computing Models in High-Performance Cloud (ParaMo 2019) was held in Göttingen, Germany. The workshop was organized in conjunction with the Euro-Par annual series of international conferences and the format of the workshop was the technical presentation of research papers. Around 20 people attended the workshop.

This year, we received six articles for review, from four countries. After a thorough peer-reviewing process, we selected four articles for presentation at the workshop. The review process focused on the quality of the papers, their innovative ideas, and the soundness of the presentation. The acceptance of the papers was the result of the reviewers' discussion and agreement. As a consequence, the quality and the relevance of the selected articles was high, despite an pretty large acceptance ratio (66%).

I would like to thank the ParaMo Steering Committee and the Program Committee, who made the workshop possible. I would also like to thank Euro-Par for hosting our community, and the Euro-Par workshop chairs Dora B. Heras, Christian Boehme, and Ulrich Schwardmann for their help and support.

Organization

Program Chairs

Sangyoon Oh	Ajou University, South Korea
Hyun-Wook Jin	Konkuk University, South Korea

Steering Committee

Geoffrey C. Fox	Indiana University, USA
Dhabaleswar K. Panda	Ohio State University, USA

Publicity Chair

Minho Bae	Ajou University, South Korea

Program Committee

Mehmet Aktas	Yildiz University, Turkey
Seung-Hee Bae	Western Michigan University, USA
Jee Choi	University of Oregon, USA
Jong Choi	Oak Ridge National Laboratory, USA
Cheol-Ho Hong	Chung-Ang University, South Korea
Xiaoyi Lu	Ohio State University, USA
Blesson Varghese	Queen's University Belfast, UK
Abhinav Vishnu	AMD, USA
Wenjun Wu	Beihang University, China
Weikuan Yu	Florida State University, USA

High Performance Queries Using Compressed Bitmap Indexes

Beytullah Yildiz$^{(\boxtimes)}$ ⓘ

Lawrence Berkeley National Laboratory, Berkeley, CA 94720, USA
byildiz@gmail.com

Abstract. Data that often contain unchanging records is becoming increasingly important. Many data sources, such as historical archives, sensor readings, health systems, and machine logs, do not change frequently but are constantly increasing. For this reason, the need to process such datasets more quickly has emerged. Bitmap index that can benefit from multicore and multiprocessor systems is designed to process data that has grown over time but does not change frequently. It has a well-known advantage, particularly in low cardinality data queries. Data such as gender, age, marital status, postal code and even date with low cardinality occupy an important place in datasets. Furthermore, the bitmap index using the compression algorithm can be applied efficiently even if the data has a high cardinality. In this study, bitmap index is introduced to improve queries and it has been shown to perform up to 20x faster queries with an appropriate encoding for data containing frequently unchanging records in a performance comparison against a commonly used relational database system.

Keywords: Data retrieval · Bitmap index · Bitmap encoding · Parallel query · Query optimization · Multicore

1 Introduction

Nowadays, data containing records that are not frequently changed are becoming increasingly important. Many sources produce data that steadily grove but do not change frequently. Health systems, Internet of Things (IoT) devices, Logging Systems produce data progressively. In general, these generated data are rarely changed. However, over time, accumulating data produce a need for faster processing.

The most common process for analyzing large data is to get a small subset of the data for further analysis. This small part, which is usually obtained by queries, opens the door to the explored answer. It is common practice to use an indexing technique to speed up queries. Database systems designed for the transactions use indexing techniques such as B-tree and hash-based indexes to increase the query speed. One of the noteworthy features of the transactional data is that it frequently changes, and hence the corresponding indexes must be

© Springer Nature Switzerland AG 2020
U. Schwardmann et al. (Eds.): Euro-Par 2019 Workshops, LNCS 11997, pp. 493–505, 2020.
https://doi.org/10.1007/978-3-030-48340-1_38

updated quickly. The use of frequently updatable indexes, therefore, has made significant contributions to database systems.

Bitmap index has been used successfully in scientific domain due to the major characteristics of scientific data such as being written once and not changing frequently [1–3]. In addition, the bitmap index provides very high performance because it can be paralleled [4,5]. Bitmap index can use parallel processing to expedite indexing and queries. This is achieved by breaking the data into non-overlapping subarrays. MPI and OpenMP can be used for communication between processes depending on the use of shared memory. For data that are not frequently changed, bitmap indices are efficient because they benefit from the stable structure of data [6,7]. A bitmap index processes queries faster than a B-tree index, but it takes longer to modify a bitmap index when an existing record is updated. Adding new records to a bitmap index usually takes less time than updating a B-tree index because the time to add to bitmap index is a linear function of the number of new records. However, the time required to update B-tree index is always higher because of sorting [8]. For these reasons, bitmap indexes are often more suitable for data that are not frequently changed.

Bitmap index technologies are very efficient because queries can be performed using bitwise logical operations that are very efficient at the hardware level. The advantages of using bitmap indexes are greatest for columns where the number of distinct values is smaller than the number of rows in the table. This ratio is called the degree of cardinality. However, thanks to the compression techniques, the bitmap index can also provide good performance in higher cardinality columns.

We use FastBit [9], an open source software tool that uses Word-Aligned Hybrid (WAH) compressed bitmaps to support SQL-like queries. FastBit 's design options have proven to be effective when compared to other bitmap indexing methods [10]. Developed in Lawrence Berkeley National Laboratory (LBNL), FastBit is software that implements most of the encoding schemes, binning methods, and compression strategies. It supports basic encoding schemes such as equality, range, and interval encoding. It also uses multi-level and multi-component encoding methods that increase query efficiency while maintaining theoretical space-time optimization.

The main contribution of this paper is the introduction of an algorithm to use the most appropriate bitmap encoding in the query process according to the most commonly used query type. The performance of the queries varies according to the bitmap index encoding scheme. Choosing the most appropriate encoding provides a great benefit in the performance of the queries. Therefore, we have created an algorithm to generate and use indexes using the optimal bitmap encoding scheme. We applied bitmap indexing to the Archive System, which contains more than 3 million unique documents. The number of documents is constantly increasing due to the addition of new documents despite the fact that the documents in the archive are not changed when they are added.

The rest of this article is organized as follows: Sect. 2 describes the related work. Detailed information about the bitmap indexing is presented in Sect. 3.

We state the experimental methodology in Sect. 4. Experiments and results are discussed in Sect. 5. We conclude in Sect. 6.

2   Related Work

In the literature, we encounter several studies using the bitmap index for different purposes. Stockinger et al. presented a strategy to effectively respond to joint queries on structured data and text data. Using an efficient compression algorithm, bitmap indexes were effectively applied to hundreds of thousands of terms over millions of documents. In the performance comparison, proposed indexing is claimed to be much faster than the full-text index utilized by a commonly used database system [8]. Madduri and Wu presented a parallel strategy to parse raw RDF data, making dictionaries of unique entities, and generate compressed bitmap indexes. In the study, bitmap indexes were used to effectively respond to SPARQL queries that simplify join evaluations. It was shown that the bitmap index-based approach runs faster than various SPARQL queries on RDF datasets [12]. Stockinger et al. evaluated the performance of the bitmap index and MySQL database index during the analysis of the e-mail traffic of the Enron dataset. Bitmap indexing provided much more performance than MySQL indexing. The join results of several tables revealed that the performance of the query increased significantly [13]. Singh and Agrawal designed an interactive focused crawler, a special purpose search engine that aimed to search the relevant pages. Bitmap indexing using WAH compression were utilized to implement the interactive focused crawler that calculated the relevance of the web pages [14]. Indexing high-speed streams of network measurement data in real-time creates significant performance challenges. Fusco et al. introduced algorithms for generating compressed bitmap indexes in real time on GPUs and showed that indexing throughputs of up to 185 million records per second could be achieved. Thus, the study claimed that achievement of wire-rate multi-10-Gbps packet indexing using commodity hardware was very likely [15].

A bitmap index is also used for data warehouse systems to improve performance. A data warehouse system often contains unchanging data. Prakash and Prathap studied different indexing strategies for data warehouses. With the experimental results, they concluded that the bitmap indexing technique was the appropriate choice for the data warehouse query operation [16]. Ni et al. proposed a new integrated index model for data warehouses. The core of the approach was an integrative index, taking the advantage of a bitmap index, b-tree index, an inverted index. The inverted index embodied by the bitmap was adopted for fast results with intersection operations. In the meantime, the tree structure was used to speed up the range queries [17]. In a data warehouse, Abdulhadi et al. measured the performance of the Bitmap indexes by comparing it with the B-tree indexes using the Oracle environment that utilizes B-tree as the default indexing. When the column had low cardinality, they showed that bitmap indexes were more efficient than B-tree indexes. In addition, bitmap indexes provided better performance than B-tree indexes when there was a combination of multiple conditions with *and/or* operators [18].

3   Bitmap Index

Bitmap indexes can provide very efficient performance for queries because of the fast bitwise logical operations over the bitmaps efficiently supported by hardware. Hardware-enabled bitwise logical operation is one of the most important features of using bitmap index. In addition, the results of bitwise logical operations can be effectively combined. Since bitwise logical operations on bitmaps create a new bitmap, the results of the logical operations can also be processed by applying bitwise logical operations.

Bitmap indexes are very effective for queries that contain multiple conditions in a *where* statement. An equality query with multiple conditions is performed by applying *and* operation to the resulting bitmap vectors of each condition. For example, finding the answer that corresponds to a query of (where $A = 1$ and $A = 2$) is only a matter of applying *and* operation to the two relevant bitmaps. Range or interval queries are executed by first applying *or* operation to all bit vectors specified by each range or interval condition and then applying *and* operation to the answers.

Each bit in a bitmap corresponds to a row id. If a bit is set, it means that the row with the corresponding row id has a matching value. A bitmap index provides the same function as a normal index because a mapping function converts the bit position to a row id. Nevertheless, there is a significant deficiency of bitmap index such that index size increases linearly with the number of distinct values. One of the procedures controlling the increase in index size due to high cardinality, and consequently the deterioration of query performance, is encoding.

Bitmap encoding is important for efficient indexing, which creates bitmaps to reduce the total number of bitmaps or the number of bitmaps needed to answer a question. There are three types of basic bitmap encoding methods: equality encoding, range encoding, and interval encoding. Equality encoding is the most basic bitmap encoding. The number of distinct values, called as cardinality, defines the number of columns. A bit for an attribute value is typically added to a bitmap vector that contains as many bits as the cardinality. Table 1 illustrates equality, range and interval encodings for 8 records. RID is the row identifier for the values of the attribute. The size of the equality encoding depends on the cardinality value c. Hence, each line requires c number bitmaps. If an attribute has n_i possible values, the bitmap size becomes $\sum_{n=1}^{c} n_i$ without any compression. The equality encoding is known as a very efficient method for an equality query because the query needs to look at only one bitmap. For example, $A = 1$ requires to check whether bitmap 1 is set to 1. Nonetheless, the size of the index can be a burden for high cardinality attributes. The second basic encoding technique is the range encoding, optimized for a one-sided query such as $A \leq 1$. The size of the bitmap index for an attribute is $\sum_{n=1}^{c} (n_i - 1)$, which is less than equality encoding. A range query takes at most 1 bitmap processing for a range encoding, which is similar the equality queries on the equality encoding. The third basic encoding technique is the interval encoding to process efficiently two-sided queries such as $2 \leq A \leq 5$ [19]. Each bitmap of interval encoding is calculated by using range encoding bitmaps; bitmap of ith bit in the internal encoding is the result from *xor* operation on the ith range encoding bitmap and $i + (\lfloor C/2 \rfloor - 1)$ range encoding bitmap. Interval encoding guaranties evaluating any interval queries by accessing at most 2 bitmaps. It also reduces the size of bitmap index almost by a factor 2 comparing to the previous basic encoding schemes.

Table 1. A sample bitmap indexes using equality, range and interval encoding

RID	A	Equality						Range					Interval		
		5	4	3	2	1	0	4	3	2	1	0	2	1	0
1	2	0	0	0	1	0	0	1	1	1	0	0	1	1	1
2	5	1	0	0	0	0	0	0	0	0	0	0	0	0	0
3	0	0	0	0	0	0	1	1	1	1	1	1	0	0	1
4	1	0	0	0	0	1	0	1	1	1	1	0	0	1	1
5	4	0	1	0	0	0	0	1	0	0	0	0	1	0	0
6	3	0	0	1	0	0	0	1	1	0	0	0	1	1	0
7	2	0	0	0	1	0	0	1	1	1	0	0	1	1	1
8	4	0	1	0	0	0	0	1	0	0	0	0	1	0	0

Chan and Ioannidis discuss the optimality of encoding schemes [19]. While the range encoding is optimal for the range query, it indicates that the equality encoding is best suited for equality queries for all cardinality values. However, the range encoding is not optimal for an interval query. The study compares equality, interval and range queries. It is stated that the range encoding is not effective for an equality query. However, it provides the best results for one-sided range queries. Interval encoding is the most space efficient between three basic schemes that require almost only half the number of bitmaps of the other two schemes.

Each bitmap index is essentially an attribute representation using a number of bits that are specific to an encoding scheme. This observation resulted in new encoding schemes to reduce index size and/or improve query performance. Almost all proposed encoding methods in the last decade can be classified as multi-level encoding or multi-component encoding. In multi-component encoding, attribute values are divided into several components. Each component that can be of different size is encoded using one of the basic encoding schemes. Single-component encoding produces the largest bitmap size similar to the basic encoding scheme. In contrast, the size of the bitmaps decreases when the number of components increases. In an earlier study of Chan and Ioannidis [20], the number of optimal components was 2. However, this may be different when using compression. Instead of fixing the number of components, the size of each component can be set to a value. For example, the size of each component can be fixed to a value of 2. This special case is also known as binary encoding and bit-sliced encoding. It constructs the least number of bitmaps, which requires

$\lceil \log_2 c \rceil$ bitmaps. The disadvantage of binary encoding is the need to access each bitmap to answer a question. Therefore, responding to a query using a binary encoding index may take more CPU time than other indexes. Another encoding is multi-level coding, worth mentioning [21,22]. Each level can be encoded using one of the three basic encoding schemes. The finest level can have a distinct value that results in the creation of a precise bitmap index for each value. Although the finest level can always answer any question, coarse levels can be used to answer a query without accessing the finest level. This results in a reduction in the amount of work for a query.

4   Experimental Methodology

We applied bitmap index using optimal encoding to an archive system that contains more than 3 million unique documents. New records that were added continuously had not been changing after they were added. We conducted the experiments on Ubuntu 16.04 LTS virtual machines having 8 Cores, 16GB Memory, and 2 TB storage. PostgreSQL 9.6 were used for the experiments. If more computing power was needed, cloud environment could be used with parallel processing procedures [23–25].

We first compared the performance of bitmap index with the PostgreSQL environment. Then, the performance comparison of bitmap indexes created by using different encoding schemes were investigated. Equality encoding, range encoding, interval coding and interval-equality multi-component encoding were used to create bitmap indexes for each database attribute. Specifically, the equality query was applied to the location attribute, and the range and interval queries were applied to the date attribute. A combination of queries such as the equality query for the location and the interval query for the date has also been tried. We created an algorithm that uses optimal encoding by monitoring the frequency of query types of each attribute and evaluating the query performance of the relevant indexes generated. Finally, we compared the number of queries that can be done using a bitmap index, B-tree index, and scanning within a second to show the improvement that our contribution brings.

5   Experimental Results

Firstly, the performance comparison of the equality query using scanning the whole data, the B-tree index and the bitmap index was conducted to show the benefit of using bitmap index, shown in Fig. 1. The query that uses the B-tree indexes has been found to work much faster than the query that scans the data. Queries that use a bitmap index generated by an equality encoding are better than queries using the PostgreSQL database either with a B-tree index or without an index. We can clearly see the advantage of the bitmap index against the B-tree index using the same hardware. The advantage lies in hardware support for bitwise logical operations, which are used very often by bitmap indexing and in parallel execution of queries. A bitmap index can be divided into subarrays

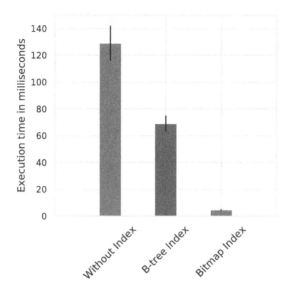

Fig. 1. Comparison of an equality query.

so that each subarray can be processed by a separate core or processor. The bitmap index execution permits the use of multiple cores or processors. There are many encoding schemes to generate a bitmap index. Equality, range and interval encoding are the basic encoding schemes. In addition, the multi-level and multi-component encodings can be formed as a combination of these three basic schemes. The difference in the number of comparisons in a query causes bitmap encoding schemes to affect the query processing time. For this reason, we have experimented to show that there is a more appropriate bitmap encoding than the reminders for a query type, such as the equality query, the range query, and the interval query. Figure 2 shows the difference between queries made on the indexes created using with equality encoding, range encoding and interval encoding, and interval-equality encoding. Depending on the type of query, execution times vary according to the type of encoding. We applied 4 different queries to the bitmap indexes created by using different encoding schemes. Equality encoding gives the best results for equality queries, while the interval encoding is faster for interval queries, as well as it provides good performance for range queries. We cannot see that the range encoding makes a much better contribution than others for any query type except for the range query. We have also observed that the multi-component interval-equality encodings gives a good result for Query 4, combining an equality and interval query.

Apparently, bitmap encoding affects query performance. Therefore, we use an algorithm to generate and store the most appropriate bitmap encoding as shown in Algorithm 1. The frequency of the query type for each attribute is maintained in the $n x m$ matrix A; where n is the number of query types and m is the number of data columns. Rows represent query types such as equality, range,

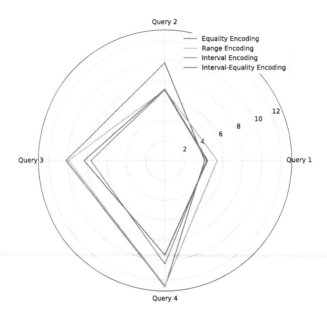

Fig. 2. Query execution times in milliseconds for various bitmap encodings.

and interval, and columns represent the attributes of data. When processing a query, the query parser determines the types of queries that apply to the attributes. For example, the query "*select* $*$ *where* $A1 = 0$ *or* $1 \leq A2 \leq 2$" includes 1 equality query in attribute $A1$ and 1 interval query in $A2$. After each query, A is updated to track the query frequency for each column. The bitmap encoding of an attribute is determined by the maximum value of the query types. For example, if an attribute has the highest value for the equality query relative to other query types, the equality encoding is selected to create an index for that attribute. This is due to the fact that the equality encoding is most suitable for the equality query. In general, basic encodings are best known for relevant queries. For example, interval encoding is best suited for interval queries, as equality encoding is best for equality queries. However, an attribute does not always encounter a single query type. An attribute that is frequently encountered with a query type may be encountered with other types of queries less frequently. For example, an attribute that is frequently encountered with a interval query may also be encountering an equality query less frequently. Therefore, it may be best to use multi-component interval-equality encoding for optimal indexing. Therefore, the performances of the encodings are measured and the indexes generated are compared to optimize the encodings.

After optimizing the bitmap indexes for each column, we measured the improvement by applying the queries continuously at a fixed rate to determine the number of queries processed per second. We evaluated three different queries that return a different number of rows as the query result and have different complexity. Each query used in the experiments consists of combined

---

Algorithm 1: Creating indexes using optimal encoding

1: **procedure** COUNTCOLUMNQUERYTYPE(A, $Query$)
2:     $i \leftarrow FindQueryType$
3:     $j \leftarrow FindQueriedColumn$
4:     $A[i][j] \leftarrow A[i][j] + 1$
5: **end procedure**

6: **procedure** CREATEINDEX(A)
7:     **for** $i \leftarrow 1, m$ **do**
8:         $columnName \leftarrow i$
9:         **for** $j \leftarrow 1, n$ **do**
10:             $mostQueryTypeOfColumn \leftarrow max(A[i][j])$
11:         **end for**
12:         Create an index according to the most frequent query type for $columnName$
13:         $EvaluateIndexes(oldIndex, createdNewIndex)$
14:     **end for**
15: **end procedure**

16: **procedure** EVALUATEINDEXES($firstIndex, secondIndex$)
17:     Run predefined benchmark queries
18:     $firstIndexPerformance \leftarrow FirstIndex$
19:     $secondIndexPerformance \leftarrow SecondIndex$
20:     **if** $firstIndexPerformance >= secondIndexPerformance$ **then**
21:         Keep the first index
22:     **else**
23:         Keep the second index
24:     **end if**
25: **end procedure**

---

equality queries and interval queries. Query number increases while the number of query results and the complexity of the query increase. Query 3 has more complexity and the highest number of query results, while query 1 has lower complexity and the smallest query results. We collected the results of the queries using bitmap indexes and PostgreSQL database, shown in Fig. 3. Bitmap indexes were generated with equality encoding, range encoding, interval encoding and interval-equality multi-component encoding. These encodings were applied to both location attribute and date attribute. We also generated bitmap index by applying equality encoding to location attribute and interval-equality encoding to date attribute. PostgreSQL queries were processed with a B-tree index as well as without an index. We use the best performing encoding among the bitmap indexes.

Bitmap indexed queries perform much better because of the advantages of bitmap indexing such as very few comparisons for a single query, hardware support and parallel execution using many cores. Equality encoding is known to be very efficient for an equality query because it is sufficient for a query to check only for one bitmap to be evaluated. Similarly, an interval query using the interval

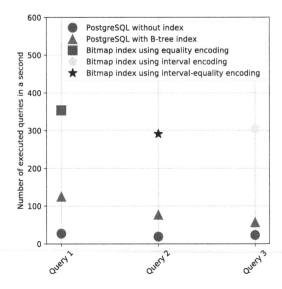

Fig. 3. Query comparison for various bitmap encodings.

encoding can be answered by accessing up to 2 bitmaps. As a result, any query that uses a bitmap index can be processed with very few comparisons so that bitmap indexed queries perform much higher than other traditional indexes such as B-tree index. The best query performance for Query 3 is achieved with the bitmap indexes using equality encoding for the location column and the interval-equality encoding for the date column. The worst performance of bitmap indexed queries happens for range encoding. This is because the range encoding is not optimal for interval and equality queries.

PostgreSQL queries perform worse than bitmap indexed queries for every type of queries. A PostgreSQL query that does not use an index cannot compete with any bitmap indexed queries. It can be clearly seen that PostgreSQL, which uses the B-tree index, scales badly as well for an increasing number of the query results and the performance degradation increases especially as the complexity of the queries increases. Therefore, we see close performance result for PostgreSQL queries using B-tree and using scanning. If an index does not provide sufficient performance improvement, PostgreSQL can choose scanning instead of using an index. However, the bitmap indexed queries are not affected that much worse from the queries that return more number of rows and have more complexity. It can be deduced that a very small performance decrease is encountered due to high I/O volume originated from the high number of return data.

6   Conclusion

Bitmap indexes provide high performance for queries because of fast bitwise logical operations supported by hardware and parallel processing ability. In addition, queries that contain multiple conditions are performed very efficiently because the results of bitwise logical operations on bitmaps are effectively combined. The use of efficient hardware and a few comparisons, which are often 1 comparison, contribute to the high performance of bitmap index. Moreover, the introduced algorithm that uses the optimal encoding for an attribute makes a significant contribution to overall performance because the execution time of a query varies according to the used encoding to create an index.

For queries that use bitmap indexes, multicore and multiprocessor environments using MPI and/or OpenMP eliminate performance barriers. With more cores or processors, performance can be improved to the point where the cost of communication exceeds the gain. Communication costs between computing nodes affect overall performance. Therefore, the shared memory option may be preferred for the parallel environment. Otherwise, virtual machines in the cloud should be carefully selected so as not to adversely affect performance.

One of the important advantages of a bitmap index is that it can be applied to an application with minor changes. This makes bitmap index very easy to use. We showed that an archive application performance can be improved almost seamlessly by using a bitmap index. We measured up to 20 times better performance comparing to PostgreSQL. Easy integration of bitmap index allows us to improve the performance of an application without introducing any new computing node.

The bitmap index is particularly suitable for queries applied to static data. Since archive data did not change frequently, we used bitmap indexing to speed up queries an archive system. There was a significant need for performance where a large number of users are querying a large number of archive documents. In this study, we achieved performance improvement using bitmap indexing for the location and date fields of documents, which were relatively low cardinality columns, that are frequently queried in an archive system. However, bitmap index does not only provide high performance for low cardinality data but is also highly efficient due to compression algorithms in high cardinality data.

References

1. Byna, S., et al.: Parallel I/O, analysis, and visualization of a trillion particle simulation. In: International Conference on High Performance Computing, Networking, Storage and Analysis, Salt Lake City, Utah, pp. 1–12 (2012)
2. Romosan, A., Shoshani, A., Wu, K., Markowitz, V., Mavrommatis, K.: Accelerating gene context analysis using bitmaps. In: The Proceedings of the 25th International Conference on Scientific and Statistical Database Management, Baltimore, Maryland, USA (2013)
3. Byna, S., Prabhat, Wehner, M.F., Wu, K.: Detecting atmospheric rivers in large climate datasets. In: The Proceedings of the 2nd International Workshop on Petascal Data Analytics: Challenges and Opportunities, Seattle, Washington, USA (2011)
4. Chou, J., Wu, K., Prabhat: FastQuery: a general indexing and querying system for scientific data. In: The 23rd International Conference Scientific and Statistical Database Management, Portland, OR, USA, pp. 573–574 (2011)

5. Yildiz, B., Wu, K., Byna, S., Shoshani, A.: Parallel membership queries on very large scientific data sets using bitmap indexes. Concurr. Comput. Pract. Exp. **31**, e5157 (2019). https://doi.org/10.1002/cpe.5157

6. Wu, K., Otoo, E.J., Shoshani, A.: Optimizing bitmap indices with efficient compression. ACM Trans. Database Syst. **31**(1), 1–38 (2006)

7. Wu, K., Otoo, E., Shoshani, A.: On the performance of bitmap indices for high cardinality attributes. In: The 13th International Conference on Very Large Databases, Toronto, Canada, pp. 24–35 (2004)

8. Stockinger, K., Cieslewicz, J., Wu, K., Rotem, D., Shoshani, A.: Using bitmap index for joint queries on structured and text data. In: Kozielski, S., Wrembel, R. (eds.) New Trends in Data Warehousing and Data Analysis. AOIS, vol. 3, pp. 1–23. Springer, Boston (2009). https://doi.org/10.1007/978-0-387-87431-9_9

9. Wu, K., et al.: FastBit: interactively searching massive data. J. Phys. Conf. Ser. **180**(1), 012053 (2009)

10. Fusco, F., Stoecklin, M.P., Vlachos, M.: NET-FLi: on-the-fly compression, archiving and indexing of streaming network traffic. Proc. VLDB Endow. **3**(1–2), 1382–1393 (2010)

11. Sharma, Y., Goyal, N.: An efficient multi-component indexing embedded bitmap compression for data reorganization. Inf. Technol. J. **7**, 160–164 (2008)

12. Madduri, K., Wu, K.: Massive-scale RDF processing using compressed bitmap indexes. In: Bayard Cushing, J., French, J., Bowers, S. (eds.) SSDBM 2011. LNCS, vol. 6809, pp. 470–479. Springer, Heidelberg (2011). https://doi.org/10.1007/978-3-642-22351-8_30

13. Stockinger, K., Rotem, D., Shoshani, A., Wu, K.: Analyzing Enron data: bitmap indexing outperforms MySQL queries by several orders of magnitude (2006). https://sdm.lbl.gov/kewu/ps/LBNL-59437.pdf

14. Singh, S.K., Agrawal, S.: Improved focused crawler using inverted WAH bitmap index. Int. J. Adv. Res. Comput. Eng. **1**(4), 407–409 (2012)

15. Fusco, F., Vlachos, M., Dimitropoulos, X., Deri, L.: Indexing million of packets per second using GPUs. In: The Proceedings of the 2013 Conference on Internet Measurement Conference, pp. 327–332 (2013)

16. Prakash, K.S., Prathap, P.M.J.: Bitmap index an efficient approach to improve performance of data warehouse queries. Int. J. Emerg. Technol. Adv. Eng. **1**(1), 164–167 (2016)

17. Ni, Z., Guo, J., Wang, L., Gao, Y.: An efficient method for improving query efficiency in data warehouse. J. Softw. **6**(5), 857–865 (2011)

18. Abdulhadi, Z.Q., Zuping, Z., Housien, H.I.: Bitmap index as effective indexing for low cardinality column in data warehouse. Int. J. Comput. Appl. **68**(24), 38–42 (2013)

19. Chan, C.Y., Ioannidis, Y.E.: An efficient bitmap encoding scheme for selection queries. In: The Proceedings of the 1999 ACM SIGMOD International Conference on Management of Data, Philadelphia, Pennsylvania, USA, pp. 215–226 (1999)

20. Chan, C.Y., Ioannidis, Y.E.: Bitmap index design and evaluation. In: The Proceedings of the 1998 ACM SIGMOD International Conference on Management of Data, Seattle, Washington, USA (1998)

21. Wu, K., Madduri, K., Canon, S.: Multi-level bitmap indexes for flash memory storage. In: The 14th International Database Engineering and Applications Symposium, Montreal, Quebec, Canada, pp. 114–116 (2010)

22. Sinha, R.R., Winslett, M.: Multi-resolution bitmap indexes for scientific data. ACM Trans. Database Syst. **32**(3), 1–38 (2007)

23. Yildiz, B., Fox, G., Pallickara, S.: An orchestration for distributed web service handlers. In: Third International Conference on Internet and Web Applications and Services, pp. 638–643 (2008)
24. Yildiz, B., Fox, G.C.: Toward a modular and efficient distribution for web service handlers. Concurr. Comput. Pract. Exp. **25**(3), 410–426 (2013)
25. Aktas, M.S.: Hybrid cloud computing monitoring software architecture. Concurr. Comput. Pract. Exp. **30**(21), e4694 (2018)

Learning Quality Improved Word Embedding with Assessment of Hyperparameters

Beytullah Yildiz[1]([⊠]) [iD] and Murat Tezgider[2]

[1] Lawrence Berkeley National Laboratory, Berkeley, CA 94720, USA
byildiz@gmail.com
[2] Hacettepe University, Ankara, Turkey
murat.tezgider@hacettepe.edu.tr

Abstract. Deep learning practices have a large impact on many areas. Big data and key hardware developments in GPU and TPU are the main reasons behind deep learning success. The recent progress in the text analysis and classification using deep learning has been significant as well. The quality of word representation that has become much better by using methods such as Word2Vec, FastText and Glove has been important in this improvement. In this study, we aimed to improve Word2Vec word representation, which is also called embedding, by tuning its hyperparameters. The minimum word count, vector size, window size, and the number of iterations were used to improve word embeddings. We introduced two approaches, which are faster than grid search and random search, to set the hyperparameters. The word embeddings were created using documents with approximately 300 million words. A deep learning classification model that uses documents consisting of 10 different classes was applied to evaluate the quality of word embeddings. A 9% increase in classification success was achieved only by improving hyperparameters.

Keywords: Deep learning · Machine learning · Text analysis · Text classification · Word embedding · Word2Vec

1 Introduction

The data produced in the digital world is increasing overwhelmingly. As a result of the development and widespread of the Internet, the data produced and served by internet applications such as social media have given a different impetus to the speed of data production. Text data have a significant share of these vast data. With the increasing volume, tasks performed on the text such as classification [1, 2], clustering, sentiment analysis, information extraction, information retrieval, and searching have become more important. Moreover, the success rate of text processing has significantly increased by deep learning methods in the advent of more data and better computing power.

Text processing requires text representation. Therefore, various methods have been introduced for text representation. One of the important obstacles of text processing has been feature extraction which has been recently eased by deep learning methods. There are different studies in which words, word grams, word roots and bodies, character

© Springer Nature Switzerland AG 2020
U. Schwardmann et al. (Eds.): Euro-Par 2019 Workshops, LNCS 11997, pp. 506–518, 2020.
https://doi.org/10.1007/978-3-030-48340-1_39

grams are used as features to represent text [3–6]. By using a set of word and context pairs extracted from the corpus, vector representations of words can be derived by applying various estimation methods, such as predicting words given their contexts (CBOW), predicting the contexts from the words (Skip-Gram), or factorizing the log of their co-occurrence matrix. Word2Vec [7, 8] implements both Continuous Bag of Words (CBOW) and Skip-Gram (SG) methods. FastText [3] also provides these two models to compute word representations. Although Word2Vec treats each word in corpus like an atomic entity and generates a vector for each word, FastText, which is essentially an extension of word2vec model, considers each word as composed of character n-grams. Therefore, the vector for a word is the sum of these character n-grams. For example, the word vector "orca" is a sum of the vectors of the n-grams such as "or", "orc", "orca", "rca", "ca". Glove [9], on the other hand, factorizes the log of the co-occurrence matrix. In these methods, picking the right context is a critical factor that affects the quality of the resulting vector representations. The most common method for defining this context is to rely on a window positioned around the word. The context window decides which contextual neighbors are taken into consideration to produce the vector representations.

The empirical variations between representation models, which is also called embedding, are basically because of differences in hyperparameters rather than differences in the embedding algorithms [10]. Hence, it is likely that different results are obtained while constructing word embedding with different corpus containing different topics in different dimensions because the size and content of the corpus will cause the words to take on semantically and syntactically different vector values [11]. Additionally, the quality of word representations is significantly affected by hyperparameters such as minimum word count, vector size, window size and the number of iterations.

In this study, we present two approaches to evaluate the important hyperparameters of Word2Vec which are faster than grid search and random search. In general, the quality of the word embedding is not enough because the default hyperparameter values are used to create the word embedding. In addition, unlike well-known deep learning models such as Convolutional Neural Networks (CNN) and Recurrent Neural Networks (RNN), hyperparameter tuning for word embedding has not been well studied. Moreover, to the best of our knowledge, there isn't a study extensively measuring the accuracy of Word2Vec representations for the Turkish language. 3 million Turkish texts which consist of totaling 300 million words were used to create Word2Vec word embedding.

To evaluate the quality of the word embedding, a deep learning model developed for text classification was used. The classification model and the data are kept unchanged to examine the effect of Word2Vec hyperparameters on the quality of word embedding. Text classification with deep learning model was performed by using different word embeddings created by changing Word2Vec hyperparameters. According to the accuracy of the classification process, the quality of the word embeddings has been measured. We used multi-core and CUDA-enabled GPU environments to create and evaluate word embeddings. Cloud base TPU and GPU can be used to accelerate word embedding, as the number of documents used and the number of unique words requires more processing power.

In the second section, related works are explained. Information about Word2Vec word embedding and used environment will be given in Sect. 3. Section 4 consists of measurements and evaluation. We conclude and give "rules of thumb" in Sect. 5.

2   Related Work

There are several studies investigating the hyperparameters of word embedding methods. Caselles-Dupré et al. investigated the importance of hyperparameters through large hyperparameter grid searches on various datasets [12]. The results revealed that optimizing the hyperparameters significantly improved the performance of a recommendation task.

Levy et al. claimed that most of the word embedding performance gains were due to specific system design choices and hyperparameter optimizations rather than embedding algorithms [10]. Although it is advisable to adjust the entire hyperparameters for the task at hand, this approach may be expensive in terms of calculation. Therefore, they provided some "thumb rules" for the solution.

In general, the quality of word representation was measured using either a model or an analogy and similarity datasets. The quality of Word2Vec word embeddings is assumed to affect the accuracy of the classification model. Embedding models often associate each word with a single vector representing its properties. Therefore, evaluation methods should analyze the accuracy and completeness of these properties. Multi-label classification is a convenient way to carry out this evaluation [13]. Nooralahzadeh et al. conducted evaluations of both general and domain-specific embeddings [14]. Evaluation of embedding models was provided by the task of domain-specific sentence classification.

Analogy and similarity datasets were often used to measure the quality of word representations, consisting of questions and answers that query the semantic and syntactic relations of words. Mikolov et al. used 8869 semantic, 10675 syntactic questions in total, consisting of 5 semantic question types and 9 syntactic question types to measure the quality of word vectors [7]. Lia et al. experimented on Word-Sim353 and the TOEFL dataset to measure semantic and syntactic relationships [11]. In their study, they compare the methods used for representing words as vectors.

3   Word2Vec Word Embedding and Used Environment

Word2Vec was proposed by Mikolov et al. in 2013 to represent a word as a vector [8]. It takes a large corpus as input and usually produces vectors of several hundreds of dimensions. Word2Vec represents words in vector space based on the unsupervised prediction. Word2Vec aims to minimize the distance value of words that are the same or semantically and syntactically close to maximize the similarity value. CBOW and SG are commonly used methods. The CBOW method estimates the center word by using adjacent words. Rather, the SG attempts to predict neighboring words using the center word. The SG model consists of input, hidden and an output layer. The input layer uses a one-hot encoding. In one-hot encoding, an index is assigned to each word.

The value corresponding to the word index in the vector is set to 1, and the others to 0. The output layer uses a softmax classifier. The number of neurons in the hidden layer determines the size of the Word2Vec vector because weights in the hidden layer are used to represent words as vectors.

Deep learning models benefit from parallel processing. However, it can be argued that no learning algorithm is really embarrassingly parallel, but some are almost embarrassingly parallel. As with previous parallel applications [15–17], procedures such as parallel processing, pipelining and orchestration should be used in the best way. In addition, deep learning, word embedding as well, is basically an optimization problem. In other words, optimizing hyperparameter is one of the most important functions.

We investigated important hyperparameters that affect the quality of Word2Vec word representation. Minimum word count, vector size, window size and number of iterations were the hyperparameters on which experimented. The quality of Word2Vec word embeddings is assumed to affect the accuracy of the classification model in which word embeddings are used. From this hypothesis, a deep learning classification model was used to evaluate the word embeddings. The classification was performed with the word embeddings created with different hyperparameter sets. The classification model and the data were kept unchanged and only the Word2Vec hyperparameters were adjusted. Based on the success of the classification model, we concluded the successful hyperparameters to create better word embeddings. Keras library and TensorFlow infrastructure were utilized for the classification. Gensim library [18] was used to construct Word2Vec word vectors. We created the word vectors by choosing combinations of 5, 10, 15, 20, 25 values as window size; 1, 2, 5, 10, 20, 30 values as the minimum word count; 50, 100, 150, 200, 250, 300 values as the vector size; 5, 10, 15, 20, 25, 30, 35, 40, 45, 50, 55, 60 values as the number of iterations.

Grid search and random search are among the well-known parameter optimization methods. In both methods, the processing can take a very long time to determine the hyperparameter values. For the grid search, when the hyperparameter values mentioned above are used, the 2160 combinations must be tried. A single word embedding can take more than a day depending on the hyperparameters. Therefore, we used two approaches to set up Word2Vec hyperparameters.

Table 1. Default values of Word2Vec model hyperparameters.

Minimum word count	5	Window size	5
Vector size	100	Number of iterations	5

In the first approach, we initially started with the default values in Table 1. In each step, only one of the Word2Vec hyperparameters was updated to create word embeddings. For a single hyperparameter, we created as many word embeddings as the number of values of the hyperparameter. After evaluating each hyperparameter, the most appropriate word embedding was obtained with the hyperparameter set using the best hyperparameter values.

The second approach similarly starts with the default hyperparameters. In each step, a hyperparameter value that produces the best result is determined and used in place of the default value of that parameter in the next steps. This model continues progressively. At the last stage, parameters that produce the best results are saved as the best hyperparameter set.

3.1 Classification Model

To investigate Word2Vec word representation using text classification, we constructed a model by using CNN, which is a deep learning model. Two convolutional layers, two maximum pooling layers, one flatten layer, two fully connected (dense) layers were used. Like the input layer, the embedding layer has dimensions of 160 x "vector size". The maximum text length was set to 160 words. For shorter texts containing fewer than 160 words, a vector of zeroes was added. In the first CNN layers, 64 filters with ReLU activation function were used. Kernel size was set to 5 for the first CNN layer, and 2 for the second CNN layer. Maximum pooling size was set to 2 for the first maximum pooling layer and was set to 3 for the second maximum pooling layer. Stride size was set to 1 for both layers. 0.5 value for the dropout layer was used to prevent overfitting. A fully connected layer of 128 units was used with ReLU activation function. Softmax activation function was used in the output layer consisting of 10 units. Adam was used as the optimization function and categorical cross entropy was used as the loss function.

3.2 Dataset

3 million Turkish texts with approximately 300 million words were used to create Word2Vec word embeddings. Corpus consists of about 2.8 million unique tokens. From the texts used for Word2Vec creation, 149504 text documents for classification were selected. The documents were labeled with 10 different classes. 104448 documents corresponding to 70% of the total documents were used for training, 22528 documents corresponding to 15% of the total documents were used for verification and 22528 documents corresponding to 15% of the total documents were used for testing purposes.

3.3 Hyperparameters

Words that appear only very few times in the hundreds of million words corpus are probably uninteresting typos or mistakes. Moreover, there is insufficient data to make a reasonable training on these words, so it is best to throw them away. Minimum word count hyperparameter is used to remove words by the number of appearance in the documents. For example, if the minimum word count parameter is set to 5, which is the default value of the Gensim library used, words that are presented less than 5 times will be discarded.

The vector size hyperparameter defines the vector dimension of Word2Vec. This hyperparameter also specifies the number of units in the hidden layer of the Word2Vec model. Therefore, the vector size also affects the cost of computation. Increasing the vector size will also increase the cost. However, the larger vector size may lead to better and more accurate models even though it may require more training data.

The window size indicates how many words to use for prediction from the left and right of the input word. The window size is the most noteworthy hyperparameter associated with the context. When it is set to 5, which is the default value of the Gensim library, 5 words will be used to the left and right of the input word for content prediction. Larger window size tends to capture more topic and domain information while smaller window size tends to capture more about 'functional' and 'synonymic' models, which may lead to better performance on similarity measurements [19, 20].

The number of iteration determines how many times the data is to be trained. Increasing the number of iterations generally improves the quality of word representation, but also significantly increases the duration of training.

4   Measurement and Evaluation

We investigated the quality of the word embedding by using a classification model. Word2Vec word embeddings created with the hyperparameters using the SG method were evaluated by using the classification model and dataset that were kept both unchanged. The classification was repeated with the word embeddings obtained by changing the value of one of the hyperparameters at a time. The optimum values of the hyperparameters were determined by evaluating the accuracy and loss values of the classification.

The two approaches mentioned in the methodology section were used for the classification to determine the hyperparameters. The results obtained by the first and second approaches will be explored below. Since the experiment of the minimum word count hyperparameter is the same for both approaches, the results are given only in the first approach. The second approach is continued using this result.

4.1   Decisive Approach

In Decisive Approach (DA), only the value of hyperparameter examined was changed. We started evaluating Word2Vec's minimum word count because it influenced the number of words of the Word2Vec dictionary. We created six models by setting the minimum word count hyperparameter to 1, 2, 5, 10, 20 and 30. The remaining parameters are fixed to the values given in Table 1.

We did not take any action to correct the misspelled words or typos because we want to make sense of the words that people wrote incorrectly. Depending on the geographical region, there are also some local forms of words that can be seen as a misspelled word. Therefore, we will use "token" instead of "word" to indicate any original word form in the documents. Because a token contains a regular word as well as a prefixed, affixed or misspelled word, the number of unique tokens may significantly exceed the number of words in a language. We saw this situation in our Word2Vec dictionary because there were 2.895.675 unique tokens. When the tokens used once or twice were examined, it was found that the vast majority of these tokens were misspelled. Very few tokens were very rarely used words.

The statistical details of the tokens for Word2Vec models using different values of minimum word count are given in Table 2. When the value of minimum word count is set to 1, all 2.895.675 unique tokens are used and the total number of tokens in the dictionary is 297.149.774. When the minimum word count is given as 2, 1.537.529 tokens that repeat once are removed from the vocabulary. The remaining 1.358.146 unique tokens correspond to about 47%. However, the total number of tokens does not change significantly. Less than 1% of all tokens are removed in the dictionary. This is better seen when the minimum word count is 30; while only 7,72% of the unique tokens remain, the percentage of the remaining total tokens is 96,97%. The sudden drop in the number of unique tokens is primarily due to misspelled words. The frequency of a word in documents used when training the Word2Vec model affects its correct positioning in the vector space. Less repetitive words in the corpus are thought to be not positioned correctly in the vector space. Accuracy and loss values of the classification model trained using the word vectors are significantly affected by the correct placement in this space. Therefore, the removal of very few repetitive words has a positive effect on classification success. When the value of minimum word count is increased, the accuracy of the classification model increases and the value of loss reduces, shown in Fig. 1.

Table 2. Word2Vec vectors and statistics

Minimum word count	Removed unique tokens	Remaining unique tokens	Percentage of remaining unique tokens	Removed total tokens	Remaining total tokens	Percentage of remaining total tokens
1	0	2.895.675	100	0	297.149.774	100
2	1.537.529	1.358.146	46,9	1.582.536	295.567.238	99,46
5	2.236.456	659.219	22,76	3.002.271	294.147.503	98,98
10	2.493.595	402.080	13,88	4.916.341	292.233.433	98,34
20	2.611.046	284.629	9,82	7.138.619	290.011.155	97,59
30	2.672.127	223.548	7,72	8.994.314	288.155.460	96,97

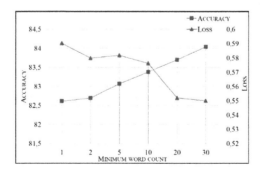

Fig. 1. Classification accuracy and loss for the various values of minimum word count

After the minimum word count, the effect of vector size hyperparameter of Word2Vec was examined. Word2Vec vectors were created by using hyperparameters of experiment 2 column in Table 3. When the classification was applied by using the same model and dataset, we obtained the accuracy and loss rates shown in Fig. 2. Keeping the vector size too large or too small affects the success of the classification negatively. It should be aimed to find an optimum vector size according to the available datasets. We observed that vector size, ranging from 50 to 300, has an impact on the classification accuracy of about 2%. The most appropriate value of the vector size for the dataset used in this study was 250. But when the amount of data is increased, using a larger-sized vector would be a more accurate approach [7].

Table 3. Hyperparameters for DA after minimum word count experiment

Parameters	Experiment 2	Experiment 3	Experiment 4
Minimum word count	5	5	5
Vector size	50, 100, 150, 200, 250, 300	100	100
Window size	5	5, 10, 15, 20 ,25	5
Number of iterations	5	5	5, 10, 15, 20, 25, 30, 35, 40, 45, 50, 55, 60

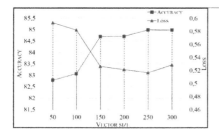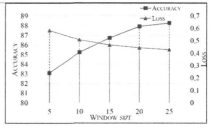

Fig. 2. Effect of vector size and window size on classification accuracy and loss for DA

Window size is an important hyperparameter to detect the context of a word. Therefore, it is expected that it will significantly affect the classification success. Using the same model and dataset, we used Word2Vec embeddings prepared using the hyperparameters of the experiment 3 column in Table 3 for classification. A higher value of window size appears to have a positive effect on the classification success shown in Fig. 2. While the value of window size increases, the classification accuracy also increases. When the window size increases from 5 to 25, a 5% improvement in classification success is achieved. Therefore, it can be deduced that context is important for classification and significantly affects the classification accuracy.

The hyperparameters of the experiment 4 column in Table 3. were used to examine the effect of the number of iterations used to train Word2Vec model. The classification results obtained using word vectors are given in Fig. 3. While the number of iterations increased from 5 to 60, the success of classification increased by about 6%. This improvement shows that the number of iterations is an important hyperparameter. However, the contribution of the number of iterations to the classification success starts to slow down after 15 iterations. Therefore, an iteration value that gives a certain success can be selected because each iteration requires extra time for training.

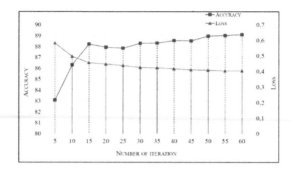

Fig. 3. Effect of number of iteration on classification accuracy and loss for DA

4.2   Progressive Approach

In Progressive Approach (PA), after determining the value of parameters that give the best result for classification, unlike DA, the best value is used instead of the default value for the subsequent steps. Since the minimum word count parameter was investigated in DA, we did not repeat this step and used the results of the minimum word count from DA. Minimum word count will be 30 as the best value for the subsequent experiments.

Table 4. Hyperparameters for PA after minimum word count experiment

Parameters	Experiment 2	Experiment 3	Experiment 4
Minimum word count	30	30	30
Vector size	50, 100, 150, 200, 250, 300	250	250
Window size	5	5, 10, 15, 20, 25	25
Number of iterations	5	5	5, 10, 15, 20, 25, 30, 35, 40, 45, 50, 55, 60

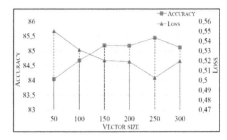 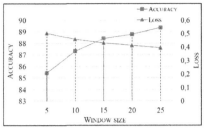

Fig. 4. Effect of vector size and window size on classification accuracy and loss for PA

The effect of vector size was examined using the hyperparameters of experiment 2 in Table 4. The results are given in Fig. 4. The best result is when the vector size is 250, which is the same as in DA. With the best minimum word count value, the vector size provides an almost 1.5% improvement with a value of 250. This was almost 2% for DA. We will use the 250 for the vector dimension parameter for the next steps.

The hyperparameters of experiment 3 in Table 4 were used to measure the effectiveness of the window size. The results are shown in Fig. 4. Increasing the window size value increases the classification success by less than 4%. In DA, the rate of improvement was 5%. As PA uses the best values in the past steps, the success of classification is seen to be increased at a lesser rate. The window size value will be used as 25 for the next steps because the best result is obtained with the value of 25.

The hyperparameters of experiment 4 in Table 4 were used to examine the effect of the number of iterations. The results are shown in Fig. 5. The increase in the number of iterations increases the success of classification by about 1%. In the first method, the contribution of the number of iterations to the classification success was about 6%. Since other parameters contribute to the improvement of classification in the previous steps, the number of iterations in this method seems to be less effective. The best result was taken at 45 iterations. However, the value of 60 also showed a very close success.

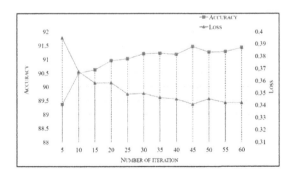

Fig. 5. Effect of iteration number on classification accuracy and loss for PA

4.3   Comparing Word2Vec Models Using the Best and Default Hyperparameters

In PA, the parameters that produce the best result in the final stage are chosen as a successor. The best parameters obtained by DA were the same as the best parameters obtained with the second method, except the number of iterations.

Table 5. Word2vec parameters set for best and worst classification accuracy

Method	Min. word count	Vector size	Window size	Number of iterations	Loss	Accuracy
Default values	5	100	5	5	0,5817	83,07
Decisive approach	30	250	25	60	0,3397	91,42
Progressive approach	30	250	25	45	0,3408	91,46

Table 5 shows the parameters for the best and worst cases in terms of the loss and accuracy of Word2Vec parameter evaluations. When we applied the classification model to classify the documents into 10 classes by using different parameters of Word2Vec, we got about 9% improvement in the classification accuracy.

5   Conclusion

In this study, we evaluated Word2Vec hyperparameters that affect the quality of word representation. A classification model was used to determine the Word2Vec hyperparameters. The results clearly show that Word2Vec hyperparameters affect the classification accuracy and thus the quality of word representation. We observed a 9% increase in the accuracy of our classification model. Considering that the classification process is done in 10 classes, the success rate achieved by setting only Word2Vec hyperparameters cannot be ignored. The Progressive Approach has been observed to offer faster convergence and more efficient performance improvement. Therefore, using the best value of each hyperparameter in the next steps is a wise choice for Word2Vec hyperparameter tuning.

We must state that there are no rules-of-thumb for a good word embedding applying to every purpose. However, we make the following conclusions for better word embedding. It was observed that the vector size, window size, and iteration number were the main hyperparameters affecting the word representation quality. Setting these parameters too large or too small can adversely affect success. The larger window size captures the topic and semantic better, but the smaller window size is more relevant to the syntactic relationship. The optimum vector size depends on the size of the datasets. Larger datasets require a larger vector size. Although the higher number of iterations requires more computing time, it is generally better for word representation quality.

The minimum word count determines the number of unique words in the dictionary and affects the amount of memory used. Very few repetitive words are often misspelled or very rare. Training these words in the Word2Vec model does not contribute to the quality of word representation. As can be seen in the results, with the small increase in the minimum word count, the number of the unique word in the dictionary is halved. This helps to remove words that are insignificant for the model. Therefore, performance gains are achieved by decreasing very rare and misspelled words.

The frequency of words affects the optimal value of hyperparameters. More frequent words may not require a larger window size for a good representation of the words. Therefore, the smaller window size value may be as good as the larger values when the dataset grows.

References

1. Deerwester, S., Dumais, S.T., Furnas, G.W., Landauer, T.K., Harshman, R.: Indexing by latent semantic analysis. J. Am. Soc. Inf. Sci. **41**(6), 391–407 (1990)
2. Pang, B., Lee, L.: Opinion mining and sentiment analysis. Found. Trends Inf. Retriev. **2**(1–2), 1–135 (2008)
3. Joulin, A., Grave, E., Bojanowski, P., Mikolov, T.: Bag of tricks for efficient text classification. arXiv preprint arXiv:1607.01759 (2016)
4. Wang, P., Xu, B., Xu, J., Tian, G., Liu, C.-L., Hao, H.: Semantic expansion using word embedding clustering and convolutional neural network for improving short text classification. Neurocomputing **174**, 806–814 (2016)
5. Liu, J., Chang, W.-C., Wu, Y., Yang, Y.: Deep learning for extreme multi-label text classification. In: Proceedings of the 40th International ACM SIGIR Conference on Research and Development in Information Retrieval, pp. 115–124 (2017)
6. Hinton, G.E.: Learning distributed representations of concepts. In: Proceedings of the 8th of the Cognitive Science Society, vol. 1, pp. 12 (1986)
7. Mikolov, T., Chen, K., Corrado, G., Dean, J.: Efficient estimation of word representations in vector space. arXiv preprint arXiv:1301.3781 (2013)
8. Mikolov, T., Sutskever, I., Chen, K., Corrado, G.S., Dean, J.: Distributed representations of words and phrases and their compositionality. In: Advances in Neural Information Processing System, pp. 3111–3119 (2013)
9. Pennington, J., Socher, R., Manning, C.: Glove: global vectors for word representation. In: Proceedings of the 2014 Conference on Empirical Methods in Natural Language Processing, pp. 1532–1543 (2014)
10. Levy, O., Goldberg, Y., Dagan, I.: Improving distributional similarity with lessons learned from word embeddings. Trans. Assoc. Comput. Linguist. **3**, 211–225 (2015)
11. Lai, S., Liu, K., He, S., Zhao, J.: How to generate a good word embedding. IEEE Intell. Syst. **31**(6), 5–14 (2016)
12. Caselles-Dupré, H., Lesaint, F., Royo-Letelier, J.: Word2Vec applied to recommendation: hyperparameters matter. arXiv preprint arXiv:1804.04212 (2018)

13. Yaghoobzadeh, Y., Kann, K., Schütze, H.: Evaluating word embeddings in multi-label classification using fine-grained name typing. In: The 3rd Workshop on Representation Learning for NLP (RepL4NLP), Melbourne, Australia, pp. 101–106 (2018)
14. Nooralahzadeh, F., Øvrelid, L., Lønning, J.T.: Evaluation of domain-specific word embeddings using knowledge resources, LREC (2018)
15. Yildiz, B., Fox, G.C.: Toward a modular and efficient distribution for web service handlers. Concurr. Comput.: Pract. Exp. **25**(3), 410–426 (2013)
16. Yildiz, B., Fox, G., Pallickara, S.: An orchestration for distributed web service handlers. In: 3th International Conference on Internet and Web Applications and Services, pp. 638–643 (2008)
17. Aktas, M.S., Kaplan, S., Abacı, H., Kalipsiz, O., Ketenci, U., Turgut, U.O.: Data imputation methods for missing values in the context of clustering. In: Big Data and Knowledge Sharing in Virtual Organizations (IGI Global, 2019), pp. 240–274 (2019)
18. Rehurek, R., Sojka, P.: Software framework for topic modelling with large corpora. In: Proceedings of the LREC 2010 Workshop on New Challenges for NLP Frameworks (2010)
19. Lison, P., Kutuzov, A.: Redefining context windows for word embedding models: an experimental study. arXiv preprint arXiv:1704.05781 (2017)
20. Goldberg, Y.: A primer on neural network models for natural language processing. J. Artif. Intell. Res. **57**, 345–420 (2016)

Hugo: A Cluster Scheduler that Efficiently Learns to Select Complementary Data-Parallel Jobs

Lauritz Thamsen[1]([✉]), Ilya Verbitskiy[1], Sasho Nedelkoski[1], Vinh Thuy Tran[1],
Vinícius Meyer[2], Miguel G. Xavier[2], Odej Kao[1], and César A. F. De Rose[2]

[1] TU Berlin, Berlin, Germany
{lauritz.thamsen,ilya.verbitskiy,sasho.nedelkoski,vinh.tran,
odej.kao}@tu-berlin.de
[2] PUCRS, Porto Alegre, Brazil
{vinicius.meyer,miguel.xavier,cesar.rose}@pucrs.br

Abstract. Distributed data processing systems like MapReduce, Spark, and Flink are popular tools for analysis of large datasets with cluster resources. Yet, users often overprovision resources for their data processing jobs, while the resource usage of these jobs also typically fluctuates considerably. Therefore, multiple jobs usually get scheduled onto the same shared resources to increase the resource utilization and throughput of clusters. However, job runtimes and the utilization of shared resources can vary significantly depending on the specific combinations of co-located jobs.

This paper presents *Hugo*, a cluster scheduler that continuously learns how efficiently jobs share resources, considering metrics for the resource utilization and interference among co-located jobs. The scheduler combines offline grouping of jobs with online reinforcement learning to provide a scheduling mechanism that efficiently generalizes from specific monitored job combinations yet also adapts to changes in workloads. Our evaluation of a prototype shows that the approach can reduce the runtimes of exemplary Spark jobs on a YARN cluster by up to 12.5%, while resource utilization is increased and waiting times can be bounded.

Keywords: Data-parallel processing · Cluster scheduling · Resource management · Distributed dataflows · Reinforcement learning

1 Introduction

Distributed data-parallel processing systems such as MapReduce [4], Spark [27], Flink [3], and Dataflow/Beam [1] enable users to take advantage of clusters of bare-metal or virtual machines for analysis of large datasets. These systems have become popular tools for workloads that range from data aggregation and search to relational queries, graph processing, and machine learning [8,9,15,17]. Jobs from these diverse domains stress different resources, while the resource demands

© Springer Nature Switzerland AG 2020
U. Schwardmann et al. (Eds.): Euro-Par 2019 Workshops, LNCS 11997, pp. 519–530, 2020.
https://doi.org/10.1007/978-3-030-48340-1_40

typically also fluctuate significantly over the runtime of jobs [16,18,21]. Therefore, multiple jobs usually share cluster resources without isolation, so they can benefit from statistical multiplexing [20,23,26]. This is implemented by using resource management systems like YARN [24] and Mesos [10]. These systems allow users to reserve fractions of cluster nodes via the notion of containers, in which users then run one or multiple jobs using the frameworks of their choice. By default the resource management systems use simple scheduling methods such as round-robin, FIFO, greedy approaches, and other reservation-based methods such as dominant-resource fairness [2,10,24,27], while low resource utilization remains a major problem in industry [6,19,20]. Yet, since jobs differ considerably in which resources they stress and how much utilization fluctuates, schedulers should actively co-locate jobs that share resources efficiently. The benefits of such approaches have been demonstrated before, including by the authors [12,22], with multiple schedulers that explicitly take combined resource utilization and interference among co-located workloads into account [5,6,16] or learn the impact of this indirectly [13,14], taking advantage of the recurrence of a majority of jobs [11]. However, previous efforts fall short in at least one of the following dimensions:

- *Learning Efficiency:* Multiple systems require extensive training data as they learn the sharing efficiency on the level of individual jobs or using completely generic learning methods [13,14,16,22].
- *Continuous Learning:* Some systems do not update their models continuously and therefore do not adapt to changes in workloads [5,12].
- *Solution Practicality:* Some systems do not incorporate objectives besides throughput [13,14,22], while others assume control over more than just job order [5,6,14] or require instrumentation not generally supported [12].

Addressing these limitations, we present Hugo, a cluster scheduler that efficiently learns from collected resource usage metrics to co-locate those jobs that have complementary resource demands and therefore share resources efficiently, building on our previous work [12,22]. Hugo first clusters jobs by their resource utilization, yielding multiple groups of jobs that contain jobs with similar resource demands. Subsequently, our scheduler uses reinforcement learning to continuously evolve its knowledge on which groups of jobs are sharing the resources of a particular cluster environment efficiently. That is, the scheduler learns for each workload and cluster from the experiences of scheduling particular job combinations onto the same cluster nodes, assessing which groups of jobs produce a high resource utilization yet low interference when co-located. This combination of generalization across a fixed number of groups of jobs with reinforcement learning of co-location benefits provides learning efficiency, a reduced scheduling complexity, and adaptation to changes in workloads. Furthermore, we show how additional scheduling requirements are integrated into Hugo with the example of balanced waiting times.

Contributions. The contributions of this paper are:

- We propose the scheduler *Hugo*, which efficiently learns how different groups of cluster jobs of a data processing workload utilize shared resources.
- We implemented a prototype of our approach as a job submission tool for Spark jobs in YARN clusters.
- We evaluated our prototype on a cluster with 34 nodes, using different workloads and in comparison to YARN's default scheduling.

Outline. The remainder of the paper is structured as follows. Section 2 discusses the related work. Section 3 explains our scheduling approach. Section 4 presents our evaluation of our approach. Section 5 concludes this paper.

2   Related Work

In this section we describe related work on scheduling distributed data-parallel workloads based on resource utilization and interference.

Paragon [5] profiles incoming jobs and matches them with jobs that are similar with regard to the impact of different hardware and interference with co-located workloads. Paragon then assigns jobs to available resources using its job classes and collaborative filtering, aiming to minimize interference and maximize resource utilization. In comparison, Hugo targets distributed data-parallel jobs and employs more resource utilization metrics for its co-location goodness.

Quasar [6] uses classification to assess the impact of resources and interference with co-located workloads when scheduling jobs. It takes performance requirements of users into account, monitors job performance at runtime, and adjusts models and allocations dynamically. Quasar does assume full control over both resource allocation and assignment, while Hugo's scope is only scheduling of distributed data-parallel jobs.

Gemini [16] uses a model that captures the tradeoff between performance improvement and fairness loss for jobs scheduled in shared clusters. The model quantifies the complementarity in the resource demands of jobs and is trained on historic workload data. Gemini then decides automatically whether the fairness loss of a computed schedule is valid under a user's setting of required fairness and in relation to Dominant Resource Fairness [7]. In comparison, Hugo uses a reinforcement learning algorithm and groups of jobs.

DeepRM [13] is a scheduler that relies on deep reinforcement learning. The scheduler models the state of a cluster system, taking into account the already allocated resources along with resource profiles for the queued jobs. It then uses a neural network to obtain a probability distribution over all possible scheduling actions, using the rewards obtained after every action to update the parameters of the neural network. In comparison, DeepRM is a generic reinforcement learning framework for job scheduling, whereas Hugo particularly targets job co-location effects. Consequently, DeepRM might require more training effort.

Similar to DeepRM, Decima [14] also uses reinforcement learning along with a neural network for job scheduling. The system focuses on dataflow jobs that are described as directed acyclic graphs. Decima does not only perform scheduling, but also learns job parameters such as task parallelism. In comparison, Hugo does not make assumptions about a job's structure and configuration options.

We used reinforcement learning to co-locate cluster jobs based on the resource usage and interference before, including the same measure of co-location goodness [22]. However, the previous approach maintains preferences of individual jobs, while Hugo learns and schedules on the level of job groups for efficiency and scalability. Other related previous results include CIAPA [12] and IntP [25]. CIAPA uses an interference- and affinity-aware performance model based on detailed system-level metrics to improve the placement of jobs. IntP is a profiling tool that extracts fine-grained resource metrics from hardware counters and system structures. Both these approaches use classification to generalize from individual jobs similar to Hugo's job groups.

3   Approach

Hugo is an adaptive cluster job scheduler that utilizes resource usage profiles of jobs to select and co-locate combinations of jobs that efficiently share the available resources. It combines offline clustering and online reinforcement learning for efficient learning, scalability, and adaptation to changes in workloads.

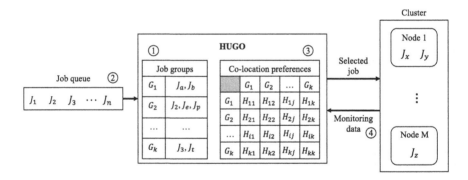

Fig. 1. Scheduling jobs onto shared cluster resources based on continuously learned co-location preferences among groups of jobs.

Figure 1 shows an overview of Hugo's approach. It consists of the following main steps as annotated by the numbers in the figure:

① Resource usage metrics of historic job runs are used to group jobs. For instance, two groups could distinguish CPU- and I/O-intensive jobs. The groups can be computed offline and can be updated periodically. Clustering methods can be used to establish a number of distinct groups automatically. Grouping provides an abstraction for the scheduling algorithm which then operates on job group level.

② Each incoming job is assigned to the job group it matches best. For this, either a profiling run on samples of the input or available historic monitoring data is used to match the job to one group.

③ Using the groups, Hugo forms and continuously updates a preference matrix that quantifies the co-location goodness for pairs of job groups. The measure of co-location goodness is based on metrics that capture the combined resource utilization and the interference of co-located jobs.

④ Based on the preference matrix, the scheduler selects those jobs from the queue that have a high co-location goodness with the currently running jobs in the cluster. The selected jobs are then scheduled onto the available resources. After a job is executed, the preference matrix is updated for the combination of jobs that were co-located via reinforcement learning.

Utilizing reinforcement learning allows to learn the efficiency of different schedules during and through actual scheduling decisions. That is, scheduling decisions can be made right away on the basis of preferences, yet the scheduler learns continuously and, therefore, adapts to changes.

3.1 Grouping Jobs Based on Resource Metrics

Grouping of the jobs is the key idea to ensure scalability and improve the learning efficiency of the scheduler, since it reduces the size of the preference matrix to k groups. Considering that we already have job resource usage statistics for all previously executed jobs we group them into k groups. Depending on the clustering method, and the job profiling information, the groups can have different meaning. For example, there could be groups for jobs that predominantly stress the CPU, memory, disks, or network, while jobs of others groups could also exhibit mixed high usage of multiple resources such as both, CPU and memory.

Once we have the initial groups formed using the historic data for a specific cluster workload, the jobs in the queue need to be assigned to these groups. Jobs in the queue can be recurring jobs or new jobs. For recurring jobs we can use the previously recorded monitoring data to match the job to one of the available k groups, for instance by averaging the utilization metrics of recent previous runs. For new jobs, a profiling run is executed on a small sample of the entire input data to collect resource usage metrics and match the jobs to the available groups. Using the resource usage profiles of the queued jobs each job is assigned to its representative group.

3.2 Learning to Schedule Job Combinations

We learn the co-location goodness on the level of job groups. Therefore, our preference matrix contains a goodness measure for pairs of job groups. The co-location goodness measure assesses how specific combinations of job groups utilize resources, using metrics that capture the resource utilization and interference among co-located jobs. We use the same measure of co-location goodness and reinforcement learning algorithm we proposed previously for cluster scheduling [22].

Typically, we have multiple jobs queued and with these jobs also multiple job groups. Simultaneously, there are jobs already running on the shared cluster. We use reinforcement learning to select the jobs for scheduling and updating the preferences in the matrix based on the currently running as well as the queued jobs. In the following we explain the job selection and the updates, which depend on each other. We denote the preference matrix as H. Its elements H_{eg} contain the preference of job group e when co-locating jobs of it with jobs of group g. The probability of picking job group g to run concurrently with an already running job of group e is denoted as $\pi_e(g) = \frac{\exp(H_{eg})}{\sum_{b \in S} \exp(H_{bg})}$. The probability of choosing a job group g to select and schedule next on the cluster then is

$$\Pi(g) = \frac{\sum_{e \in C} \Pi_e(g)}{\sum_{i \in Q} \sum_{e \in C} \Pi_e(i)}$$

where $\Pi_e(g) = \frac{\pi_e(g)}{\sum_{i \in Q} \pi_e(i)}$, C is the set of job groups with jobs currently running on the cluster, Q is the set of job groups with jobs currently in the queue and S is the set of all groups.

To represent the relative goodness among the set Q, the probability for each job group $\Pi_e(g)$ is normalized. Job group C_{next} is chosen to be scheduled next by sampling from a distribution where the probabilities of each group are proportional to their co-location goodness with the existing job groups on the cluster.

After C_{next} is chosen, the scheduler scans the waiting queue and picks the jobs assigned to C_{next}. If there is only one job match, it is scheduled next. Otherwise, if there are multiple options, a randomize function is used to choose one of the jobs in the group to schedule next. Finally, for every node n in the cluster the preferences between job groups of the co-location job pairs are subsequently updated as follows:

$$H_{ij} := \alpha(R_n - \overline{R}^i)(1 - \pi_i(j)) - \sum_{a \in \Omega_n \setminus \{i,j\}} \alpha(R_n - \overline{R}^i)\pi_i(a) \qquad \forall i, j \in \Omega_n$$

where α is the learning rate, Ω_n is the set of job groups containing jobs placed on the node n, R_n represents the co-location goodness for node n, and $\overline{R}^i$ is the mean goodness across all nodes containing jobs in the job group i.

3.3   Integrating Additional Scheduling Constraints

In practice, there are other requirements for scheduling beyond resource utilization and throughput. Examples of these are fairness among users and priorities with particularly critical jobs. To highlight the practical applicability of Hugo we integrated a mechanism that balances waiting times and prevents job starvation. As explained, when a job group is chosen as the next one to be scheduled, Hugo randomly chooses among the currently waiting jobs of that group with equal probabilities. To balance waiting times the choosing probabilities can be modified by the waiting times. The probabilities of choosing a job a within the chosen job group G is subsequently calculated by

$$\pi_a = \frac{w_a}{\sum_{i \in G} w_i}$$

where w_i is the waiting time of job i.

The above usage of job waiting time only takes effect if the job group is eventually selected to schedule next. However, if the co-location goodness preference of the job group itself is low compared to most of the other job groups, the jobs in that group are still at risk of not getting selected. We therefore further define the global parameter *waiting limit* for the scheduler. When a job's waiting time reaches this limit, it is scheduled regardless of the co-location preferences. In case of multiple jobs with waiting times above the limit, one of them is chosen with probabilities according to the waiting time using the formula as above. We denote this version of the algorithm as Hugo*.

4 Evaluation

We tested our approach with four experiments using a prototype implementation, a commodity cluster, and various exemplary jobs. In the following sections we describe the prototype implementation, the cluster setup, the test workload, and the four experiments along with the respective results.

4.1 Prototype Implementation

We implemented Hugo in Python as a job submission tool for YARN. We use the combination of Telegraf and InfluxDB to monitor and persist the CPU, memory, disk, and network usage as well I/O wait data of each node. Spark is chosen as the data processing engine. All the benchmarking jobs are implemented with Spark's APIs.

4.2 Cluster Setup

The experiments were executed on a cluster consisting of 34 nodes. Each node is equipped with an Intel Xeon E3-1230 V2 @ 3.30 GHz (4 physical cores, 8 virtual cores) and 16 GB of RAM, connected through a 1 Gbit/s Ethernet connection and running a Linux-based OS (kernel version 4.15.0).

Among the 34 nodes, one server was used to run YARN's resource manager. YARN was configured such that each container occupied one logical CPU and 1800 MB of RAM, resulting in maximum of 8 containers per node. From the 33 nodes managed by YARN, one node was used to run Spark's driver programs, while the remaining 32 nodes were used as worker nodes.

4.3   Test Workload

For simulating a mixed data processing workload, nine Spark analytic jobs are used throughout the experiment. The jobs and their datasets used for benchmarking are specified in Table 1. For further reference each job is annotated by its own letter, while a number the annotated number denotes the job's group. We grouped the jobs into six distinct groups by their utilization of CPU, disk, and memory, including groups of mixed utilization and overall low resource utilization. The sizes of the input data are chosen so that the runtime of all jobs is similar and lasts approximately ten minutes. The jobs were chosen such that they cover different application domains like machine learning (A, D, E, F), graph processing (B, C), relational queries (G), and text processing (H, I).

Table 1. Dataflow jobs used in the experiment

Job (job, group)	Data source	Data parameters
K-Means (A, 1)	KMeansDataGenerator[a]	100,000,000 points, 80 clusters
PageRank (B, 3)	Graph Challenge data sets[b]	46,656,000 edges, 2,174,640 vertices
Connected Components (C, 6)	Graph Challenge data sets[b]	38,880,000 edges, 1,812,200 vertices
Linear Regression (D, 1)	LinearDataGenerator[a]	90,000,000 samples, 20 features per sample
Logistic Regression (E, 2)	LogisticRegressionDataGenerator[a]	11,000,000 samples, 10 features per sample
SVM (F, 2)	SVMDataGenerator[a]	70,000,000 samples, 10 features per sample
TPC-H (G, 4)	DBGEN[c]	100 GB generated DB
Sort (H, 5)	DBGEN[c]	143,999,787 records
Word Count (I, 1)	Wikipedia backup data[d]	53 GB text document

[a] from the `org.apache.spark.mllib.util` package
[b] Graph Challenge datasets provided by Amazon, https://graphchallenge.mit.edu/data-sets
[c] included in TPC-H tool package, http://www.tpc.org/tpch/
[d] Wikipedia database dump, https://dumps.wikimedia.org

4.4   Experiments

We conducted four experiments. Each experiment shows how our scheduler performs in a different scenario in comparison to the baseline round-robin scheduler in terms of makespan and resource utilization. In the following we describe and motivate each of the experiments and present the results.

Learning Phase. The aim of this experiment is to gain insights into how our Hugo scheduler compares to the baseline round-robin scheduler when there is no preference data available when the scheduler starts. That is, we start with an empty preference matrix. The algorithm then populates and updates the preference matrix, continuously evaluating the resource usage of pairs of jobs. To speed up the learning process, the job queue contains a job from each job group. The jobs are placed in a repeating pattern as follows: C B G A F H × 10.

Results. Using the Hugo scheduler all queued jobs took 169 m 13 s to finish as opposed to the round-robin scheduler with 180 m 40 s, an improvement by 6.3%. This result indicates that using the Hugo scheduler is beneficial in comparison to the round-robin scheduler, even without any prior preference data and therefore while training, when the workload contains periodically recurring jobs.

Prior Preference Data. In the follow-up experiment, the preference matrix output from the first experiment is used as the input for the Hugo scheduler. However, in this experiment we exchange some of the jobs in the queue with jobs that did not appear in the queue of the previous experiment. This way, we want to evaluate how well the grouping of our scheduler generalizes to unseen jobs. The jobs are placed in a repeating pattern as follows: D E B C H G I × 5.

Results. The Hugo scheduler again yields a faster running time: 114 m 49 s compared to the running time of the round-robin scheduler of 128 m 17 s. It thus produces a schedule that needs 10.5% less time to finish all jobs. Considering the job queue in this experiment has the same diversity of job groups as in the first experiment, the result suggests that the improvement is due to the prior knowledge of preferences between job groups. Also, the result indicates that it is possible to have beneficial co-location of new jobs on the basis of the calculated co-location goodness of previously executed similar jobs.

Randomized Queues. In this experiment, we included all nine dataflow jobs. The output preference matrix from the previous experiment is used as input preference data for our Hugo scheduler in this experiment. With this experiment we want to gain insights into how our scheduler behaves with a more realistic queue as opposed to the manually created queues of the previous experiments. For this, we generated the following two randomized job queues: C B B E A E E B I H H C B I H C E G F F A F C I G D A G I C G A F F D E G D A I D B H D H (Queue 1) and E I A B C H G C A H E G C B F F G D B A C G D D H F I G C D B A F I F E I E E A H H B D I (Queue 2).

Results. The results of this experiment are summarized in Table 2. Our Hugo scheduler does not only improve the utilization for each of the resources but also results in an improvement of up to 12.42% in total processing time over the baseline round-robin scheduler. This experiment, again, indicates that our scheduling approach is capable of finding advantageous co-locations that yield shorter execution times.

Table 2. Queue processing time for randomized queues

Queue	Scheduler	CPU [%]	Mem [%]	Disk [%]	Net [%]	Duration	δ [%]
1	RR	10.44	38.52	16.86	22.65	163 m 15 s	–
	Hugo	12.45	40.74	17.36	28.85	142 m 58 s	−12.42
2	RR	10.90	39.64	17.14	23.18	158 m 48 s	–
	Hugo	12.84	41.46	18.54	25.33	141 m 06 s	−11.14

Online Job Arrival. The primary goal of the previous experiment was to assess whether our Hugo scheduler succeeds in placing those jobs onto shared nodes that run well together. With the main focus being the co-location quality, however, the experiments disregarded the waiting times of jobs in the queue. In this experiment, we evaluate how effective our extended scheduler, Hugo*, deals with job queues where jobs have different waiting times.

The preference input data for this experiment is the output of the second experiment. The job queue used for this experiment is the same randomized Job Queue 1 from the previous experiment. However, in contrast to the previous experiments, the whole queue is not known to the scheduler right away. Instead, jobs join the queue after every scheduling round. We look at two arrival patterns. With constant arrival rate (CAR), a single job is added to the queue after every scheduling round. With arbitrary arrival rate (AAR), 1 to 3 new jobs are added to the queue after every scheduling round. The exact amount of jobs added to the queue follows a probability distribution where the probability of adding 1, 2, or 3 jobs equals 60%, 20%, and 20%, respectively.

Table 3. Queue processing time with arbitrary arrival rate

Scheduler	Duration	δ [%]
RR	163 m 15 s	–
Hugo* (CAR)	145 m 44 s	−10.73
Hugo* (AAR)	154 m 29 s	−5.37

Results. Table 3 summarizes the outcome of this experiment. Our Hugo scheduler is faster than the baseline for every constellation. However, we also see a significant drop in performance with AAR. A trade-off has to be made between job starvation and efficient job order. This demonstrates the pitfall of when the scheduler is not able to submit jobs onto the cluster as fast as they arrive.

Figure 2 shows how the waiting time is distributed with Hugo and Hugo*. For Hugo there is a significantly higher number of jobs with or exceeding the waiting time limit of 20. Hugo*, on the other hand, is able to successfully reduce the amount of jobs exceeding the waiting time limit. However, since Hugo* gives jobs that are waiting longer than the global limit the highest preference, the schedules exhibit less optimal co-locations, reflected in longer total running time.

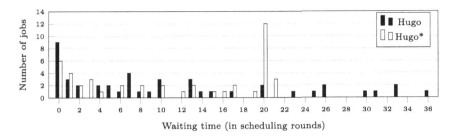

Fig. 2. Comparison of job waiting times between the Hugo and the Hugo* scheduler.

5   Conclusion

This paper presented Hugo, a cluster scheduler for distributed data-parallel processing workloads that selects jobs based on the resource usage of co-located jobs. Hugo uses a reinforcement learning algorithm to learn over time which combinations of jobs best utilize shared resources. To efficiently generalize its knowledge and thus co-locate even new jobs effectively, the approach learns preferences not for single jobs but for groups of jobs that exhibit similar resource demands. Hugo selects among the queued jobs using these learned preferences, choosing types of jobs that complement the jobs currently running on the shared infrastructure. It thereby aims to schedule those jobs jointly onto shared nodes that yield the best overall resource utilization and runtimes. We implemented a prototype of Hugo for Spark and YARN, showing that given mixed workloads with recurring jobs, our approach can reduce job runtimes, increase resource utilization, and still balance waiting times.

Acknowledgments. This work has been supported through grants by the German Ministry for Education and Research (BMBF; funding mark 01IS14013A and 01IS18025A).

References

1. Akidau, T., et al.: The dataflow model: a practical approach to balancing correctness, latency, and cost in massive-scale, unbounded, out-of-order data processing. Proc. VLDB Endow. **8**(12), 1792–1803 (2015)
2. Bao, Y., Peng, Y., Wu, C., Li, Z.: Online job scheduling in distributed machine learning clusters. In: INFOCOM 2018. IEEE, April 2018
3. Carbone, P., Katsifodimos, A., Ewen, S., Markl, V., Haridi, S., Tzoumas, K.: Apache Flink^{TM}: stream and batch processing in a single engine. IEEE Data Eng. Bull. **38**(4), 28–38 (2015)
4. Dean, J., Ghemawat, S.: MapReduce: Simplified Data Processing on Large Clusters. In: OSDI 2004. USENIX Association, January 2004
5. Delimitrou, C., Kozyrakis, C.: Paragon: QoS-aware scheduling for heterogeneous datacenters. In: ASPLOS 2013. ACM, March 2013
6. Delimitrou, C., Kozyrakis, C.: Quasar: resource-efficient and QoS-aware cluster management. In: ASPLOS 2014. ACM, March 2014

7. Ghodsi, A., Zaharia, M., Hindman, B., Konwinski, A., Shenker, S., Stoica, I.: Dominant resource fairness: fair allocation of multiple resource types. In: NSDI 2011. USENIX Association, March 2011

8. Ghoting, A., et al.: SystemML: declarative machine learning on mapreduce. In: ICDE 2011. IEEE, April 2011

9. Gonzalez, J.E., Xin, R.S., Dave, A., Crankshaw, D., Franklin, M.J., Stoica, I.: GraphX: graph processing in a distributed dataflow framework. In: OSDI 2014. USENIX Association, September 2014

10. Hindman, B., et al.: Mesos: a platform for fine-grained resource sharing in the data center. In: NSDI 2011. USENIX Association, March 2011

11. Jyothi, S.A., et al.: Morpheus: towards automated SLOs for enterprise clusters. In: OSDI 2016. USENIX Association, November 2016

12. Ludwig, U.L., Xavier, M.G., Kirchoff, D.F., Cezar, I.B., De Rose, C.A.F.: optimizing multi-tier application performance with interference and affinity-aware placement algorithms. Concurr. Comput. Pract. Exp. **31**(18), e5098 (2018)

13. Mao, H., Alizadeh, M., Menache, I., Kandula, S.: Resource management with deep reinforcement learning. In: HotNets 2016. ACM, November 2016

14. Mao, H., Schwarzkopf, M., Venkatakrishnan, S.B., Meng, Z., Alizadeh, M.: Learning Scheduling Algorithms for Data Processing Clusters. arXiv preprint arXiv:1810.01963, October 2018

15. Meng, X., et al.: MLlib: machine learning in apache spark. J. Mach. Learn. Res. **17**(1), 1235–1241 (2016)

16. Niu, Z., Tang, S., He, B.: Gemini: an adaptive performance-fairness scheduler for data-intensive cluster computing. In: CloudCom2015. IEEE, November 2015

17. Olston, C., Reed, B., Srivastava, U., Kumar, R., Tomkins, A.: Pig Latin: a not-so-foreign language for data processing. In: SIGMOD 2008. ACM, June 2008

18. Ousterhout, K., Rasti, R., Ratnasamy, S., Shenker, S., Chun, B.G.: Making sense of performance in data analytics frameworks. In: NSDI 2015. USENIX Association, March 2015

19. Rasley, J., Karanasos, K., Kandula, S., Fonseca, R., Vojnovic, M., Rao, S.: Efficient queue management for cluster scheduling. In: EuroSys 2016. ACM, April 2016

20. Reiss, C., Tumanov, A., Ganger, G.R., Katz, R.H., Kozuch, M.A.: Heterogeneity and dynamicity of clouds at scale: google trace analysis. In: SoCC 2012. ACM, October 2012

21. Renner, T., Thamsen, L., Kao, O.: Network-aware resource management for scalable data analytics frameworks. In: Big Data 2015. IEEE, October 2015

22. Thamsen, L., Rabier, B., Schmidt, F., Renner, T., Kao, O.: Scheduling recurring distributed dataflow jobs based on resource utilization and interference. In: BigData Congress. IEEE, June 2017

23. Thamsen, L., Verbitskiy, I., Rabier, B., Kao, O.: Learning efficient co-locations for scheduling distributed dataflows in shared clusters. Serv. Trans. Big Data **4**(1), 1–15 (2019)

24. Vavilapalli, V.K., et al.: Apache hadoop YARN: yet another resource negotiator. In: SOCC 2013. ACM, September 2013

25. Xavier, M.G., De Rose, C.A.: Data Processing with Cross-application Interference Control via System-level Instrumentation. Ph.D. Thesis at PUCRS, Brazil (2018)

26. Zaharia, M., Borthakur, D., Sen Sarma, J., Elmeleegy, K., Shenker, S., Stoica, I.: Delay scheduling: a simple technique for achieving locality and fairness in cluster scheduling. In: EuroSys 2010. ACM, April 2010

27. Zaharia, M., Chowdhury, M., Franklin, M.J., Shenker, S., Stoica, I.: Spark: cluster computing with working sets. In: HotCloud 2010. USENIX Association, June 2010

FLY: A Domain-Specific Language for Scientific Computing on FaaS

Gennaro Cordasco[1(✉)], Matteo D'Auria[2], Alberto Negro[2], Vittorio Scarano[2], and Carmine Spagnuolo[2]

[1] Dipartimento di Psicologia, Università degli Studi della Campania, Caserta, Italy
gennaro.cordasco@unicampania.it
[2] Dipartimento di Informatica, Università degli Studi di Salerno, Fisciano, Italy
{matdauria,alberto,vitsca,cspagnuolo}@unisa.it

Abstract. Cloud Computing is widely recognized as distributed computing paradigm for the next generation of dynamically scalable applications. Recently a novel service model, called Function-as-a-Service (FaaS), has been proposed, that enables users to exploit the computational power of cloud infrastructures, without the need to configure and manage complex computations systems. FaaS paradigm represents an opportunity to easily develop and execute extreme-scale applications as it allows fine-grain decomposition of the application with a much more efficient scheduling on cloud provider infrastructure.

We introduce FLY, a domain-specific language for designing, deploying and executing scientific computing applications by exploiting the FaaS service model on different cloud infrastructures. In this paper, we present the design and the language definition of FLY on several computing (local and FaaS) back-ends: Symmetric multiprocessing (SMP), Amazon AWS Lambda, Microsoft Azure Functions, Google Cloud Functions, and IBM Bluemix/Apache OpenWhisk. We also present the first FLY source-to-source compiler, publicly available on GitHub, which supports SMP and AWS back-ends.

Keywords: Domain-Specific Languages · Scientific computing · Parallel computing · Distributed computing · Serverless computing · Functions as a Service (FaaS)

1 Introduction

Cloud computing [2] is widely recognized as distributed computing paradigm for the next generation of dynamically scalable applications. Since the dawn of the practice of the cloud, many service models are competing to become the leading model of cloud infrastructures. Nowadays, Cloud computing is undergoing a service-model shift, moving the computation on the *Serverless computing model*, superseding the popular service-models as *Infrastructure-as-a-Service* (IaaS), *Platform-as-a-Service* (PaaS) and *Software-as-a-Service (SaaS)*. Serverless computing model is a novel paradigm for deployment of cloud applications, in which code snippets are executed over the cloud infrastructure without having to manage or configure the machines running the code.

© Springer Nature Switzerland AG 2020
U. Schwardmann et al. (Eds.): Euro-Par 2019 Workshops, LNCS 11997, pp. 531–544, 2020.
https://doi.org/10.1007/978-3-030-48340-1_41

Serverless computing architecture is the natural evolution of *microservices architecture* [3], in which the developers do not have to mind about the configuration and management of the servers executing the back-end of their applications. Cloud applications based on serverless computing are event-triggered: programmer-defined events rule the independent execution of modular pieces of code on the cloud environment. This novel service model, named Function-as-a-Service (FaaS), was first introduced and made available to the world by hook.io in late 2014 and was shortly followed by AWS Lambda, Google Cloud Functions, Microsoft Azure Functions and many others.

FaaS can be seen as a finegrained computing partitioning of a cloud applications, which enables to scale according to the provider capacity. FaaS has been designed for easily build and deploy scalable applications that are business-oriented such as Mobile and Internet of Things (IoT) Back-end, Real-time File/Stream Processing, Web Applications as well as service oriented applications.

In this work we take a novel approach by exploiting FaaS cloud service-model to develop scalable computing-intensive applications for scientific and data science. In fact, since the very beginning of Cloud, it was clear how the paradigm represented an opportunity to easily develop and execute extreme-scale applications maintaining their costs extremely low compared to High Performance Computing solutions, as shown by the experiments in [4]. On the other hand, although cloud providers offer solutions with a high level of scalability, very often the migration of a scientific application on IaaS or PaaS represents a humongous and complex task, which can conceal serious cost considerations, thereby often preventing scientific application developers to fully exploit the scalability and cost effectiveness of cloud computing in their own application domain. This work aims at reconciling Cloud and High Performance Computing by providing an efficient, effective and price-aware tool for the development of scalable scientific computing application on several FaaS environments through the design and implementation of a *domain-specific language* (DSL) named FLY. FLY is *efficient* because it enables to exploit the computing capabilities of different cloud providers at once, in a single application, and, then, the most efficient solutions can be merged together. FLY is *effective* because it consists of a user-friendly programming language that frees the programmer from the management and configuration of several complex computation systems. Finally, FLY is *price-aware* because the programmer becomes conscious of the maximum computing costs, based on the prices provided by various cloud providers. In this way, the programmer also has the possibility to choose the service that provides the best value for money, based on the characteristics of the computation that is going to perform.

1.1 The Motivations for a Parallel Language for FaaS

Cloud infrastructure provides several services in an accessible fashion through web endpoints, and/or APIs. Designing and developing scientific applications typically does not require general purposes services (for instance access to database or providing web pages), but it requires ad-hoc coding that implements algorithms, which solve specific problems.

Scientific computing applications are commonly developed using general-purposes languages or parallel languages/frameworks such as C, Java, Python, Fortran, Julia,

Table 1. Cloud Computing infrastructures API and FaaS programming languages fragmentation.

Cloud infrastructure	FaaS service	API languages	FaaS languages	Pricing and limitations
Amazon Web Services[b]	AWS Lambda function	Java, .NET, Node.js, PHP, Python, Ruby, Go, C++, REST	JavaScript, Java, Python, Go, C#	1 M functions and 400.000 GB/s of execution time free per month The execution time of a single function is limited at 300 s
Microsoft Azure[b]	Azure function	.NET, Java, Python, Go, Node.js, REST	C#, F#, JavaScript, Java	1 M functions and 400.000 GB/s of execution time free per month The execution time of a single function is limited at 300 s
Google[b]	Google function	REST, RPC	JavaScript	2 M functions, 1 M seconds of execution and 5 GB of network traffic free per month[a] The execution time of a single function is limited at 540 s
IBM Bluemix/Apache OpenWhisk[b]	Action	REST	JavaScript, Python, Java, PHP, Swift, Docker and native binaries, Go	5 M of functions and 400.000 GB/s of execution time free per month[b] The execution time of a single function is limited at 600 s
Fission[b]	Fission function	REST	C#, Go, JavaScript, PHP, Python	
Fn Project[b]	Fn function	REST	Java, Go,Ruby, Python, PHP, JavaScript	
Kubeless[b]	Kubeless function	REST	Python, JavaScript, Ruby, PHP, Go, .NET, Ballerina	

[a][1] Amazon AWS Lambda pricing. [2]Microsoft Azure Function pricing.
[3]Google Function pricing. [4]IBM Bluemix pricing.
[b]*Amazon AWS Lambda*, aws.amazon.com/lambda.
Microsoft Azure Functions, azure.microsoft.com/services/functions.
Google Cloud Functions, cloud.google.com/functions.
IBM Bluemix, www.ibm.com/cloud-computing/bluemix.
Apache OpenWhisk, openwhisk.apache.org.
Fission, docs.fission.io.
Fn Project, fnproject.io.
The Kubernetes Native Serverless Framework, kubeless.io.

Limbo, Chapel, MPI, Swift and many others (see Sect. 3 for more details). Moreover, scientific computing problems are typically computing-intensive and requires the computational power of a distributed system (clusters or HPC). Since 2017, Amazon Inc. company provides, in their IaaS offer, machines with high number of virtual processors and memory, which enables users to execute applications on a high performance cluster "de facto". According to the IaaS model, in such cases, the user is responsible for deploying and managing of such virtual clusters.

Although many cloud computing companies are recently providing MapReduce [5] programming paradigm as a cluster of machines running MapReduce compliant framework such as Apache Hadoop (e.g., AWS's *Elastic Map Reduce*), many computing-intensive problems do not fit well the MapReduce paradigm.

FLY also addresses another issue about the nature and prices of the services offered by Cloud computing providers. In fact, in some cases, it would be extremely convenient, either in terms of efficiency or cost, to be able to develop cloud scientific applications exploiting different services coming from different providers. Our result, then, enables a scientific application designer to write computing-intensive applications that can scale-up among different computing providers at the lowest costs, selecting the services that best fit the requirements of the considered problem.

2   Preliminaries

This section presents and discusses the research and state-of-the-art for the cloud computing service-models domain as well as a short introduction to domain specific languages.

2.1   Cloud Computing Service-Models

Cloud computing enables companies to use computing resources as a service (like electricity) rather than having to buy, set-up and maintain computing infrastructures in house. Several cloud computing service-models [6] has been proposed during the last two decades. Three models are mainly used by cloud providers:

- *Software-as-a-Service (SaaS)*, when applications are hosted by a cloud providers and made available on the web.
- *Platform-as-a-Service (PaaS)*, which is a paradigm for delivering applications frameworks on the Internet without downloading or installing it.
- *Infrastructure-as-a-Service (IaaS)*, which can be seen as the outsourcing of computing power required by the customers. This involves disk space, hardware, and networking components.

At a first sight, Cloud service models look promising for the Scientific Computing community, as they may take advantage of the adoption of cloud computing, in their compute-intensive applications and workflows, in each of the service models described above. It is possible, for example, to use IaaS for executing application on high performance machine or huge clusters, or a cloud computing provider can offer either PaaS or SaaS, dedicated domain specific services for scientific and data analysis purposes (like machine-learning or data-mining services, MapReduce frameworks, etc.). But the scenario does not come without effort and costs, as, for example, the developers still need to manage (complex) virtual machines (IaaS), or configure the services (PaaS and SaaS). Moreover, the scalability of these systems depends on the configuration adopted and the overall performances and costs saving are strictly dependent on the fluency and skills of the developers in the Cloud Computing realm.

Serverless computing service-model (or Function-as-a-Service, Faas) [7–9] answers to the needs of new scalable price-effective cloud applications, by providing an easy framework for deploying extremely scalable, functionally partitioned applications. FaaS enables developers to run their back-end applications on complex computing systems, without a thorough knowledge of the management and configuration of such systems. Indeed, using FaaS, the user is able to execute independent piece of code (functions), written in different languages, over the cloud infrastructure, without taking care about which is and what kind of configuration has the server running the code. FaaS service-model architecture is event-triggered, which means that developers must deploy the functions on the cloud infrastructure, and those functions are executed in response to events generated on the cloud infrastructure (e.g., insert a new record in a database, send a message on a queue, etc.). Table 1 shows some of the most popular Cloud Computing infrastructures (open-source and private companies) that provide the FaaS service-model. Our proposal is guided by the vision to adopt this service-model in a different context, that is for computing-intensive applications.

2.2 Domain-Specific Languages

Domain-Specific Languages (DSLs) are designed to provide a notation tailored toward an application domain that is based only on the concepts and features that are relevant for the domain. DSLs enable solutions to be expressed at the same level of abstraction of the problem domain and can be of significant help in shifting the development of business information systems from software developers to a larger group of domain-experts who, despite having less technical expertise, have deeper knowledge of the domain and, therefore, if an easy-to-use, tailored tool is provided, can be much more effective. Furthermore, DSLs are much easier to learn, given their limited scope. It must be said that DSLs have specific design goals that contrast with those of general-purpose languages: DSLs are much more expressive in their domain and should exhibit minimal redundancy. Examples of DSL include SQL [10] (for relational database query), HTML [11] (for website definition), R [13] (for statistics), OpenABL [12] (for simulation).

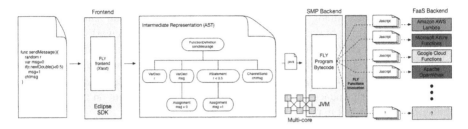

Fig. 1. FLY compilation workflow.

3   Related Work

Parallel and distributed languages have been actively investigated for decades [15]. Here we describe several languages and frameworks that are suitable for developing scalable applications in the scientific computing (SC) research area.

General-Purpose Languages. *Fortran* is a programming language designed for numeric computation and scientific computing. It is widely used in scientific fields (such as numerical weather prediction, computational dynamics and physics). Programmers are moving toward modern programming languages like *Python* [17] and *Julia* [18]

Parallel Languages. *Limbo* [19] is a programming language intended for applications running distributed systems on small computers. *Chapel* [20] is a programming language designed for productive parallel computing on large-scale systems. Its design and implementation have been undertaken with portability in mind, enabling Chapel to run on different environments. *Cilk* [21] is a general-purpose programming language designed for multithreaded parallel computing. Cilk is a C/C++ extension that supports nested data and task parallelism.

Frameworks Designed for Compute-Intensive Applications. *Apache Hadoop* [22] is a framework that enables the distributed processing of large data sets across clusters of computers using a simple programming model. *Apache Spark* [23] is a fast and general-purpose cluster computing system.

Scripting Languages for Workflow. *Swift* [24] is a featured data-flow oriented coarse grained scripting language, which is designed for scientists, engineers, and statisticians that need to execute domain-specific application programs many times on large collections of file-based data. *Swift/T* [25] is the high-performance computing version of Swift languages, in which the Swift programs are translated in MPI based programs to be executed on HPC systems. Swift and Swift/T provide set-up on cloud IaaS[1]. *OpenMole* [26] offers tools to run, explore, diagnose and optimize numerical models, taking advantage of distributed computing environments.

---

[1] http://swift-lang.org/tutorials/cloud/tutorial.html.

Listing 1.1: PI Montecarlo Estimation on Amazon AWS

```
1    var aws = [type:"aws",access_key:"amazon_aws_access_key",
         secret_key:"amazon_aws_secret_key", region:"us-east-2"]
2    var ch =  [type="channel"] on aws
3    func hit(){
4        var r =   [type="random"]
5        var x = r.nextDouble()
6        var y = r.nextDouble()
7        var msg=0
8        if( (x*x)+(y*y) < 1.0 ){ msg=1 }
9        ch!msg
10   }
11   func estimation(){
12       var sum = 0
13       var crt = 0
14       for i in [0:10000] {
15         sum += ch? as Integer
16         crt += 1
17       }
18       println "PI approximation is "+ (sum*4.0)/crt
19   }
20   fly hit in [0:10000] on aws thenall estimation
```

4   FLY Design

The goal of FLY is to provide a portable, scalable and easy-to-use programming environment for scientific computing. FLY perceives a cloud computing infrastructure as a parallel computing architecture on which it is possible to execute some parts of its execution flow in parallel. FLY enables the domain developers (i.e., domain experts with limited knowledge about complex parallel and distributed systems) to design their applications exploiting data and task parallelism on any FaaS architecture. This is achieved by a rich language that provides domain-specific constructs, that enable the developers to easily interact, using an environment abstraction, with different FaaS back-ends.

FLY provides implicit support for parallel and distributed computing paradigms and memory locality, enabling the users to manage and elaborate data on a cloud environment without the effort of knowing all the details behind cloud providers API. A FLY program is executable either on a SMP or a cloud infrastructure (supporting FaaS) without a deep knowledge of the underlying computing resources.

FLY is compiled in native code (Java code) and it is able to automatically exploit the computing resources available that better fit its computation requirements. The main innovative aspect of FLY is represented by the concept of FLY *function*. A FLY function can be seen as an independent block of code, that can be executed concurrently. FLY functions can be executed in sequential mode, in parallel on SMP or on a FaaS back-end. The language provides programming constructs for functions definition, execution, synchronization and communication. Communication among different environments/back-ends is obtained through some virtual communication path named *channels*. Along these lines FLY has been designed as an enhanced scripting language and is composed by a sequence of standard instructions integrated with a number of FLY functions invocation, which interact via channels.

Figure 1 depicts the FLY compilation workflow. On the left side, the FLY program is given in input to the compiler (written using XText). The intermediate AST representation is translated in a Java native program. Each FLY function is translated into different executable codes (one for each back-end). Therefore FLY provides compiled functions code that can be executed on each cloud infrastructure back-end (see Fig. 1).

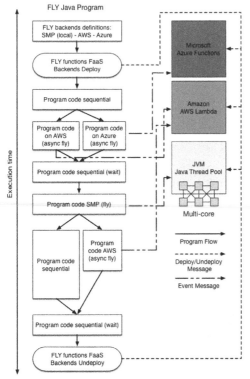

Figure 2 shows a general execution flow of a FLY program along the execution time. First of all, the program initializes all the back-ends required by the FLY code, and *deploys* the generated code on the corresponding back-end. We notice that the FLY functions are already compiled when the main FLY program is executed, thereby avoiding run-time compilation overheads. After these initialization steps, the main program is executed following the FLY code instructions. Each time the **fly** keyword is used, the program generates *events* on the corresponding SMP and/or FaaS back-end, in order to execute the FLY functions. FLY supports synchronous and asynchronous execution models.

Fig. 2. FLY execution workflow.

Before presenting the FLY language design, Listing 1.1 shows a simple example of a FLY program, which computes a PI estimation through the Montecarlo Method on an Amazon AWS Lambda back-end. Briefly, the PI Monte Carlo estimation algorithm generates a set of random points on a two dimensional Cartesian systems, and counts the number of points that are inside the positive quadrant of a circle of diameter 1.0 centered in the origin. Then, it computes the estimation of PI as $\frac{S*4.0}{N}$, where S is the number of points inside the positive quadrant of the circle and N is the total number of generated points. First of all, FLY *PI* code defines, at line 1, a new Amazon AWS FaaS back-end. Line 2 declares a new channel on the environment aws that enables the main program to communicate with the FLY function hit, defined at line 3. The hit function generates a random point and evaluates whether it belongs to the circle. This information is sent on the channel ch. Another function estimation reads the outputs of the function hit and writes on the standard output the estimation of PI. Line 20 launches 10000 hit functions synchronously on the aws back-end. When all functions terminate, the function estimation is performed on the SMP back-end. It is worth to notice that FLY functions cannot use variables declared outside the function scope, excepts for variables of type channel (see Sect. 5).

5   FLY Language Definition

The FLY syntax and concepts are inspired by different languages such as Java, JavaScript, Python, and R. This ensures familiarity with most powerful and famous general purposes/data science languages. FLY is statically, strongly typed and uses type inference to determine the initial type of all your variables (using the keyword var) and constants (using the keyword const). Moreover, FLY provides several domain specific constructs for parallel/distributed task/data based parallelism and supports inter-process (and inter-FLY-functions) communications using channels according to communicating sequential processes (CSP) definition [16].

5.1   Data Models and Types

FLY provides two sets of types named *basic* and *domain* types. Basic types, inherited by Java, comprises *boolean*, *integer*, *real* (double point precision floats) and *string*. Moreover, FLY supports one/bi/three-dimensional array definition for basic types. In addition to basic types, FLY provides several domain types that enable the users to interact and communicate with the computing back-ends.

Object Domain Type. The main domain type is the **object** type. A FLY object is a heterogeneous collection of basic and/or domain types elements. Essentially a FLY object is a mixture between an array and map data structure, which stores data in key/value pair. The value of an element can be accessed in two different ways: by position (like arrays) or by key (like maps). When a new value is assigned to a given key/position a new element is created, otherwise the new value replaces the previous one. Moreover, all FLY domain specific type are an instance of the object type, which means are build in similar fashion, specifying the object type using the parameter keyword *type = "object_type"*.

Environment Domain Type. The **Environment** type represents an abstraction of a execution environment. It provides the ability to interact with a cloud provider or a SMP system. Different environments are treated in the same way by FLY, leaving the details relating to the specific use of each execution environment to the FLY compiler.

Environments are declared as an object using several parameters that characterize a back-end. In this preliminary version of the FLY compiler, the SMP (using the type smp) and AWS back-end (using the type aws) are supported (see Sect. 6).

```
var name = [type="(smp,aws,...)", nthreads=Integer, accesskey=String,
    secretkey=String, limit=Float]
```

The first parameter specifies the desired back-end. The simplest back-end is *smp*, and enables the user to exploit the local SMP architecture. The second parameter (*threads*) indicates the maximum number of concurrent tasks allowed on the back-end. The remaining parameters are used to manage the authentication on the back-end. Eventually, the parameter *limit* enables the user to set an usage cost limit according to the used back-end.

File Domain Type. **File** object is the abstraction of file in FLY. The language supports four file formats: *csv*, *json*, *img*, and *txt*, defined by the parameter *type*. A new file object is defined using also additional parameters: *path* (the file system path) or a reference to the file, and by the separator *sep*, that is an optional parameter defined for CSV files.

The language provides two methods to access files, which depend on where the file is stored: *local* or *remote*.

```
var name = [type="(csv,json,img,txt)", path=String, sep=String] on env (optional)
```

FLY has a specific focus on *csv* files managing them as a Dataframe (similar to R language dataframes). The memory is seen as a matrix structure, allowing the user to access to rows and columns, while it provides dedicated operations for querying, filtering, random access, etc. Dataframe operations are described in details in the language documentation.

Communication Statement. Channel type is a domain type that enables the synchronization and communication between FLY functions and/or the main program, defined by the *type = "channel"*. Channels follow the Communicating Sequential Processes (CSP) definition [16]. A new channel is defined on an environment, and can be used for the communication between functions executing on the same back-end or from the main program to a back-end and viceversa. Channels are blocking message queues, that is, when the main program or a function tries to receive a message from a channel, the execution is blocked until a new message arrives on the channel. Messages are sent on a channel using the character '!' (e.g., the instruction ch!VAL sends a message VAL on the channel ch), while the character '?' is used to receive messages, (e.g., the instruction x=ch? reads a message from the channel ch and assigns the obtained value to the variable x). Channels use network infrastructures to communicate with the cloud environment and for this reason a serialization mechanism is required for sending/receiving messages. FLY defines the serialization for objects, files, images and basic types. It is not allowed to send messages containing environments, channels, and random objects.

5.2 Control Structures

FLY conditional and iterative controls structures are standard and follows the same statements of languages like Java. Two kinds of *for* loops can be used in FLY, the former uses a range definition, and enables the program to loop in a range of integer values, defined using square parenthesis ([x:y]). The latter, enables the program to iterate over a FLY object or a file.

5.3 Execution Control Structures

Functions. FLY functions are quite different from other scripting languages and follow a functional programming inspired definition. A FLY function represents a task or independent job of the main program and it is defined as a code block that can be executed concurrently. FLY functions are declared using the keyword **func**. Each FLY function can have a set of input parameters and may return a value using the word **return**. FLY functions have a private scoping, that is only function parameters and local variable are visible in the body of the function. The input parameters are passed by copy, and they are considered as immutable. However, functions can avoid this limitations using channels or constants. A channel declared in the main program or in a function running on the same environment can be directly used by a function, the same behavior is also defined for the constants.

Notice that, the FLY language does not ensure that operations are admitted: if a function is executing on a back-end B, the function can use only channels and objects available on the back-end B. FLY functions can be executed, like for standard languages, using their ID and parameters (in this case functions are executed sequentially). In order to execute functions concurrently, FLY provides the **fly** statement that will be described in the following. The **fly** statement is not admitted in the body of a function (i.e., recursion is not allowed).

Parallel/Distributed Statement. The definition of FLY functions is the consequence of the explicit parallel execution model of FLY. The language provides the keyword **fly** that enables the user to execute concurrently a set of functions (the number of concurrent functions will depend on the back-end used and the user needs). The **fly** statement is similar to the **for** statement but the **fly** statement allows to specify the back-end environment (using the keyword **on**) and, possibly, callback functions.

fly ID in [x:y]|Object|File on Env   then ID thenall ID

The **fly** statement supports two kinds of function callbacks, declared using the keywords **then** and **thenall**. The *then* callback is executed after each FLY function execution, instead the *thenall* callback is executed after all FLY function executions. *Then* and *thenall* functions have to take only one input parameter that, for *then* corresponds to the return value of a function execution, while for *thenall* is a FLY object containing all the return values obtained by all the function executions.

FLY explores synchronous and asynchronous execution models. The previous construct defines the synchronous mode, in which the main program waits all functions termination. It is possible to execute functions asynchronously using the keyword **async** before the fly construct.

Asynchronous Execution. The *async* statement returns a special FLY object, named *async-object*, that enables the user to control and interact with the asynchronous execution. The *async* FLY constructor invocation immediately returns the control to the main program and the execution can continue. The user can control the status of the asynchronous functions invoking the method status() on the *async-object* and can wait the termination of all functions using the method wait().

Types Casting. FLY uses a dynamic type checking, that is variable types are automatically inferred at run time during the first assignment. Moreover, FLY typing is strong, the type of a variable cannot change during the execution time. FLY provides support for explicit types casting as in Java and C#. Types casting is admitted on basic and domain types, but it is forbidden on environments and channels.

Native Code. FLY is also able to include external libraries (using the keyword **require**, which enables to include and install, in the selected environment, an additional library) and supports the execution of native code (using the keyword **native**). For instance, the FLY functions running on the *aws* back-end are translated in Javascript, which means that it is possible to include in these functions all JS libraries.

6   Compiler Implementation

We present, in this Section, the preliminary version of our source-to-source compiler for FLY language. An implementation of the language grammar and code generators for the SMP and AWS FaaS back-ends have been developed.

Cloud computing infrastructures expose their FaaS service model through APIs in several languages, as show in Table 1. We deployed our compiler in order to generate a Java program, which is able to support all back-ends. We decided to design our language compiler using *Xtext* [14], which enables the user to create JVM based DSL. The FLY code is translated in a pure Java program that exploits FaaS APIs in order to use FaaS services. Xtext leverages the powerful ANTLR parser which implements an LL parser.

We designed an LL grammar for FLY language that provides the complete language definition, presented in the Sect. 5. Xtext has also used to develop a code generator that, given the intermediate AST program representation (the output of the first compilation phase), generates a FLY Java program. The code generation phase is the core of our compiler, it generates different codes according to the back-end where the FLY code has to be executed. The code generation phase is designed to be specialized according to the considered back-end:

1) SMP back-end. A Java Thread Pool is used to implement the back-end for the SMP architecture. The FLY main program is executed as Java code on a JVM, which executes also the SMP back-end. In details, all FLY types are mapped on a particular Java type and the FLY functionality are provided exploiting the Java language.

2) FaaS back-ends. The back-ends for Faas architectures have been developed using the Java API of each cloud providers. In order to support different back-ends, our FLY compiler translates each FLY function in JavaScript (JS) using the specific JS cloud provider API to realize FLY operations on channels and remote files. For each back-end and each FLY function the compiler generates a binary package containing: the JS code and the used JS libraries. The generated package is used to deploy the function code on a cloud provider. The alpha release of the FLY compiler as well as the compiler guide is available for download on the GitHub github.com/spagnuolocarmine/FLY-language releases page. The FLY compiler produces: a Java Maven project including all FLY dependencies, the FLY main program (a Java class with the same name of the FLY source code), and the FLY functions code.

7   Conclusion

This paper introduces FLY, a domain specific language for scientific computing on FaaS cloud computing service model. The contributions of this paper are: (i) the design of FLY, a novel domain-specific scripting language for computing-intensive scientific applications; (ii) the language design and specification for SMP and four FaaS cloud computing architectures, and (iii) the FLY source-to-source compiler. Future works and studies are already planned to improve FLY language definition including: library and namespaces definitions, compiler optimizations (according to the FaaS execution model), derived data types (as Java class) and data visualizations. The actual version of the FLY compiler will be extended in order to support the improvements on the language definition as well as other cloud providers. We plan to extend the compiler in order to generate function code in other FaaS languages like Python. Furthermore, FLY will provide specific libraries of algorithms (optimized for FaaS environments), such as machine learning, data mining, and discrete-event simulation. In particular we will focus on graphs algorithms and mining providing support for big networks [1].

References

1. Antelmi, A., Cordasco, G., Spagnuolo, C., Vicidomini, L.: On evaluating graph partitioning algorithms for distributed agent based models on networks. In: Hunold, S., et al. (eds.) Euro-Par 2015. LNCS, vol. 9523, pp. 367–378. Springer, Cham (2015). https://doi.org/10.1007/978-3-319-27308-2_30
2. Shawish, A., Salama, M.: Cloud computing: paradigms and technologies. In: Xhafa, F., Bessis, N. (eds.) Inter-Cooperative Collective Intelligence: Techniques and Applications. Studies in Computational Intelligence, vol. 495, pp. 39–67. Springer, Heidelberg (2014). https://doi.org/10.1007/978-3-642-35016-0_2
3. Nadareishvili, I., Mitra, R., McLarty, M., Amundsen, M.: Microservice Architecture: Aligning Principles, Practices, and Culture. O'Reilly Media Inc., Sebastopol (2016)
4. Cordasco, G., Scarano, V., Spagnuolo, C.: Distributed MASON: a scalable distributed multi-agent simulation environment. Simul. Model. Pract. Theory **89**, 15–34 (2018)
5. Dean, J., Ghemawat, S.: MapReduce: simplified data processing on large clusters. Commun. ACM **51**, 107–113 (2008)
6. Hwang, K., Dongarra, J., Fox, G.C.: Distributed and Cloud Computing from Parallel Processing to the Internet of Things (2011)
7. Baldini, I., et al.: Serverless computing: current trends and open problems. In: Chaudhary, S., Somani, G., Buyya, R. (eds.) Research Advances in Cloud Computing, pp. 1–20. Springer, Singapore (2017). https://doi.org/10.1007/978-981-10-5026-8_1
8. McGrath, G., Brenner, P.R.: Serverless computing: design, implementation, and performance. In: ICDCSW 2017, pp. 405–410 (2017)
9. Stigler, M.: Beginning Serverless Computing: Developing with Amazon Web Services, Microsoft Azure, and Google Cloud. Apress (2017)
10. Groff, J., Weinberg, P.: SQL The Complete Reference (2010)
11. Graham, I.S.: The HTML SourceBook. Wiley, New York (1995)
12. Cosenza, B., et al.: OpenABL: a domain-specific language for parallel and distributed agent-based simulations. In: Aldinucci, M., Padovani, L., Torquati, M. (eds.) Euro-Par 2018. LNCS, vol. 11014, pp. 505–518. Springer, Cham (2018). https://doi.org/10.1007/978-3-319-96983-1_36
13. R Development Core Team, R: A Language and Environment for Statistical Computing (2008). www.R-project.org
14. Eclipse Project, Xtext, Language Engineering For Everyone! (2018). www.eclipse.org/Xtext
15. Thoman, P., et al.: A taxonomy of task-based parallel programming technologies for high-performance computing. J. Supercomput. **74**, 1422–1434 (2018)
16. Roscoe, A.W.: The Theory and Practice of Concurrency. Prentice Hall, London (1997)
17. Rossum, G.: Python reference manual. Technical report (1995)
18. Bezanzon, J., Karpinski, S., Shah, V., Edelman, A.: Julia: a fast dynamic language for technical computing. In: Lang.NEXT (2012)
19. Ritchie, D.M.: The limbo programming language. Technical report (2018)
20. Chamberlain, B., Callahan, D., Zima, H.: Parallel programmability and the Chapel language. Int. J. High Perform. Comput. Appl. **21**, 291–312 (2007)

21. Blumofe, R.D., Joerg, C.F., Kuszmaul, B.C., Leiserson, C.E., Randall, K.H., Zhou, Y.: Cilk: an efficient multithreaded runtime system. SIGPLAN Not. **30**, 207–216 (1995)

22. White, T.: Hadoop: The Definitive Guide. O'Reilly Media Inc., Sebastopol (2009)

23. Zaharia, M., et al.: Apache spark: a unified engine for big data processing. Commun. ACM **59**, 56–65 (2016)

24. Wilde, M., Hategan, M., Wozniak, J.M., Clifford, B., Katz, D.S., Foster, I.: Swift: a language for distributed parallel scripting. Parallel Comput. **37**, 633–652 (2011)

25. Wozniak, J., Armstrong, T., Wilde, M., Katz, D.S., Lusk, E., Foster, I.: Swift/T: large-scale application composition via distributed-memory dataflow processing. In: Proceeding of IEEE/ACM International Symposium in Cluster, Cloud, and Grid Computing (2013)

26. Reuillon, R., Leclaire, M., Rey-Coyrehourcq, S.: Openmole, a workflow engine specifically tailored for the distributed exploration of simulation models. Future Gener. Comput. Syst. **28**, 1981–1990 (2013)

PCDLifeS - Workshop on Parallel and Distributed Computing for Life Sciences: Algorithms, Methodologies and Tools

Workshop on Parallel and Distributed Computing for Life Sciences: Algorithms, Methodologies and Tools (PDCLifeS)

Workshop Description

Advances in Life Sciences are largely driven by the development of powerful technologies and computational tools. Applications range from drug discovery and personalized medical therapies to improved agricultural and green energy production. However, the solution of real-world problems requires a multidisciplinary approach and poses new challenges in the field of High Performance Computing (HPC) at different levels:

- The modeling and simulation of complex phenomena (human organ functions, evolution of diseases, sustainable energy systems, etc.)
- The processing and analysis of massive amounts of data produced by modern technologies (omics and genome sequencing, functional and anatomical imaging, High-Content Screening, etc.)
- The extracting, merging, and understanding of information from different sources (merging different types of images, bridging imaging and omics features, etc.)
- The storage, security, and availability of datasets (in order to gather information, compare results, reproduce experiments, etc.)

The main goal of the PDCLifeS workshop is to foster discussion and collaboration among researchers from different backgrounds (bioinformatics, mathematics, physics, engineering, etc.), as well as to promote interest in algorithms, methodologies, and tools of HPC to face the challenges related to different branches of the Life Sciences (Biology, Biomedicine, Bioengineering, Ecology, etc.). The first edition of PDCLifeS was held in Turin, Italy, in conjunction with Euro-Par 2018. In this second edition, the reviewing process of the PDCLifeS 2019 resulted in the selection of five high-quality papers for the workshop schedule. The accepted papers have shown the need for HPC methodologies in solving some interesting problems of the Life Sciences, for example in simulation, data processing, and testing, that require high-capability and high-capacity computing, communication, and storage resources.

Organization

Program Chairs

Laura Antonelli   CNR, Italy
Salvatore Cuomo   University of Naples Federico II, Italy

Program Committee

Andrew Adamatzky   University of the West of England, UK
Stefano Berrone   Politecnico di Torino, Italy
Mario Cannataro   Università Magna Grecia, Italy
Claudia Di Napoli   CNR, Italy
Daniela di Serafino   Università della Campania Luigi Vanvitelli, Italy
Sébastien Limet   Université d'Orléans, France
Lucia Maddalena   CNR, Italy
Mario Nicodemi   Università degli Studi di Napoli Federico II, Italy
Domenico Talia   Università della Calabria, Italy
Nicola Tonellotto   CNR, Italy
Carsten Trinitis   Technical University of Munich, Germany
Jose Carlos Valverde   University of Castilla–La Mancha, Spain
Pierangelo Veltri   Università Magna Grecia, Italy

Parallel Learning of Weighted Association Rules in Human Phenotype Ontology

Giuseppe Agapito$^{(\boxtimes)}$ ⓘ, Mario Cannataro ⓘ, Pietro Hiram Guzzi ⓘ,
and Marianna Milano ⓘ

Magna Græcia University, 88100 Catanzaro, Italy
{agapito,cannataro,hguzzi,m.milano}@unicz.it

Abstract. The Human Phenotype Ontology (HPO) is a standardized vocabulary of terms related to diseases. The importance and the specificity of HPO terms are estimated employing the Information Content (IC). Thus, the analysis of annotated data is a critical challenge for bioinformatics. There exist several approaches to support ontology curators in maintaining and analysing data. Among these, the use of Association Rules (AR) can improve the quality of annotations. In this paper, we present an algorithm for the parallel extraction of Weighted Association Rules (WAR) from HPO terms and annotations, able to face high dimension of data. Experiments performed on real and synthetic datasets show good speed-up and scalability.

Keywords: Human Phenotype Ontology · Gene Ontology · Weighted Association Rules · Parallel computing

1 Introduction

In computer science an ontology refers to a set of representational primitives employed to model a domain of knowledge [10]. In particular, bioinformatics and computational biology in the last decades made extensive use of ontologies.

For instance, Gene Ontology (GO) points to provide a common language to describe genes product [7]. More recently, the annotation efforts have also focused on the description of the relation among molecular biology and disease, leading to the introduction of different ontologies such as Human Phenotype Ontology (HPO) [21] and Disease Ontology (DO) [23].

HPO aims to provide a structured repository of phenotypic abnormalities found in human diseases. A HPO annotation links a condition with phenotypic abnormality. The Online Mendelian Inheritance in Man (OMIM) [11] provides identifiers to link diseases and phenotypic abnormality. OMIM is a broad, authoritative compendium of human genes and genetic phenotypes that are freely available and updated daily [11]. The Disease Ontology (DO) has been developed as a standardized ontology for human disease to provide stable and sustainable descriptions of human disease terms and phenotype characteristics [23].

U. Schwardmann et al. (Eds.): Euro-Par 2019 Workshops, LNCS 11997, pp. 549–559, 2020.
https://doi.org/10.1007/978-3-030-48340-1_42

The amount of annotations is regularly growing, raising new challenges to face, related to ambiguous or incomplete annotations and ontology terms [9]. The annotation task is becoming an even troublesome challenge in the genomic era, which is characterized by unprecedented growth in the production of genes, gene products, and also other information. Thus, the development of automatic computational approaches can speed up the updating and maintenance processes of ontologies, since several current strategies of annotation are carried out manually by the curators. The literature contains several computational methods developed to aid GO curators to improve GO annotations consistency [8,17,25]. Conversely to GO, in literature, there are few automatic methodologies able to support the HPO curators to improve annotations consistency and retrieve link between terms not explicitly related.

As shown in some recent works by Faria et al. [8], by Manda et al. [16], and by Agapito et al. [1–4], Association Rules (AR) may be used to improve annotations consistency and highlight correlations among terms did not appear explicitly related.

In this work, we present PHPOMiner (ParallelHPOMiner) the parallel version of our previous works in which we introduced HPO-Miner. PHPOMiner is a tool for parallel mining of weighted association rules (WAR) to control annotation consistency and to identify unknown relationships between two phenotype abnormalities from HPO. Traditional association rule methods cannot distinguish between items relevance, yielding to the generation of rules with low specificity. The information content (IC) measures the specificity of a term as reported in [12,18]. The use of IC computed for each HPO term, is a measure of the specificity of a term, producing the IC-weighted annotation as conveyed in the following: *OMIM100100: (HP:0000126, 11.18), (HP:0000144, 9.57)*. The main contributions of PHPOMiner are:

- *i)* a customized multi-threading version of PFP-Growth [15] to mine Weighted Association Rules (WAR), and
- *ii)* a novel dataset-partitioning able to produce independent computational tasks that can be run concurrently on several separate threads.

The rest of the paper is organized as follows. Section 2 introduces the AR and WAR mining main concepts, as well as describes the HPO ontology. Section 3 describes the PHPOMiner algorithm, and Sect. 4 concludes the paper.

2   Materials and Methods

2.1   The Human Phenotype Ontology

HPO is a structured and controlled vocabulary, available at the website[1], that includes more than 13,000 terms describing the phenotypic abnormalities in human diseases. HPO provides annotations of more than 15,000 human hereditary syndromes and other phenotypic abnormalities that characterize the disorders. HPO includes three independent sub-ontologies:

---

[1] https://hpo.jax.org/app/.

- the *mode of inheritance*: describes the transmission of the hereditary attributes from a generation to another;
- the *onset and clinical course*: in medicine refers to the first symptoms of sickness and the medical treatments involved to cure them;
- the *phenotypic abnormalities*: the abnormal traits of a living organism that are possible to observe;
- the *clinical modifier*: the typical modifier that are present in clinical symptoms, such as severity;
- the *frequency*: the frequency related to clinical feature presented by patient, i.e frequent/occasional.

As other ontologies, HPO presents a direct acyclic graph (DAG) terms organization. The relations among DAG's terms are modelled by means of *is_a* and *part_of* edges "relations", in order to distinguish between general or precise terms. Besides, terms are arranged hierarchically in HPO, where each path respects the *true-path-rule*. To each HPO class is provided a stable and individual identifier (e.g. *HP:00010438*), a label and a list of synonyms, describing a phenotypic abnormality i.e. *"Abnormality of the Ventricular Septum"* as depicted in Fig. 1.

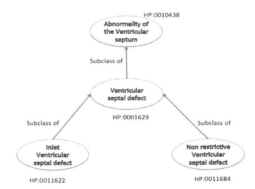

Fig. 1. HPO graph Example. The term *"Abnormality of the Ventricular Septum"* is the root and the terms *"Inlet Ventricular Septal defect"* and *"Non restrictive Ventricular Septal defect"* represent the leaves. By proceeding from the root to the leaves the information content of the terms increases, from a general term to more specific ones.

The HPO terms linked to diseases listed in the OMIM (Online Mendelian Inheritance in Man) database are available at the website. Diseases are annotated with terms of the HPO, meaning that HPO terms are used to describe all the signs, symptoms, and other phenotypic manifestations that characterize the disease in question. Since HPO contains information related to phenotypic abnormalities, the computation of semantic similarities among concepts annotated with HPO terms may enable database searches for clinical diagnostics or computational analysis of gene expression patterns associated with human diseases [14,19]. The annotations of OMIM entries are a mixture of manual annotations performed by the HPO curators team and automated matching of the OMIM Clinical Synopsis to HPO term labels. In particular, HPO is an ontology designed to provide qualitative information and not to capture quantitative data such as body weight or height. Multiple HPO terms can be used to annotate a disease, consequently the need for the definition of methodologies and tools to support HPO curators to improve annotation consistency and the structure of the ontology arises. For these reasons, we proposed in the past HPO-Miner, a data-mining strategy based on weighted-association rule mining to support HPO curators. Furthermore, the literature reports different approaches based on associative rules mining (ARM) from annotated data [1,8,17].

2.2 Association Rules

Association Rule (AR) mining is a common task in data mining; it is employed to discover hidden associations in market basket analysis and unknown relations among features in databases. Historically, it was proposed by Agrawal [5] to learning associations to support marketing decision. Formally, the association rules extraction problem may be stated as follows: let $I = \{i_1, i_2, \ldots, i_n\}$ be a set of items, and $D = \{t_1, \ldots, t_m\}$ a transactional database that contains a set of transactions, where a transaction t_j is a subset of items belonging to I. The number of items contained in a transaction is defined as *transaction width*. An association rule is a relationship of the form $A \rightarrow B$, where A and B are two disjoint sets. ARs are based on two fundamental properties to define the relevance of the mined rules, *Support* and *Confidence*. The formal Support definition is:

Definition 1.

$$S(A \rightarrow B) = \frac{\sigma(A \cup B)}{N}$$

Where N is the total number of transactions contained in D, the transactional database, and σ is called *support count*, that is the number of transactions that contain a particular item.

The Confidence is defined as:

Definition 2.

$$C(A \rightarrow B) = \frac{\sigma(A \cup B)}{\sigma(A)}.$$

Where $\sigma(A)$ is the number of transactions in D, the transactional database, containing A and $\sigma(A \cup B)$ is the number of transactions in D that contains both items A and B.

A shortcoming with the use of standard AR procedure is that it prevents the production of certain rules in which the items have very different levels of support. In several areas it does not make sense to assign equal importance to all items included in the dataset. For example in the basket market analysis, some items like computers, smartphones have much more value than small items like ice-creams or butter. Rules including smartphones or computers have less support than those involving butter or ice-cream but are much more significant in term of profit by the store. In the ontology context, the term HP:0000924 (*An abnormality of the skeletal system*) has a relevance value (IC value) lower than HP:0011803 (*Bifid nose*) although it is much more frequent. Rules involving the term HP:0000924 are less interesting (as it is a more general term) than rules involving the term HP:0011803 (as it is a more specific term) in terms of actionable knowledge.

This weakness of classical AR approach can be overcome by introducing the weighted association rules (WAR). WAR models the *importance* of a term by means of a *weight* (ω). A weight (ω) is a non-negative real number that reflects the relevance of an HPO term, for which high values represent essential items as reported in [6,24]. In our case, the relevance can be expressed by using the information content (*IC*).

Starting from the HPO dataset depicted in Fig. 2, we created a new HPO dataset by adding for each term the related value of IC as shown in Fig. 3 and called weighted HPO dataset. The weighted HPO dataset presents a transaction data structure, can easily dig with the weighted transactions of HPO terms, as depicted in Fig. 3.

```
OMIM100050 HP:0000431
OMIM100050 HP:0000484
OMIM100050 HP:0000494
OMIM100100 HP:0000126
OMIM100100 HP:0000144
```

Fig. 2. An example of HPO dataset.

OMIM100050 {HP:0000431, 10.95}, {HP:0000484, 11.36}, {HP:0000494, 11.27}
OMIM100100 {HP:0000126, 11.18}, {HP:0000144, 9.57}
OMIM302801 {HP:0002167, 7.78}, {HP:0002311, 9.72}
OMIM600175 {HP:0000006, 8.34}, {HP:0001252, 8.47}, {HP:0001265, 9.28}, {HP:0001284, 9.57}

Fig. 3. An example of weighted transaction HPO dataset.

We define as $WeightedSupport$, (ωS), obtained combining the classical formulation of the support of an item by its weight. The weighted Support ωS of a generic item x_i is defined as: $\omega S(x_i) = w_i * \sigma(x_i)$ where ω_i is the information content of the *i-th* term and $\sigma(x_i)$ is the number of transaction containing x_i. Let $I = \{i_1 \ldots i_m\}$ be a set of weighted items (HPO terms) and let WD be a set of weighted transactions database, where each transaction t_j is a sub-set of weighted items such that t_j belongs to I. We defined the *weighted minimum support (mωS)* as:

$$m\omega S = \left(\frac{\sum_{i=1}^{|WD|} \sigma(x_i) * \omega_i}{|WD|} \right) * p. \tag{1}$$

Where, $|WD|$ is the cardinality of the weighted database nominally, the number of transactions into the dataset, p is a threshold value given in input by the user in order to define which items are significant in percentage. Thus only the items for which the following constraint $wS(I) \geq mwS$ is verified, are significant and can be used as candidates to generate frequent item-sets and rules. There are different possible methods to solve the conflict between the frequency and the weight of each item. However, we have chosen to use the sum of the multiplication between weight and frequency because this balances the effects of weight and frequency.

2.3   Weighting HPO Term with Information Content

There exist different IC conceptualization that can be gathered into two classes, intrinsic and extrinsic methods. Intrinsic methods rely on the topology of the ontology graph, analyzing the positions of terms in a taxonomy. In this way, the methods define the information content for each term. Various topological characteristics as ancestors, number of children, depth (see [12] for a complete review) can be used to estimate the Intrinsic IC calculation. Instead, the extrinsic approaches involve the annotation data for a considered corpus. In literature exist different intrinsic methods proposed by Sanchez et al. [22], Harispe et al. [12], Resnick et al. [20], Seco et al. [13], Zhou et al. [26].

The measure of Sanchez employs only the number of leaves and the set of ancestors of a including itself, $subsumers(a)$ and introduce the root node as the number of leaves max_leaves in the IC assessment. Leaves are more informative than root concepts, so the leaves are more suited to describe and distinguish any concept.

$$IC_{Sanchez\,et\,al.}(a) = -log \left(\frac{\frac{|leaves(a)|}{|subsumers(a)|} + 1}{max\_leaves + 1} \right) \tag{2}$$

Harispe et al., to point out the specificity of leaves according to the number of ancestors, consider $leaves(a) = a$ concept when a is a root and assensing max_leaves as the number of enclosed ancestors of a node varying the IC assessment suggested by Sanchez et al.

$$IC_{Harispe\,et\,al.}(a) = -log \left(\frac{\frac{|leaves(a)|}{|subsumers(a)|}}{max\_leaves} \right) \tag{3}$$

The formulation provided from Resnick et al. computes the IC of a concept evaluating all the top-downs path from a concept a to the reachable leaves, $p(a)$, and then calculates the log yielding to the formula:

$$IC_{Resnik}(a) = -log(p(a)). \tag{4}$$

Seco et al. measure the IC of a term by regarding the rate between the number of hyponyms in ontology, for instance, the number of descendant with respect to the whole number of ontological concepts.

$$IC_{Seco\,et\,al.}(a) = \frac{log\left(\frac{hypo(a)+1}{max\_nodes}\right)}{log\left(\frac{1}{max\_nodes}\right)} \tag{5}$$

The formulation provided from Zhou et al. examines the depth of a term in a taxonomy, $depth(a)$, and the maximum depth of the taxonomy max_depth.

$$IC_{Zhou\,et\,al.}(a) = k - \left(1 - \frac{log(hypo(a)+1)}{log(max\_nodes)}\right) + (1-k)\left(\frac{log(depth(a))}{log(depth\_nodes)}\right) \tag{6}$$

In this formulation K is a factor which enables to weight the contribution of the two evaluated features.

In this work we used the IC implementation proposed by Harispe et al.

3   The PHPOMiner Algorithm

In this section we describe the *PHPOMiner* algorithm, developed to extract weighted association rules form HPO datasets implementing a parallel strategy, by means of a multi-thread paradigms. The target physical architecture is a multi-processor multi-core system. The main steps of PHPOMiner are summarized in Fig. 4.

Require: A weighted Transaction Database WTB, A weighted minimum support $wminSupp$.
Ensure: A set of weighted association rules $Rules$.
    Start of Concurrent Section
    for all $wi \in WTB$ **do**
        Calculation of weighted support - Split
        $ws(wi) \leftarrow computesupport$
    end for
    $frequentItemsList \leftarrow compute(wS, wminSupp)$
    End of Concurrent Section - Join
    $Rules \leftarrow FP\text{-}Tree$ {Creation of Rules}

Fig. 4. PHPOMiner pseudocode

PHPOMiner's core algorithm is based on independent Workers (threads) that allow to compute association rules in parallel. In each run of PHPOMiner, there are a supervisor worker and $c-1$ workers. We choose $c-1$ as a number of workers because, c is the real number of cores available on the machine, and 1 core is used to map the supervisor worker, avoiding to introduce overhead costs due to the physical cores saturation.

To mine association rules in parallel, it is necessary to convert the input HPO dataset in a transactional database, where the transactions are independent among them. Independent transactions makes it possible to mine AR locally to each worker. In this way, each workers can analyze its slice of dataset independently without to be necessary to share information with other workers. The supervisor worker receives as input the dataset, the minimum support *minSupp* and the *minconf* values that are used to mine association rules. Whereas, the number of available cores *#cores* is automatically detected by PHPOMiner using an opportune system call. The first step of the supervisor worker is to distribute to each worker a virtual slice of the dataset (e.g., the indexes of the starting and ending transaction) to compute the occurrences of the items, that will be stored in the OccurrencesWeightedList (OWL). OWL contains only the frequent items, for which the computed weighted-occurrences are greater than the weighted minimum support. The items within the OWL list are employed to remove the meaningless items from each transaction, to reduce the probability to generate trivial association rules.

Table 1. Independent transaction construction. weightedSupport ≥ 20

Transaction	FrequentWeightedItems	TailsDetected
{a:10}, {f:9}, {g:8}, {t:7}, {x:1}	a, f, t, g	g
{a:10}, {b:9}, {g:8}, {t:7}, {w:1}	a, b, t, g	g
{a:10}, {b:9}, {h:1}, {j:1}	a, b	b
c, {f:9}, {g:8}, {i:1}	c, f, g	g

Table 2. The execution times are obtained by analyzing an input dataset composed by 100 subjects, and using Confidence = 0 and Minimum Weighted Support = 20% respectively.

Number of processors	Execution time (sec)
1	3.198
2	1.59
4	0.793
6	0.553

In addition, the elements in each transaction are sorted in descending order of weighted-occurrence, to facilitate the creation of the independent transactions.

An independent transaction is obtained collecting together all the transactions comprising the same tail, i.e., the item with the lower value of weighted-occurrence as conveyed in Table 1.

It is worthy to note that now, each item with low value of weighted-occurrence become the identifier of a sub-set of independent transactions. Thus, the supervisor worker can partition the transactions among the workers running on the available cores (see Table 1). Then the Supervisor concurrently starts #cores-1 instances of workers and as a last step, the supervisor worker collects and merges the results.

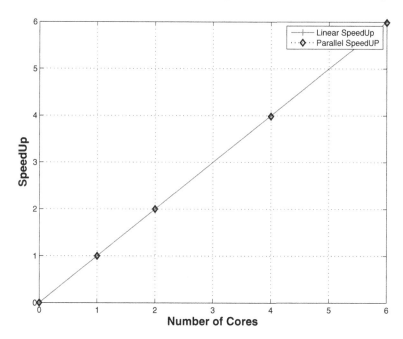

Fig. 5. Figure shows the speedup and execution times obtained by PHPOMiner for the analysis of dataset of HPO terms and annotations using 1, 2, 4, 6 cores. PHPOMiner presents good response times and speedup using 1, 2, 4, 6 slaves thread.

In detail, each worker receives a set of transactions in input, with which it can locally mine weighted association rules, and as a last step each worker returns to the supervisor worker the mined weighted association rules.

Figure 5 reports the execution times and the speedup obtained analyzing a dataset of HPO terms and annotations using 1, 2, 4, 6 cores respectively.

Table 2 shows the time obtained varying the number of cores.

Analyzing the Fig. 5 it is worthy to note that, the proposed parallel algorithm shows good response times and speedup.

4   Conclusion

We proposed PHPOMiner a multi-thread parallel algorithm for the parallel extraction of weighted association rules from HPO terms and annotations data, taking into account the relevance of a term. The significance of an HPO term by computing the IC value related to each term is obtained. PHPOMiner through an iterative process can figure out the tail of each transaction. Decomposition that makes it is possible to analyze input dataset in parallel among the available workers. In this way, workers can locally mine the weighted association rules without to be necessary to share information with the other workers. Finally, experiments performed on real and synthetic datasets show good speed-up and scalability.

Acknowledgments. This work has been partially funded by the following research project funded by the Calabrian Region: "Smart Electronic Invoices Accounting-SELINA CUP:$J28C1700016006$".

References

1. Agapito, G., Cannataro, M., Guzzi, P.H., Milano, M.: Using GO-WAR for mining cross-ontology weighted association rules. Comput. Methods Programs Biomed. **120**(2), 113–122 (2015). https://doi.org/10.1016/j.cmpb.2015.03.007. ISSN 0169-2607
2. Agapito, G., Guzzi, P.H., Cannataro, M.: Parallel and distributed association rule mining in life science: a novel parallel algorithm to mine genomics data. Inf. Sci. (2018). https://doi.org/10.1016/j.ins.2018.07.055. ISSN 0020-0255
3. Agapito, G., Milano, M., Guzzi, P.H., Cannataro, M.: Improving annotation quality in gene ontology by mining cross-ontology weighted association rules. In: 2014 IEEE International Conference on Bioinformatics and Biomedicine (BIBM), pp. 1–8. IEEE (2014). https://doi.org/10.1109/BIBM.2014.6999374
4. Agapito, G., Milano, M., Guzzi, P.H., Cannataro, M.: Extracting cross-ontology weighted association rules from gene ontology annotations. IEEE/ACM Trans. Comput. Biol. Bioinf. **13**(2), 197–208 (2015). https://doi.org/10.1109/TCBB.2015.2462348
5. Agrawal, R., Imieli, T., Swami, A.: Mining association rules between sets of items in large databases. SIGMOD Rec. **22**(2), 207–216 (1993). https://doi.org/10.1145/170036.170072
6. Cai, C., Fu, A., Cheng, C., Kwong, W.: Mining association rules with weighted items. In: 1998 Database Engineering and Applications Symposium. Proceedings, IDEAS 1998, International, pp. 68–77 (1998). https://doi.org/10.1109/IDEAS.1998.694360
7. Consortium, G.O., et al.: The Gene Ontology (GO) database and informatics resource. Nucleic Acids Res. **32**(Suppl. 1), D258–D261 (2004)
8. Faria, D., et al.: Mining go annotations for improving annotation consistency. PLoS ONE **7**(7), e40519 (2012). https://doi.org/10.1371/journal.pone.0040519
9. Flouris, G., Huang, Z., Pan, J.Z., Plexousakis, D., Wache, H.: Inconsistencies, negations and changes in ontologies. In: 1999 Proceedings of the National Conference on Artificial Intelligence, vol. 21, p. 1295 AAAI Press/MIT Press, Menlo Park/Cambridge (2006)
10. Gruber, T.: Encyclopedia of database systems. Ontology, pp. 1963–1965 (2009)
11. Hamosh, A., Scott, A.F., Amberger, J.S., Bocchini, C.A., McKusick, V.A.: Online Mendelian Inheritance in Man (OMIM), a knowledgebase of human genes and genetic disorders. Nucleic Acids Res. **33**(Suppl. 1), D514–D517 (2005)
12. Harispe, S., Sanchez, D., Ranwez, S., Janaqi, S., Montmain, J.: A framework for unifying ontology-based semantic similarity measures: a study in the biomedical domain. J. Biomed. Inform. **48**, 38–53 (2013)
13. Hermjakob, H., et al.: The HUPO PSI's molecular interaction format - a community standard for the representation of protein interaction data. Nat. Biotechnol. **22**, 177–183 (2004). https://doi.org/10.1038/nbt926

14. Kohler, S., et al.: Clinical diagnostics in human genetics with semantic similarity searches in ontologies. Am. J. Hum. Genet. **85**(4), 457–464 (2009)
15. Li, H., Wang, Y., Zhang, D., Zhang, M., Chang, E.Y.: PFP: parallel FP-Growth for query recommendation. In: Proceedings of the 2008 ACM Conference on Recommender Systems, pp. 107–114. ACM (2008)
16. Manda, P., McCarthy, F., Bridges, S.M.: Interestingness measures and strategies for mining multi-ontology multi-level association rules from gene ontology annotations for the discovery of new go relationships. J. Biomed. Inform. **46**(5), 849–856 (2013)
17. Manda, P., Ozkan, S., Wang, H., McCarthy, F., Bridges, S.M.: Cross-ontology multi-level association rule mining in the gene ontology. PLoS ONE **7**(10), e47411 (2012)
18. Milano, M., Agapito, G., Guzzi, P.H., Cannataro, M.: An experimental study of information content measurement of gene ontology terms. Int. J. Mach. Learn. Cybern. **9**(3), 427–439 (2016). https://doi.org/10.1007/s13042-015-0482-y
19. Peng, K., et al.: The disease and gene annotations (DGA): an annotation resource for human disease. Nucleic Acids Res. **41**(D1), D553–D560 (2013). https://doi.org/10.1093/nar/gks1244
20. Resnik, P.: Using information content to evaluate semantic similarity in a taxonomy. In: IJCAI, pp. 448–453 (1995), http://citeseerx.ist.psu.edu/viewdoc/summary?doi=10.1.1.55.5277
21. Robinson, P.N., Kohler, S., Bauer, S., Seelow, D., Horn, D., Mundlos, S.: The human phenotype ontology: a tool for annotating and analyzing human hereditary disease. Am. J. Hum. Genet. **83**(5), 610–615 (2008)
22. Sanchez, D., Batet, M., Isern, D.: Ontology-based information content computation. Knowl.-Based Syst. **24**(2), 297–303 (2011)
23. Schriml, L.M., et al.: Disease ontology: a backbone for disease semantic integration. Nucleic Acids Res. **40**(D1), D940–D946 (2012)
24. Wang, W., Yang, J., Yu, P.S.: Efficient mining of weighted association rules (WAR). In: Proceedings of the Sixth ACM SIGKDD International Conference on Knowledge Discovery and Data Mining, KDD 2000, pp. 270–274. ACM, New York (2000). https://doi.org/10.1145/347090.347149
25. Yeh, I., Karp, P.D., Noy, N.F., Altman, R.B.: Knowledge acquisition, consistency checking and concurrency control for Gene Ontology (GO). Bioinformatics **19**(2), 241–248 (2003)
26. Zhou, Z., Wang, Y., Gu, J.: A new model of information content for semantic similarity in wordnet. In: 2008 Future Generation Communication and Networking Symposia, FGCNS 2008, vol. 3, pp. 85–89. IEEE (2008)

Improving the Runtime Performance of Non-linear Mixed-Effects Model Estimation

Tom Haber$^{(\boxtimes)}$ and Frank van Reeth

Expertise Centre for Digital Media, Hasselt University, Hasselt, Belgium
{tom.haber,frank.reeth}@uhasselt.be

Abstract. Non-linear mixed effects models (NLMEM) are frequently used in drug development for pharmacokinetic (PK) and pharmacokinetic-pharmacodynamic (PK-PD) analyses. Parameter estimation for these models can be time-consuming due to the need for numerical integration. Additionally, the structural model is often expressed using differential equations requiring computationally intensive time-stepping ODE solvers. Overall, this often leads to long computation times in the order of hours or even days.

Combining the right mathematical tools as well as techniques from computer science, the computational cost can be significantly reduced. In this paper, several approaches are detailed for improving the performance of parameter estimation for NLMEM. Applying these, often easy, techniques can lead to an order of magnitude speedup.

Keywords: Non-linear · Mixed effects models · High-performance computing · Parallel

1 Introduction

Non-linear mixed effects models (NLMEM) are frequently used in drug development for pharmacokinetic (PK) and pharmacokinetic-pharmacodynamic (PK-PD) analyses [8]. On top of the structural model explaining the individual PK/PD observations, the statistical components allow the modeller to characterize the within-subject variability (the variability within each individual profile) as well as the between-subject variability (the variability of the individual parameters) to quantify the unexplained variability [32].

The estimation of both fixed and random effects parameters involve complex estimation methods due to non-linearity preventing closed-form solutions to the integration over the random effects. While different algorithms and software can be employed for estimating the parameters, most require repeated evaluation of the structural model for all individuals.

Additionally, the structural models are often expressed using ordinary differential equations (ODEs) as a way of describing a biological process in terms of simple input-output equations. In some cases these ODE systems cannot be

© Springer Nature Switzerland AG 2020
U. Schwardmann et al. (Eds.): Euro-Par 2019 Workshops, LNCS 11997, pp. 560–571, 2020.
https://doi.org/10.1007/978-3-030-48340-1_43

expressed with exact closed-forms due to the inclusion of non-linear terms where input or output is dependent on the response. These non-linear systems are usually solved with computationally intensive time-stepping ODE solvers, compounding the cost of the parameter estimation process.

Estimating parameters for such models in a reasonable amount of time requires the combination of the right mathematical tools as well as techniques from computer science. In this paper, several approaches are detailed for improving the performance of parameter estimation for NLMEM.

2   Non-linear Mixed-Effects Model

Mixed-effects models (MEM) can address a wide class of data, including continuous, count, categorical and time-to-event data. The following description will focus on continuous data models. A mixed-effects model is a hierarchical model: at the first level, each individual has its parametric regression model (the structural model) with unknown individual parameters. At the second level, each set of individual parameters is assumed to be randomly drawn from an unknown population distribution. The model can be defined as follows:

$$y_{ij} = f(x_{ij}; \phi_i) + g(x_{ij}; \phi_i, \Sigma)\epsilon_{ij}$$

where

- y_{ij} denotes the j-th observation from the i-th individual, $1 \leq i \leq N$ and $1 \leq j \leq n_i$.
- N is the number of individuals and n_i the number of observation for the i-th individual.
- x_{ij} denotes a vector of regression variables.
- ϕ_i is the vector of individual parameters for individual i, drawn from the same population distribution. We limit ourselves to the Gaussian model:

$$\phi_i \sim \mathcal{N}(\mu, \Omega)$$

- $\epsilon_{ij} \sim \mathcal{N}(0, 1)$ denotes the residual errors.
- f is a function describing the structural model and g a function defining the residual error model.
- $\theta = \{\mu, \Omega, \Sigma\}$ is the set of unknown population parameters.

While different estimation algorithms exist (e.g. FOCE [19], SAEM [17]), their structure is very similar: one of the main steps involves integration over the individual parameters ϕ_i for all individuals. Due to the non-linearity of the models, algorithms need to resort to approximation or numerical integration through for example Gaussian Quadrature [27] or Markov-Chain Monte Carlo [17] (MCMC). Both solutions require many evaluations of the structural model. The next step aggregates the information for all individuals and then makes an update of the population parameters θ.

Algorithm 1 gives a rough outline of the Stochastic Approximation Expectation Maximization (SAEM) algorithm from Kuhn et al. [17]. SAEM is an extension of the popular expectation-maximization (EM) algorithm for situations where the expectation step cannot be performed in closed-form. The basic idea is to split this step into a simulation and an integration step.

Algorithm 1: Stochastic Approximation Expectation Maximization

Input: $Y_1, \ldots, Y_n$, θ, f, g
Result: $\theta^\star$
$S_0, S_1, S_2 = 0$ ▷ Sufficient statistics
while not converged **do**
    for $i = 1 \ldots n$ **do**
        | $\eta_i = \text{GENERATESAMPLE}(f, g, \theta, Y_i)$
    end
    $S_0, S_1, S_2 = \text{UPDATESTATISTICS}(S_0, S_1, S_2, \{\eta_1, \ldots, \eta_n\})$
    $\theta = \text{OPTIMIZETHETA}(\theta, S_0, S_1, S_2)$
end

---

3   Load-Balanced Parallel Scheduling

Parallel computing can easily be applied to the estimation algorithms outlined in Sect. 2: the integration step can be divided into independent tasks per individual and executed in parallel [11]. This approach has been applied by several implementations, either in a multi-core (nlmixr [9] and Monolix [21]) or distributed (NONMEM [2]) setting (using MPI). However, scalability can be severely limited by statically partitioning the individuals between the processing units: it is unreasonable to assume that evaluating the structural model for some parameters takes a constant amount of time. Load imbalance is caused by the characteristics of the model itself, but also due to factors at the level of the operating system and the communication network between the processing units [35]. Consider the ratio between the sequential execution time, T_s, and the parallel execution time, T_p, with p processors [11]. For a specific integration step, the speedup is limited by Eq. 1. Here, δ_i is the time required to perform the integration for individual i and $\delta_{\max} = \max_i \{\delta_i\} = T_\infty$, is the execution time with infinite processors. Not considering the effects of load imbalance could theoretically leave a factor n/S on the table.

$$S = \frac{\Delta}{\delta_{\max}}, \quad \text{where } \Delta = \sum_{i=1}^{n} \delta_i \tag{1}$$

In the case where the structural model is expressed as a differential equation, the time-stepping ODE solvers can cause large deviations in evaluation times. Depending on the parameters, the solver might require more or less steps to

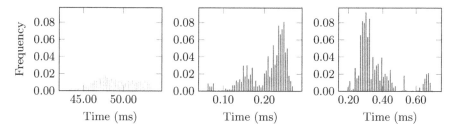

Fig. 1. Runtime distribution of the integration of ordinary differential equations in three cases: a PK-PD model with repeated administration, a PBPK model with and without repeated administration. The histograms only include the 25–75 quantiles for clarity.

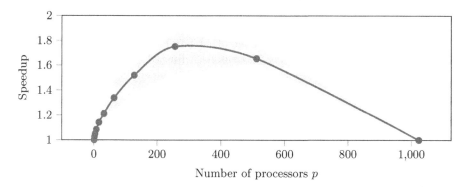

Fig. 2. Speedup due to load-balancing in terms of number of processors p. Evaluation times were simulated from the distribution of the PK-PD model with repeated administration. Mean and 95% confidence intervals are displayed.

evaluate the same model. Figure 1 shows histograms of evaluation times for three different cases and are based on actual runs using the SAEM algorithm. Firstly, a PK-PD model by Dunne et al. [37] with repeated administration. This non-linear ODE model is complicated by the fact that the solver needs to repeatedly stop to handle the administration events and therefore cannot take large steps. The distribution of evaluation times is fairly spread out with a ratio of $3\times$ between the slowest and the average. The whole-body physiologically-based pharmacokinetic (PBPK) model by Wendling et al. [36] make up the last two cases. First without and then with repeated administration. This linear ODE model is easier to solve, but also more affected by system noise. The ratio between slowest and average is $1.4\times$ and $1.9\times$ respectively.

Load-balancing in a multi-core environment can be achieved using a shared task queue (OpenMP [7]) or through work-stealing (Cilk [4], TBB [29]). In a distributed setting [6,18,33,38], it is much more involved due to the unpredictable nature of the imbalance and the network latency between the processors especially when evaluation times are in the same order as the latency.

Figure 2 demonstrates the speedup achievable due to load-balancing: $n = 1024$ evaluation times were simulated from the distribution of the PK-PD model (see Fig. 1) and speedup was computed for static partitioning versus load-balanced cases. Note that for small number of processors, the improvement is limited as the sum of tasks executed by each processor $\sum_{i \in \mathcal{P}} \delta_i$ approaches $\frac{1}{n} \sum_{i=1}^{n} \delta_i$ as $n \gg p$.

4   Adjoint-State Method

An integral part of optimization and MCMC is typically the calculation of (first and second order) derivatives. Newton or Quasi-Newton methods are popular and fast algorithms for finding local minima and maxima of functions [26]. The Laplacian approximation used in the FOCE [19] and LAPLACE methods require the maximization of the conditional individual posterior and the computation of the Hessian in the maximum. On the other hand, the MCMC step in SAEM can be efficiently performed using Metropolis Adjusted Langevin algorithm [30] (MALA) or Hamiltonian Monte Carlo [24] (HMC) which depend on the evaluation of gradients.

In the presence of differential equations, these derivatives cannot be easily derived. Statistical software therefore resorts to finite differencing (FD) or sensitivity analysis [5]. The complexity of these methods is $\mathcal{O}(p)$ and $\mathcal{O}(p^2)$ for gradients and Hessians respectively, where p is the number of parameters. This is not such an issue for models with only few parameters, but the calculation of derivatives can become a huge performance problem with increasing number of parameters. For any of the algorithms described above, the computation of the derivatives is the key operation and typically the most time-consuming step. For example, in the case of HMC, every sample requires L gradient evaluations (L might be in the order of 10 or 100). Any speedup would thus result in a direct speedup of the whole algorithm.

The adjoint-state method (ASM) allows writing the derivatives of models involving differential equations in a simpler form that is inexpensive to evaluate. In many different fields, ASM is a classical method and sometimes even the only viable method to compute gradients, such as the optimal control of partial differential equations [20]. Its application in statistics, however, is rather limited: partly due to lack of necessity given only few parameters and partly due to the discrete nature of measurements in the statistical setting. Melicher et al. [22] derive an ASM in the statistical context when discrete data is coupled with a continuous ODE model. Using this method, gradients can be computed at a cost that is independent of the number of parameters and Hessians with a linear cost instead of quadratic.

Figure 3 compares the runtime and accuracy of gradients computed using FD, sensitivity analysis and the adjoint-state method. A simple linear ODE model is used and scaled in number of parameters. The runtime of FD and sensitivity analysis is fairly similar as expected: both methods need the ODE to be simulated roughly p times. Conversely, the adjoint method requires the ODE to be solved twice: first forward in time and then backwards. Starting from around 10 parameters, the method outperforms the other methods for this model by a factor up to 10. The accuracy of the method is similar to that of sensitivity analysis. The accuracy of FD is extremely sensitive to the employed step-size.

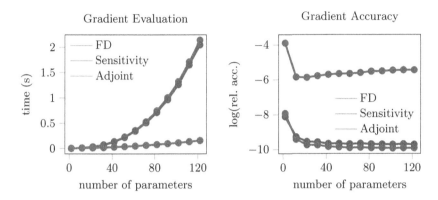

Fig. 3. Comparison of the runtime and accuracy of gradients computed using FD, sensitivity analysis and the adjoint-state method for a simple linear ODE model scaled in number of parameters.

5   Early Rejection

When derivative-free optimization or Metropolis-Hastings MCMC algorithms are employed in combination with differential equations, a simple non-approximate trick can substantially improve the model evaluation time. By inverting the order of simulation and likelihood evaluation, the evaluation can be terminated early as soon as can be concluded that the candidate will be discarded by the algorithm. While this idea has appeared previously in literature [3,25,34], it is still underutilized and yet extremely useful.

To demonstrate the idea, Metropolis-Hastings MCMC [14,23] (MH) will be used, however it can be easily extended to optimization algorithms. MH works by first proposing a candidate parameter value θ_{i+1} given the current value θ_i, and accepting the proposal with probability $\alpha = \min(1, \pi(\theta_{i+1})/\pi(\theta_i))$. Practically, a uniform random number $u \sim U(0,1)$ is drawn and θ_{i+1} is accepted when $u < \alpha$.

In general, the posterior can be written as $\pi(\theta) \propto p(\theta) \prod_{i=1}^{N} p(y_i|\theta, y_{1...i-1})$. Denoting the part of the unnormalized posterior considering only the first k measurements by $\pi_k(\theta) = p(\theta) \prod_{i=1}^{k} p(y_i|\theta, y_{1...i-1})$ and assuming that $\pi_k(\theta)$ is monotonically decreasing with respect to k, a proposal can be rejected as soon as $\pi_k(\theta_{i+1})/\pi_k(\theta_i) < u$ for some k. While monotonicity is not the case in general, many common cases exhibit this behavior. For example when measurements are independent and identically distributed with a Gaussian distribution. In other words, the sampling algorithm can be sped up by just switching up the order of the calculations: first generate u, perform the simulation and likelihood evaluation in an interleaved and part by part fashion while checking whether the proposal will be rejected and stopping early. In extreme cases, proposals can be rejected based on the prior and initial value alone without any need for expensive simulation.

Since only rejections benefit from this idea, the improvement is closely related to the acceptance rate of the sampler. Low acceptance rate due to the complexity of the posterior distribution or bad tuning of the proposal distribution can lead to potentially large performance improvements. A disadvantage of this method is that it can increase the load-imbalance discussed in Sect. 3 which can be a disadvantage in the distributed case when load-balancing is difficult/expensive.

Figure 4 demonstrates the effect of early rejection: the PK-PD model by Dunne et al. [37] was fitted using SAEM and evaluation times were recorded with and without early rejection. Speedup was computed for all 1000 individuals and the distribution is shown. Speedups of up to 6× can be observed for some individuals with an average of 1.5×. The average acceptance rate recorded was 33%. The amount of load-balance can be represented by $\frac{1/n \sum_i^n \delta_i}{\max_i \{\delta_i\}}$. A value of 1 is perfect balance whereas lower values indicate increasing degrees of imbalance. Figure 4 shows how the application of early rejection can create a shift in load-imbalance.

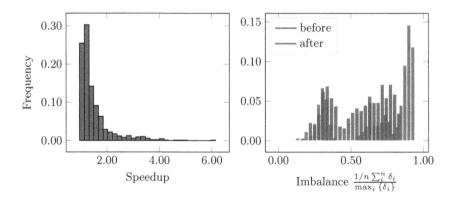

Fig. 4. Left: the distribution of the speedup of early-rejection measured on all 1000 individuals in a PK/PD study. Speedups up to 6× can be observed with an average of 1.5×. Right: the resulting shift in load-imbalance (a value of 1 representing perfect balance).

6 Avoiding Jacobian Calculation

An ordinary differential equation is defined by an initial value $y_0 \in \mathbb{R}^N$ and a function $f : \mathbb{R}^N \to \mathbb{R}^N$ describing the derivative of $y(t)$.

$$\frac{dy}{dt} = f(t, \phi, y), \quad y(t_0) = y_0$$

To compute $y(t)$, the following non-linear system must be solved at each integration step:

$$F(y^n) = y^n - y^{n-1} - h^n f(t^n, y^n) = 0$$

This equation can be solved using fixed-point iteration or Newton's method. This discussion will focus on Newton's method which requires the solution of the linear system:

$$M \times (y^m - y^{m-1}) = -F(y^{m-1}) \tag{2}$$

in which $M = (I + h^n J)$ and $J = \partial f / \partial y$, the Jacobian.

Popular packages for ODE solving such as LSODA [15] and CVODE [16] provide a way for the user to implement the Jacobian calculation, either analytically or through automatic differentiation [12]. Internally, the packages typically use direct methods to solve Eq. 2. For example, the matrix $M \in \mathbb{R}^{N \times N}$ is computed, factored and inverted. These operations have complexity $\mathcal{O}(N^3)$ and can become expensive as N increases.

Instead of direct methods, iterative methods such as Biconjugate gradient method [28] or GMRES [31] can be used. One of the powerful features of the iterative approach is that the matrix J does not need to computed and stored explicitly. Instead it requires only the matrix-vector product $J \times v$. Additionally, an iterative method might need less than N steps to reach a solution within the specified error-tolerances and therefore faster.

As demonstrated in Fig. 5, the computational cost of the matrix-vector product $J \times v$ can be much lower than computing the full matrix J. Even when repeatedly evaluating $J \times v$, the overall performance can differ significantly. The CVODE [16] package allows the use of an iterative linear solver (ILS) instead of the default direct approach. Figure 6 compares performance of solving a complete ODE system using a direct and iterative method. The package amortizes the cost of computing and factorizing the matrix M by reusing it during multiple iterations. Therefore the different methods of computing the Jacobian do not make much of a difference in runtime. As the dimensionality of the ODE system increases, it is evident that the ILS method outperforms the (default) direct approach.

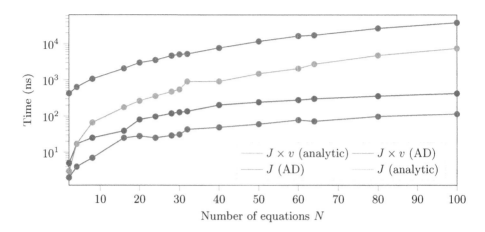

Fig. 5. Comparison of the cost (in log-scale) in terms of growing ODE complexity between the calculation of the full Jacobian J and the matrix-vector product $J \times v$ using automatic differentiation (AD) or analytically.

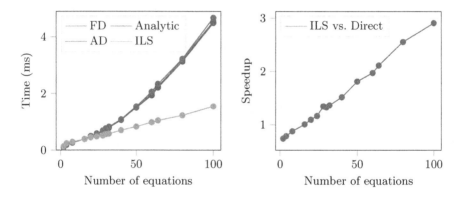

Fig. 6. Comparison in terms of growing ODE complexity between solving an ODE using the iterative linear solver (ILS) and a direct method with the matrix computed through finite-differencing (FD), analytically or automatic differentiation (AD).

7   Conclusion

Parameter estimation for non-linear mixed effects model can be an expensive and time-consuming process. Especially when structural models are expressed using differential equations, this cost can grow to hours and even days. In this paper, several ideas were presented that can significantly improve the performance of these estimation algorithms. While the ideas have appeared elsewhere in literature, they are underutilized and potentially unknown within the statistics community involved in implementing the estimation software.

The results in Sects. 4 and 6 indicate a growing computational cost of more complex models (either in number of parameters or differential equations). The methods described in this paper may help alleviate these computational problems to some extent. The increase of complexity can already be observed in whole-body physiologically-based pharmacokinetic models [36], microbiome dynamics models [10] and systems pharmacology [1].

All the methods discussed have been implemented in *DiffMEM*: an open-source package for rapid pharmacometric model estimation [13].

References

1. Balbas-Martinez, V., et al.: A systems pharmacology model for inflammatory bowel disease. PLOS ONE **13**(3), e0192949 (2018)
2. Beal, S., LB Sheiner, A.B., Bauer, R.: NONMEM User's Guides. Icon Development Solutions, Ellicott City (1989–2009)
3. Beskos, A., Papaspiliopoulos, O., Roberts, G.O.: Retrospective exact simulation of diffusion sample paths with applications. Bernoulli **12**(6), 1077–1098 (2006)
4. Blumofe, R.D., Joerg, C.F., Kuszmaul, B.C., Leiserson, C.E., Randall, K.H., Zhou, Y.: Cilk: an efficient multithreaded runtime system. In: Proceedings of the Fifth ACM SIGPLAN Symposium on Principles and Practice of Parallel Programming, PPOPP 1995, pp. 207–216. ACM, New York (1995)
5. Cesari, L.: Optimization Theory and Applications: Problems with Ordinary Differential Equations. Applications of Mathematics, vol. 17. Springer, New York (1983). https://doi.org/10.1007/978-1-4613-8165-5
6. Cybenko, G.: Dynamic load balancing for distributed memory multiprocessors. J. Parallel Distrib. Comput. **7**(2), 279–301 (1989)
7. Dagum, L., Menon, R.: OpenMP: an industry standard API for shared-memory programming. Comput. Sci. Eng. **5**(1), 46–55 (1998)
8. Ette, E.I., Williams, P.J.: Population pharmacokinetics I: background, concepts, and models. Ann. Pharmacother. **38**(10), 1702–1706 (2004)
9. Fidler, M., Xiong, Y., Schoemaker, R., Wilkins, J., Trame, M., Wang, W.: nlmixr: nonlinear mixed effects models in population pharmacokinetics and pharmacodynamics (2017)
10. Gibson, T., Gerber, G.: Robust and scalable models of microbiome dynamics. In: Dy, J., Krause, A. (eds.) Proceedings of the 35th International Conference on Machine Learning. Proceedings of Machine Learning Research, Stockholm smässan, Stockholm Sweden, 10–15 July 2018, vol. 80, pp. 1763–1772. PMLR (2018). http://proceedings.mlr.press/v80/gibson18a.html
11. Grama, A., Karypis, G., Kumar, V., Gupta, A.: Introduction to Parallel Computing, 2nd edn. Pearson Addison Wesley (2003)
12. Griewank, A., Walther, A.: Evaluating Derivatives. Society for Industrial and Applied Mathematics (2008)
13. Haber, T., Melicher, V., Kovac, T., Nemeth, B., Claes, J.: Diffmem (2018). https://bitbucket.org/tomhaber/diffmem
14. Hastings, W.K.: Monte Carlo sampling methods using Markov chains and their applications. Biometrika **57**(1), 97–109 (1970)
15. Hindmarsh, A.C.: Odepack, a systematized collection of ODE solvers. In: Stepleman, R. (ed.) Scientific Computing. Applications of Mathematics and Computing to the Physical Sciences, pp. 55–64. IMACS/North-Holland, Amsterdam (1983)
16. Hindmarsh, A.C., et al.: SUNDIALS: Suite of nonlinear and differential/algebraic equation solvers. ACM Trans. Math. Softw. (TOMS) **31**(3), 363–396 (2005)

17. Kuhn, E., Lavielle, M.: Coupling a stochastic approximation version of EM with an MCMC procedure. ESAIM: Prob. Stat. **8**, 115–131 (2004)
18. Kumar, V., Murthy, K., Sarkar, V., Zheng, Y.: Optimized distributed work-stealing. In: 2016 6th Workshop on Irregular Applications: Architecture and Algorithms (IA3). IEEE, November 2016
19. Lindstrom, M.J., Bates, D.M.: Nonlinear mixed effects models for repeated measures data. Biometrics **46**(3), 673 (1990)
20. Lions, J.L.: Optimal Control of Systems Governed by Partial Differential Equations. Springer, Berlin (1971)
21. Lixoft: Monolix 2018 user guide (2018). http://monolix.lixoft.com/single-page/
22. Melicher, V., Haber, T., Vanroose, W.: Fast derivatives of likelihood functionals for ODE based models using adjoint-state method. Comput. Stat. **32**(4), 1621–1643 (2017)
23. Metropolis, N., Rosenbluth, A.W., Rosenbluth, M.N., Teller, A.H., Teller, E.: Equation of state calculations by fast computing machines. J. Chem. Phys. **21**(6), 1087–1092 (1953)
24. Neal, R.: MCMC using Hamiltonian dynamics. In: Chapman & Hall/CRC Handbooks of Modern Statistical Methods. Chapman and Hall/CRC, May 2011
25. Nemeth, B., Haber, T., Liesenborgs, J., Lamotte, W.: Relaxing scalability limits with speculative parallelism in sequential Monte Carlo. In: 2018 IEEE International Conference on Cluster Computing (CLUSTER). IEEE, September 2018
26. Nocedal, J., Wright, S.J. (eds.): Numerical Optimization. Springer, Heidelberg (1999)
27. Pinheiro, J.C., Bates, D.M., Pinheiro, J.C.: Approximations to the log-likelihood function in the nonlinear mixed-effects model. J. Comput. Graph. Stat. **4**(1), 12 (1995)
28. Press, W.H., Teukolsky, S.A., Vetterling, W.T., Flannery, B.P.: Numerical Recipes 3rd Edition: The Art of Scientific Computing, 3rd edn. Cambridge University Press, New York (2007)
29. Reinders, J.: Intel Threading Building Blocks, 1st edn. O'Reilly & Associates Inc., Sebastopol (2007)
30. Roberts, G.O., Tweedie, R.L.: Exponential convergence of Langevin distributions and their discrete approximations. Bernoulli **2**(4), 341–363 (1996). https://projecteuclid.org:443/euclid.bj/1178291835
31. Saad, Y., Schultz, M.H.: GMRES: a generalized minimal residual algorithm for solving nonsymmetric linear systems. SIAM J. Sci. Stat. Comput. **7**(3), 856–869 (1986)
32. Sheiner, L.B., Rosenberg, B., Marathe, V.V.: Estimation of population characteristics of pharmacokinetic parameters from routine clinical data. J. Pharmacokinet. Biopharm. **5**(5), 445–479 (1977)
33. Shivaratri, N., Krueger, P., Singhal, M.: Load distributing for locally distributed systems. Computer **25**(12), 33–44 (1992)
34. Solonen, A., Ollinaho, P., Laine, M., Haario, H., Tamminen, J., Järvinen, H., et al.: Efficient MCMC for climate model parameter estimation: parallel adaptive chains and early rejection. Bayesian Anal. **7**(3), 715–736 (2012)
35. Tsafrir, D., Etsion, Y., Feitelson, D.G., Kirkpatrick, S.: System noise, OS clock ticks, and fine-grained parallel applications. In: Proceedings of the 19th Annual International Conference on Supercomputing, ICS 2005, pp. 303–312. ACM, New York (2005)

36. Wendling, T., Dumitras, S., Ogungbenro, K., Aarons, L.: Application of a Bayesian approach to physiological modelling of mavoglurant population pharmacokinetics. J. Pharmacokinet. Pharmacodyn. **42**(6), 639–657 (2015)
37. de Winter, W., et al.: Dynamic population pharmacokinetic-pharmacodynamic modelling and simulation supports similar efficacy in glycosylated haemoglobin response with once or twice-daily dosing of canagliflozin. Br. J. Clin. Pharmacol. **83**(5), 1072–1081 (2017)
38. Wozniak, J.M., et al.: Dataflow coordination of data-parallel tasks via MPI 3.0. In: Proceedings of the 20th European MPI Users Group Meeting on - EuroMPI. ACM Press (2013)

Hybrid Machine Learning and Polymer Physics Approach to Investigate 3D Chromatin Structure

Mattia Conte[1], Andrea Esposito[1,2] ![ORCID], Luca Fiorillo[1],
Carlo Annunziatella[1], Alfonso Corrado[1], Francesco Musella[1],
Renato Sciarretta[1], Andrea Maria Chiariello[1(✉)] ![ORCID],
and Simona Bianco[1(✉)] ![ORCID]

[1] Dipartimento di Fisica, Università di Napoli Federico II, and INFN Napoli,
Complesso Universitario di Monte Sant'Angelo, 80126 Naples, Italy
{chiariello,simona.bianco}@na.infn.it
[2] Berlin Institute for Medical Systems Biology, Max-Delbrück Centre
(MDC) for Molecular Medicine, Berlin, Germany

Abstract. Innovative experimental protocols from Molecular Biology provided in recent years quantitative data about the structure of the cell nucleus. These technologies, such as Hi-C, GAM or SPRITE, revealed that the genome has a non-random three-dimensional (3D) spatial organization, which serves functional purposes. In order to dissect the complexity of chromosome folding, models from Polymer Physics have been employed, highlighting many key aspects of large-scale chromatin organization. A deep understanding of the molecular mechanisms underlying the genome architecture is currently a crucial problem in Biology, since chromatin misfolding or structural variants can reconfigure chromatin domains, thereby resulting in pathogenic phenotypes and disease. Here, we discuss a numerical Polymer-Physics-based approach (PRISMR), able to model 3D chromatin folding by using Machine Learning strategies informed with experimental data. Using as a case study the *Pitx1* locus, a genomic region critically involved in hindlimb development, we show that the PRISMR algorithm reproduces in silico with high accuracy the experimental contact data, thus providing a powerful computational tool for analyzing and predicting the 3D chromatin structure.

Keywords: Polymer Physics · Machine Learning · Chromatin organization

1 Introduction

Understanding the three-dimensional (3D) structure of the genome is one of the most challenging problems in Biology, currently open and debated. Innovative experimental technologies that measure genome-wide contact frequencies between distal DNA regions, such as Hi-C [1], GAM [2] or SPRITE [3], envisaged a scenario where the

---

M. Conte and A. Esposito—Equal contribution.

© Springer Nature Switzerland AG 2020
U. Schwardmann et al. (Eds.): Euro-Par 2019 Workshops, LNCS 11997, pp. 572–582, 2020.
https://doi.org/10.1007/978-3-030-48340-1_44

chromatin folds non-randomly within the cell nucleus, giving rise to spatial conformations deeply linked to gene activity and transcriptional regulation [4–7]. Indeed, genome-wide Hi-C data have shown that mammalian genomes are compartmentalized in topologically associating domains (TADs) [8, 9], megabase-sized genomic regions displaying an interaction enrichment and largely conserved across species, cell types, and tissue types. Moreover, TADs exhibit a hierarchical higher-order organization, spanning across genomic scales up to the range of entire chromosomes. These higher-order interactions, called metaTADs, are relatively conserved through cell differentiation and their rearrangement is linked to gene expression changes [10–12]. Therefore, the genome-folding problem goes far beyond the simple need for packing efficiency, due the intimate link between chromosome spatial organization and gene activity. In this framework, models from Polymer Physics have been successfully employed to dissect the organization of chromosomes within the cell nucleus [13–18], highlighting the possible molecular mechanisms driving the folding of the genome [19–29].

In the present work, we focus on the Strings and Binders Switch (SBS) model [19, 20], a polymer physics approach able to recapitulate a great variety of experimental data [2, 20, 26, 30–32]. In this model, briefly recalled in Sect. 2, chromatin is represented as a polymer chain and the chromosome conformations arise through attachment of diffusible molecular factors to binding sites arranged along the polymer. To estimate the minimal number of model parameters needed to explain the experimental datasets, we developed a Polymer-Physics-based algorithm [33], named PRISMR, discussed in detail in Sect. 3. PRISMR is a numerical method based on a standard simulated annealing Monte Carlo optimization procedure that minimizes the distance between the predicted polymer model and the input experimental data, thereby returning the best SBS model describing a given genomic region. In Sect. 4, we illustrate an application of our model to a real DNA locus, known as *Pitx1*, which plays a critical role in hindlimb development [34]. Here, we consider experimental data from mouse forelimb and hindlimb tissues and we show that the PRISMR algorithm recapitulates with high accuracy in both cases the different *Pitx1* functional conformations observed in the experiments [35]. Moreover, we discuss how, by implementing massive parallel Molecular Dynamics (MD) simulations of the PRISMR polymer, ensembles of single-molecule 3D structures of the locus can be produced, that reveal biological key aspects of the regulation of the *Pitx1* gene in the two different tissues. In this context, we highlight the benefit obtained by adopting High-Performance-Computing (HPC) approaches, which allow to efficiently simulate polymer models with increasing level of complexity. Notably, as recently shown [33], our hybrid Machine Learning and Polymer Physics approach allows not only dissecting chromatin tissue-specific arrangements (such as gene-enhancer interaction), but also predicting the effects of genomic mutations, i.e. deletions, inversions or duplications, on chromatin architecture.

2 Overview of the Strings and Binders Switch (SBS) Polymer Model

In this section, we review some key features of the Strings and Binders Switch (SBS) model, a phase-separation based polymer model broadly discussed in previous works [20, 26, 27]. In the SBS framework, the chromatin is represented as a Self-Avoiding-Walk (SAW) chain having attachment points for diffusing binding molecules, called "binders", which can form loops by bridging pairs of polymer sites (Fig. 1a). Therefore, the model envisages a scenario where the architecture of chromosomes is shaped by their interactions with other molecular factors, biologically related to DNA binding molecules (e.g., Transcription Factors), the nuclear envelope or other nuclear bodies (e.g., the lamina). In our SBS model, the polymer sites, called "beads", and the binders are subject to a Brownian motion, described by the Langevin equation. Given the huge number of interacting particles (about ten thousand for the modeling of a real genomic region), we numerically integrate the motion equations by using the Verlet algorithm, a symplectic integrator [36], in the LAMMPS package [37]. The binders are placed in the box simulation at a given concentration and their interaction with the polymer beads is described by an energy affinity. Quantitative details concerning the interaction potentials between beads and binders can be found in [38].

The SBS model provides a phase diagram where different folding classes emerge [16]. In fact, by varying the molecular concentration of the binders and their affinity to the polymer, distinct thermodynamic phases are established (Fig. 1b). These stable emergent phases correspond to different conformational classes of Polymer Physics [39], ranging from open-SAW to compact-closed conformations in a switch-like transition. Conformation changes can be obtained by crossing the phase boundary, with no need of parameter fine-tuning. In the SBS view, a given polymer model is fully assigned by the arrangement of binding sites along the chain. In order to explain the complexity of the experimental data, as Hi-C contact frequencies of real genomic loci, it is necessary to introduce different types of binding sites along the polymer, each one interacting with only a "cognate" (i.e., same-type) binder. We schematically represent different types of beads, and correspondingly cognate binders, by different colors, giving rise to a complex "multicolor" SBS polymer model [26, 33]. In the next section, we describe a hybrid Machine Learning and Polymer-Physics based approach [33] to estimate the minimal number of colors and parameters for a given SBS model able to describe with high accuracy a real genomic region.

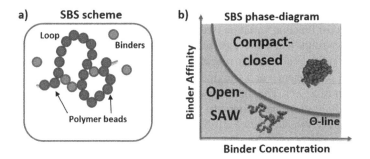

Fig. 1. a) Schematic overview of the SBS model: a chromatin filament is represented by a Self-Avoiding-Walk (SAW) chain having binding sites for Brownian diffusing binders. The interaction between the polymer and the molecular binders can produce loops, shaping in this way the chromosome spatial organization. Adapted from [26]. b) The SBS phase-diagram includes a phase where the polymer folds in a random-open conformation (in the SAW universality class) and a phase where it spontaneously folds into a compact-closed conformation. At the phase transition point, there is the Θ-point state. Adapted from [26].

3 PRISMR: A Machine Learning Strategy to Identify the Optimum SBS Polymer Model

PRISMR (Polymer-based RecursIve Statistical inference Method) [33] is a Machine Learning procedure developed in order to infer the factors that shape chromatin folding. Based on polymer physics principles, it aims to find the polymer model best describing an input contact matrix, obtained e.g. by Hi-C, GAM or SPRITE experiment. Although our method can be readily generalized to a wide range of different paradigms, here we focus on its application to the previously described SBS polymer model.

A crucial parameter of the PRISMR method is the number n of different types of allowed interactions (different SBS colors). Given n, the algorithm scans through the huge space of all possible polymer models via a Simulated Annealing Monte Carlo optimization procedure to find the model with the colors arrangement, i.e. the distribution of the different binding sites, best describing the contact matrix given as input (INPUT in Fig. 2). This is performed by searching for the minimum of a specific cost function $H = H_0 + H_\lambda$, where H_0 considers the distance between the experimental and the model-predicted contact matrices, while H_λ is a Bayesian term proportional to the number of colored sites of the polymer through a parameter λ. The first term only accounts for the necessity to fit well the input data, and it gets small when the predicted frequencies are similar to the experimental ones. The second term penalizes the addition of new colored beads, and it is needed to avoid overfitting, i.e. to select the minimum number of interacting beads required to explain the input within a fixed accuracy [33].

The PRISMR procedure starts with an initial configuration of the SBS polymer where the beads have been randomly colored. At each Monte Carlo step, we select at random a polymer bead, change its color, compute the average contact matrix of the new polymer, evaluate the new cost function and accept or reject the color change based on the cost function variation (see Fig. 2). This step is replicated many times and the simulation stops when the cost function reaches the convergence (OUTPUT in Fig. 2). The entire procedure is repeated (varying the polymer initial configuration) with different parameters n and λ to find their optimal value (the minimum of n, n^* and the maximum of λ, λ^*). The final output of PRISMR is the best positioning of the n^* different binding site types along the SBS polymer that describe the experimental matrix within a given accuracy [33] (Fig. 2).

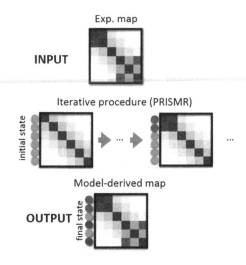

Fig. 2. Key steps of the PRISMR minimization procedure. An experimental contact matrix is given in input to the algorithm. Once initialized the polymer in a random state, the colors of the different beads are changed to find the best distribution of binding sites able to reproduce the input. Adapted from [33]

4   A Case Study: The *Pitx1* Gene Region

4.1   PRISMR Optimal Polymer Models

As a case study, here we review the application of PRISMR on a real genomic locus, *Pitx1*, located on the chromosome 13 of the mouse genome. The *Pitx1* gene regulation is crucial to ensure a correct identity and differentiation of hindlimbs [34] (limbs that are found in the back part of an animal's body). Indeed, during limb development, *Pitx1* is only expressed in hindlimbs, but not expressed in forelimbs (limbs that are found in the front part of an animal's body). In ref [35] we showed that the *Pitx1* regulatory landscape extends over 400 kb and forms several chromatin loops termed regulatory anchors (RA) 1–5. In particular, *Pitx1* activity is mainly regulated by the genomic element RA5/Pen, located about 300 kb downstream [35]. The DNA sequences which control the activation of genes are called enhancers and they carry out their function by coming into physical proximity with the genes they activate [7].

In order to study the spatial conformation of such a system we considered a 1 Mb wide genomic sequence encompassing the *Pitx1* regulatory region where the differences between the forelimb and hindlimb contact patterns are marked. To obtain the 3D structures of these loci, we first derived our best SBS polymer models running PRISMR on forelimb and hindlimb pair-wise contact data from capture Hi-C (cHi-C, a variant of Hi-C) experiments. In both cases we obtained as best estimate of the number of different colors $n^* = 14$ [33]. Our results are summarized in Fig. 3 where we show the experimental contact matrices (panel a top), the matrices inferred from the model (panel a bottom) and the position and abundance of the 14 different binding domains in each studied case (panel b). The contact pattern is well recapitulated by our model in both cases, as also shown by the high values of the Pearson correlation coefficient r between the experimental and model matrices ($r = 0.98$ in both forelimb and in hindlimb).

4.2 3D Structures by Molecular Dynamics Simulations and the Role of High Performance Computing

Next, to simulate such complex biological systems in 3D space, we ran massive parallel Molecular Dynamics simulations of our inferred SBS polymers using LAMMPS (Large-scale Atomic/Molecular Massively Parallel Simulator), a broadly used efficient MD open-source software. Model interaction potentials were set as in classical studies of polymer physics [40] and previous works [26, 37]. The initial state of the polymer was a Self-Avoiding Walk (SAW) and the binders were randomly distributed in the simulation box whose size was at least two times larger than the self-avoiding polymer gyration radius to minimize finite-size effects [26]. LAMMPS was built to run in parallel using the MPI (message-passing interface) protocol and parallelization achieved by domain decomposition, i.e. by partitioning the simulation box into cells, each assigned to a different processor. In general, the optimum number of processors depends on the complexity of the polymer model in the first place, but also on other factors such as queuing time and resource availability [41]. Here we used 8 MPI processes, gaining a speed-up of approximately 10x, for both forelimb and hindlimb cases. Simulations were run on the CINECA HPC "MARCONI Broadwell" infrastructure. In both tissues, we obtained at least 10^2 independent configurations, each evolved up to 5×10^8 simulation time steps to reach stationarity, as monitored by the gyration radius R_g of the polymer [20, 38, 39], that is the radius of a sphere enclosing the polymer 3D structure (Fig. 4a). All the details about the interaction energies and binder concentrations can be found in ref [35].

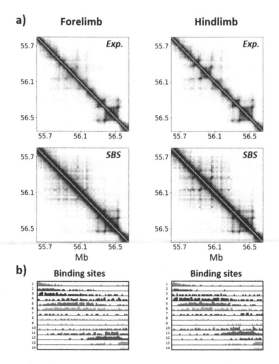

Fig. 3. a) Top: Experimental cHi-C maps [35] of forelimb and hindlimb E11.5 tissues restricted to the considered genomic region. Bottom: SBS model-derived contact maps show high similarity to the experimental ones. The Pearson correlation values are $r = 0.98$ in forelimb and $r = 0.98$ in hindlimb. b) Histograms displaying the abundance and position along the genome of the different binding site types in forelimbs (left) and hindlimbs (right). Each binding domain is represented with a different color. Adapted from [35].

The 3D structures, produced by POV-Ray software [42], give rise to a clear bio-logical interpretation. As we can see from Fig. 4b, in forelimb the locus segregates into two chromatin hubs, one containing *Pitx1*, *RA3* and *Neurog1* (blue, pink and red spheres, respectively) and the other one containing *Pen* and *RA4* (dark green and light green spheres, respectively). In such a spatial conformation *Pen* and *Pitx1* are separated from each other and the repressed gene *Neurog1* is close to *Pitx1*, so preventing its activation. Conversely, the hindlimb 3D structure is organized in three major hubs, one containing *RA1*, another one containing *Pitx1* and *RA3*, and the last one *RA4*, *Pen* and *Neurog1* (see Fig. 4b). In this conformation, the *Pitx1* gene and its enhancer *Pen* are physically closer, so ensuring a correct activation of the gene in hindlimb.

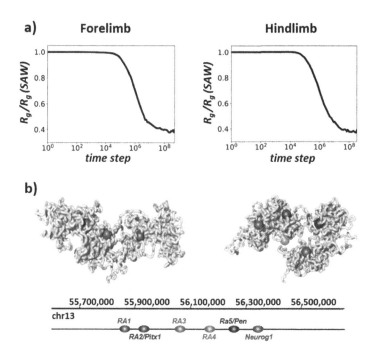

Fig. 4. a) Folding dynamics of the forelimb and hindlimb SBS polymer models. Equilibrium is reached at nearly 10^8 time steps in both cases as measured by the plateauing of gyration radius (R_g) of the system. b) Representative 3D structure of the locus in each studied case showing the two-hub structure in forelimb (left) and the three-hub structure in hindlimb (right). The colored spheres represent the key regulatory regions whose genomic positions are showed in the bar below. Adapted from [35]. (Color figure online)

The spatial reconstruction obtained by the PRISMR method enables us to interpret the different behavior of the *Pitx1* locus in the forelimb and hindlimb tissues. The key point is the different spatial positioning of the gene relative to its enhancer *Pen* and the repressed *Neurog1* gene. While in hindlimb *Pitx1* is in close spatial vicinity of *Pen* and segregated from *Neurog1*, an opposite situation turns out in forelimb, where *Pitx1* is physically disconnected from its enhancer and associated with *Neurog1*. These tissue-specific arrangements of the *Pitx1* landscape can restrict (forelimb) or assist (hindlimb) the enhancer activity, playing an important role in the correct development of the tissue.

5 Conclusions

Polymer Physics models are becoming an important tool to study the complex genome spatial organization [20, 21, 23, 25, 29, 30]. Here, we focused on the Strings and Binders Switch (SBS) model, a phase-separation based polymer model where the folding of real genomic loci is driven by a specific arrangement of binding domains and molecular factors along the polymer chain [26, 27, 33, 43]. We described a Machine-Learning-based algorithm, named PRISMR, to infer the best SBS polymer explaining a given input experimental data, typically chromosome conformation capture data. We took as a case study the *Pitx1* genomic region in mouse, deeply involved in hindlimb development, and we showed that our model recapitulates with high accuracy (Pearson correlation >95%) the experimental contact data of the locus. Furthermore, we discussed how massive parallel Molecular Dynamics simulation have been employed in order to provide the 3D structure of the *Pitx1* locus, highlighting key biological aspects of the *Pitx1* gene regulation.

Due to the progressive increase in the number of published databases and their available resolution, Polymer Physics models describing the 3D genome organization could take into account finer details in order to provide increasingly accurate predictions. Indeed, novel experimental technologies [2, 3, 44–46], such as super-resolution chromatin imaging approaches, are allowing to dissect the genome well beyond the population level, revealing TAD-like structures and multiway interactions also in single-cells. To refine the biological realism of the models, strong computational efforts are needed in order to manage the major complexity of the simulated systems. Therefore, High-Performance-Computing resources are crucial to model datasets with higher resolution and to highlight new insights on the structure and molecular mechanisms underlying the spatial organization of chromosomes in the cell nucleus.

References

1. Lieberman-Aiden, E., et al.: Comprehensive mapping of long-range interactions reveals folding principles of the human genome. Science (80-.) (2009). https://doi.org/10.1126/science.1181369
2. Beagrie, R., Scialdone, A., Schueler, M., et al.: Complex multi-enhancer contacts captured by genome architecture mapping. Nature **543**, 519–524 (2017). https://doi.org/10.1038/nature21411
3. Quinodoz, S.A., et al.: Higher-order inter-chromosomal hubs shape 3D genome organization in the nucleus. Cell **174**(3), 744–757.e24 (2018). https://doi.org/10.1016/j.cell.2018.05.024
4. Misteli, T.: Beyond the sequence: cellular organization of genome function. Cell **128**(4), 787–800 (2007). https://doi.org/10.1016/j.cell.2007.01.028
5. Bickmore, W.A., van Steensel, B.: Genome architecture: domain organization of interphase chromosomes. Cell **152**(6), 1270–1284 (2013). https://doi.org/10.1016/j.cell.2013.02.001
6. Tanay, A., Cavalli, G.: Chromosomal domains: epigenetic contexts and functional implications of genomic compartmentalization. Curr. Opin. Genet. Dev. **23**(2), 197–203 (2013). https://doi.org/10.1016/j.gde.2012.12.009
7. Dekker, J., Mirny, L.: The 3D genome as moderator of chromosomal communication. Cell **164**(6), 1110–1121 (2016). https://doi.org/10.1016/j.cell.2016.02.007
8. Dixon, J.R., et al.: Topological domains in mammalian genomes identified by analysis of chromatin interactions. Nature **485**, 376–380 (2012). https://doi.org/10.1038/nature11082
9. Nora, E.P., et al.: Spatial partitioning of the regulatory landscape of the X-inactivation centre. Nature **485**, 381–385 (2012). https://doi.org/10.1038/nature11049
10. Fraser, J., et al.: Hierarchical folding and reorganization of chromosomes are linked to transcriptional changes in cellular differentiation. Mol. Syst. Biol. **11**, 852 (2015). https://doi.org/10.15252/msb.20156492

11. Chiariello, A.M., Bianco, S., Annunziatella, C., Esposito, A., Nicodemi, M.: The scaling features of the 3D organization of chromosomes are highlighted by a transformation a la Kadanoff of Hi-C data. EPL **120**, 40004 (2017). https://doi.org/10.1209/0295-5075/120/40004

12. Bianco, S., Chiariello, A.M., Annunziatella, C., et al.: Predicting chromatin architecture from models of polymer physics. Chromosome Res. **25**, 25–34 (2017). https://doi.org/10.1007/s10577-016-9545-5

13. Emanuel, M., Radja, N.H., Henriksson, A., Schiessel, H.: The physics behind the larger scale organization of DNA in eukaryotes. Phys. Biol. **6**, 025008 (2009). https://doi.org/10.1088/1478-3975/6/2/025008

14. Tark-Dame, M., Driel, R., Heermann, D.: Chromatin folding - from biology to polymer models and back. J. Cell Sci. **124**, 839–45 (2011). https://doi.org/10.1242/jcs.077628

15. Barbieri, M., Scialdone, A., Gamba, A., Pombo, A., Nicodemi, M.: Polymer physics, scaling and heterogeneity in the spatial organisation of chromosomes in the cell nucleus. Soft Matter. **9**, 8631 (2013). https://doi.org/10.1039/c3sm51436f

16. Nicodemi, M., Pombo, A.: Models of chromosome structure. Curr. Opin. cell Bio. **28C**, 90–95 (2014). https://doi.org/10.1016/j.ceb.2014.04.004

17. Chiariello, A.M., et al.: Polymer models of the organization of chromosomes in the nucleus of cells. Mod. Phys. Lett. B. **29**(9), 1530003 (2015). https://doi.org/10.1142/S0217984915300033

18. Esposito, A., Annunziatella, C., Bianco, S., Chiariello, A.M., Fiorillo, L., Nicodemi, M.: Models of polymer physics for the architecture of the cell nucleus. WIREs Syst. Biol. Med. **11**, e14442019 (2019). https://doi.org/10.1002/wsbm.1444

19. Nicodemi, M., Prisco, A.: Thermodynamic pathways to genome spatial organization in the cell nucleus. Biophys. J. **96**, 2168–2177 (2009). https://doi.org/10.1016/j.bpj.2008.12.3919

20. Barbieri, M., et al.: Complexity of chromatin folding is captured by the strings and binders switch model. Proc. Nat. Acad. Sci. **109**(40), 16173–16178 (2012). https://doi.org/10.1073/pnas.1204799109

21. Jost, D., Carrivain, P., Cavalli, G., Vaillant, C.: Modeling epigenome folding: formation and dynamics of topologically associated chromatin domains. Nucleic Acids Res. **42**, 9553–9561 (2014). https://doi.org/10.1093/nar/gku698

22. Bohn, M., Heermann, D.W.: Diffusion-driven looping provides a consistent framework for chromatin organization. PLoS One **5**(8), e12218 (2010). https://doi.org/10.1371/journal.pone.0012218

23. Sanborn, A.L., et al.: Chromatin extrusion explains key features of loop and domain formation in wild-type and engineered genomes. Proc. Natl. Acad. Sci. **112**, E6456–E6465 (2015). https://doi.org/10.1073/pnas.1518552112

24. Fudenberg, G., Imakaev, M., Lu, C., Goloborodko, A., Abdennur, N., Mirny, L.A.: Formation of chromosomal domains by loop extrusion. Cell Rep. **15**, 2038–2049 (2016). https://doi.org/10.1016/j.celrep.2016.04.085

25. Brackley, C.A., et al.: Nonequilibrium chromosome looping via molecular slip links. Phys. Rev. Lett. **119**, 138101 (2017). https://doi.org/10.1103/PhysRevLett.119.138101

26. Chiariello, A., Annunziatella, C., Bianco, S., et al.: Polymer physics of chromosome large-scale 3D organisation. Sci. Rep. **6**, 29775 (2016). https://doi.org/10.1038/srep29775

27. Annunziatella, C., Chiariello, A.M., Bianco, S., Nicodemi, M.: Polymer models of the hierarchical folding of the Hox-B chromosomal locus. Phys. Rev. E. **94**, 042402 (2016). https://doi.org/10.1103/PhysRevE.94.042402

28. Rosa, A., Everaers, R.: Structure and dynamics of interphase chromosomes. PLoS Comput. Biol. **4**(8), e1000153 (2008). https://doi.org/10.1371/journal.pcbi.1000153

29. Brackley, C.A., Taylor, S., Papantonis, A., Cook, P.R., Marenduzzo, D.: Nonspecific bridging-induced attraction drives clustering of DNA-binding proteins and genome organization. Proc. Nat. Acad. Sci. **110**(38), E3605–E3611 (2013). https://doi.org/10.1073/pnas.1302950110

30. Barbieri, M., Xie, S., Torlai Triglia, E., et al.: Active and poised promoter states drive folding of the extended HoxB locus in mouse embryonic stem cells. Nat. Struct. Mol. Biol. **24**, 515–524 (2017). https://doi.org/10.1038/nsmb.3402

31. Paliou, C., et al.: Preformed chromatin topology assists transcriptional robustness of Shh during limb development. Proc. Nat. Acad. Sci. **116**(25), 12390–12399 (2019). https://doi.org/10.1073/pnas.1900672116

32. Bianco, S., et al.: Modeling single-molecule conformations of the HoxD region in mouse embryonic stem and cortical neuronal cells. Cell Reports **28**(6), 1574–1583.e4 (2019). https://doi.org/10.1016/j.celrep.2019.07.013. ISSN 2211-1247

33. Bianco, S., Lupiáñez, D.G., Chiariello, A.M., et al.: Polymer physics predicts the effects of structural variants on chromatin architecture. Nat. Genet. **50**, 662–667 (2018). https://doi.org/10.1038/s41588-018-0098-8

34. DeLaurier, A., Schweitzer, R., Logan, M.: Pitx1 determines the morphology of muscle, tendon, and bones of the hindlimb. Dev. Biol. **299**, 22–34 (2006). https://doi.org/10.1016/j.ydbio.2006.06.055

35. Kragesteen, B.K., et al.: Dynamic 3D chromatin architecture contributes to enhancer specificity and limb morphogenesis. Nat. Genet. **50**, 1463–1473 (2018). https://doi.org/10.1038/s41588-018-0221-x

36. Allen, M.P., Tildesley, D.J.: Computer Simulation of Liquids (Oxford Science Publications) SE - Oxford science publications. Oxford Univ. Press (1989)

37. Plimpton, S.: Fast parallel algorithms for short-range molecular dynamics. J. Comput. Phys. **117**, 1–19 (1995). https://doi.org/10.1006/jcph.1995.1039

38. Annunziatella, C., Chiariello, A.M., Esposito, A., Bianco, S., Fiorillo, L., Nicodemi, M.: Molecular dynamics simulations of the strings and binders switch model of chromatin. Methods **142**, 81–88 (2018). https://doi.org/10.1016/j.ymeth.2018.02.024

39. De Gennes, P.G.: Scaling Concepts in Polymer Physics. Cornell University Press, Ithaca (1979). https://doi.org/10.1163/_q3_SIM_00374

40. Kremer, K., Grest, G.S.: Dynamics of entangled linear polymer melts: a molecular-dynamics simulation. J. Chem. Phys. **92**(8), 5057–5086 (1990). https://doi.org/10.1063/1.458541

41. Conte, M., et al.: Efficient computational implementation of polymer physics models to explore chromatin structure. Int. J. Parallel Emergent Distrib. Syst. 1–12 (2019). https://doi.org/10.1080/17445760.2019.1643020

42. Persistence of Vision Pty. Ltd.: Persistence of Vision Raytracer (2004)

43. Chiariello, A.M., et al.: A polymer physics investigation of the architecture of the murine orthologue of the 7q11.23 Human Locus. Front Neurosci. **11**, 559 (2017). https://doi.org/10.3389/fnins.2017.00559

44. Allahyar, A., Vermeulen, C., Bouwman, B.A.M., et al.: Enhancer hubs and loop collisions identified from single-allele topologies. Nat. Genet. **50**, 1151–1160 (2018). https://doi.org/10.1038/s41588-018-0161-5

45. Oudelaar, A.M., Davies, J.O.J., Hanssen, L.L.P., et al.: Single-allele chromatin interactions identify regulatory hubs in dynamic compartmentalized domains. Nat. Genet. **50**(12), 1744–1751 (2018). https://doi.org/10.1038/s41588-018-0253-2

46. Bintu, B., et al.: Super-resolution chromatin tracing reveals domains and cooperative interactions in single cells. Science (80-). 362, eaau1783 (2018). https://doi.org/10.1126/science.aau1783

Adaptive Domain Decomposition for Effective Data Assimilation

Rossella Arcucci[1(✉)], Laetitia Mottet[2], César A. Quilodrán Casas[1],
Florian Guitton[1], Christopher Pain[2], and Yi-Ke Guo[1]

[1] Data Science Institute, Department of Computing, Imperial College London,
London, UK
r.arcucci@imperial.ac.uk
[2] Department of Earth Science and Engineering, Imperial College London,
London, UK

Abstract. We present a parallel Data Assimilation model based on an Adaptive Domain Decomposition (ADD-DA) coupled with the open-source, finite-element, fluid dynamics model Fluidity. The model we present is defined on a partition of the domain in sub-domains without overlapping regions. This choice allows to avoid communications among the processes during the Data Assimilation phase. However, during the balance phase, the model exploits the domain decomposition implemented in Fluidity which balances the results among the processes exploiting overlapping regions. Also, the model exploits the technology provided by the mesh adaptivity to generate an optimal mesh we name *supermesh*. The *supermesh* is the one used in ADD-DA process. We prove that the ADD-DA model provides the same numerical solution of the corresponding sequential DA model. We also show that the ADD approach reduces the execution time even when the implementation is not on a parallel computing environment. Experimental results are provided for pollutant dispersion within an urban environment.

Keywords: Data Assimilation · Fluidity · Domain Decomposition · Adaptive mesh · Big data

1 Introduction and Motivation

Numerical simulations are widely used as a predictive tool to better understand complex air flows and pollution transport at the scale of individual buildings, city blocks and entire cities. The strongly nonlinear character of many physical processes results in the dramatic amplification of even small input uncertainties producing large uncertainties in the system behavior [7]. To reduce these uncertainties and increase the accuracy of predictions, Data Assimilation (DA) techniques are used [15]. Data Assimilation (DA) is the approximation of the true state of some physical system at a given time by combining time-distributed observations with a dynamic model in an optimal way. DA can be classically

© Springer Nature Switzerland AG 2020
U. Schwardmann et al. (Eds.): Euro-Par 2019 Workshops, LNCS 11997, pp. 583–595, 2020.
https://doi.org/10.1007/978-3-030-48340-1_45

approached in two ways: as variational DA [6] and as filtering, such that Kalman Filter (KF) [14]. In both cases, the methods are computed as an optimal solution: statistically, KF methods try to find a solution with minimum variance, while variational methods compute a solution that minimises a suitable cost function. In certain cases, the two approaches are identical and provide exactly the same solution [15]. While the statistical approach it is often complex and time-consuming, it can provide a richer information structure. Variational approaches are relatively rapid and robust instead [6]. In DA, one makes repeated corrections to data during a single run, to bring the code output into agreement with the latest observed data. In operational forecasting there is insufficient time to restart a run from the beginning with new data then, DA should enable real-time utilisation of data to improve predictions. This mandates the choice of efficient methods to opportunely develop and implement DA models.

Due to the necessity to have DA in real time, we introduce in this paper an efficient Adaptive Domain Decomposition approach for variational Data Assimilation (ADD-DA). The ADD-DA model is presented to assimilate data from sensors into the open-source, parallelised fluid dynamics model Fluidity (http://fluidityproject.github.io/). It is estimated that by 2050, around four-million deaths per year will be attributable to outdoor air pollution (twice the current mortality rate) [16]. This mandates the development of techniques that can be used for emergency response, real-time operational prediction and management. A variational DA model (VarDA) to assimilate air pollution data has been introduced in [4] in which it has been shown that the use of an optimal space for solving DA can reduce the execution-time. However, the interface between this VarDA and Fluidity present a big bottleneck due to the gathering of the data after Fluidity to run DA (as shown in Fig. 1-left).

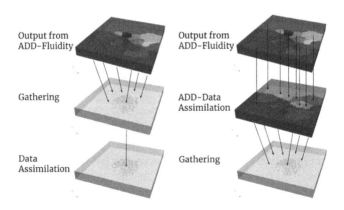

Fig. 1. Comparison of the sequential VarDA coupled with Fluidity (left) and ADD-DA coupled with Fluidity (right)

Parallelisation of data assimilation has been previously used in oceanography, however its application for urban air pollution is novel. Previous works on parallelised data assimilation include domain decomposition (DD) in a regional ocean model of Australia [20] and a parallel implementation of data assimilation for operational oceanography by [9,22]. A different approach which introduce a reduction on the execution time is presented in [10] where the authors use a recursive filter (RF) with the third order of accuracy (3rd-RF) to approximate horizontal Gaussian covariances. A domain decomposition approach for data assimilation has been presented in [2] where the authors implemented a geographical decomposition made of sub-domains (of fixed same sizes) with overlapping.

In this paper, we developed a DA model based on the same domain decomposition (DD) implemented in Fluidity such that the DA process can be coupled with Fluidity in a straight forward way (Fig. 1-right). We propose a DD approach which does not include any interaction/communication among the sub-domains, thus removing the interaction/communication overhead. We prove that the solution of the ADD-DA model is the same of the VarDA model without any decomposition introduced in [4]. We also show that the approach reduces the execution time even when the implementation is not on a parallel computing environment.

This paper is structured as follows. The ADD-DA model is presented in Sect. 2. The set-up of the test case is detailed in Sect. 3 where results using ADD-DA to improve the results of the pollutant concentration are presented. The scalability of the ADD-DA approach is also discussed in Sect. 3. Finally, conclusions and future work are provided in Sect. 4.

2   The ADD-DA Model

In this section we present a Data Assimilation model based on an Adaptive Domain Decomposition to be coupled with Fluidity.

One of the key and innovative aspects of Fluidity is its mesh-adaptivity capability on unstructured meshes. The use of the mesh-adaptivity allows to have fine mesh in regions where small-scale and important physical processes occur, while keeping a coarser mesh elsewhere, and then allowing to considerably reduce the total computation time [21]. Fluidity was running with mesh adaptivity for an enough long time for the flow statistics to reach a quasi-steady state. From this point onwards, the mesh is fixed and considered as the optimal mesh. This mesh will be referred as the *supermesh* in the following.

Let $\Omega = \{x_j\}_{j=1,...,n}$ be the discrete spatial domain representing the *supermesh* and let $\mathcal{P}(\Omega) = \{\Omega_i\}_{i=1,...,s}$ be a partition of Ω in subdomains as implemented in Fluidity [1]. In Fluidity, the decomposition of the domain into subdomains is based on the number of nodes x_j. The number of nodes assigned to a partition/processor is assumed to be a good proxy for the expected computational load on that processor and, hence, one aim of the algorithm is to equidistribute the nodes. Other requirements include a minimization of edge cut and data migration. The number of nodes is balanced to be more or less the same on each processor, even if it is not a strict constraint.

For a fixed time t, according to this decomposition, let

$$u_i^{\mathcal{M}} \equiv u_i(t) \tag{1}$$

be the vector denoting the state of the dynamical system. At time t, we get $u(t) = \mathcal{M}\left(u(t-1)\right)$ where $\mathcal{M}$ is the forecasting model, in our case represented by Fluidity. Let be

$$v_i = H_i(u_i) \tag{2}$$

the vector of observations where H_i is an interpolation operator collecting the observations at time t. The aim of DA problem is to find an optimal trade-off between the current estimate of the system state (the background) in (Eq. 1) and the available observations v_k in (Eq. 2).

ADD-DA computational model is a system of s non-linear least square problems:

$$u_i^{ADD-DA} = argmin_{u_i} \|u_i - u_i^{\mathcal{M}}\|_{\mathbf{B}_i}^2 + \|H_i(u_i) - v_i\|_{\mathbf{R}_i}^2 \tag{3}$$

where $\mathbf{R_i}$ and $\mathbf{B_i}$ are the covariance matrices providing the estimate of the errors on v_i and on $u_i^{\mathcal{M}}$, respectively.

As the background error covariance matrix $\mathbf{B_i}$ is ill-conditioned [19], in order to improve the conditioning, only Empirical Orthogonal Functions (EOFs) of the first largest eigenvalues of the error covariance matrix are considered. Since its introduction to meteorology [18], EOFs analysis has become a fundamental tool in atmosphere, ocean, and climate science for data diagnostics and dynamical mode reduction. Each of these applications basically exploits the fact that EOFs allow a decomposition of a data function into a set of orthogonal functions, which are designed in such a way that only a few of these functions are needed in lower-dimensional approximations [13]. Furthermore, since EOFs are the eigenvectors of the error covariance matrix [12], its condition number is reduced as well. Nevertheless, the accuracy of the solution obtained by truncating EOFs exhibits a severe sensibility to the variation of the value of the truncation parameter, so that a suitably choice of the number of EOFs is strongly recommended. This issue introduces a severe drawback to the reliability of EOFs truncation, hence to the usability of the operative software in different scenarios [3,12]. In this paper, we set the optimal choice of the truncation parameter as a trade-off between efficiency and accuracy of the DA algorithm as introduced in [4]. The Optimal ADD-DA model as implemented in this paper is summarised in Algorithm 1. Eq. (3) is linearised around the background state [17]:

$$u_i = u_i^{\mathcal{M}} + \delta u_i \tag{4}$$

where $\delta u_i = u_i - u_i^{\mathcal{M}}$ denotes the increments. The ADD-DA problem can then be re-formulated by the following form:

$$\delta u_i^{ADD-DA} = argmin_{\delta u_i} \left\{ \frac{1}{2}\delta u_i^T \mathbf{B}_i^{-1}\delta u_i + \frac{1}{2}(\mathbf{H}\delta u_i - d_i)^T \mathbf{R}_i^{-1}(\mathbf{H}\delta u_i - d_i) \right\} \tag{5}$$

where

$$d_i = [v_i - H\left(u_i^{\mathcal{M}}\right)] \tag{6}$$

is the misfit between the observation and the solution computed by Fluidity and

$$H\left(u_i\right) \simeq H\left(u_i^{\mathcal{M}}\right) + \mathbf{H}\delta u_i \tag{7}$$

denotes the linearised observational and model operators evaluated at $u_i = u_i^{\mathcal{M}}$ where $\mathbf{H}$ is the Hessian of H.

In Eq. (5), the minimisation problem is defined on the field of increments [8]. In order to avoid the inversion of $\mathbf{B}_i$, as $\mathbf{B}_i = \mathbf{V}_i\mathbf{V}_i^T$, the minimisation is computed with respect to a new variable [17] $w_i = \mathbf{V}_i^+\delta u_i$, where $\mathbf{V}_i^+$ denotes the generalised inverse of $\mathbf{V}_i$, yielding to:

$$w_i^{ADD-DA} = argmin_{w_i} J_i(w_i)$$

$$= argmin_{w_i} \left\{ \frac{1}{2}w_i^T w_i + \frac{1}{2}(\mathbf{H}\mathbf{V}_i w_i - d_i)^T \mathbf{R}_i^{-1}(\mathbf{H}\mathbf{V}_i w_i - d_i) \right\} \tag{8}$$

The ADD-DA process, on each sub-domain of the partition, is described in Algorithm 1.

Algorithm 1: ADD-DA

    Input: v_i and $u_i^{\mathcal{M}}$

1   Define H_i ▷ interpolation operator

2   Compute $d_i \leftarrow v_i - H_i u_i^{\mathcal{M}}$ ▷ compute the misfit

3   Define R_i ▷ covariance matrix of the observed data v_i

4   Define V_i ▷ deviance matrix of background data

5   Define the initial value of δu_i^{ADD-DA}

6   Compute $V_i \leftarrow TSVD(V_i, m)$ ▷ m is the truncation parameter

7   Compute $w_i \leftarrow V_i^T \delta u_i^{ADD-DA}$

8   **while** *Convergence on w_i is obtained* **do**

9   Compute $J_i \leftarrow J_i(w_i)$

10   Compute $gradJ_i \leftarrow \nabla J_i(w_i)$

11   Compute new values for w_i ▷ L-BFGS step

12   **end**

13   Compute $u_i^{ADD-DA} \leftarrow u_i^{\mathcal{M}} + V_i w_i$

     Output: u^{ADD-DA}

We prove that the solution computed on this partitioning does not affect the accuracy of the DA process as the solution of the ADD-DA problem is the same than the DA algorithm coupled with Fluidity in [4]. In the following, w^{DA} denotes the solution of the DA process computed without any decomposition [4], i.e. defined on the whole domain Ω and such that:

$$w^{DA} = argmin_w J(w) = argmin_w \left\{ \frac{1}{2}w^T w + \frac{1}{2}(\mathbf{H}\mathbf{V}w - d)^T \mathbf{R}^{-1}(\mathbf{H}\mathbf{V}w - d) \right\} \tag{9}$$

The functionals $J_i(w_i)$ (for $i = 1, \ldots, s$) defined in Eq. (8) are restrictions of the functional $J(w)$ in Eq. (9), i.e. $J(w)/\Omega_i = J_i(w_i)$. It has also to be noted that the functionals $J(w)$ and $J_i(w_i)$ are convex [6]. Hence, the following result helds.

Theorem 1. *Let w^{DA} be the solution of the DA process computed without any decomposition and let w_i^{ADD-DA} be the solution of ADD-DA as defined in Eq. (3), we have:*

$$w^{DA}/\Omega_i = w_i^{ADD-DA}, \ \forall i = 1, \ldots, s. \tag{10}$$

Proof: *As w^{DA} is the minimum of $J(w)$ as defined in Eq. (9), it yields:*

$$\nabla J(w^{DA}) = 0 \Leftrightarrow \nabla J/\Omega_i \left(w^{DA}/\Omega_i\right) = 0, \ \forall i = 1, \ldots, s$$

As $J/\Omega_i = J_i$, we have:

$$\nabla J_i \left(w^{DA}/\Omega_i\right) = 0, \ \forall i = 1, \ldots, s$$

As J_i is a convex function, the minimum is unique. Then the Eq. (10) is satisfied.

The Eq. (10) ensures that the accuracy obtained by the decomposition is maintained.

In Sect. 3, we validate the results provided in this section. We also show that the ADD approach reduces the execution time even if the implementation is not on a parallel computing environment.

3   Experimental Test Case

This work uses the three dimensional incompressible Navier-Stokes equations: continuity of mass (Eq. (11)) and momentum equations (Eq. (12)) as the full physical system.

$$\nabla \cdot \mathbf{u} = 0, \tag{11}$$

$$\frac{\partial \mathbf{u}}{\partial t} + \mathbf{u} \cdot \nabla \mathbf{u} = -\frac{1}{\rho}\nabla p + \nabla \cdot \tau \tag{12}$$

where $\mathbf{u} \equiv (u, v, w)^T$ is the velocity, $p = \tilde{p}/\rho_0$ is the normalised pressure ($\tilde{p}$ being the pressure and ρ_0 the constant reference density) and τ denotes the stress tensor. Further details of the equations solved and their implementation can be found in [1,5,11]. The dispersion of the pollution is described by the classic advection-diffusion equation such that the concentration of the pollution is seen as a passive scalar (Eq. (13)).

$$\frac{\partial c}{\partial t} + \nabla.(\mathbf{u}c) = \nabla. \left(\overline{\overline{\kappa}}\nabla c\right) + F \tag{13}$$

where $\overline{\overline{\kappa}}$ is the diffusivity tensor (m^2/s) and F represents the source terms (kg/m^3/s), i.e. the pollution generated by a source point for example.

The capability of ADD-DA has been estimated using a realistic case representing a real urban area located in London South Bank University (LSBU) in Elephant and Castle, South London, UK (Fig. 2). The computational domain includes 767,559 nodes (Fig. 2b). In air pollution problems, we are interested in optimising the concentration field of the pollutant as well as the spread of it into the domain. In this work, a point source of pollution, mimicking pollution generated by traffic in a busy intersection, is located into the domain (red sphere in Fig. 2a) with a source term equal to 1 kg/m^3/s and the dispersion behaviour of it is simulated for a westerly wind (blue arrows in Fig. 2a). Observed values of the state variable are provided by sensors from positions randomly located among the buildings.

(a)   (b)

Fig. 2. (a) Computational domain and (b) surface mesh of the test site: the London South Bank University (LSBU), London (UK) area. In (a) the red sphere denotes the location of the source and the blue arrows the wind direction. (Color figure online)

ADD-DA combined with Fluidity is a fully-parallel program, using the Message Passing Interface (MPI) library to communicate information between processors. The *supermesh* is decomposed into sub-domains *.vtu* files and *.halo* files, the latest ones containing information on overlapping regions. The *.vtu* files are read in the ADD-DA algorithm. In each of these sub-domains, ADD-DA computes the background covariance matrices (Step 4 in Algorithm 1) and computes the solution of the assimilation process (Steps 9-13 in Algorithm 1). Algorithm 1 has been implemented and tested on 3 high performance nodes equipped with bi-Xeon E5-2650 v3 CPU and 250 GB of RAM.

The accuracy of the ADD-DA results is evaluated by the mean squared error on each subdomain:

$$MSE(u_i) = \frac{\|u_i - u_i^C\|_{L^2}}{\|u_i^C\|_{L^2}} \tag{14}$$

computed with respect to a control variable u_i^C, for $i = 1, \ldots, s$ and s still denotes the number of sub-domains. The global mean squared error is then defined by: $MSE(u) = mean_i\{MSE(u_i)\}$.

Figure 3a shows the values of $MSE(u^{\mathcal{M}})$ and $MSE(u^{ADD-DA})$ as a function of the number of sub-domains which constitute the decomposition. The sub-domains are labeled by the ID of processors p, i.e. $s = p$. For each domain decomposition made of $p = 4, 8, 16, 32$ sub-domains, the value of $MSE(u^{\mathcal{M}})$ is greater than the $MSE(u^{ADD-DA})$. It has also confirmed in Fig. 3b which shows the values of the difference between $MSE(u^{\mathcal{M}})$ and $MSE(u^{DA})$.

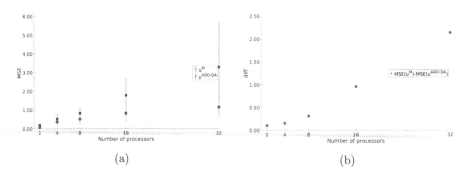

(a)   (b)

Fig. 3. (a) MSE of model background $(u^{\mathcal{M}})$ and ADD-DA (u^{ADD-DA}) as a function of the number of processors. The markers depict the MSE, and the error bars their standard deviations, for the assimilation of pollutant concentration, and (b) Error reduction as a function of the number of processors.

We evaluated the execution time needed to compute the solution of the ADD-DA model by Algorithm 1. Let $T_s(n)$ denotes the execution time of the Algorithm 1 for a domain decomposition made of s sub-domains. We still assume that $p = s$, where p denotes the number of processors and we pose

$$T_s(n) = max\{T_{s_i}(n_i)\}_{i=1,\dots,s} \tag{15}$$

where $T_{s_i}(n_i)$ denotes the execution time for each processor on each sub-domain. The total execution time is shown in Table 1. There is a clear decreasing trend in the total execution time with the increase of number of processors. Is is also confirmed by the values of speed-up computed as $S_s = T_1(n)/T_s(n)$.

Table 1. Execution times for $s = p$.

p	T_p (seconds)	S_s	$\hat{S}_p$
1	2.80×10^3	–	–
4	8.04×10^2	3.48	4
8	3.63×10^2	7.71	8
10	3.06×10^2	9.15	10
16	1.96×10^2	14.3	16
32	3.35×10^2	11.9	32

As described in the Fluidity manual [1], it is suggested to have at least $50,000$ nodes per processor in Fluidity to have full advantage of the parallelisation. It is due to the surface-to-volume ratio [2] which becomes too big for small sub-domains. As the number of nodes in our simulation is $n = 767,559$, the optimal number of processors to use to run Fluidity is supposed to be less than $p = \frac{767,559}{50,000} \simeq 15$. The optimal number of processors computed and suggested by Fluidity [1], for the computational domain in Fig. 2b, is made of $p = 10$ sub-domains. This constraint affects the ADD-DA execution time as confirmed by the results of speed-up in Table 1. In fact, the total execution time of ADD-DA using 10 processors is 306 s, while using one processor is 2800 s with a speed-up of 9.15. Increasing the number of processors, we start to lose gain in terms of speed-up compared with the theoretical one $\hat{S}_p = p$. We observed a reduction of the execution time even if ADD-DA implements a decomposition of s sub-domains but Algorithm 1 runs on one processor, i.e. $s \neq p$. In fact, we tested ADD-DA implementing a First In First Out (FIFO) queue processing the sub-domains of the decomposition on $p = 1$ processor and we have seen that the total execution time of ADD-DA for a decomposition of $s = 32$ sub-domains is 9.48×10^2 s. Even if the gain in terms of Speed-Up is only 2.95, this result underlines the gain we have in introducing Adaptive Domain Decomposition on top of the math stack, i.e. in the mathematical model. This results is due to the complexity of the numerical model which decreases when we introduce the ADD. In fact, the time complexity of Algorithm 1 is $\tau(n) \simeq m \times n^2$ where m is the truncation parameter for the TSVD (Step 6 of Algorithm 1) and n is the number of points of the *supermesh*. If we assume that the time needed to perform $\tau(n)$ floating point operations is $T(n) = \tau(n) \times t_{flop}$, where t_{flop} denotes the unitary time required for the execution of one floating point operation, we have in our case

$$T(n) = m \times n^2 \times t_{flop} \tag{16}$$

Assumed that $n = \sum_{i=1}^{s} n_i$ and assuming a fixed truncation parameter m, the (16) gives:

$$T(n) = m \times \left(\sum_{i=1}^{s} n_i \right)^2 \times t_{flop} \tag{17}$$

Due to the properties of the square of a polynomial, the (17) gives

$$T(n) = m \times \left(\sum_{i=1}^{s} n_i \right)^2 \times t_{flop} > m \times \sum_{i=1}^{s} n_i^2 \times t_{flop} \tag{18}$$

$$= \sum_{i=1}^{s} m \times n_i^2 \times t_{flop} = \sum_{i=1}^{s} T_{s_i}(n_i) > max\{T_{s_i}(n_i)\} = T_s(n)$$

which gives $T_s(n) < T(n)$ where $T_s(n)$ still denotes the execution time defined in (15) and $T(n)$ is the execution time when the algorithm does not implement any decomposition.

(a) $u^{\mathcal{M}}$: predicted pollutant concentration field

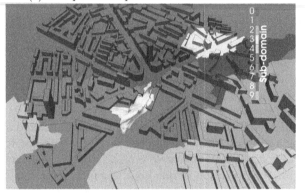

(b) v: observed pollutant concentration field

(c) u^{DA}: assimilated pollutant concentration field

Fig. 4. Iso-surface, in white, of the pollutant concentration for 5.10^{-1} kg/m^3 computed in parallel with $p = 10$ and generated by a point source.

Figure 4 shows the impact of ADD-DA on the iso-surface of the pollutant concentration for 5.10^{-1} kg/m^3 computed in parallel with $p = 10$ processors and generated by a point source. Figure 4a shows the results predicted by Fluidity, i.e. $u^{\mathcal{M}}$, while Fig. 4b shows the observed data, i.e. v. Values v are assimilated in parallel by ADD-DA to correct the forecasting data $u^{\mathcal{M}}$. The assimilated data after the ADD-DA process, i.e. u^{ADD-DA}, are then obtained (Fig. 4c).

Conclusions and future works are presented in next section where we propose the next steps towards the development of a scalable data assimilation software for accurate air pollution prediction in big cities.

4 Conclusions and Future Work

We presented a parallel Data Assimilation model based on Adaptive Domain Decomposition (ADD-DA) coupled with the open-source, finite-element, fluid dynamics model Fluidity. The model is defined on a partition of the domain in sub-domains without overlapping regions. We provided experimental results for pollutant dispersion within an urban environment. We proved that the ADD-DA model provides the same numerical solution of the sequential model. We have also shown that the ADD approach reduces the execution time even when the implementation is not on a parallel computing environment. An implementation of ADD-DA for improving air pollution prediction in big boroughs of London (as the one shown in Fig. 5) has been developed as future work. In that case we are implementing a multi-level parallelism. Starting from the Adaptive Domain Decomposition, the sub-domains are distributed on parallel processing units and, each sub-domain, is decomposed in sub-sub-domains to implement a First In First Out (FIFO) queue as we have seen it provides a further improvements in terms of reduction of the execution time.

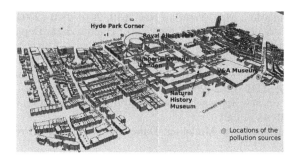

Fig. 5. Computational domain in the South West London area. The corresponding surface mesh is made of 12,9 millions of nodes.

Acknowledgments. This work is supported by the EPSRC Grand Challenge grant "Managing Air for Green Inner Cities" (MAGIC) EP/N010221/1, by the EPSRC Centre for Mathematics of Precision Healthcare EP/N0145291/1 and the EP/T003189/1 Health assessment across biological length scales for personal pollution exposure and its mitigation (INHALE).

References

1. I.C.L. AMCG: Fluidity manual v4.1.12 (2015). https://figshare.com/articles/Fluidity_Manual/1387713
2. Arcucci, R., D'Amore, L., Carracciuolo, L., Scotti, G., Laccetti, G.: A decomposition of the Tikhonov regularization functional oriented to exploit hybrid multilevel parallelism. Int. J. Parallel Program., pp. 1214–1235. (2016). https://doi.org/10.1007/s10766-016-0460-3
3. Arcucci, R., D'Amore, L., Pistoia, J., Toumi, R., Murli, A.: On the variational data assimilation problem solving and sensitivity analysis. J. Comput. Phys. **335**, 311–326 (2017)
4. Arcucci, R., Mottet, L., Pain, C., Guo, Y.K.: Optimal reduced space for variational data assimilation. J. Comput. Phys. **379**, 51–69 (2019)
5. Aristodemou, E., Bentham, T., Pain, C., Robins, A.: A comparison of Mesh-adaptive les with wind tunnel data for flow past buildings: mean flows and velocity fluctuations. Atmos. Environ. J. **43**, 6238–6253 (2009)
6. Asch, M., Bocquet, M., Nodet, M.: Data Assimilation: Methods, Algorithms, and Applications, vol. 11. SIAM, University City (2016)
7. Christie, M.A., Glimm, J., Grove, J.W., Higdon, D.M., Sharp, D.H., Wood-Schultz, M.M.: Error analysis and simulations of complex phenomena. Los Alamos Sci. **29** (2005)
8. Courtier, J.: A strategy for operational implementation of 4D-Var, using an incremental approach. Q. J. R. Meteorol. Soc. **120**(519), 1367–1387 (1994)
9. D'Amore, L., Arcucci, R., Marcellino, L., Murli, A.: A parallel three-dimensional variational data assimilation scheme. In: AIP Conference Proceedings, vol. 1389, pp. 1829–1831. AIP (2011)
10. Farina, R., Dobricic, S., Storto, A., Masina, S., Cuomo, S.: A revised scheme to compute horizontal covariances in an oceanographic 3D-Var assimilation system. J. Comput. Phys. **284**, 631–647 (2015)
11. Ford, R., Pain, C.C., Goddard, A.J.H., De Oliveira, C.R.E., Umpleby, A.P.: A non-hydrostatic finite-element model for three-dimensional stratified oceanic flows. Part I: model formulation. Mon. Weather Rev. **132**, 2816–2831 (2004)
12. Hannachi, A.: A primer for EOF analysis of climate data. Department of Meteorology, University of Reading, UK (2004)
13. Hannachi, A., Jolliffe, I., Stephenson, D.: Empirical orthogonal functions and related techniques in atmospheric science: a review. Int. J. Climatol.:J. R. Meteorol. Soc. **27**(9), 1119–1152 (2007)
14. Kalman, R.E.: A new approach to linear filtering and prediction problems. J. Basic Eng. **82**(1), 35–45 (1960)
15. Kalnay, E.: Atmospheric Modeling, Data Assimilation and Predictability. Cambridge (2003)
16. Lelieveld, J., Evans, J.S., Fnais, M., Giannadaki, D., Pozzer, A.: The contribution of outdoor air pollution sources to premature mortality on a global scale. Nature **525**(7569), 367 (2015)
17. Lorenc, A.: Development of an operational variational assimilation scheme. J. Meteorol. Soc. Jpn **75**, 339–346 (1997)
18. Lorenz, E.N.: Empirical orthogonal functions and statistical weather prediction (1956)
19. Nichols, N.K.: Mathematical concepts of data assimilation. In: Lahoz, W., Khattatov, B., Menard, R. (eds.) Data Assimilation, pp. 13–39. Springer, Heidelberg (2010). https://doi.org/10.1007/978-3-540-74703-1_2

20. Oke, P.R., Brassington, G.B., Griffin, D.A., Schiller, A.: The bluelink ocean data assimilation system (BODAS). Ocean Model. **21**(1–2), 46–70 (2008)
21. Pain, C., Umpleby, A., De Oliveira, C., Goddard, A.: Tetrahedral mesh optimisation and adaptivity for steady-state and transient finite element calculations. Comput. Methods Appl. Mech. Eng. **190**, 3771–3796 (2001)
22. Teruzzi, A., Di Cerbo, P., Cossarini, G., Pascolo, E., Salon, S.: Parallel implementation of a data assimilation scheme for operational oceanography: the case of the medbfm model system. Comput. Geosci. **124**, 103–114 (2019)

PMACS - Performance Monitoring and Analysis of Cluster Systems

Workshop on Performance Monitoring
and Analysis of Cluster Systems (PMACS)

Workshop Description

For a long time, hardware performance monitoring was used on a small scale to measure and analyze data of single application runs in order to detect performance limitations caused by hardware and/or software. Monitoring the whole cluster system for observing hardware failures has been the duty of system administrators with emphasis on operating the system and changes in the system parameters. In recent years, many HPC providers have extended or replaced their monitoring system to additionally track performance data from hardware monitoring facilities and even from the applications. The analysis of the data provides deeper insight in resource utilization and the quality of software. In addition, system administrators use performance data to track the causes of system instabilities to specific user codes. Due to the diversity of HPC centers, many tailored solutions for collection, storage, evaluation, and visualization exist today.

The goal of this workshop was the exchange of experience about various solutions on the collection, transmission, storage, evaluation, and visualization of runtime data about the hard- and software of whole cluster systems. Indeed, the presentations covered a lot of aspects:

- Luka Stanisic et al. presented MPCDF, a performance monitoring system that offers a lightweight open-source middleware to collect hardware and software performance monitoring data on compute nodes. After collecting the data, the system can aggregate and process it, enabling detailed per-cluster and per-job interactive analysis in a web browser. Additionally, the system can generate performance reports as PDF files so that users, system administrators, application support, and management can obtain and study the information.
- Philipp Neumann described a method for predicting run-times of simulation codes based on sparse grid regression. The ultimate goal of such prediction is to improve balance in the execution of parallel multi-model codes on HPC clusters. The runtime prediction uses on various dynamic and runtime-dependent parameters. Based on measurements using three applications in the domains of molecular dynamics and weather & climate, the approach shows good runtime prediction for up to five-dimensional parameter spaces using only a relatively low number of training samples.
- Gence Ozer et al. developed a resource-aware scheduling mechanism that can balance performance and fairness even in the presence of complex inter-job dependencies and highly variable resource requirements, as is the case in Electronic Design Automation workloads.
- Saurav Nanda et al. presented a supervised learning model which enables optimal selection of CPU frequency during the execution of a job, with the objective of minimizing the energy consumption of a HPC system.

These systems address different aspects of the monitoring and analysis challenges described above, yet all are related to performance evaluation, data management, and analytics, which were the main focus of the PMACS workshop. Hopefully, by bringing together the developers and users of such infrastructure we enabled ways for them to collaborate and exchange ideas for further developments.

We like to thank the Euro-Par Organization Committee and Program Committee for their support. A retake of the workshop is planned for Euro-Par 2020.

Organization

Program Chairs

Thomas Gruber	University Erlangen-Nuremberg, Germany
Anthony Danalis	University of Tennessee, USA

Program Committee

Ann Gentile	Sandia National Laboratories (SNL), USA
Michael Klemm	Intel Cooperation, Germany
Sameer Shende	Univesity of Oregon, USA
Julian Kunkel	University of Reading, UK
Heike Jagode	University of Tennessee, USA
Zhang Yang	Institute of Applied Physics and Computational Mathematics, China
Josef Weidendorfer	Technische Universität München, Leibniz Rechenzentrum der Bayerischen Akademie der Wissenschaften, Germany
Robert Dietrich	Technische Universität Dresden, Germany
Jack Deslippe	National Energy Research Scientific Computing Center, USA
Jonas Hahnfeld	RWTH Aachen, Germany
Erich Focht	NEC, Germany
Axel Auweter	Megware, Germany
Stephane Eranian	Google LLC, USA
Dmitry Nikitenko	Lomonosov Moscow State University, Russia

Sparse Grid Regression for Performance Prediction Using High-Dimensional Run Time Data

Philipp Neumann[1,2,3]($\boxtimes$) (iD)

[1] Universität Hamburg, Bundesstr. 45a, 20146 Hamburg, Germany
[2] Deutsches Klimarechenzentrum, Bundesstr. 45a, 20146 Hamburg, Germany
[3] Helmut-Schmidt-Universität, Holstenhofweg 85, 22043 Hamburg, Germany
`philipp.neumann@hsu-hh.de`

Abstract. We employ sparse grid regression to predict the run time in three types of numerical simulation: molecular dynamics (MD), weather and climate simulation. The impact of algorithmic, OpenMP/MPI and hardware-aware optimization parameters on performance is studied. We show that normalization of run time data via algorithmic complexity arguments significantly improves prediction accuracy. Mean relative prediction errors are in the range of few percent; in MD, a five-dimensional parameter space exploration results in mean relative prediction errors of ca. 15% using ca. 178 run time samples.

Keywords: Performance modeling · Sparse grids · Regression

1 Introduction

Increasing complexity of simulation software is observed in various science and and engineering disciplines. Examples comprise multi-component million-lines-of-code climate models [1] or multiscale multi-model simulations which combine several solver components with applications in biology [2], fusion [3], or fluid dynamics [4]. This complexity translates into a multitude of run time-relevant parameters and parameter dependencies, such as

- algorithmic parameters (convergence criteria, mesh sizes, time steps, etc.),
- hardware-aware optimization parameters (blocking parameters for cache reuse, contiguous data alignment settings, etc.),
- parallelization settings (number of MPI processes/OpenMP threads, etc.),
- scenario-dependent parameters (domain size, number of particles, etc.).

For example, sampling vapor-liquid equilibria in molecular dynamics (MD) requires parallelized simulations, executed at various density values and particle numbers. This already yields three dependencies (parallelization, density, particle number). Knowledge and prediction of the actual run time is beneficial in this case to optimally distribute the required MD simulation ensembles on

© Springer Nature Switzerland AG 2020
U. Schwardmann et al. (Eds.): Euro-Par 2019 Workshops, LNCS 11997, pp. 601–612, 2020.
https://doi.org/10.1007/978-3-030-48340-1_46

a HPC cluster. Another example is given by high-resolution weather ensemble simulations. These simulations come with many physical and technical parameters influencing performance, and they require extreme-scale HPC capacity for execution. Also, accurate performance predictions allow to efficiently distribute and schedule the ensembles on a supercomputer, while still obeying to tight production schedules of, e.g., the underlying systems of a weather service.

In the following, we show that regression on sparse grids combined with local refinement allows to sufficiently discretize high-dimensional parameter spaces and yields accurate run time predictions.

We present sparse grid regression in Sect. 2 which follows the methodology from [5]. Related work on performance prediction and sparse grid regression is discussed in Sect. 3. We detail our parametrization and evaluation procedure for the performance prediction in Sect. 4.1 and provide the analysis for the MD simulation *SimpleMD* [4] and a weather/climate model *ICON* [6] in Sects. 4.2, 4.3. We summarize our findings and give an outlook to future work in Sect. 5.

2   Sparse Grids

2.1   Regular Sparse Grids

In the following, the space spanned by the performance-relevant parameters is scaled to the unit hyper-cube. The native form of d-dimensional sparse grids arises from a smart combination of anisotropic Cartesian grids and d-linear hat functions $\varphi_{l,i}$ as basis functions, with the latter defined over the Cartesian grid points $\boldsymbol{x}_{l,i} := (2^{-l_1}i_1, ..., 2^{-l_d}i_d)$ [5,7]. Given subspaces $W_l := span\{\varphi_{l,i}(x) : i \in I_l\}$ and index vectors $I_l := \{\boldsymbol{i} : 1 \leq i_j \leq 2^{l_j} - 1, i_j \text{ odd}, 1 \leq j \leq d\}$, a level-$n$ *sparse grid* arises from the following combination of the subspaces:

$$V_n := \bigoplus_{|l|_1 \leq n+d-1} W_l. \tag{1}$$

The finest grid point distance (i.e., mesh size) in V_n is given by $h_n := 2^{-n}$. Figure 1(a) illustrates this discretization for a level-3 grid (i.e., showing V_3 in terms of grid points). In the following, $\boldsymbol{x}$ contains the run time-relevant parameters, and we search for a function $u(\boldsymbol{x}) \in V_n$ which approximates the run time of a program $t(\boldsymbol{x}) \approx u(\boldsymbol{x})$. Sparse grids are powerful for *high-dimensional, sufficiently smooth* problems: while the number of grid points and hat functions at level n is $O(h_n^{-d})$ for a regular Cartesian grid, sparse grids only require $O(h_n^{-1}(\log h_n^{-1})^{d-1})$ functions while still exhibiting accurate approximation properties [5,7].

The given discretization only covers inner parts of the hyper-cube and, thus, results in zero boundary values. We follow [5] by defining the constant basis function $1 =: \varphi_{1,1} \in W_1$ and extrapolating values towards the outer boundaries for all other basis functions that are closest to it.

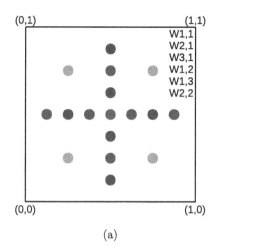 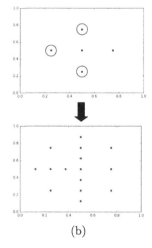

(a)   (b)

Fig. 1. (a) Two-dimensional, level-3 sparse grid. The grid points are colored according to their basis function's subspace W_l. (b) Local refinement for a 2D, level-2 sparse grid. One refinement step is carried out in which $m = 3$ marked grid points are refined (Color figure online)

2.2 Regression

Given a set of simulation run times y_j for parametrizations $\boldsymbol{x}_j$, $j = 1, ..., M$, we aim at training the sparse grid and optimizing a function $v(\boldsymbol{x}) := \sum_i \alpha_i \varphi_i(\boldsymbol{x})$, with i looping over the span of V_n (for simplicity, $\varphi_i(\boldsymbol{x})$ corresponds to each hat function), to match the run times:

$$u = \arg\min_{v \in V_n} \left(\frac{1}{M} \sum_{j=1}^{M} (y_j - v(\boldsymbol{x}_j))^2 + \lambda C(v) \right), \tag{2}$$

with regularization terms $C(v)$, $\lambda \in \mathbb{R}^+$, to enforce smoothness of the solution; we use $C(v) := \|\alpha\|_2^2$ due to its simplicity and effectiveness [5]. Minimization in Eq.(2) results in a linear system

$$\left(\frac{1}{M} BB^\top + \lambda \mathbb{1} \right) \alpha = \frac{1}{M} B\boldsymbol{y}, \tag{3}$$

with $B_{i,j} := \varphi_i(\boldsymbol{x}_j)$ and identity matrix $\mathbb{1}$.

2.3 Adaptivity

To further improve function approximations, sparse grids can be extended by adaptivity [8,9]. We employ local adaptivity [9]: given training data points $\boldsymbol{x}_j$, the pointwise error $e_j := t(\boldsymbol{x}_j) - v(\boldsymbol{x}_j) = t(\boldsymbol{x}_j) - \sum_i \alpha_i \varphi_i(\boldsymbol{x}_j)$ is computed and the contribution of each basis function $c_i := \sum_{j=1}^{M} |\varphi_i(\boldsymbol{x}_j) \alpha_i e_j^2|$ is calculated.

Given a number of local refinements m per iteration, m grid points are refined, which exhibit the largest contributions c_i. A refinement example is shown in Fig. 1(b). Instead of searching for $u \in V_n$, we thus search in the following for $u \in V_n^{r,m}$, with $V_n^{r,m}$ denoting all spaces that arise from r successive refinement steps applied to V_n with m grid point refinements per step.

3   Related Work

Performance modeling for individual applications based on hardware and software characteristics is widely employed, see amongst others [10,11]. Generating and combining performance models for different hardware and software components via a performance modeling framework is presented in [12], with a focus rather on predicting the performance of a complex application on another hardware than under different parameter settings. Cache miss counts and run times are predicted in [13] across different pieces of hardware through a toolkit, which semi-automatically measures and models application characteristics. Analytical performance models and their automatic generation are addressed in [14] to detect scalability bugs in complex applications. Regression methods and neural networks for performance prediction are discussed in [15–18], achieving prediction errors of typically few percent—a similar accuracy as targeted in this work, yet it is hard to compare the methods due to different applications under consideration. Neural networks have further been used predict the run time for combinatorial problems in artificial intelligence, which is a highly non-trivial task due to high run time variations [19]. Deep learning has been shown to yield accurate run time predictions over a multitude of applications running on a HPC cluster, considering a dataset with 300,000 job executions [20]. In the following, sparse grid-based run time predictions are particularly considered for single applications that respond rather smoothly to parameter changes.

The motivation to consider locally refined sparse grids for performance data regression is two-fold. First, sparse grids hierarchically cover the parameter space and, thus, locally adapt their resolution to run time features. Sparse grid-based regression [5,21] has been used in various applications, including option pricing [5,22], or the photometric estimation of cosmological redshifts [5]. Second, convergence rates and upper error bounds for least squares regression on sparse grids have been investigated in [23], allowing for a mathematical explicability of, in our case, the runtime predictions. A variant of sparse grid regression based on the optimized combination technique is presented in [24].

4   Results

4.1   Evaluation Procedure

We evaluate the regression methodology from Sect. 2 in three cases: *SimpleMD*, *ICON Node-Level* and *ICON Multi-Node*. All run time samples were measured on a system equipped with dual-socket Broadwell nodes, each node comprising

2×18 cores at 2.1 GHz. We make use of the sparse grid toolbox SG++ [5], version 2.1.0, and its Python bindings to implement the regression. To avoid overfitting, we set the maximum number of sparse grid points to $\leq 50\%$ of the number of run time samples $t(\boldsymbol{x}_j)$ that are used for training. We further restrict our initial grids to level-2 and level-3 grids, which are subsequently locally refined. Level-3 grids are only considered for bigger sample counts. We set the number of points to be refined to $m = 3$ which provides–given rather small-sized sparse grid structures–a compromise between improved accuracy while (mostly) abstaining from creating regular level-n grids through the refinement procedure. The maximum number of refinement steps is set to $r = 3$. The adaptivity criterion and the 50%-rule from above imply that a level-2 or level-3 grid may be refined once or several times, or not at all. For example, given a number of run time samples for training (named *learning size* in the following), a level-2 solution might be based on a level-2 grid with several levels of refinement and thus a rather high level of local accuracy, while a corresponding level-3 grid might not have been refined at all and thus does not feature any kind of local improvements. We solve the linear system from Eq. (3) with the CG solver provided by SG++. Its accuracy parameter is set to $1e - 4$, and we allow a maximum of 1000 CG iteration steps to ensure that convergence errors are negligible in all experiments. Sensitivity studies for the smoothing parameter λ did not reveal significant influence on the solutions (not reported in the following); we use $\lambda = 1e - 6$.

Given a number of samples, we split this set into a fraction $0.1 \leq s < 0.9$ to train our sparse grid by solving the regression problem. The remaining fraction $1 - s$ is used for validation. To investigate the prediction accuracy, we evaluate the relative error on validation and training samples and compute the *average relative error* (averaged over all samples in either validation or training set). Average relative errors on training/validation set are considered separately to check for potential overfitting/accuracy. To assess the effects of the random splitting, we carry out this evaluation 10 times for different splittings and compute the mean of the average relative error, referred to as *mean relative error*, and its standard deviation. Consecutive random splittings will automatically result in differently refined grids. Therefore, we report on two takes *Take1* and *Take2* of this procedure, with each take consisting of 10 repetitions of the sparse grid regression on randomly split data with mean and standard deviation evaluation.

4.2   SimpleMD

This case considers the parallel execution of the single-site Lennard-Jones short-range MD simulation *SimpleMD* [4]. Particles within a prescribed *cut-off radius* r_c interact via force fields. This procedure is implemend in *SimpleMD* through the linked cell algorithm [25]. Considerations are restricted to homogeneous 3D particle systems in a cubic, periodic domain. Although simplistic, this scenario allows to study the influence of various important parameters on performance:

Density ρ: the particle density corresponds to the number of molecules per volume. Linearly increasing the number of particles (and, thus, density) within the cut-off region implies a locally linear increase in computational cost and run time t, $t \propto \rho$. However, depending on the vectorization and underlying implementation, other scalings may be observed, see, e.g., [26].

Number of molecules N: The linked-cell method results in an $O(N)$ algorithm with N being the number of molecules, suggesting a run time $t \propto N$. Yet, performance may deviate from the linear behavior due to cache effects or threading (the latter is not considered in this work).

Cut-off radius r_c: Increasing r_c is similar to increasing density, implying a run time $t \propto r_c^3$. Yet, the actual application and its accuracy constraints dictate how r_c and ρ must actually be chosen.

Blocksize: this parameter determines the level of contiguous memory allocation and denotes the number of molecules that are allocated en bloque. If additional particles need to be inserted (for example due to boundary conditions) and all blocks are entirely filled, at least one block of *blocksize* particles is allocated.

Number of MPI processes P: SimpleMD employs a regular domain decomposition. Optimal parallel efficiency suggests a run time dependency $t \propto 1/P$.

We generated 357 random configurations for this parameter space, see Table 1; min/max run times per time step reach from 7.3e-4 s to 1.1 s. Each configuration was executed 3× and run times were averaged to provide denoised run time data.

Table 1. Randomized sampling procedure for the case *SimpleMD*

Parameter	Parameter range	Random sampling
Density	$[0.3; 0.9]$	Uniform distribution
Number of molecules	$[1\,000; 100\,000]$	Uniform distribution
Cut-off radius	$[1.2; 4.5]$	Uniform distribution
Block size	$[10; 1\,000]$	Uniform distribution
Processes	$\{1, 2, 4, 8\}$	Uniform sampling from index set $\{0, 1, 2, 3\}$

Performing regression directly on the run time data resulted in very poor approximations due to the high ratio of max/min run time $1.1\,s/7.3e - 4\,s = 1507$. We therefore normalized the run time t according to all aforementioned proportionalities and use these values $t_c := t\rho^{-1}r_c^{-3}N^{-1}P$ in the regression process. This results in a max/min run time ratio of 7 and a much smoother, sparse grid-friendly run time representation. The mean relative errors for two takes in Fig. 2 indicate minor variability between the takes. The mean relative error (incl. standard deviation bars) on the validation data drops below 15% for a learning size of ca. 50%, corresponding to ca. 178 training samples to approximate the 5-dimensional parameter space. Differences between level-2 and level-3 adaptively refined sparse grids are rather marginal for larger training sets, with the level-3 grid performing worse for smaller training sets.

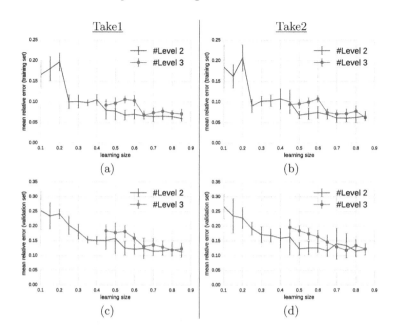

Fig. 2. Mean relative error analysis for two takes of *SimpleMD*. The errors on train-
ing/validation sets and their standard deviations are shown in (a),(b)/(c),(d) with
regard to 10 repetitions per take. Each plot shows the dependency of the errors on the
learning size s for spatially adaptive sparse grids, that are locally refined from either
level 2 or level 3

We compared the sparse grid regression to polynomial regression with first-
and second-order polynomials using Python's module sklearn, cf. Fig. 3. Expect-
edly, polynomial and sparse grid regression perform equally well on small learning
sizes. For bigger learning sizes, sparse grids outperform the other two approaches.
Note that the degree of approximation remains fixed in the polynomial regressions (with 5/20 degrees of freedom for first- and second-order polynomials),
while the number of sparse grid points increases with increasing learning size: a
learning size $s \leq 20\%, 45\%$ resulted in 11, 38–39 grid points.

4.3   ICON

The ICOsahedral Nonhydrostatic (ICON) model [6] is used for climate and
weather predictions, amongst others in the production schedules of the German Weather Service. ICON computes these predictions on triangular horizontal
meshes that arise from a successive refinement of an icosahedron. The horizontal grid cells are blown up to prism-like columns of cells to incorporate vertical
physics. We restrict considerations to configurations of global atmosphere-only
simulations, employing the dynamical core to solve the atmospheric equations
of motion, radiation, and particular physics parametrizations.

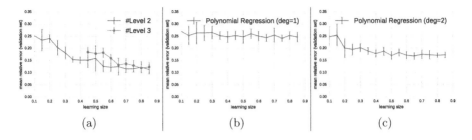

Fig. 3. Comparison of different regression techniques for *SimpleMD*, considering the mean relative error on the validation set. (a) Take 1 of the sparse grid regression, (b) regression with first-order polynomials, (c) regression with quadratic polynomials

ICON Single-Node. The climate case *ICON Single-Node* uses the ICON V16.0 benchmark[1] and considers an Earth-like planet without any land mass. The planet is resolved horizontally with a mesh size of 160 km and its atmosphere (i.e., vertically) by 90 levels. We consider (1) the number of OpenMP threads (1/2/4/6/8/12/18/36 threads) and (2) the parameter *nproma* $\in \{8, 16, 24, 32\}$, which is an ICON-specific blocking parameter for the vertical columns. Every configuration was executed twice, and the averaged run time was used for the regression. We saturate one full dual-socket Broadwell node including hyper-threading in every experiment (the choice of OpenMP threads prescribes the number of MPI processes). Such experiments are useful to determine the optimal node-level configuration, which would outperform the other potential configurations typically by few percent. The full node saturation implies a rather flat (smooth) performance profile over all 32 configurations. Note that, in contrast to *SimpleMD* which aims to explore the entire parameter space, *ICON Single-Node* shall rather investigate, if and to what extent the sparse grid regression can accurately predict marginal performance differences: while errors of 10–20% are perfectly acceptable in *SimpleMD*, such accuracies would not deliver any insight into the performance data of *ICON Single-Node* which exhibit a max/min run time ratio of 1.14. Due to the small number of *ICON Single-Node* configurations, the prescribed sparse grid parametrization for spatial adaptivity always results in a two-dimensional, level-3 sparse grid. Figure 4 shows that mean relative errors decay to ≤3%. More run time data (i.e., bigger learning sizes) only marginally improve accuracy since the overall number of available data is very limited.

ICON Multi-node. This case corresponds to a global high-resolution weather simulation using a horizontal 5 km mesh; this is a cutting-edge simulation setup in terms of resolution and corresponding physics parametrization [11,27] and it is subject to current research and analysis. We consider the following parameters in our performance prediction method:

---

[1] https://redmine.dkrz.de/projects/icon-benchmark/wiki/Instructions_on_download_execution_and_analysis_ICON_Benchmark_v160.

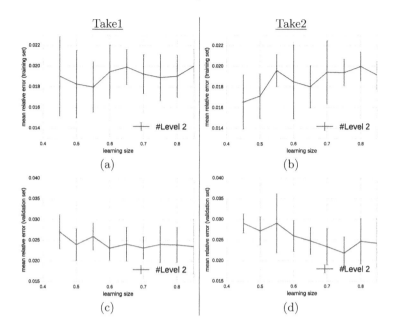

Fig. 4. Mean relative error analysis for two takes of *ICON Node-Level*. The errors on training/validation sets and their standard deviations are shown in (a),(b)/(c),(d). Each plot shows the dependency of the errors on the learning size s for level-3, non-adaptive sparse grids (created through the refinement applied to level-2 grids)

Number of OpenMP threads: the number of threads $(1/2/4/6/12/18$ threads) is varied. To fully saturate each compute node, the number of MPI ranks is adapted correspondingly as in *ICON Single-Node*.

Total number of nodes P: the number of nodes is varied in the strong scaling sense, $P \in \{100, 200, 300, 400\}$, resulting in a run time $t \propto 1/P$.

Number of vertical levels L: approaching the kilometer-resolving regime in these weather simulations, it is unclear how many vertical levels are required for an accurate representation of atmospheric physics. We varied $L \in \{60, 70, 80, 90\}$ and assume a linear relation to run time, $t \propto L$.

The parameter nproma: a blocking parameter, cf. *ICON Single-Node*.

Every configuration was executed twice, and the averaged, normalized run time $t_c = tL^{-1}P$ was used for the regression, showing a max/min run time ratio of 1.94. Training with only 40 configurations (that is a learning size $s = 0.1$) is sufficient to achieve mean relative errors (incl. standard deviation bars) of $\leq 10\%$, cf. Fig. 5. The errors basically drop to 6% for >200 training configurations.

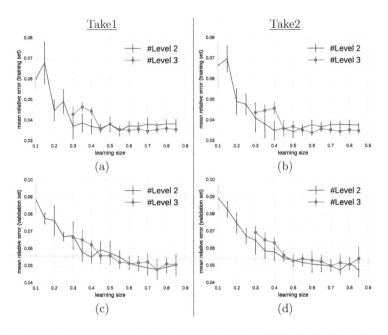

Fig. 5. Mean relative error analysis for two takes of *ICON Multi-Node*. The errors on training/validation sets and their standard deviations are shown in (a),(b)/(c),(d). Each plot shows the dependency of the errors on the learning size s for spatially adaptive sparse grids, that are successively refined from either level 2 or level 3

5   Conclusions and Future Work

We have investigated sparse grid regression to predict run times for numerical simulations that depend on the choice of algorithmic, MPI/OpenMP and hardware-aware optimization parameters, resulting in a (potentially) high-dimensional parameter space. Considering single- and multi-node experiments, we are confident that the sparse grid regression is an effective approach for a variety of prediction problems. To obtain sufficiently smooth run time data to make sparse grids feasible, we normalized the run times according to complexity arguments, which is similar to dimensional analysis. This normalization can be substantial—for the case *SimpleMD* with a five-dimensional parameter space, it reduced the max/min run time ratio by more than two orders of magnitude. Most regressions yielded mean relative run time prediction errors of few percent–which is more than sufficient for applications such as efficient scheduling and distribution of simulation ensembles, considering the fact that performance reproducibility is a difficult topic on its own. Compared to polynomial regression, sparse grids performed equally well for moderate numbers of training samples. They do, however, pay off for bigger numbers of samples and in higher-dimensional problem settings such as the case *SimpleMD*, since they allow to locally adapt to the given run time data at acceptable discretization cost. Locally refined level-2 grids slightly outperformed refined level-3 grids, as level-2 grids feature a higher level of local adaptation to the run time profiles while using the same order of number of grid points.

Future work comprises, amongst others, comparisons with other methods such as neural networks, random forests or Gaussian process regression. Current work concentrates on collecting performance data on-the-fly and augmenting a sparse grid predictor with this information, resulting in a dynamically refining sparse grid and a continuously improving predictor.

Acknowledgements. Financial support by the Federal Ministry of Education and Research, Germany, grant number 01IH16008B (project TaLPas), and by the European project ESiWACE is acknowledged. ESiWACE has received funding from the European Union's Horizon 2020 research and innovation programme under grant agreement No 675191. P. Neumann thanks K. Brusch, R. Brown and P. Harder for initial works on sparse grid-based performance evaluations.

References

1. Flato, G.: Earth system models: an overview. Wiley Interdisc. Rev. Clim. Change **2**(6), 783–800 (2011)
2. Southern, J., et al.: Multi-scale computational modelling in biology and physiology. Prog. Biophys. Mol. Biol. **96**(1), 60–89 (2008)
3. Frauel, Y., et al.: Easy use of high performance computers for fusion simulations. Fusion Eng. Des. **87**(12), 2057–2062 (2012)
4. Neumann, P., Flohr, H., Arora, R., Jarmatz, P., Tchipev, N., Bungartz, H.J.: MaMiCo: software design for parallel molecular-continuum flow simulations. Comput. Phys. Commun. **200**, 324–335 (2016)
5. Pflüger, D.: Spatially Adaptive Sparse Grids for High-Dimensional Problems. Dr, Hut, Munich (2010)
6. Giorgetta, M., et al.: ICON-A, the atmosphere component of the ICON Earth System Model: I. Model description. J. Adv. Model. Earth Syst. **10**(7), 1613–1637 (2018)
7. Garcke, J.: Sparse grids in a nutshell. In: Garcke, J., Griebel, M. (eds.) Sparse Grids and Applications, pp. 57–80. Springer, Heidelberg (2013). https://doi.org/10.1007/978-3-642-31703-3_3
8. Gerstner, T., Griebel, M.: Dimension-adaptive tensor-product quadrature. Computing **71**, 65–87 (2003). https://doi.org/10.1007/s00607-003-0015-5
9. Pflüger, D.: Spatially adaptive refinement. In: Garcke, J., Griebel, M. (eds.) Sparse Grids and Applications, pp. 243–262. Springer, Heidelberg (2013). https://doi.org/10.1007/978-3-642-31703-3_12
10. Kerbyson, D., Alme, H., Hoisie, A., Petrini, F., Wasserman, H., Gittings, M.: Predictive performance and scalability modeling of a large-scale application. In: Proceedings of the 2001 ACM/IEEE Conference on Supercomputing, p. 39. ACM, New York (2001)
11. Neumann, P., et al.: Assessing the scales in numerical weather and climate predictions: will exascale be the rescue? Philos. Trans. R. Soc. A **377**(2142), 20180148 (2019)
12. Carrington, L., Snavely, A., Wolter, N.: A performance prediction framework for scientific applications. Future Gener. Comput. Syst. **22**(3), 336–346 (2006)

13. Marin, G., Mellor-Crummey, J.: Cross-architecture performance predictions for scientific applications using parameterized models. In: Proceedings of the Joint International Conference on Measurement and Modeling of Computer Systems SIGMETRICS 2004/Performance 2004, pp. 2–13. ACM, New York (2004)

14. Calotoiu, A., Hoefler, T., Poke, M., Wolf, F.: Using automated performance modeling to find scalability bugs in complex codes. In: Proceedings of the International Conference on High Performance Computing, Networking, Storage and Analysis, pp. 45:1–45:12. ACM, New York (2013)

15. Barnes, B., Rountree, B., Lowenthal, D., Reeves, J., de Supinski, B., Schulz, M.: A regression-based approach to scalability prediction. In: Proceedings of the 22nd Annual International Conference on Supercomputing, pp. 368–377. ACM, New York (2008)

16. Ipek, E., de Supinski, B.R., Schulz, M., McKee, S.A.: An approach to performance prediction for parallel applications. In: Cunha, J.C., Medeiros, P.D. (eds.) Euro-Par 2005. LNCS, vol. 3648, pp. 196–205. Springer, Heidelberg (2005). https://doi.org/10.1007/11549468_24

17. Singh, K., et al.: Comparing scalability prediction strategies on an SMP of CMPs. In: D'Ambra, P., Guarracino, M., Talia, D. (eds.) Euro-Par 2010. LNCS, vol. 6271, pp. 143–155. Springer, Heidelberg (2010). https://doi.org/10.1007/978-3-642-15277-1_14

18. Lee, B., Brooks, D., de Supinski, B., Schulz, M., Singh, K., McKee, S.: Methods of inference and learning for performance modeling of parallel applications. In: Proceedings of the 12th ACM SIGPLAN Symposium on Principles and Practice of Parallel Programming, pp. 249–258. ACM, New York (2007)

19. Eggensperger, K., Lindauer, M., Hutter, F.: Neural networks for predicting algorithm runtime distributions. In: Proceedings of the Twenty-Seventh International Joint Conference on Artificial Intelligence (IJCAI 2018), pp. 1442–1448. International Joint Conferences on Artificial Intelligence Organization (2018)

20. Wyatt, M.R., Herbein, S., Gamblin, T., Moody, A., Ahn, D., Taufer, M.: PRIONN: predicting runtime and IO using neural networks. In: Proceedings of the 47th International Conference on Parallel Processing (ICPP 2018), pp. 46:1–46:12. ACM, New York (2018)

21. Garcke, J.: Maschinelles Lernen durch Funktionsrekonstruktion mit verallgemeinerten dnnen Gittern. Ph.D. thesis, University of Bonn (2004)

22. Dirnstorfer, S., Grau, A., Zagst, R.: High-dimensional regression on sparse grids applied to pricing moving window Asian options. Open J. Stat. **3**, 427–440 (2013)

23. Bohn, B.: On the convergence rate of sparse grid least squares regression. In: Garcke, J., Pflüger, D., Webster, C.G., Zhang, G. (eds.) Sparse Grids and Applications – Miami 2016. LNCSE, vol. 123, pp. 19–41. Springer, Cham (2018). https://doi.org/10.1007/978-3-319-75426-0_2

24. Garcke, J.: Regression with the optimised combination technique. In: Proceedings of the 23rd International Conference on Machine Learning, pp. 321–328. ACM, New York (2006)

25. Griebel, M., Knapek, S., Zumbusch, G.: Numerical Simulation in Molecular Dynamics - Numerics, Algorithms, Parallelization, Applications. Springer, Heidelberg (2007). https://doi.org/10.1007/978-3-540-68095-6

26. Tchipev, N., et al.: TweTriS: twenty trillion-atom simulation. Int. J. High Perform. Comput. Appl. **33**, 838–854 (2019)

27. Klocke, D., Brueck, M., Hohenegger, C., Stevens, B.: Rediscovery of the doldrums in storm-resolving simulations over the tropical Atlantic. Nat. Geosci. **10**, 891–896 (2017)

MPCDF HPC Performance Monitoring System: Enabling Insight via Job-Specific Analysis

Luka Stanisic[(✉)] and Klaus Reuter

Max Planck Computing and Data Facility,
Gießenbachstraße 2, 85748 Garching, Germany
{luka.stanisic,klaus.reuter}@mpcdf.mpg.de

Abstract. This paper reports on the design and implementation of the HPC performance monitoring system deployed to continuously monitor performance metrics of all jobs on the HPC systems at the Max Planck Computing and Data Facility (MPCDF). Thereby it reveals important information to various stakeholders, in particular to users, application support, system administrators, and management. On each compute node, hardware and software performance monitoring data is collected by our newly developed lightweight open-source *hpcmd* middleware which builds upon standard Linux tools. The data is transported via rsyslog, and aggregated and processed by a Splunk system, enabling detailed per-cluster and per-job interactive analysis in a web browser. Additionally, performance reports are provided to the users as PDF files. Finally, we report on practical experience and benefits from large-scale deployments on MPCDF HPC systems, demonstrating how our solution can be useful to any HPC center.

Keywords: HPC · Cluster monitoring · Performance analysis

1 Introduction

HPC systems are highly expensive facilities that are rapidly evolving with respect to computational power, complexity, and size. More and more scientific disciplines use HPC resources in their research process to gain insight from numerical simulations or from data analytics. Hence, it is essential to strive to maximize the performance of the applications running on these precious resources. However, an efficient usage requires expert knowledge in parallel algorithms and programming, and a lot of effort spent on optimization and parameter tuning. This point became more important in recent years with the advent of processors with many cores and accelerators, which made parallel programming even more complex. Having performance numbers available for each job is therefore essential for the stakeholders of the HPC system, first, to make them aware of potentially suboptimal usage of resources, and second, to enable them to take action to improve the way these resources are used.

© Springer Nature Switzerland AG 2020
U. Schwardmann et al. (Eds.): Euro-Par 2019 Workshops, LNCS 11997, pp. 613–625, 2020.
https://doi.org/10.1007/978-3-030-48340-1_47

Jobs on a HPC cluster are commonly orchestrated by a batch scheduler, which can easily provide usage statistics based on *allocated* resources. These are often quantified in terms of CPU or GPU hours, and have proven useful for accounting purposes. However, these numbers do not carry information about the actual resource *utilization*. Performance metrics measured for each job are therefore crucial to learn, e.g., about under-utilization of allocated resources (idle vector units, or idle cores and accelerators), or other problematic usage patterns.

Modern hardware provides a plethora of counters that can be used for performance monitoring. In addition to the arithmetic units, CPUs have performance monitoring units (PMUs) that can be programmed to count certain instructions (e.g., scalar and vectorized floating point operations) with very little performance overhead. Hardware such as GPUs and network adapters provides similar counters. These hardware-related metrics can be complemented by software-related metrics, obtainable from the Linux kernel or from system tools. Such metrics include information on the running processes, their memory footprint, filesystem-related counters, etc.

Selecting and efficiently collecting these metrics is a challenge which we address in the present work. We developed a new lightweight software daemon, *hpcmd*[1], that runs on each node, performs measurements periodically in the background, and finally writes the data to the syslog. The syslog lines from all nodes are then propagated to the Splunk framework, for which we have developed special dashboards to perform advanced interactive data analysis. As a service to the users, we also provide PDF reports downloadable for each job. These two main components, *hpcmd* and Splunk dashboards together with few additional scripts compose a comprehensive suite designed to continuously monitor the performance of all jobs on the HPC systems at the MPCDF. We believe that other centers could also benefit from our system.

In the following, we first elaborate on the insight and benefits the various stakeholders of an HPC system may draw from a performance monitoring system. Second, we discuss related work before we describe in detail our solution in the main part of the paper. Finally, we illustrate several cases in which our system has already proven very useful, before closing with a summary.

2   Benefits from an HPC Performance Monitoring System

The following four groups of key stakeholders of an HPC system benefit from the insight enabled by HPC performance monitoring data.

Computational scientists and other users who run jobs on an HPC system typically have to apply for CPU hours. They have a strong intrinsic motivation to use the resources as efficiently as possible, in order to maximize the scientific knowledge they can obtain from the results. Based on HPC monitoring data, experienced users are often capable of identifying and fixing issues themselves, e.g., by applying appropriate compiler optimization for a specific architecture.

---

[1] hpcmd stands for HPC monitoring daemon.

Less skilled users might be motivated to approach application support when facing poor performance indicated by monitoring data.

Application support at a computing center provides technical support and is in charge of porting and optimizing applications for the HPC systems. HPC performance monitoring data enables application support to detect problematic jobs, and consequently, to proactively approach users who are potentially in need of assistance.

System administrators may benefit from performance monitoring data, e.g., to better judge the impact of software updates, security patches, and hardware settings. Potential changes in application performance after some maintenance work can be traced in an objective way based on current and historical performance data.

Management is interested in learning performance numbers that represent the actual resource utilization in addition to knowing the allocation of plain CPU hours, a metric that has been widely used up to now to quantify the resource share. Moreover, performance data gathered on present systems can be used to steer decisions for the procurement of future HPC clusters. For example, looking at a roofline plot with measurement data from most used applications enables decision makers to judge quickly if these applications are limited by the memory bandwidth or by the peak floating-point performance, and thereby if investing in new architectures with higher memory bandwidths would pay off. Similarly, analysis of network traffic may hint at applications that would benefit, e.g., from higher network bandwidth or lower latency. Finally, performance data documents to which degree GPUs are actually used, especially on multi-GPU nodes. In these respects, HPC performance monitoring data helps to close important information gaps.

3   Related Work

There are at least two big challenges regarding the implementation of a HPC performance monitoring system that have been addressed by various solutions in recent years.

The first, data-related, challenge is to choose which metrics should be tracked, how to interpret the collected data, how to identify performance bottlenecks, and how to ultimately detect if there is a significant problem in an application code. There are several software tools that can be used to analyze the performance of a running job. For example, for CPU codes, there are Linux perf [15], PAPI [3], LIKWID [14], and VTune [7], among others. These tools provide access to hardware counters which are then often analyzed using a "top-down" method [17]. One compares the counter values to the theoretical peak values of the machine and deduces how well the compute resources are utilized. However, there are cases when utilization values appear rather low even for well-optimized applications, e.g., due to the nature of the problem the code is solving or the required data structures. Hence, looking only at the utilization numbers can be misleading, and one needs to be careful before declaring that a job has a performance issue. To alleviate this effect, some researchers prefer to rely on cross-comparisons between different runs and applications [5], recently proposing machine learning techniques for such analysis [2,9].

The second, technical, challenge is to design and deploy a system that works reliably on (multiple) large HPC clusters while introducing minimal overhead, efficiently collects the data from many nodes into a centralized database, and provides a powerful framework for analysis and visualization. For example, the *TACC stat* framework has been developed to achieve these goals [4,5]. It combines information collected by various standard Linux tools and some custom tools, e.g., *REMORA* [10], to monitor resource utilization at the Texas Advanced Computing Center. Next, the *PerSyst* monitoring system developed at the Leibnitz Supercomputing Center comprises a hierarchical system of collectors and aggregators, a central database and a web interface to monitor large-scale HPC systems [6]. Thanks to the data aggregation using quantiles, this tool is well suited for jobs that run on a large number of nodes. The *LIKWID Monitoring Stack* targets small to medium scale systems [11]. It is partly based on the LIKWID performance tool suite developed by the same group of authors [14]. Finally, the *Lightweight Distributed Metric Service (LDMS)* was developed for performance monitoring at Sandia National Labs [1]. This framework provided very useful information for the system administrators and users, while having minimal impact on the application performance.

All the aforementioned solutions gave us valuable ideas and helped us to better define the goals for our approach. However, there are several reasons why we decided to develop our own system. Most importantly, all of these systems either rely on data-measurement software or on infrastructure setups (e.g., batch system configuration) that are specific to the center where they have been developed, and hence, would be difficult to adapt and maintain. Moreover, many of the existing approaches appear to rely on complex hierarchical communication layers and custom web-based visualization platforms, while we found ourselves in the convenient position to use rsyslog and Splunk systems that had already been deployed at the MPCDF for other monitoring purposes, e.g., the monitoring of the system "health" status.

4   Solution Architecture

In this section, we detail on how our system can obtain, collect, analyze, and present performance data from HPC clusters, addressing the needs of all stakeholder groups mentioned in Sect. 2.

Figure 1 presents a schematic overview on the architecture of the MPCDF HPC monitoring system. The design was motivated by the principle of simplicity and the focus on key questions which implied the reuse of existing infrastructure. To this end, our programming efforts focused on two major components (shown with red background in Fig. 1).

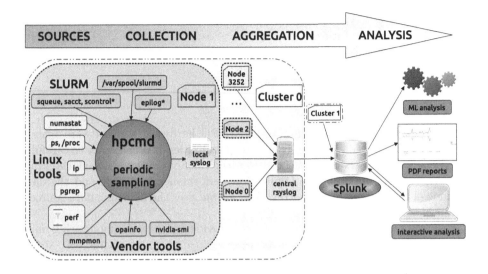

Fig. 1. Schematic showing the architecture of the MPCDF HPC monitoring system. The *hpcmd* middleware and various Splunk analysis dashboards were written by the authors, while the other infrastructure had already been existing. Automatic analysis using machine learning techniques is under development. (Color figure online)

The first component, labeled *hpcmd*, is a lightweight middleware that runs as a daemon in the background on each compute node, performs measurements at regular intervals, and computes derived metrics if necessary. A thorough evaluation of the overhead of *hpcmd* showed that the impact on the application performance is negligible, e.g., being much smaller than the influence of unavoidable machine and OS jitter on the application runtime. *hpcmd* is written in plain Python (both versions 2.7 and 3 are supported) and configurable via a flexible, hierarchical YAML configuration file. Measured values are simply written by *hpcmd* to syslog messages, forwarded via rsyslog, and finally fed into a Splunk repository.

The second major component are dashboards for Splunk written in XML, that we have developed for performance data analysis and visualization. The Splunk [12] platform excels in the analysis of large volumes of temporally ordered log-line data via a powerful query language. Hence, Splunk is suitable for crunching performance data collected from many nodes over long periods of time. After having collected performance data for nearly one year now, we do not notice any performance degradation and do not see any reason to limit the storage lifetime of the data. There are several viable alternatives to Splunk which could be used similarly, such as the open-source ELK (Elasticsearch, Logstash, Kibana) stack, the InfluxDB-Grafana stack, or even custom frameworks. However, the Splunk infrastructure was already installed and used at MPCDF systems for system monitoring, and thus it was the natural choice to employ it for performance monitoring as well. We are considering the aforementioned alternative solutions for evaluation in the future.

In the rest of this section, we detail on the different aspects of the data flow as depicted on the top of Fig. 1.

4.1   Data Sources

From a technical point of view, today's HPC hardware and software offer a plethora of metrics to look at. Given these possibilities, it is necessary to carefully choose a set of observables essential to yield valuable insight, and at the same time, keep the impact on the application performance negligible and the data volume of the measured values tractable. *hpcmd* uses the following data sources.

CPU Core Events: State-of-the-art CPUs provide performance monitoring units (PMUs) for each core. These can be programmed to count events, e.g., scalar and vector instructions, cache misses, and many more. Since the PMUs are additional programmable hardware units, the event counting induces only minimal overhead, typically not noticeable for the running scientific application.

CPU Uncore Events: In addition to the core PMUs, modern CPUs provide uncore PMUs that enable to monitor, e.g., the memory controller traffic and the traffic between different sockets. To access the core and uncore counters, the Linux *perf* subsystem is used.

GPU: At present, monitoring GPUs is much more difficult than CPUs due to the dependencies on proprietary tools and APIs from hardware vendors, as well as due to the lack of publicly available counter specifications. Nevertheless, it is possible to track some values, such as the memory occupation and the overall utilization, which we do using the *nvidia-smi* tool.

I/O: Large parallel file systems are crucial components of any HPC system. They are a shared resource, and wrong usage may affect not only a single problematic job but potentially even the whole system. Monitoring the I/O traffic and characteristics per node can give valuable hints at harmful use patterns. Since Spectrum Scale (GPFS) is the preferred file system at MPCDF, its CLI tools are used for monitoring.

Network: High-speed networks represent the backbone of an HPC system. Communication characteristics at per-node resolution complement many other metrics with valuable insight. Relevant counters can be queried using the CLI tools that come with InfiniBand or OmniPath network adapters.

Software: The Linux kernel complemented by various system tools gives access to a rich set of application-related metrics, e.g., the number of tasks (processes and threads) actually launched by the job, the pinning of these tasks, the memory usage, the job's environment variables, and many more. The *hpcmd* software accesses this kind of information using the *ps* and *numastat* tools, and the */proc* virtual filesystem in some cases.

Any of these observables can be sampled at regular intervals by *hpcmd* and used directly or after some arithmetic manipulation (e.g., computing the GFLOP/s) as performance metrics.

4.2 Data Collection

On each compute node, an instance of the *hpcmd* middleware is running in the background as a systemd service, measuring at regular intervals and sequentially collecting data from the aforementioned sources. The measurements are synchronized across the nodes via the system clock, avoiding any communication between nodes. In addition to a continuous operation mode, the *hpcmd* daemon supports the widely used SLURM batch system [8], and determines the state of a node (allocated, idle, shared) and job information automatically. We are typically monitoring only nodes which have a single job running on them, i.e., data is not collected for nodes that are currently idle or shared, as such cases are considered less relevant in our context and would be much harder to interpret. *hpcmd* allows for a highly flexible configuration, e.g., to perform more frequent sampling or per-core monitoring of performance counters. Moreover, users may suspend the *hpcmd* systemd service during the runtime of a job to get exclusive access to hardware counters, e.g., for running performance profilers such as VTUNE or using libraries such as PAPI. Measured values and derived metrics are written as log lines containing key-value pairs to the local syslog file. For further details, we kindly refer the reader to the documentation of *hpcmd* [13].

4.3 Data Aggregation

From each monitored node, the *hpcmd* log lines are transported via rsyslog, collected, and finally fed into a central Splunk system. At MPCDF, HPC systems are configured such that the rsyslog traffic goes via the Ethernet link, not putting any load on the high performance network reserved for the applications. For large HPC systems, there may be intermediate (per-"island") rsyslog servers. Operating at sampling intervals on the order of minutes we do not see any scalability issues for our present and future HPC cluster sizes. See Sect. 5 for some practical experience.

4.4 Data Visualization and Interactive Analysis

Data visualization and analysis takes place in the Splunk system, for which we have developed several dashboards providing views at different levels of detail.

Roofline View: The roofline model is a simple yet intuitive performance model widely used in performance engineering [16]. This type of overview is suitable in particular when the performance of a job needs to be condensed into only

Fig. 2. Overview on a selection of jobs from the previous 24 h in a roofline plot on a specific HPC system. Each circle represents a job with its average performance, where the circle sizes are scaled by the actual CPU core hours of the jobs.

two numbers and related to the theoretical peak values of the machine. In a 2d system of coordinates, the horizontal axis denotes the arithmetic intensity in FLOP/Byte, while the vertical axis denotes the performance in GFLOP/s. We pragmatically chose to solely rely on CPU-RAM memory bandwidth for the roofline plot, computed from CPU uncore events. For the application support staff, the entry point for the inspection of performance data in Splunk is a roofline-type of overview plot, as shown in Fig. 2. All finished jobs that fall into a certain time frame and satisfy certain constraints, which are specified by the user using drop-downs on the top of the web-page, are displayed as colored circles, scaled in size by their consumption of CPU hours. This dashboard represents an intuitive performance map showing the current or historic utilization status of the system. Clicking on a circle in the plot or on a line in the data table below forwards to the detailed job view.

Detailed Job Views: This dashboard provides a detailed view on the job's performance characteristics through temporal plots of the performance metrics described in Subsect. 4.1. An excerpt from the dashboard is shown in Fig. 3. To make the data from large jobs more comprehensible, a second dashboard is provided that displays the data using statistical variables such as maximum, median, and minimum curves, taken from all nodes or sockets. These two dashboards are intended to be used by the application support staff through the interactive Splunk web interface. For the users, static PDF reports are provided for download containing the same information. Based on these detailed job views it is typically possible to draw well-grounded conclusions about performance issues of application codes.

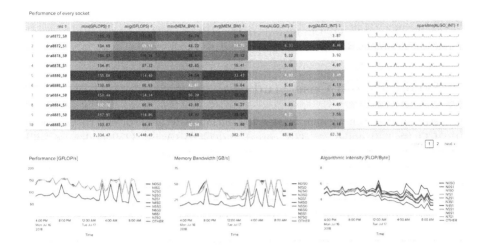

Fig. 3. Excerpt from a detailed view on a specific job, showing the achieved performance in GFLOP/s, the memory bandwidth, and the algorithmic intensity for each socket. In addition to the averaged and maximum values shown in the table, plots over time are available per socket. Moreover, the Splunk dashboard contains about 30 more plots for other CPU, GPU, network, filesystem, and software metrics (not shown here).

Specialized Views: System administrators and the management of a computing center are often interested in specific analysis of many jobs. To obtain such information, they can submit custom queries to the Splunk database. As some of their questions are recurrent, we have developed several dashboards to ease their access to the data. Currently we are providing plots that show the most executed applications by core hours, jobs that reserved GPU nodes without using GPUs, jobs that reserved large memory nodes without using much memory, and jobs that use less than half of the available CPU cores.

4.5   Per-job Reports for Users

To make the performance data accessible to the users, a performance report can be generated for each job and provided as a PDF file for download via a web server after login. We decided not to grant the users access to Splunk directly for security, data protection, and administrative reasons.

4.6   Data Analytics and Automation

On the MPCDF HPC systems, several thousands of jobs are typically run per day. To be able to cope with these numbers and the massive amount of generated data, an automatic data analytics system is indispensable in order to identify problematic jobs on the systems, and notify both support staff and users in critical cases. The data analytics module of the HPC monitoring system is currently under development, but goes beyond the scope of this paper.

5   Scenario- and Case-Studies

The HPC monitoring system is used to continuously monitor the HPC systems DRACO ($\approx$ 940 nodes, $\approx$ 32K cores) and COBRA ($\approx$ 3250 nodes, $\approx$ 130K cores) at the MPCDF. These HPC systems are heterogeneous, containing nodes with different CPU micro-architectures, with different RAM sizes, and with or without GPU accelerators of different models. The system is configured to write performance data every 10 min which generates up to 3 KiB of raw log line data per node. Hence, the total data volume per sample for both machines is about 12.5 MiB, which amounts to about 1.8 GiB per day in total. Note that the rsyslog system is able to easily cope with that data volume, making complex custom hierarchical transport agents unnecessary in our case. In the following, we illustrate with 4 examples how the HPC monitoring system already proved to be helpful in practice at the MPCDF.

Suboptimal Job Scripts: We provide users with a detailed job-specific report (see Subsect. 4.5 for more details), based on which they can quickly spot potential errors related to their job scripts. We are aware of several cases where HPC monitoring was already helpful in this respect.

Hanging Jobs: Even though HPC clusters are supposed to be used to run stable programs, there are still jobs that encounter problems at runtime without shutting down in a controlled manner. For example, in cases of livelocks or deadlocks, the processes of a job continue to run without actually executing any useful instructions, thereby occupying the reserved resources. This can potentially waste a large number of CPU hours. Such "hanging" jobs are typically manifested by very low values in certain performance metrics, especially in GFLOP/s and IPC. To report on a specific example, it was observed from the HPC monitoring data that jobs from a particular user often demonstrated the aforementioned behavior. We contacted the user and showed the plots that illustrated the performance problem. The user then investigated the code and fixed the issue. Catching this particular case was achieved unintentionally, by manual inspection of the data, however an automatic detection system for such types of jobs is under development.

Verification of the Utilization of Extra Resources: To satisfy the compute needs for a broad spectrum of users, computing centers often equip parts of their HPC systems with nodes that contain very large amounts of RAM memory or with nodes that contain GPU accelerators. Sometimes, users with applications that require only moderate amounts of memory or lack GPU support, by mistake or by convenience, allocate such nodes with extra resources instead of regular ones.

This is not a problem if these nodes would otherwise be idle, but if not, such allocations mean a waste of resources and increased queueing times for legitimate users. HPC monitoring can easily detect this type of wrong usage and warn staff or the users directly.

Coarse-Grain Overview for Experts: The HPC monitoring system has not been designed for in-depth code profiling. Nevertheless, it can still provide coarse-grain performance information that can be useful to code developers and application support. Indeed, several members of the application support group at the MPCDF routinely use HPC monitoring to inspect the performance of applications they personally contributed to during development. In most cases, HPC monitoring confirmed their expectations. Interestingly, there were some occasions when even these experts were surprised. In fact, the Splunk analysis of the data showed that the performance in some stages of the application was much worse than expected, which had notable influence on the overall runtimes of the programs. The reason was the lack of code vectorization for some code blocks that were initially considered less relevant. As a next step, the developers profiled the code with more specialized tools which confirmed the observation from the Splunk dashboards and were able to point to the exact lines of code that caused the performance issue.

6   Summary and Outlook

This paper reports on the requirement analysis, the design, and the implementation of the MPCDF HPC performance monitoring system. Our solution is simple, modular, lightweight, mostly based on standard Linux tools, and thus it can easily be adopted by other HPC centers. The system is in operation to comprehensively monitor the performance of all jobs running on two large HPC systems at the MPCDF with about 4200 nodes and more than 160.000 CPU cores in total. After several months of production we have collected a large amount of job-related performance data, and doing data analytics on it will be the main topic of our future work. Additionally, we plan to extend the deployment of our performance monitoring system to more (medium-sized) clusters at the MPCDF, and will continue to develop and maintain the *hpcmd* middleware.

Software: The *hpcmd* software is free of charge and publicly available for download at https://gitlab.mpcdf.mpg.de/mpcdf/hpcmd. Online documentation is available at http://mpcdf.pages.mpcdf.de/hpcmd. The software is licensed under the permissive MIT license. We kindly request to cite this paper in case the software is used and reported on in publications.

Acknowledgements. We are grateful to Christof Hanke for the continuous support with Splunk and the implementation of major parts of the PDF generation web service. We are indebted to Alexis Huxley and Christian Guggenberger for the regular (re)installation of the HPC monitoring software on the HPC systems at short notice. Finally, we thank Lorenz Hüdepohl, Andreas Marek, Pavel Kus, Sebastian Ohlmann, and Markus Rampp from the application support group for many valuable suggestions and fruitful discussions.

References

1. Agelastos, A., et al.: The lightweight distributed metric service: a scalable infrastructure for continuous monitoring of large scale computing systems and applications. In: SC 2014 Proceedings of the International Conference for High Performance Computing, Networking, Storage and Analysis, pp. 154–165, November 2014
2. Borghesi, A., et al.: Online Anomaly Detection in HPC Systems. Preprint, February 2019. http://arxiv.org/abs/1902.08447
3. Browne, S., et al.: PAPI: a portable interface to hardware performance counters. In: Proceedings of Department of Defense HPCMP Users Group Conference, June 1999
4. Evans, R.T., et al.: Understanding application and system performance through system-wide monitoring. In: 2016 IEEE International Parallel and Distributed Processing Symposium Workshops (IPDPSW), pp. 1702–1710, May 2016
5. Evans, T., et al.: Comprehensive resource use monitoring for HPC systems with TACC stats. In: 2014 First International Workshop on HPC User Support Tools, pp. 13–21, November 2014
6. Guillen, C., Hesse, W., Brehm, M.: The persyst monitoring tool. In: Lopes, L., et al. (eds.) Euro-Par 2014. LNCS, vol. 8806, pp. 363–374. Springer, Cham (2014). https://doi.org/10.1007/978-3-319-14313-2_31
7. Intel: Intel VTune Performance Analyzer (2008). http://www.intel.com/cd/software/products/asmo-na/eng/vtune/239144.htm
8. Yoo, A.B., Jette, M.A., Grondona, M.: SLURM: simple linux utility for resource management. In: Feitelson, D., Rudolph, L., Schwiegelshohn, U. (eds.) JSSPP 2003. LNCS, vol. 2862, pp. 44–60. Springer, Heidelberg (2003). https://doi.org/10.1007/10968987_3
9. Park, B.H., et al.: Big data meets HPC log analytics: scalable approach to understanding systems at extreme scale. In: CoRR (2017)
10. Rosales, C., et al.: Remora: a resource monitoring tool for everyone. In: Proceedings of the Second International Workshop on HPC User Support Tools (HUST 2015), pp. 3:1–3:8. ACM, New York, NY, USA (2015)
11. Röhl, T., et al.: Likwid monitoring stack: a flexible framework enabling job specific performance monitoring for the masses. In: 2017 IEEE International Conference on Cluster Computing (CLUSTER), pp. 781–784, September 2017
12. Splunk: SIEM, AIOps, Application Management, Log Management, Machine Learning, and Compliance (2019). https://www.splunk.com/
13. Stanisic, L., Reuter, K.: MPCDF HPC Performance Monitoring System (2019). http://mpcdf.pages.mpcdf.de/hpcmd/
14. Treibig, J., et al.: LIKWID: a lightweight performance-oriented tool suite for x86 multicore environments. In: 2010 39th International Conference on Parallel Processing Workshops, pp. 207–216, September 2010
15. Weaver, V.M.: Linux perf_event features and overhead. In: The 2nd International Workshop on Performance Analysis of Workload Optimized Systems, FastPath (2013)

16. Williams, S., et al.: Roofline: an insightful visual performance model for multicore architectures. Commun. ACM **54**, 65–76 (2009)
17. Yasin, A.: A top-down method for performance analysis and counters architecture. In: 2014 IEEE International Symposium on Performance Analysis of Systems and Software (ISPASS), pp. 35–44, March 2014

Towards a Predictive Energy Model for HPC Runtime Systems Using Supervised Learning

Gence Ozer[1], Sarthak Garg[1], Neda Davoudi[1], Gabrielle Poerwawinata[1],
Matthias Maiterth[2], Alessio Netti[1,3], and Daniele Tafani[3(✉)]

[1] Technische Universität München, Boltzmannstr. 3, 85748 Garching, Germany
{gence.ozer,sarthak.garg,neda.davoudi,gw.poerwawinata}@tum.de
[2] Intel Deutschland GmbH, Dornacher Str. 1, 85622 Feldkirchen, Germany
matthias.maiterth@intel.com
[3] Leibniz-Rechenzentrum, Boltzmannstr. 1, 85748 Garching, Germany
{alessio.netti,daniele.tafani}@lrz.de

Abstract. High-Performance Computing systems collect vast amounts
of operational data with the employment of monitoring frameworks, often
augmented with additional information from schedulers and runtime systems. This amount of data can be used and turned into a benefit for
operational requirements, rather than being a data pool for post-mortem
analysis. This work focuses on deriving a model with supervised learning
which enables optimal selection of CPU frequency during the execution
of a job, with the objective of minimizing the energy consumption of a
HPC system. Our model is trained utilizing sensor data and performance
metrics collected with two distinct open-source frameworks for monitoring and runtime optimization. Our results show good prediction of CPU
power draw and number of instructions retired on realistic dynamic runtime settings within a relatively low error margin.

Keywords: Energy efficiency · Monitoring systems · Random forest ·
DVFS · Runtime systems

1 Introduction

The primary goal of High-Performance Computing (HPC) centers is to provide
computational resources to their users, a feat that is paid proportional to the
center's size in terms of energy consumption. Over the past decade, relevant
concerns have arisen for the massive amount of power necessary for operating
such systems at all levels, from the building infrastructure, past the hardware
and software layers, to the application code run by users [5–7,18]. Significant
emphasis has been placed into optimization of the software stack layer, particularly with the development and adoption of comprehensive sensor monitoring
tools and efficient optimization mechanisms for scheduling and runtime systems [1,2,4]. Improvements in processor design made CPU-level measurements

© Springer Nature Switzerland AG 2020
U. Schwardmann et al. (Eds.): Euro-Par 2019 Workshops, LNCS 11997, pp. 626–638, 2020.
https://doi.org/10.1007/978-3-030-48340-1_48

and tuning widely available, thanks to different power management techniques, such as Dynamic Voltage and Frequency Scaling (DVFS) and the Intel's Running Average Power Limit (RAPL) interface. Combined with fine-granularity acquisition of sensor and hardware counter data, the features offered by these technologies can support both scheduling systems and runtime frameworks. The measurements are mapped to characteristics of the running application to adapt operational modes (i.e., selecting an optimal CPU frequency) appropriate for optimizing objectives such as power consumption, thus reducing operational costs. In this regard, machine learning techniques have been very promising for forecasting and evaluating hardware metrics and ultimately optimize such decisions [16,19].

Related Work. Amongst the different proposed machine learning techniques to forecast hardware metrics for power management, reinforcement learning is often regarded as one of the most promising and widely adopted [10,12,15]. Despite its advantages, as the state-space expands exponentially with the core count, most of the traditional models trained with this technique are limited to a single processor and a small number of cores. Improvements in this direction have been achieved using modular reinforcement learning [16]. However, the training process in these models is *online*, which is significantly challenging outside of a full system simulator. In this regard, alternative approaches based on supervised learning introduce less overhead and may be more suitable for implementations in realistic scenarios. Yang et. al. [19] developed a runtime model using linear regression to map an application task on a computing resource during runtime, ensuring minimum energy consumption for a given application performance requirement. A branch of research employs time series analysis to characterize the history of an application and forecast its behavior. This research shows that time series analysis with Autoregressive Moving Average and Singular Spectrum Analysis can be used with runtime traces to achieve good prediction [8]. Kunkel et al. [9] analyzed the quality of monitoring data and applied Principal Component Analysis to identify the counters required for power prediction.

Wang et. al. [14] have built and evaluated a model for performance prediction for power-capped applications. This approach is very valuable and shows the feasibility of modeling approaches of performance with variable power. Tuncer et al. [13] applied supervised machine learning for anomaly detection using statistical features of monitoring data. While our model is similar, its scope is different: the former work focuses on classification of system states at coarse time scales, while we perform time series regression at a very fine scale, in the order of milliseconds, using high-fidelity data both from monitoring and runtime systems.

Contributions. In this paper we propose a case study for predicting hardware metrics with supervised learning in HPC systems. Specifically, we derive a machine learning model based on random forest regression focusing on the prediction of *CPU power* and total number of *instructions retired*. Data acquisition is performed by using two distinct data sources, specifically the Intel GEOPM runtime framework and the Data Center Database (DCDB) monitoring tool of the Leibniz Supercomputing Center (LRZ). We demonstrate that our model is capable of predicting the selected hardware metrics with high accuracy. Results are obtained by executing a set of benchmarks covering a wide range of HPC application behaviours of interest to LRZ in terms of compute intensity and memory utilization. We then propose a theoretical model to use the predictions as input to support runtime decisions for selecting efficient CPU frequencies, with the objective of reducing the energy consumption of a HPC system.

Organization. The remainder of the paper is organized as follows: the adopted methodology, along with a description of the modeling process, are described in detail in Sect. 2. In Sect. 3 we briefly introduce the tools employed for collecting data while Sect. 4 presents an experimental evaluation of our model. Finally, conclusions and future work are discussed in Sect. 5.

2 Methodology and Modeling

In the following, we propose a conceptual framework to adapt CPU frequency during the execution of an application using hardware metrics. First, we convert the problem to the forecasting of two hardware metrics, namely *CPU power* and *instructions retired*: these are used as an overall power consumption and performance indicator respectively. We then develop a machine learning model to forecast these metrics using the high-granularity sensor data made available by GEOPM and DCDB. The DVFS control mechanism allows to realize a feedback loop, by changing the CPU frequency at runtime, and subsequently making efficient frequency decisions which reduce energy consumption. Figure 1 shows the framework's workflow from feature processing up to training of the model, while Fig. 2 outlines how online inference at runtime can be performed.

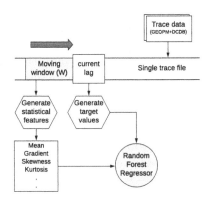

Fig. 1. Training (offline)

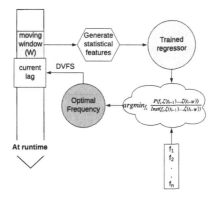

Fig. 2. Inference (at runtime)

2.1 Overview

We consider the problem of energy minimization for an application with arbitrary execution time, running on a fully-saturated single node. Our domain of control is the CPU and the node level. All other energy consumers can be considered static or directly proportional to CPU usage, for safe operation of the system. Under such assumption, the total energy consumed by an application is the total power consumed integrated over the execution time. We further simplify the problem by assuming that node-level hardware metrics are enough to sufficiently characterize the application behavior, greatly reducing the dimensionality of data, since DVFS usually operates at the node level.

Supervised learning techniques are well-suited for real-time, online implementations, due to their low computational overhead in training and inference. This work focuses on the training and validation of such a model. Specifically, we explore an *offline* training approach, in which the machine learning model is trained "a priori", and can later be used for online inference of power and instructions. Such a model can also be re-trained online, with recent data, so as to cope with changing system behavior over time. The evaluation of real-time inference against new data is left for future work.

2.2 Mathematical Model

We quantify the efficiency of frequency decisions for each point in time based on the following model: first, we assume that a generic application, with total execution time T, is divided into N time intervals (also referred to as *lags*) of equal duration $\delta t = \frac{T}{N}$. Such δt duration is assumed to be independent from the current CPU frequency setting, and is calculated from a clock source such as NTP. We then define the *power consumption* for each interval i at time t_i as the function $P(f_i, \zeta(t_{i-1}), \zeta(t_{i-2}), ..., \zeta(t_{i-W}))$, where $\zeta(t_k)$ is a vector of hardware metrics for time interval k at time $t_k \in [t_{i-W}, t_{i-1}]$. W is the length of the historical time window used to determine P at time t_i, and its value depends on the application and system being analyzed. f_i is the CPU *frequency* to be used at time t_i: since frequency decisions are taken at each time interval i using DVFS, affecting the power consumed by the CPU as well as the time taken to progress in the application, observed frequency will also change.

Given the above, in this work we focus on minimizing the energy of each time interval i separately, instead of the application as a whole, neglecting the influence of different decisions on one another. This simplifies the underlying optimization process, at the expense of sub-optimal solutions which do not consider long-term effects. Application throughput at each time interval can potentially decrease when decreasing frequency as the application executes less instructions per unit of time. We approximate this relation by assuming that the throughput of an application in a time interval is inversely proportional to the number of retired instructions. We thus use the latter to compute the energy associated with time interval i by introducing the *Inst* function, which depends on the same variables as P. The minimum energy for a time interval i is then given by:

$$MinEnergy(i) = min_{f_i} \frac{P(f_i, \zeta(t_{i-1}), \zeta(t_{i-2}), ..., \zeta(t_{i-W}))}{Inst(f_i, \zeta(t_{i-1}), \zeta(t_{i-2}), ..., \zeta(t_{i-W}))} \quad (1)$$

Using the mathematical formulation of minimum energy above, we can estimate the most efficient frequency of a time interval i by finding which frequency f_i minimizes the function in Eq. 1. This is expressed as the following:

$$f_i^{opt} = argmin_{f_i} \frac{P(f_i, \zeta(t_{i-1}), \zeta(t_{i-2}), ..., \zeta(t_{i-W}))}{Inst(f_i, \zeta(t_{i-1}), \zeta(t_{i-2}), ..., \zeta(t_{i-W}))} \quad (2)$$

Given that frequency lies in a small discrete space of values, online tuning can be performed by evaluating the P and $Inst$ functions for all available frequency values and picking the one which generates the lowest energy value.

2.3   Machine Learning Model

We assume the CPU power (P) and Instructions retired ($Inst$) for any interval i at time t_i in Eq. 1 to be functions of the frequency at time t_i, and of the sequence of hardware metrics in the historical time window $[t_{i-1}, t_{i-2}, ..., t_{i-W}]$ of size W. After statistical analysis of traces, partial auto-correlation [3] of power and instructions retired indicated that only the most recent 3–5 lags in the sequence are significant. In general, a temporal machine learning model must be used to capture the causal relationships existing in sequence data, which is assumed to be non-independent. Auto-regressive time series models are not suitable as the series is non-stationary. However, instead of using the sequence of time lags as input in our model, we can generate statistical features from the time series of each hardware metric, preserving information content in the temporal dimension. The main benefit is that a simpler supervised learning model can be used, which comes at an expense of generating the features from data before actual inference can be performed. Since our machine learning model should predict the optimum frequency in real-time, the computational effort of generating the features should be as low as possible. Due to this limitation, feature set selection was done prior to evaluation, instead of performing exhaustive generation and "a posteriori" elimination.

The features used in this work are exponentially weighted mean, exponentially weighted gradient, standard deviation, skewness, kurtosis, quantiles (0.25, 0.5 and 0.75), absolute sum of changes and sample entropy. The mean and gradient values are exponentially weighted to give more importance to recent data, which is fundamental for performing regression, as opposed to classification tasks [13]. Extracted features were then employed to train a model for estimating the power consumption and instruction retired metrics for the corresponding set of input features. Considering the non-linearity of the problem, a multi-output random forest regressor was used as learning method. Random forests were chosen due to their robustness against unbalanced, noisy and non-normalized data, and because of their efficient operation in the presence of large feature vectors. Moreover, random forests supply information about the importance of each single feature in the regression process, which is useful for our study.

3   Data Collection

In the following we introduce two tools used at LRZ which we employ for data acquisition. Both have a slightly different scope: GEOPM, a runtime system designed for monitoring and optimizing performance and power control at job execution, and DCDB, a continuous monitoring system collecting operational data with complete compute clusters as scope.

3.1   GEOPM

The Global Extensible Open Power Manager (GEOPM) is a framework designed to provide scalable abstractions to hardware controls and performance counters for power and energy optimization [4]. The GEOPM runtime executes alongside a regular MPI job to observe application and hardware characteristics, which serve as input for GEOPM's optimization algorithms, called "agents". The operating agent can be selected from a set of readily available or self-implemented plugins for center-specific use-cases. It was crucial for our models to observe the behavior of applications under different frequencies to make correct energy and work load predictions. Thus, for this work we implemented a GEOPM agent that samples hardware metrics every 50 ms and changes the frequency to a random available setting every third sampling (150 ms). The benchmarks are run with this GEOPM agent multiple times so as to extract characteristics arising from the different frequencies in the same section of an application.

3.2   DCDB

LRZ researchers developed DCDB with the objective of providing a holistic solution for fine-grained monitoring of sensor and performance metrics in HPC systems [11]. Support for large cluster deployments is ensured by storing data in a NoSQL wide-column database, while low latency and minimal overhead are achieved by transmitting telemetry data with MQTT messages. DCDB is designed following a plugin-based architecture, with each plugin supporting a specific type of protocol for retrieving data. In the scope of this work, we used DCDB to collect sensor data (through SysFS) and in-band performance metrics (through perfevents [17] and ProcFS[1]). Applications that are executed alongside GEOPM were monitored by DCDB, by sampling each metric every 100 ms.

3.3 Fitting Two Data Sources

DCDB and GEOPM originally have two different scopes. GEOPM is job-centric, and is able to sample CPU hardware counters at rates of ~10 ms. DCDB's intent is to persistently store time series data of the complete cluster, including hardware counters from compute nodes, but also information from the operating system. Since the tools access different counters via different methods exposed by the kernel or directly by the hardware, and at different time resolutions, the respective readings are not synchronized. To be able to utilize both data sets for evaluation of a job execution the excess readings before and after the actual run had to be removed. The sliced time series set of DCDB was then upsampled via linear interpolation to fit the GEOPM sampling rate to complete the dataset. Linear interpolation was also used to fit the DCDB data points to the GEOPM time stamps, and to have consistently-aligned and evenly-spaced data. By using both DCDB and GEOPM, we can assess how useful the combination of different metrics collected from different tools is and if these can be brought together for a specific use-case.

4 Experimental Evaluation

In this section we evaluate the performance of our model when predicting the CPU power and instruction retired metrics. We first present our experimental setup and methodology, and then give insights on our results.

4.1 Experimental Setup

The collection of data was performed by monitoring different runs of a set of benchmarks from the Coral-2[2] suite on the CooLMUC-3[3] system hosted by LRZ.

---

[1] http://man7.org/linux/man-pages/man5/proc.5.html.

[2] https://asc.llnl.gov/coral-2-benchmarks/.

[3] https://www.lrz.de/services/compute/linux-cluster/coolmuc3/.

Test Environment. CoolMUC-3 consists of 148 nodes each equipped with Intel Xeon Phi CPU 7210 processors, operating at frequencies ranging from 1.0 GHz to 1.5 GHz, 96 GB of RAM and Intel OmniPath network interfaces. We designated a single node for data acquisition, to ensure consistency of measurements. Each node runs SUSE Linux Enterprise Server 12 SP3 and comes with Intel performance libraries and compilers, which were used to compile the applications. Intel GEOPM 0.6.0, MPI 17.0.6 and an early version of DCDB were used during our experiments. All models were implemented with the open-source Scikit-learn library for Python.

Applications. In order to obtain organic data reflecting the behavior of real HPC workloads and exhibiting different application characteristics, we employed a series of applications from the Coral-2 suite. These are *AMG, Kripke, LAMMPS, Quicksilver* and *Nekbone.* All applications are configured to run with one MPI rank and 62 threads for full node saturation, with two cores reserved for the operating system and the GEOPM controller, and are tuned for an execution time of approximately 8 min. For the purpose of this initial model evaluation, and thanks to the diversity of the benchmark programs, we assume these single-node runs to be representative enough of the large-scale runs done at LRZ.

Table 1. Summary of the two approaches with the corresponding relative error values.

	GEOPM	GEOPM + DCDB
Number of features	81	417
Overall training error	3.9%	2.4%
Overall validation error	9.1%	6%
Validation error (Power package)	3%	2.2%
Validation error (Instruction retired)	15.3%	9.7%

Model Configuration. The random forest regressor chosen for our application was trained using two distinct approaches: first, we train the model using only features from GEOPM data, whereas in the second case we enrich the dataset with DCDB data for further analysis, as discussed in Sect. 3.3. In both cases, we used data from 5 traces of each application and 5-fold cross validation to test the model's performance, with 53 k training samples and 23 k validation samples for each combination of folds. We report average results from each pair of training and test sets. When DCDB data is included, the size of input feature vectors to the model was significantly increased. The input statistical features composing the feature vectors at each time step were built using a sliding, overlapping temporal window of the most recent 9 lags, whereas the target CPU power (in the following referred to as *power package*) and instruction retired values are the average of the next 3 lags. We also supply the average CPU frequency of the next 3 lags as an input feature to make the model suitable for the control algorithm described in Sect. 2.2. The details of the datasets used to train the model with the two approaches described above are outlined in Table 1.

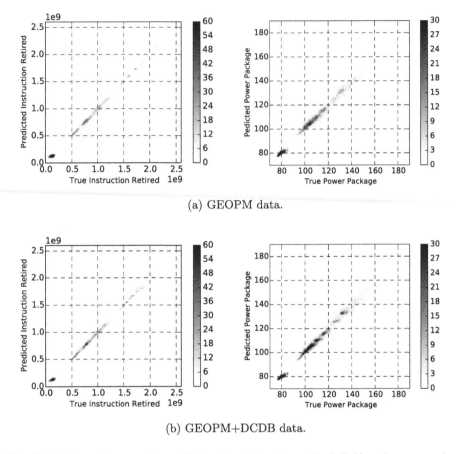

(a) GEOPM data.

(b) GEOPM+DCDB data.

Fig. 3. Model performance in predicting the instruction retired (left) and power package (right) with different data sources.

4.2   Overview of the Results

Results for regression on acquired data are presented in Fig. 3. Specifically, the heatmaps indicate the predicted values from the regressor for instruction retired (left) or power package (right), compared to the actual values, when using only GEOPM data (Fig. 3a) or DCDB data as well (Fig. 3b). Darker areas indicate higher density of points. In Table 1 we also show the average relative training error and validation error for each separate target as well as combined.

It can be seen that in all cases the results are very positive, with an average relative error lower than 15.3%, and metric values are predicted correctly across the whole range. The power package metric is predicted more accurately than the instruction retired metric, likely because the latter corresponds to an inherently noisier sequence, and is influenced by unpredictable factors such as OS interference. Moreover, adding DCDB data leads to slightly more precise prediction. This last result is more pronounced when observing the average relative error for each target, which is shown in Table 1. For comparative purposes we also implemented a *baseline* predictor, which uses the average of the latest three lags as prediction for the power package and instruction retired metrics. Using this naive implementation, we observed an average relative error of 23.7% and 168.6% respectively, proving the intrinsic complexity of this regression problem.

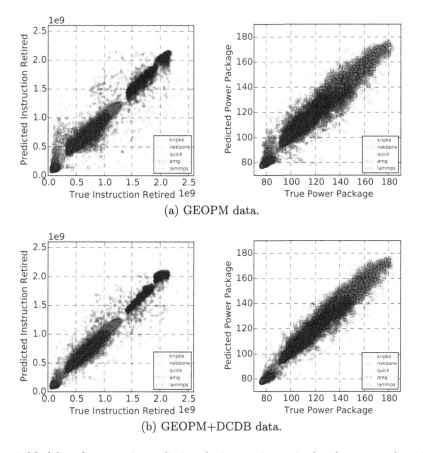

(a) GEOPM data.

(b) GEOPM+DCDB data.

Fig. 4. Model performance in predicting the instruction retired and power package for each benchmark.

4.3   Per-application Analysis

Here we show regression results for each application in the dataset separately, so as to expose artifacts and effects that may be associated to their behavior.

Results are shown in Fig. 4: the scatter plots depict predicted values against the actual ones, like in Fig. 3, and are color-coded for each application.

The results reflect those discussed in Sect. 4.2. However, some interesting effects can be observed: the LAMMPS and AMG applications, for example, show two distinct operational behaviors, which translate into two separate clusters visible in the scatter plots. This behavior is successfully captured by our model. It can also be seen that the Kripke application shows a comparatively higher spread in the predicted instruction retired values, which is mitigated when using both GEOPM and DCDB data. However, it can be seen that overall performance for our model is equally good for all applications, implying that it is generic enough to characterize the diversity of HPC work loads.

Table 2. Most important features as quantified by a random forest regressor.

GEOPM		GEOPM + DCDB	
Score	Name	Score	Name
0.208	geopm inst-retired mean exp weighted	0.376	geopm inst-retired mean exp weighted
0.171	geopm cycles thread kurtosis	0.144	dcdb hfi0temp grad exp weighted
0.071	geopm cycles reference quantile 0.25	0.121	dcdb col idle grad exp weighted
0.060	geopm frequency	0.098	dcdb hfi0temp diff sum
0.048	geopm energy dram quantile 0.25	0.055	dcdb references quantile 0.5
0.047	geopm energy pkg quantile 0.75	0.052	dcdb energy quantile 0.75
0.045	geopm power pkg quantile 0.75	0.042	dcdb hfi1temp grad exp weighted
0.044	geopm power pkg quantile 0.5	0.040	dcdb intr quantile 0.25
0.040	geopm power pkg kurtosis	0.022	dcdb col idle diff sum
0.038	geopm inst-retired quantile 0.5	0.014	geopm frequency

4.4   Evaluation of Feature Importance

As mentioned in Sect. 2.3, random forest regressors are capable of extracting the most dominant features for generating the model. Table 2 indicates the most important features in training the model with the corresponding weight, when using only GEOPM data (left) and DCDB data as well (right).

As it can be seen, the most important feature in both cases is associated to past instruction retired observations, which is expected. The average CPU frequency of the next 3 lags (*frequency*) also plays an important role, proving the validity of the model discussed in Sect. 2.2. When using GEOPM data alone, the remaining most important features are mostly related to past observations of the power package and energy metrics. When using DCDB data as well, the set of important features is more heterogeneous: metrics indicating time spent by the CPU in idle (*col idle*) operation can be seen, as well as temperature sensors (*hfi0temp* and *hfi1temp*) and interrupt counters (*intr*). This, coupled with the results discussed in Sect. 4.2, shows the importance of using diverse monitoring data for our regression problem.

5 Conclusions

In this paper we developed a machine learning model to predict the CPU power and instruction retired metrics, designed to support efficient frequency decision during the execution of HPC applications. We first collected data by running a set of applications on a production HPC system using the DCDB and GEOPM frameworks, which was later combined. We then derived a mathematical model to predict CPU power draw and instructions retired, based on the hardware metrics available, and thus make appropriate frequency decisions to minimize energy consumption. The model is suitable for online training and inference. For this study, we evaluated the generated model offline using training data obtained on LRZ's CooLMUC-3 system, using various applications from the Coral-2 suite.

The results show that the model is generic, with high accuracy in both predicted power as well as instructions retired across all applications. Moreover, we show the effectiveness of combining data from cluster monitoring and high-fidelity runtime systems: the monitoring system has access to data not accessible by the runtime and, on the other hand, the runtime system brings a scalable infrastructure to implement agents for online optimization. As future work, we plan to evaluate our model with data from multiple HPC nodes, and further test its effectiveness by implementing an agent for online frequency tuning using predictions from new data as captured in real time.

Acknowledgements.. This work originated from the TUM Data Innovation Lab, and was further supported by Intel Deutschland GmbH and LRZ.

References

1. Agelastos, A., Allan, B., Brandt, J., Cassella, P., et al.: The lightweight distributed metric service: a scalable infrastructure for continuous monitoring of large scale computing systems and applications. In: Proceedings of SC 2014, pp. 154–165 (2014)
2. Auweter, A., Bode, A., Brehm, M., Brochard, L., Hammer, N., et al.: A case study of energy aware scheduling on SuperMUC. In: Kunkel, J.M., Ludwig, T., Meuer, H.W. (eds.) ISC 2014. LNCS, vol. 8488, pp. 394–409. Springer, Cham (2014). https://doi.org/10.1007/978-3-319-07518-1_25
3. Box, G.E.P., Jenkins, G.M., Reinsel, G.C.: Time Series Analysis, Forecasting and Control, 4th edn, p. Chapter 3.2. Wiley, Hoboken (2008)
4. Eastep, J., Sylvester, S., Cantalupo, C., Geltz, B., Ardanaz, F., et al.: Global extensible open power manager: a vehicle for HPC community collaboration on co-designed energy management solutions. In: Kunkel, J.M., Yokota, R., Balaji, P., Keyes, D. (eds.) ISC 2017. LNCS, vol. 10266, pp. 394–412. Springer, Cham (2017). https://doi.org/10.1007/978-3-319-58667-0_21
5. Jones, N.: How to stop data centres from gobbling up the worlds electricity. Nature **561**, 163–166 (2018)
6. Koomey, J.G.: Worldwide electricity used in data centers. Environ. Res. Lett. **3**(3), 034008 (2008)
7. Koomey, J.G.: Growth in data center electricity use 2005 to 2010. Analytics Press, New york (2011). http://www.analyticspress.com/datacenters.html

8. Kumar, A.S., Mazumdar, S.: Forecasting HPC workload using ARMA models and SSA. In: 2016 Proceedings of ICIT, pp. 294–297 (2016)
9. Kunkel, J., Dolz, M.F.: Understanding hardware and software metrics with respect to power consumption. Sustain. Comput. Inf. Syst. **17**, 43–54 (2018)
10. Lin, X., Wang, Y., Pedram, M.: A reinforcement learning-based power management framework for green computing data centers. In: 2016 Proceedings of IC2E, pp. 135–138. IEEE (2016)
11. Netti, A., Mueller, M., Auweter, A., Guillen, C., et al.: From facility to application sensor data: modular, continuous and holistic monitoring with DCDB. In: 2019 Proceedings of SC. ACM (2019)
12. Triki, M., Wang, Y., Ammari, A., Pedram, M.: Hierarchical power management of a system with autonomously power-managed components using reinforcement learning. Integr. VLSI J. **48**(C), 10–20 (2015)
13. Tuncer, O., Ates, E., Zhang, Y., Turk, A., et al.: Online diagnosis of performance variation in HPC systems using machine learning. IEEE Trans. Para. Distrib. Syst. **30**(04), 883–896 (2018)
14. Wang, B., Terboven, C., Mller, M.S.: Performance prediction under power capping. In: 2018 Proceedings of HPCS, pp. 308–313. IEEE (2018)
15. Wang, Y., Xie, Q., Ammari, A., Pedram, M.: Deriving a near-optimal power management policy using model-free reinforcement learning and bayesian classification. In: 2011 Proceedings of DAC, pp. 41–46 (2011)
16. Wang, Z., Tian, Z., Xu, J., Maeda, R.K.V., Li, H., et al.: Modular reinforcement learning for self-adaptive energy efficiency optimization in multicore system. In: 2017 Proceedings of ASP-DAC, pp. 684–689. IEEE (2017)
17. Weaver, V.M.: Linux perf_event features and overhead. In: 2013 Proceedings of the FastPath Workshop, vol. 13 (2013)
18. Wilde, T., Auweter, A., Shoukourian, H.: The 4 pillar framework for energy efficient HPC data centers. Comput. Sci. - R&D **29**(3–4), 241–251 (2014)
19. Yang, S., Shafik, R.A., Merrett, G.V., Stott, E., Levine, J.M., et al.: Adaptive energy minimization of embedded heterogeneous systems using regression-based learning. In: 2017 Proceedings of the PATMOS Workshop (2015)

Resource Aware Scheduling for EDA Regression Jobs

Saurav Nanda[(⊠)], Ganapathy Parthasarathy, Parivesh Choudhary,
and Arun Venkatachar

Synopsys Inc., Mountain View, CA, USA
{sauravn,gpartha,parivesh,arunv}@synopsys.com

Abstract. Typical Integrated Circuit (IC) design projects use Electronic Design Automation (EDA) tool flows to launch thousands of regressions every day on shared compute grids to complete the IC design verification process. These regressions in turn launch compute jobs with varied resource requirements and inter-job dependency constraints. Traditional grid schedulers, such as the Univa Grid Engine (UGE) [12] prioritize fairness over performance to maximize the number of jobs run with equal distribution of resources at any time. A constant challenge in day-to-day operations is to schedule these jobs for minimum overall job completion time so that developers can expect predictable regression turn-around time (TAT).

We propose a resource-aware scheduling mechanism that balances performance and fairness for real-word EDA-centric workloads. We present an analysis of historical profile information from a set of regressions with complex inter-job dependencies and highly variable resource requirements to show that many of these regression jobs are well suited for efficient packing on grid machines.

We formulate the regression scheduling problem as a variant of the *bin packing problem*, where the size of bins and balls may vary according to job-resource requirements and differing server configurations on the grid. We propose using two analytic techniques – namely *k-means* clustering [8] and adaptive binning [10], to solve this problem. We then evaluate the performance of our proposed solution using real workloads from daily regressions on an enterprise compute grid.

Keywords: Job scheduling · Machine learning · K-means · Adaptive binning · Regression testing · Electronic Design Automation

1 Introduction

Compute and license resources are the two prime elements of infrastructure and resources to enable the full cycle of the chip design process in a large-scale electronic design automation (EDA) company as described by Hao et al. [3]. These resources include hardware infrastructure (CPU, storage, memory, and network) set up as a shared pool of compute resources (compute-grid),

© Springer Nature Switzerland AG 2020
U. Schwardmann et al. (Eds.): Euro-Par 2019 Workshops, LNCS 11997, pp. 639–651, 2020.
https://doi.org/10.1007/978-3-030-48340-1_49

software licenses, and other software/hardware utilities. The amount of compute resources needed by an end-to-end chip design and verification process is directly proportional to the complexity of design and to the challenges related to final stage of shipping these designs for manufacturing. Figure 1 shows a simplified flow of the Integrated Chip (IC) design process. The design described in *Register-Transfer Logic* (RTL) code goes through iterative simulation steps that also takes input from pre-silicon validation. Verified RTL code goes through gate-level synthesis with various libraries as collateral and is also an input to the formal verification process. Typical next steps are static timing analysis among other low-level design analysis and verification steps; and finally, floor planning and routing steps before moving from the gate-level to a silicon implementation process. Various tools used in these steps employ significant parallelization (as shown in the Fig. 1). The parallel jobs related to this IC design flow differ from standard HPC jobs since many of them have various dependencies between stages in the flow. Jobs spawned in a typical IC design flow form a directed acyclic graph (DAG) as opposed to pipelines seen in typical HPC jobs.

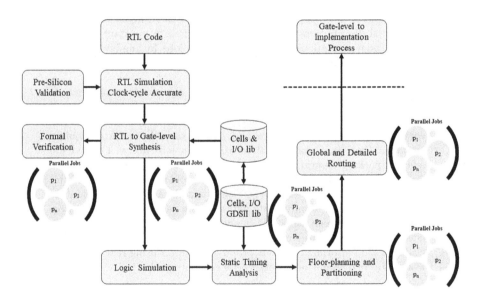

Fig. 1. Simplified view of a modern Integrated Circuit design flow

This illustrates one of the main challenges in any large-scale IC design company with large EDA tool flows – i.e., efficient utilization of compute resources to conduct chip design and verification processes in parallel. This problem has grown to be a significant cost driver in today's competitive IC design market [6].

CPU run-time (i.e. sum of user time and system time) and memory utilization are the two main metrics of any job execution. Optimal use of these resources is critical to enhance the overall performance of the design/verification process and maintain the turnaround time within tight *service level agreements* (SLA). If a regression job requests more memory than the available memory on any machine in the compute grid, it stops other jobs and pushes them to a pending state. Similarly, a regression job may abort abruptly due to system constraints if it tries to consume more memory than that currently available on the machine. Hence, an effective job scheduling technique is necessary to ensure that all the jobs get their expected memory requirement for proper execution, while balancing machine utilization and TAT.

We map the regression job scheduling problem to the classic *job-shop* scheduling problem with precedence and resource constraints. This is an NP-hard problem and a great deal of research has gone into finding tractable variants and solutions to these variants, as described by Lawler et al. [7] and Gen et al. [1]. In this paper, we first analyze historical resource consumption of regression jobs for a sample IC design flow and construct a predictive model of resource utilization using a classic statistical method of adaptive binning [10]. We then use a greedy bin-packing method to develop a job scheduling system on a compute grid, based on the predictions from the statistical model. Our model is capable of handling large volumes of data in near real-time so that we can schedule jobs at scheduler speed.

2 Motivation

The motivation behind this work is based on the amount of reduction that we can bring in overall job completion time (*makespan*). We assume that the infrastructure is designed such that these jobs are placed on a grid machine using Univa Grid Engine (UGE) that schedules each mapper and reducer task as per the resource requirement. Our goal is to construct and evaluate a scheduling algorithm that packs these jobs efficiently and places them on suitable grid machines.

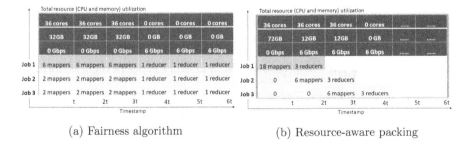

(a) Fairness algorithm   (b) Resource-aware packing

Fig. 2. Job scheduling using fairness versus multi-resource packing methods

We explain our motivation using an example inspired by Grandl et al. [2]. Consider a cluster with a total resource capacity of 36 CPU cores, 72 GB of memory, and 6 Gbps of network bandwidth. Also consider a scenario where the cluster is used to execute 3 map-reduce jobs job-1, job-2 and job-3. Job-1 has 18 mapper tasks, job-2 and job-3 have 6 mapper tasks each, and each of them has 3 reducer tasks. Each mapper task for job-1 needs 2 CPUs and 4 GB memory, and 6 CPUs and 2 GB memory for job-2 and job-3. Each reducer task also needs a negligible amount of CPU and memory but requires 2 Gbps of network resources.

Typical fairness algorithms schedule these jobs such that every job gets an equal amount of resources, so the 6 mappers of job-1, the 2 mappers of job-2 and the 2 mappers of job-3. Therefore, all mapper tasks are completed by time $3t$. However, this results in 40 GB of unused memory in the mapper phase. The fair scheduler runs one reducer from each job during the execution of reducer tasks, such that each job gets an equal network resources and all reducer tasks complete by time $6t$ as shown in Fig. 2a.

Now consider a scheduler that packs these jobs/containers based on their resource requirement rather than fairness. We see the following based on resource-aware scheduling:

1. All 36 mappers of job-1 are scheduled first so that all available memory in the cluster is utilized
2. All 12 mapper tasks of job-2 are scheduled along with 6 reducer tasks job-1
3. All jobs complete by time $4t$ as shown in Fig. 2b

Hence, such a resource-aware packing algorithm can reduce the total job completion time of the cluster by 33%. In addition, we can free up more physical machines by consolidating these mappers and reducers tasks.

3   Problem Formulation

In this section, we formulate the problem statement using a list of variables and assumptions related to resource-aware packing of jobs placing them optimally on grid machines to minimize the *makespan*, which is defined as the time taken to complete the processing of all jobs. The derivation steps we present below for our multi-resource bin-packing problem follows the derivation developed and described by Grandl et al. [2] to solve a job scheduling problem using their *Tetris* scheduler. We consider a grid computing center responsible for executing multiple jobs, such as batch jobs, map-reduce jobs, and other types of high-performance compute jobs.

Our work primarily focuses on compute jobs for EDA regression test-cases for an IC design flow that takes an RTL design from synthesis to hardware. Every job may be executed on a local machine or on a remote machine assigned by the UGE job scheduler. Our target is to schedule these jobs so that the *makespan* is minimal which is equivalent to maximizing the efficiency of packing these jobs. Current grid schedulers tend to schedule these jobs based on a *fair-share* algorithm so that each job gets an equal amount of computing resources. However, fair schedulers are inefficient when given dynamically changing resource demands as they do not consider the individual resource demands of each job.

EDA regression jobs typically have different resource requirements – some of them are CPU intensive, some are memory intensive, some are I/O intensive, some are network intensive jobs, and some need some combination of each resource. Current job scheduling algorithms do not consider the resource demands of individual jobs, which leads to resource fragmentation and over allocation of resources. Thus, current scheduling algorithms based on fairness can schedule all jobs of comparable size (example: pack of all memory intensive jobs) on the same physical machine to maintain fairness, but may block other resources, such as CPU. Prior scheduling algorithms, such as *Smallest Remaining Time First* (SRTF) [4] do not have an optimal job packing process and *Fair Schedulers* have a higher job completion time. Also, these prior scheduling techniques does not consider the size of job and the overhead of launching it on a remote machine. The problem we target differs from the classic bin packing problem since the resource demands of all the jobs may vary slightly vary from one regression to another due to minor changes in the actual test-case and/or code changes in the underlying EDA tools. This may also depend upon the actual physical machine that is allocated. Therefore, we have twin goals, i.e., 1) *Adaptive learning of resource requirements of each job*, and 2) *Monitoring of available resources*.

Hence, we need a scheduling algorithm that is packing efficient and can dynamically decide whether the job should be launched on the local machine or on the remote machine depending upon the job size. In addition, we consider the practical case where the number of machines in the grid may change because of system failures, new additions/removals, and routine IT maintenance. We discount network latency effects in our model by assuming that network resources are uniform throughout the grid.

Table 1. Functionality of current state-of-the-art scheduling techniques and the proposed approach.

	LoadLeveler	PBS	SLURM	Our proposed approach
Job characterization	✓	✓	✓	✓
Inter-dependent Jobs (DAG)				✓
Scheduling based on historical job utilization data				✓
Resource aware job packing				✓

State-of-the-art grid engines, such as IBM LoadLeveler[1], PBS[2], SLURM[3] and UGE/SGE[4] are currently used by many HPC data centers effectively. They can manage both single and batch jobs efficiently in the HPC world. However, the EDA workload is different from regular HPC workloads as we described in Sect. 1. Table 1 presents a functional comparison between default job scheduling techniques available in various grid management engines, such as IBM LoadLeveler, PBS, SLURM, and our proposed approach that is agnostic to any specific grid engine. We have implemented our proposed approach and demonstrate experimental results in UGE, but not all the described grid engines. We believe that the experimental results in UGE should transport well to all the above-mentioned systems.

4   System Architecture

In this section, we describe our resource-aware *adaptive binning* approach to solve this job scheduling problem for EDA regression jobs. Figure 3 shows the overall architecture of our system that uses a *Feature Manager* to analyze the profile logs related to regression runs. A regression run is defined as a standardized set of test-cases selected from a pool of test-cases maintained for an IC tool-flow. The feature manager collects and processes all the profile logs from regression runs. These logs are parsed to extract test-case names along with the job-level resource utilization parameters per regression run. The log parser also captures the job name and execution command from the *qrsh* command used in the profile logs for each job, which are hashed to create a hash-value. The hash-value provides a unique key corresponding to each job as related to a specific test-case that is stored in an in-memory database (*Redis*[5]).

When a list of test-cases runs in real time, each test-case spawns multiple jobs that goes through the UGE grid scheduler, which allocates an appropriate machine from a pre-allocated pool to each job. We implement a separate UGE driver that reads all the incoming jobs from any given test-case and replaces the actual *qrsh* command with a custom command script that does the following:

1. Parse the incoming grid command to create a hash in the same manner used to populate data in our feature manager;
2. Probe the computed hash value from in-memory database; and
3. If the hash value of current grid command matches the hash value stored in in-memory database that contains all the small job instances (less than 1 s CPU/100 Mb mem), then we launch these jobs on the local machine. Otherwise we use the standard UGE schedule to launch the job on a remote machine.

---

[1] https://www.ibm.com/support/knowledgecenter/en/SSFJTW_5.1.0.

[2] https://www.pbspro.org/.

[3] https://slurm.schedmd.com/.

[4] http://www.univa.com/products/.

[5] https://redis.io/.

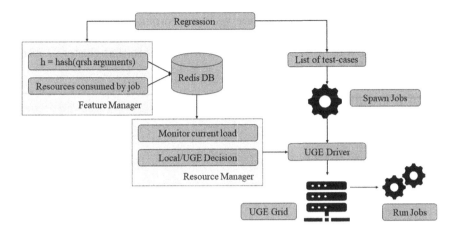

Fig. 3. Simplified flow of the proposed approach.

Finally, we have a *resource manager* module that is responsible for reporting the resource utilization of each physical host and the total number of available hosts. If the current host does not have enough resources to accommodate the predicted resources for an incoming job (however small), then the resource manager forces the customized driver script to send the job directly to the standard UGE scheduler.

5   Adaptive Packing and Scheduling Techniques

Given resource requirement estimates, we should ideally be able to place jobs precisely on those machine that meet those resource requirements. However, the majority of the jobs in our target data-set that need to be placed require less than 5 cpu-seconds of run-time. It would be prohibitively expensive to measure the current state of machines in the grid at such fine-grain intervals using UGE or other commonly available monitoring infrastructure, such as metricbeat[6].

In absence of such infrastructure, we cluster similar jobs into buckets such that we can dedicate machines to jobs with similar resource requirement characteristics. This must be done dynamically since job characteristics can change from run to run depending on the state of the tools in the EDA flow. Therefore, we investigate fast unsupervised learning techniques to bucketize historical job run-time features – namely *k-means* clustering and *discretization*-techniques.

5.1   K-means Clustering

The *k-means* method of clustering [8] is one of the simplest and most popular unsupervised learning algorithms to solve the clustering problem since it is intuitive and computationally efficient as compared to other clustering methods. It

---

[6] https://www.elastic.co/products/beats/metricbeat.

operates on distances between feature vectors in n-dimensional space. *k-means* generates a fixed number of centroids, k, that it uses to define clusters. A data point is considered to be in a given cluster if it is closer to that cluster's centroid than the centroid of any other cluster.

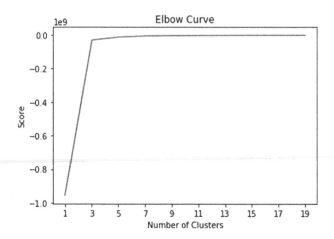

Fig. 4. K-means clustering using elbow method to verify the number of bins

However, in general, the optimal value of k is unknown and often difficult to estimate. We cannot simply use the centroid distance as a measure of cluster quality since increasing k will always decrease the centroid distance used in the clustering step to the limit of zero when k is the same as the number of data points. Therefore, we use the well-known *elbow*-method where mean distance to the centroid as a function of k is plotted and the *elbow point*, where the rate of decrease sharply shifts, is used to estimate the optimal value of k. Based on the elbow point shown in Fig. 4, we see that the value k lies between 3 and 4, which implies that we should either bin the jobs in this data-set into 3 or 4 bins. Other methods such as the *gap-statistic* method [11] are also reliable in cases where the shifts in the rate of decrease are well defined.

5.2 Adaptive Binning

As we saw in the previous section, a straight-forward application of *k-means* seems to work well in determining a close-to optimal number of clusters. Therefore, we use a method traditionally used in machine learning – *discretization*, (also known as quantization or binning), which partitions continuous valued features into discrete labels or bins. We use a variant of one of the simplest methods of descretization – that of Holte [5], which greedily divides the observed values of a continuous feature into bins that contain instances of one particular class, such that each bin contains a strong majority of that class. The variant is simply using the metric that all values in each bin have the same nearest center of a 1D *k-means* cluster in this procedure.

We use the python-based open-source *KBinsDiscretizer* package in *scikit* [9] for our experiments. This implements the discretization method described above with some additional heuristics such as removing buckets that are too small to be useful. Figure 5 shows the final output from *KBinsDiscretizer* algorithm to generate unequal-width bins that covers all the jobs. As we can see, the bulk of the jobs are placed in four bins. This is similar to the results from the result from iterative *k-means*-clustering that produced a well-defined elbow at 4 clusters.

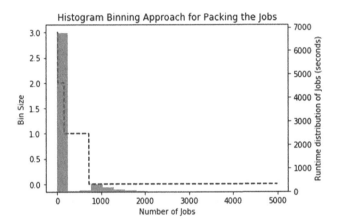

Fig. 5. Adaptive Binning approach to find the near-optimal number of bins

6   Experimental Results

In this section, we describe our experiments that demonstrate the results of our adaptive binning approach. The UGE driver and all other components of our proposed approach are implemented in Python-3.

6.1   Initial Validation

We conducted an initial set of experiments using 10 homogeneous physical hosts of 200 CPU slots, 2.5 TB of memory, and 20 TB of disk storage set up as a private UGE grid project to validate our approach in a controlled setting.

We evaluated our system by conducting a set of experiments to present the preliminary results. Initially, we collected profile log data for a sample set of test-cases (400) for training our model. After parsing the profile logs, we collected all the resource utilization features, such as CPU and memory utilization. We created clusters based on the resource requirements of these jobs. For example, the data-set in the prior discussion resulted in four different categories: ≤ 1 s, ≤ 2 s, ≤ 5 s, and ≥ 5 s. As discussed in Sect. 5, we have already verified these four

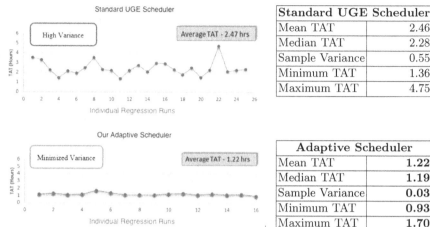

Fig. 6. Adaptive scheduler v/s the standard UGE scheduler in isolated grid.

bins using the elbow-based *k-means* clustering method. We also found that more than 50% of jobs are in the category of ≤1 s. Based on our historical training information, the UGE driver in our architecture checks the incoming job and chooses to run it locally (which is a separate pool of machines) or pass it directly to UGE grid machines based on the other bins that we have calculated. We also reduce the load on grid queue as this approach reduces the submission rate of jobs on the UGE scheduler, which significantly improves the overall job scheduling efficiency.

We started with two fundamental goals: 1) achieve near-optimal job packing/scheduling to improvise the total turn-around time; and 2) improve the overall grid machine utilization. We conducted our experiment in two different grid environments to ensure that the solution works well in a controlled environment as well as on real life grid infrastructure. In the first experiment, we ran ≈550 test-cases in a controlled grid environment, where no other jobs were running, with standard UGE scheduler (without our enhancement) and then with our adaptive scheduler.

Figure 6 shows that the total turn-around time (TAT) has significantly more variance if we use standard UGE scheduler (0.55) compared to our adaptive scheduler (0.03). In addition, we see a major improvement (almost half) in the average TAT using our adaptive scheduler. We note that this kind of improvement is not practical in real-world scenarios when the grid is loaded with multiple users running thousands of jobs at any time.

6.2   Real-World Workload Evaluation

Next, we conducted an evaluation of real workloads comprising regressions of ≈550 EDA test-cases submitted by different users asynchronously on a

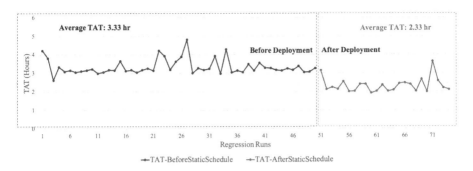

Fig. 7. TAT comparison of adaptive scheduler v/s the standard UGE scheduler

multi-user shared-resource real-world grid. The grid consists of 49 heterogeneous physical hosts that provides compute resources of 900 CPU slots, 12 TB of memory and 80 TB of disk storage.

Figure 7 shows the overall performance improvement in the real-world grid environment that we have achieved using our adaptive scheduling technique over standard UGE scheduler for running ≈550 test cases in each iteration. The total execution time of running these test-cases using adaptive scheduler is 2.33 h, whereas the total execution of the running same number of test-cases with only UGE scheduler is 3.33 h and that shows a promising improvement of ≈40%, which completes our first goal. Now, we present the data on overall grid utilization in Fig. 8 that shows a major improvement in resource utilization. Figure 8a shows that we can maintain an average CPU utilization (user time) of ≈41% using our adaptive job scheduling approach, whereas the standard UGE scheduler maintains an average CPU utilization (user time) of ≈26% – which is a promising improvement of more than 50%.

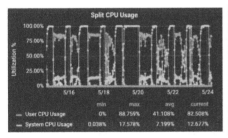   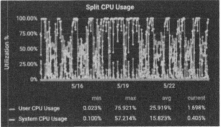

(a) Utilization with our optimization   (b) Utilization without our optimization

Fig. 8. Improvement in grid resource utilization with the proposed approach.

7   Conclusion

In this paper, we proposed a method to track job resource requirement history and use this data to pack jobs having highly diverse resource requirements into unequal size bins so that they can be efficiently placed on a partitioning of the machines in the grid. The assumption behind the approach is that job packings with similar resource requirements will yield lower variance in TAT, and higher resource utilization than those from a traditional round-robin scheduler. This is borne out by our experimental results.

The placement is lazy in the sense that machines in a set are selected by the initial placement of the job in the EDA tool flow for a design. Additional jobs in the flow for that design are placed either on the local machine based on estimated resource consumption and currently available resources or on remote machines if the estimated resources overflow current resources on the local machine. This prevents over/under-allocation problems that arise from a static partitioning of the machines in the grid. Based on preliminary results, we observe that our resource aware static scheduling algorithm achieves an improvement of ≈34% compared to standard algorithm used by UGE job scheduler.

However, there are several limitations in our work. The current work restricts the freedom of the adaptive scheduler to choose machines in the grid, while we will need true dynamic partitioning and placement to achieve maximum efficiency. This cannot be done without accurate measurement of resource utilization across the grid whenever we need to spawn a job. This necessitates building custom low-overhead measurement utilities outside the standard grid infrastructure and methods to generate close-to-optimal packing given the dynamic state of the grid. We will address this as part of our future work.

References

1. Gen, M., Cheng, R.: Genetic Algorithms and Engineering Optimization, vol. 7. Wiley, Hoboken (2000)
2. Grandl, R., Ananthanarayanan, G., Kandula, S., Rao, S., Akella, A.: Multi-resource packing for cluster schedulers. ACM SIGCOMM **44**(4), 455–466 (2015)
3. Hao, X., Lin, L., Gen, M., Ohno, K.: Effective estimation of distribution algorithm for stochastic job shop scheduling problem. Procedia Comput. Sci. **20**, 102–107 (2013)
4. Harchol-Balter, M., Schroeder, B., Agrawal, M., Bansal, N.: Size-based scheduling to improve web performance. ACM Trans. Comput. Syst. **21**, 207–233 (2003)
5. Holte, R.C.: Very simple classification rules perform well on most commonly used datasets. Mach. Learn. **11**, 63–91 (1993). https://doi.org/10.1023/A:1022631118932
6. Kamath, V., Giri, R., Muralidhar, R.: Experiences with a private enterprise cloud: providing fault tolerance and high availability for interactive EDA applications. In: Sixth IEEE International Conference on Cloud Computing (CLOUD), pp. 770–777, June 2013. https://doi.org/10.1109/CLOUD.2013.72
7. Lawler, E.L., Lenstra, J.K., Kan, A.H.R., Shmoys, D.B.: Sequencing and scheduling: algorithms and complexity. Handb. Oper. Res. Manag. Sci. **4**, 445–522 (1993)

8. Macqueen, J.: Some methods for classification and analysis of multivariate observations. In: 5th Berkeley Symposium on Mathematical Statistics and Probability, pp. 281–297 (1967)
9. Pedregosa, F., et al.: Scikit-learn: machine learning in Python. J. Mach. Learn. Res. **12**, 2825–2830 (2011)
10. Poli, R., Woodward, J., Burke, E.K.: A histogram-matching approach to the evolution of bin-packing strategies. In: 2007 IEEE Congress on Evolutionary Computation, pp. 3500–3507. IEEE (2007)
11. Tibshirani, R., Walther, G., Hastie, T.: Estimating the number of clusters in a dataset via the gap statistic. J. R. Stat. Soc.: Ser. B (Stat. Methodol.) **63**, 411–423 (2000)
12. Univa Corporation: Univa® grid engine®. http://www.univa.com/. http://www.univa.com/products

Resilience - Workshop on Resiliency in High Performance Computing with Clouds, Grids, and Cluster

Workshop on Resiliency in High Performance Computing in Clouds, Grids, and Clusters (Resilience)

Workshop Description

Clouds, Grids, and Clusters are three different computational paradigms with the potential to support High Performance Computing (HPC) and enterprise IT infrastructure. Currently, they consist of hardware, management, and usage models particular to different computational regimes (e.g., high performance cluster systems designed to support tightly coupled scientific simulation codes that typically utilize high-speed interconnects and commercial cloud systems designed to support software as a service (SAS) which typically do not). However, in order to support HPC, all must at least utilize large numbers of resources and hence effective HPC in any of these paradigms must address the same issue of resiliency at a very large-scale.

Recent trends in HPC systems have clearly indicated that future increases in performance, in excess of those resulting from improvements in single-processor performance, will be achieved through corresponding increases in system scale, i.e., using a significantly larger component count. As the raw computational performance of the world's fastest HPC systems increases from today's current multi-petascale to next-generation exascale capability and beyond, their number of computational, networking, and storage components will grow from the ten-to-one-hundred thousand compute nodes of today's systems to several hundreds of thousands of compute nodes in the foreseeable future. This substantial growth in system scale, and the resulting component count, poses a challenge for HPC system and application software with respect to reliability, availability, and serviceability (RAS).

Resilience is a critical challenge as HPC systems continue to increase component counts, individual component reliability decreases, and software complexity increases. Application correctness and execution efficiency, in spite of frequent faults, errors, and failures, is essential to ensure the success of the extreme-scale HPC systems, cluster computing environments, Grid computing infrastructures, and Cloud computing services.

Resilience for HPC systems encompasses a wide spectrum of fundamental and applied research and development, including theoretical foundations, fault detection and prediction, monitoring and control, end-to-end data integrity, enabling infrastructure, and resilient solvers and algorithm-based fault tolerance. This workshop brings together experts in the community to further research and development in HPC resilience and to facilitate exchanges across the computational paradigms of extreme-scale HPC, cluster computing, Grid computing, and Cloud computing.

The goal of this workshop is to bring together experts in the area of fault tolerance and resilience for HPC to present the latest achievements and to discuss the challenges ahead. The Resilience 2019 workshop program included presentations of four high-quality peer-reviewed papers as well as an opportunity for discussions among the participants from research, academia, and industry.

Organization

Workshop Chairs

Stephen L. Scott   Tennessee Tech University, USA
Chokchai (Box) Leangsuksun   Louisiana Tech University, USA

Workshop Program Chairs

Patrick G. Bridges   University of New Mexico, USA
Christian Engelmann   Oak Ridge National Laboratory, USA

Program Committee

Ferrol Aderholdt   Middle Tennessee State University, USA
Rizwan Ashraf   Oak Ridge National Laboratory, USA
Wesley Bland   Intel Corporation, USA
Hans-Joachim Bungartz   Technical University of Munich, Germany
Marc Casas   Barcelona Supercomputer Center, Spain
Zizhong Chen   University of California at Riverside, USA
Robert Clay   Sandia National Laboratories, USA
Nathan DeBardeleben   Los Alamos National Laboratory, USA
James Elliott   Sandia National Laboratories, USA
Kurt Ferreira   Sandia National Laboratories, USA
Saurabh Hukerikar   NVIDIA, USA
Dieter Kranzlmueller   Ludwig-Maximilians University of Munich,
                                   Germany
Ignacio Laguna   Lawrence Livermore National Laboratory, USA
Scott Levy   University of New Mexico, USA
Dirk Pflueger   University of Stuttgart, Germany
Alexander Reinefeld   Zuse Institute Berlin, Germany
Rolf Riesen   Intel Corporation, USA
Yves Robert   ENS Lyon, France
Thomas Ropars   Université Grenoble Alpes, France
Martin Schulz   Lawrence Livermore National Laboratory, USA
Keita Teranishi   Sandia National Laboratories, USA

Space-Efficient Reed-Solomon Encoding to Detect and Correct Pointer Corruption

Scott Levy$^{(\boxtimes)}$ and Kurt B. Ferreira

Center for Computing Research, Sandia National Laboratories, Albuquerque, Mexico
{sllevy,kbferre}@sandia.gov

Abstract. Concern about memory errors has been widespread in high-performance computing (HPC) for decades. These concerns have led to significant research on detecting and correcting memory errors to improve performance and provide strong guarantees about the correctness of the memory contents of scientific simulations. However, power concerns and changes in memory architectures threaten the viability of current approaches to protecting memory (e.g., Chipkill). Returning to less protective error-correcting codes (ECC), e.g., single-error correction, double-error detection (SECDED), may increase the frequency of memory errors, including silent data corruption (SDC). SDC has the potential to silently cause applications to produce incorrect results and mislead domain scientists. We propose an approach for exploiting unnecessary bits in pointer values to support encoding the pointer with a Reed-Solomon code. Encoding the pointer allows us to provides strong capabilities for correcting and detecting corruption of pointer values.

In this paper, we provide a detailed description of how we can exploit unnecessary pointer bits to store Reed-Solomon parity symbols. We evaluate the performance impacts of this approach and examine the effectiveness of the approach against corruption. Our results demonstrate that encoding and decoding is fast (less than 45 μs per event) and that the protection it provides is robust (the rate of miscorrection is less than 5% even for significant corruption). The data and analysis presented in this paper demonstrates the power of our approach. It is fast, tunable, requires no additional per-pointer storage resources, and provides robust protection against pointer corruption.

Keywords: Resilience · Error-correcting codes · Silent data corruption

1 Introduction

Concern about memory errors has been widespread in high-performance computing (HPC) for decades, *see e.g.,* [15]. As result, significant research has been dedicated to detecting and correcting memory errors to improve performance and

U. Schwardmann et al. (Eds.): Euro-Par 2019 Workshops, LNCS 11997, pp. 657–668, 2020.
https://doi.org/10.1007/978-3-030-48340-1_50

to provide strong guarantees about the correctness of the memory contents of scientific simulations. In HPC systems, powerful error-correcting codes (ECC), e.g., Chipkill [8], have been widely deployed. However, power concerns and changes in emerging memory architectures threaten their continued viability.

Chipkill can protect against the loss of a complete memory device, but at the cost of 4 times as many memory devices as less protective ECC[1]. Reducing the number of activated memory devices from 36 to 9 can reduce memory power by up to 45% [14]. Given the increasing total memory capacity of next-generation HPC systems, it is not clear that there will continue to be room in the power budget for Chipkill. Moreover, the emergence of new categories of memory devices, e.g., high-bandwidth memory (HBM), that may not easily support Chipkill may also limit its use.

Returning to less protective ECC, e.g., single-error correct, double-error detect (SECDED), may increase the frequency of memory errors, including silent data corruption (SDC), cf. [18]. SDC occurs when a memory corruption is not corrected or detected by the hardware (e.g., hardware ECC). SDC is particularly pernicious because it has the potential to silently produce incorrect results, thereby misleading the domain scientists that rely on data from simulations to understand important physical phenomena. SDC also has the potential to result in poor resource utilization because the application terminates abnormally (i.e., it crashes) and has to be restarted. Moreover, many existing techniques that can tolerate data corruption, e.g., [5,9], remain vulnerable to pointer corruption.

Pointer corruption can result in abnormal application termination (e.g., if the corrupted value no longer refers to a valid memory address) or in the wrong answer (e.g., if the corrupted value refers to an incorrect, but valid, memory address). C/C++ pointer values are distinct from other data types in that their semantics are clear: they contain a memory address. As a result, we can exploit the structure in memory addresses to repurpose bits that are easily reconstructed. We therefore propose an approach for using unnecessary bits in pointer values to provide correction and detection of silent data corruption of pointer values.

In this paper, we describe our proposed approach and evaluate its performance characteristics. Specifically, we make the following contributions:

- We provide a detailed description of how we can use Reed-Solomon encoding to protect against pointer corruption by repurposing unnecessary pointer bits to store parity symbols[2] Sect. 3;
- We evaluate the time required to encode and decode pointers using this approach, Sect. 4.2; and
- We demonstrate that for some encodings, we can reduce the rate of miscorrection (silent data corruption) to less than 5% even when significant corruption is introduced, Sect. 4.3.

---

[1] 36 × 4 devices for Chipkill compared to 9 × 8 devices for single-error correct, double-error detect (SECDED).

[2] A small, constant amount of memory, less than 1 KiB per process, is required but it is independent of the number of pointers included.

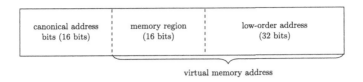

Fig. 1. Illustration of Linux C pointer values.

The data and analysis presented in this paper demonstrates the potential of our proposed approach to provide significant protection against pointer corruption. Our approach is fast, tunable, and requires no additional per-pointer storage resources.

2   Background

2.1   Linux Virtual Memory Addresses and C Pointers

In the C and C++ programming languages, pointers are used to store virtual memory addresses. Linux currently uses 48-bit virtual memory addresses for 64-bit processors. Because instruction sets of modern CPUs are designed to manipulate data in powers-of-2 numbers of bytes, pointers are stored as 64-bit quantities. Figure 1 illustrates the breakdown of a Linux C pointer. For x86 and ARM processors operating in 64-bit mode, addresses must be in *canonical* form: the most significant 16 bits must be set equal to bit 47 (i.e., all ones or all zeros), *see* [13, §3.3.7.1], [3,4]. The least significant 48 bits contain the actual virtual memory address. For the purposes of this paper, we have subdivided the virtual memory address into the *memory region*, the most significant 16 bits of the virtual memory address; and the *low-order address*, the least significant 32 bits of the virtual memory address. In Linux, the stack and the heap have discoverable[3] addresses. Additionally, anonymously mapped memory (e.g., acquired by calling `mmap()`[4]) are, in many cases, assigned to a discoverable range of addresses. As a practical matter, many memory addresses will have many of their most significant bits in common. We can potentially exploit this fact to repurpose additional bits of the pointer for error protection.

2.2   Reed-Solomon Codes

Reed-Solomon Codes are linear block codes that are commonly used for error correction. A Reed-Solomon Code operates on m-bit symbols to generate a codeword whose length can be no longer than $2^m - 1$ symbols long. A Reed-Solomon

---

[3] Because of the widespread use of address space layout randomization (ASLR) to guard against exploits by malicious code, the range of the stack and heap are discoverable at runtime but are not known in advance.

[4] Standard memory allocators (e.g., `malloc()`) will also map memory to satisfy large, e.g., more than 128 KiB, memory allocation requests.

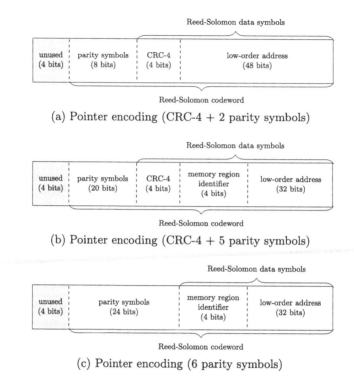

(a) Pointer encoding (CRC-4 + 2 parity symbols)

(b) Pointer encoding (CRC-4 + 5 parity symbols)

(c) Pointer encoding (6 parity symbols)

Fig. 2. Illustration of leveraging unnecessary bits in pointer values to provide additional protection against memory errors.

Code, $RS(n,k)$, transforms a k-symbol message into an n-symbol codeword by adding $n-k$ parity symbols.[5] An n-symbol codeword is $n \times m$ bits long (e.g., an $RS(15,4)$ code will generate 60-bit codewords). Errors affecting $\lfloor \frac{(n-k)}{2} \rfloor$ or fewer symbols can be corrected. In principle, errors affecting $(n-k)$ or fewer symbols can be detected. As a practical matter, open source Reed-Solomon decoders cannot always meet this theoretical limit. In particular, errors that affect between $\lfloor \frac{(n-k)}{2} \rfloor$ and $(n-k)$ symbols are not always detected as errors.[6]

3   Approach

Our proposed approach is to use the unnecessary bits in pointer values to store parity symbols generated by a Reed-Solomon Code. The basic idea is that a programmer can encode a pointer when it is not being frequently de-referenced and

---

[5] Generally, n is the maximum codeword length. Shorter codewords can be obtained by padding the message with well-known symbols (e.g., zeroes) during encoding, dropping the pad symbols to transmit/store the codeword, and then adding the pad symbols back during decoding.

[6] For example, we have demonstrated that cases exist for $RS(15,10)$ where both Schifra [1] and EZPWD [2] miscorrect codewords with four or five corrupted symbols.

decode it when it needs to be dereferenced. By leveraging these unnecessary bits, we can provide protection without requiring additional storage resources.[7] The protective benefit of this approach is in addition to existing hardware protection (e.g., error correcting codes (ECC)). The benefit of this additional protection will only be realized when the hardware protection is exceeded (e.g., when a detected, uncorrectable error (DUE)[8] or SDC occurs).

Figure 2a illustrates the simplest and most widely applicable approach. In this case, we simply leverage the unused bits that occupy the 16 most significant bits of the pointer. We use an $RS(15, 13)$ code as our error-correcting code and divide the pointer value into the following fields:

– **Unused (bits 63-60)**: An $RS(15, 13)$ code uses 15 4-bit symbols to create 60-bit codewords. Because the codeword contains fewer bits than the pointer value, the most significant 4 bits are left unused. However, because these bits are unnecessary to reconstruct the pointer, errors that occur in these four bits do not affect our ability to successfully decode the pointer value.
– **Parity Symbols (bits 59-52)**: The two parity symbols generated by our $RS(15, 13)$ code. Two parity symbols means that we can correct any error that is confined to a single symbol and detect any set of errors that affect no more than two symbols.
– **CRC-4 (bits 51-48)**: Given the practical limitations of existing open source Reed-Solomon decoders (*see* Sect. 2.2) and the difficultly of detecting errors when the number of erroneous symbols exceeds $(n - k)$, including a 4-bit cyclic redundancy check (CRC) adds additional detection capabilities. The CRC-4 is included as one of the Reed-Solomon data symbols. As a result, it is itself protected against errors. If the codeword is successfully decoded (i.e., the Reed-Solomon decoder believes that all errors have been successfully corrected), the CRC-4 provides an additional check of the correctness of the decoded value, *cf.* [19].
– **Low-order Address Bits (bits 47-0)**: The least significant bits of the virtual memory address.

By exploiting additional information about the way that virtual memory addresses are assigned, we can potentially provide even more protection. As a practical matter, the most significant bits of a virtual memory address will frequently take on a small number of values based on how the memory was allocated. By grouping similarly valued addresses we can reduce the number of low-order address bits that we need to store. Exploiting virtual memory addresses in this way allows us to encode pointer values as shown in Fig. 2b. In this format, the low-order address has been reduced to 32 bits, the number of parity symbols has been increased to 5, and an additional 4-bit field has been added:

---

[7] A small (less than 1 KiB), constant amount of additional storage is required, additional storage is not necessary when a pointer is "at rest". During encoding and decoding, additional memory *will* be required, likely in the form of stack memory.

[8] In the case of a DUE, our approach may enable the underlying error to be corrected. The detailed mechanisms for making this approach work are beyond the scope of this paper.

– **Memory Region (bits 35-32)**: We currently identify three memory regions: *stack*, *heap*, and *anonymous mappings*. The region that a particular pointer belongs to is recorded in this field. The 16 most significant bits of the base virtual memory address are stored separately (e.g., in a global variable). As a result, pointers can refer to up to 4 GiB of memory in each of these regions. Although it is not implemented in our current prototype, it is also possible to add additional memory regions dynamically. Up to 16 different memory regions can be identified with this field.

In our prototype implementation, we discover the addresses of the stack and heap by parsing `/proc/<pid>/maps`. We discover the virtual address of anonymous mappings by calling `mmap()` and extracting the most significant bits from the assigned address. Reducing the number of bits required to store the memory region[9] allows for the addition of 3 parity symbols. As a result, this encoding can correct errors that affect two or fewer symbols and detect errors that affect five or fewer symbols.

Adding a CRC to the encoding reduces the number of parity symbols that we can include. To understand the implications of trading a parity symbol for a CRC, we examine a third encoding, *see* Fig. 2c, that uses 6 parity symbols to protect the pointer.

4   Experimental Results

4.1   Prototype Implementation

To evaluate the potential costs and benefits of this approach, we created a prototype implementation using Schifra [1], an open-source Reed-Solomon library and CRC-4 source taken from Linux kernel version 4.20.4.[10]

4.2   Performance Evaluation

To evaluate the performance of our approach, we constructed a benchmark that obtains a pointer value, encodes it, corrupts it, and then attempts to decode it. We encode the pointer using each of the three encodings shown in Fig. 2 and discussed in Sect. 3. We corrupt the pointer by corrupting n symbols of the codeword, for $0 \leq n \leq 15$.[11] Each symbol is corrupted by changing the value of every bit in the symbol (i.e., XORing the 4-bit symbol with $0xF$). We also consider all $\binom{15}{k}$ combinations of corruptions, for $0 \leq k \leq 15$. For each combination of corruptions we encode and decode at least $100,000$ pointers; the

---

[9] Storage for the 16 bits that identify the memory region are effectively amortized over all of the virtual memory addresses in the region.

[10] The CRC4 source is available in `lib/crc4.c` and `lib/crc4.h` of the Linux kernel source.

[11] We do not corrupt the four most significant bits, since their contents are entirely ignored during decoding, i.e., we can tolerate any combination of errors in these bits without affecting our ability to correctly decode the codeword.

actual number is the smallest multiple of $\binom{15}{k}$ that is greater than $100,000$.[12] Each pointer is obtained by requesting $1\,\mathrm{KiB}$ of memory using `malloc()`.[13]

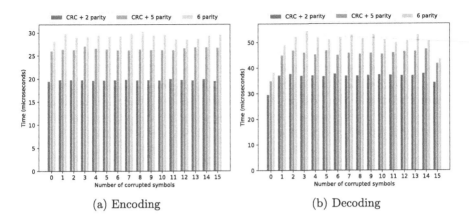

(a) Encoding   (b) Decoding

Fig. 3. Arithmetic mean of time required to encode and decode pointers (Color figure online)

4.3 Encoding and Decoding Performance

In this subsection, we consider the time required to encode a pointer and to decode the resulting codeword as a function of the number of symbols that are corrupted. All performance measurements were obtained from a Linux workstation with a $3.30\,\mathrm{GHz}$, quad-core Intel Core i5 (Sandy Bridge) processor that is running Red Hat Enterprise Linux (RHEL) version 6.10.

Figure 3 shows the arithmetic mean of the time to encode a pointer using a CRC-4 and 5 parity symbols (blue bars), and to decode corrupted versions of the resulting codewords (orange bars) as a function of the number of corrupted symbols. These data show that the time to encode a pointer is (unsurprisingly) consistent across trials: approximately $26.4\,\mu\mathrm{s}$ per encoding with less than a 4% difference between the minimum and maximum mean values. Encoding a pointer with 6 parity symbols is approximately 10.5% slower. Encoding a pointer with a CRC-4 and 2 parity symbols is approximately 25.5% faster.

The time required to decode a corrupted codeword is slower on average than encoding, averaging approximately $45.0\,\mu\mathrm{s}$ per decoding event, and is dependent on the number of corrupted symbols. Decoding an uncorrupted symbol is approximately 29.1% faster than the overall average. Uncorrupted symbols allows for the bypass of the algorithms that attempt to identify the nearest

---

[12] The reason for this is to ensure that our results weight the different arrangements of corrupted symbols equally.

[13] Because of memory limits, we periodically free the acquired memory. As a result, it is possible that multiple trials use the same pointer value.

codeword to the corrupted value. Additionally, decoding a codeword with all 15 symbols corrupted is approximately 8% faster. We have not been able to identify the precise reason for this speedup. Decoding a pointer with 6 parity symbols is 11.7% slower on average. Encoding a pointer with a CRC-4 and 2 parity symbols is 18.9% faster on average.

These performance results show that this approach to encoding and decoding pointers is fast; the overhead of a Corrected Machine Check Interrupt (CMCI) in response to a memory error corrected in hardware (775 μs) [11] is many times greater. However, the total overhead is tunable: the programmer chooses when to encode and decode the pointer. The benefit of this approach will be maximized when a pointer is encoded at the beginning of an interval when it is unlikely to be accessed and decodes it when a period of likely access begins.

4.4   Decoding Outcomes

Decoding may result in one of three possible outcomes: (i) *corrected*, the decoded pointer exactly matches the original pointer value; (ii) *detected*, the decoded pointer cannot be decoded but the error is detected; or (iii) *miscorrected*, the decoded pointer does not match the original pointer value and the error was not detected during decoding. Further, decoding errors can be *detected* in one of three ways, depending on the encoding that is used: (i) the Reed-Solomon algorithm will return an error (e.g., because the error appears to exceed its correction and detection capability); (ii) the CRC-4 in the decoded codeword (if present) is not consistent with the contents of the remainder of the codeword; or (iii) the memory region field (if present) does not represent a valid value. Currently, we support three memory regions, *see* Sect. 3. As a result, we know that the memory region in a valid codeword will match one of those three values.[14]

Figures 4, 5, and 6 show the breakdown of outcomes for decoding corrupted codewords. Outcomes are each assigned a color, the length of each colored region represents the fraction of our trials that resulted in a particular outcome. Each stacked bar corresponds to the number of symbols that were corrupted.

Figure 4 shows the breakdown of outcomes for decoding codewords that were encoded using a CRC-4 and two parity symbols, *see* Fig. 2a. With zero or one corrupted symbols, the Reed-Solomon algorithm matches its theoretical capabilities and successfully reconstructs the pointer. With two corrupted symbols, it detects all of the corrupted codewords. In this case, corrupting three or more symbols exceeds the theoretical limits of the algorithm. However, if we corrupt between 3 and 13 symbols, the Reed-Solomon algorithm is still able to detect the corruption in many cases (e.g., more than 94% of the trials with eight corrupted symbols). In this case, the Reed-Solomon algorithm appears to be much more effective at detecting an even number of corrupted symbols than an odd number of corrupted symbols. However, even for an odd number of corrupted

---

[14] This approach is potentially fragile because it may become necessary to support more memory regions. As a result, the number of invalid values will decrease and limit the effectiveness of this approach.

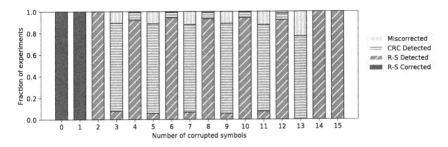

Fig. 4. Outcomes of decoding corrupted codewords (CRC + 2 parity symbols). (Color figure online)

symbols, verification of the CRC-4 detects many of the instances of corruption that the Reed-Solomon algorithm does not. For example, more than 83% of trials with five corrupted symbols are detected by the CRC-4, in fewer than 6% of these trials is the corruption detected by the Reed-Solomon algorithm itself. For a large number of corrupted symbols, a non-trivial number of miscorrections are possible, e.g., more than 22% of our trials with thirteen corrupted symbols resulted in a miscorrection. All of the trials with extreme corruption (i.e., 14 or 15 corrupted symbols) resulted in detection by the Reed-Solomon algorithm.

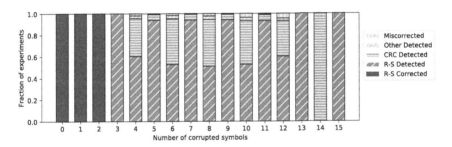

Fig. 5. Outcomes of decoding corrupted codewords (CRC + 5 parity symbols). (Color figure online)

Figure 5 shows the breakdown of outcomes for decoding codewords that were encoded using a CRC-4 and five parity symbols, *see* Fig. 2b. With zero to two corrupted symbols, the Reed-Solomon algorithm successfully recovers the pointer. The trials with three corrupted symbols all result in detection by the Reed-Solomon algorithm. For the trials with four or five corrupted symbols, the Reed-Solomon is theoretically capable of detecting all of the corruption but these results show that, in practice, the algorithm falls short of the theoretical limit, *cf.* Sect. 2.2. We also observe that the algorithm in this configuration is much better at detecting corruption in trials with an odd number of corrupted symbols than in trials with an even number of corruptions. However, the fraction of trials in which corruption is detected is, on the whole much higher than we observed for CRC-4 and two parity symbols, *see* Fig. 4. Additionally, for this encoding (CRC-4 and five parity symbols) it is also possible to detect corruption by checking for a valid memory region. For example, with eight corrupted symbols, corruption is detected using this method for approximately 3% of the trials. Overall, this encoding significantly reduces the miscorrection rate relative to CRC-4 and 2 parity symbols: no more than 4.5% of trials for a given number of corrupted symbols result in miscorrection.

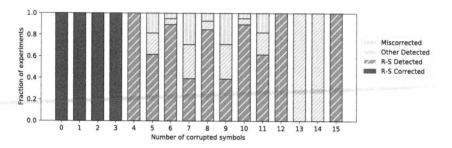

Fig. 6. Outcomes of decoding corrupted codewords (6 parity symbols). (Color figure online)

Figure 5 shows the breakdown of outcomes for decoding codewords that were encoded using six parity symbols, *see* Fig. 2c. Fundamentally, these data allow us to compare the relative protective benefit of using 4 bits for a CRC-4 with using those 4 bits for an additional parity symbol. As these data show, adding a parity symbol allows the Reed-Solomon algorithm to correct up to three corrupted symbols. However, the frequency of miscorrection is much greater than for the CRC-4 and 5 parity symbols encoding: more than 29% of trials with 7 corrupted symbols resulted in miscorrection. For many trials, corruption can be detected by checking for a valid memory region encoding, but the value of this approach may diminish if more than three memory regions have to be supported. Although this encoding has a higher rate of miscorrection when significant corruption (i.e., 5 or more corrupted symbols) occurs, if DUEs are a larger concern than SDC then its ability to correct a larger number of corrupted symbols may recommend it over CRC-4 and 5 parity symbols.

5   Related Work

FlipSphere [10] uses a hash and ECC to detect SDC. When an application accesses a memory page that has not been recently accessed, the integrity of its contents are verified using a CRC-32 detect unexpected modifications. Single-bit errors are corrected with SECDED. While FlipSphere provides strong protection, it is expensive (every protected page requires 516 additional bytes of memory) and slow (up to 70% runtime overhead).

PointGuard [7] protects pointers against malicious corruption by using a compiler extension to XOR pointers with a random, fixed key each time they are transferred to, or from, memory. This prevents attackers from reliably corrupting pointers (e.g., return addresses) to get the target to execute malicious code. Similarly, Watchdoglite [16] protects against malicious pointer corruption by maintaining metadata to verify its validity (e.g., the bounds of the memory region it can refer to). These approaches detect some pointer corruption, but they can not correct corrupted pointers. Moreover, Watchdoglite requires additional per-pointer memory to store metadata. Casas et al. [6] uses pointer triplication to detect and correct pointer corruption. While this approach can detect and correct corrupted pointers, it triples the memory required to store each pointer.

Gottscho et al. [12] and Poulos et al. [17] have proposed strategies for using knowledge about the hardware ECC to correct DUEs. Our approach can also potentially correct DUEs, but also provides strong protection against SDC. Moreover, it may be possible to combine our approach with theirs to provide additional protection.

6 Future Work

Based on the promising results presented in this paper, we intend to construct a software framework to simplify developer use of these ideas. Given this infrastructure, we intend to study the performance impact of this approach on important scientific workloads. A compiler extension may also be able to automate the encoding and decoding of pointers.

7 Conclusion

In this paper, we provide a detailed description of a space-efficient approach to using Reed-Solomon encoding to protect against pointer corruption. We demonstrate that our approach is *fast*, less than $45\,\mu s$ per encoding/decoding event, *robust*, the rate of miscorrection (silent data corruption) is less than 5% even when significant corruption is introduced, *space-efficient*, no additional per-pointer memory is required, and *tunable*, the programmer (or perhaps the compiler) uses program knowledge to decide when to encode and decode pointers.

References

1. GitHub - ArashPartow/schifra: C++ Reed Solomon error correcting library. http://github.com/ArashPartow/schifra/, commit b493921465840ef28ad8e4b8445569f624f11d92
2. GitHub - pjkundert/ezpwd-reed-solomon: Reed-Solomon & BCH encoding and decoding. https://github.com/pjkundert/ezpwd-reed-solomon, commit 6b5af65efd31a494245eb1dc84336eba41cdefa7
3. AMD: BIOS and kernel developer guide (BKDG) for AMD family 16h models 00h–0fh processors. http://support.amd.com/TechDocs/48751_16h_bkdg.pdf

4. ARM: ARMv8-A address translation: Translating a virtual address to a physical address. https://developer.arm.com/docs/100940/latest/translating-a-virtual-address-to-a-physical-address

5. Bosilca, G., Delmas, R., Dongarra, J., Langou, J.: Algorithm-based fault tolerance applied to high performance computing. J. Parallel Distrib. Comput. **69**(4), 410–416 (2009)

6. Casas, M., de Supinski, B.R., Bronevetsky, G., Schulz, M.: Fault resilience of the algebraic multi-grid solver. In: Proceedings of the 26th ACM International Conference on Supercomputing, pp. 91–100. ACM (2012)

7. Cowan, C., Beattie, S., Johansen, J., Wagle, P.: PointGuard^{TM}: protecting pointers from buffer overflow vulnerabilities. In: Proceedings of the 12th Conference on USENIX Security Symposium, vol. 12, pp. 91–104 (2003)

8. Dell, T.J.: A white paper on the benefits of chipkill-correct ECC for PC server main memory. IBM Microelectron. Div. **11**, 1–23 (1997)

9. Elliott, J., Hoemmen, M., Mueller, F.: Evaluating the impact of SDC on the GMRES iterative solver. In: 2014 IEEE 28th International Parallel and Distributed Processing Symposium, pp. 1193–1202. IEEE (2014)

10. Fiala, D., Mueller, F., Ferreira, K.B.: FlipSphere: a software-based DRAM error detection and correction library for HPC. In: 2016 IEEE/ACM 20th International Symposium on Distributed Simulation and Real Time Applications (DS-RT), pp. 19–28. IEEE (2016)

11. Gottscho, M., Shoaib, M., Govindan, S., Sharma, B., Wang, D., Gupta, P.: Measuring the impact of memory errors on application performance. IEEE Comput. Archit. Lett. **16**(1), 51–55 (2017)

12. Gottscho, M., Schoeny, C., Dolecek, L., Gupta, P.: Software-defined error-correcting codes. In: 2016 46th Annual IEEE/IFIP International Conference on Dependable Systems and Networks Workshop (DSN-W), pp. 276–282. IEEE (2016)

13. Intel: Intel 64 and IA-32 architectures software developer's manual, January 2019. http://www.intel.com/content/www/us/en/processors/architectures-software-developer-manuals.html

14. Jian, X., Duwe, H., Sartori, J., Sridharan, V., Kumar, R.: Low-power, low-storage-overhead chipkill correct via multi-line error correction. In: Proceedings of the International Conference on High Performance Computing, Networking, Storage and Analysis, p. 24. ACM (2013)

15. May, T.C., Woods, M.H.: Alpha-particle-induced soft errors in dynamic memories. IEEE Trans. Electron Devices **26**(1), 2–9 (1979)

16. Nagarakatte, S., Martin, M.M., Zdancewic, S.: WatchdogLite: hardware-accelerated compiler-based pointer checking. In: Proceedings of Annual IEEE/ACM International Symposium on Code Generation and Optimization, p. 175. ACM (2014)

17. Poulos, A., et al.: Improving application resilience by extending error correction with contextual information. In: 2018 IEEE/ACM 8th Workshop on Fault Tolerance for HPC at eXtreme Scale (FTXS), pp. 19–28. IEEE (2018)

18. Sridharan, V., et al.: Memory errors in modern systems: the good, the bad, and the ugly. ACM SIGPLAN Not. **50**(4), 297–310 (2015)

19. Yang, C.Q., Hossain, E., Bhargava, V.K.: On adaptive hybrid error control in wireless networks using Reed-Solomon codes. IEEE Trans. Wireless Commun. **4**(3), 835–840 (2005)

Improving Reliability for Provisioning of Virtual Machines in Desktop Clouds

Carlos E. Gómez[1,2]($\boxtimes$) (ID), Jaime Chavarriaga[1] (ID), Andrei Tchernykh[3,4] (ID),
and Harold E. Castro[1] (ID)

[1] Systems and Computing Engineering Department, Universidad de los Andes,
Bogotá, Colombia
{ce.gomez10,ja.chavarriaga908,hcastro}@uniandes.edu.co
[2] Universidad del Quindío, Armenia, Colombia
[3] CICESE Research Center, Ensenada, Mexico
chernykh@cicese.mx
[4] South Ural State University, Chelyabinsk, Russia

Abstract. Desktop clouds (DC) provide services in non-stationary environments that face reliability and performance threats not found in traditional clusters and datacenters. The idle resources available on computers can be claimed by users, turned off and faulted any time. For instance, platforms such as CernVM and UnaCloud harvest idle resources on computer labs to run virtual machines and support scientific applications. These platforms deal with interruptions and interferences caused by both users and applications. This non-stationarity is one of the main sources of issues in the design of reliable desktop cloud infrastructures that are capable of mitigating their own faults and errors. Based on a fault analysis that we have been carrying out and refining for a couple of years, we have found that reliability problems begin as the number of virtual machines that are going to be executed increases; these virtual machines must first be provisioned in the physical machines where they will be hosted. On the one hand, the main factors that can affect the provisioning of virtual machines in a DC are: the use of disk space, and the transmission of virtual images over the network. On the other hand, the applications and actions performed by users in the desktops may cause the virtual machine malfunction. In this paper, we propose an strategy based on known techniques applied to a particular environment: the scalable provisioning of virtual machines in desktop clouds. In addition, we describe the implementation and analyze its effectiveness.

Keywords: Reliability · VM provisioning · Fault tolerance · Chain of threats

1 Introduction

Desktop clouds (DC) are opportunistic platforms based on virtualization that offer cloud computing services on common desktop computers [2]. They take

U. Schwardmann et al. (Eds.): Euro-Par 2019 Workshops, LNCS 11997, pp. 669–680, 2020.
https://doi.org/10.1007/978-3-030-48340-1_51

advantage of idle resources in computers when their users perform regular activities. A DC manages these resources to execute virtual machines (VMs), with their operating systems and applications, without the users of these physical machines (PMs) perceiving a slowdown in the performance of the computer or feeling that their security is compromised. DC is a rugged platform in which resources (computing capacity, network and disk), are shared with the user of the physical machine.

DCs, such as $CernVM^1$ [13] and $UnaCloud^2$ [12], execute VMs on desktop computers located on university or business campuses where the aggregate capacity of idle resources is significant [7]. Typically, these DCs offer a subset of the infrastructure services provided by private and public cloud platforms based on dedicated infrastructure, such as $OpenStack^3$ and $Amazon\ Web\ Services^4$. Researchers can use DCs to execute scientific and academic tasks just like they use traditional cloud platforms. These tasks run on VMs on desktops, at the same time as the programs launched by the users of these computers [8].

DCs are more susceptible to failures than other cloud platforms because their infrastructure is not based on dedicated data centers nor on dedicated hardware. Considering our analysis of faults in a DC, presented in [9], we have found that the faults that affect the reliability of this class of systems occur mainly in two moments: in the provisioning, and in the execution of the VMs. On the one hand, provisioning of VMs has significant limitations in its scalability. The disk images used by the VMs, a.k.a. virtual images (VI), are large files whose transmission may take a while and is failure-prone. On the other hand, executing VMs in the presence of users in the same computers may affect their normal operation. Tasks executed by a DC can be interrupted by applications run by the users. As a result, the DC user may lose the work done so far.

Typically, a DC offers a *best effort* service without warranties on the execution of the tasks sent to the platform. The cloud users must check if the tasks were executed satisfactorily and, if necessary, start again their execution. The platform reliability is one of its most important aspects to improve in DCs.

This paper revisits our previous work [9] characterizing the faults that could occur in DC platforms. Here, we present a more comprehensive analysis that considers, not only the *UnaCloud* platform, but also other DC platforms such as *BOINC*, *cuCloud* and *CernVM*. We propose an improved mitigation strategy to overcome the detected failures. This paper describes a new approach for provisioning VMs by using pre-loaded templates of virtual images and customized images configured as multiattach disks. These techniques are well known and used in other contexts. Now, we are going to apply them in the provisioning of VMs in DCs. According to our preliminary evaluation, this strategy reduces the required transmission time and disk space, which allows us to provision and deploy multiple VMs for each host in a very short time and without failures.

---

[1] https://cernvm.cern.ch/.

[2] https://sistemasproyectos.uniandes.edu.co/iniciativas/unacloud/.

[3] https://www.openstack.org/.

[4] https://aws.amazon.com/.

The rest of this paper is organized as follows. Section 2, gives a background, describing how the DC platforms work. Section 3 includes related work regarding reliability on DC systems. With respect to our contributions, Sect. 4 talks about our revisited fault analysis, Sect. 5 introduces a new approach for scalable provisioning of VMs, and Sect. 6 presents the preliminary evaluation. Finally, Sect. 7, concludes the paper and discusses the future work.

2 Background About Desktop Cloud Systems

Desktop clouds take advantage of the idle capacity in a set of computers to provide Infrastructure as a Service (IaaS), a form of cloud computing. For DC users, the system offers infrastructure just like any other cloud platform. Behind the scenes, DCs run VMs on desktop computers, such as those found in university computer labs [4]. This section presents a background on the DCs and their operation.

DC is a computational paradigm that combines volunteer computing and cloud computing [2,6,12]. Its goal is to make shared resources available to users in order to provide cloud computing services without using dedicated resources. DCs use idle computing resources of the participant computers to provide services for processing, storage, networking, and applications using VMs running operating systems and their respective applications.

In contrast to traditional cloud platforms, DCs do not rely on specialized hardware or data centers. They use non-dedicated resources, typically heterogeneous, obtained from diverse computers such as those found in the computer labs and offices in a university. In addition, DCs typically do not offer solutions aimed to meet service-level agreements (SLA), nor do they offer advanced tools for monitoring or billing. Traditionally, a DC offers a *best effort* service that may run computing tasks at lower costs than other dedicated platforms [1].

Operation of a Desktop Cloud. Typically, a DC uses a client-server architecture: there is a *DC server* program in charge of receiving and processing requests from users and a *DC client* program running on each desktop computer. The DC server has (or builds) an inventory of PMs that can be used and a mechanism for allocating VMs on these machines. Basically, each PM has a computational capacity in use and an idle computational capacity that can be exploited. When a request for deploying VMs is received, the DC server determines which PMs can run them. The DC client software on each PM receives instructions from the DC server to copy the required files, create, configure and execute the requested VMs.

The functioning of a DC comprises two phases: (1) a conditioning phase and, (2) an operation phase. The *conditioning phase* groups four activities: (1.1) Preparing the virtual images. It consists in the creation of the virtual images, including the operating system, libraries and the applications properly configured and customized by the user for its execution. (1.2) Requesting the deployment of one or more VMs from a virtual image. (1.3) Scheduling the resource allocation. The system selects, by means of a location algorithm, the PMs that will be used for the execution of the VMs. As a result, multiple VMs can be assigned to the same PM. (1.4) Provisioning the VMs. The DC copies the virtual images in the PMs, creates the VMs and then configures them. During the *operation phase*, the DC platform (2.1) controls the VMs, e.g. starting, pausing or stopping a VM; and (2.2) monitors their execution.

There are many problems that may occur at provisioning the VMs. Provisioning implies tasks such as transmitting the virtual image to the desktop, creating the VM o VMs based on that virtual image, configuring the hypervisor to use that virtual image, starting the VM and copying data and installing additional software in that VM. Any of these tasks may fail. In a previous work [5] we noted a large number of requested machines that were not deployed by a DC. We are interested in analyzing the failures that may occur in that phase and provide means to detect, at runtime, the type of problem that is occurring and the proper strategy that must be used.

3   Related Work

Many authors have analyzed reliability problems that occur on DC platforms at provisioning VMs. This section presents some extensions and strategies that overcome these limitations.

Volunteer based DC platforms are systems where desktop users donate their idle computing resources. An agent in each computer, when detecting some idle capacity, requests a task to the platform and runs a VM to do it. These systems have inherent problems of volatility and availability because users on the desktops may claim idle resources and stop assigned tasks at anytime [10]. These systems typically replicate the same tasks for running on multiple desktops. If one desktop fails, the other desktops may report results.

Appliance based DC platforms are volunteer based platforms where desktop computers run optimized virtual images. Instead of using typical virtual images that must be transmitted each time, these platforms use custom images and specialized provisioning software to reduce transmission and improve starting time. Unlike other platforms that must transmit large virtual images before running VMs, appliance based systems such as *CernVM* [13] use the same small-sized virtual image for all the users and run any additional software using *CernVM-FS*, a set of remote read-only file-systems. These solutions reduce the space required in each desktop, but increase the use of the network and require a team responsible for maintaining and configuring the virtual image and the file-systems with the software.

Private-cloud based DC platforms extend existing cloud platforms to integrate physical computers when they are idle. Private-cloud based DCs must manage the volatility of these physical machines. Several works have extended the monitoring tools existing in the private-cloud platforms to support different strategies. *cuCloud* [11], for instance, predicts future availability and reliability based on historical information from volunteers to allocate the VMs considering its probability to fail.

Opportunistic DC platforms are systems designed to run VMs on desktops while the users on these computers do not notice it. *UnaCloud*, for instance, runs one or more VMs on the same PM at the lowest possible priority to minimize interference to applications started by the desktop users. *UnaCloud* has been used to run *HPC* and grid computing applications, and this platform has experienced problems related to the VMs provisioning. To overcome them, for instance, *UnaCloud* has been extended to transmit virtual images using *peer-to-peer* protocols [5]. They found that using protocols such as BitTorrent it is possible to reduce the time required to transmit files and the number of failures caused by transmission errors and timeouts.

4 A Revisited Fault Analysis for Desktop Cloud Platforms

Recently, we have updated our fault analysis [9] regarding the provisioning of VMs, considering not only *UnaCloud* but also other of DC platforms. We used the *extended chain of threats* to analyze faults, errors, failures and mitigation strategies. As a result, we identified two main types of errors: when (1) the DC cannot copy the virtual image to the desktop and when (2) DC cannot configure and start the VM.

E_1: The DC can not copy the virtual image. It can fail due to communication errors, timeouts and insufficient disk space in the desktop. Network congestion and the large size of the files to transmit, i.e. the files for the virtual image and the software packages to install, are some of the causes. Figure 1 shows the extended chain of threats for the error E_1. *Mitigation strategies* include:

- M_1: Using efficient transmission protocols, such as *P2P* file sharing implemented in *UnaCloud* [5].
- M_2: Using mechanisms to reduce the files to transmit, such as the use of small-sized virtual images used in *CernVM* [13].
- M_3: Using mechanisms to reduce the need for transmitting files, such as the caching of frequently used virtual images, used in *CernVM* [13].

In addition, we are proposing other two strategies distilled from some experiments performed on *UnaCloud*:

- M_4: Using efficient disk space management, such as the linked clone disks and the multiattach virtual disks available on hypervisors such as *VirtualBox*[5], *KVM*[6] and *VMware*[7]. These techniques can be used to run multiple VMs sharing disks among them and, therefore, to optimize disk space on desktops.
- M_5: Using allocation methods that considers disk space, that prevent the systems to assign desktops without enough space.

---

[5] https://www.virtualbox.org/.
[6] https://www.linux-kvm.org/.
[7] https://www.vmware.com/products/workstation-pro.html.

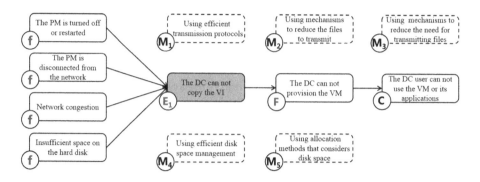

Fig. 1. Fault propagation: *The desktop cloud cannot copy the virtual image.*

E₂: The DC cannot configure and start the VM. It can fail when the virtual image is incompatible with the hypervisor installed in the desktop or does not include some required software. In some DCs such as *UnaCloud* and *BOINC*, the configuration may fail if the virtual image does not satisfy some requirements or does not have configured some predefined user accounts. For instance, these DCs use special types of networking and require specific settings in the virtual image. If the virtual image does not satisfy these requirements, the VMs cannot be configured nor started. Figure 2 shows the extended chain of threats for the error E₂. *Mitigation strategies* include:

- M₆: Using preconfigured templates of virtual images, already tested by DC administrators and staff, instead of arbitrary images customized by cloud users. For instance, this strategy is used by *CernVM* and *cuCloud*, platforms that offer catalogs of images that the users may select to create their VMs.
- M₇: Provision additional VMs than those needed to have backup VMs in case that some VMs can not be configured and started correctly. This strategy is used, for instance, by *BOINC* [3]. It assigns the same task to many nodes expecting that some, probably not all of them, may process the task and provide a response.

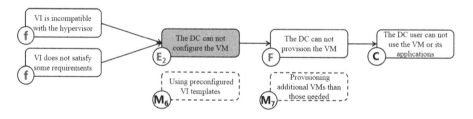

Fig. 2. Fault propagation: *The desktop cloud cannot provision the VM.*

5   Implementing Strategies to Improve *UnaCloud* Reliability at Provisioning Virtual Machines

Based on our fault analysis, we have extended *UnaCloud* to implement three strategies to improve the reliability during the provisioning of VMs. Previously, we implemented the use of efficient transmission protocols [5]. Now, we are implementing: (1) using preconfigured virtual images, (2) using efficient disk space management by running VMs using multiattach disks, and (3) using mechanisms to reduce the files to transmit, by preloading base images in the desktops where the VMs will run. The implementation of these strategies is described below.

5.1   Using Preconfigured Templates of Virtual Images

We reviewed the diverse applications we are running on *UnaCloud*. Nowadays, our users create clusters of VMs to run MPI-based applications, especially GRO-MACS for computational chemistry and other HPC custom applications. Almost all the users run Debian or Ubuntu Linux Operating System, using some distribution of MPI. Instead of requiring users to create their own virtual image, we created a single virtual image that can be used by them.

We created a customized virtual image based on Ubuntu 16.04 by installing software such as NFS servers and clients, MPI libraries and some other utility programs. We defined some scripts that run at startup and that can be used to request data from servers or to install additional software when a VM starts.

5.2   Using Efficient Disk Space Management Mechanisms

Instead of having multiple copies of the same virtual image, one for each VM running on a desktop, we are using multiattach virtual disks. Using this writing mode, we define a single virtual disk that is shared across multiple VMs running at the same time. The content of the shared disk is not modified. Each VM creates a differential disk storing only its own changes. Typically, because our DC users only creates some configuration files and connect to different NFS remote disks to obtain their data, this results in relatively small files that do not consume large amounts of disk space on the desktops.

Note that this strategy, which we did not found in the other DCs, help to minimize problems related to consuming unnecessary disk space in the desktops.

5.3   Using Mechanisms to Reduce the Need for Transmitting Files

As a complement to the two previous strategies, we propose to copy, in advance, the files of the template virtual image in the desktops where the VMs will run. Considering that almost all the users can run MPI-applications using our template and we use the computers in the labs of the university. We copied the templates in these computers and modified the *UnaCloud* agents to check the existence of templates before requesting a copy.

We implemented this copying process as an on-demand task. We are considering a new extension where the most-used templates or the required templates for scheduled experiments are copied automatically at low-congestion times. *UnaCloud* may determine upfront the templates to be used in some labs and perform the copies at night or at times where the network has low usage rates.

6   Preliminary Evaluation

We have been working on improving the *UnaCloud* reliability at provisioning VMs. In the past we had many difficulties to achieve successful implementations of more than 20 machines. In 2017, after some improvements, we provisioned clusters of 100 nodes with 98% success [5]. Now, by applying the proposed strategies, we can deploy consistently, and without failures, fully successful deployments of up to 400 VMs.

6.1   Provisioning Large Clusters Using Our Approach

To analyze the time and errors provisioning clusters in *UnaCloud*, we conducted an experiment using up to 50 desktop computers and provisioned up to 200 VMs. We used a 3.51 GB Ubuntu Server 16.04 virtual image to deploy VMs with 1 GB RAM, 5 GB of virtual hard disk and 1 processing core. The VMs ran on desktops with an Intel Core i7-4770 processor, 20 GB of RAM and 500 GB of hard disk. We used a computer lab with 78 desktops. All of them connected to a 1 GB Ethernet network.

Table 1 shows the average provision time. Since when using the proposed strategies, it is not necessary to transmit files to the desktop, the provisioning time is the time used in creating the VM and making the necessary configuration so that it is ready for execution. It is important to note that in our experiments we created up to four VMs in the same PM, and 100% of the VMs were provisioned successfully, without failures during the process.

Table 1. *UnaCloud* behavior after implementing the mitigation strategies

#V/PMs	Time	#V/PMs	Time	#V/PMs	Time	#V/PMs	Time
1/1	0,98	2/1	9,45	3/1	18,55	4/1	28,38
2/2	1,04	4/2	10,32	6/2	19,90	8/2	28,98
5/5	1,02	10/5	10,24	15/5	20,89	20/5	30,72
10/10	1,09	20/10	11,33	30/10	20,40	40/10	31,09
20/20	1,10	40/20	11,32	60/20	21,27	80/20	31,39
50/50	1,10	100/50	11,38	150/50	21,75	200/50	31,38
(a)		(b)		(c)		(d)	

Table 1 includes the maximum provision time of the experiment. In (a), we see the time from 1 to 50 VMs using 1 PM to host 1 VM. In (b), (c) and (d), the ratios are 2 VMs in 1 PM, 3 VMs in 1 PM and 4 VMs in 1 PM. Using a 1VM/1PM ratio, we can note that provisioning from 1 to 50 VMs vary from 0.98 to 1.10 s.

Table 1 (b) shows that when changing the proportion of VMs/PMs, the times increase, because a VM is first created and connected with a preloaded disk in multiattach mode, and subsequently the following VMs are created one by one on the same host. When the ratio is 2 VMs on 1 host, the VMs can be provisioned between 9.45 and 11.38 s. It is remarkable that we can provision 100 VMs in 50 PMs in just 11.38 s, using a classic 1 Gbps Ethernet shared with the students' regular browsing activities.

Table 1 (c) presents the provisioning time of 3 to 150 VMs in 1 to 50 PMs with a ratio of 3 VMs in each 1 host. The times obtained were from 18.55 to 21.75 s. In this experiment, the provisioning time for 150 VMs was only 21.75 s.

Finally, Table 1 (d) reports the provisioning times by using a ratio of 4 VMs in each PM, supplying between 4 and 200 VMs in times between 28.38 and 31.38 s.

6.2 Errors at Provisioning Virtual Machines

Regretfully, our previous monitoring systems reported failed deployments but did not identify the errors that caused the failures. We are implementing now a new monitoring system that identifies, with some level of confidence, the cause of the errors. However, we cannot compare the efficiency of our strategies. This section presents a discussion of the errors prevented by the three strategies implemented in *UnaCloud* and reported in this paper. The following are the faults described in the extended chain of threats in Sect. 4.

Network congestion and errors. The mentioned strategies reduce (or eliminate) the need of transmitting virtual images. Typical users can start VMs using a preloaded templates of a virtual images in the desktops. These deployments do not need to transfer any files.

Insufficient space on desktop's hard disks. Considering that VMs use mutiattach disks, the space required in the desktops is reduced. For instance, according to the results obtained in our experiments, instead of requiring 3.51 GB for each VM running in a desktop, using the mutiattach disks requires 0.29 GB for each additional VM running in the same desktop.

The virtual image does not meet required specifications. Given that we provide a tested virtual image for running the VMs, we are assuring that it will meet all the requirements of the system. In our tests, we have been able to configure and start all the VMs using our predefined virtual image.

There are two faults that cannot be prevented by the strategies discussed in this paper: (1) when desktops are turned off or restarted and (2) when desktops are disconnected from the network at that same time that some virtual images are being copied or VMs are being configured. These faults are inevitable given the not-dedicated nature of the hardware used in DCs.

6.3   Discussion

The proposed strategies are easy to apply and the benefits can be obtained by carrying them out together.

The preload of a disk implies that it contains a virtual image. Although a normal disk can be preloaded, and thus prevent the network consumption that would be used in the transfer of the virtual image, this type of disk requires cloning mechanisms that consume time in the creation of VMs and inefficiently occupy the disk space.

We suggest that the same platform provide the virtual images in the form of a catalog with images ready to be used in the provisioning of VMs. Although it is a task that seems simple, it is necessary to have a team in charge of creating the images and implementing the changes when necessary. Modifications to the virtual image are a challenge due to the impact that the modifications can have on the VMs that have been created. Therefore, we understand that in the future it will be necessary to develop a version control system to deal with this circumstance.

By using multiattach writing mode disks preloaded with preconfigured virtual images, that can be connected to multiple VMs at runtime, we not only manage the space more efficiently, but we also prevent the transfer of voluminous files over the same network through which users access the Internet.

This, on the one hand, decreases the provisioning time and, on the other, significantly improves the performance of the network for users.

In addition, since after creating a VM, it is connected to the disk with the operating system and the applications installed and configured, the VM is quickly ready for execution. Therefore, the creation of one or more VMs in the same PM is a much faster process, compared to the equivalent process of creating VMs by cloning existing ones.

In addition, to have virtual images ready to use on disks in multiattach writing mode, our strategies enable the possibility of migrating VMs at run time. In this case it is sufficient to move the files of the differential disks to the PM in which a VM will run and it will quickly be running again.

Finally, to implement this strategy in *Oracle VirtualBox*, it was necessary to develop applications not available in the hypervisor. The created applications allow us to preload the disk in the PM and register it at the hypervisor, create a virtual machine from an image stored in a multiattach disk, and create an VM from another one that is connected to a disk multiattach, among other tools.

7   Conclusion and Future Work

In this paper, we present (1) a revisited reliability analysis for desktop cloud systems and (2) a *UnaCloud* extension that implements strategies to improve reliability at provisioning VMs.

On the one hand, we extended our analysis of faults experienced in *UnaCloud* to consider faults and mitigation strategies that occur in desktop cloud platforms such as *BOINC, CernVM* and *cuCloud*. Our analysis, based on *extended chains of threats*, includes information not only of failures, errors and faults, but also of the mitigation strategies that can help us face these faults. With respect to the analysis published a year ago, this time we have included new mitigation strategies and redefined others. For instance, *using efficient disk space management*, such as the linked-clones and the multiattach disks, is a new strategy, and *educate the desktop cloud user in the creation of their virtual images* was redefined.

On the other hand, we implemented the following three strategies in *UnaCloud*. We (1) defined a template of a virtual image that can be used by almost all the users, (2) used multiattach disks to efficiently manage the disk space in desktops, and (3) preloaded the virtual image in the desktops to reduce the need for transmitting files.

As future work, we are considering to use the information gathered in monitoring to improve decisions regarding VMs allocation and scheduling. We are also considering new analyses and experiments to validate the findings presented in this paper and to improve the strategies already implemented.

Acknowledgments. We would like to thank *David Camilo Bonilla Verdugo* for all his collaboration running the experiments discussed in this paper.

References

1. Alwabel, A., Walters, R., Wills, G.: Towards a volunteer cloud architecture. In: Tribastone, M., Gilmore, S. (eds.) EPEW 2012. LNCS, vol. 7587, pp. 248–251. Springer, Heidelberg (2013). https://doi.org/10.1007/978-3-642-36781-6_18

2. Alwabel, A., Walters, R.J., Wills, G.B.: A view at desktop clouds. In: International Workshop on Emerging Software as a Service and Analytics (ESaaSA 2014), pp. 55–61. ScitePress, Barcelona (2014)

3. Anderson, D.P.: Boinc: A system for public-resource computing and storage. In: Proceedings of the 5th IEEE/ACM International Workshop on Grid Computing, pp. 4–10. IEEE Computer Society (2004)

4. Anderson, D.P.: Volunteer computing: the ultimate cloud. ACM Crossroads **16**(3), 7–10 (2010)

5. Chavarriaga, J., Forero-González, C., Padilla-Agudelo, J., Muñoz, A., Cáliz-Ospino, R., Castro, H.: Scaling the deployment of virtual machines in UnaCloud. In: Mocskos, E., Nesmachnow, S. (eds.) CARLA 2017. CCIS, vol. 796, pp. 399–413. Springer, Cham (2018). https://doi.org/10.1007/978-3-319-73353-1_28

6. Cunsolo, V.D., Distefano, S., Puliafito, A., Scarpa, M.: Volunteer computing and desktop cloud: the cloud@ home paradigm. In: Eighth IEEE International Symposium on Network Computing and Applications (NCA 2009), Cambridge, MA, USA, pp. 134–139. IEEE (2009)

7. Gómez, C.E., Díaz, C.O., Forero, C.A., Rosales, E., Castro, H.: Determining the real capacity of a desktop cloud. In: Osthoff, C., Navaux, P.O.A., Barrios Hernandez, C.J., Silva Dias, P.L. (eds.) CARLA 2015. CCIS, vol. 565, pp. 62–72. Springer, Cham (2015). https://doi.org/10.1007/978-3-319-26928-3_5

8. Gómez, C.E., Chavarriaga, J., Bonilla, D.C., Castro, H.E.: Global snapshot file tracker. In: Florez, H., Diaz, C., Chavarriaga, J. (eds.) ICAI 2018. CCIS, vol. 942, pp. 90–104. Springer, Cham (2018). https://doi.org/10.1007/978-3-030-01535-0_7

9. Gómez, C.E., Chavarriaga, J., Castro, H.E.: Fault characterization and mitigation strategies in desktop cloud systems. In: Meneses, E., Castro, H., Barrios Hernández, C.J., Ramos-Pollan, R. (eds.) CARLA 2018. CCIS, vol. 979, pp. 322–335. Springer, Cham (2019). https://doi.org/10.1007/978-3-030-16205-4_24

10. Marosi, A., Kovács, J., Kacsuk, P.: Towards a volunteer cloud system. Futur. Gener. Comput. Syst. **29**(6), 1442–1451 (2013)

11. Mengistu, T.M., Alahmadi, A.M., Alsenani, Y., Albuali, A., Che, D.: cuCloud: volunteer computing as a service (VCaaS) system. In: Luo, M., Zhang, L.-J. (eds.) CLOUD 2018. LNCS, vol. 10967, pp. 251–264. Springer, Cham (2018). https://doi.org/10.1007/978-3-319-94295-7_17

12. Rosales, E., Castro, H., Villamizar, M.: UnaCloud: opportunistic cloud computing infrastructure as a service. In: Second International Conferences on Cloud Computing, GRIDs, and Virtualization (CLOUD COMPUTING 2011), pp. 187–194. ThinkMind (2011)

13. Segal, B., et al.: LHC cloud computing with CernVM. In: 13th International Workshop on Advanced Computing and Analysis Techniques in Physics Research (ACAT2010), Jaipur, India, p. 004. PoS (2010)

Physics-Based Checksums for Silent-Error Detection in PDE Solvers

Maher Salloum, Jackson R. Mayo$^{(\boxtimes)}$, and Robert C. Armstrong

Sandia National Laboratories, P.O. Box 969, Livermore, CA 94551, USA
{mnsallo,jmayo,rob}@sandia.gov

Abstract. We discuss techniques for efficient local detection of silent data corruption in parallel scientific computations, leveraging physical quantities such as momentum and energy that may be conserved by discretized PDEs. The conserved quantities are analogous to "algorithm-based fault tolerance" checksums for linear algebra but, due to their physical foundation, are applicable to both linear and nonlinear equations and have efficient local updates based on fluxes between subdomains. These physics-based checksums enable precise intermittent detection of errors and recovery by rollback to a checkpoint, with very low overhead when errors are rare. We present applications to both explicit hyperbolic and iterative elliptic (unstructured finite-element) solvers with injected memory bit flips.

Keywords: Silent errors · Partial differential equations · Linear algebra · Algorithm-based fault tolerance · Checkpoint/restart

1 Introduction

The effects of faults at extreme scale are a growing concern for high-performance computing (HPC) applied to scientific simulation [4]. Much resilience work deals with recovery from hard failures, such as a node that crashes. However, erroneous behavior can manifest in other ways. For example, an error may not immediately cause a crash, but may lead to an insidious wrong answer or cascade to a costly wider failure, which could be avoided if caught earlier. Thus, detecting errors with locality in space and time provides the best opportunity to mitigate them.

In scientific computations, error detection at the application level is facilitated by properties that are common in these simulations and are typically violated when errors occur: smoothness, conservation, and other numerical characteristics. In the face of uncertainty about likely error types and rates at extreme scale, improved algorithmic detection can aid both diagnosis and recovery.

Silent hardware errors, such as silent data corruption, are a prime example where precise detection is important. The future prevalence of these errors is

Under the terms of Contract DE-NA0003525, there is a non-exclusive license for use of this work by or on behalf of the U.S. Government.

unclear, but there is concern that they will be significant at extreme scale [4]. In addition, improved algorithmic detection could help diagnose and localize subtle software issues such as numerical instability and race conditions [2,9].

Existing work on algorithm-based fault tolerance (ABFT) has developed approaches for application-level error detection. Generic ABFT for linear algebra solvers can be achieved using checksums [13]. In addition, scientific computations often feature physical conserved quantities such as energy or momentum, which can be viewed as a type of checksum, even for nonlinear problems. Such checksums and conserved quantities enable detecting errors reliably. However, in their standard form, they are defined globally, so in a parallel solver they require expensive collective communication [1] and do not localize errors to specific processes or tasks.

Spatially local error detection offers the potential for greater scalability of resilience, reducing communication and allowing more efficient local (rather than global) recovery, just as is sought for other localized failures in parallel programming models [6,14]. Techniques explored for detecting errors locally in scientific computations include machine learning [12], comparison between different numerical methods [2], and outlier detection [11], but these techniques are empirical and inexact, with significant risk of false positives and false negatives.

Here we present a "physics-based checksum" (PBC) approach that builds on ABFT checksums and physical conservation laws applicable to scientific computations, and enables precise and efficient local error detection when such conserved quantities exist. As long as some form of checkpoint/restart remains viable, focusing purely on detection can allow recovering from occasional silent errors by rollback, as for hard failures. This is efficient for rare errors because it avoids the cost of more complex checksums that would support not only detection but also correction (roll-forward).

While the greatest expected benefit of the PBC approach is in conjunction with local recovery (restarting only the processes or tasks with errors) [14], the present work uses global checkpoint/restart (driven by local PBC detection) to illustrate the effectiveness in a familiar resilience setting. We demonstrate the approach in simple MPI-based solvers for partial differential equations (PDEs) and evaluate the effect on solver completion time and accuracy in the presence of emulated silent errors.

An abstract of this work was presented previously [10].

2   Checksum Approaches for Resilience

2.1   Error Detection Concepts

Checksums aim to introduce efficient redundancy in a solver via a smaller "side" computation that remains consistent with the solver state if all computations are correct (Fig. 1). State-of-the-art linear algebra checksums (LACs) [13], when verified after a series of linear algebra operations, can indicate with very high probability whether an error (processor or memory error) occurred somewhere in those operations (including in the checksum itself). Even if multiple errors occur, precise cancellation of their effects so that the checksum still matches is very unlikely. Thus, the verification of consistency can be performed intermittently, e.g., just before each checkpoint.

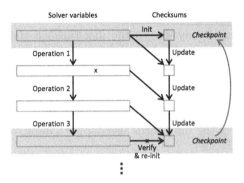

Fig. 1. Data flow in a solver using checksums. An error introduced in an intermediate step (red x) can be detected when the checksums are verified, and the solver can then restart from a valid state. (Color figure online)

The checksum for a floating-point vector u is typically taken as the sum of its entries, $Q(u) = e^T u$, where $e = \{1, \ldots, 1\}$. When an operation is performed on u, the linearity of such a checksum allows it to be updated in a way other than directly recomputing it, thus providing the redundant error check. Even with correctly functioning hardware and software, algebraic checksum relations hold numerically only to the level of floating-point roundoff. Silent errors in low-order bits whose numerical magnitude is within the roundoff level will be false negatives (undetected). When a checksum is verified by recomputing it from the underlying data, it is prudent to re-initialize (refresh) the checksum to remove accumulated roundoff drift.

From a different perspective, physical conserved quantities can be used in a similar way. Global conservation laws of the form

$$Q = \int_{\text{space}} dV \, \rho = \text{const}, \tag{1}$$

where ρ is a density expressible in terms of solver variables, are an exact property of many continuum equations, including nonlinear ones. We here consider the preferred case of a "conservative discretization", where a version of the conservation law holds independent of the mesh size or time step and is exact up to roundoff. As with standard LACs, these conserved quantities can detect errors reliably (via comparison of Q at an initial time and a later time) but involve global communication and do not localize errors in space.

To better leverage the benefits of conservation laws and create efficient local PBCs, we consider the more fundamental, local form of a continuum conservation law, $\partial \rho / \partial t = -\nabla \cdot \mathbf{J}$, where $\mathbf{J}$ is the flux density of the conserved quantity. Then, defining the conserved quantity in a spatial region R (e.g., a computational subdomain), $Q(R) = \int_R dV \, \rho$, we find the integrated conservation law

$$\frac{dQ(R)}{dt} = - \oint_{\partial R} d\mathbf{S} \cdot \mathbf{J}. \tag{2}$$

Thus, $Q(R)$ changes only due to the flux through the boundary ∂R. The flux is much faster to compute than $Q(R)$ itself because the integral in (2) is lower-dimensional. When a discretized form of the local conservation law holds, $Q(R)$ is a local PBC that can be updated efficiently and verified intermittently, in contrast to generic LACs [13] that are as costly to update as to verify. While this conservation derivation applies to time-dependent problems, we show in Sect. 4.1 that PBCs of the same form also apply to iterative elliptic solvers.

2.2   Injecting and Recovering from Errors

To demonstrate the practical effectiveness of PBC error detection, we test parallel solvers in a simple resilience framework with emulated silent errors. As in previous work [11], each solver process includes a concurrent thread that performs asynchronous, uniformly distributed bit flips in the large memory regions in use (floating-point data arrays) at an adjustable rate. Such a memory error model is representative of other error types also [3], such as processor errors.

We use a simple global checkpoint/restart scheme where verification of local checksums and writing of checkpoints occur periodically after a certain number of solver time steps or iterations, termed the verification interval. In our solvers, to establish a baseline given ideal checkpoint reliability and performance, checkpoints are stored in memory and are not subject to error injection, and time spent in checkpointing is not included in our measurements of resilience overhead. Rather, we measure the cost of updating and verifying the checksums and of redoing the computations from the previous checkpoint (global rollback) when an error is detected by any process based on a local checksum discrepancy. Checksum verification occurs together with each checkpoint, so the verification cost has the same effect as checkpointing cost. The cost could be adjusted to reflect any specific checkpoint storage technology. We seek resilience efficiency similar to that seen in standard global checkpoint/restart usage, which can achieve very low overhead using long intervals when failures are rare [5].

The impact of silent errors should be judged in relation to existing numerical inaccuracies (roundoff, discretization, and incomplete convergence) that solvers exhibit even on perfect hardware. An error rate is considered tolerated by a solver, and overhead results are reported, only when the solver reliably finishes with accuracy similar to that of an error-free run. Silent errors are stochastic and vary from run to run, so the results must be considered as a distribution. A solver is deemed to fail in the presence of errors if, in >10% of runs, it takes longer than a cutoff time or returns a solution for which the residual or error compared to an analytic solution is more than 3 times that obtained by a run without error injection.

3   Application to 1D Hyperbolic Solvers

We describe the application of PBCs to a linear advection equation and to the nonlinear Burgers equation, and present test results for the latter.

3.1   Algorithm

The 1D linear advection equation is written as

$$\frac{\partial \phi(t,x)}{\partial t} + \nu \frac{\partial \phi(t,x)}{\partial x} = 0, \tag{3}$$

where ν is a constant. The explicit finite-difference Lax-Wendroff scheme for the linear advection equation is determined by the stencil

$$\phi_j^{n+1} = \frac{c(c+1)}{2}\phi_{j-1}^n + (1-c^2)\phi_j^n + \frac{c(c-1)}{2}\phi_{j+1}^n, \quad 0 \le j \le N-1, \tag{4}$$

where the CFL number is $c = \nu\,\Delta t/\Delta x$. This can be thought of as a linear algebra operation, a sparse matrix-vector product $\phi^{n+1} = A\phi^n$, where the tridiagonal matrix A is not explicitly stored.

The vector checksum $Q(\phi) = e^T \phi = \sum_j \phi_j$, where e is a vector of ones, is the discrete version of the quantity $\int dx\, \phi$ conserved by the continuum PDE (3). The checksum computed for each update ϕ^{n+1} should correspond to the matrix-vector product. A general LAC formula for such a checksum update is

$$Q(\phi^{n+1}) = \left(e^T A - d e^T\right)\phi^n + d\,Q(\phi^n), \tag{5}$$

where d is an arbitrary scalar constant, whose choice may affect the detectability of propagated errors [13]. In general, this approach incurs the cost of the dot product of $(e^T A - d e^T)$ with ϕ^n, the former being a constant precomputed vector.

However, based on our physical reasoning, it must be possible to compute the update more efficiently. The natural PBC is obtained with the choice $d = 1$. For global conservation (e.g., a periodic closed domain), all columns of A have sum 1, as is seen by adding the coefficients of the three terms in (4); so $(e^T A - e^T) = 0$ and the update is trivial: $Q(\phi^{n+1}) = Q(\phi^n)$. For local conservation (e.g., a subdomain within a parallel computation), the column sums of the local matrix A differ from 1 only at the boundaries where fluxes occur, i.e., $(e^T A - e^T)$ is a sparse vector, and the update is much more efficient than a general dot product. For the parallel Lax-Wendroff scheme, the local PBC update is

$$Q(\phi^{n+1}) = Q(\phi^n) + \frac{c(c+1)}{2}(\phi_{-1}^n - \phi_{N-1}^n) + \frac{c(c-1)}{2}(\phi_N^n - \phi_0^n), \tag{6}$$

where ϕ_{-1}^n and ϕ_N^n are values communicated from neighboring subdomains.

PBCs can also be constructed for nonlinear equations where LACs do not apply. The 1D inviscid Burgers equation is written as

$$\frac{\partial u(t,x)}{\partial t} + \nu\, u(t,x)\frac{\partial u(t,x)}{\partial x} = 0. \tag{7}$$

The explicit finite-difference MacCormack scheme for the Burgers equation is determined by the stencil

$$u_j^{n+1} = \frac{1}{2}(u_j^n + u_j^*) - \frac{c}{4}\left((u_j^*)^2 - (u_{j-1}^*)^2\right), \quad 0 \le j \le N,$$

$$u_j^* = u_j^n - \frac{c}{2}\left((u_{j+1}^n)^2 - (u_j^n)^2\right). \tag{8}$$

This stencil cannot be cast purely in terms of linear algebra operations. However, the conservation principle is still valid for the MacCormack scheme, which is conservative by construction. The checksum $Q(u) = e^T u = \sum_j u_j$ corresponds to the momentum $\int dx\, u$ conserved by the Burgers equation, with the continuum flux density $J = \frac{1}{2}\nu u^2$. The corresponding PBC update is

$$Q(u^{n+1}) = Q(u^n) + \frac{c}{4}\left((u_{-1}^*)^2 + (u_0^n)^2\right) - \frac{c}{4}\left((u_{N-1}^*)^2 + (u_N^n)^2\right). \tag{9}$$

Here again, the checksum can be updated from the previous time step by only adding contributions from boundary terms.

3.2 Evaluation

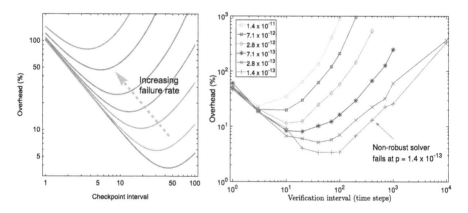

Fig. 2. Left: Example overhead behavior of global checkpoint/restart predicted by an analytic model [5]. Checkpointing and restarting each have a cost of 1 time unit, and the global failure rate per time unit varies from 10^{-3} (bottom curve) to 10^{-1} (top curve). Right: Overhead due to the detection algorithm and additional computations upon restarts when the PBC technique is used in solving the 1D Burgers equation. Results are reported for runs performed on 1024 cores with 100,000 mesh points per core for 25,000 time steps, at several bit-flip rates expressed as probability p per bit per standard time step.

Alongside a typical behavior of global checkpoint/restart for hard failures as a comparison, the overhead results for the Burgers equation are shown in Fig. 2. Upon completing a given verification interval (VI), a global restart is performed if any subdomain's recomputed "true" checksum Q_t differs from its efficiently updated checksum Q by more than 10^{-2}. The cost of checksum verification is reduced with a longer VI, leading to the initial decreasing trend of overhead with VI, but as VI increases further, the overhead increases due to more restarts and more wasted work. The optimal VI increases at lower error rates. Error injection is also performed on the non-robust version of the solver without error detection, to determine the maximum error rate tolerated. As shown, error rates significantly higher than this level can be tolerated by the robust solver with overhead of ~10% or less.

4 Application to 3D Elliptic Solver

To illustrate the applicability of PBCs to iterative unstructured applications, we consider a conjugate gradient solver modeled on the HPCCG and MiniFE mini-apps [7].

4.1 Algorithm

The 3D Laplace equation is a linear elliptic PDE often solved using a finite-element method. The solution is represented as a vector x encoding a superposition of basis functions (elements) defined on a mesh, and the PDE is discretized as a linear system $Ax = b$. Here A is a sparse, symmetric "stiffness matrix" determined by the basis functions, and b is a vector determined by the boundary conditions. In a parallel solver, the mesh is partitioned into subdomains and the corresponding blocks of A, b, and x are distributed among the processes. A typical iterative solver approach is the conjugate gradient method, which repeatedly updates an estimate of the solution x using linear algebra operations until the residual $b - Ax$ becomes sufficiently small. HPCCG implements an unpreconditioned conjugate gradient solver for the Laplace equation using a notional hexahedral mesh.

A key operation in the conjugate gradient solver is a sparse matrix-vector product Ap, where p is a vector generated within the algorithm. As discussed in Sect. 3.1, the generic LAC update for this operation is

$$Q(Ap) = \left(e^T A - de^T\right) p + d\, Q(p), \qquad (10)$$

requiring a dot product that is as costly as recomputing the checksum. Again, a more efficient update is possible with the PBC approach. In our problem, e (a vector of ones) represents a superposition of elements into a constant function, and A represents a differential operator constructed from gradients; thus $e^T A$, corresponding to the derivative of a constant, is a sparse vector (zero except at boundaries). We can take $d = 0$ and obtain the simpler PBC update

$$Q(Ap) = \left(e^T A\right) p. \qquad (11)$$

Even though elliptic equations do not involve time advancement and so a conservation law does not literally apply, the solver operations are mathematically analogous to time steps and PBCs can still be used.

To obtain a somewhat more generic example, we replace HPCCG's simple cubic mesh by a cylinder composed of wafers with an unstructured cross-section. Our solver reads in a corresponding stiffness matrix computed offline using basis functions that interpolate between values assigned to each mesh node (trilinear hexahedral elements). Each process operates on a subset of the wafers. The curved surface of the cylinder uses a standard Neumann zero-flux boundary condition, so fluxes in and out of subdomains occur on the boundaries between wafers. The mesh, stiffness matrix, and PBC update are visualized in Fig. 3.

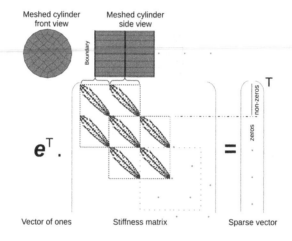

Fig. 3. Top: Schematic 3D unstructured mesh of a cylinder; each wafer (side view not to scale) corresponds to a block in the stiffness matrix. Bottom: In the physics-based approach, the vector of ones (e) is used to form the checksum of solution vectors; the vector on the right is used to update checksums when performing matrix-vector products. The vector on the right is nonzero only on the boundary where fluxes occur, reflecting conservation properties of the Laplace operator.

In this case, due the uniformity of the cylinder, the above-diagonal blocks are copies of a square matrix B and the below-diagonal blocks are B^T. The nonzero entries in $e^T A$ arise from these B and B^T blocks that couple adjacent subdomains. If p_i denotes the part of the vector p on process i, which can span several wafers, then let $p_{i,l}$ and $p_{i,r}$ be the sub-vectors corresponding to the leftmost and rightmost of these wafers. The local PBC update on process i for the vector $q = Ap$ is then

$$Q_q = (e^T B^T)p_{i-1,r} + (e^T B)p_{i+1,l} - (e^T B^T)p_{i,l} - (e^T B)p_{i,r}. \tag{12}$$

The full conjugate gradient method including local error detection and global checkpoint/restart is shown in Algorithm 1. Steps in blue are PBC updates performed during every iteration, while steps in green are error detection and checkpointing operations performed only after each verification interval. The basis for detection is the relative discrepancy in each local checksum, e.g., $\eta_x = (Q_x - Q_{x,t})/\|x_i\|_1$, upon computing the true checksum $Q_{x,t} = e^T x_i$ on process i.

Algorithm 1. Conjugate gradient method with PBCs. Checksums Q_x, Q_p, Q_q, and Q_r correspond to local portion of vectors on each process i.

$x_0 := 0$ {Initial guess of solution}
$r_0 := b - Ax_0$, $p_0 := r_0$ {Initial residual and direction vectors}
$(R_0)^2 := r_0^T r_0$
for $n = 0, 1, \dots$ until convergence **do**
  $q_n := Ap_n$
  $Q_q := (e^T B^T)p_{n,i-1,r} + (e^T B)p_{n,i+1,l} - (e^T B^T)p_{n,i,l} - (e^T B)p_{n,i,r}$
  $\alpha := (R_n)^2 / \left(p_n^T q_n\right)$
  $x_{n+1} := x_n + \alpha p_n$
  $Q_x \mathrel{+}= \alpha Q_p$
  $r_{n+1} := r_n - \alpha q_n$
  $Q_r \mathrel{-}= \alpha Q_q$
  $(R_{n+1})^2 := r_{n+1}^T r_{n+1}$
  $\beta := (R_{n+1})^2/(R_n)^2$
  $p_{n+1} := r_{n+1} + \beta p_n$
  $Q_p := Q_r + \beta Q_p$
  if $\mathrm{mod}(n+1, vi) = 0$ **then**
    $Q_{x,t} := e^T x_{n+1}$, $Q_{p,t} := e^T p_{n+1}$, $Q_{r,t} := e^T r_{n+1}$ {Recompute checksums}
    Compute errors η between recomputed and separately updated checksums
    if $\eta \geq \epsilon$ on any process **then**
      $n :=$ [illegible] {Restart}
      Read x_{n+1}, p_{n+1}, and r_{n+1} from checkpoint
      Read Q_x, Q_p, and Q_r from checkpoint
    else
      Checkpoint x_{n+1}, p_{n+1}, and r_{n+1}
      Checkpoint Q_x, Q_p, and Q_r
      Refresh checksums
    end if
  end if
end for
Return x_n

We note several details of error detection:

- Verifying the x, p, and r checksums is sufficient because an error in q propagates to an error in r that remains detectable.
- The PBC update (11) does not itself preserve the detectability of an error in p, because Q_p is not used in computing Q_q. However, because a multiple of p is subsequently added to x, the consequence would still be a detectable error in x. Our results support that errors are detected well with $d = 0$.

- The dot products $p^T q$ and $r^T r$ require special consideration because dot products do not have checksums [13]. In our memory error model, this is not a problem because an existing error in p, q, or r that affects a dot product will also affect the subsequent use of the same vectors in a detectable way.
- Error injection is not performed on the stiffness matrix A itself. If corruption of static data like A is a concern, then there are simple protection schemes that can be used [8], but we do not consider this here.

4.2   Evaluation

Error detection thresholds are chosen based on the maximum roundoff-induced checksum discrepancies observed in the solver in the absence of any injected errors. These accumulated errors in the checksum updates increase with VI due to the nonlinear feedback in the conjugate gradient algorithm over iterations and between processes. We have fitted thresholds for our cylinder example as a function of subdomain size and VI.

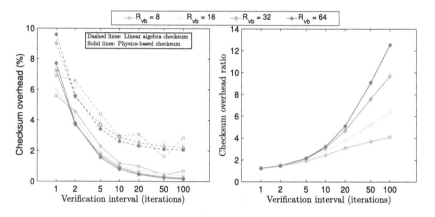

Fig. 4. Error detection overhead is plotted for LACs and PBCs (percent overhead of each technique on left, ratio of LAC to PBC overhead on right) in the conjugate gradient solver on 32 processes with no bit flips injected. Different subdomain sizes are indicated by the volume-to-boundary ratio R_{vb}.

We now examine the overhead induced by our error detection mechanism. With no error injection, we compare the overhead of PBC-based detection to a version where the LAC with $d > 0$ [13], but computed locally, is used for the matrix-vector product. As shown in Fig. 4, the PBC approach has significantly lower overhead for larger computational subdomains and larger VI (infrequent verification, expected to be feasible for low error rates). This difference occurs because the LAC update requires a dot product with cost proportional to the subdomain volume at every iteration, whereas the PBC update requires computations only along the subdomain boundaries, which are smaller by a ratio R_{vb}.

In the remaining results, we set $R_{\rm vb} = 8$, corresponding to a subdomain size of 8840 mesh points per process.

The results of overhead measurements with error injection and local PBC detection, shown in Fig. 5, are similar to the those for explicit solvers and likewise reflect the similarity to hard-failure checkpoint/restart (left plot in Fig. 2). A difference is that the conjugate gradient solver cannot afford as large a VI, because roundoff in the checksum updates propagates more strongly through the algorithm and error detection becomes less precise. Error rates and VIs plotted in Fig. 5 are those for which the accuracy criteria in Sect. 2.2 are met.

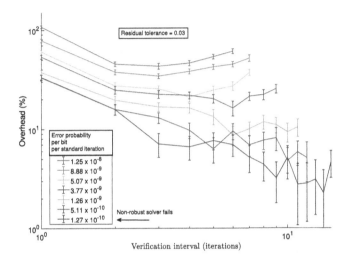

Fig. 5. For the conjugate gradient solver on 32 processes, overhead is plotted versus VI for several rates of memory bit flips. At relatively low error rates, the overhead is <10% for suitable VI. At larger error rates, the optimal VI decreases and overhead increases due to greater rollback costs, but the solver can still complete.

5   Conclusion

We have demonstrated a streamlined approach to silent-error detection that shows promise for physics simulations. Physics-based checksums (PBCs) enable precise and efficient local error detection with intermittent verification. In conjunction with recovery by rollback, PBCs fit into a typical checkpoint/restart resilience technique. Moreover, PBCs can apply to a range of solvers and error types that may occur at extreme scale. The approach has generality for scientific computing due to its physical foundation.

While existing ABFT linear algebra checksums correspond to conserved quantities in special cases, the conservation viewpoint leads to a general and efficient method for updating subdomain checksums using boundary fluxes, including for nonlinear equations. The local detection provided by these checksums can be further leveraged with local recovery [14].

Reliable algorithmic error detection provides a risk mitigation for future HPC systems and opens a broader space for co-design in which hardware reliability requirements could be relaxed. The conditions under which resilience techniques are effective can provide useful guidance for these future system designs.

Acknowledgments. Sandia National Laboratories is a multimission laboratory managed and operated by National Technology & Engineering Solutions of Sandia, LLC, a wholly owned subsidiary of Honeywell International Inc., for the U.S. Department of Energy's National Nuclear Security Administration (NNSA) under contract DE-NA0003525. This work was funded by NNSA's Advanced Simulation and Computing (ASC) Program. This paper describes objective technical results and analysis. Any subjective views or opinions that might be expressed in the paper do not necessarily represent the views of the U.S. Department of Energy or the United States Government.

References

1. Bautista-Gomez, L., Benoit, A., Cavelan, A., Raina, S.K., Robert, Y., Sun, H.: Which verification for soft error detection? In: Proceedings of the 22nd IEEE International Conference on High Performance Computing (HiPC) (2015)
2. Benson, A.R., Schmit, S., Schreiber, R.: Silent error detection in numerical time-stepping schemes. Int. J. High Perform. Comput. Appl. **29**(4), 403–421 (2015)
3. Bridges, P.G., Ferreira, K.B., Heroux, M.A., Hoemmen, M.: Fault-tolerant linear solvers via selective reliability (2012). https://arxiv.org/abs/1206.1390
4. Cappello, F., Geist, A., Gropp, W., Kale, S., Kramer, B., Snir, M.: Toward exascale resilience: 2014 update. Supercomput. Front. Innov. **1**(1), 5–28 (2014)
5. Daly, J.: A model for predicting the optimum checkpoint interval for restart dumps. In: Proceedings of the International Conference on Computational Science (2003)
6. Gamell, M., et al.: Local recovery and failure masking for stencil-based applications at extreme scales. In: Proceedings of the International Conference for High Performance Computing, Networking, Storage and Analysis (2015)
7. Heroux, M.A., et al.: Improving performance via mini-applications. Report SAND2009-5574, Sandia National Laboratories (2009)
8. Hukerikar, S., Engelmann, C.: Resilience design patterns: a structured approach to resilience at extreme scale. Supercomput. Front. Innov. **4**(3), 4–42 (2017)
9. Rinard, M.: Parallel synchronization-free approximate data structure construction. In: Proceedings of the 5th USENIX Workshop on Hot Topics in Parallelism (2013)
10. Salloum, M., Mayo, J., Armstrong, R.: Physics-based checksums for silent-error detection in PDE solvers. In: SIAM Conference on Computational Science and Engineering (2019)
11. Salloum, M., Mayo, J.R., Armstrong, R.C.: In-situ mitigation of silent data corruption in PDE solvers. In: Proceedings of the 6th Workshop on Fault-Tolerance for HPC at Extreme Scale (2016)
12. Subasi, O., et al.: MACORD: online adaptive machine learning framework for silent error detection. In: Proceedings of the IEEE International Conference on Cluster Computing (2017)

13. Tao, D., et al.: New-sum: a novel online ABFT scheme for general iterative methods. In: Proceedings of the 25th ACM International Symposium on High-Performance Parallel and Distributed Computing (2016)
14. Teranishi, K., et al.: ASC CSSE level 2 milestone #6362: resilient asynchronous many-task programming model. Report SAND2018-9672, Sandia National Laboratories (2018)

Checkpointing Kernel Executions
of MPI+CUDA Applications

Max Baird[1]([envelope]), Sven-Bodo Scholz[1], Artjoms Šinkarovs[1],
and Leonardo Bautista-Gomez[2]

[1] Heriot-Watt University, Edinburgh, UK
{mmb1,s.scholz,a.sinkarovs}@hw.ac.uk
[2] Barcelona Supercomputing Center, Barcelona, Spain
leonardo.bautista@bsc.es

Abstract. This paper proposes a new approach to checkpointing MPI
applications that use long-running CUDA kernels. It becomes possible to
take snapshots of data residing on the GPUs without waiting for kernels
to complete. The proposed technique is implemented in the context of the
state of the art high performance fault tolerance library FTI. As a result
we get an elegant solution to the problem of developing resilient MPI
applications where GPU kernels run longer than the mean time between
hardware failures. We describe in detail how we checkpoint/restart collaborative MPI-CUDA applications, and we provide an initial evaluation
of the proposed approach using the Livermore Unstructured Lagrangian
Explicit Shock Hydrodynamics (LULESH) application as a case study.

Keywords: HPC · MPI · GPU · Snapshots · Checkpoints · Resilience

1 Introduction

The use of GPUs for scientific applications is on the rise. High levels of parallelism
of GPU architectures offer impressive performance and naturally fits the domain.
When incorporating the use of GPUs into MPI programs, which is the de-facto
standard when using clusters, making such applications resilient becomes even
more challenging than before.

As the architecture of GPUs is based on the idea of CPU-managed non-
interruptible kernel executions, current checkpointing practice assumes that all
data has been taken off the GPUs and kernel execution is finished. Such a
restriction does not constitute a major problem when applications only have
short-running kernels all of which are being run synchronously. However, as
kernels become more complex, we can observe that data increasingly often is
maintained on the GPU only, and multiple kernels are launched asynchronously.
Typical cluster designs provide fewer GPUs than CPU cores at individual nodes.
Consequently, MPI+CUDA applications usually require several MPI processes
to share GPUs, which increases their utilisation. Such high GPU utilisations

© Springer Nature Switzerland AG 2020
U. Schwardmann et al. (Eds.): Euro-Par 2019 Workshops, LNCS 11997, pp. 694–706, 2020.
https://doi.org/10.1007/978-3-030-48340-1_53

make it more challenging to identify or create application states where all relevant data is on the host and no kernel is running. If these states occur less frequently than the Meantime Between Failure (MBTF) of the given hardware, resilience becomes problematic.

In this paper we propose a novel approach to deal with this challenge. We enable checkpointing of MPI+CUDA applications in a way that allows snapshots to happen in states where kernels are only partially finished and where snapshot-relevant data still resides on the GPUs of the system. We achieve this by extending the MPI checkpointing library Fault Tolerance Interface (FTI) [2] with a mechanism[1] for soft interrupts for GPU kernels proposed in [1]. The individual contributions of the paper are:

- we extend FTI to enable data on GPUs to be part of checkpoints;
- we extend FTI to mark kernels so that checkpoints can be performed before those kernels are completed;
- we demonstrate the practical applicability of the proposed approach[2] on a given MPI+CUDA implementation of the Livermore Unstructured Lagrange Explicit Shock Hydrodynamics (LULESH) application [9];
- we provide some indicative performance evaluations quantifying the effects of the proposed extensions on the LULESH MPI+CUDA application.

2 Interrupting a Kernel

Checkpointing with a GPU kernel comes with two problems: saving/restoring the GPU context and interrupting a long-running kernel. The CUDA runtime implicitly creates an underlying context for communication between the host process and device. Once created, the context remains attached to the host process for its lifetime. If a process is checkpointed with an active context, restart from that checkpoint will fail because the restored context will be invalid. FTI does not preserve process states, so this work is not concerned with the GPU context save/restore problem and CUDA does not facilitate the interruption of a running GPU thread. Nevertheless, threads can be instrumented to interrupt themselves; this is done by ensuring that the first step of a thread's execution is to check a host-controlled flag for permission to continue or to return. At runtime, CUDA threads are partitioned into groups called *blocks*, so a boolean array is used to keep track of executed blocks and is examined after the kernel returns. If all blocks have executed then the kernel is complete; otherwise, the kernel is relaunched. Figure 1 illustrates how a kernel is transformed into an interruptible one. For more details refer to [1]. Note that this approach does not work for kernels with explicit intra-block synchronisation.

---

[1] Available at https://bitbucket.org/maxbaird/cuda_backup.
[2] The FTI extension is available at https://github.com/leobago/fti/tree/cuda-dev-kernel-interrupt.

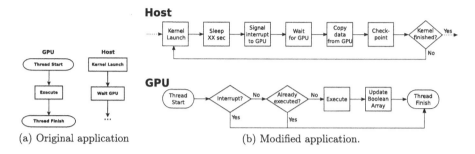

(a) Original application   (b) Modified application.

Fig. 1. How to apply the technique to an original application.

3   FTI

FTI is a multilevel checkpointing library for large scale supercomputers. At extreme scale, supercomputers suffer from frequent failures due to the increased number of components. As scientific applications grow in scale, they are more prone to failures forcing to restart the execution. At the same time, they also use more data, and therefore the state to be saved upon a checkpoint is also increasing. This leads to an I/O bottleneck that could render scientific applications unable to make progress. To alleviate this problem, FTI makes use of multiple storage levels, including the global parallel file system (GPFS), as well as local storage inside the compute nodes. In particular FTI has four levels of checkpointing, providing a good trade-off between resilience and performance.

All the complexity of erasure coding, asynchronous transfer and managing multiple storage levels is hidden by FTI behind a simple interface that can be summarized in only four functions:

- FTI_Init: This function initializes FTI with the configuration provided by the user in the configuration file.
- FTI_Protect: This function is used to tell to FTI which are the variables that need to be checkpointed.
- FTI_Snapshot: This function actually takes the checkpoint according to the frequency provided in the configuration file.
- FTI_Finalize: This function frees the memory and clean up the different storage levels.

For most MPI applications, it suffices to insert calls to these FTI functions in order to render unprotected codes resilient against the majority of possible faults. Most scientific applications have one or more long running iterative computations at their core where over 90% of the runtime is being spent. These loops typically successively recompute the values of several key data structures until either a pre-determined number of iterations or a certain degree of data stability is being reached. The LULESH application that we use as our case study throughout this paper is no different. Consequently, adding resilience using FTI can be achieved by means of a few added function calls. The full FTI

enabled code can be found at https://github.com/maxbaird/luleshMultiGPU_
MPI/blob/integrating-fti/lulesh.cu. The core structure of that code looks like
this:

```
int main(int argc, char *argv[])
{
  ...
  MPI_Init(&argc, &argv) ;
  FTI_Init(fti_config_path, MPI_COMM_WORLD);
  ...

  FTI_Protect(1, its, 1, FTI_INTG);
  ...
  FTI_Protect(19, domain->elemBC.raw(), domain->numElem, FTI_INTG);
  ...

  while(locDom->time_h < locDom->stoptime)
  {
    res = FTI_Snapshot();
    LagrangeLeapFrog(locDom) ;
    checkErrors(locDom,its);
    its++;
  }
  FTI_Finalize();
  MPI_Finalize();
  return 0 ;
}
```

The calls to **FTI_protect** inform FTI which data needs to be checkpointed.
Here, we only show the protection of the iteration variable **its** as well as one of
the data carrying arrays **elemBC.raw()**. Within the main computational loop,
FTI_Snapshot is being called. It globally synchronises all MPI ranks to establish a global time and, provided the checkpoint interval has been exhausted, it
triggers the actual checkpointing operation.

In case a failure happens, the same program is started. However, during the
execution of **FTI_Init** the library notices that this is actually a restart and the
data is restored to the latest checkpoint values, effectively skipping the loop
iterations that had been completed before the fault had occurred. More details
on FTI can be found in [2].

4   Extending FTI

4.1   Checkpointing GPU Data

The first extension enables the checkpointing of data that reside on the GPU
rather than the CPU. This extension does not require any new FTI functions;
instead, it suffices to extend the functionality of **FTI_protect**.

FTI_protect obtains a pointer to the data to be saved whenever a snapshot is
being taken. Therefore, handling data residing on the GPU requires determining
whether such a pointer is a valid host or device pointer. Conveniently, the CUDA
API provides the **cudaPointerGetAttributes** function which makes it possible
to distinguish host and device pointers. For device pointers, a device to host
transfer is made prior to making a snapshot, and correspondingly on restart, the
data is copied back to the device.

Things get slightly more involved due to the variety of memory models that CUDA supports. Unified Virtual Addressing (UVA) and Unified Memory (UM) introduced in CUDA versions 4.0 and 6.0 correspondingly, present a programmer with a coherent view of host and device memory [12]. In those cases explicit transfers are not required. Our extension to FTI_protect reflects this through further pointer attribute inspections.

4.2   Adding Kernel Suspension to FTI

Our second extension adds the ability to perform checkpoints during kernel execution. This constitutes the main technical contribution.

The key challenge here is that the underlying concept of FTI_Snapshot cannot easily be extended so that it could be used within GPU kernels. In comparison to MPI ranks, GPU kernels have several orders of magnitude higher levels of parallelism. Executions through millions or billions of threads on single GPUs are the norm and not the exception. Running the equivalent of FTI_Snapshot as part of such a massively parallel kernel would introduce massive overheads due to the increased synchronisation and the need to transfer back control to the host. Therefore, we execute FTI_Snapshot on the host, asynchronously to the kernel executions on the GPU. In case a snapshot needs to be performed, we use a technique for soft-interrupts of GPU-kernels as described in [1] to stop the current kernel and to initiate the snapshot process which is performed on the host.

To achieve this with a suitably simple interface extension of FTI, we add three new API functions:

1. FTI_Protect_Kernel: replaces the normal kernel launch;
2. FTI_Kernel_Def: wraps around the kernel header; and
3. FTI_Continue: needs to be inserted into the beginning of each protected kernel.

FTI_Protect_Kernel is responsible for the host-side code that manages the kernel launch. It triggers the initial kernel launch, potentially issues an interrupt from the host followed by the execution of a snapshot and repeats this activity until the kernel is completed.

FTI_Kernel_Def rewrites the kernel's definition to add some extra parameters to handle the soft interrupts. Lastly, FTI_Continue_check adds code that is needed inside the kernel to enable soft-interrupts.

For the LULESH example, this means that we replace kernel invocations such as

```
CalcVolumeForceForElems_kernel <true >
    <<<dimGrid ,block_size ,0 , domain ->streams [1] >>>(...);
```
by a call

```
FTI_Protect_Kernel (&domain ->snapshotCount , 1, 0.08 ,
    ( CalcVolumeForceForElems_kernel <true >),
    dimGrid ,block_size ,0 , domain ->streams [1] , ...);
```

From the user's perspective this is merely the addition of a wrapping function call with three additional parameters. Our complete version of LULESH with kernel protection can be found at https://github.com/maxbaird/luleshMultiGPU_MPI/blob/integrating-fti-protecting-kernels/lulesh.cu.

4.3   Implementing FTI_Protect_Kernel

Roughly, FTI_Protect_Kernel translates into the following pseudo code:

```
FTI_Protect_Kernel (delta_t, kernel)
{
  FTI_kernel_init ();
  while (!all_complete) {
    if (!my_rank_complete) {
      <<<kernel>>>;
      FTI_wait (delta_t);
      FTI_stop_kernel ();
    }
    FTI_Snapshot ( );
    MPI_allgather (all_complete);
  }
}
```

FTI_Protect_Kernel first makes a call to FTI_kernel_init which initializes an object of type FTIT_KernelInfo with information on how to interrupt, checkpoint and restart the kernel. For efficiency, a kernel's metadata is initialized once and cleared and reused as necessary if the kernel with same ID is launched again. The initialisation call is made irrespective of normal application execution or failure, if a kernel has associated metadata, this metadata will be restored.

After initialisation we have the kernel launch in a loop which only terminates after it has been executed by all MPI processes. This ensures consistency as it guarantees that all snapshot images stem from the same call to FTI_Snapshot across all MPI ranks. Once the kernel has been asynchronously launched the host waits for some period δ_t (delta_t) before stopping the kernel and invoking FTI_Snapshot. The choice of δ_t is tricky. The smaller δ_t is the finer granular is the capability to stop protected kernels. While this is desirable, it comes for a price: whenever we invoke FTI_Snapshot, we synchronise across all MPI ranks which introduces noticeable overhead. On the other hand, choosing a large δ_t could mean that (a) we heavily overrun our checkpointing interval or (b) the host is idly waiting while the kernel has already terminated. The former can be avoided by choosing δ_t as a sufficiently small fraction of the checkpoint interval. We avoid the latter by implementing the waiting through an internal function FTI_wait which polls the GPU for the kernel's completion status every 0.5 ms. Finally, after FTI_Snapshot has terminated, a call to MPI_allgather ensures that all ranks know about the completion status of all other MPI ranks.

4.4   What Happens at Checkpoint Time

Additional to the data that have been declared by the user for protection, FTI also saves metadata that contain information about the state of execution. For GPU kernels, this entails information about the degree of kernel completion which needs to be transferred from the GPU to the CPU and accumulated in the standard way of FTI.

4.5   What Happens at Restart Time

A previously failed application may be restored if at least one checkpoint was successful prior to failure. When executed, FTI will detect the execution as a restart and try to recover the most recent checkpoint data. The corresponding metadata of the recovered checkpoint is also loaded as part of the restart. The initialization phase of FTI triggers the restart process and subsequently calls a setup function for kernel protection. If the setup function detects the application is in recovery mode it attempts to load the metadata for all protected kernels. For an interruptible kernel, `FTI_Protect_Kernel` will rewrite the kernel launch as described, this time however, the kernel's associated metadata will be restored instead of newly allocated. The restored metadata contains information about the kernel execution state which the kernel uses to accurately resume.

A previously complete kernel will have its metadata reset so that it can be launched again. However, If there are multiple kernels to be restored, a check is performed to ensure that *all* protected kernels are complete. Since at this point, whether the kernel is being relaunched immediately after failure or again through iteration cannot be determined. For the former case, execution must resume from the incomplete kernel. For the latter case, complete kernels that are not reset will still launch but do nothing since all blocks are marked as complete.

5   Experimental Setup

From LULESH we used a kernel that is called once for each iteration of its main executing loop and sufficiently oversubscribes the GPU. For our experiments only level 1 checkpoints were permitted. The other levels were effectively disabled by configuring their interval to be greater than longest running experiment, this was done as the time taken for checkpointing is not consistent for each level. Interruptions were simulated by prematurely terminating the application (via `ctrl + c`) during its execution with a minimum of one successful checkpoint. The amount of data captured at each checkpoint varies in relation to the application's input, for our experiments the checkpoint data size ranged from 500 MB to 1 GB.

All experiments were executed using an AMD Opteron 6376 CPU running Scientific Linux Release 7.6 (Nitrogen), kernel version 3.10.0. The system has 1024 GB of RAM and an NVIDIA TITAN-XP GPU with 12 GB of global memory connected via PCIE x16. For our experiments CUDA version 10.0 was used with driver version 410.79.

6   Case Study

In this section we seek to examine the practical impact of our extension on the use case of LULESH. To this end, we have run experiments to examine three effects, the first experiment is aimed at figuring out whether we can stop a kernel prematurely. The second experiment demonstrates how much more interruptibility is possible with our proposed approach and the final experiment looks at the incurred overhead.

Restarting after the Checkpoint. Our first experiment is a sanity check for the extended FTI. We verify that when protecting a single kernel of our test application, which includes snapshotting of the data residing only on a GPU, we can use the saved data to successfully restart. We verified that the modified application successfully restarted, and that the result it computes is identical to the one computed by the original application. We also verified that the snapshot happened before the kernel completed, and that the GPU data have been actually stored in the snapshot. This raises our confidence that the proposed implementation works as expected.

Counting Snapshots. Our second experiment is concerned with the changes in the minimal snapshotting interval. The method used to verify this change is by counting the number of snapshots that we can do after we have protected the kernel. If the minimal snapshotting interval is determined by the runtime of the kernel, then the factor we decrease that interval is exactly the same as the factor by which the number of taken snapshots increased. This experiment includes two separate parts. In Fig. 2a we explore the limit case—how many more snapshots we could possibly do after protecting one kernel. In Fig. 2b we investigate a more realistic scenario when running resilient version of our application.

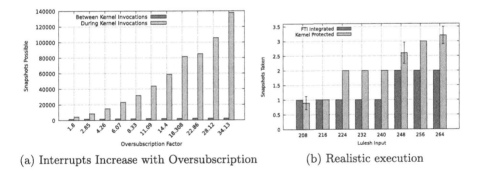

(a) Interrupts Increase with Oversubscription   (b) Realistic execution

Fig. 2. Reducing checkpoint interval

Let us assume a simplistic execution model of the application with one protected kernel, one MPI process, and all the kernel launches are synchronous. In this case, the snapshot count is determined by the number of kernel interrupts we can make. The latter is determined by the oversubscription factor of a kernel—the number of threads divided by the number of threads the GPU can simultaneously execute. Therefore, in Fig. 2a we have related the number of snapshots we can possibly take with the oversubscription factor. For that we set δt to a very small value of 1 ms. We can observe two things. First we can clearly see that with more kernel oversubscription, more snapshots are possible. Secondly, the number of snapshots is noticeably larger than the oversubscription factor. This becomes possible due to asynchronous kernel launch. As kernel launches are queued, the actual launch on the GPU is delayed, and it might happen so that the interrupt comes *before* the kernel managed to execute any blocks. This means that in the asynchronous case, the kernel interrupts may happen even in the undersubscribed cases.

In Fig. 2b we investigate the snapshot increase when running our application with a realistic snapshotting interval of 4 min. We observe a similar pattern: the larger data set we use, the more threads we allocate per GPU kernels, therefore the number of snapshots we do increases as we would expect. The graphs shows average increase after running the same application 10 times.

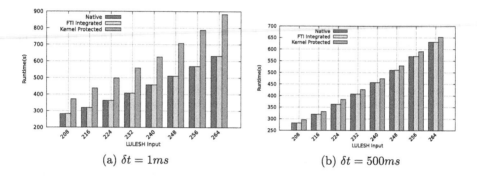

(a) $\delta t = 1ms$ (b) $\delta t = 500ms$

Fig. 3. Overhead analysis

Overhead Analysis. Our third experiment examines the overhead that comes with our extension. As it turns out, measuring the overhead is tricky because it very much depends on the value chosen for δt. As Fig. 3a shows, if δt is very small the overhead is quite noticeable. This is due to the MPI synchronization that must occur for the call to `FTI_Snapshot` at each interrupt. However, Fig. 3b shows that if δt increases this overhead is significantly reduced. The remaining observable overhead is attributed to each kernel thread always having to first check for the host's permission to continue.

7   Related Work

GPU Proxies CRUM [4] achieves transparent CR by using a proxy process to decouple the application process' state from the device driver state. This allows for checkpoints to be made without recording any active driver state. CRUM is geared toward applications with large memory footprints which make use of Unified Virtual Memory (UVM). The proxy process creates a shadow UVM region for each allocation made by the application process and then makes a corresponding real allocation via the CUDA driver. This setup is necessary because

UVM has no API calls that can be intercepted. However, the restart process is based on the assumption of deterministic memory allocations that are made by the CUDA driver libraries which is not guaranteed by CUDA. It also raises the question of what happens if a restart needs to occur on a different device; while the allocations may be deterministic it does not mean they are consistent across devices. CRCUDA [17] and CheCL [19] are proxy based approaches that target CUDA and OpenCL respectively. Like CRUM, CRCUDA is transparent to the application process. Unlike CRUM, CRCUDA does not rely on deterministic memory allocations. Instead, it logs and replays CUDA API calls where BLCR [7] is responsible for saving and restoring the application's state. CRCUDA does not support MPI or applications that make use of UVM. CheCL provides its own OpenCL library to intercept and redirect API calls to decouple the process from the OpenCL runtime.

GPU Virtualisation. A lot of related work is based on GPU Virtualisation such as [3,5,6,13]. Virtual Machines (VMs) are attractive as they inherently serve as a buffer between the application and the physical device. This decoupling from the hardware makes checkpointing easier especially in the realm of CUDA where the GPU context cannot be checkpointed along with the application. VMGL [10] is marketed as an OpenGL cross-platform GPU independent virtualisation solution with suspend and resume capabilities. Suspend and resume is enabled through a shadow driver which keeps track of OpenGL's context state. While OpenGL is supported by all GPU vendors, in reality it is used chiefly for rendering and not well suited for general purpose GPU computing. vCUDA [16] follows the identical approach of VMGL using CUDA instead of OpenGL. Unfortunately, VMs typically add more overhead via extra communication ultimately degrading performance.

Application Specific. CheCUDA [18] and NVCR [11] are currently obsolete CUDA based libraries because they depend on the CUDA context detaching cleanly before a checkpoint. Recent versions of CUDA no longer have this property. Consequently, correct restarts can not be guaranteed. CudaCR [15] is a CR library that is capable of capturing and rolling back the state within kernels in the event of a soft error. Similarly for soft errors, VOCL-FT [14] offers resilience against silent data corruption for OpenCL-accelerated applications. VOCL-FT is a library that virtualises the layer between the application and the accelerators to log commands issued to OpenCL so that they may be replayed later in case of failure. HiAL-Ckpt [20] is a checkpointing tool for the Brook+ language with directives to indicate where checkpoints should be made. However the development on Brook+ seems to have stopped with the last official release in 2004. HeteroCheckpoint [8] is a CUDA library and mainly focuses on how efficient checkpoints can be made by optimising the transfer of device data.

8   Conclusions and Future Work

This paper demonstrates a system that makes it possible to checkpoint/restore MPI applications with long running GPU kernels. Its distinctive feature is the ability to take snapshots without the necessity to wait for kernels completion. To our knowledge, none of the existing resilience tools can do this automatically.

The system is based on the FTI library—one of the standard resilience tools; and it is extended with the kernel interruption mechanism that we have described in [1]. As a result, by using the proposed tool, we significantly reduce the minimal interval at which the snapshots can be taken, making it possible to align the snapshot frequency with the MTBF of the system of interest. We apply our system to the real-word numerical MPI/CUDA application named LULESH. We verify that the proposed system is operational by running a number of snapshot/restores that include GPU data; and we demonstrate that the minimal snapshotting interval actually decreases.

Despite our system being fully operational and production-ready, it comes with a few limitations that immediately guide our future work. Currently, we do not verify that automatic kernel interruption mechanism is safe, assuming that this is a job of a programmer. For example, if a kernel uses explicit intrablock synchronisation, our mechanism may introduce a deadlock. This is less of a problem for CUDA systems prior to the version 9, as intra-block synchronisation was not supported, and use of manual spinlocks are not advised by the manual. Latest CUDA architectures allow for such synchronisations which we would like to attempt to detect by means of analysing CUDA kernels. Work is also required to identify and reduce the overhead observed from our extension.

Currently, the time we have to wait to interrupt the running kernel is equal to the time it takes to execute one thread of a kernel. If this time happens to be too large, we need to make our interruption mechanism smarter—we can check for interrupts not only at the beginning of each block, but also while the thread is running. This would require a more sophisticated analysis of kernels, that would take into account dataflow and controlflow.

Acknowledgement. This work was supported in part by grants EP/N028201/1 and EP/L00058X/1 from the Engineering and Physical Sciences Research Council (EPSRC) and partially sponsored by the European Union's Horizon 2020 Programme under the LEGaTO Project (www.legato-project.eu), grant agreement 780681.

References

1. Baird, M., Fensch, C., Scholz, S.-B., Šinkarovs, A.: A lightweight approach to gpu resilience. In: Mencagli, G., et al. (eds.) Euro-Par 2018. LNCS, vol. 11339, pp. 826–838. Springer, Cham (2019). https://doi.org/10.1007/978-3-030-10549-5_64
2. Bautista-Gomez, L., Tsuboi, S., et al.: FTI: high performance fault tolerance interface for hybrid systems. In: SC 2011, pp. 1–12 (2011). https://doi.org/10.1145/2063384.2063427
3. Duato, J., Peña, A.J., et al.: rCUDA: reducing the number of GPU-based accelerators in high performance clusters. In: 2010 International Conference on High Performance Computing Simulation, pp. 224–231 (2010). https://doi.org/10.1109/HPCS.2010.5547126

4. Garg, R., Mohan, A., et al.: CRUM: checkpoint-restart support for CUDA's unified memory. In: CLUSTER 2018, pp. 302–313 (2018). https://doi.org/10.1109/CLUSTER.2018.00047

5. Giunta, G., Montella, R., Agrillo, G., Coviello, G.: A GPGPU transparent virtualization component for high performance computing clouds. In: D'Ambra, P., Guarracino, M., Talia, D. (eds.) Euro-Par 2010, Part I. LNCS, vol. 6271, pp. 379–391. Springer, Heidelberg (2010). https://doi.org/10.1007/978-3-642-15277-1_37

6. Gupta, V., Gavrilovska, A., et al.: GViM: GPU-accelerated virtual machines. In: ACM Workshop on System-level Virtualization for High Performance Computing, pp. 17–24. ACM (2009), https://doi.org/10.1145/1519138.1519141

7. Hargrove, P.H., Duell, J.C.: Berkeley lab checkpoint/restart (BLCR) for linux clusters. J. Phys. Conf. Ser. **46**, 494–499 (2006). https://doi.org/10.1088/1742-6596/46/1/067

8. Kannan, S., Farooqui, N., et al.: HeteroCheckpoint: efficient checkpointing for accelerator-based systems. In: 2014 44th Annual IEEE/IFIP International Conference on Dependable Systems and Networks, pp. 738–743 (2014). https://doi.org/10.1109/DSN.2014.76

9. Karlin, I., et al.: LULESH Programming Model and Performance Ports Overview. Technical report. LLNL-TR-608824, December 2012. https://computing.llnl.gov/projects/co-design/lulesh_ports1.pdf

10. Lagar-Cavilla, H.A., et al.: VMM-independent graphics acceleration. In: Proceedings of the 3rd International Conference on Virtual Execution Environments, pp. 33–43. ACM (2007). https://doi.org/10.1145/1254810.1254816

11. Nukada, A., Takizawa, H., et al.: NVCR: a transparent checkpoint-restart library for NVIDIA CUDA. In: 2011 IEEE International Symposium on Parallel and Distributed Processing Workshops and PhD Forum, pp. 104–113 (2011). https://doi.org/10.1109/IPDPS.2011.131

12. NVIDIA Corporation: NVIDIA CUDA Compute Unified Device Architecture Programming Guide version 10.1.105 (2019). https://bit.ly/2EcQ4hN

13. Oikawa, M., Kawai, A., et al.: DS-CUDA: a middleware to use many GPUs in the cloud environment. In: 2012 SC Companion: High Performance Computing, Networking Storage and Analysis, pp. 1207–1214 (2012). https://doi.org/10.1109/SC.Companion.2012.146

14. Peña, A.J., Bland, W., et al.: VOCL-FT: introducing techniques for efficient soft error coprocessor recovery. In: SC 2015: Proceedings of the International Conference for High Performance Computing, Networking, Storage and Analysis, pp. 1–12 (2015). https://doi.org/10.1145/2807591.2807640

15. Pourghassemi, B., Chandramowlishwaran, A.: cudaCR: an In-Kernel application-level checkpoint/restart scheme for CUDA-enabled GPUs. In: CLUSTER 2017, pp. 725–732 (2017). https://doi.org/10.1109/CLUSTER.2017.100

16. Shi, L., Chen, H., Sun, J., et al.: vCUDA: GPU-accelerated high-performance computing in virtual machines. IEEE Trans. Comput. **61**(6), 804–816 (2012). https://doi.org/10.1109/TC.2011.112

17. Suzuki, T., Akira Nukada, S.M.: Transparent Checkpoint and Restart Technology for CUDA applications (2016). https://bit.ly/2DzHGbO. Accessed 25 April 2019

18. Takizawa, H., Sato, K., et al.: CheCUDA: a checkpoint/restart tool for CUDA applications. In: 2009 International Conference on Parallel and Distributed Computing, Applications and Technologies, pp. 408–413 (2009). https://doi.org/10.1109/PDCAT.2009.78

19. Takizawa, H., et al.: CheCL: transparent checkpointing and process migration of OpenCL applications. In: 2011 IEEE International, IPDPS. IEEE (2011). https://doi.org/10.1109/IPDPS.2011.85
20. Xu, X., et al.: HiAL-Ckpt: a hierarchical application-level checkpointing for CPU-GPU hybrid systems, pp. 1895–1899 (2010). https://doi.org/10.1109/ICCSE.2010.5593819

Poster Papers

Poster Papers

Description

Euro-Par 2019 introduced a Poster Track as a new format to the conference series. We invited short papers presenting ongoing projects in novel and original research covering subjects of parallel and distributed computing. The poster call was aimed especially at young scientists and was accompanied by a mentoring session, which provided young contributors the opportunity to discuss their research findings with established researchers.

Organization

Program Chair

Ramin Yahyapour   GWDG, Germany

Program Committee

Luc Bougé   ENS Renne, France
Fernando Silva   University of Porto, Portugal

MPI+OpenMP Parallelization for Elastic Wave Simulation with an Iterative Solver

Mikhail Belonosov[1(✉)], Vladimir Tcheverda[2], Victor Kostin[2], and Dmitry Neklyudov[2]

[1] Aramco Research Center - Delft, Aramco Overseas Company B.V., Delft, The Netherlands
mikhail.belonosov@aramcooverseas.com
[2] Institute of Petroleum Geology and Geophysics SB RAS, Novosibirsk, Russia
{cheverdava,kostinvi,neklyudovda}@ipgg.sbras.ru

Abstract. In this paper, we propose and study the hybrid (MPI and OpenMP) parallelization for our novel approach to 3D numerical simulation of elastic waves with Krylov-type iteration method. The quality of the parallelization is justified by weak and strong scaling analysis.

Keywords: Parallelization · MPI · OpenMP · Elastic equation

1 Introduction

Accurate and fast estimation of the subsurface parameters is of vital importance in the oil and gas industry. A potential candidate to handle this task is a frequency-domain full waveform inversion (FWI) (see e.g. [6]) that has been actively developing in the last decades. Due to advances in supercomputing technology, even 3D elastic inversion, that may bring the most valuable information about the subsurface, seems to be feasible. The most time consuming part of this process is the forward modeling performed several times at each iteration. The efficiency of this process is strongly dependent on how optimally the process is parallelized.

In this effort, we consider a frequency-domain elastic iterative solver proposed in [3]. It is based on a Krylov-type iteration method [5] with a special preconditioner. This method demonstrates a fast convergence at low frequencies, needed for FWI applications. In this paper, we explain an approach to parallelize it using a hybrid parallelization: MPI and OpenMP. Its quality is justified by weak and strong scaling analysis. We also illustrate, that this parallel method allows simulation in big models, including a modified 2.5D Marmousi model comprising 90 million cells, for a feasible time.

The original version of this chapter was revised: The abstract was updated. The correction to this chapter is available at https://doi.org/10.1007/978-3-030-48340-1_64

U. Schwardmann et al. (Eds.): Euro-Par 2019 Workshops, LNCS 11997, pp. 709–714, 2020.
https://doi.org/10.1007/978-3-030-48340-1_54

2   A Preconditioned 3D Elastic Equation

Consider an elastic equation written in the velocity-stress form, describing propagation of a monochromatic component of a wave in a 3D isotropic heterogeneous medium

$$\left[i\omega \begin{pmatrix} \rho I_{3\times3} & 0 \\ 0 & S_{6\times6} \end{pmatrix} - \begin{pmatrix} 0 & \hat{P} \\ \hat{P}^T & 0 \end{pmatrix} \frac{\partial}{\partial x} - \begin{pmatrix} 0 & \hat{Q} \\ \hat{Q}^T & 0 \end{pmatrix} \frac{\partial}{\partial y} - \gamma(z) \begin{pmatrix} 0 & \hat{R} \\ \hat{R}^T & 0 \end{pmatrix} \frac{\partial}{\partial z} \right] v = f, \quad (1)$$

where vector of unknowns v comprises nine components. These components include the displacement velocities and components of the stress tensor. ω is the real time frequency, $\rho(x, y, z)$ is the density, $I_{3\times3}$ is 3 by 3 identity matrix, $\hat{P}$, $\hat{Q}$ and $\hat{R}$ are constant matrices, $S_{6\times6}(x, y, z) = \begin{pmatrix} A & 0 \\ 0 & C \end{pmatrix}$ is 6 by 6 compliance matrix, and

$$A = \begin{pmatrix} a & -b & -b \\ -b & a & -b \\ -b & -b & a \end{pmatrix}, C = \begin{pmatrix} c & 0 & 0 \\ 0 & c & 0 \\ 0 & 0 & c \end{pmatrix}. \quad (2)$$

Coefficients $a(x, y, z)$, $b(x, y, z)$ and $c(x, y, z)$ are related to the Lame parameters. f is the right-hand side representing the seismic source. $\gamma(z)$ is an attenuation function. Equation (1) is solved in a cuboid domain of $N_x \times N_y \times N_z$ points with free surface top boundary and attenuation layers on the other boundaries.

Introducing preconditioner L_0 (for details refer to [3]), we arrive at equation

$$\left(I - \delta L L_0^{-1} \right) \tilde{v} = f, \text{ with } v = L_0^{-1}\tilde{v}, \ \delta L = L - L_0, \quad (3)$$

We solve Eq. (3) via the biconjugate gradient stabilized method (BiCGSTAB) [7]. This assumes computing several times per iteration the product of the left-hand side operator of Eq. (3) by a particular vector w, i.e. computing $\left[w - \delta L L_0^{-1} w \right]$. Computations of $L_0^{-1}w$ takes the most of runtime. To solve $L_0 q_1 = w$ we assume that function $w(x, y, z)$ is expanded into a Fourier series with respect to x and y with coefficients $\hat{w}\left(k_x, k_y, z \right)$, where k_x and k_y - spatial frequencies. $\hat{w}$ are solutions to equation

$$\left[i\omega \begin{pmatrix} \rho_0 I_{3\times3} & 0 \\ 0 & S_0 \end{pmatrix} - ik_x \begin{pmatrix} 0 & \hat{P} \\ \hat{P}^T & 0 \end{pmatrix} - ik_y \begin{pmatrix} 0 & \hat{Q} \\ \hat{Q}^T & 0 \end{pmatrix} - \gamma(z) \begin{pmatrix} 0 & \hat{R} \\ \hat{R}^T & 0 \end{pmatrix} \frac{\partial}{\partial z} \right] \hat{v} = \hat{w},$$

$$(4)$$

with the same boundary conditions as for Eq. (1). Here ρ_0 and S_0 are some averaging of ρ and S. We solve it numerically, applying a finite-difference approximation, resulting in a system of linear algebraic equations with a banded matrix. Computation of $\hat{w}$ we perform via the 2D Fast Fourier Transform (FFT) and after $\hat{v}$ are found, $L_0^{-1}w$ is computed via the inverse 2D FFT.

3   Parallelization

Four computational processes including BiCGSTAB, the 2D FFTs and solving (4), mainly drive the solver. We decompose the computational domain along one of the horizontal coordinates and parallelize these processes via MPI: using parallel BiCG-STAB function from PETSc [2], 2D FFT from Intel Math Kernel Library [4], and each MPI process, corresponding to a certain subdomain, solves boundary value problems (4) for its own set of spatial frequencies k_x and k_y, independently of other MPI processes. The main exchanges between the MPI processes are while performing FFTs.

Following this strategy, each MPI process would independently solve its own set of $N_x \cdot N_y / N$ (N – number of MPI processes) problems. We solve them in a loop, parallelized via OpenMP. Schematically, our parallelization strategy is presented in Fig. 1.

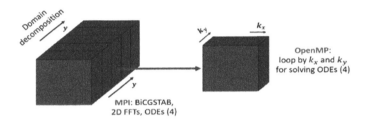

Fig. 1. Parallelization scheme.

To investigate the properties of this parallelization we construct a 2.5D land model (left image of Fig. 2) from the open source 2D Marmousi model. It is discretized with a uniform grid of $551 \times 700 \times 235$ points. In the right image of Fig. 2 we illustrate the 10 Hz monochromatic component of the computed wavefield for this model. Using 9 nodes with 7 MPI processes per node and 4 cores per process, the total computation time is 348 min.

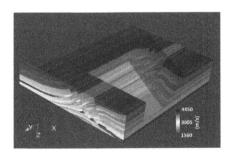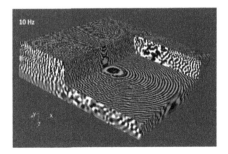

Fig. 2. Left - 2.5D P-velocity model; right - 3D view of a computed wavefield.

MPI strong scalability of the solver is defined as ratio t_M/t_N, where t_M and t_N are elapsed run times to solve the problem with N and $M > N$ MPI processes each corresponding to a different CPU. Using MPI, we parallelize two types of processes. First, those scaling ideally (solving problems (4)), for which the computational time with N processes is $\frac{T}{N}$. Second, the FFT, that scales as $\frac{T_{FFT}}{\alpha(N)}$, with coefficient $1 < \alpha(N) < N$. The total computational time becomes $\frac{T}{N} + \frac{T_{FFT}}{\alpha(N)}$ (here we simplify, assuming no need of synchronization) with scaling coefficient $\frac{T+T_{FFT}}{\frac{T}{N}+\frac{T_{FFT}}{\alpha(N)}}$, that is greater than $\alpha(N)$. This is why, we expect very good scalability of the algorithm, somewhere between the scalability of the FFT and the ideal scalability. We did not take into account OpenMP, which can be switched on for extra speed-up. It is worth noting, that we can not use MPI instead of OpenMp here, since then the scaling would degrade. MPI may have worked well if $T \gg T_{FFT}$, but this is not the case.

We estimate the strong scaling for modeling in two different models, both of $200 \times 600 \times 155$ points: a subset of depicted in Fig. 2 and the overthrust model [1]. From the left image of Fig. 3 we conclude that our solver scales very well up to 64 MPI processes.

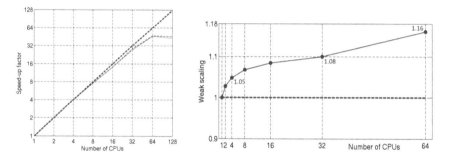

Fig. 3. Left - strong MPI scaling of the solver: blue dashed line - for the Marmousi model, red line - for the overthrust model, the dashed grey line - ideal scalability; right - weak MPI scaling measurements: the blue line - the solver and the dashed grey - ideal weak scaling. (Color figure online)

For weak scaling estimation, we assign the computational domain to one MPI process and then extend the size of the computational domain along the y-direction, while increasing the number of MPI processes. Here, we use one MPI process per CPU. The load per CPU is fixed. For the weak scaling, we use function $f_{weak}(N) = \frac{T(N)}{T(1)}$, where $T(N)$ is the average computational runtime per iteration with N MPI processes. The ideal weak scalability corresponds to $f_{weak}(N) = 1$.

To estimate it in our case, we considered a part of the model presented in Fig. 2 of size $200 \times 25 \times 200$ points with a decreased 4 m step along the y-coordinate. After extending the model in the y-direction 64 times, we arrive at a model of size $200 \times 1600 \times 150$ points. The right image of Fig. 3 demonstrates that for up to 64 MPI processes, weak scaling of our solver has small variations around the ideal weak scaling.

With OpenMP we parallelize the loop over spatial frequencies for solving (4). To estimate the scalability of this part of our solver, we performed simulations in a small part of the overthrust model comprising $660 \times 50 \times 155$ points on a single CPU having 14 cores with hyper-threading switched off and without using MPI. Figure 4 shows that our solver scales well for all threads involved in this example. It is worth mentioning, that we use OpenMP as an extra option applied when further increasing of the number of MPI processes doesn't improve performance any more, but the computational system is not fully loaded, i.e., there are free cores.

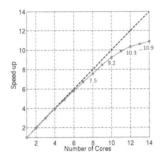

Fig. 4. Strong scalability on one CPU: blue line - ideal and red line is the solver scalability. (Color figure online)

4   Conclusions

Further improvement of the MPI scaling may be achieved by incorporating a domain decomposition along two horizontal directions into the current MPI parallelization scheme. Moreover, the parallelization using domain decomposition along the vertical direction for solving boundary value problems 4 may be applied for accelerating the computational runtime.

Acknowledgments. Two of the authors (Dmitry Neklyudov and Vladimir Tcheverda) have been sponsored by the Russian Science Foundation grant 17-17-01128.

References

1. Aminzadeh, F., Brac, J., Kuntz, T.: 3-D Salt and Overthrust Models: SEG/EAGE Modelling Series, no. 1, SEG Book Series, Tulsa, Oklahoma (1997)
2. Balay, S., Abhyankar, S., Adams, M. et al.: PETSc Users Manual. Argonne National Laboratory, ANL-95/11 - Revision 3.11 (2019). https://www.mcs.anl.gov/petsc
3. Belonosov, M., Kostin, V., Dmitriev, M., Tcheverda, V.: 3D numerical simulation of elastic waves with a frequency-domain iterative solver. Geophysics **83**(6), 1–52 (2018)

4. Intel: Intel®Math Kernel Library (Intel®MKL) (2018). https://software.intel.com/en-us/intel-mkl
5. Saad, Y.: Iterative Methods for Sparse Linear Systems, 2nd edn. SIAM, Philadelphia (2003)
6. Symes, W.W.: Migration velocity analysis and waveform inversion. Geophys. Prospect. **56** (6), 765–790 (2008)
7. Van Der Vorst, H.A.: BI-CGSTAB: a fast and smoothly converging variant of BI-CG for the solution of nonsymmetric linear systems. SIAM J. Sci. Stat. Comput. **13**(2), 631–644 (1992)

Active-Code Replacement
in the OODIDA Data Analytics Platform

Gregor Ulm[1,2(✉)] ⓘ, Emil Gustavsson[1,2] ⓘ, and Mats Jirstrand[1,2] ⓘ

[1] Fraunhofer-Chalmers Research Centre for Industrial Mathematics,
Chalmers Science Park, 412 88 Gothenburg, Sweden
{gregor.ulm,emil.gustavsson,mats.jirstrand}@fcc.chalmers.se
[2] Fraunhofer Center for Machine Learning,
Chalmers Science Park, 412 88 Gothenburg, Sweden
http://www.fcc.chalmers.se/

Abstract. OODIDA (On-board/Off-board Distributed Data Analytics) is a platform for distributing and executing concurrent data analytics tasks. It targets fleets of reference vehicles in the automotive industry and has a particular focus on rapid prototyping. Its underlying message-passing infrastructure has been implemented in Erlang/OTP. External Python applications perform data analytics tasks. Most work is performed by clients (on-board). A central cloud server performs supplementary tasks (off-board). OODIDA can be automatically packaged and deployed, which necessitates restarting parts of the system, or all of it. This is potentially disruptive. To address this issue, we added the ability to execute user-defined Python modules on clients as well as the server. These modules can be replaced without restarting any part of the system and they can even be replaced between iterations of an ongoing assignment. This facilitates use cases such as iterative A/B testing of machine learning algorithms or modifying experimental algorithms on-the-fly.

Keywords: Distributed computing · Code replacement · Erlang

1 Introduction

OODIDA is a modular system for concurrent distributed data analytics for the automotive domain, targeting fleets of reference vehicles [5]. Its main purpose is to process telemetry data at its source as opposed to transferring all data over the network and processing it on a central cloud server (cf. Fig. 1). A data analyst interacting with this system uses a Python library that assists in creating and validating assignment specifications. Updating this system with new computational methods necessitates terminating and redeploying software. However, we would like to perform updates without terminating ongoing tasks. We have therefore extended our system with the ability to execute user-defined code both on client devices (on-board) and the cloud server (off-board), without having to redeploy any part of it. As a consequence, OODIDA is now highly suited

© Springer Nature Switzerland AG 2020
U. Schwardmann et al. (Eds.): Euro-Par 2019 Workshops, LNCS 11997, pp. 715–719, 2020.
https://doi.org/10.1007/978-3-030-48340-1_55

for rapid prototyping. The key aspect of our work is that active-code replacement of Python modules piggybacks on the existing Erlang/OTP infrastructure of OODIDA for sending assignments to clients, leading to a clean design. This paper is a condensed version of a work-in-progress paper [6], giving an overview of our problem (Sect. 2) and its solution (Sect. 3), followed by an evaluation (Sect. 4) and related work (Sect. 5).

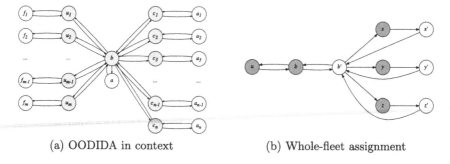

(a) OODIDA in context   (b) Whole-fleet assignment

Fig. 1. OODIDA overview and details: In (a) user nodes u connect to a central cloud b, which connects to clients c. The shaded nodes are implemented in Erlang/OTP; the other nodes are external Python applications, i.e. the user front-ends f, the external server application a, and external client applications a. In (b) the core of OODIDA is shown with permanent nodes (dark) and temporary handlers (light) in an instance of a whole-fleet assignment. Cloud node b spawned an assignment handler b'. After receiving an incoming task, clients x, y and z spawned task handlers x', y', and z' that interact with external applications. Nodes x and x' correspond to c_1 in (a) etc.

2   Problem

OODIDA has been designed for rapid prototyping, which implies that it frequently needs to be extended with new computational methods, both for on-board and off-board data processing. To achieve this goal, Python applications on the cloud and clients have to be updated. Assuming that we update both, the following steps are required: The user front-end f needs to be modified to recognize the new off-board and on-board keywords for the added methods, including checks of assignment parameter values. In addition, the cloud and client applications have to be extended with the new methods. All ongoing assignments need to be terminated and the cloud and clients shut down. Afterwards, we can redeploy and restart the system. This is disruptive, even without taking into account potentially long-winded software development processes in large organizations. On the other hand, the turn-around time for adding custom methods would be much shorter if we could do so at runtime. Active-code replacement targets this particular problem, with the goal of further improving the suitability of OODIDA for rapid prototyping.

3   Solution

With active-code replacement, the user can define a custom Python module for the cloud and for client devices. It is implemented as a special case of an assignment. The front-end f performs static and dynamic checks, attempting to verify correctness of syntax and data types. If these checks succeed, the provided code is turned into a JSON object and ingested by user node u for further processing. Within this JSON object, the user-defined code is stored as an encoded text string. It is forwarded to cloud node b, which spawns an assignment handler b' for this particular assignment. Custom code can be used on the cloud and/or clients. Assuming clients have been targeted with active-code replacement, node b' turns the assignment specification into tasks for all clients c specified in the assignment. Afterwards, task specifications are sent to the specified client devices. There, the client process spawns a task handler for the current task, which monitors task completion. The task handler sends the task specification in JSON to an external Python application, which turns the given code into a file, thus recreating the Python module the data analyst initially provided. The resulting files are tied to the ID of the user who provided it. After the task handler is done, it notifies the assignment handler b' and terminates. Similarly, once the assignment handler has received responses from all task handlers, it sends a status message to the cloud node and terminates. The cloud node sends a status message to inform the user that their custom code has been successfully deployed. Deploying custom code to the cloud is similar, the main difference being that b' communicates with the external Python application on the cloud.

If a custom on-board or off-board computation is triggered by a special keyword in an assignment specification, Python loads the user-provided module. The user-specified module is located at a predefined path, which is known to the Python application. The custom function is applied to the available data after the user-specified number of values has been collected. When an assignment uses custom code, external applications reload the custom module with each iteration of an assignment. This leads to greater flexibility: Consider an assignment that runs for an indefinite number of iterations. As external applications can process tasks concurrently, and code replacement is just another task, the data analyst can react to intermediate results of an ongoing assignment by deploying custom code with modified algorithmic parameters while this assignment is ongoing. As custom code is tied to a user ID, there is furthermore no interference due to custom code that was deployed by other users. The description of active-code replacement so far indicates that the user can execute custom code on the cloud server and clients, as long as the correct inputs and outputs are consumed and produced. What may not be immediately obvious, however, is that we can now create *ad hoc* implementations of even the most complex OODIDA use cases in custom code, such as federated learning [3].

Inconsistent updates are a problem in practice, i.e. results sent from clients may have been produced with different custom code modules in the same iteration of an assignment. This happens if not all clients receive the updated custom code before the end of the current iteration. To solve this problem, each provided module with custom code is tagged with its md5 hash signature, which is reported together with the results from the clients. The cloud only uses the results tagged with the signature that achieves a majority. Consequently, results are never tainted by using different versions of custom code in the same iteration.

4   Evaluation

The main benefit of active-code replacement is that code for new computational methods can be deployed right away and executed almost instantly, without affecting other ongoing tasks. In contrast, a standard update of the cloud or client installation necessitates redeploying and restarting the respective components of the system. In an idealized test setup, where the various workstations that run the user, cloud and client components of OODIDA are connected via Ethernet, it takes a fraction of a second for a custom on-board or off-board method to be available for the user to call when deployed with active-code replacement, as shown in Table 1. On the other hand, automated redeployment of the cloud and client installation takes roughly 20 and 40 s, respectively. The runtime difference between a standard update and active-code replacement amounts to three orders of magnitude. Of course, real-world deployment via a wireless or 4G connection would be slower as well as error-prone. Yet, the idealized evaluation environment reveals the relative performance difference of both approaches, eliminating potentially unreliable data transmission as a source of error.

This comparison neglects that, compared to a standard update, active-code replacement is less bureaucratic and less intrusive as it does not require interrupting any currently ongoing assignments. Also, in a realistic industry scenario, an update could take days or even weeks due to software development and organizational processes. However, it is not the case that active-code replacement fully sidesteps the need to update the library of computational methods on the cloud or on clients as OODIDA enforces restrictions on custom code. For instance, some parts of the Python standard library are off-limits. Also, the user cannot install external libraries. Yet, for typical algorithmic explorations, which users of our system regularly conduct, active-code replacement is a vital feature that increases user productivity far more than the previous comparison may imply. That being said, due to the limitations of active-code replacement, it is complementary to the standard update procedure rather than a competitive approach.

5   Related Work

The feature described in this paper is an extension of the OODIDA platform [5], which originated from `ffl-erl`, a framework for federated learning in Erlang/OTP [4]. In terms of descriptions of systems that perform active-code replacement, Polus by Chen et al. [1] deserves mention. A significant difference is that it replaces larger units of code instead of isolated modules. It also operates in a multi-threading environment instead of the highly concurrent message-passing environment of OODIDA. We also noticed a similarity between our approach

Table 1. Runtime comparison of active-code replacement of a moderately long Python module versus regular redeployment in an idealized setting. The former has a significant advantage. Yet, this does not factor in that a standard update is more invasive but can also be more comprehensive. The provided figures are the averages of five runs.

	Cloud	Client
Active-code replacement	20.3 ms	45.4 ms
Standard redeployment	23.6 s	40.8 s

and Javelus by Gu et al. [2]. Even though they focus on updating a stand-alone Java application as opposed to a distributed system, their described "lazy update mechanism" likewise only has an effect if a module is indeed used. This mirrors our approach of only loading a custom module when it is needed.

Acknowledgements. This research was financially supported by the project On-board/Off-board Distributed Data Analytics (OODIDA) in the funding program FFI: Strategic Vehicle Research and Innovation (DNR 2016-04260), which is administered by VINNOVA, the Swedish Government Agency for Innovation Systems. It took place in the Fraunhofer Cluster of Excellence "Cognitive Internet Technologies". Simon Smith and Adrian Nilsson helped with a supplementary part of the implementation of this feature and carried out the performance evaluation. Ramin Yahyapour (University of Göttingen) provided insightful comments during a poster presentation.

References

1. Chen, H., Yu, J., Chen, R., Zang, B., Yew, P.C.: Polus: a powerful live updating system. In: 29th International Conference on Software Engineering (ICSE 2007), pp. 271–281. IEEE (2007)
2. Gu, T., Cao, C., Xu, C., Ma, X., Zhang, L., Lu, J.: Javelus: a low disruptive approach to dynamic software updates. In: 2012 19th Asia-Pacific Software Engineering Conference, vol. 1, pp. 527–536. IEEE (2012)
3. McMahan, H.B., Moore, E., Ramage, D., Hampson, S., et al.: Communication-efficient learning of deep networks from decentralized data. arXiv preprint arXiv:1602.05629 (2016)
4. Ulm, G., Gustavsson, E., Jirstrand, M.: Functional federated learning in Erlang (ffl-erl). In: Silva, J. (ed.) WFLP 2018. LNCS, vol. 11285, pp. 162–178. Springer, Cham (2019). https://doi.org/10.1007/978-3-030-16202-3_10
5. Ulm, G., Gustavsson, E., Jirstrand, M.: OODIDA: On-board/off-board distributed data analytics for connected vehicles. arXiv preprint arXiv:1902.00319 (2019)
6. Ulm, G., Smith, S., Nilsson, A., Gustavsson, E., Jirstrand, M.: Facilitating rapid prototyping in the OODIDA data analytics platform via active-code replacement. arXiv preprint arXiv:1903.09477 (2019)

CNN-SIM: A Detailed Arquitectural Simulator of CNN Accelerators

Francisco Muñoz-Martínez[1]([✉]), José L. Abellán[2], and Manuel E. Acacio[1]

[1] Universidad de Murcia, 30100 Murcia, Spain
{francisco.munoz2,meacacio}@um.es
[2] Universidad Católica San Antonio de Murcia, 30107 Murcia, Spain
jlabellan@ucam.edu

Abstract. In this work we provide a quick overview of our ongoing effort to derive an open-source framework for detailed architectural simulation of the inference procedure of CNN hardware accelerators. Our tool, called *CNN-SIM*, exposes the values computed during the inference procedure of any CNN model using real inputs, which allows the investigation of architectural techniques for optimized inference. As a use case, we show the percentage of communicated zero values for two possible dataflows.

Keywords: Convolutional Neural Network · DNN accelerators · Simulation · Hardware architecture · Scale-Sim

1 Introduction and Motivation

The recent popularity of Deep Neural Networks (DNNs) in general, and convolutional Neural Networks (CNNs) in particular, to solve very complex problems such as image classification and object recognition in real time [5], has given birth to a fruitful research field on the design of novel architectures to ensure efficient support for their entailed computational load. Thus, several accelerator architectures have appeared in the literature, such as the Google's TPU [2], the MIT's Eyeriss [1], or more recently, the MAERI fabric that ensures adaption to a variety of DNN partitions and mappings [3].

These accelerators are typically designed as spatial architectures based on systolic arrays, as they have long been proved to excel at matrix-matrix/vector multiplications – integral operations in CNN processing. A systolic array is typically composed of a 2D-mesh network of processing elements or PEs, where each PE is equipped with an ALU, local memory and control logic, and implements some flavor of dataflow processing (e.g., output stationary or weight stationary [5]) in order to maximize data reuse within the network, thereby saving costly memory accesses and energy consumption.

Traditionally, one of the first steps in the design, implementation and optimization of a new computer architecture has been to simulate it in great detail. Unlike what happens for traditional general-purpose architectures, there is still no detailed simulation tool that can be employed to analyze the behavior of

U. Schwardmann et al. (Eds.): Euro-Par 2019 Workshops, LNCS 11997, pp. 720–724, 2020.
https://doi.org/10.1007/978-3-030-48340-1_56

such CNN accelerator architectures. The only CNN accelerator simulator publicly available to date is *SCALE-Sim* [4]. However, its limitations (explained in Sect. 2) impede using it for exploration of architectural techniques to improve the efficiency of the training and inference procedures based on the computed values. To fill this gap, in this work we provide a quick overview of our ongoing effort to derive an open-source framework for detailed architectural simulation of the inference procedure of hardware CNN accelerators. As an example of use, we show the percentage of communicated zero values for two possible dataflows.

2   CNN-Sim

As already mentioned, *CNN-Sim* is based on *SCALE-Sim*, which is a cycle-accurate simulator written in Python that allows insight into design trade-offs and mapping strategies for systolic-array based CNN accelerators. This simulator can conduct experiments based on the weight stationary (WS), output stationary (OS) and input stationary (IS) dataflows [5]. To do so, *SCALE-Sim* models an array of PEs and three SRAM modules to read in and write out the three data types (i.e., input activations, weights and output activations) used by each CNN.

For the design-space exploration of this accelerator model, the tool is setup with a user-defined configuration file where users can specify architectural details such as the number of PEs (i.e., the array shape), the SRAM memory size for each type of data, and the dataflow to use. Based on these inputs and a CNN layer specification provided through a separate network configuration file, *SCALE-Sim* simulates the processing of the CNN layer and reports some statistics such as the resulting latency (i.e., number of cycles), array utilization, number of SRAM accesses and DRAM accesses, as well as the demand of DRAM bandwidth.

However, since the tool is just designed to gain insight into the impact of a certain dataflow in the context of a configured accelerator design, these outputs cannot be utilized to truly understand the actual inference procedure of a CNN processing for a given input from the real world (e.g., an image). Another important limitation of *SCALE-sim* is that users cannot analyze the particular computed values during the processing of the CNN's layers, i.e., the layers are not actually executed but they rely on an analytic model that simply outputs the number of processing cycles per convolution layer. This fact seriously limits the design-space exploration of CNN accelerators since value-based architectural techniques, such as those based on skipping the useless multiplications by zero [1], cannot be explored. To fill this gap, we present *CNN-SIM*, an extended version of *SCALE-Sim* that allows the research community to truly simulate the actual inference procedure of a certain CNN with different dataflows.

With this aim, we first extend the well-known Caffe DL framework so that users can now choose *SCALE-Sim* as the target computing platform to execute the inference. More specifically, as illustrated in Fig. 1, users can setup any inference procedure by means of the typical configuration files in Caffe: the CNN model with the `model.prototxt` file, the values of the learned CNN's weights in `weights.caffemodel` file, and the real input data to predict (e.g., an `Image Database`). Besides, users need to configure the desired accelerator architecture

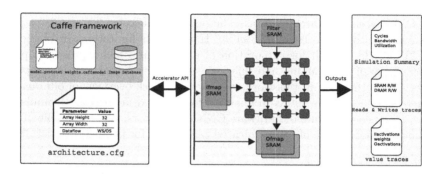

Fig. 1. High level description of CNN-Sim.

with the very same input parameters from *SCALE-Sim*: as shown in the figure, the `architecture.cfg` file that lists the array dimensions of PEs and type of dataflow (e.g., OS). On the other hand, we modify *SCALE-Sim* to truly execute the arithmetic operations involved when processing a CNN. In particular, while *CNN-Sim* is running, each PE is modeled and its particular operation computed, so that the real dataflow is simulated (the user can know at any time the result of the operation executed by each PE, as well as the input data being used).

Once *CNN-Sim* is configured, the interaction between Caffe and our tool works as follows: First, Caffe starts the execution of the first image from the `Image Database` loading the input data needed into the SRAM modules of the simulator. After that, the simulator runs the entire dataflow and tracks the data that passes through the PE array. After the simulator finishes the computation for all the output activations, it sends the results back to Caffe, allowing it to continue normally. Apart from the original *SCALE-Sim*'s output statistics (see `Simulation Summary` and `Read&Writes traces`), *CNN-Sim* is also capable of reporting all the values passed through the network per clock cycle in three different files (i.e., input activations, weights and output activations).

3   Case Study: Dataflows and Useless Network Traffic

The existence of useless operations (i.e., multiplications by zero) in the execution of the inference procedure of a CNN is widely demonstrated by the state-of-the-art. However, studying the resulting network traffic composed of zeroes across the array of PEs depending on a dataflow has not been thoroughly studied yet. The reason is that, before *CNN-SIM*, the research community lacked an accurate simulator capable of analyzing computed values in different dataflows.

To show the potential of our tool, we carry out a case study in which we utilize the third convolution layer of AlexNet CNN (i.e., an input of size $256 \times 27 \times 27$ and 384 filters of size $256 \times 3 \times 3$) and an accelerator consisting of a 32×32 array of PEs. Then, we analyze the useless network traffic for both WS and OS dataflows using one particular input image.

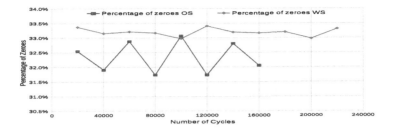

Fig. 2. Percentage of zeroes passed through the interconnection network when the 3rd layer of AlexNet CNN is executed on *CNN-SIM* using both WS and OS dataflows.

Figure 2 depicts the percentage of zeroes that are read and written through the network of PEs for both OS and WS dataflows at 20,000-cycle time intervals. More specifically, we plot the percentage of zeroes that all the PEs in the array receive either from memory or from other PE neighbors. As it can be noticed, zero values account for a significant fraction of the network traffic, ranging from 31% to 34%. Also, it is worth noting that the amount of zeroes tends to be superior for WS dataflow. This is due to it keeps the weights stationary in the PEs, thus reducing the total memory traffic while the amount of traffic due to activations (which contain most of the zeroes) is kept. Note also that the number of cycles required by WS is noticeably higher than that of OS.

4   Conclusions and Ongoing Work

We have presented *CNN-SIM*, a simulation tool aimed to ease the exploration of architectural techniques for optimized inference procedures in CNN hardware accelerators. Inspired by MAERI [3], we are currently extending the type of hardware elements that are supported. The ultimate goal is to provide the user with a framework that can be employed to configure and simulate a myriad of CNN architectures, so that direct comparisons between them can be carried out, also fostering the exploration of CNN design-oriented optimizations.

Acknowledgments. The authors would like to thank the anonymous reviewers for their critical assessment of our work and constructive comments that have helped improve the manuscript. This work has been supported by the Spanish MCIU and AEI, as well as European Commission FEDER funds, under grants "RTI2018-098156-B-C53" and "TIN2016-78799-P". Francisco Muñoz-Martínez is supported by fellowship 20749/FPI/18 from Fundación Séneca, Agencia Regional de Ciencia y Tecnología de la Región de Murcia.

References

1. Chen, Y.H., et al.: Eyeriss: An energy-efficient reconfigurable accelerator for deep convolutional neural networks. IEEE J. Solid-State Circ. **52**(1), 127–138 (2017)
2. Jouppi, N.P., et al.: In-datacenter performance analysis of a tensor processing unit. In: 44th International Symposium on Computer Architecture (ISCA), pp. 1–12 (2017)
3. Kwon, H., Samajdar, A., Krishna, T.: MAERI: enabling flexible dataflow mapping over DNN accelerators via reconfigurable interconnects. In: 23rd ASPLOS, pp. 461–475 (2018)
4. Samajdar, A., Zhu, Y., Whatmough, P., Mattina, M., Krishna, T.: SCALE-Sim: Systolic CNN Accelerator Simulator. arXiv:1811.02883v2 (2019)
5. Sze, V., Chen, Y.H., Yang, T.J., Emer, J.: Efficient processing of deep neural networks: A tutorial and survey. arXiv preprint arXiv: 1703.09039v2 (2017)

Duality-Based Locality-Aware Stream Partitioning in Distributed Stream Processing Engines

Siwoon Son and Yang-Sae Moon[✉]

Kangwon National University, Chuncheon, Korea
{ssw5176,ysmoon}@kangwon.ac.kr

Abstract. In this paper, we propose duality-based locality-aware stream partitioning (LSP) in distributed *stream* processing engines (DSPEs). In general, LSP directly uses the locality concept of distributed *batch* processing engines (DBPEs). This concept does not fully take into account the characteristics of DSPEs and therefore does not maximize cluster resource utilization. To solve this problem, we first explain the limitations of existing LSP, and we then propose a *duality* relationship between DBPEs and DSPEs. We finally propose a simple but efficient *ping*-based mechanism to maximize the locality of DSPEs based on the duality. The insights uncovered in this paper can maximize the throughput and minimize the latency in stream partitioning.

Keywords: Distributed processing · Data stream · Locality · Duality

1 Introduction

A distributed *stream* processing engine (DSPE) is a real-time processing framework that guarantees high throughput and low latency by processing continuously generated data streams in a cluster of multiple servers. Each DSPE application is defined as a directed acyclic graph (DAG). Figure 1 shows an example of such a DAG. In the example, $Sample_n$ receives a data stream, $Extract_n$ extracts a keyword, and $Count_n$ aggregates the number of keywords. In the DAG, vertices are processing operators (POs), and they transmit the data stream through edges. Each PO replicates multiple instances (POIs), and they are deployed on a distributed server. If there are multiple receiver POIs, the sender POI changes the edges frequently. Therefore, DSPEs require a stream partitioner for sender POIs to select receiver POIs. In this case, the receiver POIs may be deployed in the local machines as well as the remote machines. The basic idea for reducing the network communication cost, which is the largest proportion of the turnaround time in stream processing, is to select the PO placed on the local machine as the receiver. This idea is called *locality-aware* stream partitioning (LSP).

© Springer Nature Switzerland AG 2020
U. Schwardmann et al. (Eds.): Euro-Par 2019 Workshops, LNCS 11997, pp. 725–730, 2020.
https://doi.org/10.1007/978-3-030-48340-1_57

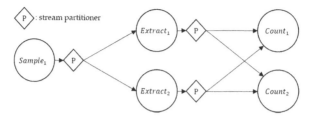

Fig. 1. An illustration of duality between DBPEs and DSPEs.

Many studies have already introduced locality and achieved high-performance benefits. In particular, Apache Hadoop [1], a representative distributed *batch* processing engine (DBPE), introduces locality into the MapReduce framework [2–5]. The advantage of this locality can also be applied to DSPEs, and a few studies deal with LSP [6–8]. However, most studies do not fully exploit the characteristics of DSPEs because they apply the locality of DBPEs to DSPEs in the same way. In this paper, we define the relationship between DBPEs and DSPEs as *duality*. The contributions of this paper can be summarized as follows. First, we theoretically analyze the use cases of existing LSP methods. Second, we present the duality relationship between DBPEs and DSPEs and explain the limitation of stream partitioning methods considering only locality in DSPEs. Third, we present a simple but efficient *ping*-based mechanism for the duality-based LSP.

2 Related Work

Apache Hadoop [1] is a widely used DBPE that stores large data blocks on HDFS servers and allocates multiple tasks to each server to process the data. If the required blocks are not on the same server as the task, the task copies the blocks from the other server over the network. To reduce this network bottleneck, many works introduce locality to task partitioning. In particular, binary locality [2, 3] and discrete locality [4, 5] are proposed according to the locality-awareness. This locality concept of DBPE is well adapted to the characteristics of processing large data, and thus leads very high performance.

As a representative DSPE, Apache Storm [9] provides several stream partitioning methods [6][1]. Among them, Local-or-Shuffle Grouping (hereinafter referred to as *LoSG*) does not generate network communication since sender POIs select receiver POIs operating in the same process by introducing binary locality of DBPEs. However, due to the lack of consideration of the characteristics of DSPEs, the locality is reduced or cluster utilization is lowered. Caneill *et al.* [7] propose an LSP method for *stateful* applications. However, since stateful partitioning requires a lot of user knowledge and restricts applications, we focus on *stateless* partitioning. We have studied the LSP of the ping-based mechanism in the previous work [8], and this paper presents its rationale in terms of locality and duality.

---

[1] Apache Storm describes stream partitioning as grouping method.

3 Duality-Based Locality-Aware Stream Partitioning

In this section, we show how to apply locality effectively in DSPEs based on the duality concept between DBPEs and DSPEs. First, we classify the existing LSP of DSPEs (i.e. LoSG) into four use cases. To this end, we assume the followings: (1) only a single process runs per server, and (2) all tasks are allocated as evenly as possible. These assumptions are for simple modeling of use cases and do not affect the duality described below. If we denote the number of sender POIs as S, the number of receiver POIs as R, and the number of servers as N, LoSG can be classified into four use cases:

1. *Best locality*: locality and load balancing are maximized,
   if $S \bmod N = 0 \, and \, R \bmod N = 0$.
2. *Strong locality*: locality is maximized but load balancing is not,
   if $(R \bmod N \neq 0 \, and \, R > N) or (R \bmod N = 0 \, and \, S \bmod N \neq 0)$.
3. *Weak locality*: only partial locality is guaranteed, if $R < N \, and \, S + R > N$.
4. *Worst locality*: no node guarantees locality, if $S + R \leq N$.

Best locality and strong locality show high performance because no network communication occurs in data transmission. On the contrary, weak locality and worst locality have relatively low performance because they require network communication. Based on this observation, DSPE applications can place S and R in best locality or strong locality according to N for high performance. However, these use cases are extremely classified to show the benefits of locality, and only horizontal task partitioning is considered.

Next, we explain the duality concept between DBPEs and DSPEs. DBPEs require *task partitioning* which distributes tasks to each server in order to process the data distributed and stored in the cluster. On the contrary, DSPEs require *stream partitioning* which selects the task to transmit data among the tasks distributed in the cluster. Thus, DBPEs and DSPEs are similar but have a *duality* relationship with each other. Figure 2 shows their duality relationship, and Table 1 describes the duality between DBPEs and DSPEs in terms of locality.

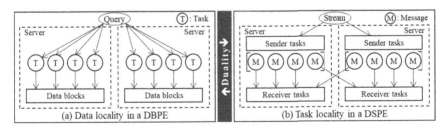

Fig. 2. An illustration of duality between DBPEs and DSPEs.

Table 1. Duality between DBPEs and DSPEs for supporting locality.

	DBPE	DSPE
Static object	Data (block)	Task (POI)
Dynamic object	Task (map or reduce)	Data stream (messages)
Data unit size	Large (hundreds of MB to GB)	Small (hundreds of bytes to MB)
Partitioning policy	Task partitioning	Stream partitioning
Optimization factor	Data locality	Task locality

By considering data locality, DBPEs deploy the tasks on the server where the data requested by each task is located. This approach is used where the data blocks that DBPE handles are very large (e.g. the default block size of HDFS is 128 MB), which requires a high communication cost. Similar to DBPEs, DSPEs can also select the receiver POI located in the same server as the sender POI, taking into account the task locality (i.e. LoSG). However, the data size of DSPEs is relatively small compared to DBPEs (e.g. Twit messages are less than 1 KB). This characteristic of DSPEs increases the load of the receiver POI and wastes computing power of the other receiver POI if we transmit the messages only to the receiver POI of the same server. In addition, the following variables can cause performance degradation despite best locality due to high load on the receiver POI:

1. TA: vertical, horizontal, and hierarchical task allocation in a job.
2. MJ: multiple job assignment in a distributed stream processing engine.
3. NC: network capacity in a hierarchical cluster.
4. OP: other CPU- and memory-bounded processes in a cluster.
5. FS: fluctuation of message size and occurrence interval of data stream.
6. HS: heterogeneity of resources among servers in a cluster.

These variables have a significant effect on stream partitioning considering only locality. In other words, although it is efficient to transmit the messages to the idle receiver POI of another server, the messages are transmitted only to the receiver POI of the same server. Therefore, based on the duality relationship between DBPEs and DSPEs, the LSP should be able to select an optimal receiver including not only the same server but also other servers considering various variables at the time of transmitting messages.

We classify the six variables described above into two categories in terms of stream processing. First, TA, MJ, and NC are classified as Network Distance (ND), which represents the relative distance between a sender POI and receiver POIs. Second, OP, FS, and HS are classified as Receiver Load (RL), which represents the computing power of each receiver POI. Therefore, we need ND and RL measurements for optimal stream partitioning. We can estimate ND as discrete locality [4, 5], but ND may be changed from time to time in large clusters. We can estimate the RL by local load estimation [10], where each sender POI aggregates the amount of transmission locally, but cannot accurately measure the load by considering only a part of the RL of the receiver POI. Therefore, the most accurate way is for the stream partitioner to measure ND and RL directly.

The simplest and most efficient way to measure both ND and RL is to use *ping*. Ping measures the round-trip time (RTT) by sending and receiving packets small enough to not affect the system to the remote server, and this RTT includes ND and RL. In other words, with ND, RTT of the same server is the lowest, and RTT increases as the number of network hops increases. Also, with RL, the higher the server's computing power, the lower the RTT. Therefore, the ping-based RTT measurement is very suitable for duality-based LSP. In actual preliminary experiments [8], the ping-based method showed up to 1.6 times faster transmission time than Shuffle grouping [6] in the best locality, and 8.6 times higher resource utilization than LoSG in the strong locality.

4 Conclusions and Future Work

In this paper, we presented the duality between DBPEs and DSPEs in LSP. The existing LSP, LoSG, applied the locality of DBPEs as it was, and transmitted the messages only to the receiver POI of the same server. This did not take into account the characteristics of the DSPEs. Therefore, we analyzed the duality relationship between DBPEs and DSPEs, and explained that it was efficient to transmit some messages to the receiver POIs of other servers in DSPEs. We also proposed a ping-based mechanism to solve the limitations of existing LSP. In future work, we will (1) theoretically present the optimal model for performing stream partitioning, and (2) analyze the effect of the ping-based mechanism on LSP and the comparison with existing stream partitioning.

Acknowledgements. This research was supported by Korea Electric Power Corporation. (Grant number: R18XA05).

References

1. Apache Hadoop. https://hadoop.apache.org/
2. Ibrahim, S., et al.: LEEN: locality/fairness-aware key partitioning for MapReduce in the cloud. In: Proceedings of the 2nd IEEE International Conference on Cloud Computing Technology and Science, Indianapolis, IN, pp. 17–24, November 2010
3. Wang, W., et al.: MapTask scheduling in MapReduce with data locality: throughput and heavy-traffic optimality. IEEE/ACM Trans. Netw. **24**(1), 190–203 (2016)
4. Zaharia, M., et al.: Delay scheduling: a simple technique for achieving locality and fairness in cluster scheduling. In: Proceedings of the 5th European Conference on Computer Systems, Paris, France, pp. 265–278, April 2010
5. Bu, X., et al.: Interference and locality-aware task scheduling for MapReduce applications in virtual clusters. In: Proceedings of the 22nd International Symposium on High-performance Parallel and Distributed Computing, New York, NY, pp. 227–238, June 2013
6. Apache Storm Concepts. http://storm.apache.org/releases/1.2.2/Concepts.html
7. Caneill, M., et al.: Locality-aware routing in stateful streaming applications. In: Proceedings of the 17th International Middleware Conference, Trento, Italy, pp. 4:1–4:13, December 2016

8. Son, S., et al.: Locality aware traffic distribution in apache storm for energy analytics platform. In: Proceedings of the 6th IEEE International Conference on Big Data and Smart Computing, Shanghai, China, pp. 721–724, January 2018

9. Toshniwal, A., et al.: Storm @Twitter. In: Proceedings of the International Conference on Management of Data, Snowbird, UT, pp. 147–156, June 2014

10. Nasir, M., et al.: The power of both choices: practical load balancing for distributed stream processing engines. In: Proceedings of the 31st IEEE International Conference on Data Engineering (ICDE), Seoul, South Korea, pp. 137–148, 13–17 April 2015

Message Latency-Based Load Shedding Mechanism in Apache Kafka

Hajin Kim, Jiwon Bang, Siwoon Son, Namsoo Joo, Mi-Jung Choi,
and Yang-Sae Moon[(⊠)]

Kangwon National University, Chuncheon, Korea
{hajinkim,jiwonbang,ssw5176,nsju,mjchoi,ysmoon}@kangwon.ac.kr

Abstract. Apache Kafka is a distributed message queuing platform that
delivers data streams in real time. Through the distributed processing
technology, Kafka has the advantage of delivering very large data streams
very fast. However, when the data explosion occurs, the message latency
largely increases and the system might be interrupted. This paper proposes a load shedding engine of Kafka that solves this message latency
problem. The load shedding engine solves the data explosion problem by
introducing a simple mechanism that restricts the transmission of some
messages when the latency exceeds the given threshold in the Kafka's
producer. Experiments with Apache Storm-based real-time applications
show that the latency does not continuously increase due to the load
shedding function in both single and multiple data streams, and maintains a constant level. This is the first attempt to apply a load shedding
technique to Kafka-based real-time stream processing, providing simple
and efficient data explosion control.

Keywords: Big data · Data stream · Apache Kafka · Load shedding

1 Introduction

Apache Kafka [1] is a distributed message queuing platform that delivers large
data streams [6] very fast across multiple servers, ensuring scalability and high
availability [5]. However, when data explosion occurs, there is a problem that
the latency of messages loaded on Kafka gradually increases. If this situation
continues, there would be a lot of messages waiting on Kafka and the real time
nature of data streams could not be guaranteed, and in the worst case, the
system might be shut down. Therefore, in this paper, we apply a load shedding
mechanism to the Kafka-based real-time processing environment. Load shedding
[7] is a overload control technique that discards some messages so that the system
is not overloaded if the data stream instantly explodes and exceeds the processing
capacity of the system.

The proposed load shedding technique uses a simple concept that measures
message latency in Kafka and discards some messages based on the latency. That
is, when the latency exceeds the user-given threshold (ϵ), the Kafka's producer

© Springer Nature Switzerland AG 2020
U. Schwardmann et al. (Eds.): Euro-Par 2019 Workshops, LNCS 11997, pp. 731–736, 2020.
https://doi.org/10.1007/978-3-030-48340-1_58

restricts the transmission of some messages. The latency threshold and message transmission ratio are determined by the system administrator who knows the data characteristics well. This latency-based mechanism has the advantage of easy implementation with the simple concept while performing the load shedding function efficiently.

In the experiment, we use Apache Storm [3,4] for processing real-time applications. Storm is a real-time distributed stream processing platform, and in the experiment it runs a sorting application for continuous array streams. Experimental results show that the latency increases gradually in the existing system, while the latency does not continuously increase in load shedding applied system and maintains a constant level. In addition, even for multiple input sources, it performs load shedding of each source in parallel correctly. This is the first attempt to apply load shedding to Kafka-based real-time data stream processing, providing simple and efficient data explosion control.

2 Related Work

In this section, we explain the concept of load shedding and its recent technologies. Load shedding maintains an appropriate load by ignoring some of the input data when more data than the system's processing capacity is introduced. Load shedding techniques are classified into two categories: random selection and semantic-based techniques. Random selection load shedding randomly ignores the input data regardless of the data content. On the other hand, semantic-based load shedding weights to the data and ignores some data based on their importance. In this paper, we use random selection because all input data are assumed to be equivalent.

Recent load shedding techniques consider the relationship between data items, computation processing time, and system power consumption. CoD [8] estimates the relationship between input data items and ignores relatively irrelevant items. LAS [9] calculates the latency based on the computation processing time and the amount of tuples. After then, if the total latency of the input data stream is longer than a user-specified threshold, it ignores some data of the stream. E-DLS [10] is effective in reducing the power consumption and communication bandwidth, and it reduces the usage of system resources while maintaining the maximum throughput.

The above recent techniques have advantages and disadvantages compared to the random selection load shedding used in this paper. First, CoD shows better results in latency and relative error ratios than the random selection, but is complex to process and implement. Also, CoD has an additional overhead, which requires a separate implementation of the window sample and the data buffer. Second, LAS yields better results than the random selection at average processing time and average queuing time. But, it is difficult to implement without sufficient experience with the system because it needs to know the processing time and the data characteristics. Third, E-DLS uses power and communication bandwidth efficiently, but due to use of the cluster, we need to know exactly the role of the cluster nodes. In particular, Kafka, which manages the cluster through Zookeeper, doesn't know exact roles of cluster nodes. Based on the above observations, we use simple and efficient random selection despite the advantages of the new techniques.

3   Latency-Based Load Shedding Engine in Apache Kafka

This section describes the load-shedding mechanism in Apache Kafka-based real-time processing systems. The proposed engine determines the three major issues [7] of load shedding as follows. First, the *load shedding time* is determined when the message latency exceeds the given load shedding threshold. Since the input rates of data streams change dynamically, we need to keep the message latency below a certain level to guarantee real-time processing. Thus, the proposed load shedding engine measures message latency and starts load shedding when the latency exceeds a given threshold. Second, the *load shedding position* is determined as a Kafka producer delivering the data stream between the data stream source and the real-time processing system. This is because the real-time system does not perform unnecessary processing by discarding the message before handling the data stream. Third, the *load shedding quantity* is determined by the system administrator. This is to maintain the load of the whole system constantly by setting an approprite load shedding ratio under the recognition of the system administrator.

Figure 1 shows an example architecture of the proposed Kafka-based load shedding engine. As shown in the figure, the data input and output of the real-time message processing system correspond to Kafka's producer and consumer. It then processes and analyzes stream data through a real-time message processing system such as Apache Storm [3,4] and Apache Spark Streaming [2]. The load shedding manager operates independently of the real-time message processing system and cooperates with the Kafka consumer to determine whether the data explosion occurs. If data explosion occurs, it discards message at a preset load shedding rate. In Fig. 1, steps ① to ⑧ show the procedures for message processing and load shedding.

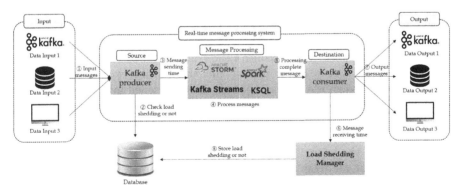

Fig. 1. A real-time processing system adopting the Kafka-based load shedding engine.

Our load shedding engine manages the data stream on a source basis, so it can support load shedding function for each source for multiple sources. Figure 2 shows the operation procedure for handling multi-source streams. First, when the Kafka consumer requests a socket communication to the load shedding manager, the manager accepts the request (①), passes the connected socket, and creates a managing thread (②). After establishing the communication, the consumer delivers message sending/receiving times to the managing thread (③). Each thread computes the latency from the sending/receiving times and determines whether load shedding is required for the corresponding source.

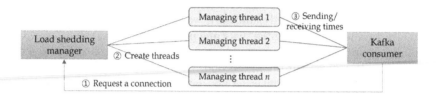

Fig. 2. Operation procedure of handling multiple sources in the load shedding manager.

4   Experimental Evaluation

The experimental application is to input an array of real numbers as a stream, sort it and output it again. We use Apache Storm as a real-time processing system and construct a Storm topology for sorting the arrays. The hardware platform consists of one master and eight slave nodes, each equipped with Xeon E5-2630V3 2.4 GHz 8Core CPU and 32 GB RAM. We configure the load shedding manager on an HP workstation with Intel i7 3.60 GHz CPU and 8.0 GB RAM.

The first experiment is the latency comparison in a single source. We set the latency threshold (ϵ) to 5 s and the load shedding ratio to 0.01. We then input an array of 1000 real numbers every 1 ms. Figure 3(a) shows the latency of the system with and without load shedding. In the figure, if load shedding is not applied, the unprocessed messages continue to accumulate, and the latency also continues to increase. In this case, the latency reaches several tens of seconds, and the real-time property cannot be guaranteed at all. On the other hand, if load shedding is applied, we can control the system load by temporarily limiting the messages. The latency is continuously increased until it exceeds the threshold of 5 seconds, but when it exceeds 5 seconds, it is shortened by the load shedding and it is increasing again. By applying load shedding in this way, we can control the latency below the threshold, although it discards some messages.

Figure 3(b) shows the latency for each source for multiple input sources. Similarly, we set the latency threshold to 5 seconds and the load shedding ratio to 0.01. We input an array of 700, 1,000, and 1,500 real numbers every 1 ms to Src1, Src2, and Src3, respectively. As shown the figure, although there is a slight difference depending on the array size, the latency of all sources tends to repeat increasing and decreasing without increasing continuously. It means that the load shedding engine works well for multiple sources as well as a single source.

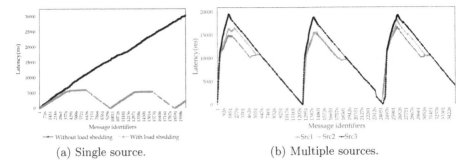

(a) Single source.   (b) Multiple sources.

Fig. 3. Comparison of latency with and without load shedding.

5   Conclusions

In this paper, we proposed a Kafka-based load shedding engine in a data stream environment. Our method performed load shedding when the latency exceeded the threshold, and discarded messages in the Kafka producer for quick overload control. Experiments using Apache Storm showed that load shedding worked efficiently for both single and multiple sources. Future research will explore an intelligent mechanism for self-tuning the load shedding ratio for non-experts.

Acknowledgements. This work was supported by the National Research Foundation of Korea(NRF) grant funded by the Korea government(MSIT) (No. 2017R 1A2B4008991).

References

1. Apache Kafka. http://kafka.apache.org/
2. Apache Spark Streaming. http://spark.apache.org/streaming/
3. Apache Storm. http://storm.apache.org/
4. Goetz, P., O'Neill, B.: Storm Blueprints: Patterns for Distributed Real-time Computation. Packt Publishing, Birmingham (2014)
5. Kreps, J., Narkhede, N., Rao, J.: Kafka: a distributed messaging system for log processing. In: Proceedings of the NetDB, Athens, Greece, pp. 1–7, June 2011
6. Leskovec, J., Rajaraman, A., Ullman, J.D., et al.: Mining of Massive Datasets. Cambridge University Press, Cambridge (2014)
7. Tatbul, N., Çetintemel, U., Zdonik, S., Cherniack, M., Stonebraker, M.: Load shedding in a data streams. In: Proceedings of the 29th International Conferences on Very Large Data Bases, Berlin, Germany, pp. 309–320 (2013)

8. Katsipoulakis, N.R., Labrindis, A., Chrysanthis, P.K.: Concept-driven load shedding: reducing size and error of voluminous and variable data streams. In: Proceedings of the International Conference on Big Data, Seattle, WA, pp. 418–427 (2018)
9. Rivetti, N., Busnel, Y., Querzoni, L.: Load-aware shedding in stream processing systems. In: Proceedings of the 10th International Conference on Distributed and Event-Based Systems, Irvine, CA, pp. 61–68 (2016)
10. Choumas, K., Paschos, G.S., Korakis, T., Tassiulas, L.: Distributed load shedding with minimum energy. In: Proceedings of the International Conference on Computer Communications, San Francisco, CA, pp. 1–9 (2016)

Enhancing Block-Wise Transfer
with Network Coding in CoAP

Cao Vien Phung$^{(\boxtimes)}$, Jasenka Dizdarevic, and Admela Jukan

Technische Universität Braunschweig, Braunschweig, Germany
{c.phung,j.dizdarevic,a.jukan}@tu-bs.de

Abstract. CoAP (Constrained Application Protocol) with block-wise transfer (BWT) option is a known protocol choice for large data transfer in general lossy IoT network environments. Lossy transmission environments on the other hand lead to CoAP resending multiple blocks, which creates overheads. To tackle this problem, we design a BWT with network coding (NC), with the goal to reducing the number of unnecessary retransmissions. The results show the reduction in the number of block retransmissions for different values of block size, implying the reduced transfer time. For the maximum block size of 1024 bytes and total loss probability of 0.5, CoAP with NC can resend up to 5 times less blocks.

Keywords: CoAP · Block-wise transfer · REST HTTP

1 Introduction

One of the most known IoT (Internet of Thing) protocols, CoAP [2], integrates BWT [1] as a good choice to transmit large amount of data. Since CoAP operates over User Datagram Protocol (UDP) and is thus fundamentally unreliable, it introduces a mode operation *confirmable* where a message is considered delivered once the acknowledgment has been received. This mode is often combined with BWT implementation where a large resources are divided into blocks for transferring. The receiver needs to send an acknowledgment after each received block. In lossy environments, which is typically the case in IoT, these acknowledgments can fail to arrive at the client, resulting in unnecessary retransmissions.

This paper addresses this problem of unnecessary retransmission by combining BWT in CoAP with NC (NC_BWT). Similar approach has been done for REST HTTP in [5]. Since REST HTTP and CoAP follow the same request-reply paradigm, the REST HTTP algorithm was modified for the specific CoAP requirements. Instead of adding a NC layer for REST, in this paper we introduce a novel design which adds NC technique in form of a so called *option value* for BWT. It is a simple coding scheme with only XOR operations for the normal

This work has been partially performed in the framework of mF2C project funded by the European Union's H2020 research and innovation programme under grant agreement 730929.

© Springer Nature Switzerland AG 2020
U. Schwardmann et al. (Eds.): Euro-Par 2019 Workshops, LNCS 11997, pp. 737–741, 2020.
https://doi.org/10.1007/978-3-030-48340-1_59

coded blocks, except the additional blocks using random linear network coding (RLNC) to better operate in constrained devices and environments. The numerical results show that additional retransmission of blocks can be reduced.

2   Related Work

The authors in [3] extend BWT using NC, while authors in [4] propose a scheme where multiple blocks can be retrieved by one request, focusing more on the problem of reducing latency. The goal of these schemes is to reduce communication time. Our paper focuses on another approach, combining NC and BWT based on the work in [5] to reduce the amount of traffic that needs to be resent, therefore improving bandwidth utilization.

3   System Design

3.1   Scenario

This section shows our scenario using NC method to apply for BWT in CoAP. Our scenario considers a CoAP client-server communication as shown in Fig. 1a. The client sends a large resource divided into 5 blocks. Our scheme uses BWT with stop-and-wait mechanism. BWT without NC in Fig. 1a.1 allows the blocks to be retransmitted when the client does not receive their acknowledgment in timeout interval. However, resending blocks p_1 is unnecessary because it has arrived at the server. To address this issue, we design a NC scheme in Fig. 1a.2. We observe the acknowledgment of block p_1 is lost, but the client is unaware of what is happening at the server. So, the client should perform NC among blocks after each timeout. In our scenario, one new block is only presented by one coded block at a time. Therefore, coded blocks are always linearly independent [6]. Taking advantage of this feature, we perform NC with only XOR operations, instead of RLNC as [5], to reduce coding/decoding overhead. With simple XOR operations, we can remove coding coeffcients from the option value. As a result, we can dramatically reduce the protocol overhead. At the time of arriving coded block $(p_1 + p_2 + p_3 + p_4)$, along with block p_1 received before, the server operates Gauss Jordan Elimination(GJE) to identify seen blocks p_1 and p_2 (please refer to [5] to understand seen packets). The acknowledgment R(sn,htp,rdt_s)=(2,4,2) can be responded even when the original blocks have not been decoded yet, where $sn = 2$, $htp = 4$ and $rdt_s = 2$ are the newest seen block, highest block ID that the server has, and number of additional blocks, respectively. The two additional blocks $(\delta_1 p_3 + \delta_2 p_4)$ and $(\delta_3 p_3 + \delta_4 p_4)$ are resent using RLNC, since they are coded from the previous blocks. Observe Fig. 1a.2, the first additional block is lost. When R(3,4,1) comes, based on the option value presented below, the client can identify this one responded from the second additional block with the symbol of two stars in the figure, and decide to send the native block p_4 instead of coded block $\delta_5 p_4 + \delta_6 p_5$ as [5] to decrease coding/decoding complexity. Observe that BWT with NC can shorten 1 block cycles compared to BWT.

3.2   Option Value

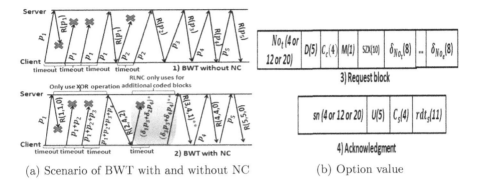

(a) Scenario of BWT with and without NC   (b) Option value

Fig. 1. Scenario BWT with and without NC, and option value for BWT with NC.

Figure 1b.3 shows the option value of request block. The typical sizes (in bits) of various fields are written inside. No_t and No_e are the minimum and maximum block index, respectively, involved in the random linear combination (RLC), where $No_e = D + No_t$. C_c is the number tagged for each coded block to distinguish the acknowledgment of which the transferred block is. M denotes more flag, $M = 0$ and $M = 1$ show the coded block contains and does not contain the last block, respectively. SZX is the block size. δ_i is the coding coefficient of ith block involved in RLC.

Figure 1b.4 represents the option value of acknowledgment. C_s is copied from C_c received from the client side. sn is the newest seen block. rdt_s denotes the number of additional blocks. The highest block index htp exists at the server, which is indirectly represented via U, where $htp = U + sn$.

3.3   Coding and Decoding, and Computing Additional Blocks

The coding process is similarly performed as [5], but one new feature of Algorithm 1 is added to distinguish which acknowledgement responds for corresponding block. Note that all blocks of a resource are only dropped from the buffer when that resource is successfully transacted.

if *Acknowledgement (Ack) received for the additional blocks* **then**
    if $C_s < C_c$ **then**
        | Ack of previous additional block; perform as [5], but use XOR;
    else
        | **if** $rdt_s > 0$, detect losses; Resend using RLNC as [5];
    end
else
    | **if** $htp < No_e$, Ack of previous normal block: No transmission;
end

Algorithm 1: Acknowledgement identification.

For decoding process, acknowledgement method, decoding and delivery method, buffer management method are similarly performed same as [5].

Let N, R and B be the total number of blocks of a resource, size of a resource and size of each block, respectively. The total number of blocks sent is $N = \lceil \frac{R}{B} \rceil$. Based on analysis in [5], the number of additional blocks of BWT $A_{WoNC} = \frac{N}{1-p} - N$ and of NC_BWT $A_{WNC} = \frac{N}{1-(\alpha \cdot p)} - N$, where p is the total loss probability for both request block and acknowledgement, and α is the loss rate when the client transfers block to the server.

4   Numerical Results

This section shows numerical results to compare block-wise transfer in CoAP with network coding (NC_BWT) with traditional block-wise transfer in CoAP (BWT) in term of the number of redundant blocks in Fig. 2. For our example, we consider an application with size $R = 512000$ bytes, where three types of block size B are chosen: 1024 bytes, 512 bytes, and 256 bytes. With an application size $R = 512000$ bytes, the number of blocks for block size $B = 1024$ bytes is $N = \lceil \frac{R}{B} \rceil = \lceil \frac{512000}{1024} \rceil = 500$ blocks, for block size $B = 512$ bytes is $N = \lceil \frac{R}{B} \rceil = \lceil \frac{512000}{512} \rceil = 1000$ blocks, for block size $B = 256$ bytes is $N = \lceil \frac{R}{B} \rceil = \lceil \frac{512000}{256} \rceil = 2000$ blocks. The total loss probability p is considered in $[0; 0.9]$. We assume that all types of block size B have the same total loss probability p. Three values of the request block loss rate $\alpha = 0.3$; 0.7 and 1 are selected. $A_{WoNC} = \frac{N}{1-p} - N$ and $A_{WNC} = \frac{N}{1-(\alpha \cdot p)} - N$ are used to compute the number of redundant blocks for BWT and NC_BWT, respectively.

Examples of NC_BWT and BWT in term of the number of redundant blocks shown in Fig. 2. Figure 2a, Fig. 2b and Fig. 2c present the scenario with request block loss rate $\alpha = 0.3$, $\alpha = 0.7$ and $\alpha = 1$, respectively. We see that for both BWT and NC_BWT when the total block loss probability p increases, the number of redundant blocks also increases because the higher total block loss probability p is, the more retransmissions happen. We also observe that the number of retransmissions with block size $B = 256$ bytes is the highest for both BWT and NC_BWT because under the impact of block loss, if a smaller block size is selected, the resource is divided into more blocks, therefore leading to more block losses, and resulting in more retransmissions. NC_BWT always outperforms BWT term of the number of redundant blocks. We consider an example of $p = 0.5$, $B = 1024$ bytes, BWT needs to resend 500 blocks for all values of request block loss rate α, but NC_BWT only resends 88.235 blocks for $\alpha = 0.3$, and 269.231 blocks for $\alpha = 0.7$. In addition, we observe that the smaller the loss rate value α, the more the benefit from NC_BWT is. We can explain for this that the client with NC_BWT only performs to re-dispatch for the lost request blocks. As a result, the request block loss rate $\alpha = 0.3$ is the best case for using network coding, compared to $\alpha = 0.7$ and $\alpha = 1$. Figure 2c with the request block loss rate $\alpha = 1$ shows that NC_BWT does not have any benefit from NC for all total loss probability p, it even makes bandwidth utilization worse, if we take coding coefficients in the option value into account when sending redundant

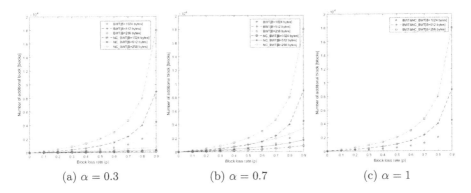

(a) $\alpha = 0.3$ (b) $\alpha = 0.7$ (c) $\alpha = 1$

Fig. 2. Number of additional blocks with network coding NC_BWT and without BWT

blocks. With these analyses, we can give a conclusion that NC_BWT is totally better than BWT for all cases, except the request block loss rate of $\alpha = 1$.

5   Conclusion

Network coding is a concept for enhancing bandwidth utilization. In this paper, we consider a combination between block-wise transfer with network coding in CoAP. We shows how our algorithm can reduce the number of redundant blocks and enhance bandwidth utilization in lossy and unreliable environments. In future works, we will do simulation for our design to see the impact of network coding on large resource transfer.

References

1. Bormann, C., Shelby, Z.: Block-wise transfers in the constrained application protocol (CoAP). RFC Editor, RFC **7959** (2016)
2. Shelby, Z., Hartke, K., Bormann, C.: The constrained application protocol (CoAP). RFC Editor, RFC **7252** (2014)
3. Schutz, B., Aschenbruck, N.: Adding a network coding extension to CoAP for large resource transfer. In: 2016 IEEE 41st Conference on Local Computer Networks (2016)
4. Choi, G., Kim, D., Yeom, I.: Efficient streaming over CoAP Gyuhong. In: International Conference on Information Networking (2016)
5. Phung, C.V., Dizdarevic, J., Carpio, F., Jukan, A.: Enhancing REST HTTP with random linear network coding in dynamic edge computing environments. In: 42nd International Convention on Information and Communication Technology, Opatija, Electronics and Microelectronics (MIPRO) (2019)
6. Van Vu, T., Boukhatem, N., Nguyen, T.M.T., Pujolle, G.: Dynamic coding for TCP transmission reliability in multi-hop wireless networks. In: WoWMoM, pp. 1–6 (2014)

A Classification of Resource Heterogeneity in Multiprocessing Systems

Andreas Grapentin$^{(\boxtimes)}$ and Andreas Polze

Operating Systems and Middleware Group, Hasso Plattner Institute for Digital
Engineering, University of Potsdam, Potsdam, Germany
{andreas.grapentin,andreas.polze}@hpi.uni-potsdam.de

Abstract. There is a disconnect between the structure and behavior of computer systems, and the way they are described and instructed in applications and system software. To each application, the structure of the system is presented as a homogeneous collection of memory and compute resources and peripherals to be utilized in full, while the operating system attempts to provide a layer of abstraction from the specifics of the devices, and the resource contention inherent to multiprocessing systems. This simplified and abstract view allows applications to function correctly with little regard to the specifics of the underlying hardware, and scale up with relative ease. However, disregarding the inherent heterogeneity of the hardware comes at the cost of degraded performance and reduced interoperability.

This work attempts to identify sources of heterogeneity common in multiprocessing systems, or emerging through new hardware or interaction paradigms, and discusses how these effects impact the performance and interoperability of applications on such systems.

Keywords: Heterogeneity · Multiprocessing · Classification

1 Introduction

In this work, we focus on the effects of heterogeneity in resources where software either expects homogeneity, or is presented the illusion thereof by the operating system. Traditional *Symmetric Multiprocessing* (SMP) systems contain two types of resources with that property. The first instance is main memory, where through the ubiquitous virtual memory abstraction to the application all bytes are presented equally, forming an isolated, apparently homogeneous virtual address space for each process. The second instance is compute resources, or *Cores*, on the homogeneity of which the *symmetry* of SMP relies.

Both of these types of resources have in common that their apparent homogeneity as presented to the application is disconnected from properties of the real hardware, and no portable standard operating system APIs for resource discovery exists, making the creation of portable applications capable of mitigating or even utilizing the heterogeneity of the hardware exceedingly difficult, which is especially egregious in cases where the mitigation that an operating system abstraction can provide is limited.

© Springer Nature Switzerland AG 2020
U. Schwardmann et al. (Eds.): Euro-Par 2019 Workshops, LNCS 11997, pp. 742–745, 2020.
https://doi.org/10.1007/978-3-030-48340-1_60

2   Classification

The following sections outline four types of resource heterogeneity, two of which are concerning main memory, and two are concerning the systems compute resources. We build on the term *Non-Uniform Memory Access* (NUMA), which is already well established in literature, and introduce the similar terms *Non-Uniform Memory Segments*, *Non-Uniform Compute Capabilities* and *Non-Uniform Instruction Set Architecture* to describe other types of heterogeneity.

2.1   Non-Uniform Memory Segments

Each addressable physical memory cell has functional and non-functional properties that are caused by the hardware memory module that backs it. Some of these properties, such as access throughput and latency, directly impact the performance of the application process, while others, such as error correction (ECC), change how the overall system responds to external events.

In systems with Non-Uniform Memory Segments, the hardware modules backing physical memory cells differ in their functional and non-functional properties in a way that is not mitigated by the systems hardware and firmware. A currently emerging example for such a configuration is a system that contains both volatile, and non-volatile memory DIMMs that share the same physical address space. Further examples can be found in the *Internet of Things* (IoT) domain, where the main memory of embedded controllers may be backed by modules with differing access latency behaviour, for example as it is found in Flash and SDRAM technology.

Historically, this issue is solved in the operating system through a virtual memory abstraction and the knowledge of the operating system about the memory layout, or in systems without that abstraction through explicit references to memory locations in the embedded application. This is possible because the different types of memory have specific purposes and their properties are leveraged accordingly, for example by directing all dynamic memory allocations of application processes to heap space located in SDRAM, which restores the illusion of homogeneity.

With the availability of non-volatile memory technologies, this is starting to change. In systems with general-purpose heterogeneous memory modules, the application process needs to indicate what types of memory are suitable for each allocation, which is not possible with existing standard memory allocation interfaces, and while Schwalb et al. and others are working on new APIs for NVRAM allocations [3,6], no approach has yet been adopted into the *Portable Operating System Interface* (POSIX) standard to fill this gap.

2.2   Non-Uniform Memory Access

Beyond backing separate regions of the physical main memory with modules of different properties, the distribution of these modules in the system also introduces access heterogeneity, as described by the well established NUMA architecture that is widespread in modern SMP systems.

NUMA was created to mitigate the starvation effects in memory access in multiprocessing systems with a shared memory bus, where resource contention is a limiting factor for scalability [1]. In NUMA systems the memory is distributed across the compute nodes and access to memory not local to the compute node is provided through the processor interconnect.

While this approach reduces the congestion on the memory bus and as a consequence improves the memory throughput of multiprocessing systems, it introduces heterogeneity into the memory access, where the latency and throughput of memory access for a process depends on the locality of the physical memory cell with respect to the executing processor. An unaware parallel application can be caught off-guard by these effects and suffer severe performance degradation, to the extent that it performs worse and consumes more resources than an instance of the same program run on a smaller machine.

Operating systems try to mitigate these issues through predictive task and memory placement and migration to increase data locality. Additionally, a wealth of approaches trying to establish NUMA-aware allocation APIs exists, such as the PGASUS Project by Hagen et al. [2] and `libnuma` by Kleen [5], but again none have been adopted into POSIX.

Lastly, the emerging *GenZ* architecture specification introduces more degrees of freedom into the structure of the memory communication, which is expected to further complicate the existing problems by introducing even more levels of locality.

2.3 Non-Uniform Computing Capabilities

The mobile and IoT ecosystem has given rise to the ARM *big.LITTLE* architecture, in response to conflicting demands for high peak performance in contrast with battery efficiency during phases of low utilization. In this configuration, a system contains processing units with varying performance and energy consumption characteristics, allowing the operating system to switch between a power-hungry high performance mode, and a battery saving mode on demand.

In big.LITTLE, the operating system can switch between pairs of cores, or between the entire cluster at runtime, but it is also possible to operate all of the cores at once in a heterogeneous multiprocessing configuration. The successor of this architecture is ARM *DynamIQ*, which provides more degrees of freedom in the configuration of the cores. Additionally, Intel has announced a similar architecture with *Lakefield*.

Scheduling on heterogeneous multiprocessing systems faces unique problems, since tasks behave differently on the heterogeneous cores, and optimal placement is difficult to predict. A task waiting for IO completion in a spinlock will waste resources on a faster core, while a task busy with calculations will have a longer turnaround time on a smaller core. As a consequence, the throughput and the energy efficiency of the system will degrade unless a heterogeneity aware scheduler is used, which constantly monitors and migrates workload to appropriate cores.

While work on improving scheduling on heterogeneous systems is ongoing, for example by Kim et al. [4], POSIX and the C standard again provide no means to explicitly annotate a program or a subroutine with regards to its requirements to the executing compute unit.

2.4 Non-Uniform Instruction Set Architectures

The technologies discussed in the previous section rely on cores that are binary compatible, to enable seamless migration of tasks between the cores. It is also possible to configure a system with heterogeneous cores that are not binary compatible, and that have different *Instruction Set Architectures* (ISAs).

This includes many types of accelerators, where tasks are explicitly offloaded, and interoperability with applications often achieved through message passing and shared memory. However, devices with cores adhering to separate ISAs that could be operated in a true SMP configuration do exist, such as the RV32M1 SoC, which contains an ARM and a RISC-V core, or the parallella SoC, which contains an FPGA that can be configured as a soft core running in an SMP configuration with the boards ARM core. This poses even more unique challenges to the operating system scheduler and kernel in maintaining interoperability between the ISAs and is worthy of further investigation.

3 Conclusions and Future Work

In this work, we have distinguished four types of heterogeneity that are existing in multiprocessing system, as well as their relevance for applications and system software. We have shown that operating systems interface standards are not suitably adapted to these effects to allow portable applications to behave optimally on both homogeneous and heterogeneous systems, but that new programming approaches and APIs are emerging to mitigate the issues and allow applications to utilize the strengths of the heterogeneous hardware.

References

1. Gustavson, D.B.: The scalable coherent interface and related standards projects. IEEE Micro **12**(1), 10–22 (1992)
2. Hagen, W., Plauth, M., Eberhardt, F., Feinbube, F., Polze, A.: Pgasus: a framework for c++ application development on numa architectures. In: 2016 Fourth International Symposium on Computing and Networking (CANDAR), pp. 368–374. IEEE (2016)
3. Hwang, T., Lee, D., Noh, Y., Won, Y.: Designing persistent heap for byte addressable nvram. In: 2017 IEEE 6th Non-Volatile Memory Systems and Applications Symposium (NVMSA), pp. 1–6. IEEE (2017)
4. Kim, M., Kim, K., Geraci, J.R., Hong, S.: Utilization-aware load balancing for the energy efficient operation of the big. little processor. In: 2014 Design, Automation & Test in Europe Conference & Exhibition (DATE), pp. 1–4. IEEE (2014)
5. Kleen, A.: A numa api for linux. Novel Inc. (2005)
6. Schwalb, D., Berning, T., Faust, M., Dreseler, M., Plattner, H.: nvm malloc: Memory allocation for nvram. ADMS@ VLDB **15**, 61–72 (2015)

Abstract Decision Engine for Task Scheduling in Linux Based Operating Systems

Sreeram Sadasivam[1]([⊠]) [ID], Malin Ewering[1,2] [ID], and Horst Schwichtenberg[1] [ID]

[1] Fraunhofer SCAI, Schloss Birlinghoven, 53757 Sankt Augustin, Germany
{sreeram.sadasivam,malin.ewering,horst.schwichtenberg}@scai.fraunhofer.de
[2] University of Köln, Weyertal 86-90, 50931 Köln, Germany

Abstract. Schedulers have improved and optimized the performance of various multi-threaded applications over many years. Schedulers are conceived as a part of user space task or realized as an algorithmic implementation within the operating system scheduler. However, there is no generic design in place to enforce a scheduler design targeting a selected group of tasks in the operating system.

In this paper, we present a novel approach to generalize an abstract decision engine, which would select the appropriate scheduler design based on the user and system constraints. This paper also provides a case study on IRS(Iterative Relaxed Scheduling) framework. The evaluation of this case study provides a foundation for the generic decision engine, which would alter the behavior of selected tasks in the operating system.

1 Motivation

In operating system, we have process scheduling and thread scheduling. Task is the generic term used within Linux based operating system to refer to a process or a thread [7]. In the rest of this document, we would use the terms process and thread inferring the same, which is task.

Thread scheduling is a method used to exhibit efficient resource sharing among multiple threads on a single machine. A scheduler is a thread in the operating system, which deals with scheduling. A scheduler is evaluated based on the following metrics: throughput, waiting time, response time, fairness [7]. There are many working models and designs addressing thread scheduling in an operating system. However, those models/designs are primarily aimed at addressing the entire system rather than tailor-made for each multi-threaded application. In this proposal, we mainly focus on a design, which is motivated from using two design paradigms. These paradigms are based on user-level and kernel-level scheduling designs. In user-level scheduling, we have a scheduler designed in the user land primarily as a user level thread, which makes scheduling decisions for a given multi-thread application. However, there are many limitations

© Springer Nature Switzerland AG 2020
U. Schwardmann et al. (Eds.): Euro-Par 2019 Workshops, LNCS 11997, pp. 746–750, 2020.
https://doi.org/10.1007/978-3-030-48340-1_61

to such an approach. One disadvantage is the possibility of getting context-switched by the operating system scheduler. In Linux operating system, we have the ability to design kernel modules which has the capability to be used as a plug-and-play feature. There are many publications, which address the ability to use this plug-in-play feature for enabling custom process scheduling in Linux [2,4]. LKM(Loadable Kernel Module) based scheduler implementation is motivated from the above idea [5]. LKM based scheduler was adapted to be used in the thesis work, which dealt on software verification for multi-threaded applications [6]. Preliminary evaluations and conclusions from this work suggest a need for an abstract decision engine to get the best out of both the design choices.

An abstract decision engine is a novel engine, which makes a single selection between two scheduling designs based on the user's multi-threaded program and the scheduling constraints persistent with the given program.

2   Case Study

The idea presented in this paper is validated by implementing a proof of concept on the IRS framework [6]. The proof of concept works as a case study for this paper. Iterative Relaxed Scheduling(IRS) is a software verification framework designed for verifying multi-threaded applications for concurrency bugs [3]. Figure 1 depicts a comparison between IRS and conventional verification approach.

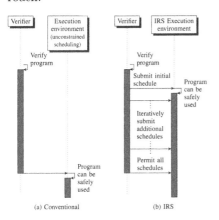

(a) Conventional   (b) IRS

Fig. 1. Comparison between conventional and IRS approach [3]

IRS consists of a scheduler and a verifier. The scheduler in IRS is intended to enforce schedules generated from the verifier on a multithreaded program. The verifier generates safe schedules (Schedules which are deemed to be safe from concurrency bugs) for a given multithreaded program. The scheduler within IRS enforces the above mentioned safe schedules on a given multithreaded program. The scheduler for IRS is implemented in three different ways: user space scheduler, kernel space scheduler and kernel space scheduler with a proxy decision making in the user space [6]. Different evaluations are conducted on top of these three design choices to determine the best option among them. Execution overhead is the metric used in these evaluations. The execution overhead is the additional execution time consumed by the benchmark when enforcing the scheduling constraints over plain execution of the benchmark(benchmark run without any scheduling constraints). The scheduling constraints are primarily the constraints provided in the safe schedules.

Table 1. Fibonacci - execution overhead(%)

mem_const	user_sched	kernel_sched(no proxy)	kernel_sched(with proxy)
24	381.5	333.704	152.425
44	1220.398	352.506	160.266
98	2078.221	385.416	277.793

Evaluations are conducted with benchmarking programs such as Indexer, LastZero, Dining Philosopher's Problem and Fibonacci. These evaluations are conducted with varying number of processor cores with core count of 2, 4 and 8. Table 1 depicts the evaluation of the Fibonacci benchmark. The evaluations are performed over two threads, where the first 200 fibonacci numbers are generated among the two threads. The number of memory constraints considered for this benchmark include 24, 44 and 98. From Table 1, it is clearly evident that with increase in the number of memory constraints(mem_const) the overhead becomes larger for user space scheduler design. Similarly, with decrease in the number of memory constraints the kernel space solution creates overhead due to unnecessary communication to the kernel space. From this evaluation, it is abundantly clear to formulate a solution with the best of two worlds(user space and kernel space) [6]. Kernel space with proxy is one such solution, which uses a proxy checking for a valid memory event and the validity of the event with the provided memory constraints. Based on Table 1, this solution(kernel_sched with proxy) showcases a very low execution overhead compared to the other scheduler designs.

A scaled evaluation of different scheduling approaches for the dining philosopher's problem(number of threads = 16) is depicted in Fig. 2 with different number of processor cores. The evaluation clearly shows that the user level scheduler is better than LKM based scheduler when the number of scheduling constraints (Constraints are decision parameters, based on which scheduling decisions are made. For example, these constraints can be shared-memory access of a variable in a multi-threaded application. Here we have considered memory constraints.) were negligible compared

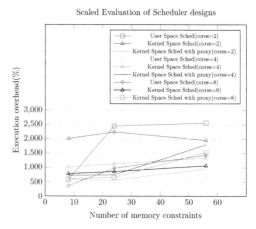

Fig. 2. Dining philosopher's problem

to overall shared memory events. However, user-level scheduler performed poorly when the number of scheduling constraints were increased. For detailed information about the evaluations kindly refer the thesis work [6].

3   Design

In this paper, we address an abstract decision engine perceived with a decision function for assisting the selection of a right scheduling design in place for a given multi-threaded application. The design overview is visualized in Fig. 3.

Let C be the context space for all possible context information, which is available from a given computational node N and a given multi-threaded application a_m. An element $c \in C$ states one of the relevant information, which is obtained from N or a_m.

For example, c can be the number of processor cores available in the computational node N, number of threads for the application a_m, CPU load exerted by other processes on the node N, or the number of relevant dependency constraints within the application a_m.

Let us consider p_m as the program used for running the application a_m. Let us consider n_r as the number of relevant shared memory constraints provided for a multi-threaded program p_m and n_t is the total number of shared memory events within the multithreaded program p_m. If the condition depicted in equation (1) holds for an application a_m, this is an indicator that usage of user space scheduler provides a better execution overhead. Whereas, if condition does not hold, such a scenario implies the use of a LKM based scheduler.

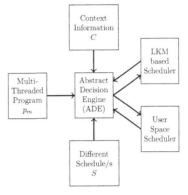

Fig. 3. Design overview

$$n_r << n_t \tag{1}$$

Let us consider S as the set of schedules deemed consistent with the execution of program p_m and the selection set $G = \{$"$LKM\ based\ Scheduler$", "$User\ Space\ Scheduler$"$\}$. G corresponds to the set, which contains the available scheduler choices for an application a_m. The abstract decision engine can be realized as a mathematical function making use of inputs C, S, p_m to provide an inference $g \in G$. The target function of this mathematical design is to select the scheduler design g, which has relatively less execution overhead. Other possible context information include the amount of spread for relevant dependencies across the application a_m.

Such an engine would serve the user to alter execution pattern of his multi-threaded application without affecting the entire operating system. The engine would be able to adapt to various system load and resource constraints. The efficiency of the engine depends upon the amount of evaluations done during the empirical study. This engine would aid many multi-threaded application developers to develop their applications without worrying about the underlying scheduler.

4 Conclusion and Future Outlook

The evaluation of IRS [6] showcased a need for a design, which could exploit the benefits of both the worlds(user space and kernel space). In this paper, we have showcased a novel idea of using the combination of different scheduler designs based on a mathematical formulation. To built an extensive mathematical function, it is needed to conduct an empirical study of both the scheduler designs. Such an empirical study requires an extensive use of different benchmarking frameworks. Benchmarking frameworks include PARSEC, Splash2 [1,8]. A mathematical function would be derived from the recordings obtained for different performance metrics associated with different bench-marking frameworks and additional thread conditional programs. The future objective is to find the right scheduling design, which can minimize the execution overhead.

References

1. Bienia, C., Kumar, S., Singh, J.P., Li, K.: The parsec benchmark suite: characterization and architectural implications. In: Proceedings of the 17th international conference on Parallel architectures and compilation techniques, pp. 72–81. ACM (2008)
2. Kato, S., Rajkumar, R., Ishikawa, Y.: A loadable real-time scheduler framework for multicore platforms. In: Submitted to Real-Time Computing Systems and Applications, RTCSA (2010)
3. Metzler, P., Saissi, H., Bokor, P., Suri, N.: Quick verification of concurrent programs by iteratively relaxed scheduling. In: Proceedings of the 32nd IEEE/ACM International Conference on Automated Software Engineering, pp. 776–781. IEEE Press (2017)
4. Regehr, J., Stankovic, J.A.: Hls: a framework for composing soft real-time schedulers. In: Proceedings 22nd IEEE Real-Time Systems Symposium, RTSS 2001, pp. 3–14. IEEE (2001)
5. Sadasivam, S.: Loadable kernel module based scheduler (2017). https://github.com/m4n1c22/Loadable-Scheduler
6. Sadasivam, S.: Realizing Iterative Relaxed Scheduler in Kernel Space. Master's thesis, Technische Universität Darmstadt (2018)
7. Silberschatz, A., Galvin, P.B., Gagne, G.: Operating System Concepts Essentials. Wiley, Hoboken (2014)
8. Woo, S.C., Ohara, M., Torrie, E., Singh, J.P., Gupta, A.: The splash-2 programs: characterization and methodological considerations. In: Proceedings 22nd Annual International Symposium on Computer Architecture, pp. 24–36. IEEE (1995)

Transparent Data Access for Scientific Workflows Across Clouds

Michał Orzechowski[1(✉)], Bartosz Baliś[1], Łukasz Dutka[2], Renata G. Słota[1], and Jacek Kitowski[1,2]

[1] Department of Computer Science, AGH University of Science and Technology, Krakow, Poland
{morzech,balis,rena,kito}@agh.edu.pl
[2] AGH University of Science and Technology, ACK Cyfronet AGH, Krakow, Poland

Abstract. We present a scientific workflow data management solution that combines global data access with a block-level optimization of data transfer, wherein only the data blocks that are used by a remote job are transferred over the network, significantly reducing data movement for specific common data access patterns. We propose the implementation of the solution based on the HyperFlow workflow management system and the Onedata data management platform. Preliminary results confirm the advantages of the proposed solution.

Keywords: Scientific workflow management · Scientific data management · Container clouds

1 Introduction

Deployment and execution of scientific workflows across multiple distributed computing infrastructures such as clouds benefit greatly when considering cost and infrastructure requirements. Private and public cloud infrastructures are the first choice when compute resources are needed temporarily and immediately and for running a computation. A common approach for data-intensive distributed computing is to stage the needed data to a remote computing infrastructure's local storage [3]. Depending on the data access patterns this may result in needless transfers large data sets, even if the computational jobs will only use a fraction of it – a pattern typical for data-parallel algorithms. However, transferring only the required portion of a file may not be trivial if the legacy application running the jobs (a common case in scientific computing) expects the entire file to be provided. Re-engineering the legacy application could be the solution, but it may not always be trivial or even possible. In the worst case, the exact data access pattern may only be known at run-time, so dividing some data sets into chunks before the execution is impossible. The problem grows linearly when adding additional nodes or even computing infrastructures – each of them may need a replica of a large input file.

© Springer Nature Switzerland AG 2020
U. Schwardmann et al. (Eds.): Euro-Par 2019 Workshops, LNCS 11997, pp. 751–755, 2020.
https://doi.org/10.1007/978-3-030-48340-1_62

In this paper, we report on a work in progress solution for scientific workflow data management providing a transparent global data access and block-level optimization of data transfer. We implement the solution based on the Hyper-Flow workflow management system [1] and Onedata data management platform [5] deployed in a Kubernetes cluster. The main contributions can be summarized as follows:

- we propose a solution for scientific workflow data management that offers transparent global data access and block-level data transfer optimization;
- we present initial integration of the Hyperflow WMS and Onedata running on multiple distributed Kubernetes clusters;
- we report preliminary results evaluating the optimized data transfer method.

2   Related Work

Scientific workflow data management is a multi-aspect problem with a variety of existing approaches. In a typical system, exemplified by Pegasus [4], data either exists on a shared file system, or the WMS tracks all files produced in a workflow run and transfers them between nodes. Pegasus has a dedicated catalog for this and adds special data-transfer nodes into the executable workflow graph. In [7], a tiered storage architecture is proposed for scientific workflow data management. Data placement strategies are also developed to minimize data movement [6]. Some general studies of data access patterns in scientific workflows and their consequences for data management design include [8] and [2]. Overall, none the existing works we are aware of studies data access patterns of scientific workflows at the block level and uses this mechanism for optimization of data access.

3   Solution Description

An example deployment diagram of the proposed solution is depicted in Fig. 1. The solution spans across three cloud infrastructures: in-house Openstack cloud infrastructure; an Amazon AWS and EGI Cloud. On Openstack and Amazon Kubernetes clusters are deployed using Terraform to provide a uniform infrastructure layer. On Kubernetes on Openstack, we setup core services including monitoring services, high-speed CEPH storage and the Hyperflow workflow management system. Hyperflow can schedule workflow tasks on a Kubernetes – main Hyperflow service is deployed on a Openstack Kubernetes and the task can be deployed on either Kubernetes cluster. Each task is deployed with a monitoring agent and accompanying Oneclient – which provides transparent data access by mounting a POSIX FUSE virtual filesystem. Global data access layer is realized by deploying two Oneproviders – one on each Kubernetes cluster. Oneproviders provide an abstraction layer over physical storage: CEPH and S3. Oneclient connects to a local Oneprovider instance and transfers data from a Oneprovider to a task. Both Oneproviders are registered with EGI Onezone service, which provides authentication, authorization over data access.

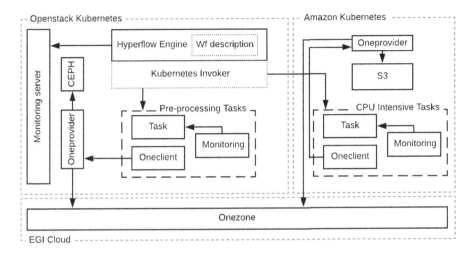

Fig. 1. Scientific workflow execution in hybrid cloud environment.

Upon workflow execution, a Workflow Description is loaded into Hyperflow. Workflow tasks are labelled which is to be scheduled on which Kubernetes cluster. For example, less resource-intensive pre- and post-processing tasks are executed on in-house Openstack Kubernetes cluster, while CPU and data-intensive tasks are scheduled to a remote cloud. Initially, all the data needed by the workflow is stored on a CEPH storage and no data is present on Amazon S3. When a CPU intensive task is scheduled on a remote cloud and tries to access the data, Oneclient connected to a Oneprovider on the remote cloud requests data transparently. Data is transferred from the Openstack Oneprovider to the Amazon Oneprovider in a P2P fashion.

Table 1. Comparison of execution times of a job reading 25% of a 1 GB file with and without block-level data transfer optimization. Without the optimization, the entire file is transferred. With the optimization, only the required 25% is transparently transferred; two cases are shown: data in continuous block vs. data scattered throughout the file.

Test case	Exec time (s)
100% file data transfer	71
25% continuous block read data transfer	19
25% random read data transfer	22

Onedata operates on blocks, not entire files, so in the case when a job reads part of a file, only the appropriate blocks are transferred from Oneprovider to Oneclient (or, in the case of remote data access, between Oneproviders). This may lead to a significant reduction of data transfer, depending on the job's data access patterns. Table 1 shows a comparison of execution times of a job reading 25% of a 1 GB file in three cases: transfer of the entire file, transfer of 25% of the file data in a continuous block, and transfer of 25% of the file data scattered randomly. Note that the mechanism is fully transparent: the job accesses the file as if it existed in a local file system. However, the actual data blocks are only transferred just-in-time, when requested through read operations.

4 Conclusions and Future Work

The proposed transparent data access for scientific workflows across multi-cloud offers significant advantages for scientific workflow data management. The global data access layer allows the execution components to use the POSIX interface for file operations transparently. The block-level data transfer allows optimizing data movement for specific common data access patterns.

Future work includes experimental studies involving running different real scientific workflows characterized by various data access patterns to evaluate advantages of Onedata block-based data access integrated with the HyperFlow scientific workflow management system.

Acknowledgements. This work is supported by the following grants. BB: National Science Centre, Poland, grant 2016/21/B/ST6/01497. LD: 2018–2020's research funds in the scope of the co-financed international projects framework (projects: XDC 3958/H2020/2018/2 and EOSC-hub 3905/H2020/2018/2). This work was partially supported by the Polish Ministry of Science and Higher Education under subvention funds for the AGH University of Science and Technology.

References

1. Balis, B.: Hyperflow: a model of computation, programming approach and enactment engine for complex distributed workflows. Future Gener. Comput. Syst. **55**, 147–162 (2016)
2. Costa, L.B., et al.: The case for workflow-aware storage:an opportunity study. J. Grid Comput. **13**(1), 95–113 (2014). https://doi.org/10.1007/s10723-014-9307-6
3. Deelman, E., Chervenak, A.: Data management challenges of data-intensive scientific workflows. In: 2008 Eighth IEEE International Symposium on Cluster Computing and the Grid, CCGRID, pp. 687–692. IEEE (2008)
4. Deelman, E., Vahi, K., Juve, G., et al.: Pegasus, a workflow management system for science automation. Future Gener. Comput. Syst. **46**, 17–35 (2015)
5. Dutka, L., et al.: Onedata–a step forward towards globalization of data access for computing infrastructures. Proc. Comput. Sci. **51**, 2843–2847 (2015). https://doi.org/10.1016/j.procs.2015.05.445
6. Ebrahimi, M., Mohan, A., Kashlev, A., Lu, S.: Bdap: a big data placement strategy for cloud-based scientific workflows. In: 2015 IEEE First International Conference on Big Data Computing Service and Applications, pp. 105–114. IEEE (2015)

7. Ghoshal, D., Ramakrishnan, L.: Madats: managing data on tiered storage for scientific workflows. In: Proceedings of the 26th International Symposium on High-Performance Parallel and Distributed Computing, pp. 41–52. ACM (2017)
8. Shibata, T., Choi, S., Taura, K.: File-access patterns of data-intensive workflow applications and their implications to distributed filesystems, pp. 746–755. ACM (2010)

Time-Based Consensus

Hasan Heydari$^{(\boxtimes)}$, Guthemberg Silvestre, Nicolas Larrieu, and Alain Pirovano

ENAC, Université de Toulouse, Toulouse, France
heydari@enac.fr

Abstract. Reaching consensus is fundamental in distributed computing. For each execution of a consensus algorithm, there is no difference
between the proposed values by different nodes with respect to their
proposed times. By presenting a realistic application scenario related to
distributed asynchronous mobile robots in dynamic environments, we
argue some safety-critical, real-time systems require reaching consensus
on the *newest proposed values* when the old proposed values may not be
valid anymore. Afterward, we formulate a new type of consensus problem called time-based consensus, which requires to take into account the
times of proposed values. Finally, to tackle such a consensus problem, we
determine an essential characteristic which should be considered.

Keywords: Consensus algorithm · Distributed mobile robot ·
Safety-critical application · Real-time system · Dynamic environment

1 Introduction

Reaching consensus is a primitive of distributed computing [3]. Consensus, informally, refers to an agreement among a group of nodes in which each node proposes a value, and the goal is to agree on exactly one value. There are several
reasons why, in distributed systems, consensus is required, like to agree on who
is the leader, to agree on who gets access to a shared resource, synchronizing
nodes' clocks, to agree on an ordering of events/operations among nodes, or
achieving formation control [2].

There are different types of consensus problems. Each type is presented for
specific purposes and has its own characteristics but satisfying agreement and
termination properties is common among all the types. Based on validity property, which means the decided value is one of the proposed values, the consensus
problems can be divided in two types. The first type satisfies validity property
which is the case in distributed data stores. For the other type of consensus problems, validity property is stated differently or not defined. For example, validity
property for average consensus [1] and max-min consensus [8], which are mostly
used in robotics, is not defined. In this paper, we focus on a subset of the first
type which is subject to FLP [4] (it is leader-based and should provide strong
consistency in addition to satisfying validity).

Formally, a consensus algorithm which is subject to FLP is correct when it
satisfies three properties– *agreement, termination,* and *validity* [3]. Also, it has

© Springer Nature Switzerland AG 2020
U. Schwardmann et al. (Eds.): Euro-Par 2019 Workshops, LNCS 11997, pp. 756–759, 2020.
https://doi.org/10.1007/978-3-030-48340-1_63

some characteristics– each node proposes exactly one value, all the proposed values should be taken into account to reach consensus, there is no difference between the proposed values with respect to their proposed times because the system's model is asynchronous and failures eventually occur, and if the nodes want to propose other values, they have to execute the algorithm again. Paxos [6] and Raft [7] are two well-known examples for such an algorithm.

For some safety-critical, real-time systems, the nodes have to consider the times of proposed values and reach consensus on the *newest proposed values*. Note that determining which proposed values are new is a challenging problem in asynchronous distributed systems when occurring failures are possible. In this paper, we formulate a new type of consensus problem called time-based consensus, which requires to take into account the times of proposed values. The structure of the paper is as follows. In Sect. 2, we argue that having such a time-based consensus is crucial for some safety-critical, real-time systems, like distributed asynchronous mobile robots in dynamic environments. We explain the limitations of consensus algorithms that lead to not reaching consensus on the newest proposed values in Sect. 3. Finally, (i) we formulate time-based consensus problem and (ii) finish the paper by presenting ongoing works to tackle such a problem.

2 Motivation

There are some safety-critical, real-time systems in which consensus is required, and in the process of reaching consensus, it is important to consider the times of proposed values. For an instance of such systems, suppose that there are n mobile heterogeneous robots located in a burned building in which some persons need help to rescue (Fig. 1(a)). The robots have two responsibilities– detecting and counting the persons and rescue some of them by creating a formation. Since the robots are mobile, and the environment is dynamic (which means if there are n_t detected persons at time t, it is possible that at time t' $(t' > t)$, there are $n_{t'}$ $(n_t \neq n_{t'})$ detected ones due to finding new alive ones, dying some of them, etc.), the number of detected persons can be different for each robot and is not constant during the rescue process (Fig. 1(b)). Control formation means that some of the robots create a determined formation around the detected persons (Fig. 1(c)). After creating a formation, they spread fire extinguishers to rescue the persons.

To create a formation for rescuing p persons, n_p robots is required. Robots for creating the formation need to reach consensus on the number of detected persons. Its reason is two-fold. First, some of the robots do not know the correct number of detected persons (Fig. 1(b)). Thus, when a robot detects a new person, it needs to broadcast the number of persons. Second, if more than n_p robots are allocated, it is not optimized. Note that the number of robots is limited, and here, taking into account optimization is crucial because what robots are doing is a critical task, and the remaining non-allocated robots can continue the rescue process. Therefore, the robots need to know the exact number of persons to decide how many of them have to participate in creating the formation.

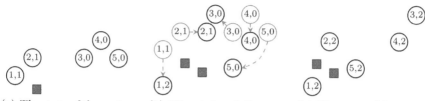

(a) The state of the system at time t.

(b) The state of the system at time t'. Robots moved to new positions.

(c) The state of the system at time t''. Robots 1,2, and 5 create a formation.

Fig. 1. Circles and squares correspond to robots and persons respectively. The first and second digits written in each circle are its unique identifier and detected persons respectively $t < t' < t''$.

3   Consensus Algorithms' Limitations

Suppose that two nodes n_1 and n_2 execute a consensus algorithm (for the sake of generality, suppose that the algorithm is Paxos) and are measuring/sensing a *critical data*. In what follows, by presenting two scenarios, we show Paxos' limitations that lead to not reaching consensus on the newest measured values. Consider x_1^i and x_2^j $(i, j \in \mathbb{N})$ are the measured values by n_1 and n_2 respectively. n_1 and n_2 measure two values– x_1^1 and x_2^1. n_1 by sending a prepare message to n_2 starts a consensus execution. In the first scenario, suppose that they reach consensus on x_1^1. Then, n_1 measures a new value, x_1^2 $(x_1^2 \neq x_2^1)$. It is clear that if they execute the algorithm for another time, they can reach consensus on x_2^1 while it is not correct (i.e, they have to reach consensus on x_1^2 because it is the newest measured value). This scenario is depicted in Fig. 2(a).

In another scenario which is depicted in Fig. 2(b), n_1 measures a value like x_1^2 $(x_1^2 \neq x_2^1)$ in the time period t_2 started after receiving some prepare message of n_2. They can reach consensus on x_2^1 which is not correct. Indeed, what we can do to distinguish the measured values with respect to their proposed times is using the executions and phases of a consensus algorithm.

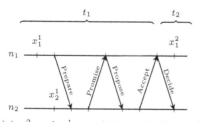
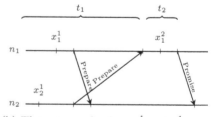

(a) x_1^2 and x_2^1 are distinguishable with respect to their proposed times but Paxos does not consider it.

(b) The measured values x_1^1 and x_2^1 are not distinguishable with respect to their proposed times for n_1 but x_1^2 and x_2^1 are.

Fig. 2. Executing Paxos on two nodes.

4   Time-Based Consensus and Ongoing Works

To tackle the problem explained in the previous sections, we model the system by a dynamic asynchronous distributed system with n nodes, where each node is a mobile robot. Each node has a sensor, which can be used to measure/sense some *critical data*, and can send (receive) messages to (from) the other nodes located in its communication range. Crash and link failures are possible. A correct node and link is a non-failed one. Being dynamic, here, means the set of correct nodes and links between a correct node and other correct nodes are not constant during the rescue process. Here, we formulate time-based consensus. When an algorithm satisfies three following properties, we say it can solve time-based consensus.

- *Termination.* Each node eventually should decide a value.
- *Agreement.* The decided values of all nodes should be the same. **The decided value is the last distinguishable proposed value (or among the last distinguishable proposed values) before deciding a value.**
- *Validity.* **Each node can propose one or more than one values before deciding a value by all nodes.** The decided value should be proposed by at least one node.

To tackle time-based consensus, we are using Paxos as a baseline because most consensus algorithms which are subject to FLP are variants of Paxos [5]. By changing some of its phases and adding an (some) additional phase(s) to it, we want to present an algorithm for time-based consensus. One of the essential characteristics of this algorithm is when a leader proposes a value measured at pth phase of eth execution to some node, and the measured value of the node was measured at p'th phase of e'th execution, the node cannot propose its measured value where $e' < e$ or $(e' = e) \wedge (p' < p)$.

References

1. Acciani, F., Frasca, P., Heijenk, G., Stoorvogel, A.A.: Achieving robust average consensus over lossy wireless networks. IEEE Trans. Control Netw. Syst. **6**, 127–137 (2019)
2. Alonso-Mora, J., Montijano, E., Nägeli, T., Hilliges, O., Schwager, M., Rus, D.: Distributed multi-robot formation control in dynamic environments. Auton. Rob. **43**(5), 1079–1100 (2018). https://doi.org/10.1007/s10514-018-9783-9
3. Attiya, H., Welch, J., Zomaya, A.Y.: Distributed Computing. Wiley, Hoboken (2004)
4. Fischer, M.J., Lynch, N.A., Paterson, M.S.: Impossibility of distributed consensus with one faulty process. J. ACM **32**, 374–382 (1985)
5. Hao, Z., Yi, S., Li, Q.: Edgecons: achieving efficient consensus in edge computing networks (2018)
6. Lamport, L.: Paxos made simple. ACM SIGACT News **32**, 18–25 (2001)
7. Ongaro, D., Ousterhout, J.: In search of an understandable consensus algorithm (2014)
8. Shi, G., Xia, W., Johansson, K.H.: Convergence of max-min consensus algorithms. Automatica **62**, 11–17 (2015)

Correction to: Euro-Par 2019: Parallel Processing Workshops

Ulrich Schwardmann (ID), Christian Boehme, Dora B. Heras,
Valeria Cardellini, Emmanuel Jeannot, Antonio Salis,
Claudio Schifanella, Ravi Reddy Manumachu, Dieter Schwamborn,
Laura Ricci, Oh Sangyoon, Thomas Gruber, Laura Antonelli,
and Stephen L. Scott

Correction to:
U. Schwardmann et al. (Eds.): *Euro-Par 2019:*
***Parallel Processing Workshops*, LNCS 11997,**
https://doi.org/10.1007/978-3-030-48340-1

The original version of the book was revised; the following corrections have been incorporated:

In chapter "In Situ Visualization of Performance-Related Data in Parallel CFD Applications":
The chapter was inadvertently published without the two videos. The two videos were added.

In chapter "MPI+OpenMP Parallelization for Elastic Wave Simulation with an Iterative Solver":
The chapter was inadvertently published with the wrong abstract. The abstract was updated.

The updated version of these chapters can be found at
https://doi.org/10.1007/978-3-030-48340-1_31
https://doi.org/10.1007/978-3-030-48340-1_54

Author Index

Printed in the United States
By Bookmasters